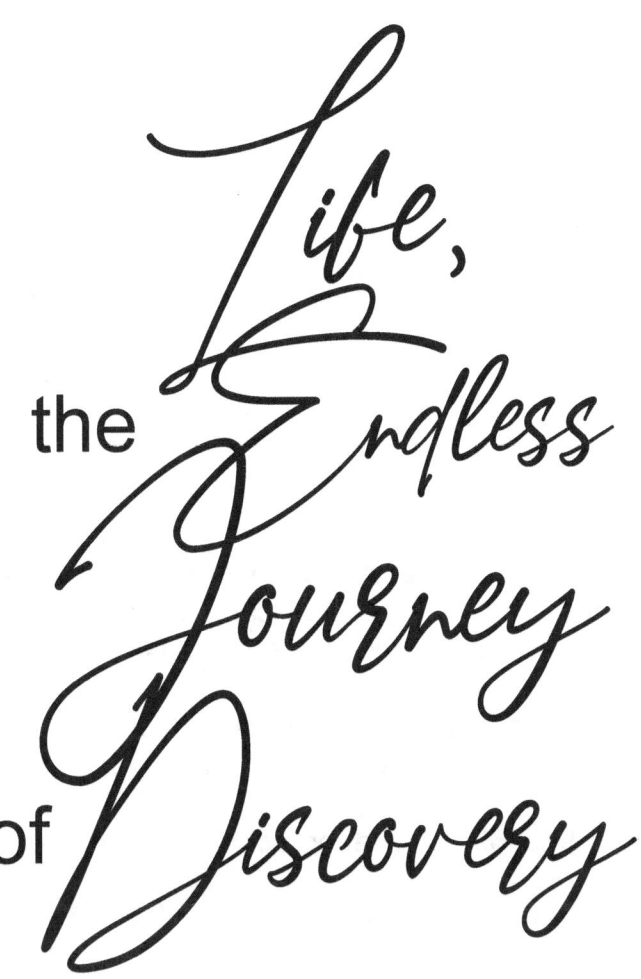

Life, the Endless Journey of Discovery

JIM WONDERS

Life, the Endless Journey of Discovery
© Jim Wonders 2024

All rights reserved. No part of this publication may be reproduced, stored in a retrieval system, or transmitted in any form or by any means, electronic, mechanical, photocopying, recording or otherwise, without the prior written permission of the author.

Jim Wonders is recognised as the creator of this content and has asserted the right to be identified as the author of this work.

ISBN: 978-1-92328931-4 (Paperback)

 A catalogue record for this book is available from the National Library of Australia

Cover Design: Jim Wonders and Clark & Mackay
Format and Typeset: Jim Wonders and Clark & Mackay
Published by Jim Wonders and Clark & Mackay

Proudly printed in Australia by Clark & Mackay

Contents

Author's Welcome iv
Introduction viii

Chapter 1   Living a Better Life 1
Chapter 2   Revealing Experience 79
Chapter 3   Life Is More Than It Appears To Be 93
Chapter 4   Social Situations 124
Chapter 5   The Meaning of Life 140
Chapter 6   The Nature of Our Eternal Existence 156
Chapter 7   Integrating Our Consciousness 196
Chapter 8   A Consciousness Integration Experience 260
Chapter 9   Human Nature Issues 283
Chapter 10 Evolved Life Forms and the Nature of Soul 542
Chapter 11 Life Continues After Earthly Life 651
Chapter 12 Focus Upon the Positive 715

Author's Welcome

Thank YOU for making the decision to join me on our mutual journey of discovery.

Humanity is now entering a new phase in its' progressive transformation into 'higher states' of consciousness by becoming increasingly capable of achieving our dreams to create a better life. EVERY individual; each in their own unique circumstances, is fortunate to be participating in this amazing process. The numerous challenges we all experience are assisting every one of us to become our best possible self, throughout the eons of passing time within multiple reality systems. We each and ALL do indeed 'stand upon the shoulders of giants', both figuratively and literally.

This lengthy book is a compilation of a lifetime of astute observations and reflective consideration upon my part, with focused intent to assist and inspire YOU to access additional valid information that will clarify and confirm numerous aspects of life. Proceed at a comfortable pace that you choose, as this is not 'a race' or competition of any type. This is simply you and I sharing 'our reality', from YOUR perspectives.

As the year 2024 (thankfully) comes to an end; here we are TOGETHER, bravely acknowledging the cumulative results of our combined efforts to create a global society that is worthy of self-respect, admiration and love within the seemingly infinite cosmos of life. The history of Humanity upon Earth is ancient beyond one's wildest imagination, contrary to the false history we have been taught to wrongly believe.

As you read these ideas, you will find countless things to consider or ignore, as you choose at the time. Many of us will find these concepts familiar, almost as though we wrote them ourselves. Other concepts and personal experiences will appear to be unlikely, seemingly impossible, improbable, or alien to your existing beliefs.

You will see that I have intentionally 'skipped' many years of earthly activity and ignored making personal comments on many international events and characters that are prominent within our global culture. Trust there are valid reasons for my doing so, as the book is comprehensive in its assessment of life's complex realities. Know and accept that it will be far more challenging for you to read and comprehend the entire book; if you choose and are mentally, emotionally and spiritually capable of doing so, than it was for me to write every word that is contained herein.

Chapter 1, "Living a Better Life" was written in early 2022. It is a 'summary introduction' to the entire book. Many people will understandably not read the entire book for countless valid reasons, so they will ideally receive sufficient 'value' by reading as much of it as possible, as they wish.

Numerous observations here may be contrary to your attitudes and belief systems, yet other ideas will 'find a home' within your heart, mind and Soul. You may find places where there are minor errors or seemingly inaccurate opinions. Admittedly, I am far from being a truly enlightened person; however, it is a relative thing.

This current 'self-published' edition is the fourth version of twenty years' intermittent efforts to 'speak my truth' to the best of my verbose abilities. You will find many locations where I mention the year the thoughts were written or re-edited to update the information to the (then) 'present moment', without expressing further opinions on debateable issues and socially influential individual personalities. Some parts are tediously repetitive and intentionally applying lengthy convoluted sentence structures for reasons that will become self-evident, if you are able to endure and persevere in the ongoing process of (slowly) reading the entire book. Other parts of the book will 'trigger' whatever levels of joy, inner peace and gratitude you possess to magnify the appreciation you have in being alive within your human physical body, regardless of your unique circumstances. Please know and accept the fact that we ALL have been 'damaged' by the prevailing social, cultural and religious realities.

There are subtle reasons for the way things are expressed here and I choose to use the Australian spelling, although American born. I have intentionally ignored some punctuation and grammatical 'rules', yet ideally this proclivity will not upset, annoy or distract you. You are encouraged to read (and reread, as necessary) this information with healthy scepticism or total denial, in whatever areas that contradict or surpass your own beliefs and experiences. Simply be aware that each and every one of us is evidently doing whatever they 'think is best' in this earthly life, although clearly some dysfunctional, delusional and inappropriate behaviours are inherent within me and almost everyone, to various degrees.

You will find that your mind will react adversely in ways that may surprise you. Anticipate that you will sometimes need to set the book aside for various periods of time to reflect upon its' content and your inner responses to the information here. It is NOT recommended that you 'skip around'; however, please do as you wish. Often you will find that you will simply 'go to sleep', or mentally 'drift off' into your own thoughts and emotional journeys; then wonder whatever relevance what you were reading at the time prompted that to occur unexpectedly. Other times, intuitions of unusual beneficial ideas or emotions will suddenly 'come to mind' that are seemingly totally unrelated, or inexplicable, or long-forgotten events that served to help make you the unique individual that you have progressively become throughout your lifetime. I intentionally waited many 'extra' decades to author my first book, to attain sufficient experiences and abilities to become worthy of your consideration. I am virtually unknown to 'mainstream' society, although this may change soon.

This book is written specifically for YOU !!!

Reading it is 'a process' by which you are assisted to progressively become the best possible YOU, regardless of the level of your personal and spiritual development !!!

If various things are so unusual, 'beyond', contrary, or repugnant and offensive to your belief systems, then please do simply inwardly acknowledge the fact and view the information as fiction or delusions on my part, which is fine with me.

Wishing and hoping for the best to occur in YOUR lifetime and for us ALL existing upon Mother Earth, here TOGETHER within Humanity !!!

May the Blessings Be

Introduction

*"The waters of your rushing mind need
to be like a quiet spring."*

Did you ever ask the question "Why?" as a child, only to receive answers that did not exactly seem to fully make sense or instead you were told: "because that is the way life is", "it is too difficult to explain", "you don't need to know that at your age", "you would not understand", or other such evasive, non-informative responses? Can you still recall how that made you feel as you tried to figure what made the sky blue, the rain fall, day and night, how far away the stars were from Earth, what the sun was made of that made it shine so brightly or how it could make us warm so far away, why birds laid eggs to have babies and could fly, or why cookies were only considered to be a treat for special occasions whereas things like potatoes, corn and rice were things you could eat as much of as you wanted at dinner until they were all gone, and countless other such questions? You may have tried to learn these things and many others from your parents and later in life, your teachers at school or others who you hoped would provide clear answers to your life's questions and various curiosities.

As you grew older you became better able to think for yourself and to intuitively perceive more deeply into significant life issues. Like me, you may recall wondering why some people acted happy outwardly, yet inwardly some of them seemed to feel sad, as though they were crying inside, whereas some other people seldom smiled at all. Other people seemed to be genuinely happy, very alert, and somehow much more intelligent, perceptive and alive. You gradually discovered that people are all quite unique in their thinking patterns, emotions and actions. You grew to learn the same was true of yourself too, in that there were some times when you had mostly happy, kind thoughts and other times your attitudes changed, generally because of what happened around you, so that life did not seem quite so good or joyous in various ways. You may have also been curious why the older kids did not usually play with the little children or teach them many of the secrets about life that they were learning. As a result, you may have gradually begun to stop asking other people "Why?" so often and began to seek your own experiences and information to provide the actual answers to life's mysteries. Some of us at an early age began to cease asking these more difficult types of questions, even to ourselves, since other normal daily things seemed more important, interesting, more fun and much easier to comprehend. Some of us to various degrees gradually found that our curious nature began to withdraw more deeply into ourselves for differing reasons. As children living in a sometimes strange world, we attempted to fully understand everything and to get along well with other people and cope with life's circumstances. Most of us eventually sought various forms of distraction or inner escape from the confusing, uncertain or even frightening aspects of life that we experienced.

Some of us began a conscious determined quest to discover the truth to as many of life's mysteries as we could, then share the results with our young friends, brothers and sisters, our parents, grandparents and any other people that we thought would care or benefit from our unique knowledge. Sometimes we would ask other children questions that we already knew our parents or teachers would not or could not answer. "Do your parents argue a lot?" or perhaps some of us asked "Do your parents punish you often or ever tell you not to cry so loudly the neighbours can hear you?" You may have also asked other kids, "Have you seen Santa Claus, the Tooth Fairy, the Easter Bunny or God?" You may have asked your father why he went away to work and only got to stay home one or two days a week, or why he was away from home for days, weeks or months at a time, or why he needed to work so hard on the farm or ranch every day from dawn until dark. Others of us never knew our father and looked at strangers in the street or the men that visited our mothers, wondering "Is he my Dad?" Some of us never knew our birth parents and felt very alone in the world at times, yet we may have had an inner sense of security and comfort anyway. Others of us saw our parents every day for most of our lives, yet never actually realised who they truly were, what they loved doing or wanted to do in life, or what their dreams were as a child long before they became an adult, or if their dreams ever came true. Some of us were fortunate enough to have joyously ideal childhoods filled with loving, happy times that were shared with well-balanced, financially secure parents and extended families that protected us from experiencing the less blissful aspects of reality that sometimes characterise most people's lives.

Regardless of the nature of our infinitely unique different upbringings, some of us took the conscious decision to travel an inner journey of discovery to determine life's meaning for ourselves. Others of us began to slowly close our minds, hearts and body away from life mostly out of a lonely desperation to find a sense of peace and calm that our external lives seldom revealed in the company of others. Some as children had quite blissful, happy, contented, loving childhoods that at first fostered a surreal image and understanding of this world and the thought that all other people were pleasant, polite, kind, happy, decent, and trustworthy, with plenty to eat, living in nice homes. As children, most of us were sooner or later warned to be wary of strangers, without anyone seeming to realise that most of the people we meet in life are initially strangers; not that we now seek to disagree with that advice upon fully considering some of our life's experiences as adults.

Can you now begin to vaguely or more vividly recall the paths of your inner and outer knowing that you began to choose as a child? You may be asking yourself, "What has any of this got to do with my life now?" or "How would those memories make any difference to my happiness, lifestyle, or perceptions now?" You may not be able to recall much of your childhood, aside from hazy distant recollections and glimpses as from a long-forgotten black and white movie, almost as if some of those events were never really lived by your present self at all. Others of us may never seem able to extinguish or forget various vivid memories, whether we wish to recall them or not. Some events and emotions will be clearly recalled while others are forgotten for no apparent reasons and some of our memories of events will differ greatly from those who shared those times with us. Those past memories and realisations continue to exist within us, if we will simply take the time and make the efforts to see them within our mind's inner vision. In this process we each are seeking to gradually inquire and re-discover aspects of ourselves, our past, our thoughts, our imaginings, and our hopes and dreams as well as even some of the terrors and nightmares, all in order to better comprehend ourselves and the lives we now create together upon our Earth.

Some of us learned to stop asking questions or to accept whatever we were told as being factual information at a very early age. Others of us began to seriously consider and even doubt some of the information and answers we received from various sources, in relation to our own experiences. As we entered into our teens and young adulthood, most of us found life's realities to be an inexplicable odd mixture of seemingly unproven, often contradictory and frustratingly confusing groups of discordant so-called 'facts'. Many of life's most important realities apparently had no clear, definitive, proven, absolute truth upon which all people could conclusively agree. That situation concerned and bothered some of us, yet mostly we generally tended to accept this situation as being inherent in the nature of life and earthly reality.

Your own unique set of experiences, thoughts, opinions, perceptions, beliefs, dreams, hopes, needs, desires, feelings, emotions, and life goals are the only ones that truly matter now in the context of our further discussions here. This is true of me as well, since we will share these written thoughts, mental images and life experiences throughout this discussion. We will be primarily seeking to create a 'meeting of the minds, hearts, and souls' in our journey to re-discover who we have become through our life's experiences and to realise more fully what and who we seek to 'be' as our life progresses from this time forward. Please feel as though we are gradually becoming closer friends, who will confide together in the privacy of your own inner being, a variety of life experiences, feelings, emotions, thoughts, perceptions, and beliefs that have created the unique, innately precious individuals that we are today. The primary aspect that will be shared between us is that we are all independent, free-thinking, human beings. We each and all live closely together upon this Earth as self-aware, exceptionally perceptive life forms that mutually share the same basic realities, in drastically individualised circumstances, possessing unique experiences, perceptions and attitudes. Throughout this discussion, we will periodically focus our attention upon the fact that we all possess additional aspects of ourselves that exist simultaneously upon higher, eternal levels of existence than that we now see here on this earthly planet.

In our communications here, it is intended that we share an intimacy of interaction that you have seldom experienced in any book previously. You are encouraged to choose to consider the subjects discussed here with an open-minded attitude, while doing your best to clearly recall and closely examine your own set of life events and the resulting emotions, lessons, realisations, choices and actions. Perhaps you have not really wanted to confide various events, thoughts, or feelings with any other human being. Sometimes when you did tell people private things about yourself, they did not fully understand the situation's meaning for you. None of us can really truly understand what other people's life events mean to them; yet sharing similar experiences, thoughts and emotions certainly helps create a better sense of empathy with one another. What is most special about our communications here is that I will share many experiences, beliefs, opinions, perceptions, events, historical and cultural realities in unique ways to prompt and clarify your own recall of your life's significant events, even some of those seemingly forgotten events and the related thoughts, emotions, intuitive impressions, and higher mental processes that compose your overall state of being. All of your past experiences and the resulting perceptions will then remain completely private, unspoken and secure, if you wish to keep them confidential in this manner. Alternatively, you could discuss some of these concepts, your experiences, thoughts, reactions and feelings with others that may have similar interests or even with some people that have completely different perspectives to your own or those mentioned here.

This book is intended to be much like an interpersonal private discussion between you and I. Please frequently pause in your reading to reflect upon your own life and attitudes, in response to various things stated here, and to examine closely the resulting ideas and images which seem to pop into your mind. Your own personal inner consideration will lead to further realisations and ideally ultimately that process of self-discovery will then create some positive focused action in your own life, as seems appropriate for you at the time. You are also welcome to mentally discuss various ideas mentally with me, as though I was a friend of yours' who did not speak much, except in the form of this discussion. In so doing, you will begin to directly contact aspects of yourself that will ideally be most helpful in clarifying the various issues in your life.

Some of what is included here is very likely going to seem to be unacceptable, unbelievable, impossible, simply irrelevant, or starkly opposed to your own set of beliefs, yet there will be other ideas that you can agree with completely from your own set of experiences. We will develop a process of mutual discovery by presenting a quite limited range of my life's important events, realisations and perceptions, including some major references to significant historical events, modern events and additional pertinent information that is relevant to the topics here. This will be done in a manner that serves as a catalytic stimulus to your own thoughts and experiences regarding the entire scope of your life, so that your own memories, experiences, realisations, revelations, hopes and dreams will assume additional meaning and clarity in your life. We will focus upon fundamental factors that confirm and integrate aspects of your own life and inner knowingness regarding many of life's most important issues and realities. Your own experiences, beliefs, opinions, and realisations are vastly more real, more sacred, more significantly illuminating to you than even my most treasured, inspirational experiences will be to you.

Please always consciously realise that this is YOUR life story we are discovering here! It is essential that you often pause on this mutual journey of self-discovery to consider, reflect and contemplate upon your own experiences, thoughts, reactions, responses, emotions, opinions, beliefs, perceptions, inner knowingness; as the images of your unique past begin to replay significant aspects of themselves upon your conscious mind and feeling heart. As we communicate here, you will begin to relive and recall some key aspects of your life privately with me. Be absolutely assured that in this process of interaction the ideas and emotions shared between us will remain completely confidential due to the nature of this discussion. Over the course of this communication, you will feel the development of our mutual shared sense of being within the privacy, autonomy and security of your own mind and heart, so that every important thought, realisation and decision will remain based firmly upon your own set of experiences, perceptions and judgements. What is stated here will often trigger memory recalls, mental images and emotions that may have no apparent direct relationship to what subject is being addressed at the time in the discussion. Please allow yourself to periodically 'shut down' your normal mental processes by taking a quick nap, meditating to clear one's mind, contemplating silently on the issues discussed here in relation to your own thoughts and experiences, or simply put the book aside for a while and perhaps go for a walk. Understand this unusual free mental and emotional association within your self is intended to be the situation throughout this communication. In this manner, your state of being can better express its own reality, with these words and ideas only serving to provide some structure and to stimulate the occurrence of that process within us both. This book serves the same purpose in my life as it is intended to serve for you. The cumulative life experiences of countless billions of people throughout history have assisted me greatly in the preparation and presentation of our mutual shared experiences and realisations over the eons of time we human beings have existed on this Earth.

It matters little if you care to believe or even seriously consider what is given here so long as you seek often to pause and think your own thoughts, to feel your own heart and Soul speak to you in the language and emotions that you best understand and respond within your own process of development. This will be our journey together, yet it is your own destination that is the actual reason we are travelling on this path together now, in the form of this shared set of ideals and events. We each will reach our own individual conclusions, learn our own independent lessons, and continually develop according to our own pace, in our own unique ways in this earthly and eternal life. Deep aspects of one's self are eagerly waiting to express themselves through this process. Are you ready to begin the next step in our journey of awakening to the higher aspects within ourselves now, in a way that will ideally improve your daily life and that of those people around you ?

Chapter 1

Living a Better Life

Living a better life is the primary focus of our attention. This will be somewhat different for each individual and community, although key basic simular needs apply that are related to one's circumstances, culture and attitudes.

There are many attitudes, actions, and value systems that (falsely) claim to be done 'in God's name' by various religions, nations, organisations and people.

Throughout human history, divinely inspired Human Beings have brought God's messages of divine love, peace and better ways to live into the public awareness. None of these prophets (falsely) claimed to possess any special divine status that placed them 'above' other Human Beings. They all stated in their own unique ways that our basic birth right as Human Beings is that each of us is Divine Soul; and are all as equals within the Consciousness of God/Creator; regardless of one's creed (beliefs/culture), race (skin colour or genetic traits), gender (sexual status), 'caste' (social/financial status/group/tribe), nation, religion, or age, or Species of life.

The magnificent words of wisdom and the noble deeds exemplified by these monumental spiritual humans have been recorded by others throughout history in religious books, on stone, clay, bone and sacred scrolls for the upliftment, betterment and enlightenment of Humanity. For example, "By their acts, ye (you) will know them." was stated to enable Humanity to be aware of the true ways (deeds/actions) of all life forms, regardless of their words.

In spite of any and all appearances to the contrary, earthly Humanity is now entering a new and better stage of progressive cooperative development in becoming a truly civilised, more peaceful, loving, compassionate Species of life within this Universe.

YOUR states of being; happiness, health, mental/emotional condition, daily lifestyle, social status, appearance, beliefs, profession (or lack of one), financial capabilities and various other aspects of life are most important to YOU !!!

The basic intention of sharing the information in this book is to enable YOU to live a better, happier, more enjoyable, truly meaningful, productive and beneficial life; ideally doing whatever it is that YOU LOVE or like DOING that to some extent benefits you, others and/or earthly environments and causes no harm, detriment or damage to others in the process of your chosen lifestyle.

Obviously, not everyone thinks or acts in this idealistic, utopian, loving, kindly visionary manner within this clearly insane, evil, genocidal, unjust, corrupted, dysfunctional 'world government system' that is now existing upon Earth in 2024.

This first chapter is to clarify specific, proven successful, simple ways that you can achieve greatly improved conditions in every area of YOUR life. This chapter is written to inspire and assist us all with some timely 'truth telling', yet primarily to provide VALUE immediately to the people that only read this 'preface/update' chapter, being unable or unwilling to read the entire book for various reasons.

The listing of a few proven health 'cures' and spiritual 'exercises' are included here for YOUR consideration. These are not issues to debate, or be approved or denied by some corporation, scientific organisation, government agency, university, or religious authorities. They are for

YOU and your family and friends to consider; try or not, as you freely choose over passing time.

Optimum health and longevity with peace of mind, a joyful Spirit while accomplishing meaningful enjoyable activities in harmonious cooperation with others are optional, self-responsible lifestyle choices provided to EACH Soul within Humanity by our Creator. Currently, these pleasant states of being are intentionally being selectively denied, thwarted and aggressively attacked by a predatorial, parasitic, malignant, autocratic, evil, inhumane, murderous, oppressive, genocidal, globalistic, 'corporate system' that assertively seeks to deny and control all basic human rights, eliminate personal freedoms, limit creativity, oppose individuality, deny/ignore the existence of a Creator/God and negate sanity for its' own self-serving purposes. It openly expresses an adversarial intent to prevent one's inner peace, and to forcefully eliminate one's right to make personal or cultural and religious choices that are already granted to us as individual Souls within our existing physical bodies in this particular lifetime on Earth, by our Creator.

For those amazingly wonderful people who still will be reading along here; congratulations to YOU and to ALL of US in Humanity !!!

Our Freedom Day to improve our lives as individuals and as a Species (of 'aggregated humanoid gene pools' or 'useless eaters', as some few evil self-serving 'elite creeps' define Humanity) has finally 'officially' arrived here upon Mother Earth !!!!!

The publication of this book and YOU reading it is one indicative confirmation that these events are actually occurring at this time. YOU reading this book now is a culmination of major and minor miracles. We each have our own unique, 'one and only' life journey, which is eternal and infinite in nature; so let's make the **best** of it.

The entire purported 'mainstream' history of life on this planet is certainly an accumulation of absurd fiction and blatant lies of the self-limiting variety; as some of the information in this book will (falsely) be perceived by people with differing perspectives. Fortunately, we live within a self-evident reality system where 'direct knowing' is attainable with moderate dedicated efforts over passing time. We (as individuals, communities and as Humanity as a global civilisation of diverse cultures) are now deeply into the ongoing process of massively changing our attitudes, perceptions and actions for the betterment of ALL life upon and within Mother Earth.

Let's start with experiencing inner peace with a blissful quiet mind ... 'FREE' of all concerns, worries, fears, resentments, guilt, traumas, dramas, blame, self-loathing, hate, abuse, desires for vengeance or retribution, denial of the obvious, unpleasant imaginings, unkind intentions, greedy gluttonous lustful, 'never enough' tendencies, anger, frustrations, jealousy, limitations and many more of the same types of unpleasant emotions and degrading painful realisations. We clearly perceive the self-evident realities in global earthly societies within every nation and creed upon this beautiful, life-nourishing planet.

Beyond Humanity's normal daily awareness; co-existing here upon, within and relatively nearby the Earth within and beyond this solar system are many so-called "extra-terrestrial' (ET) 'races' commonly known by various descriptive names such as Reptilians, Draconians, Greys, Nordics, Martians, etc. who tend to attempt to dominate earthly conditions for primarily their own benefits and advantage. Those ETs of a spiritual benevolent compassionate nature are far less well-known, yet are vastly more numerous than those mentioned previously, and their amazing abilities can sometimes surpass our wildest imaginations, as many of us already KNOW by our own personal experiences with them.

Additionally, numerous other highly intelligent evolved life forms exist here, yet most are relatively unknown to modern science or Humanity. A few of these Species are being progressively acknowledged; such as 'orbs', or 'nature spirits', devas, 'little people', Forest People/Sasquatch/Yowies, Sea People, inner Earth realm inhabitants, Angels, Fairy

People, Pixies, etc. Many earthly humans choose to basically ignore such 'little-known' realities and deny the existence of unknown Beings and Species of life that also call the Earth 'home'. Whales and porpoise are certainly highly intelligent spiritually-evolved life forms, as are elephants, gorillas, canines, lions, tigers, and many other species of creatures. It is imperatively important that we do NOT 'blindly' attribute human socio-cultural ways, innate tendencies and our various motives, attitudes and self-serving actions upon other Species of life that we do not (yet) know or understand at this point in our evolution of conscious perceptive awareness.

My sharing this widely mixed set of mental/emotional 'imagery' is to clarify the diverse scope of highly-aware life forms that are now living here upon and within the Earth and its' vast uncharted oceans. Can any of us know exactly what the life or consciousness of an ant, or an eagle, or a chimpanzee, an orca, or any other life form actually is; unless we ourselves as Soul in a physical form actually experience it in a lifetime of one's own existence ? Most of us are vastly older Souls than our normal human conscious minds could possible comprehend or acknowledge as even being a possibility. Therefore, the various choices and potential capabilities potentially existing within each and all of us are unlimited by APPLYING one's independent self-will, experiences and unique inherent abilities.

YOU, as a uniquely 'one of a kind' individual Being within a physical body, are an eternally-aware, conscious Divine Soul (the ENTIRE YOU) that can make specific beneficial choices on where and how to apply your mental, emotional, spiritual energetic focus into ACTION within the infinite 'parameters' of Life Itself.

One optional personal choice is to be intent and totally focused upon manifesting various beneficial activities by working upon self-fulfilling plans that improve aspects of one's life to attain ongoing, uplifting, edifying realisations and various progressive life-style developments as being your personal moment-to-moment, relaxing, enjoyable reality.

Or, simply 'go along as you are' and see how that works out for you, which is a reasonable viable option too.

Repeating old patterns of thought and action usually results in more ongoing repetition in habitually 'programmed' routines that are mostly of the self-limiting variety. Many people in all types of living conditions and cultures have simply 'given up' on the idea of creating a 'better life', or never truly had the conscious 'dream' (inner-imagined intention) to improve their circumstances, as though the possibility and methods to accomplish it, does NOT actually exist for them. They primarily accept whatever society and life presents them with as being their 'reality'.

We are 'here together' now with clear mutual intent to IMPROVE the lives of ALL life, by focusing upon improving the ways that Humanity functions on Earth. That process involves you and me.

Most of us that are interested in self-improvement and spiritual unfoldment are already doing some of the things that will be recommended here, or have been previously experienced uniquely within your life, to some extent. Therefore, much of this information and my personal experience will simply be a confirmation and validation of whatever YOU already know, or believe, or have already experienced yourself in various unique ways. If you can derive even one key realisation or benefit that improves your life, and consequently the lives of ALL within Humanity, then this book is meaningful for YOU. Here we go !!!

'Peace of mind' and Spirit is attainable for YOU !!!

Some of us already live 'here' every day, at all times and truly love life deeply.

For the majority of Humanity, this appears to be another 'seemingly impossible dream'. Therefore, let's focus upon what is attainable and worthy of one's efforts.

The experience of inner peace, deep true contentment, joy, feeling 'at-one with all that is', and directly knowing one's divine aspects of love with gratitude by the 'comfort of resting in God's heart', and other gloriously delightful uplifting states of existence, such as 'the Silence', or the Bliss are euphoric types of spiritual (Divine) feelings.

The related benefits of these experiences are among life's most precious cherished gifts, along with good health, intimate human love, affection and earthly happiness. Bliss states of being can be achieved to various degrees of realisation in many of the following ways: sitting quietly reflecting on whatever runs through one's mind for minutes or hours, perhaps with eyes open or closed watching dappled sunlight through moving leaves while observing the vividly colourful patterns on your mind's inner screen; or a more contemplative quieter calm relaxed mind with no inner chatter or distractive mental/emotional imagery or external distractions, as Soul consciousness integrates Itself with daily awareness in an easy-flowing, connected, spontaneous manner.

Other methods include whatever unique spiritual practices that inspire YOU into a wide variety of indescribable inner feelings of bliss, 'at one-ment' within Self as Soul within the human consciousness, peace-filled comfort/relaxation, love for self/others/life, immense gratitude for 'all that is', and deeply loving <u>feeling</u> an interactive, uplifting, powerful, all-encompassing, fulfilling, transformative 'inner connection' with one's Creator that many call "God", by various names.

The spiritual practices that you most enjoy can be varied with new ones that are appealing and beneficial, as will be mentioned here or elsewhere. Many people simply want to feel better without much effort on their part and that may work very well, if that is your intention and are able to manifest it to whatever 'levels' are ideal for you. Some of us wish to excel and continually progressively improve ourselves, as best as we are able, in a relaxed accepting manner over eons of passing time. Regardless of your personal pace, abilities or desires; to align and harmonise one's self with Creator/God is a wise choice, for those choosing freely to do so in patient, perceptive, receptive ongoing ways.

The adverse alternatives of NOT doing so are obviously self-evident everywhere within the 'materialist', 'service to self' types of individuals and cultures now.

God/Creator IS about kindness, peace, respect for all life, gratitude, humility, love and compassion for self and others, with the freedom to be creative, joyful, giving and receiving.

True God/Creator is NOT about endless wars, abuse, murder, drama, discord, terrorism, poverty, suffering, degradation, destruction of the environment, oppressive systems of slavery, deceit, genocide, injustice, corruption, greed and many of the self-evident 'evil' aspects of our 'civilisation' such as over-crowded cities, limited opportunities, dictatorial policies and ineffective, inequitable social and economic systems that urgently need widespread improvement globally.

Because health is a significant aspect of reality that influences everyone, it is inspiring to be able to share a few 'cures' that work well for others, without endorsing any specific products or companies. A few proven successful ones will be listed here for your consideration, yet unlimited others are being discovered and proven daily, so please do 'research the research' as you wish or need.

Simply knowing that others have successfully fully 'recovered' from illnesses that were purportedly 'deemed' to be "incurable" is very encouraging and edifying. These common diseases include; arthritis, cancer, heart disease, obesity, diabetes, depression, high-anxiety or 'panic attacks', suicidal and self-abusive tendencies, addictions to harmful substances and virtually every type of disease and health misfortune; including being comatose or declared 'officially dead' in some amazing cases. One's healing could result from a simple mental, emotional, spiritual or lifestyle adjustment; such as not allowing external circumstances or other's opinions and actions to adversely affect one in detrimental unpleasant ways. Some healings occur due to a powerful life-altering realisation, or even a fortunate amazing miracle that triggers healing to occur.

At about age 63, I was diagnosed by my doctor of 30 years as having arthritis in many joints from years of basketball and intense manual labour. I was told the weakness in my body was normal and would continue to worsen. It did indeed worsen from relatively mild stiffness to much more severe and undeniable weakness and discomfort. A few falls onto the rocks and over passing time circumstances deteriorated to the extent that I found it difficult to hold the relatively light weight of a full 1 litre drink bottle of water. By then I knew I was in real trouble and was only able to climb stairs x1 at a time.

The grinding, clicking and popping in my weak knees was a real problem. I lived in a remote location about 20 kilometres from town, where I had to walk home from where I parked my vehicle, 'off the grid' nearly x1 kilometre uphill, over uneven mountainous terrain, across three creek crossings, often in the dark by flashlight with enough food in my backpack for several days to a week. I lived (and happily live now) in a comfortable large tent covered by a strong good tarp to remain dry and shaded under nice nearby trees that I had planted there 30 years earlier. Here in Queensland, Australia it is a tropical climate where it never freezes, so I am very fortunate in many ways.

In earlier years, my adult children had kindly reminded me that when I was unable to care for myself, that I would be immediately going into an 'aged-care facility'. I had clearly understood and totally agreed; so that upsetting possibility was the only motivation required to become increasingly focused upon health solutions to my worsening arthritis, loss of cartilage and mildly diminishing brain functions. The evidence for the causes of my 'suffering' were primarily; inadequate nutrition, over-exposure to multiple sources of harmful man-made radiations, cumulative internal poisons such as mercury from my teeth fillings, other toxic metals and environmental poisons, stress, rotten teeth, pathogenic microbes (like parasites, intestinal worms, etc.), Candida and many others that are too numerous and annoying to list here. The many detrimental unhealthy conditions that are adversely influencing most of us now upon Earth are well-known to Humanity, as are the vast number of potential cures.

My experienced doctor did the standard medical procedures and confirmed that x2 knee replacements would be required. There was virtually no cartilage in my knees, so the chance of them locking or collapsing was increasingly likely, as the x-rays showed in detail. By the time I was able to see the 'specialist' doctor; it was about x3 months later. I was curious what he would say or do, as my knees were already feeling significantly BETTER due to natural health remedies I had been creating myself by blending many ingredients together in a food processor. These inexpensive, natural items included; fresh ginger, garlic, turmeric, cinnamon, coconut oil, black and red pepper, sea salt, lemon and lime juiced, onions of several types, and a few other anti-inflammation, high-nutrition herbs, such as moringa tree powder and small amounts of highly-beneficial apple cider vinegar, olive oil, etc. and ingesting and/or applying them in a topical manner daily.

The additional other key other thing I did, was begin taking an extract tincture (only about x5 drops per day) of a native Australian medicinal tree called 'Gumby Gumby' tree (scientific name *Pittosorum angustifollum*), which seemed to help noticeably within only a few DAYS !!! Gumby Gumby extracts of a quality type do help improve overall health, vitality, mental/emotional function, etc. Thanks to the supplier of my Gumby Gumby extract, I am now growing about x50 Gumby Gumby trees from seeds they generously supplied to me at no cost. They are located in Rockhampton, Australia and ship globally. Their kindness will be returned (ideally soon), as they have been creating a natural safe health product range from Gumby Gumby trees for decades to help many people. The Gumby Gumby topical salve is excellent for skin problems and relieves pain too.

Those ongoing humanitarian efforts qualify as being a viable project that is worthy of humanitarian aid funding, as are others who are helping Humanity in various ways. Gumby Gumby helps improve health and has been proven to safely assist the body in 'curing' (into "remission" ha ha !!!) cancer and other serious diseases that other 'medically prescribed' treatments fail to help improve at all.

I also began to consciously <u>avoid exposure to radiation</u> from various sources, as such as my phone, computers, etc. that is virtually impossible in today's highly contaminated, man-made radiation 'energy fields'; so using crystals (tourmaline, quartz, etc.) and other forms of energetic protection are very helpful. I'm <u>not</u> recommending wearing a pyramid-shaped silver hat with a propeller on top; however, those could become self-identifying 'trendy fashion statements', as could 'funny face' masks become good 'fun fashion statements' for some 'real oddballs'.

A key herbal extract that I began making is 'full spectrum' CBD oil made from quality outdoor, organically-grown cannabis. I was unable to financially afford or locate reliable suppliers of quality CBD oil, so we began to research and experiment with various methods of processing over a few years. We now use a low-temperature extraction method of under 45C degrees and above 40C degrees, using MCT oil that is a quality organic oil derived from 'cold-pressed' coconuts. The finely processed herbal material, which can be fresh or dried, is 'cooked' and occasionally stirred for about 40+ hours to accomplish a reliable 'slow extraction' method. It can be extended and/or placed into direct sunlight, with crystals for additional potency and enhanced energetic qualities. Various other processing methods exist at higher temperatures, etc. The increase of healthy oils in my diet with many natural phyto-nutrients evidently created a healing 'entourage effect' of these synergistically beneficial, immune-boosting nutritional ingredients; so significant definitive improvement had already occurred within the x3 months of self-applied health treatments BEFORE my appointment with the specialist doctor to further assess the condition of both my knees.

The specialist doctor was accompanied by x2 medical students for the examination. I did NOT mention how much better my knees and I were feeling, to see what he had to observe. Before the exam in greeting me, he immediately asked, "How are you feeling?" and I pleasantly replied, "Much better." He looked at me with incredulous disbelief, and had a sideways glance at the students, as they thought and could SEE: "Here we have 'another one', with missing teeth and a 'care less' attitude, who obviously smokes cannabis regularly, that is a self-evident poverty-case 'dope head' (misfit/retard), who is obliviously in denial".

He proficiently did a thorough knee examination within minutes and progressively became increasingly confused; repeatedly looking at the x-rays he already had for months. He then had me to do a few increasingly strenuous leg exercises, touching the knees as they moved, while 'listening with his fingers' for the grinding, clicking and popping noises that used to occur with every movement. There was very little of it. The strength in my entire body was back to about 40% of reasonable previous capacity, which for me was fantastic, as the decline required many years of slow deterioration to be at about 10% (or less) of my original physical capabilities.

Within about 10 minutes, he plainly and honestly said, "You no longer require the knee replacements. Whatever you are doing ... (I try to tell him and he stops me from doing so) ... keep doing it." His quick response was very revealing for those x4 of us attending. Before I could say more than to thank him for the great unexpected news, I was out of the room and on my way home feeling very relieved and happy.

What really helped my improving health (increased alkalinity) most at that point in time was NOT yet in my life. Please allow us to digress as I explain how this key information has 'come into' my normal daily conscious awareness by a series of synchronous events and clearly 'delivered' intuitions that are seemingly divinely inspired or intentionally created by Creator/Source/God for our benefits.

Intuition (quiet inner 'voice' of truth, reason, wisdom and protection) has been a blessing of enhanced awareness and perception in my life from a young age. Intuition (inner knowing) has 'saved me' repeatedly, so I DO listen attentively when It 'speaks' inwardly (not audible to my ordinary hearing or to others nearby), as that only occurs in times of need and personal benefit. Intuition has never 'steered me wrong' and It never 'speaks' unless there is a specific timely need or benefit to doing so. The amazing ways intuition functions are simple, reliable, and subtle, yet definitive to those familiar with Its functions. Ideally, you will know exactly what I am referring to about intuition within your own life.

If not, then you can with effort over passing time, acquire these and other capabilities. Life will present its realities to the astute receptive attentive patient observer.

Because enhanced/expanded perception is among the qualities of character that occur among spiritually aware people/beings; I habitually apply my full attention to all events and people around me. My social interactions are relatively limited and it has been a life-long tendency that serves me well. Being somewhat introverted while observing reality closely does divert my attention into unwanted areas of reality at times. Inner balance with relaxed attentive focus is required and the cumulative benefits and advantages are substantial and pervasive.

Quite unexpectedly in x1 day I got x2 different reliable sources of information that were unrelated to one another; BOTH basically saying that 'baking soda' (also known as 'bi-carb soda', as one gets at the grocery store for cleaning/cooking) had a very beneficial effect upon eliminating arthritis, cramps and many other disease conditions. Both times that the information came to my attention that day (hours apart), intuition immediately simply inwardly said, "Do it."

Ok, I did it daily and in x3 WEEKS ... seriously, in only x3 weeks, I was walking down the mountain to my vehicle and suddenly realised that I felt as though I was walking on cushions or soft padding of some type. There was NO pressure feeling upon my knees or legs and my gait was longer, stronger, and more well-balanced and springy, with no grinding or clicking with each movement !!!

Astounded and perplexed, I immediately stopped walking and felt the knees for the usual moderate grinding or clicking as I flexed them in every direction, doing my own quick exam; well-aware and deeply grateful in knowing they had been improving for months. There was absolutely NO noise or weakness in any of my joints. My feet and ankles felt as though they were 'cushioned' somehow and vastly stronger than only weeks before. I would have estimated being at nearly 70% of original capacity, although it seems untrue even to my own assessments at this time. 50% is likely to be more generous than fully accurate. What is far more unusual and inexplicable is my ability to move very large rocks, as well as daily volumes that I would never have attempted in my youth, with ease and no soreness resulting from the activities, while building my 'peace foundations' to create flat areas on my land.

In more recent times, nearly x5 YEARS into the over-all healing processes with the many ongoing health challenges that we ALL are experiencing now; I am doing exceedingly well in all ways, as evidenced by my enhanced happiness and physical abilities. We can all improve our mental, emotional, physical, spiritual self.

Some of the unnecessary, adversely-integrated, exponentially-increasing health challenges that are now confronting Humanity are: the intentional over-exposure to harmful man-made radiations (radar, microwaves, radio waves, x-rays etc.), environmental poisons (chemtrails, toxic food/water additives, residual poisons, and widespread use of neuro-toxins such as artificial sweeteners, MSG, chlorine, aluminium. mercury, lead, fluoride, etc.), harmful pharmaceutical drugs and ineffective medical procedures, over-crowding within stressful anxiety-producing unpleasant living conditions, etc. These are the detrimental aspects of society that we seek to IMPROVE !!! Others are focused upon manifesting scarcity, disease, misery, discord, conflict and evil autocratic control for self-serving materialistic motives.

In 2021 I finished carrying countless basket loads of rocks into building my 5th 'peace foundation' to create flat sitting and living areas on steep mountain slopes. Much to my delight, it was completed as a big fun job that took me about one year, working at least several days per week from between only an hour or two, to almost all day whenever I (rarely) felt like doing so. This large construction of many tons of stacked 'rubble' rocks confirms my healing processes at age 68 now. Arthritis and excessive weakness are GONE !!! Full function is at about 80% of my youthful abilities; however, realistically there are no reasonably accurate, verifiable comparisons. I recently finished my 1st 'peace and prosperity pathway' that is x33 metres in length and it progressed much faster than the others, as the rocks were mostly already in piles, segregated from the nearby artifacts and crystals.

Additional physiological confirmations of my definite improvement are that I am again playing chess, basketball, playing in pool shooting tournaments, running, skipping my 'heavy rope', stretching, swimming and body surfing, jogging in soft sand and other fun and meditative activities without any weakness, discomfort or soreness after my moderate 'fitness training' lifestyle. I have another health challenge in that I was poisoned in September 2021 by a little-known (thallium) toxic substance(s) that had the same x9 symptoms as arsenic poisoning, including about 90% loss of feeling (neuropathy) below my knees. Evidently zeolite is good for detoxification, so we will see. Whatever YOUR challenges are; simply trust that you can resolve and improve them over passing time, with effort and wisdom.

Here (to follow) are a few of the many obvious health benefits that I and others have experienced by regularly using the mixture of baking soda (bicarb soda) x1 teaspoon, with 100% pure maple syrup (x1+ tablespoon to taste) mixed in drinking water (500ml) on empty stomach in the morning, to basically increase the alkalinity within their body. The quality pure baking soda sold in health food shops is far superior and tastes better than the inferior (somewhat toxic) baking soda that is available in grocery stores. I sometimes also add 'diatomaceous earth' (powdered sea shells that are beneficial in detoxification) of about a half of x1 teaspoon and about x5 drops of 'stabilised oxygen' to this mixture for additional benefits in blood flow, detoxification, better immune function, along with various herb teas, and herbal extracts, etc. You may create your own uniquely useful health mixtures, as you learn more, by adding crystals, flower essences, essential oils, herbal infusions and other energetic technologies, such as 'violet ray tube' types of healing devices, to YOUR healing remedies.

An increase in the alkalinity (pH) of the body (if it is too acidic, as modern 'diets' and lifestyles create) evidently 'prompts' the following physiological benefits: (1) allows the red blood cells to carry more healthy oxygen throughout the body, (2) improved inner-cellular communication with greatly enhanced immune activities, (3) reduced inflammation, (4) more energy, (5) deeper better sleep with awakening more 'refreshed', alert and feeling better in every way, (6) enhanced relaxation states of being, so a reduction in tension and stress occurs naturally, (7) safely reduces/eliminates internal pathogenic micro-organisms of many types, (8) creates an 'oxygen rich' internal physiological environment that is NOT conducive to cancer and other disease states, such as poor blood flow, poor elimination of waste from the body, gout, inner tension, anxiety, depression, etc. (9) regrowth of cartilage in all joints to various extents, (10) improved mental and emotional function, with eyesight, hearing and other debilitated physical conditions can also recover (somewhat), (11) diminished 'brain fog' and less prevalent forgetfulness or dementia symptoms will occur in most people, especially over months and years of regular moderate use, (12) greater clarity of perception, thought and focus, among many additional self-evident benefits, (13) skin looks better and feels smoother, hair and nails grow faster, sores heal faster, enhanced sense of well-being, others comment that you are looking well, etc. that YOU may experience over passing time and improving circumstances.

Recently a new herb came to my attention, named very appropriately Self Heal (scientific name: *Prunella vulgaris* and has 28+ 'common names' and various sub-species), which is growing wild on my land and abundantly in the surrounding areas. It is a perennial (grows more than a year or more survives winter in temperate climates) and the research of the research indicates it as being among the best of the best self-healing herbs growing upon Earth. Another of the best is turmeric, which contains curcumin and many other beneficial plant compounds that reduce inflammation possesses countless additional health benefits. Another three are cinnamon, Ginkgo biloba, and Olive Leaf extract (*Olea europaea*). These and countless more are readily available to all and probably growing nearby you, so you can grow YOUR favourites. Most medicinal herbs or underground 'bulbs', like garlic, ginseng and ginger, grow easily from 'seed' and are not 'pest' types of plants.

It seems to be divinely synchronous that this amazing healing plant information, along with it growing upon my land and nearby would 'present itself' to me and now to you and your family, friends and associates. The first batch of Self Heal extract using moderate heat (over 60C to under 100C) using MCT oil (derived from coconuts) has proven to be excellent and will be ideal to mix with both Gumby Gumby and CBD oil extracts for the optimum results in healing the body safely, reliably and relatively rapidly in ideal situations. The lower temperature extraction method used for CBD oil seems to be preferable to the higher temperature, yet thorough ongoing testing needs to occur. Another declared 'pest' with amazing immune boosting medicinal properties is 'cat's claw vine' (bark and roots are used for many healing remedies) that is native to the Amazon rainforest and also is growing prolifically near my land in Australia and maybe growing somewhere near you too.

Traditional confirmed health benefits of Self Heal include: Chinese herbalists consider Self Heal useful for changing the course of chronic diseases for the better. It can be an expectorant (useful for lung problems and improved oxygenation of the entire body); reducing inflammation throughout the body, and thereby significantly reducing pain in many people, assists female reproductive disorders and thereby improves intercellular communication; as a skin treatment, astringent, antiseptic, with proven antibacterial effects; treat colic, stomach upsets and gastroenteritis; internally used as tea for sore throats, fevers, wounds, internal bleeding and weakness of the heart and liver, as well as improving health within the overall intestinal and circulatory (blood and lymph) systems. Interestingly, it is also reducing symptoms of dementia in some older people, as well as diminishing 'brain fog' and improving health in some younger people. It is abundant in Vitamins A, C and K as well as having many (unknown) phytonutrients, flavonoids and alkaloids, and includes thiamine, rutin, betulinic acid, rosmarinic acid, myristic acid and (bitter) tannins (that can be moderated by washing leaves in water before use).

I had intended to list many of the most effective beneficial herbs and trees (there are thousands globally), yet other significant topics here are higher priorities. Likewise effective is the use of the thousands of crystals and minerals that have healing and beneficial effects, as do plant and flower essences, essential oils, and countless energetic healing technologies and modalities. Do YOUR own research of the research and join us in making your own improving health and happiness an ongoing priority in your life.

Our intention is to shift one's focus of daily attention toward optimising health, improving one's dietary choices, while reducing or eliminating disease creating substances and conditions from one's lifestyle choices, if necessary. Additionally, to do meditation and deep breathing for stress relief and better oxygenation along with one's regular daily spiritual practices creates enhanced peace of mind and happiness. There is no benefit to waiting until one already has heart disease, cancer, auto-immune diseases, obesity or is chronically depressed or anxiety debilitated before applying these simple, safe, inexpensive, readily available and easily applicable health and 'peace of mind' solutions.

Now that we have considered a few aspects of physical healing, let's briefly delve into how one can reliably experience inner peace, healthy self-love with self-respect, true joy, gratitude and a genuinely enthusiastic exuberant love of life. I generally refer to these uplifting inner conditions as being in one's Bliss states of existence within daily life. These relaxed calm inner feelings do NOT rely upon positive peace-filled external circumstances to reliably experience, acknowledge and benefit by FEELING 'the Bliss' inwardly.

As a member of Eckankar, my spiritual path for over 30 years, we sing 'Hu' (aloud or silently), which is an ancient name for God/Creator. This enjoyable relaxing Hu song helps harmonise one with Divinity and Mother Earth vibrations to various degrees over passing time. Divine 'grace' will assist one in their progressive 'endless' spiritual journey, every step of the way. We 'quiet the mind' of one's own inner chatter by focusing upon singing the Hu (Hhhhhuuuuuuu that is pronounced like the name Hugh, or the word 'hue') in a long drawn-out manner, on the out-breath, with one's inner attention upon the colours and images visible 'inwardly' via the '3rd eye' above/between the physical eyes in a relaxed attentive manner. This can be an active contemplative progressive process of ongoing spontaneous discovery, applied to experience inner peace, an inner connection with the Divine, or sung aloud or silently in times of need, or pain or suffering of any type, or with people whose Soul is in the process of leaving their physical body; for a few moments, or lengthy periods of time, or as a daily experience for as long as you wish to continue the (silent or audible) Hu Song.

Many cumulative benefits occur within the divine relationship that develops of its' own accord throughout this ongoing process. It is simple and can be done a few times when stressed or 'in danger', or regularly for extended time periods (20 minutes is ideal for some, yet others such as myself, find this far too lengthy and tedious), as you wish and feel comfortable. You will experience various levels of awareness and definitive confirming indications of YOUR expanding consciousness and enhanced 'direct knowing' capabilities, in due course. Attentive receptive patience without any specific expectations, while 'letting go' ('releasing'/transformation of one's 'little ego self'), to 'let God' develop one as Soul via the human body experiences, is a wise way into this expansive miraculous realm of 'higher', more all-inclusive reality.

Or, ignore that and watch plenty tv, play with your devices, take your mandatory vaccinations as often as the evil genocidal creeps want and see how things go.

Another beneficial connection/relaxation technique involves enjoying more time in nature; IF the annoying biting insects are not eating you alive, ha ha !!!!

By observing life closely in nature or doing things you love and enjoy doing, one can easily soon experience heightened states of being more inwardly/deeply connected with Source/Creator/God and all nature that is in harmony with It. The best confirmation is the quieting of one's inner mental chatter, and/or the end to relentless self-questioning and/or being overly-critical of one's self/others, and/or requesting prayers of divine assistance and the manifestation of preferred life events, as some people are prone to do for obvious reasons. This process awakens one as Soul, while the normal human mind consciousness gradually (or rapidly, or in variable cycles, as your situations may be) reduces its' 'control' or domination of one's overall conscious states of being aware upon a moment to moment basis. Soul consciousness gradually becomes increasingly more relevant, noticeable and applicable within normal daily life through the progressive, yet often-reluctant 'acceptance' of the conscious mind.

For example, in such states of being, one would be vastly LESS prone to 'replay' previously occurring events of a traumatic or unpleasant nature, or concern one's self with the dire purported events that are threatening to destroy life on Earth, or other distractive, temporal, relatively meaningless/irrelevant hypothetical events within one's mind repetitively, along with the 'attached' emotional content. How many typical Hollywood movies or tv/internet advertisements can you watch and endure before you have simply 'had enough' ?!!

By placing the focus of your attention basically upon your nature as eternal Soul that is now consciously aware within your existing human body, that is patiently seeking to inwardly 'connect with' your Creator/Source, then you simply 'be' and 'see' what happens. Sometimes it will be a relaxing, ordinary-seeming event without any discernable results. However, at other times there may be amazing expansion of consciousness experiences or other miraculous events that occur; such as seeing orbs, getting amazing realisations, deep gratitude for life's many blessings, or feeling the incredible Divine Love and/or Bliss. This calm, joyful, contented, relaxed, peace-filled state of being could be accompanied by beautiful inner musical or energetic soothing sounds, bright vivid colours and images of unlimited variety, as you and divinity merge in various ways. These 'higher' states of being help shift your inner focus OUT of the usual limited, self-deceptive states of being that normal human social conditions tend to evoke within many of us by subtle, yet pervasive methods. You can literally journey into the unknown within yourself, and then do so externally as well, as we are doing here now.

Another technique is to know that as Soul existing within a human form, YOU exist WITHIN Source/Creator/God. Therefore, with sincere trusting ongoing receptive patient intent and energetic harmonious capability; YOU can consciously 'connect with' Divine energies and 'frequencies of being' that enable you to 'encompass' ('draw in') these Divine energies (also known as 'the Holy Spirit', 'ECK', or 'prana') into yourself in much the same way (energetically) as one would drink water or eat food to nourish one's physical body. Divine energies are highly beneficial and transformative !!!

Reality Therapy Experiences

Throughout my current lifetime from a very early age as an American, there have been many unique circumstances that have fortunately and inexplicably provided my inquisitive, highly observant, perceptive, deductive traits as a relatively aware person with a vast amount of valid, undeniable, verified, well-integrated information about the entire scope of activities occurring upon and within Earth, from the 'civilised human' perspectives. (However, it is a 'relative thing' Ha ha !!!)

This bold, curious, seemingly unsubstantiated, unlikely statement is NOT simply an egoistic, wishful, supposition, nor a haughty opinion, or a fictitious lie being applied here to exaggerate my access to information and direct personal experiences that surpasses my comprehensive understanding at the magnitude of it all. I have many sources and ways of accessing information, primarily by 'direct knowing' methods.

These facts are provided here to preface the following information that was kindly provided to me by my father, Lt. Col. 'Doc' Wonders (retired/deceased) USAF, SAC (Strategic Air Command). Dad astutely decided to share the following key information as he lay painfully upon his deathbed in Roswell, New Mexico; being 'eaten alive' by cancers caused from exposure to Agent Orange, nuclear contamination, years of alcoholism, and a 'hurting heart' that was being continually ravaged mentally and emotionally by what America had clearly become, with Bill Clinton as the then 'acting' President of the USA in about 1999.

He wisely shared these almost unbelievable FACTS with considerable emotion, focusing intently while speaking his astounding TRUTHS with firm, brave, succinct conviction through the emaciated 'shell' of the shrunken body that still housed his great astute capable Spirit. "Son, if you ever SEE the U.S. military attacking its' OWN PEOPLE, then you MUST first speak YOUR TRUTH, and then you must DO something, but stay AWAY from the people with guns."

As these highly unexpected, shocking and seemingly incomprehensible ideas and unbelievable words entered my unprepared consciousness; I immediately thought he was deluded by his painful suffering, his tragic experiences in Vietnam as Commander of AWACs during 1967/68 and other traumatic things that he had experienced. I immediately DOUBTED the validity, veracity and sanity of his clear, succinct message. This memorable event was BEFORE 9/11 in New York and Washington D.C., before countless other acts of 'state sponsored' terrorism, before Hurricane Katrina in New Orleans, or the wars in Iraq, Libya, Syria, Somalia, etc. This event was during the totally corrupt, self-evident 'war of drugs' upon the American people, started well-before the Reagan administration. This deathbed testimony pre-dated many other self-evident genocidal, 'war crimes' by the USA, Israel, and their 'allies' of 'state sponsored' terrorism, unjust wars, government and corporate frauds and theft in monumental proportions, such as the 'savings and loan' (banking) and the 'fixed' corrupted stock, bullion and Fx market frauds involving members of the Bush family and their associates internationally. Listing these proven financial crimes, such as in Iraq would require many pages and we will identify some of the major ones here, in brief form as we proceed.

Please allow me to digress to provide additional information to help PROVE my Dad was an impeccable, valid source of reliable information on all issues related to the U.S. military and government. Dad was first stationed in Roswell, New Mexico after joining the U.S. Air Force (USAF) in about 1950 to do his initial pilot training. While there he met and married my mother Ann, a long-time local resident. After completing his pilot training program, Doc was assigned to duties related to UFO field investigations. I only learned about his UFO research activities many decades later when I was asked by USAF (Retired) Col. Jim and Coral Lorenzen, the Directors of the Aerial Phenomena Research Organization (APRO) located in Tucson, Arizona to, "Please ask your Dad about the Roswell UFO crash in 1947".

At the time, it was in the early 1980's and my parents had already retired from the USAF and permanently settled in Roswell. My role in APRO was as their "Field Investigator" with numerous duties being assigned to me over the nearly 8 years that I worked closely with them from Baton Rouge, Louisiana. Later, I moved to Tucson to finish some of my APRO assignments there and to read all of the approximately 20,000 UFO related case files in their possession to analyse the data of over x30 year's scientific research and witness testimonies to gain a relatively comprehensive assessment of the phenomena. I was assigned to write and conduct a UFO related opinion survey (300 respondents) and also organise a UFO book with about 12 prominent knowledgeable UFO authors, each writing one chapter upon their primary area of expertise.

My 'assigned' chapter, as a sociologist with a Bachelor of Science Degree from LSU in 1976, was titled, "The Socio-cultural Implications of UFO Phenomena" and it was 24 pages in length. Neither the UFO Survey, nor the APRO UFO Book were ever published because "Humanity is not (yet) ready for these truths." according to the Lorenzens. They both soon died of cancer. That dismissive, curiously self-evident, unfortunate attitude and their apparent intentional mis-application of my diligent efforts disappointed me greatly at the time and assisted my decision to immigrate permanently to Australia in 1986.

My first interactions with APRO were with Coral Lorenzen by letter and phone related to Billy Meir, the experienced Swiss UFO researcher who was in possession of hundreds of quality UFO photos and videos. The Lorenzens confirmed the case was genuine and they had direct ongoing communications with Billy. We progressively gained one another's confidence through many ongoing investigations and amazing UFO related events, such as the Travis Walton case in Arizona and others too numerous to mention here. The Lorenzens also were in direct communication with Betty and Barney Hill for many years. At the time, APRO was the most professional, capable and well-informed 'civilian' UFO research organisation globally and existed for about 33 years.

After about 5 years proving my reliability, I was assigned the official role as the APRO "Field Investigator" whereby the Lorenzens provided me with introductions to reputable knowledgeable UFO researchers and organisations internationally that 'contributed' their personal 'off the public record' reports and testimony regarding their OWN personal UFO experiences. I too had countless such inexplicable, yet definitive UFO events occurring in many locations. I also heard amazing testimony among people I already knew, such as them saying "I thought you were crazy saying things about UFOs (as they had never seen one previously), but we do believe you now", after seeing an undeniable one. Also people seemed prone to volunteer their UFO experiences or convey stories told to them by others, such as by reliable family or friends, or heard about locally; wherever I travelled internationally. APRO enabled me to associate with highly aware Directors of other UFO groups internationally (and independent UFO researchers) to confirm the scope of their organisation's reports and their own personal experiences for 'background' and information integration purposes. Those events would be worthy of a book in themselves.

A revealing statistic the Lorenzens kindly provided to me follows: By extrapolating statistical data of only the publicly reported confirmed INEXPLICABLE UFO events (less than 5% of total reported possible UFO sightings), then including the minimal under-reported UFO-related statistics (where no 'official' UFO reports are made to public authorities), they concluded there were "at least 25 MILLION seemingly authentic UFO types of 'reports' within only the past 100 years globally".

They defined UFO types of events as being similar to those recorded in their case files, then included authentic historical documents, such as the Bible, UFOs and ETs being visible in old paintings, descriptions of alien races and advanced technologies written about in ancient scrolls, historical books, ancient drawings, stone and clay tablets, rock carvings, etc. They estimated that only a small percentage of the actual total number of UFO sightings were ever publicly recorded, so they calculated a vastly higher number of sightings, landings, crashes and definitive UFO-related cases had definitely happened over recorded history. This was definitely NOT a recent series of inexplicable UFO types of events. This establishes a fact there are BILLIONS of unknown events occurring, that we can acknowledge, with a vastly larger unknown number occurring beyond our comprehension or abilities to make a thorough accurate assessment.

In my role as 'Field Investigator' for APRO, I learned that EVERY UFO researcher that I spoke with (at least 10, yet 20 would be an under-estimate) had experienced multiple UFO sightings PERSONALLY themselves, many from a close range. Additionally, some researchers acknowledged they had additional 'encounters' they preferred to remain private, by saying 'there was more they did NOT care to discuss with me'. I always accepted their responses, as I had similar experiences myself. Many were definitely "inexplicable" or at least unknown types of events with no reasonable explanation being possible. These do include 'missing time' with no apparent lapses in conscious awareness, with or without UFOs being visible at the time. Others report having lengthy-seeming events happen within very short time periods that defy comprehension or explanation. For example, a person would be taken to another planet to visit for days, months or years; then be returned to Earth and find that virtually no time had passed since they departed and were 'returned'. These types of events are inexplicable, unless the 'visitors' possessed time travel or 'portal' capabilities. Many of these UFO 'sightings' were from within distances of less than 100 metres to much further away, such as some reported by pilots and astronauts, law enforcement, military personnel, etc. that definitively were identified by expert witnesses to be reliably classified within the 'unknown' category because they did 90 degree turns at enormous speeds, disappearing, re-appearing, silent flight while hovering, impossible changes in appearance, speeds, light, colour, etc., as sometimes confirmed by radar and multiple reliable witnesses. My experience of growing up as a child in the USAF enabled me to identify planes relatively easily and usually differentiate them from UFO types of activities. Some reported being taken aboard these UFOs for various purposes, including flights into outer space and experiencing various types of unknown alien beings that were interacting with them using telepathy, who were in possession of amazing technological devices and other abilities.

When I asked Dad about the Roswell UFO crash, I had never heard of it as it was before the case had re-entered the public awareness in the early 1980's. He immediately confirmed that it had happened before he arrived in Roswell, and that he flew with 'Pappy' Henderson for many years. Pappy confirmed privately that he had flown the UFO wreckage from Roswell to Wright-Patterson Air Force Base and that small 'grey' aliens' bodies had been recovered dead, with one still being alive. From various such 'reports', Doc was able to obtain from other military personnel there at the time the crash site(s) was 'sanitised' by the U.S. military located in Roswell (about 50km from the primary crash site), he knew it was real although he had not been there at the time.

Nuclear weapon research and experimental bomb detonation activities were occurring in New Mexico at various locations before, during and after World War 2. Dad told me that his security oath prevented him from telling me any specific information about the Roswell UFO case, or any events during his time doing UFO field investigations as a military officer. He confirmed the entire subject of UFOs as being 'Above Top Secret'. Instead, he provided me with a book on the event and said, "This is as close to the truth about what happened at Roswell in 1947 as you will ever get, so read it." I am tempted to mention the title of the book, yet for those people 'in the know', they will already be aware of the book that I refer to here, implicitly as being the basic truths about Roswell UFO crash(es) near Roswell. This is only one example of information that has come to my attention that is related to UFO activity in relation to the USAF and its' complicity with some 'agencies' within the U.S. government.

Dad then referred me to the USAF Public Information Officer (retired), who lived nearby in Roswell, who (reluctantly at first) then shared the information that the event was real and had ruined his military career. After our discussion, years later he founded and opened the Roswell UFO Museum. Know the Roswell UFO 'crash' case is real.

Additionally, I recall in years earlier, after I was in university, Dad told me about a few revealing events from his 'tour of duty' in Vietnam as the Commander of AWACs during the Tet Offensive in early 1968. I already knew that Dad had been emotionally damaged by unknown circumstances that lead to the end of his military career relatively abruptly in 1969. He immediately retired prematurely and went to work with General Wade (retired) in Louisiana to reduce corruption within the State Police there (??!!). I was curious to know more, so he shared some facts that I had no way to know otherwise. In about 1974 I may have asked him something akin to, "Why did the USA not win the Vietnam war ?" while we were watching a football game on tv at Christmas. Dad and I did NOT do a lot of talking in those days, thankfully for us both ha ha !!

This is when I began to obtain 'lower-level', 'top secret' information that was beyond my ability to assess it, as corroborative information was not available then to the extent that such information is known to some aware people within the public domain in 2024. To share some of this information now is relevant to providing more potent, subsequent, timely examples of these types of information that has come to my attention from many many many reliable, well-informed, honest people upon an international basis for the past 45 years.

Dad was initially reluctant to share his personal experiences in Vietnam with me. The emotional process when I briefly visited Roswell every year from Louisiana for Christmas reminded me of how I was feeling; looking backwards into the past times. I clearly recalled at the age of about 12 when Dad was standing on the windswept, almost vacant military runway with the family, wishing my Mother and younger brother and I to have a good year while he was away in Vietnam. There were NO hugs and kisses for the boys, only a firm handshake and then he was gone, to fly himself to Vietnam on the nearby military Lear jet. He had volunteered a 'tour of duty' in Vietnam shortly after the 'sudden' retirement of the 'four star' USAF General David Wade. Dad had served as pilot and Aide for over 15 years, while General Wade was the Commander of the Strategic Air Command (SAC), which included the U.S. nuclear weapons capabilities, B-52s, and various other advanced weapon systems.

Dad said these memorable, yet confusing words to us all, standing there 'at attention' wearing our little suits with skinny ties, with Mom trying her best not to burst out in hysterical crying as she had been recently diagnosed with breast cancer, with Dad saying directly to us boys, "I am going to do my service and hopefully you boys' service as well."

I was totally confused and baffled at his parting comment to us; thinking silently to myself, "I am only 12 years old now, so does he think the Vietnam war will still be going on when I turn 18 ?" Please understand that the 6 years before I became 18 was the equivalent of half of my entire life at that time.

I was very surprised, somewhat shocked actually; to hear those words coming out of his mouth while standing on the military runway, feeling it to be seemingly impossible, or surreal or untrue. This feeling is very similar to the feeling and awareness I have now in regard to our 'point of discussion' here. Currently, the covid fraud and 'war crimes' against Humanity are occurring globally to further apply fascist autocratic military rule according to the evil, corrupted, inequitable, self-serving, war-mongering, terrorist-sponsoring 'New World Order' (NWO) nazi-style/communist methodologies that President George Bush(s) had bragged about years ago, that are progressively becoming increasingly true and self-evident now.

I had always staunchly REFUSED to consider the military (or 'law enforcement') as a potential occupation. This firm decision from about age 4 was much to the dismay, annoyance and chagrin (embarrassment and frustration) of both my parents, who 'planned' a successful military career within the USAF for both my younger brother and I, as officer military pilots. Their vision included us ideally becoming USAF generals someday; thereby 'serving' to manifest American-style 'freedom', throughout the world by whatever methods were required to do so. I wanted nothing to do with killing people, nor wearing uniforms, nor marching, or standing 'at attention', 'taking orders', or such things. By inwardly resisting the social agenda relentlessly applied upon me by my loving parents and an impersonal predatorial-seeming society; I progressively developed self-direction, inner awareness, perceptive, inquisitive, self-confident, 'no nonsense', spiritually focused character. My military upbringing definitely did influence me in various ways, yet I have never killed, aggressively attacked, nor raped anyone.

Years later after Dad had retired, he gradually 'found' his 'inner peace' with the deep true love that he and my mother shared; and the prominent role socially within the Roswell community, where Ann served as President of the Roswell Symphony for at least 10 years. He quietly applied his 'medicine of choice', his daily alcohol consumption, to ease his ongoing emotional turmoil, along with his great sense of (mostly unexpected) humour. Dad was always was up early, cleanly shaven and active every day. We never saw him 'falling down' drunk, as he could 'handle' his copious alcohol consumption, as most military people do to some extent or another.

Over the years around Christmas time, especially after I became a UFO researcher 'officially' as my 'profession', we would watch football or basketball on tv and chat calmly together alone. It was a new experience for us, as I had already earned a modest amount of savings from growing cannabis in remote areas after university and had already 'retired' to avoid going to prison or 'going missing'. Dad told me a variety of confirming events related to Vietnam and his roles there. He sometimes included other related relevant information that was far too specific to be created within an overly-active imagination or a finely concocted set of fabricated lies that were insidiously 'designed' to confuse, frighten or somehow to 'impress' me. Everything was consistent and the diverse sets of information integrated together quite well, especially over passing time and self-evident revealing circumstances.

As stated previously, the facts began to be presented in stark, brutally clear, military-style terms of description with only the related specific FACTS, when I asked him basically, "Why did the USA not win the Vietnam war ?" There were NO short simplistic responses to direct questions with Dad. He always had an extremely strict definition as to what was accurate information. What constituted a lie included many variables that many people do not consider relevant, such as the withholding of ANY relevant information was a form of a lie, or for misconstruing the facts to create a false impression in any ways, was a lie.

Like how the candy bar 'found its' way' into my pocket about age 8, the one and only time at the grocery store and did not get properly purchased before it was found at home (??!!). I had to return to the store, apologise sincerely while being closely observed, then pay for it and ask them if they wanted to spank me with a stiff fly swatter. The store manager kindly declined with a straight face and it was a memorable lesson. Such transgressions were minimal, yet the inevitable resulting physical beating (usually with a leather belt) was not designed to cause permanent injuries and did almost always apply instantly, or soon after the 'interrogation' was completed, ha ha !!! There is a lesson in this for ALL of us.

My point being, it was 'the whole truth and nothing except the truth', with NO excuses allowed for inappropriate attitudes or actions. So, Dad's reply about how the USA 'lost' the Vietnam war was very explicit in specific minimal detail. Over several years, more and more of the actual events that happened were revealed to me, yet most were far beyond my ability to assess them adequately due to limited direct knowledge. I simply listened and trusted that my Dad had never lied to me about anything and he never accepted any of my 'lies of convenience' and let me know accordingly in many memorable instances, as being my 'always 100% reliable' Dad.

Here in brief form is the basic response to what Dad told me about Vietnam. It includes minimal relevant detail that I was UNABLE to confirm by direct inner knowing, as I am able to do far better here now in this timely, effective, 'for the public record' manner. Dad said: (1) "We were NOT allowed to win the war." (2) "The Rockefeller and Rothschild families owned all the oil refineries and munitions factories located in North Vietnam, so we were NOT allowed to bomb those military targets." (3) "We were not allowed to bomb their levees (holding back rivers or lakes, etc.) to flood their supply lines into South Vietnam or flood their underground cave systems that protected Viet Cong and North Vietnamese troops from our air attacks." (4) "The Vietnam war was strictly designed to test our weapons systems, make money, kill off unwanted (poor or 'lower class') Americans, and get those troops serving there addicted to 'hard' drugs such as heroin, opium and others, as well as to import drugs into the USA by the CIA to make money and make drug addicts of other Americans." (5) "We were concerned about China and Russia entering the war aggressively, if they saw we were intent upon 'winning' the war, so we simply did not attempt to do so for many reasons." (6) Other facts could be included, yet you get the idea in a better perspective due to events currently.

After I had a number of years to consider that basic information, then Dad also shared additional key information about his role as Commander of AWACs during his tour of duty at a key time in the war. AWACs are large jet airplanes that are basically 'flying command centers' that have communications, radar, surveillance systems, electronic 'jamming' equipment, and other similar types of technologies that enable the crew to 'conduct' the entire war effort, directly above whatever location they selected for the day, in 12 hour shifts from various altitudes, usually at least 20,000 to 30,000+ feet in elevation. There were only 3 AWACs stationed in Vietnam and the crews rotated 24/7 every day in 12 hour shifts, often being continually 'buffeted' by nearby exploding anti-aircraft weapons fired upwards from the ground. They also had U.S. jet fighter 'escorts' as airborne defenders, against potential North Vietnamese fighter jets. Their base was initially located near the 'demilitarised zone' (??!!) near North Vietnam and was heavily fortified by the best methods available at the time. The AWACs base was surrounded by multiple circles of tall barbed wire fences topped with rolls of 'razor wire', with mine fields throughout the enclosed areas surrounding the base, with machine gun turrets positioned all around and within the base in key locations. It contained a large runway and other facilities, like any small important U.S. military base.

It was not comfortable for Dad to share various events for many reasons. I am reluctant to share some of this information, yet it needs to be done now, so here it is: Dad said many things about the Tet Offensive in early 1968 and other events in Vietnam, yet here are the basics only: (1) "The CIA reports (wrongly) said that 'our' troops (Australian, other 'allies' and South Vietnamese were included) were 'only' out-numbered by about 3 enemy troops per 1 allied troop on the ground, located in mostly upon remote 'hill-top' bases within South Vietnam. Our own information was that in many locations (just before the annual 'Tet Offensive' in early 1968) our ground troops were out-numbered by up to 12+ enemy troops to every 1 allied soldier. We were asking for re-enforcements and for some vulnerable bases to be re-deployed out of those remote, unprotected areas, into safer, more well-protected areas with easier access to protective helicopters and navy/USAF jet air-strikes." (2) "All of our requests were denied by our Commanders and the CIA." (3) "When the Tet Offensive began in early 1968, we immediately requested permission to bomb many key military targets and most of those requests for bombing missions were denied and therefore were prevented through 'official' channels of Command." (4) "When one of our 3 AWACs was stuck on the ground (plane's wing was blown off) while sitting on the runway within the AWAC base by mortar fire from the surrounding hordes of attacking North Vietnamese army soldiers, I had already been ordered to 'ground' the 2 planes (the 3rd AWAC jet was in the air at the time). However, the runway surface was rapidly being destroyed by intensive mortar fire, creating craters that would soon prevent any further plane landings or take-offs from that vital runway. So, I had to DISOBEY my orders (military 'legal grounds' for immediate court martial arrest and prosecution, by the 'death penalty' or life in prison) and take off with the crew and I ordered the other AWAC to fly to a safe location in Thailand." (5) "We then fought the air-war for about 3 days non-stop and continued to disobey ongoing orders to land our plane to submit to certain court martial arrest for disobeying a direct order, repeatedly. We continued to refuse to do so. USAF and U.S. Navy airborne troops that were loyal to our mission to save as many of our people as we were able, did continually re-fuel and protect our AWAC as we continued to direct the air-war in support of the (otherwise) unprotected ground troops in small remote bases throughout South Vietnam as best we could. Using bombing runs and helicopter gunships, we directed jet fighters to and from various locations, as we did our missions." (6) Dad decided NOT to share the actual situation when he and his crew finally landed the AWAC that he was in command of for those 3 days, as obviously he and his crew were then immediately detained and imprisoned. Later, Dad was later awarded with a number of medals for his service in saving countless lives, yet he kept them in a box in the garage and never showed them to us. The medals were later stolen by convicts on a 'work-release' program where we lived in New Orleans, while he worked with the retired General Wade, trying to 'clean up' corruption within the Louisiana State Police (?!!), while I attended high school at Holy Cross.

What he did say was deeply upsetting and emotional for us both, as YOU may imagine: (7) "EVERY man we left at my base DIED there (or was captured by the North Vietnamese). I spoke with them by radio periodically, and eventually their machine gun barrels melted due to the volume of rounds they fired. The North Vietnamese troops literally ran over their dead and dying soldiers that were piled up higher than the tops of the tall barbed wire fences, with some holes in the fences having been blown 'open' to enable the attacking troops to enter the base." Dad emotionally said he felt that "I should have ended my life along with the men at our base", yet his ultimate duty was to save the lives of otherwise undefended soldiers throughout South Vietnam, Therefore, traumatic circumstances and Life Itself had 'other ideas' about how his life would end.

So it is for us as well now !!! Many of us have 'fallen along the way', yet we will endure and win FREEDOM for Humanity soon (and ongoing).

We can thankfully digress 'back' to events about what my Dad shared with me upon his 'deathbed' in 1999 in Roswell: Please recall his basic comment that I was UNABLE to comprehend or believe could ever occur: "Son, if you ever SEE the U.S. military attacking its' OWN PEOPLE, then you

MUST first speak YOUR TRUTH, and then you must DO something, but stay AWAY from the people with guns."

You have your own perspectives about life's events; yet please consider current events within the factual context of what you are about to read here. Consider the source of this information, from a 'mystery person' that virtually no one has heard of publicly before (me), via my Dad's wise perceptive truths when he was prepared to 'step off' into the 'other side of life'.

I responded to Dad, "What do you mean, the U.S. military is going to attack its own people ?!! It is NEVER going to happen !!!" He replied words to the effect, "Nazis have taken control of America and world governments and they plan to 'kill off' a lot of people."

Imagine a world before 9/11, yet knowing the assassinations of J.F. Kennedy, R.F. Kennedy and M.L. King and the 'curious deaths' of others such as Princess Diana and John Lennon have occurred, the unfair imprisonment of Julian Assange and the assassination-style murders of many 'whistle blowers' and genuine health doctors, inventors, UFO researchers, scientists, and even 'insiders' such as Supreme Court Judge Scalia, etc.; then you can better 'add in' your own realisations.

My next question was more of a statement of my (wrong) truth at that time. I said, "Dad, I simply can NOT believe this will ever happen in America. I need to know specifics about what you are saying here. You mean, like dropping bombs on people or using helicopter gunships on them ?"

He replied, "No, there are many ways planned." The following information was not limited to a single discussion, as we had a month to share together without interruptions or other visitors, aside from my mother briefly at times. I left Roswell to return to Australia only about 2 weeks before he died (to provide 'alone time' for Dad and Mom) and then the miracles continued ha ha !!! That is another lovely story that proved Dad was able to be with us in Spirit. Here we are now.

Dad shared about 20 individual major specific areas of 'activity'. I will summarise them to the best of my ability, as they were etched clearly within my disbelieving sceptical mind, with each area having multiple aspects, or integrated components. He had to explain them simplistically within the limited terms of my awareness; often wisely including other additional information that we had already confirmed as being valid, truthful facts from other circumstances. You too may be a sceptic at this point in time, yet if so (?!!); then exactly what valid information that you did NOT hear upon television or read about in newspapers are you considering, in relation to the types of information provided here?

I will identify the basic areas in summary form and provide a few of the specific applications now being experienced in general terms for the purposes of brevity. Your own experience and research can provide further detail. Additional information I could provide here would be inconclusive or remains unidentified to keep our focus somewhat coherent and logical.

Dad made a point of observing: "Sometimes what you identify as things you do NOT know (limitations in information or experience), can reveal more than aspects of what you 'think' you know." Likewise, Doc observed, "If they are directing your attention in one location, be sure there are other things happening they are trying to distract your attention away from." We see this situation by INTENTIONALLY creating problems of many types (Doc mentioned migration from war and poverty areas, financial depravation, religious intolerances, 'state sponsored' terrorism, racial/national issues, fraudulent elections, fictitious 'mainstream' propaganda, etc.) and promoting chaos/discord, as we observe currently. Now there is so much corruption and evil abuse being revealed that it is truly 'over' (finished) for them. The 'nwo elites' are desperately resisting justice to promote distractions leading nowhere, except to intensified versions of military-enforced 'martial law' (autocratic military 'rule') in many nations globally.

For example, Doc showed me how to read satellite photos of the Moon and Mars when decent resolution enabled proper visibility and scrutiny of whatever was located there (?!!!); as compared with now the intentionally limited clarity of resolution on many forms of 'Google' Earth, Moon or Mars, or various forms of media etc. Another bit of wisdom he shared that is relevant to our discussion is, "Never try to understand the mind of a psychopath."

Another simular type of observation was at a time when I was having difficulty in math at school and asked Dad for help. He started showing me how to do math mentally instead of on paper. I declined and said, "We need to show our work". He replied, "It will only take me a little while to teach you." but again I declined and he accepted. He then calmly made a subtle comment that I never forgot, "You need to think about WHY you do not want to know." and never again mentioned the issue. As a pilot of exceptional abilities, somehow Dad conveying the basic awareness that other better easier faster ways of doing mathematics or other physics calculations and assessments do exist. Now this is a highly encouraging fact of life. That I never asked him to teach me to do rapid complex mental math is like-wise deeply revealing and somewhat unfortunate.

The following specific general areas of activity are now being progressively synergistically applied together in a well-integrated evil plan to enslave Humanity by self-serving, nazi-style, communistic, fascist, 'new world order' (NWO) people and organisations that have 'infiltrated' themselves within nearly every nation and culture upon Earth, to some degree or another. Most of the military technologies that Dad referred to were unknown to me at the time and much was classified 'above top secret'. He wisely advised me to "Permanently leave UFO research" (as a profession in 1986), "or end up dead." Great advice Dad. Thanks !!!

This is a self-evident evil genocidal predatorial plague of militaristic totalitarian fascism upon Humanity that is openly intent upon reducing the global population by many combined murderous genocidal destructive methods such as endless war and terrorism and by making obedient slaves of everyone remaining alive, as dictated and controlled by the 'chosen' few elitist families and cultures. We SEE this exact event occurring now in whatever nation or community you may live in globally.

For nations and people that the USA has deemed to be 'enemies' (??!!), they see there is NO conscience, mercy, pity or compassion when the bombs rain from the sky and helicopter/drone gunships patrol their communities, destroy their national resources and mass-murder their people including the elderly, women and children with impunity, and call it 'collateral damage' instead of genocidal mass-murder war crimes. <u>These wars are intentionally staged genocidal events to create financial 'income' at the cost of others' suffering, losses and murder</u>.

Deadly pathogens (virus, fungi, artificially created harmful 'nanobots', etc.) causing diseases have been intentionally created in government and corporate laboratories for decades (HIV/AIDS, ebola, sars, corona, covid, etc.) to damage people's health, kill millions, then billions of people over passing time, at great suffering to us all. So, between intentionally created wars, diseases, terrorism, financial chaos, deteriorating social services, etc.; <u>we SEE 'enough now'</u>.

At the time, I simply was unable to believe that an elitist, divisive, nazi-style, nwo globalist USA corporate government' would ever attack its' own people. Here are some of the ways they are doing it NOW, as we see clearly in the past as well.

Let's start by mentioning one of those toward the end of our list: (13) "Endless pandemics." Does this one sound relevant and familiar to YOU today in 2022 ?!!!

Here is a condensed list of what Doc Wonders told me over several weeks in 1999 about the various ways the U.S. military would attack (mass-murder) and control its' own citizens. It also applies in other nations internationally, as we can all recognise. We must peacefully RESIST this militaristic oppression and evil, unnecessary, planned, global genocide. Otherwise, in due course, 'other ways' will subsequently need to be 'applied'.

"USAF military <u>use</u> of these weapons systems upon Americans and others:"

    1.   "Directed Energy Weapons (DEWs)"

'High technology' weapons systems of diverse types with many differing applications, depending upon the desired 'targets' and circumstances involved. Some weapons looking somewhat like a 'laser beam' are used to start 'fires' that burn hotter than ordinary forest fires, that simply 'appear out of nowhere' and 'level' (totally destroy) homes and buildings; including steel, glass and bricks, yet mysteriously (DEWs) sometimes do NOT burn nearby plastic items such as trash bins, and (sometimes) the trees, grass and nearby bushes are not burned (initially) !!! These genocidal acts have been witnessed, photographed and videoed in many nations including the USA, Australia, Indonesia, Brazil and many other locations. These are genocidal, fraudulent, treasonous events that are a 'high tech' type of genocidal intentional arson being applied globally in many locations. Some people are being 'employed' as arsonists to start these destructive fires in conventional ways.

    Other types of DEWs are used to create earthquakes, cyclones/hurricanes, and other extreme weather events such as tornadoes, or even snow in normally warm desert climates, for example.

    4G and 5G microwave 'communications' technologies are now being used in communications devices that could potentially 'deliver' an energetic 'kill shot' from multiple triangulated positions to 'targeted' individuals (or communities). This can occur by various methods; as the Patent records and 'top secret' documents do reveal in detail. The harmful deadly energies can be 'fired' remotely from high-flying satellites or low-flying drones, and/or local 'towers' or from various types of energy-pulse 'guns' (simular to a gun that fires bullets) being able to 'target' and 'shoot' the harmful destructive energies to a specific electronic device (phone, computer, tv, vehicle etc.) or location to attack a person(s) directly for unethical, murderous or debilitating reasons, without any obvious nearby assailant being visible.

All communities within so-called 'civilised societies' now contain DEW technologies installed as 'communications towers', or 'radar speed traps' for "safety purposes", associated camera surveillance technologies, 'radio waves', microwaves, x-rays and numerous other 'top secret' types of harmful radiations, etc. All these electronic devices receive and emit potentially harmful radiations in a widely variable set of frequencies that can be 'directed' by various methods to 'target' specific devices and/or locations from multiple locations. These are potential war crimes being prepared intentionally now by complicit people and interconnected corporations, along with corrupt nwo governments and militaries.

These harmful energy emissions also damage other life forms, such as the location detection and communication abilities of bees, whales, porpoise, birds and countless other life forms. People are intentionally being 'dumbed down' too.

For other DEWs, a Patent search will reveal many thousands of potential harmful military applications, being used commercially and militarily now to our detriment.

Knowing that proven lethal and harmful military weapons systems are now being used for public applications in communications and other domestic uses is revealing in itself, especially as things progress. The Patents prove these intentional war crimes and self-identify those responsible. They will be <u>unable</u> to wrongly say, "We did not know" as they hold and license the Patents and own the corporations that are directly responsible. Therefore, 'by their acts we DO know them' and Humanity (and Divinity) will prosecute them accordingly soon.

2. "Endless wars"

This category 'pains me' too much to list any of them here now, as I would omit many from the listing because they were never revealed to the American public or the world. The same is true of all their countless assassinations and political destabilisation operations. Please simply recall the wars that the USA has been involved in since you became aware of such things, and the wars since America began with the genocides of millions in the Native American (Indian) Tribes. Consider how many murdered millions died in Russia under Stalin (20M+), or Mao in China (20M+), or Pol Pot in Cambodia or in Iraq, in Lebanon, Afghanistan and in South America, South East Asia and countless more. Then look closely at the destruction of their national economies, the mass-murder, suffering and deprivation of their people and the theft of their lands and resources; then consider the same thing happening within YOUR communities. Not a good image to consider, yet this awful 'nightmare reality' is the actual legacy these evil creeps intend to create 'endlessly' for the ENTIRE world, aside from within their cosy, secure 'retreats' and well-protected 'sanctuaries'.

Consider the financial implications and FRAUDS of these two wars alone:

When the USA attacked Vietnam, the Vietnamese Dong ($) was twice as valuable as the U.S. Dollar. It required x2 USA Dollars to buy x1 Vietnamese Dong ($). (!!!)

When the USA attacked Iraq, it required x3 and one half USA Dollars to purchase x1 Iraqi Dinar ($), making it about 3 and a half times more valuable than the U.S. Dollar. (!!!)

Currently, for many years, about $500 USD ($700 AUD) would buy about 10 Million Vietnamese Dong. For about $1,200 USD one could buy about 1 Million Iraqi Dinar, which the U.S. government has been printing in the trillions as 'controllers' of Iraq for nearly x2 decades (massive frauds). Therefore, we can see how the predatorial attacks by the USA destroyed these two nations' valuable currencies, stole and destroyed their national treasures, ruined natural environments, bombed infrastructure and historical sites with intentional criminal vengeance, robbed precious resources such as oil, gas and minerals, and mass-murdered millions of people for greedy controlling evil motives. Now consider the 'bigger picture' involving other nations and U.S. military bases globally. <u>This destructive insanity must stop now.</u>

    3.   "Endless terrorism"

These areas of genocidal activity were identified by Doc BEFORE 9/11 events in New York City and the associated 'false flag' attack on the Pentagon in Washington D.C. by a USA military launched 'cruise missile'. Terrorism would be primarily a government covert (hidden or secret) or overt ongoing series of 'operations' intended to falsely create the purported reasons to apply various levels of surveillance and 'martial law', which is another term for autocratic fascist totalitarian oppressive rule 'enforced' by murder and terrorism by a relative few self-serving 'elites' and their compliant docile slaves, 'law enforcement' and military forces, 'against' unarmed, peaceful, non-combatant, defenceless people.

    Ample proof exists that the USA and its' allies have consistently provided financial support to known actual terrorist organisations, as well as being involved in the creation of terrorist organisations and then paying wages ($) to combatants, 'suicide bombers', beheading (cutting people's heads off in a vicious display to upset and frighten the victim and other people) etc. and supplying training and weapons, as well as various forms of 'protection' and ongoing financial aid.

    This vile agenda has been to intentionally create misery, deprivation, chaos, fear, and mass-murder by vicious methods to intentionally terrify people by ongoing carefully-controlled, theatrical, hugely destructive, evil mass-murder events, such as 9/11, in various locations. This evil, purposefully contrived situation also creates a significant ongoing refugee problem, as we see in Europe and elsewhere; where cultural, racial, national and religious differences and relentless poverty tend to provoke divisiveness, encourage lawlessness and criminal behaviours that are in epidemic proportions in many locations globally.

Because an aware, well-informed, free-thinking, productive, prosperous population is unwanted by these evil nwo fascist people; we now clearly SEE them by their ACTIONS and attitudes. We see NO politicians and nwo government or corrupt banking or taxation institutions have been suffering from terrorism or poverty related 'hard times'; rather only the 'common folks'. So-called 'law enforcement' and the international and national 'intelligence services' seem UNABLE to PREVENT these so-called 'terrorist attacks', or strange shootings, and endless supply of socially created misfits to 'blame things upon'.

Look at the suicide rates and realise that life on Earth is so upsetting that many despondent people choose self-murder (suicide), rather than to endure the abuse, oppression, self-loathing and suffering any longer.

Therefore ... can YOU deny or ignore this now ?!!

Do NOT be beguiled or confused by the total nonsense and lies with some half-truths that are expressed publicly by politicians and so-called 'world leaders'; President Putin excepted.

4. "Create any excuse or reasons to apply and strengthen 'martial law', which is nazi-style, oppressive, totalitarian fascism and steadily apply widespread selective genocide, abuse and enslavement and the destruction of natural environments."

This includes and relates with intentionally promoting and financing acts of 'government sponsored' or 'conducted' terrorism. Consider the militaristic 'terrorist sponsoring' USA diplomats could not agree upon an international definition of what exactly 'terrorism' is, in their 'fascist nwo reality'. However, they continually accuse others without proof, while ignoring and supporting Israeli war crimes, as well as those by the USA's allies. Consider corrupt 'acting President' Biden has insanely openly labelled Trump and Republicans as 'enemies of America', as well as publicly threatening to attack Russia with nuclear weapons.

This totalitarian insanity also involves intentionally creating immigration and migration problems, and divisive social issues resulting in socio-cultural 'unrest' and potential conflicts due to religious and/or cultural, racial or national reasons, as well as unemployment and socio-economic 'disaster areas' with widespread homelessness. Clearly, we see George Soros and his many associates, such as Clintons, Bushs, Obamas, Rothschilds, other members of 'royalty' and the Vatican in many nations, etc.; doing these disruptive criminal activities blatantly for decades. It must end now.

These illegitimate criminal activities are intentionally creating ambiguous identity issues, so that more invasive identity requirements such as finger prints, facial recognition, voice prints, DNA scans, and various gender issues, etc. to purposefully create chaos and discord. These multiple types of draconian fascist methods are being synergistically integrated to easily enable institutionalised fraud/theft and coercion (force) to be conducted by 'elites', through complicit 'law enforcement', while normal people are criminalised and being 'legally robbed' for almost anything being 'deemed' as a crime, such as tax evasion, money laundering, staying healthy, walking your dog, feeding the homeless, or even earning an honest productive living Ha ha !!! Never enough money to repair or replace deteriorating roads and infrastructure, yet trillions constantly 'invested in' war equipment and personnel.

On August 18, 2021, in some locations in Australia, to walk out of your home for 'unapproved reasons', due to the covid martial law 'lockdowns', one could be fined ' on the spot' $5000 by the police (or military). In China it was far worse.

Now the covid FRAUD is revealed and PROVEN factual by corporations owned by Bill Gates' 'entities' that have been: (1) granted Patents of 'exclusive ownership' on both the purported 'virus', which conveniently evidently may not exist at all in any verifiable detectable form; plus (2) 'vaccines' that are highly toxic and infectious and damaging in nature, were Patented in about 2002, BEFORE the 'pandemic' was 'released', along with known-harmful 5G radiation technologies.

These premeditated CRIMINAL ACTS were intended to create another EXCUSE to do exactly what has happened already: strengthen and expand existing 'martial law'. This entire situation is an international treasonous criminal fraud, and a definitive 'war crime' by clearly established historical legal statutes that apply to these cases of intending and conducting genocidal mass-murder of civilian populations (as the Nazis and Communists have done and now the USA too) without their knowledge or fully-informed consent; as some of these highly toxic 'vaccines' are being PROVEN to harm and kill people.

The use of DEWs to damage properties, the natural environment and mass murder by arson, flood, severe earthquakes, etc. is likewise an intentional war crime, along with the chemtrails as another self-evident application of known poisons and pathogens by airplanes and other methods. Public water supplies and vital water resources are being poisoned and polluted. <u>This criminal insanity must stop now</u>.

5. "Multiple ways to set people against one another (by religion, nationality, culture, race, age, gender, financial status, genetics, etc.) and destroy families and local communities' autonomy (which is a word for 'freedom to choose)."

Can you perceive ways this is occurring ?!! Divorce and suicide rates, emotional mental and addiction problems, relentless financial difficulties, and on and on ...

6. "Multiple ways to collapse the world and local economies and deprive people of access to money, productive work and owning their own homes and land."

We see this happening with all public businesses and international 'markets'. Consider the frauds in the banking industry, stock markets, bullion markets, commodity markets, and foreign currency exchange (Fx) markets, 'derivatives' markets, and the theft of retirement funds, the squandering of taxation income upon weapons, wars and terrorism. There is an intention to create misery through poor health, degraded food, a predatorial dysfunctional social system that applies a minimalist 'fixed' inequitable slave-wage upon the majority of people, along with inequitable taxation systems, with a constantly increasing 'cost of living', with fraudulent bankruptcy laws, fixed real estate markets and many many other well-integrated, 'organised crime' financial situations.

Again, I could write a book on this topic alone.

Let's quickly run through a few of the major frauds for clarity. All national currencies (Fx/$) are variable in the 'assessed value' when compared with other nations, understanding that money itself is a mutually agreed fictional, yet 'real' exchangeable commodity, like gold, land, one's home, food, etc. Over a decade ago, about 4 trillion dollars per day (averaged) was the reported Fx/$ of total daily 'exchange', which is <u>a lot of potential **income** ($) to those controlling those markets in various ways</u>.

The international Fx/$ market is totally controlled. It is seemingly complex, yet very simple actually. These people do NOT want solutions for Humanity. This is among the reasons for the closure of many (corrupt/insolvent) banks, and far less access to cash or even ATM cash machines. The entire situation is currently being 'tightly controlled' by those 'insider' people, corporations, governments and 'entities' that created them. Frauds on a massive unimaginable scale have been occurring historically, yet that is an issue for another time.

Humanity demands 'the return' of some of the wealth that 'we' have **earned** already.

Aside from the 'fixed' market frauds mentioned previously, the long-awaited 'revaluation' (RV/GCR) of the world Fx/$ currencies was supposed to happen. Trillions of 'real dollars' in existing international currencies were 'invested' in buying many different foreign currencies, with the USA 'government' in Iraq, printing trillions of Iraqi Dinar, then selling them at various rates of exchange into the global investment markets; including to corporations, governments, banks, institutions/'entities', wealthy 'insiders', and then progressively into a gullible, uninformed 'public market'. They take your 'real money' and give you recently printed or other 'hard currency' cash and sell you at various prices and exchange rates, 'foreign currencies' that the banking system NEVER intends to 'exchange' or redeem by any methods. They 'cash in' their money at prime rates, as they wish; while others wait forever or are fortunate to get some of their money back in some form or another.

Now, we SEE the same frauds with crypto-currencies. You pay your 'real money' to 'receive' on-line crypto-currency 'credits', which are numbers on a computer screen that may go up or down in actual redeemable value (someday, ideally ... Ha ha !!!). Of course, surely yes they want you doing 'banking' with your 'hacked' communications devices, trying to access your own 'credits' or 'crypto-nana'.

With EVERYTHING being computerised these days, are you 'betting' these online internet financial systems and their records are NOT going to ever CRASH ?!!! Ha ha !!! Try to remove an unwanted online payment plan on your credit card or report a fraudulent transaction, for example. They want control of your money in whatever forms it may be. Then what ?!!

The old expression, "Can you smell a (dead) rat?" applies now. Can you SEE the rat droppings ??!!

By using organised criminal controls of commodity markets like oil and gas, bullion markets, mining etc. along with the ongoing 'war and terror machine'; the evil system promotes and rewards (and destroys) itself massively, as it self-evident for those willing to view the evidence. This global covid nwo scam fraud is an attempt to make money and gain further fascist control by 'collapsing' the world economic system and/or adversely affecting it in multitudinous ways.

A key priority is to eliminate local access to cash money from any source, with continual 'updates' to 'securitise' currencies to prevent them being 'counterfeited', when that is exactly what is happening already upon an 'official basis' constantly by organised criminals within 'corporate governments' globally, as we see now.

'Social distancing' and rampant blatant pervasive censorship is about stopping people commenting about these events while destroying local businesses and economies by intentional design to further apply their existing dysfunctional, self-serving control systems.

The biggest frauds are within the military and governmental budgets, along with the banking and finance-related industries. An example would be investing in war-related corporations, and then starting ongoing wars globally, as we see now. Those responsible need to be treated as war criminals, and qualify as being involved in clearly defined, self-evident 'organised crime' activities of many types. I want to say more, and name names, yet you can assess this very well yourself, if you wish to do so.

The other primary international banking frauds ALL involve the Federal Reserve Bank (FED) and they are exceedingly well established in the industry known as "off ledger bank trading programs" or Private Placement Programs (PPPs). Here is where the system devised a financial process to (criminally) 'sequester' people's money in large amounts over lengthy periods of time while giving them nothing in return, except promises and threats until the fund's owner(s) realised their money was stolen or made 'unavailable' to the rightful owners by 'the system'. My knowledge on that 'industry' is extensive, so again Doc was correct. When I discovered George Bush (senior/deceased) was the 'top trader' within the PPP industry, I left just before the 2008 intentionally planned and designed 'collapse'. I was NEVER paid for any of the work I did over those x10 years, which is revealing.

The financial damages (known as 'civil damages' in legal terms) now being 'owed to' Humanity are beyond the total of purported 'money' existing upon this planet. There is NO way they can 'pay up' or exterminate us, so **they must GO NOW**.

7. "Mind control programs ('psyops') integrated within normal society."

This is clearly seen in the mass media 'outlets' in every form; on television, in newspapers, magazines, books, movies, government self-promotion activities at taxpayers' expense, mandatory 'deemed' social compliance with onerous, dysfunctional and inequitable, unsustainable, unconstitutional governmental legislation and absurd policies enacted by corrupted, self-serving, dishonest politicians and bureaucrats without public discussion, consent or approval.

When the facts are presented, there are simply denials, distractions, excuses, false promises of improved circumstances and new policies, etc.; while the endemic dysfunctional corruption continues and worsens considerably over passing time.

In other words, 'nwo society' says to you and us all, "Everything is fine. Your needs will be cared for, yet get ready to die suddenly of anything like cancer, heart attack, stroke, terrorist attack, HIV/AIDS, vehicle accident, or a sudden fire, or maybe an earthquake or meteorite. Your insurance will be unlikely to pay for your hospital bills or cover funeral costs, so keep working if you can find one or more jobs, pay your 'layers upon layers' of unfair inequitable taxes and trust in us to 'care for' you and your family. News alert: hear this now; we intend to mandate that you and your children receive toxic poisonous immune-damaging harmful 'vaccines' or be 'punished' in various ways in the near future, such as by having your financial records become inaccessible or your ability to travel denied temporarily or permanently. Resistance is futile and freedom to choose is illegal."

Really ?!! They want YOU to 'freely' accept this fate. This is simply NOT going to happen; evil satanic fascist nwo globalist inbred elitist 'retards' (people of diminished intellect).

8. "International corrupt nazi-style autocratic, satanic/ungodly, materialistic 'new world order' (nwo) globalist evil governments have joined 'forces' as one ruling ('faceless heartless') 'entity' seeking to assert themselves as being 'in control' of all, in all locations."

This is a summation of the over-all evil nwo plan. It encompasses all international organisations such as the United Nations (UN), the International Monetary Fund (IMF), the International Bank of Settlements (IBS), most major so-called 'humanitarian foundations', charities, trusts; the Federal Reserve Bank (FED) and many other such 'high level' international organisations such as the Vatican in Rome and various royal families; and (ideally) every national government to the state and local levels by the intended autocratic rule of a few secretive wealthy 'elites', also known as 'the illuminati'.

One key is to destroy the worlds' existing religions and cultures, in preference of creating a new and vastly more unpleasant set of social and cultural practices related to endless war, terrorism, fear, willingness to murder others or one's self, creating new and unknown incurable diseases, ongoing social unrest, accepting abuse, 'social distancing' and financial uncertainty and deprivation. Their clearly stated intent is the destruction of people's innate beliefs in a loving kind Creator/God/Source of life and replace those beneficial realities with total blind-allegiance to the 'state religion' of godless materialism, totalitarian nwo evil satanic dogma and selfless scarcity 'in service to community', nation and others as ordered, until death.

When a 90 year old Florida man can be arrested for feeding homeless people in his community, or the military can use DEWs to intentionally and repeatedly start fires by airborne arson from afar (USA and Australia, etc.); <u>it is time to make a few major **beneficial changes** to the ways things are 'progressing'</u>.

Examples include 'political correctness' and 'code of conduct violations' for speaking or revealing truths not appreciated by others that are 'in control' so that censorship is standard procedure, even of one's own thoughts, needs and reasonable appropriate desires. Another example is the needless focus upon 'gender issues' among children and 'sexual proclivity' issues among adults.

9. "Destruction of environments and resources (such as clean water, oceans, rivers, lakes, 'old growth' forests, wetlands, etc.) intentionally by various methods for insane psychopathic reasons that I am not fully aware of now."

Studying the environmental effects of long-term 'civilised human' habitation proves Humanity could be correctly identified as being the 'termite people' by seeing the results of only a couple thousand years of ongoing settlement. Evidently the lands of Earth were previously covered in many locations by giant-sized trees and vast forests and wetlands. Now de-forestation and pollution typify the destructive results of those responsible, as we know from examples too numerous and pervasive to fully comprehend.

People have been aware of the problems created by environmental destruction, yet very little has been done to stop those practices, so this is self-evident too.

To realise that an insane evil-minded group of elitist 'supremacist' people and their war and disease-related businesses, divisive predatorial militant religions and corrupted corporate governments would perpetuate and accelerate intentional environmental destruction and massive human genocide is a clear obvious 'warning sign' for us all at this key time in history now.

Perhaps those RESPONSIBLE will soon get the full, ongoing opportunity to explain clearly and precisely exactly WHY they sought to do whatever evil it is they wrongly and foolishly sought to 'enforce' upon Humanity and natural earthly environments of every description. Oh yes, so be it now.

10. "Create civil war within America and other nations."

In the USA it is easy to SEE the differences between the world we thought we grew up in and what has actually been created by the ways things are regressing and deteriorating massively now.

'Vested interests' (evil self-serving predatorial parasitic fascist abusive paedophilic nwo murderous creeps, via their many 'organisations') have been intentionally creating chaotic unstable unreliable inequitable financial circumstances for the vast majority of people for a long while within so-called 'civilised societies'. The workers/slaves were to own their own homes, or rent them at a reasonable affordable price, until homes became 'investment properties'. Then collusion between banks, real estate agents and appraisers, with government and taxation rogues (all on the same team) became 'normal' in capitalistic nations. Their criminal plan being to increase the purported values to the extent that they were unaffordable (as wage earning capacity would be 'fixed' and relatively limited for most people), so with variable unfair bank/ FED 'interest rates', the bankruptcies inevitably occurred in cycles; with homelessness and empty abandoned homes of little to no value to anyone, as evidenced by them being vacant. Deteriorating neighbourhoods have resulted in many locations, as the dysfunctional systems fails in an increasingly escalating manner, as is self-evident. Conversely, unknown millions of fine luxury 'prestige homes' (and buildings) are mostly vacant and used simply as investment properties or rented occasionally for about $10,000 per week to those few people that can afford such luxuries.

Bringing in overseas investors or corporations like banks and investment groups into suppressed real estate markets results in exactly what we are seeing now. Vast amounts of EMPTY UNWANTED commercial space and many large homes being unoccupied/vacant, because only the wealthier few can afford the prices that are well-beyond any normal people's dreams. Farms and ranches are being forced by deteriorating circumstances into bankruptcy, to then be bought at inexpensive prices by the wealthy and large corporations to no productive benefit. High rents for limited accommodation (or costly 'camping' options) are the situation in many communities, resulting in more homeless people with fewer and fewer non-government related jobs becoming the daily 'normal' now. With NO 'relief' in the foreseeable future; politicians publicly assert this unacceptable, deplorable, unnecessary, dire situation as being "the new normal".

Create the circumstances for disaster, then ignore people's plight; while creating additional problems, health challenges, wars, ongoing drama ... is standard procedure with these evil organised criminals, who are desperately attempting to create chaos and discord by utilising financial issues, (or contrived racial, or religion, or gender issues) to 'fuel the fire' of people's discontent and suffering, for primarily self-benefit and increased fascist 'controls'.

By creating difficult dire financial conditions, this system sets people apart from one another by financial, racial, cultural, ethnic, religion, status, etc., then 'plays upon' the challenging circumstances. We see many totally unacceptable situations whereby travesty of justice is standard procedure. The person phoning police for help is soon murdered by police or by an attacker in their own home, or a person cooking dinner in their own apartment is shot to death by an 'off-duty' insane police officer that accidentally walked into the wrong apartment, thinking it was their apartment (evidently). Or a man lying prone and motionless on the ground with arms and legs spread, as ordered by 'law enforcement officers' is then shot to death or beaten into retardation, or a deaf man is shot to death for failing to stop walking on the sidewalk of a city street by himself when verbally ordered to do so by a passing police officer in a vehicle.

Of course these chaotic social and economic conditions, along with poor health and an inadequate nutritious diet are INTENTIONALLY created, for their own insane psychopathic self-serving reasons.

These and other vile criminal events by those in positions of social responsibility are being encouraged, approved and rewarded by those nwo fascist types of evil self-serving autocrats. This promotes divisions between all aspects of society and with difficult financial situations; this is <u>intended</u> to create civil war and mental/emotional instabilities, suicides, murders, etc. among the emotionally, mentally and spiritually damaged people.

Indigenous Peoples globally have systematically been fraudulently and militarily dispossessed (robbed) of their native ancestral lands globally by this corrupt evil system, as well as been genocidally exterminated in the millions (billions actually) and enslaved by many methods. <u>This must end now</u>.

Another covert ploy is to pay 'rioters' or 'terrorists' to create damage and conflict between groups of people simply to engender chaos, mutual hatred, anger and desires for vengeance and promote an increased 'law enforcement' and military presence. Again, the list of those responsible, with sufficient money to pay rioters, terrorists, suicide bombers, give away and/or sell weapons internationally, train and deploy military personnel, etc. is limited to those few 'at the top', such as we see mentioned here later.

Thankfully, that stupid evil plan is NOT working either, in spite of the deprivation, suffering, extensive unnecessary homelessness, massive illegal immigration, rampant drug addiction and violent crime problems and the fact that mentally/emotionally damaged and elderly people are increasingly being ignored and denied opportunities to improve their circumstances, etc. The people of America and the entire world are joining TOGETHER to demand improved ways and are already happily working to achieve them in most locations. So it is now.

    11. "End all true freedom of choice."

Can you see it happening in ways that YOU can reliably identify ? Would you wear a (toxic) health-debilitating mask or take a poisoned 'vaccine' if you KNEW it was going to KILL YOU, slowly or quickly ? For example, would you 'accept' being coerced or 'forced' to comply simply to be able to use your bank account, travel, work, or shop at your local grocery store, etc. without being detained and taken to a 'infection detection centre' by local 'health enforcement authorities' ?

    Who do YOU vote for when only x2 or more totally unworthy choices exist ?!! A purported 'choice' between x2 or more unacceptable options is NO choice at all. Voter fraud is rife.

    What would you think if you were officially identified as being a 'terrorist' or threat to society for NOT willingly wearing a mask or 'willingly' accepting a poisonous 'kill shot' vaccine ? Does this wildly hypothetical, absurdly unlikely scenario seem impossible to you now ?!!!

    Think very carefully again whether or not YOU would you 'freely consent' (?!!!) to limitations on YOUR freedoms to stay alive, or travel away from home, be granted a functional bank account, be allowed to drive and shop publicly, or to attend school, work or social events, etc. to avoid being forcefully detained in a 'non-compliance camp', or to save the lives of your children or to prevent them being permanently removed from your parental care by 'health authorities' ?!!

    When you KNOW people are trying to injure and/or KILL YOU and your family, it is one's personal and spiritual responsibility and duty to RESIST that by whatever (ideally) peaceful assertive methods are required. Existing society seems intent upon DENYING us that right to resist evil peacefully; then to identify those objecting in any way as being 'terrorists' or unwanted dangerous dissenters, and/or as being criminals needing to be silenced in various ways.

Be prepared to assert YOUR RIGHT to self-expression in protecting yourself and family.

12. "Declare and 'officially deem' there to be NO real Creator/God, aside from materialism with a viciously autocratic rule by known (and unknown) predatorial elitist people and 'entities' of multiple types and origins, as we see within satanic organisations, 'religions' and 'corporate governments' that are now active globally. There are evil ETs involved too."

We can see many so-called 'religions' both in the 'mainstream' and as cults of many types that openly serve materialistic values, select perverse egoistic leaders and often condone mass-murder and cruel prejudicial attitudes and abusive predatorial actions (rape, torture, imprisonment, etc.) as 'standard procedure'. They are NOT truly spiritual and seek to exterminate the Soul qualities of genuinely humane, loving, compassionate, kindly values and characteristics that are innate to Divinity and most of our human Species and all other non-predatorial life forms.

So, they must 'cease and desist' and 'go' now. Clearly, they refuse to do so and this is self-evident to all of Humanity now in November 2024.

Satanic demonic worshiping religions, such as the Catholic Church in Rome, and other vicious cults are responsible for the global epidemic of missing children and adults, as well as sponsoring and 'protecting' those involved in organised 'people trafficking' that has recently come into the public awareness more so than in past decades. The ceremonial satanic abuse and mass-murder of children and adults and rampant paedophilia is mostly 'hidden' from the normal general public awareness, for obvious reasons.

Many of the DISTRACTIONS we see in the public media and by politicians are simply 'cover-up' efforts seeking to focus attention AWAY from these terrible truths for THEIR self-preservation reasons.

Most sane normal (oblivious) people are completely and blissfully unaware of these facts. Most of these seek to remain so (ignorant and in denial of wider awful realities) and would be content to receive their vaccination 'kill shot' without much worry or complaint. Now it is necessary to bring these totally unacceptable realities into the public awareness, so that those evil elitists planning and conducting these murderous oppressive activities are STOPPED from completing their vile, cruel ungodly plans.

Amazingly, perhaps (?) these vile types of people will basically 'take their own poisonous medicines' to kill themselves, or mysteriously 'drop off' of the planet. Perhaps they will form 'suicide clubs' when confronted with inescapable public accountability based upon their own admissions of guilt and knowing that criminal and civil prosecutions await them. Wow !!!

> 13. "Endless pandemics (HIV/AIDS, ebola, sars, swine flu, bird flu, corona, covid, etc.) and diseases (**without** widely applying ANY of the many natural safe effective health solutions that are **already available**)."

Wow, what more can we say here ?!!! Plenty.

Most of these 'unknown' diseases are now Patented 'viruses' (like covid, etc. evidently) are PROVEN to originate from various government and corporate scientific laboratories. For example, the unique strain of anthrax that was sent to a few people through the mail in letters after the 9/11 attacks was later 'traced back' to an East Coast U.S. military laboratory. These are 'war crimes'. The toxic poisonous 'vaccines' being supplied to children, adults and the elderly globally are likewise 'war crimes' against Humanity.

Those responsible will be treated accordingly, very soon ideally. In fact, as these words are being written for future publication, the beneficial forces of positive change are truly 'in the action' now, as we will see. So be it now.

My Dad said, "Never accept any vaccinations of ANY types, as they will be a slow 'kill shot', or a fast 'kill shot', or a 'do nothing' shot, <u>until they decide to get rid of you</u>."

He made it known they "happily kill their own people, regardless of their loyalty", if and when they decide to do so for any reasons, as Americans witnessed with Judge Scalia's assassination-style murder (or that of the Kennedy brothers) by the Bush family and their associates, on both 'sides' of American politics. They eagerly kill others they consider to be victims or enemies with vicious callousness; yet plenty of us survive, as you too do know for sure.

No one should be coerced, fooled or forced into accepting the injection of poisonous, carcinogenic, toxic, contaminated, debilitating, harmful, unnecessary, immune system destroying 'vaccines' that are untested and unproven to be beneficial in any ways. Falsely fabricated, so-called 'evidence' of purported vaccine benefits are almost non-existent, even by the 'vested interests' responsible for creating these proven harmful 'medications'. They openly admit to devastating potential 'side effects' that are actually 'direct effects', as the medical/scientific evidence does PROVE.

There will be NO indemnity from prosecution or culpable financial responsibility for those creating these intentionally devastating, 'costly' war crimes. There will be no statute of limitations for medical murder and malpractice. Humanity can indeed begin to reduce the world population by legally executing these murderous proven 'war criminals'. So be it now.

This category (along with endless 'high level' corporate and government frauds) is the stuff that quality successful 'class action' lawsuits are made of (!!!), so 'stay tuned' for the results of these cases and other unexpected amazing miraculous events, that are far too numerous to fully identify here now.

Fortunately, many health solutions and immune boosting options exist that are natural, safe and rapidly effective for most people that are fortunate enough to receive them, who are genuinely wishing and attempting to improve their health and longevity. Others seem to accept disease and a pre-mature death as their fate by their poor food and unhealthy lifestyle choices. To each, their own ways.

No one needs to consent to others that are attempting to harm or murder them. We see in many nations like Australia the nazi-style corrupted 'globalist' nwo government created a 'reason' ('terrorist' shooting in Port Arthur, Tasmania) to remove most people's ability to defend themselves with guns, as we see happening now elsewhere while the police and law enforcement receive many types of weapons and equipment to attack its' own citizens. These evil creeps seek to prevent people from being able to make a 'free-choice' to defend one's self, family and communities, unless they do so with sticks, stones and kitchen knives evidently. Even 'slingshots' are now 'illegal'; as are metallic straws, for hygienic reasons purportedly (??!!!).

What will YOU be doing ... until 'they' show up at YOUR door ?!!

> 14. "Use of various technologies to kill people slowly or rapidly, as they require."

This is the all-inclusive category of activity that Dad spoke most about in the last few weeks of our ongoing conversations before I returned to Australia and he died within about x2 weeks of cancer.

Over a decade earlier in the early 1980's, we had already thoroughly discussed the basic events occurring at Roswell related to the UFO crash there in 1947, as he flew with Pappy Henderson (who flew the UFO wreckage from Roswell to Wright-Patterson Air Force Base). Dad personally knew various other military officers that were stationed at Roswell, including some that served on the x2 crash locations as investigators, and/or the remove crash debris and the few grey 'aliens' that were found dead within and nearby the crashed small UFO. Evidently one was still alive and was 'recovered' in that condition by the military. Quality UFO research has subsequently conclusively proven that Dad shared key facts that enabled me to do my own corroborative research of this factual event as a UFO researcher, as reliable information continues to be 'made public'.

Likewise in the 1970's, upon my request about "why did the USA not win the Vietnam war?" Dad had thoroughly explained the circumstances he encountered there as Commander of AWACs, while withholding much specificity that he decided I did not need to know, which I gladly accepted at the time. Now, I wish I knew more; however, what we do know is 'more than enough' to make decisions.

Dad was adamant about everything he said to me. There was no confusion or hesitation in whatever he decided was acceptable to share with me, while he withheld other information upon a 'need to know' basis, as is standard procedure.

When Doc said words to the effect that "Nazis have taken over America", he was certain of his facts by personal experiences, as we all can observe now in 2024. Here are some of the primary well-integrated categories that he stated to me:

Directed Energy Weapons (DEWs) of many types do exist, as revealed within the Patent records: DEWs are now being used illegally in a ' war crime' and an 'organised crime' manner against non-combatant civilian populations in many locations globally. These also include: sonic (sound-producing) weapons systems (if only noisy vehicles on nearby roads, airplanes and helicopters overhead, electronic devices within homes, offices, businesses etc.) and ultra-sonic (inaudible noise/sound/energy) weapons systems of countless variety that were designed and manufactured with malicious intent. Now we are seeing some of the devastating consequences in various ways, such as:

sudden inexplicable 'fires', earthquakes, storms, blizzards and curious weather events that are not normally occurring historically in these locations.

Phones, computers, televisions and various other household items are also now being used in nefarious insidious invasive and unconstitutional/criminal ways; such as to obtain private information and utilise some of it for unscrupulous and basically criminal purposes, such as to obtain private banking and other personal information, as has been proven to be factual in an ongoing manner globally. 5G systems are recent attempts to further monitor, control, enslave, and potentially to injure and kill people through their electronic devices, as mentioned previously.

'Death shot' (slow or faster) 'vaccines' and intentionally created pandemics, such as covid, HIV/AIDS, etc. are an ongoing self-evident fact. Corrupt evil nwo international 'agencies' and organisations are seeking to make these harmful 'vaccines' MANDATORY to all people, as they so 'deem' and apply at their own choice, without public knowledge or consent. This is obviously happening within national, state and other areas (locally). Killing defenceless 'civilian' non-combatant people with 'medications'/drugs, or by other murderous methods (execution, cremation, drowning, suffocation, starvation, etc.) is a war crime, punishable by the 'death penalty' for those responsible for ordering and applying those criminal genocidal actions. Those responsible are now self-identifying themselves as 'war criminals' and there will be NO indemnity from prosecutions.

Poisonous toxic food and water additives, such as chlorine, fluoride, and others leeched from contaminated sites, such as lead, mercury; 'artificial sweeteners' are proven known neurotoxins; 'MSG' is another toxic food additive and so on, seemingly endlessly.

'Chemtrails' are being intentionally 'released' (sprayed from special-purpose military jet airplanes at high altitudes) of poisonous and fire-producing chemicals (such as aluminium) that include a mixture of known and potential pathogens (bacteria, fungi, microbes, artificial intelligence (AI) 'nanobots', etc.) and other harmful and known carcinogenic additives. These are also 'war crimes' against Humanity and the Earth. It is an 'organised crime' activity globally with an insane self-serving financial benefit.

Proven harmful 'microwave' man-made radiations including: all man-made energy frequencies currently being used in communications of phones and computers, multitudes of radio frequencies, radar frequencies, x-ray and many other (unknown to public) debilitating frequencies and all are INVISIBLE to most normal human senses. These are proven conclusively to be detrimental to human health, yet virtually nothing (except warning people to avoid excessive radiation exposure), is being done to improve or prevent widespread radiation over-exposure within 'civilised society' locations internationally.

People living in or near cities are being intentionally immersed continuously with over-exposure to these invisible harmful fields of man-made radiations. This too is an 'organised crime' activity and an intentional ongoing 'war crime' globally.

Dad said, "These radio waves ('microwaves') will slowly cook you, just like a lobster or a frog in hot water; just you will not know because it will be gradual." Doc suggested, "When you can see your mental and physical abilities deteriorating rapidly, then you will know it is happening." The self-evident unpleasant confirming evidence is clearly presenting itself for acknowledgement now and will become increasingly so, until the causative factors are eliminated by decisive wise actions to improve matters. So be it now.

You, your family and friends will be able to confirm these events for yourselves now.

15. "Create a 'no escape' scenario with nazi-style 'concentration' (extermination or mass murder or genocidal) prisons to transport unwanted, objectionable and/or 'infected' people to their immediate deaths.

Others would be imprisoned in slave labour camps until they are worked to death or are later shipped to 'death camps' when unable or unwilling to continue working as ordered."

These high-security prisons are already built in most locations globally, as can be seen via the internet on videos of the facilities that include gas chambers and crematoriums (furnaces for burning corpses or those still alive perhaps). The newly constructed prisons are always near railways, airports, major roads and other easily accessible locations for prisoner transportation purposes. All these empty prisons are surrounded by tall razor wire fences, limited access points, guard towers for potential armed marksmen to position themselves, extensive camera surveillance, and contain segregated confined imprisonment areas with small to large-sized 'cells'.

Other videos show hundreds of thousands of large-sized thick plastic coffins that can hold at least five to ten deceased people or more, located within enclosed areas relatively nearby these unoccupied newly constructed prisons. Guillotines for beheading people have been produced for centuries and are planned for use upon Humanity and most other species of life living naturally here too. Evil elitist people, allied with Artificial Intelligence (AI), demonic 'entities' and malevolent ETs (Draconians, Greys etc.) seek to prevail here. This is factual now in the USA, Australia, China, the EU and countless other locations upon Mother Earth.

The current 'health pandemic' is INTENTIONALLY CREATED and is being used as an EXCUSE to do exactly what is being described here. Those RESPONSIBLE have now clearly and repeatedly self-identified themselves, very boldly and proudly. Now comes the times where true justice will be 'served to' those intending mass-murder, oppression, slavery and genocide and ongoing environmental devastation. NOT going to happen that way 'evil nwo creeps'.

Humanity has SEEN how people imprisoned in Guantanamo Bay ('GITMO') have been mistreated. That is 'nothing', compared to the evil treatment and torture that some receive.

It is highly probable that those responsible will choose suicide (self-murder) instead of openly admitting their crimes in the process of various types of ongoing 'investigations' and the public trials that will subsequently occur, as circumstances continue to 'shift in favour' of the 'freeing of Humanity'.

You may be involved, if only as an interested observer. Others will serve in whatever ways are required, as I am doing here now and ongoing. I have NO suicidal tendencies whatsoever. My recent repeated poisonings and the resulting premature death of my partner is the 'final wakeup call' and confirmation that my Dad warned me about, saying, "These psychopaths kill their 'own' and LAUGH about it." This happened to Maura and I in 2021.

Vast amounts of additional information is available to me, related to UFO, ET activities and other 'higher dimensional' spiritually capable Beings that are so diverse/numerous that only many self-evident miracles and accomplishing the seemingly impossible with ease often over the passing years provide confirmations and confidence in knowing these events are occurring.

'We the People' will win our freedom now and ongoing. So be it.

16. "Use various types of drugs to control and make drug-addicted 'zombies' to create 'programmed', robotic-types of reduced-intelligence, or hyper-active to exceedingly docile, or psychotic and mentally emotionally unbalanced (insane), or simply oblivious, unobservant, mindless states of being, etc. for most people."

Dad was a very intelligent, capable, perceptive person and among the best pilots in the USAF. He insisted I learn to play chess at about 8 years old. He did not enjoy playing the game, having been taught by his demanding father and we never played again after I was about 15. That was a relief for us both !!! When I adamantly refused to consider joining the military (beginning at about age 4), my sanity was always a matter of scrutiny and debate within the family.

Playing a quality chess game proved I could think coherently, although the doubts about my sanity continued. I am again playing chess at a 'high level' for various reasons, after 40 years without playing the game and am enjoying chess much more than I did previously, as it is relevant to us all now.

After Dad returned from Vietnam (1969), it was either join ROTC (preliminary military educational service training to become an officer upon graduation from officer training school) at Holy Cross High School in New Orleans (wear the uniform and enlist in the USAF military upon graduation as an 'officer trainee'), or play basketball and wear 'street clothes' at school. Then, if 'drafted' in 1972, I would be going to mandatory military service as an 'enlisted man' (not good options from my perspective ha ha !!!), so I wisely decided to stay true to my personal ethics and staunchly refuse military service of any type.

This consistent unacceptable personal choice led to new options, presented by my Dad: (1) re-consider, or (2) visit a psychiatrist who would fully assess my sanity, and (3) perhaps give me medications to assist in my decision processes to become more amenable and agreeable to the preferred choice for my future career; being in the military for 4 or more years. I replied, "If the drugs do not work, what comes next, the electro-shocks ?!!" The look in my face with the intense reality of it all after over 10 years of ongoing discord on the issue, along with his recent 'tour of duty' in Vietnam was enough 'reality therapy' for us to both instantly be transformed into a mutual silent truce. My decisively beating Dad in the last chess game we ever played at age 15, as we discussed the issue in an amicable manner, was illuminating and definitive for us both. In 1972, my 'draft number' was about 250, yet they stopped 'taking' people that year (except 'volunteers'); so basketball at university was my future, rather than a trip to Vietnam. Great choice Jim !!!

My point being, many people have decided to be upon MEDICATIONS (drugs) of various types too numerous to mention. You may be participating too. I prefer cannabis, yet mostly in the form of 'full spectrum' CBD oil orally in drops. I do not drink alcohol or take any drugs or medications ever and I have stopped smoking cannabis by 'free choice'.

Some people who have lived in the same locations for many years, now rely upon their vehicle navigation device to drive in areas they already know very well because they are on drugs, addicted to their electronic devices, functioning on pathetically dulled senses of perception, getting senile, unable to focus the mind reliably, or just like the robotic voice talking to them constantly, etc. ... and are contently thinking, 'I'm fine." (and everyone else 'has a problem').

The 'warning signs' are literally SCREAMING at us now !!! I am basically 'the canary in the cage' (not yet dead), now publicly clearly saying here, "Houston, we have a problem." For those of you that are not aware of the x2 analogies I am making, they relate to revealing existing potentially dangerous deadly situations.

These electronic devices and the so-called entertainment with advertising is a habitual drug-type of distractive destructive condition that is afflicting many people within modern civilised cultures to the detriment of all life upon the Earth.

How are YOU doing in these times of self-evident criminal insanity among those in key positions of social and financial responsibility now ? Your best possible response is to know YOUR truths, be prepared to make ongoing wise decisions to create YOUR 'better' earthly reality, or suffer accordingly over passing time.

Suicide (self-murder) is NOT an option for ANY of us who are seeking freedom for Humanity. 'We the People' have a beautiful planet to 'save' for future generations of life upon Mother Earth, to live within a peaceful enjoyable reality.

Are YOU ready to truly start doing YOUR STUFF in a peaceful productive way ?

Many of us are already doing so now and FEELING the Bliss too !!!

17. "Faked ET Invasion"

Dad said, "And if all of that is not working well enough or fast enough, then they will do a FAKED ET (extra-terrestrial/alien) invasion. They will have dead Reptilian and Grey bodies and crashed UFOs to make a theatrical war 'show' with their ET allies, to make it look good. Then, back to business as usual."

You can imagine I was shocked and somewhat mentally disorientated by the seemingly impossible, surreal 'Twilight Zone' scenario; having been a UFO researcher previously, then suddenly leaving that occupation in 1986 and permanently immigrating to Australia to try to stay alive and have enjoyable life, while earthly events continued to unfold globally.

This information was presented to me BEFORE 9/11 !!! Did 9/11 events look 'real' to you ?!!! Please consider it in relation to the other facts you already know.

9/11 was a U.S. 'false flag' military operation to intentionally mass-murder people and create what we are now enduring in 2024. It is an ongoing situation that is 'playing itself out' now.

Dad was NOT kidding. Fortunately for Humanity, the wonderfully fantastic news is the evil satanic nwo creeps and their controlling predatorial ET allies (that have apparently been here on Earth for millions of years and/or have time travel and/or 'portal' abilities) have already repeatedly missed their key 'time lines'. The ongoing military and spiritual energetic battles have NOT gone in their favour strategically or logistically. These faked ET attacks and invasion scenarios have NOT happened as planned, and the resulting devastation has been mostly UNKNOWN to human surface populations.

The falsely-fabricated inaccurate myth that earthly military scalar anti-UFO weapons will be able to 'shoot them all down' is hysterically funny (to some of us), as many UFOs and other 'entities' are operating upon astral or etheric levels, as well as applying unknown technologies and capabilities constantly. Most of the underground military bases of the existing nwo fascist system have been destroyed or compromised in various ways. Mars is ALREADY occupied by humans, and various other life forms and they are NOT eager for new immigrants from Earth to arrive there.

Peace-seeking forces are in the action now on every level here upon Earth, while the alternatives are clearly before us now (and will likely continue to be so); however, miracles do occur often during these 'end times'. Peaceful UFOs are being seen by millions globally.

Surrender now, and be held accountable is the only way forward, yet the existing evil nwo system prefers to viciously 'fight on', as they reveal themselves to all. So be it.

Many such efforts to attack Humanity by advanced technologies were assertively thwarted (this time in our history, whereas Tartaria and other civilisations were not so fortunate) with excellent results, thankfully for Humanity and Mother Earth. There will be NO nuclear war.

Countless species of benevolent, highly evolved ET races and beings are collaborating with aspects of Divinity Itself, to defeat (and 'remove' by various methods) the evil 'forces of darkness'. Inclusive in this monumental effort are multitudinous 'channels' or 'co-workers' that include those in physical bodies of various types, possessing technologies and capabilities that are totally unimaginable to our evil aggressive, predatorial, self-identifying adversaries.

This is indeed a war between good and evil; between freedom with love and peace, verses oppressive slavery with hatred, anger, fear, mass murder and war. It is an imposed choice between benevolent bountiful meaningful creative productivity; versus an evil tyrannical insane 'scarcity system' characterised by terrorism, insecurity and dogmatic corrupt fascism.

These are the possible options for the future of human life on Mother Earth now. All are involved to some extent within these ongoing conflicts to 'free' Humanity upon Earth now. Yes, I am 'loving it' (somewhat Ha ha !!) and this is why I am here now, as are YOU.

Many loud booms, with earth-shaking power and strange deep earthquakes with no after-shocks or lightening or clouds in the sky, etc. do reveal the ongoing destruction of the predatorial 'dark ones' many under-ground military and imprisonment 'bases'. Most are now the permanent tombs for those responsible that refuse to surrender their evil predatorial ways to peaceful freedom, with true opportunities for productive prosperity for us all.

Countless (earth-based) UFOs have been seen to be attacked by other (unseen or visible) UFOs or simply come crashing earthwards as though unable to fly. Most are already partly destroyed and non-functional, usually coming down on fire at about a 45 degree angle, to then rapidly disintegrate into only smoke or vapour before impacting the ground, so no damage is done to the ground or people located there in those instances. I saw a video with at least x15 such amazingly revealing UFO 'crashes' from recent times. Almost none of these self-evident videos are making the 'mass media' news. The superior Beings and their incredible abilities and technologies are truly allied with Humanity; along with the 'good guys' in their billions upon trillions, including those seeking freedom and peace from other galaxies, dimensions and reality systems, for reasons that are beyond our imagination.

So it is.

We in Humanity, along with our allies from many locations, now in the action too; are hereby clearly, politely, peacefully and calmly in late 2024 are saying, "NO thanks and NO way, evil nwo-corrupted, treasonous, unconstitutional, baby-killing, blood-drinking, murderous, people-enslaving, abusive, satanic, proudly-demonic, militaristic, fascist creeps !!!"

It is our spiritual role and obligation to resolutely resist evil now and ongoing.

Their final reply is not yet forthcoming, except they obviously intend more of the same and much much worse to come. However, they have explained their perspectives openly to some extent and clearly demonstrated their evil ways. <u>Humanity has clearly peacefully and firmly now said, "No, thank you"</u>.

We know exactly who 'they' are, and exactly where they live and who their families and friends and work associates are globally. Now, "all the kings' horses and all the kings' men will NOT be putting 'Humpty Dumpty' back together again", AFTER Humanity gets finished 'taking care of business', ideally peacefully; with true justice for all concerned here on Earth and in other locations.

The Global Mission of Peace

The Global Mission of Peace (GMOP) is a recently established international humanitarian foundation that is identifying and funding quality projects that will create improved circumstances that characterise the divine qualities of God's presence here on Earth. People of all nations, races, religions and cultures are already working harmoniously and peacefully together to manifest their vision of better ways to do things is the primary focus of GMOP.

Most aware people recognise the self-evident existence of the current oppressive, evil fascist 'nwo globalist system' that is now pervasively seeking to assert its' dysfunctional, corrupt, inequitable, insane, pathologically destructive, unsustainable ways upon all life forms living upon Earth. This volatile, chaotic, unacceptable social circumstance has resulted in international 'martial law' being applied to restrict travel, destabilise the international economy, reduce the population by numerous inhumane ways and promote fearful insanity as 'global public policy'. This totalitarian scenario has been planned for many decades. The fictional books "Brave New World" and "1984" were intentionally created documents that clearly explained what has been intended for centuries. These events appear to be a repetitive cycle that has occurred previously. (Please see the available online information that is related to "Tartaria", a pre-existing global civilisation (destroyed, then 'reset') in relatively recent times.)

While these unpleasant events may not have seemed possible 30 or 50 years ago; we now are distinctively seeing it happening every single day in pervasive ways. A diverse range of adverse circumstances intentionally exist to basically destroy societies, nations, local communities, families, cultural groups and businesses with a clearly stated intent to promote endless war, terrorism, economic inequities, environmental destruction, selective population control (by 'sanctioned', inhumane/brutal mass-murder/genocidal methods) with intended widespread deprivation/suffering for the majority of people for inexplicable, insane 'reasons'. They say it is to 'help the environment', yet we know otherwise.

To pathologically eliminate freedoms and negate (prevent) opportunities for achieving prosperity for most people by a few greedy predatorial autocratic (satanic) evil people is simply unacceptable now. This untenable deplorable situation places Humanity into the ultimate challenge, whereby the ability of our global civilisation to create improved conditions and attitudes, or fail in dramatic chaos; are our only future options now. This is exactly what the evil organised crime organisations intend for their own self-serving unconscionable insane reasons, to the detriment of us all.

The aspiration and intention of the Global Mission of Peace is to improve the lives of every living being here upon Earth by our own wise actions and transform the natural environment into its' optimum circumstances. This will include re-forestation, the stopping of clear-cutting any old growth forests, 'cleaning up' the pollution of all water sources and the oceans on Earth, improving food quality and availability, as well as many other necessary beneficial remedial activities. Limiting environmentally destructive mining practices and replacing them with more environmentally sustainable methods will also be primary GMOP activities globally. Likewise, this includes applying beneficial organic farming and improved health opportunities for all life upon this beautiful, life-sustaining planet.

In this ongoing process, it is necessary to differentiate between what is truly God's Law (Divine ways) and what activities are likely to be Man's Law (mankind's ways), as perceived by the attitudes and self-evident actions existing now and in our past history.

The Law of Love characterises Creator/God's ways and are creative, productive, beneficial and life enhancing. Compassion for others ('the golden rule', do onto others as you would have them do onto you) is a key foundation principle within every genuine religion and spiritual path now existing upon this planet. This is a universally specific 'command' or God's Law that is consistently provided to us. It is that we all learn to "treat others as you wish to be treated"; with respectful kindness, compassion, understanding, peace and love. This is at the heart of all of God's Law. Live in harmonious freedom and let others live peacefully as they choose too.

For centuries Humanity has witnessed the ugly awful evil alternatives.

Man's Law is vastly different in fundamental ways. Man's laws do allow (or even encourage and officially condone/approve) the murder and enslavement of others for many reasons. They seek to legislate codes of legal conduct that enable the 'enforced' violent theft and destruction of other people's land, possessions, culture and freedoms by war, outright 'legalised' theft/fraud and many other unethical unkind adversarial predatorial circumstances. Man's Laws are often 'in conflict' with (opposed to) God's Laws, as any perceptive observer of current reality and history can confidently realise by examining the facts.

Unfortunately, the long ugly painful history of Humanity on Earth is written in the blood and tears of the suffering butchered people and creatures who were unable to defend themselves from the ungodly ones with equal or greater violence. This is NOT God/Creator's intended way for us, truly.

Some of us are already highly aware of external events and are 'at peace' inwardly, in spite of these onerous pervasive challenges. We are rapidly learning that an unhappy, stressful, dysfunctional 'way' of existence is no longer 'acceptable'. The option to create our new and better lives and future is here on Mother Earth now, for Humanity and all the Divine Beings with whom we share this beautiful planet.

We are focused on what we DO wish, intend and dream to create to improve our attitudes, circumstances and actions; so that we manifest and exemplify the best Divine qualities that our Saviours and Prophets have repeatedly demonstrated to us throughout human history in every continent and race, or Species upon Earth.

Divine qualities include those that characterise our Saviours, Prophets, Saints and Messengers: love for all of life, peaceful desires in lifestyle, productive lives to create abundance, acceptance of other's unique ways, freedom to pursue one's dreams of creating a better life through one's ongoing efforts, forgiveness of other's and one's own errors in judgement, compassion and patience for one's self and others, acknowledgment and surrender to God's ways and direction in our lives, and an awareness that we shall generally 'reap as we sow' (receive what we give/create) in earthly life and beyond, as we travel the infinite Divine paths throughout endless eternal realities and realms.

Man's qualities include a vastly less beneficial or enjoyable set of characteristics, as are clearly revealed in the history books and by thoroughly examining daily global events and our personal lives. We see many examples where man's ways are wrongly included or inaccurately interpreted within religious texts and are then perpetrated upon others within Humanity. These include: in the intentional senseless destruction of other people's property and lives; the murder and enslavement of others by brute force and often without mercy or conscience; many forms of abuse, degradation, deprivation (such as forced starvation), and the needless killing of innocent old people, women, children, and even domestic animals; endless examples of greed, corruption, lies, manipulation, deceit and the violent domination of others for self-interest by many of those that are in positions of power and social responsibility, as well as promoting discord, conflict and hate among people; instead of peace, love and productivity. This would include being highly and unreasonably critical or violent toward other groups of people simply because they may disagree with one's perspectives, or be of a differing culture, nationality, race, gender, religion or age.

To wrongly attribute the mistreatment and murder of other humans and life forms as being acceptable or advocated by God through man's religious books is insane and totally unacceptable within a truly civilised society. No Saviour, Prophet, Saint or Messenger has ever encouraged the murder or enslavement or abuse of peaceful defenceless good people, or the destruction of, or theft of their property or homes for any reasons.

However, currently we see some so-called 'extremist' religions and 'war-like' nations, such as the USA and its' allies, are constantly involved in violent predatorial actions with impunity, unconscionable aggression, relentless merciless brutal consistency, and absolutely no remorse or human compassion, nor any genuine peace-seeking, nor any sense of forgiveness for the wrongly perceived transgressions of those they deem to be their enemies. This is mankind's way; NOT God's way.

For example, the Vatican Catholic Church in Rome has deemed itself with the 'ownership' of the entire Earth, its' life forms, etc. and has openly conspired to apply military and financial aggression by governments and corporations in producing the current 'status quo' for thousands of years, according to our contrived false misleading 'history' books. Therefore, it is urgent and imperative that the Vatican recant ('give up', disclaim and disavow) its' claims in this regard.

The Vatican Church is basically an 'organised crime' business that urgently needs to be identified as such and 'closed' immediately, with ALL its' assets, financial wealth and historical treasures being immediately 'assigned to', transferred 'officially' and fairly/wisely 'disbursed' to Humanity over an extended time period, through worthy effective genuinely productive equitable viable ongoing humanitarian activities.

Global Mission of Peace (GMOP) exists to help manifest PEACE within the hearts and minds of ALL people here on Mother Earth; so that LOVE becomes the predominate reality; NOT fear, hate, power and its' other unpleasant 'associates'.

Perhaps someday YOU would like to become a member of GMOP as your 'tribe'.

Our Way Forward

Life is revealing Itself to us all upon Earth in an infinite variety of ways. Many of the ongoing miracles and realisations involved in our individual and collective upliftment and transformation are being presented to each and all of us within Humanity, as well as to other life forms. Amazing events are happening often, including many from unknown sources of which we are only somewhat aware. Other miraculous events and realisations originate from aspects of reality that supersede (go beyond) our current levels of understanding and awareness. We must not dismiss or ignore whatever we do not believe, know or understand at this point in our ongoing evolution as individuals or collectively, as Humanity.

The information within this book, as well as the resulting expansion of your own awareness and capabilities, will ideally serve us all very well. These ideas, experiences and observations are simply a new 'beginning point' for you to verify, confirm and describe things with reference to a few events from my perspectives in ways that ideally will assist YOU, your family, friends and associates and Humanity itself to progress into new areas and better ways of living life to the fullest. This progressive process is to the mutual benefit of us all.

What follows is intended to assist YOU in your journey of discovery through life, in whatever manner exists for you. Because some of this information may seem unlikely, impossible, or a mixture of unbelievable, lengthy comments; please feel free to go slowly and think clearly about all of the events, feelings, and realities that you are aware of existing within YOUR OWN life (and your 'eternal Life', as Soul).

Direct 'inner knowing' by your own 'external events'; will always be your best source of reliable, proven-correct information and experience. Trust and truly learn to LOVE and appreciate yourself, by being worthy of those uplifting wonderful FEELINGS !!!

You may feel unsure of your own nature/being, seemingly alone even while surrounded by others, or unable to 'find your tribe' of compatible harmonious people, or feel 'stuck between a rock and a hard spot' within the current external man-created events and unkindly evil attitudes adversely influencing us all. This 'reality therapy' lesson is to be appreciated and expected, for Earth is the 'school of hard knocks' for most of us here now. Those people that are doing very well and feeling great about life are unlikely to read this book, nor consider its' contents at all. It is all ok now. We have seen the awful truths of these earthly realities and will definitely adjust accordingly now (ha ha !!!).

Enjoy YOUR life, by being as happy/well-adjusted as humanly possible, within this volatile crazy inequitable corrupt world. You may feel the need and benefit of leaving the prevailing human social consciousness 'behind', as you re-discover and creatively improve yourself within this rapidly changing 'reality system'. Be kind to yourself and others; as you live life with grace, relaxed ease, deep joy, gratitude, genuine love, mutual affection and the resulting 'inner bliss', as your 'new way' to be. We can achieve our dreams of creating a better world, simply by going forward into 'better times' peacefully TOGETHER !!!

Just because we 'peace lovers' do not like to argue or fight, does NOT mean that we are cowardly, willing slaves, nor incapable of fighting and defeating the evil, fascist, predatorial, nazi-style, nwo globalist plague upon Humanity. We clearly recognise this is all an aspect of a Divinely created series of circumstances; whereby evil violent people and 'entities' are clearly proudly openly self-identifying themselves over passing time, without any conscience, regret, remorse or true intention to change, or ever stop their vicious, murderous, destructive, dysfunctional, useless, insane, predatorial ways and unkind attitudes. We go forward with this acute helpful awareness and it is one's spiritual obligation to resist evil. We are. We will prevail. We are doing so, now and ongoing...

YOU are now aware of some of my personal well-informed 'testimony', as well as key information wisely provided to me by my astute 'peace loving' father, 'Doc' Wonders.

If you wish, please feel encouraged to read the following previously written book which is predominantly intended for one's spiritual unfoldment (as tedious and painful as it will be in some sections, ha ha !!!) and for the benefit YOU and ALL of Humanity.

'May the Blessings Be' ... and these miraculous events are HAPPENING NOW !!!

Chapter 2

Revealing Experience

Life reveals itself in infinite ways to those of us who seek answers and revelations through our experiences, thoughts and realisations. Over the course of our discussions a wide variety of events will be presented for consideration that conclusively taught me that life's reality is vastly more complex, comprehensive, incredible, fantastic, unknown, and exciting than our normal conscious mind can easily comprehend in logical, analytical terms. The main thing to continually be aware of here is to observe your own mind's responses and reactions, as well as your own similar, yet unique and different life experiences, thoughts and perceptions as these varied events and opinions are being shared.

You may think what is said in some cases is absurd, pure fiction, or absolute nonsense, while in other situations you may share a similar type experience or realisation from such an event in your own life. The most important thing here is to carefully observe your own mind and heart's responses and reactions to the various events expressed, as you search your own mind for any experiences, thoughts, realisations or revelations that become conscious at that time or later. Subsequently, as the discussion progresses, we will more fully analyse some of the implications that these events and realisations have in our lives. In the beginning you may simply wish to read this information on another level, such as being some sort of science fiction novel and that will be fine too, if that is your individual choice. This journey of discovery is about you, my friend; not about me; since most of my lessons came in the living of these events along with the associated realisations at those times, as well as later upon further reflection, and in the writing of our discussion here. Now I am only serving as the 'tool' or 'vehicle' that helps to take you from where and who you now appear to be, a bit closer toward the destination you will choose to reach by the end of our mutual journey of discovery. Then you will once again be travelling your sometimes lonely, yet thrilling eternal journey of discovery on your own. Always know that your loyal travelling companions accompany you, sometimes going their own directions upon their own individual paths, yet always we are all ultimately heading in the same direction; into increasingly greater levels of awareness, wisdom and true love. Everything in life is a matter of individual choice and perception, so please keep this fact in mind as we examine these life circumstances together. It will be quite helpful to temporarily defer deciding what to acknowledge as a possibility, or what you find too difficult to accept as being factual, because this will prevent the tendency for you to reject various concepts when at first they may seem too odd, impossible, or irrelevant to even seriously consider.

Let's begin by examining a few of the bigger issues in life. As a young boy I heard about God from somewhere unknown to me, probably from my parents, since we had no television until I was twelve years old. I gave the issue of God's existence or nature very little thought initially and had no conscious recollection of what I was told on the subject, since at the time I was about a four year old boy. My thoughts focused mainly upon nothing much more than chasing the quick birds, catching little lizards, and the odd harmless snake that lived in our yard, with hopes of getting a cookie when I was deemed to be a good boy.

One of my most vivid, truly conscious memories as a child occurred a short while after my brother was born, which I will now recall and share with you. The experience was then and still remains as one of the most unusual, memorable events of my entire life, which is now about half a century at this point in time. My mother told me to go outside to play in the yard, since she was taking care of my brother, who was a relatively newborn baby. I was always pleased to be outside in our large yard, with trees, bushes, and seemingly lots of wildlife that were unable to evade my inquisitive capture, affection, which would then be released to hopefully be caught again on another day. The day of the most memorable event in my childhood was at that moment; normal, very common and actually quite forgettable in every way, yet what followed was not. Those moments almost fifty years ago still remain as clear in my mind's eye as though they were happening upon an old home movie one would watch to reminisce of bygone days too distant to recall. As I relive them in this writing, they again become vibrantly alive, exceedingly special, delightful and exceedingly fulfilling in my heart, mind, and Soul.

On this memorable day I recall walking outside into the yard by myself, enjoying a brilliant beautiful afternoon, birds singing, breeze gently swaying the treetops, a few puffy clouds in the otherwise clear blue sky. Suddenly I heard someone call my name, "Jim" in a pleasant, somewhat longer than usual, drawn out in length manner, phonetically sounding like "Jiieemm". I immediately stopped observing nature to look to see the source of who was calling my name in such an evocative, somewhat unusual manner, in a voice that seemed vaguely familiar, yet was not recognised by me. As I looked around, I could see no one; nothing was visible in the yard, nor in the bushes, and Mom was upstairs inside and it was not her voice. A few moments later, after I was sure there was no one visible anywhere in the yard, the same voice softly, clearly, and quite distinctly called my name, sounding like "Jiieemm" again. Once again I quickly looked around, but could see no one in the yard, or nearby, so I then looked upwards, thinking that the voice was perhaps from someone upstairs or in a tree. As I did so, a puffy white cloud altered its shape quite rapidly, as if it were a man turning the back of his head to face me. The cloud almost instantly transformed in appearance to become like a large distinct smiling face with rosy cheeks and sparkling intense blue eyes that connected deeply with mine. The most striking feature was the brilliance of the vibrantly blue shining eyes on the wide smiling, very happy face that was looking directly at me, very intently into my own receptive amazed eyes. Immediately I felt an overwhelmingly powerful, incredible sense of the intense mixed emotions of love, joy and peace within myself that vastly surpassed anything I had ever known. Instantly I became so indescribably happy to experience such an incredible state of joyous bliss that I felt 'light' enough to have literally floated off the ground to move closer to this inexplicable, unknown presence in the sky. I had never before, nor ever since, experienced such indescribable happiness, sheer joy, deep true love, and secure comfort that I did feel for those few brief moments. Nothing more was said to me. I simply experienced true divine love for the first time in my earthly life; the dramatic extent to which has not been repeated again in my conscious recollection, in spite of many amazing experiences occurring since that time. Then the face instantly dissolved into a cloud again, as if the head turned away from me. The vividly powerful, indescribably intense, spontaneously unexpected, undeniable feelings of joy, peace, love and comfort were still very much alive and vibrant within me, as though the experience were still continuing, but without the face smiling at me.

I clearly recall the entire event, in spite of my young age at the time, as among one of the most lucid, memorable, undeniable, defining moments in my entire life. It was one experience I will never forget, ignore or confuse as being unreal, imagined, nor was it contrived in any way by any earthly human beings.

I distinctly recall running as fast as any four year old could, up the stairs to my mother and very excitedly and joyously trying to explain to her what I had seen and felt only moments before. After a few confused attempts to express the event so she was able to understand the significance, I simply said, "I saw God! I saw God in the sky!" I can vividly recall the perplexed, mystified look of confused concern and worry upon my mother's face. I knew immediately from her expression and relative emotional apathy that she did not fully understand what I was saying, or what I saw. Otherwise, I was absolutely sure that she would have been smiling and very happy to hear about the event. I was somewhat stunned by her inability to mentally comprehend and emotionally empathise with the joy, peace, and amazingly powerful love that I had briefly experienced. I then immediately became quite concerned and somewhat frustrated about her inability to fully understand my joy and excitement in that moment or to later gain an appreciation of the event, even after I sought to adequately explain the entire experience to her in as much detail as a four year old could do in a few minutes.

Then I clearly recall my mother, the wisest, most loving person I knew, begin to explain to me something about someone dying on a cross to save us all and that his name was Jesus. I did not even know what a cross was at the time. All I knew was that whatever I saw in the sky was definitely alive in some mysterious way, although not in a body as we know them to be, and that it was pure love, that it called my name, then somehow contacted me directly to enable me to know through my own experience what true love, joy, peace and inner comfort were all about. As I watched my mother's face full of concern, telling me of someone's death with no joy, peace, love, or comfort showing in her expression, nor such feelings in her voice or heart at the time, I immediately knew absolutely in that moment that she did not know what or whom I had seen. It then also became quite obvious to me that she had never witnessed such an event herself, otherwise her responses and reactions would have been different, more joyous, delighted and excited for me. I then recalled feeling quite disappointed and sorry for her unaware state of mind, as she tried in vain to explain away any possibility that I had seen God in a cloud in the sky. For me it was not a matter to be debated or explained in any terms aside from those of the experience itself, which were self-evident then and will always remain so in my mind. I then experienced the poignant realisation that my mother, who was someone I would need to depend upon to teach me many things in life, definitely had no real understanding of my life's most important, intensely vivid, meaningful experience. As Mom continued speaking and explaining about her version of God which made almost no sense at all to me then, I first fully realised that the most significant, loved adult that I knew perceived life differently to me. This knowledge concerned me greatly, yet at such a relatively young age it also helped me to better understand our individual natures as people. That pivotal early experience definitely taught me in an illuminating, easy to comprehend manner that adults actually did not know everything, nor were they infallible, as they often appeared to us while we were children.

That event began immediately to have an effect on my mind as the myths of my childhood were revealed over the following few years to be mostly false. Subsequently, I spent the next few years trying to find or see the Easter Bunny, Santa Claus, the Tooth Fairy, and even to see God again, with no luck. I already knew conclusively in my mind, heart, and spirit that God did indeed exist and that the Creator of the universe and I were not likely to be personified by a long-dead man named Jesus Christ, as I had been told. Gradually I began to seriously doubt the purported factual existence of the mythical Easter Bunny, Tooth Fairy and even Santa Claus, as well as 'the boogie man', although I was unsure about the tales of elves, witches and ghosts and other such entities at that time. These events and realisations were among many others that began my life-long search for the truth as revealed by my own experiences. Fact for me became distinct from what I was told, taught or read in books. Facts from my perspective were only to be ultimately accepted as such when they were clearly, distinctly revealed and ideally repeatedly confirmed by my own experiences.

A relevant confirming subsequent postscript to this event happened about forty years later. One day I was working in the yard when my two young sons, who were about four and five years old at the time, ran up to me very excitedly saying to me, "Did you see him?!" then repeated, "Did you see him?!" I was much less excited than they obviously were and calmly replied, "See who?" They took turns saying, "It was just like you said, we didn't believe you, but we both saw him!" My older son, Nathan first told me of seeing the happy face in the sky and told me that he then had pointed it out to his brother Kevin, who also saw it. They both were quite elated with excitement, joy and delight and added that they had also experienced the positive, loving good feelings as well. When I asked what they were referring to, they looked amazed at my momentary confusion both saying at the same time, "It was just like you said happened to you when you were a little boy. We saw God's face in the sky smiling at us! We both saw it and it made us feel really good and happy!"

Only in that moment did I truly begin to relate with my Mom's perceptions and emotions because initially before the magnitude of the unexpected event became more apparent to me, I could only express in words how happy I was for them both. I then became much more excited for them, said it was great, and that I wished that I had seen it with them too. I was acutely aware that I was indeed very happy for them, yet nowhere near as happy as they were at the time because I had not actually experienced those incredible feelings myself in that moment. I can clearly now recall struggling to try to actually feel the sheer joy that they were obviously emotionally feeling at the time. I was truly delighted, then and now, in knowing that they had also experienced that special, profoundly meaningful event so early in their lives. I asked them why they did not call me to look too and they replied that it was only there for a few moments and that they did not think to do so, or have time because it was gone so quickly. I fondly recall the amazed look on their smiling, excited little faces, with their experience and the related emotions still fresh in their minds and hearts. At the time I was quite aware and somewhat frustrated that I was not able to empathetically share the full degree of their emotionally joyful experience in my heart at that moment. I then recalled how difficult it had been for my mother to comprehend my own experience of seeing God in a similar manner as a youngster. That vivid memory further then lead to the more inclusive appreciative realisation that to experience something one's self is vastly superior and quite different than hearing about it, even if one has experienced the same thing or something similar themselves, as I had. This is an essential concept to carefully consider and accept throughout our discussion, especially as it progresses, so please reflect upon this fact.

One reason in sharing the experience of my two boys is that I had told them previously of my own childhood experience of seeing God in the sky. They later confided in me after seeing a similar event themselves, in spite of their young age, that they had privately both discussed having some serious doubts regarding whether their father, as a four year old, could have possibly seen God in the sky. With both boys having had the unexpected, spontaneous, undeniable, powerful experience together of actually seeing and feeling the same event confirmed one another's perceptions of astounded amazement and better enabled both of them to intellectually accept, understand and empathise with my own similar experience as a child. In this process, I was primarily intellectually aware of the actual nature of the event upon hearing their explanation, yet still not able to be fully conscious emotionally and spiritually aware of its magnitude to the extent that they were experiencing that situation. Please consider the fact the boys were only about twenty meters from where I was working in the yard and that it was distinctly like my own experience as a young child. My ability to empathise with them at that time was significantly diminished when compared to the actual magnitude of the emotional, enormously significant event for them both. It is essential to realise there is no way for me to fully convey or express to you the fantastically intense, sublime, unforgettable feelings and emotions inherent in the similar event I had experienced as a child in this written form nor in spoken language to another person. This event demonstrates a key principal related to the power and meaning of analysing the nature of our own experiences or those reported by other people, while realising that our own experiences are by far the most important to each of us, as individuals.

Your experiences are what really and truly matter most to you. You can mentally intellectualise upon my story of the events described previously, or other events that will be recorded here, yet nothing that others experience will even approximate reality or properly convey the full set of information as would experiencing such an amazing event for yourself. This process will be further clarified as we reveal that life is vastly more interesting, complex and infinitely diverse than any human mind can ever fully comprehend or consciously be aware of in this earthly life.

As the long past event of seeing God is being vibrantly relived in my mind, another consideration is the intense emotions I felt and knew very deeply at the time. About fifty years have passed since my own childhood experience with what I perceived to be God. There is an undeniable sadness or longing arising from reliving those dynamic stimulating memories; to once again experience the joy, peace and divine love now. It is compelling to share this fact with you. We can ask ourselves, why does this odd mixture of happy sadness co-exist together now when this experience seems to be the ultimate superlative, the greatest event in my life's memory? Such issues are matters of deliberation, reflection, curiosity, and wonder. Examining our entire state of being, as revealed through our experiences, is the foremost relevant key issue at the core of our quest to better understand and more fully integrate the various aspects of our human character with our total, eternal levels of self-awareness.

Specifically, it seems the intensity of the sadness and longing referred to here when reliving those events of seeing God is somewhat akin to the loss of a close loved one. It is a combination of mixed feelings of fond love, with a sense of loss, of separation, of being somewhat disconnected from the much loved event or person in one's life and one's true emotional, spiritual essence. The intensity, sheer joy, deep true love and comfort that I momentarily experienced as a toddler remains alive within me as an adult; however, the event has now seemingly become a bit more intellectualised; somewhat less vibrant, a bit less of an illuminating transcendent moment of pure reality than it was at the time it actually happened. Even now, the magnitude of the powerful, life-changing event is still astounding to me, especially in examining the sequential influences and further implications that the event created throughout my lifetime. The fact remains that at the time it occurred there was absolutely no sadness, feelings of separation or disconnectedness between my self-awareness and what I perceived to be God, which I witnessed as a smiling face in the sky. Yet now I inevitably experience the intense flood of mixed emotions upon vividly recalling that extraordinary event.

So, what is the possible nature, source or cause of the odd and seemingly out of place or unrelated emotions of sadness, longing and a somewhat disconnected feeling or awareness at the fond thoughts of my life's most precious, loving, happy event? Your opinion, guess, or assumptions are very likely to be every bit as valid and relevant as my own would be. You may have recalled some event in your past that evokes similar emotions and realisations, even if that event seems completely unlike the ones mentioned here for our consideration. One of many possible responses to the previous question is that as an adult, I have realised how remote, estranged, and distant my present life and state of being has become since that event occurred, as evidenced by the fact such a dramatic event has not yet been repeated in my conscious, awake, living memory as an adult. The emotion of sadness seems to originate from a sense of apparent alienation or separation from that source of life that I experienced or believed to be an aspect or revealed characteristic of my Creator. The odd, seemingly out of place, mild feeling of sadness when considering the joyful event may be related to my (false) perception now that God seems far more remote and distant from my daily conscious awareness than was the situation in those few brief moments of lucid, aware, shared higher consciousness as a child. To consciously realise that situation exists within various aspects of my mind, heart and Soul results in the mixed emotions that seek on some levels to re-create, find, and again experience that same blissful, vibrantly alive state of joyous, truly loving being.

Life's realities apparently have their own sense of timing, purpose and action, which often seems independent or unaffected to some degree by our personal volition, free-will, wishes, prayers, preferences, best intentions and efforts. Most people have an inner knowingness or faith of God's existence that may originate from various sources or their own types of definitive experiences. I was fortunate enough to distinctly witness what my present level of consciousness would define or assume to be an aware aspect of God, or my Creator. This could be an inaccurate assumption upon my part regarding the alive-appearing face or being that contacted me briefly, which could simply be one type of the many 'higher' manifestations that God's consciousness inhabits within its cosmic creations. In the context of our discussion here we are defining the concept of God as being synonymous in principal with the Creative Force that somehow brought into existence all life and consciousness in this universe.

Accompanying the brilliant recollection of that special event is the intense desire and virtual 'need' to reconnect consciously with that being or consciousness that I perceive to be God. It is important to acknowledge that I am unable to conclusively know whether or not that particular manifestation was actually an aspect of God, or instead simply could have been a higher species of life that my level of consciousness would naturally assume (possibly somewhat incorrectly) to be God, the Creator of life as we know it. Such intellectualisations are basically irrelevant, unprovable, unsubstantiated assumptions based upon limited evidence and pure conjecture; so we shall not further address them now. However, the issue goes to the core of what is actually factual, from a given perspective, at a certain point in time. For example, some of the early South American Indians falsely perceived the technologically superior European explorers as some form of gods. It took them some time to later determine that these unusual looking people were simply normal human beings originating from another earthly civilisation whose conquest over several centuries would lead to their indigenous civilisation's destruction. Therefore, obviously here in this earthly life we must be very careful, deliberate and thorough in deciding what we choose to believe and how we act upon that information in various ways.

It is of critical relevance to our inquiry to acknowledge that most people are attracted to experiences that express true love, joy, comfort, bliss, peace and heightened awareness in our lives, minds and hearts. Once we experience these states of higher consciousness, then subsequently we seek them again and again in the various ways possible for us. Our earthly inability to reliably create, sustain, or re-experience these sublime, delightful, joyous, aware states of human existence within our usual ordinary life conditions tends to upset and frustrate us to some degree, even if only on a subconscious basis. On a deep intuitive level we innately know the highest possible positive states of being exist within us. These heightened states of consciousness are relatively seldom experienced in this earthly life by most of us in our normal daily lives. Nevertheless, most people are well-aware that these joyous, highly perceptive states of being are eternal realities. Those of us who have experienced blissful, sublime levels of awareness in one form or another seek to do so as often as possible, so long as not too much effort or inconvenience to our material lifestyle is required. A distinct minority of people throughout recorded history have been and continue to remain willing to adjust their attitudes and activities to encourage these higher states of being within themselves and to manifest them through the activities of their daily lives. All people living in our global society owe a great debt of gratitude and appreciation for the example provided by such true leaders because they have improved our world in countless ways. Our quest here is to describe specific methods that enable each of us, as individuals and as groups of like-minded people, to become the best people and global society that we can possibly be.

Please take the time and make a serious effort to reflect upon and recall some of your childhood's most pleasant, happy, unique and sublime experiences. You may be surprised with what will reveal itself through your relaxed contemplation, idle daydreams, night's dreams, or to otherwise stimulate the memory of long forgotten events in this manner. If less pleasant memories from your childhood are prone to assert themselves, then acknowledge them and simply focus more upon your happier experiences even if they were of a favourite pet, school friendship, enjoyable pastime, nice family outing or whatever gave you a sense of joy as a young child, to the best of your memory's ability. If not much comes to mind after ten or twenty minutes, then focus more upon what you enjoy doing now or what positive activities you believe that you would like to do now to improve your happiness, peace of mind, and inner comfort. This is a very important process to begin now at this particular point in our evolving discussion, so please make the time available to do this personal assessment of your childhood's most enjoyable experiences. If this process requires a few focused attempts over an extended time period to familiarise your mind with these mental visits into your distant past, then be patient and persistent because the resulting achievements are well worth the efforts. It is essential that you reconnect to some degree with the happier, inner self that most of us were more consciously aware of when we were youngsters. Since this may not necessarily be the situation in your life, focus your recall on whatever has made you happiest in your life or even imagine what you believe would make you happiest and most fulfilled and visualise that occurring, if you wish to do so. We will develop an increased awareness of our ability to experience inner happiness, joy and peace of mind in various ways throughout our discussion.

Often many years would pass between my conscious recall of that youthful experience with what my human mind can only interpret, describe, and define that unknown entity, which at the time seemed to be God, for lack of a better description, then or now. Creative conscious life forces or 'higher beings' manifest in various ways; just as do life forms of less evolved natures, such as humans, animals, sea creatures, plants and so on. Whomever or whatever type of Being that the ultimate Creator of all of existence may actually be, I am unable and unwilling to further speculate upon my own unsubstantiated ideals as to Its nature, purpose or intent in this existence we know as life on Earth. All I do know is that the infinite aspects of life gradually do reveal themselves to those who seek truth for truth's sake, to better comprehend the nature of reality and quest for the ultimate meaning of life through examining the multifarious processes of their own mental, emotional, and spiritual states of being.

We shall continue to share a wide range of ways this mysterious process of discovery can and does occur, as you examine your own life experiences and beliefs to determine your own realisations, similar, yet quite unique to my own.

Chapter 3

Life Is More Than It Appears To Be

If we genuinely seek answers in life, then they are provided to us. Often these answers or solutions to various issues do not present themselves the way or when we expect them, yet they do eventually arrive, if we are receptive, persistent and observant. Almost always our most difficult, challenging circumstances, especially when later viewed retrospectively, prove to be some of our greatest lessons that tend to build strength of character and are catalysts for important life-changing realisations. Reflecting back into one's life's multitude of experiences, some will reveal themselves as being essential in creating critical positive or negative turning points in one's life. Usually, these significant moments in our lives result from one's conscious realisations and decisions at the time, which subsequently lead to significant growth, adaptation and beneficial change in one's perceptions, lifestyle and personal choices. Alternatively, our poor choices tend to make life more difficult and overly complex, until we make improved choices to get our lives functioning in a better manner again.

To fully accept and lucidly realise that we are indeed the creators and masters of our own destiny and to respond accordingly with clear intent regarding what we seek to accomplish is quite advantageous. Some of us tend to allow and even encourage other people to influence, control, and determine our fate; whereas other types of people are more self-reliant, independent-minded, and seek to consciously make their own decisions in life. This self-responsibility of perception and choice enable this latter type of person to maintain a greater degree of self-control, inner direction, and a sense of purpose that manifests in ways that seem to present more autonomy, freedom and opportunity for personal growth and individualistic expression than other types of people, who tend to primarily rely upon others for their direction, purpose and needs. This generalisation is surely not to categorically state that either type of person will be happier, more successful or better integrated in society than another idealised stereotypic person, for the sake of our consideration here.

Actually most people exhibit some of both type tendencies, depending upon the circumstances. For example, one may function as a relatively pliant, conformist type of personality within their occupational role and at other times by an entirely different set of unique characteristics in their personal private life. Conversely, one may be individualistic and creative in their work, yet quite socially controlled and group focused in their family life, religious practices and in their other social contexts. Also, one can fluctuate to some degree between these tendencies based upon one's experiences in life, such as the submissive spouse becoming the rugged individualist after a difficult marriage ends, or when one career path ends and another begins that presents a new set of personal character prerequisites. The core issue we are considering here is that social and economic needs and specific circumstances can definitely affect one's attitudes and actions and life in diverse ways that have a real impact upon one's manifested character. For example, if one were to work in a sensitive public government job, then various personal and public comments and actions of the controversial nature may not be acceptable avenues of expression; regardless of one's personal belief system, if publicly expressing one's opinions or disclosing confidential information were against government policy, procedures or regulations. Therefore, if one had a personal proclivity or compulsion to fully and honestly express themselves and in all cases to act according to their own inner conscience and personal opinion; then, for example, the role of a government official such as a diplomat or press secretary would not be an ideal or acceptable role in public life for such an individualistic, self-expressive person. However, these character traits may be ideal as a novelist, artist, philosopher, social scientist or other such profession. Alternatively, after a career in one field of activity, one may retire or otherwise be encouraged by life's events to pursue a more personally fulfilling, self-controlled occupation or hobby.

While this brief introduction to our topical matter in this chapter will seem somewhat irrelevant, it is actually vitally important that we reflect back before we proceed to consider some of what follows here. When one began to form their viewpoint in order to determine their perspective and system of beliefs, they also began making a huge number of conscious and unconscious value assessments and judgments, which greatly influenced their entire lives and state of mind. As a child in school and later in the process of selecting one's career path and through adjusting to one's adult life in roles as a spouse, parent, employee, etc; we all are to some degree making choices on how we perceive the world. Subsequently, over time this process greatly affects our attitudes, beliefs, activities and roles in life in many ways.

Some experiences in life demonstrate quite obviously and unforgettably a variety of factors that leave a lasting, powerful influence in one's mind. In many such cases, the experiences are so dramatic, unpleasant or contrary to one's system of beliefs that they are ignored, denied or suppressed. Part of our journey of self-discovery is to extensively examine a multitude of personal and cultural factors, attitudes, tendencies, characteristics, beliefs, responses, reactions, and social conditioning influences. At times, such a self-analysis process can be quite uncomfortable, very confusing, upsetting, frightening or absolutely delightful, or any other set of descriptive qualifiers, depending on the circumstances and one's responses and attitudes to those events, experiences and realisations. To exemplify this process, we will refer to an unusual, amazing event experienced in fully conscious alert awareness that definitely defies one's normal logical, rational, intelligent mind. Such an inexplicable event would be experienced, analysed and ordinarily be concluded as being "impossible", when considered according to one's own prior existing perspective of the natural laws of this universe as we have been taught in school, by science and society, as well as by our own previous life events and knowledge.

Examining these unique events along with the associated emotions and life altering realisations is one of our key foundation themes here. This mutual interaction of our experience will lead us to more fully consider our true shared nature as human beings. Therefore, aspects of these types of unusual, sometimes unbelievable experiences in many varied forms are included and alluded to throughout our discussion. The most important set of incredible experiences are the ones that you will recall from your own personal experiences in life. What is recorded here for your consideration has great meaning, symbolism and significance in my system of knowledge and belief, yet is primarily intended to trigger aspects of your own life memories and to provide examples that you relate to personally in various ways. Some of your memories may be long-forgotten or were perceived at the time they occurred as being curious occasional oddities that had relatively little meaning to you then. Such experiences may have been "explained away" by others in your life as figments of your overly active imagination, or which you completely or partly discounted and ignored as being impossible mistaken perceptions that did not actually occur as it seemed or appeared to you at the time, and so on. Some of these events to follow in our discussion will seem impossible, improbable, pure fiction, or total imagination; yet they actually occurred to me exactly as is stated here, to the best of one's ability to relate such incidents into written words. These unusual experiences are not included to undermine my credibility by creating doubt, or antagonism in your mind. Neither am I attempting to add excitement to what some people would consider to be a rather boring, mundane, meaningless topic, nor am I seeking to appear to be someone with a more unique or inexplicable life to that of any other ordinary human being. Some of my own special experiences are included for a variety of reasons that may not seem readily apparent. Likewise, it was perplexing that I chose to intentionally omit other equally amazing events of incredible personal revelation, including some of a highly controversial nature that I was quite tempted to include, yet did not. The primary reason for including my own personal experiences is that they actually happened to me and therefore I am acutely aware of the circumstances involved in the example events that I will share here in our discussion. Another reason is to reveal that all of our lives, including your own range of personal life experiences, do clearly demonstrate that various events, responses, and realisations considerably supersede our standard, traditional understanding, awareness and interpretations that we as individuals, societies, religions, and science are presently able to intellectually acknowledge in earthly existence.

To experience something that is highly unusual, unexpected, and spontaneous while one is fully alert and consciously aware tends to transcend the normal function of the human intellect. In such incredible events, quite often a higher form of vivid perception occurs, that is associated with strong, clear, intuitive feelings, a definitive inner knowingness, resolute conviction, and sometimes a deep understanding, followed by faith in one's experiences, based upon the revelations of these inexplicable events. It is through the process of examining these unique, special, sometimes amazing, often inexplicable, yet undeniable events and perceptions that each of us can better recognize and eventually come to accept, in our own time and ways, that there is vastly more reality in existence than we, as human beings on this Earth at this stage of our evolutionary history, are now aware of through our five ordinary senses of perception. So much of our daily lives are filled with what seem to be the standard norms, the sometimes boring repetitions of 'the same old things' in our awareness, that our full set of perceptive systems become somewhat dulled; to some extent desensitized, blocked and significantly overloaded by too much superfluous, mundane seeming information. Our higher senses of perception thereby cease to function as efficiently and effectively as innately possible for all of us. Therefore, among our goals here is to improve the functional nature of our higher set of capabilities.

Throughout our communication here various events, experiences, perceptions, thoughts, realisations, and philosophical opinions will be presented to stimulate various responses and to assist in the recall of events within your past, as well reveal much additional information about your current beliefs and attitudes. What matters here is what you have experienced and what those events, perceptions, realisations, attitudes, beliefs, actions, and life responses mean to you. These vital factors influence and create the life you now live and will progressively choose to create over passing time, as the result of all of these integrated factors. The only aspect we are able to share here is our experience, beliefs, opinions and attitudes. Our discussion may at times seem to be basically 'one-way traffic' in the process of my sharing my own ideas, experiences, perceptions and opinions with you here. However, this process is ideal in some ways because ultimately speaking; the only events and perceptions that really matter are yours, not mine. I am no different than you are, except as being a different individual. My human bodily experiences, beliefs, opinions, attitudes, responses, and life choices are as individually unique to me, as are yours to you; as is true for each and all human beings. So my experiences here are only used to serve as examples of various types of events. The result of these personal experiences has been the establishment of a wide range of assumptions, perceptions, opinions, beliefs, and responses that resulted within me and some of these events will relate to you and your own experiences, perceptions, beliefs, inner explanations, and responses. Please remain conscious that these events in most cases are not always intended to prompt similar memories of the same types of events or perceptions in your own life. In some situations this may occur, yet it is far more likely that you will recall seemingly unrelated events through these mental and emotional associations that sometimes will be far different and quite unlike what I am then describing as you read these events, concepts, and perceptions. As these basic ideas and events are written here, countless other personal experiences, realisations and a few revelations crowd into my mind, which seek expression, relevance, integration, and imply greater meaning.

Much of the human intellect is relatively limited by 'either/or' type mental contrasts, and 'like this', or 'opposed to that' type thinking processes and situations. So, while one concept is being referred to here, please do not be concerned or opposed to your own mind presenting many seemingly unrelated or alternative memories, thoughts, experiences, or just distracting your attention to other issues of your daily life, past, and so on. You may wish to be read through some of this information, or even the entire book more than once, if you wish or need to do so for greater clarity. Or you may skim through it as being some sort of curious science fiction novel written by someone who is overly imaginative or perceives things in life much differently than you currently do. I repeat this encouragement because there will be issues raised and discussed that will make you, and even myself, quite uncomfortable in some cases. Please feel free to respond to what follows in any reasonable way that you feel appropriate for you, since this journey of discovery is primarily your own life's story.

Some of these events are the most real, significant experiences in my life, which assisted me toward making some relatively profound realisations that enabled me to more accurately comprehend the nature and meaning of existence, from my own perspective. Other events and realisations that will also be included here are much more common, basic and unimpressive; with some almost seeming mundane, until or unless perceived from another, more integrated perspective or attitude. Then, in this wider, more inclusive, expansive context, even common events, emotions and conclusions are quite meaningful in the larger context of our eternal life, which is another key theme in our discussion here.

The following experience is selected now because it is relatively basic and is explicable in terms of the event being open to various interpretations, to avoid it seeming too unbelievable in your mind. It could seem to you as being the wishful imagining of a young boy. Yet, the facts prove otherwise to me and the person whose life I saved at that time. What is most revealing and significant for discussion here is not the event itself; rather it is the application of higher mental capabilities that dramatically prove the existence of an intuitive, inner mental connection that established an urgent form of telepathic communication between mother and son in a time of great need. The key concept here is to acknowledge the existence of non-verbal, telepathic, mind to mind communication occurring between people; not the relatively obvious manner that this factual reality was demonstrated to me as a youngster by this event.

At about the age of ten, I was playing football with a few of the local children about hundred meters from my home. As I ran out to receive a pass, I heard my mother urgently and distinctly call me, "Jim come home now." The call audibly sounded as though it was her voice, which was clearly heard by me and characterised by being made in a somewhat loud, immediately urgent, insistent manner. Normally I would have either caught the pass or at least said, "I have to go home now" and said goodbye to my friends. However in this extremely unusual case, I never looked back and urgently sprinted as fast as I could possibly run to the back door of our home. As I rounded the corner in view of the back door, my mother was in the process of opening the back door and she literally fell out of the door upon her hands and knees. Her face was a vivid bright reddish purple colour and she looked in helpless horror at me to do something. I immediately knew somehow that she was choking, although she did not have time to gesture about the fact to me as I now recall the event. I immediately hit her very sharply on the back with my open hand as she reached for her throat to indicate her choking situation. Immediately, a huge piece of chicken breast flew out of her mouth, with a broken bit of wishbone in it which had lodged itself firmly in her throat, totally blocking her air supply.

When Mom recovered, she profusely thanked me and asked me why I had come running home as, she had seen the abnormal speed of my approach around the house and up the stairs as she fell out of the doorway. I explained that I had heard her call me urgently, so I had run home. We both well-knew that was quite unusual for me in any previous event. She fairly calmly explained to me that she had been alone in the kitchen and by the time she realised how severely she was choking and that she could not dislodge the chicken in her throat herself, that she was already near losing consciousness due to lack of oxygen and was completely unable to verbally call for help. Her last effort was to try to get outside where I or someone may see and help her before she lost consciousness and choked to death. I explained that I distinctly heard her call me in what seemed to be in an auditory voice, to very urgently come home. Mom again explained that she was not able to breathe, nor able to speak, much less call out from inside the kitchen loudly enough for me to hear her about 100 meters away.

The fact that I had run home so quickly before she could even get outside to try and get my attention was undeniable. She then encouraged me to consider the full situation, to not ignore my experience as being simple coincidence, and allow myself to consider the possibility that I may have telepathically somehow "heard" her desperate initial cry for help when she first realised she was in real danger of choking to death. Mom said her main mental focus was to exert her willpower to remain conscious long enough to exit the house before passing out. Mom said she was aware that to lapse into unconsciousness inside the house with no one home would have likely resulted in her death by the time she was found by anyone. It was well before our normal dinner time, so my father was not due home for at least another hour.

As I reflect upon the event periodically over the years, I also have the opportunity to consider how difficult, different and lonely my life would have been if my mother had died on that day. Also, the realisation of one's mortality and the resultant effects of acting intuitively and instinctively with great urgency in times of emergency for one's self and others tended to impress itself periodically upon me in a multitude of ways. It was almost impossible to deny the event occurred in that way because I was forced by the obvious circumstances to accept that I had heard her call to me telepathically, since she was unable to verbally call to me loudly while choking inside the home 100 meters away, as anyone who has choked can attest. Nor could I ignore and forget about the event since it periodically replayed itself upon my mind, asking the question, "How did that happen?" Over the passing months and years, I gradually finally knew and accepted that I really "heard" Mom call me on an internal, intuitive level, that we term telepathic, mind to mind, nonverbal, non-auditory, mental communication. Now, after about 40 years of reconsidering all aspects of the event, including my instant response in that critical moment, along with recalling it was the only time I ever recall running home with such speed and urgency results in my considering the experience as an example of telepathic communication in an emergency situation. Since that event I have experienced countless other examples of telepathic communication on various levels, yet none have been this dramatic or urgent in my conscious recollection. These events have proven to me that human beings can occasionally consciously communicate by purely non-verbal, clearly understood, mind to mind mental telepathy, especially when the need to do so is extremely urgent and necessary. Some of us use this form of communication periodically or upon a normal conscious, subconscious, or unconscious basis.

Another brief story proves to me that this is not limited to human to human communications. I shared many good years with a fine large dog, named Bandit, who was outstanding in every respect. One of his unique traits was to let me know that he needed to go out to the bathroom or to meet his canine friends at night when I was asleep by putting his paw upon my bed, or upon my arm or upon my chest. During the day he would simply walk to the door and look at it, then again look at me, then again at the door, until I let him go outside. One night I may have been quite slow to awaken; and somehow mistakenly Bandit put his rough large paw across my eyes and nose, scratching them somewhat abruptly. Out of a deep sleep, I came up swinging like a man fighting for his life. By the time I awakened enough to realise what had happened, unfortunately I had punched Bandit several times in the head quite hard. Quickly, I realised what happened and immediately stopped, apologizing most sincerely for my actions, before letting him outside. From that night onwards, Bandit would awaken me, not putting his paw upon my bed nor upon my body, but rather he would simply sit by my bedside and apparently stare at me to awaken me. He would arouse me from sleep me by mentally calling my name somehow, or by getting my sleeping attention to awaken me in an unknown manner. Sometimes Bandit would actually appear in my dream, simply looking at me inquisitively. In these events, I would awaken and see

Bandit sitting patiently in the dim light, several feet from my bed, looking at me. Is this coincidence or chance? Perhaps, yet I think not!

The simple fact is animals are life forms possessing a level of intelligence and capabilities that are beyond present human scientific documentation. Countless examples of intelligent interactions between various other life forms and my self have confirmed this reality. Scientific proof is now beginning to emerge that acknowledge some animals, such as chimpanzees, dolphins and whales, definitely have their own manner of auditory communication, as well as various facial and eye expressions that transmit a level of understanding among their own species and social groups. There is also much accumulating evidence for a high degree of auditory communication occurring between various species of higher life forms. It is also obvious that humans have been communicating with many domesticated animals for thousands of years already. The issue here is there are various levels and means of communication between Earth's life forms, some depending upon one's own level of consciousness and the ability to communicate in this manner so that one is aware of such events. For example, I am unable to communicate with elephants even though I know they have a high level of conscious awareness, yet communication between a domesticated work elephant and its handler is accomplished with ease and positive effect, as evidenced by the work they mutually accomplish through these communications. Additionally, some animals communicate with one another, such as when some bird species use specific warning calls to alert various other species of animals, like monkeys or antelope, that a predator like a lion or leopard is stalking in the area and to be wary of their presence. Various types of communication between mankind and countless other types of life forms have existed for ages among our primal ancestors and will likely continue into the future, perhaps at an improved level than we are currently able to accomplish. Human beings are making progress toward improving communications with various dolphin and whale species, as well as various higher species of trained apes, who now communicate with researchers by using sign language and by computer. This process could expand human's understanding and appreciation that other life forms indeed possess higher perceptions, emotions and a highly developed state of consciousness which vastly surpasses the range of capabilities that most of us currently would believe is possible.

A foundation theme within our discussion of life is that there are numerous aspects of existence that are beyond ordinary levels of human awareness and our basic comprehension. Life's human experiences, observations, spiritual abilities and scientific research often can dramatically reveal and confirm previously unrecognised facets of existence. These experiences and perceptions result in our greater understanding, enhanced capabilities and promote the evolution of our developing individual, social and environmental state of existence. While we may tend to take for granted this increased levels of knowledge, awareness and capability; such cumulative progress is actually a vital key attribute and characteristic trait of humanity's complex successful civilisation. Humanity's progressive development exists at the current level of expansion due to the accumulative efforts, wisdom and the constructive activities of countless generations of innovative, perceptive, hard-working, committed individuals and groups of people working together. The progressive intellectual achievement necessary to develop spoken and written languages to communicate our thoughts, ideas, emotions and work together to build and improve our technological civilisation is an amazing accomplishment. This fact is something we, as individuals and as a world society, cannot simply take for granted or ignore at this critical time in our history. Honest communication is among the essential factors that can potentially salvage our struggling civilisation.

You may think to yourself, "What does this observation really have to do with improving my own state of being or lifestyle options?" We will get around to discussing those ideas, yet initially our focus is to begin to more fully realise and accept that human beings' progress is reliant upon many factors. Society's progressive achievements depend upon creative, perceptive, observant, innovative, constructive, free-thinking, independent, self-willed individuals and groups of them, all interacting with various types of people to re-create and sustain our civilization. This process requires workers to put ideas into practice, engineers to design and build innovative and creative ideas into functional equipment, financiers to analyse and fund project developments, accountants to manage the finances and a multitude of other talented people interacting in an integrated, goal focused fashion. All these people work together to create our entire civilization's system reality, as we know it today.

A key consideration in any quality communication is concisely defining one's literal meaning, such as addressing the concept of "our system of reality as we know it today". This includes your personal circumstances, your attitudes and beliefs, along with that of your community, nation, cultural group, as well as our global civilization. The perceptions of reality and its applications in daily life tend to continuously fluctuate between cycles of progression, regression and then further progression. Ideally, this continual cyclic progress occurs by making incremental adaptations, improvements and increasing knowledge and capability over passing time, be it on an individual or societal basis. The incredible variety of mixed human motivations and belief systems often tend to create various opposing viewpoints and actions that can sometimes lead to divisive situations which are detrimental to our civilization. The complexities involved in this subject could consume an enormous amount of our attention, so we will deal with this issue in further detail subsequently.

Now we reach a conclusive point in our discussion. Life, as we know it, is actually an aspect of a far greater reality within which we all exist on Earth. Our civilization is composed of individuals at various levels of awareness and capabilities, working within alliances of people forming various social, cultural, economic, intellectual, and philosophical groups. The entire complex process of inter-related interactions that compose this reality system vastly surpasses our present level of perception and understanding, although some gifted and highly intelligent, perceptive, capable individuals' awareness provide important clues for the rest of us to gain greater insights through our own life experiences. In more simplistic terms, there is vastly more to life and reality than human beings, on any level of development, are currently able to be fully aware of or understand. This is going to be an issue addressed in some depth and detail, only as a prerequisite for further, more meaningful communications as our discussion proceeds. Our purpose here is to stimulate a conscious recall of one another's unique experiences, perceptions, and thoughts in order to better examine them in closer detail to see what we can learn from them. Please take this opportunity to reach your own conclusions through this process based entirely upon the wealth of your own personal experiences, knowledge, wisdom and understanding. While I am unable to respond here specifically to your uniquely individual, independent thoughts about your own life's events, be assured I will address many of your foremost considerations regarding life. Much of what is revealed in this process of self-discovery will prompt further reflection upon your personal experiences that can serve as clear, undeniable examples of life's greater realities for you. These progressive realisations will further develop our overall understanding, peace of mind and ideally enable each of us to achieve a greater level of accomplishment, happiness, love and true purpose in our lives.

It is necessary to specify the interactive nature of our communication here so you are encouraged to primarily recall and focus upon your own life's unique and most memorable experiences and realisations. "Why is he doing this?" you may ask, somewhat annoyed by this ongoing irritating reminder of your responsibility to continually search and analyse your own thoughts, memories, feelings, perceptions, experiences and reactions to this information. You have aspects of your own mind that respond to my promptings in ways which are challenging to identify or explain at this point in our discussion. The key realisation now required is to become more aware that various aspects or levels of your mind are gradually being evoked in this process of communication. It is imperative to stimulate various levels within your total mind and perceptions to become more actively and intimately involved, connected and integrated through the nature and content of our discussion here. Remember, this discussion is all about you and your own experiences, some of which you may not now be aware of from your ordinary life perspective. This developmental process will necessarily contain many of my ideas, thoughts and experiences, yet please attempt to always consciously (or unconsciously) recall the primary purpose of these topics of discussion is intended to stimulate your own thinking and awareness capabilities, as they apply to your own life.

My personal life's examples will serve to explain the nature of this interpersonal integration that is a preliminary progressive development for aspects of the successive stages of our discussion here. These experiences are specifically intended to typify integral concepts and aspects of overall reality that likely do not presently play a significant role in one's daily consciousness or life plan. Some of us will be well-aware of these issues and may find this process a bit tedious, so you have my sincere apologies. Ideally we will benefit by re-examining what we already believe and know to gain a consensus of opinion and perception.

Various unique, sometimes surprising personal experiences have clearly revealed in quite obvious and dramatic circumstances that there are aspects of life and reality that I was not fully aware of at the time the event occurred. When the various unusual events occurred in an undeniable manner, I became well-aware of them, yet in some cases was consequently quite unable to adequately understand or explain them, even to myself. In such situations, only the factual sequence of the events along with my mental, emotional and physical reactions and subsequent responses remained to enable me to analyse these experiences at the time and later periodically throughout the years of my life. One's acknowledgment, evaluation and integration of those multitudinous unique events and realisations in one's life are of permanent significance, in a cumulative manner. When the total of all the unusual, interesting, sometimes amazing, often inexplicable, odd type events that periodically occur in one's life are viewed as a whole; then these events clearly reveal various extraordinary aspects of life and one's entire state of being. Such experiences could generally be characterised by their ability to inexplicably defy and confound one's ordinary understanding. Many such events would contradict the normally accepted nature of reality and greatly surpass one's basic normal human capabilities. As one analyses and contemplates the full spectrum of these predominantly unusual events, then patterns of higher levels of awareness and capability begin to emerge. These realisations often occur unexpectedly and over the years of one's lifetime, as the ongoing integration of this information and experience becomes progressively beneficial to one's overall level of awareness and its development.

One of the most obvious, undeniable personal experiences in my life enabled me to fully understand that the physical laws of life, such as gravity and momentum, can in rare instances be "flexible" or not apply in a normal manner, under certain circumstances. This following particular event happened in such a serious life-threatening way that I was left with absolutely no doubt in my mind or body of the reality of the experience. Additionally, the event created considerable interest, concern, inexplicable curiosity and profound amazement for those people who were with me at the time, mountain climbing as novices.

When I was about twenty years old, a group of about four of us were hiking up a fairly steep mountain trail and

I foolishly decided to take a more vertical route by myself while the other guys continued without me up the trail. Quite quickly the ascent became a sheer vertical rock wall and there were many good foot and hand holds available. I had neither safety equipment, nor ropes and only wore tennis shoes. Obviously in such a situation I was indeed "an accident waiting to happen" and life kindly provided me with an incredible lesson that I will never forget, explain away or otherwise ignore. Being an inexperienced mountain climber, I went straight up the 90° vertical sheer rock wall with deliberate care, knowing it was a potentially fatal situation. I did quite well for about 50 meters until reaching a point where the vertical wall became a 45° slope. There was unexpectedly a large pile of loose rubble rock blocking my way upwards. I had a moment to look downwards to see where I could reposition my feet and hands to attempt to somehow go around this large pile of loose, small, slippery, unattached rocks. Without warning, one then both of my footholds broke free, leaving me hanging by my two good finger holds, again giving me a few brief seconds to look down for a foothold further down the wall somewhere. None were visible at that visual angle, yet what caught my attention was about 10 meters down there was a narrow horizontal ledge about 6 inches wide and a couple feet in length and about another 15 meters down was a much wider dirt ledge. As my feet blindly searched the rock wall for any foothold, I was quite aware of the seriousness of my situation and vividly noted every detail of the two narrow ledges below me. The lower ledge was about 1 meter wide and 3 meters in horizontal length directly under me, with a large boulder jutting out along the outside edge.

In the five or so seconds I had to look downwards to survey the scene, my mind very calmly, somewhat detached of any emotion at all, instantly analysed the situation with thoughts to the obvious effect of "This is a very difficult, dangerous situation". That was my only mental thought which was virtually devoid of any fear, oddly enough. Within a couple seconds of a foothold's breaking loose and the quick glance downwards, then almost simultaneously both of my insufficiently adequate hand holds gave away. I was facing toward the sheer 90° cliff falling freely, making no physical contact with the rock wall as I fell. My immediate thought was to attempt to land upon the 6 inch wide ledge with both feet and then somehow hold onto the rock wall with my hands. I was amazed to feel how relatively slowly I seemed to be falling downwards. It was almost as if one was sinking quickly into water with a modest amount of negative buoyancy, like a scuba diver with a very heavy weight belt on. As I landed on the 6 inch wide ledge, my left foot seemed to land solidly while the right foot landed with a more uneven impact, causing my right knee to "pop" (dislocated somewhat loudly), as my fingernails dug futilely upon the featureless rock face for non-existent hand holds. The right leg that made the loud popping noise upon impact slipped immediately off the ledge, as the other left foot somehow remained firmly upon the ledge, as I fell backwards away from the cliff with my upper body. Amazingly, the left foot still maintained its place on the rock ledge where it had initially landed. As I rolled backwards, my mind unemotionally said, "broken leg". I was quite conscious as I rolled backwards to remain as close to the vertical wall as possible, yet not to bounce against it as I fell, which would have made me drift out away from the wall, causing me to land upon the large boulder.

As I slowly fell backwards off the first ledge, I focused my attention upon the dirt section of the ledge below that was about one meter wide and three meters in length. As my left foot released from the narrow ledge above me, I was again free falling in a slow seeming manner, yet this time my back was toward the sheer rock wall and my head was pointing downwards, like a diver about to enter the water in a pool. The slow seeming nature of the downward fall allowed me plenty of time to see the likely impact area clearly, which was quite thankfully all relatively soft dirt. The large boulder was about 3 meters wide on the ledge's edge, away from the cliff face. I could vividly see that was the last ledge before a 200 meter free fall to the rock pile below. I was still strangely unafraid and unemotional, yet acutely aware of the extremely life-threatening nature of the situation. As I fell slowly downwards, I adjusted my body's position to land lengthwise, parallel to the cliff face, fully flat on my back, intending to hold my head upwards so that I would not be knocked unconscious by the impact. Due to how slowly I seemed to be falling at the time, I incorrectly assessed the enormous force of impact upon my landing, wrongly anticipating it would be relatively minor. I had exactly enough time to roll my body side-ways and onto my back, without even brushing the wall of the cliff face. I landed quite solidly on the dirt, fully on my back, avoiding a boulder completely and not allowing the back of my head to impact the dirt ledge too severely. As I landed, the terrific force of the relatively painless impact from such a height caused me to bounce upwards far higher than expected. My plan as I then bounced upwards was to again land on the dirt part of the second ledge, avoiding landing on the boulder, if possible.

Imagine my shock, intense concern and extreme disappointment to slowly see the life-saving ledge and rock boulder moving slowly away from underneath me! My body travelled into a prone, relatively horizontal position, as if in a Superman flying position, with my head facing directly downwards, so I could clearly see the rocks far below me. There was no longer any part of the potentially life-saving final ledge remaining underneath me at that point in time, with every detail of the rocks a couple hundred meters below very vividly in my unobstructed vision. I then quickly glanced further backwards to see the ledge a couple meters behind my feet and slightly below me. I realized in that moment that the force of the landing had caused me to bounce a couple of meters beyond the boulder and there was nothing below me except about 200 meters of free fall to the rocks below.

Then matters immediately got very interesting indeed. Upon relatively calmly and instantly acknowledging my dire situation with virtually no emotion; mentally I simply internally intensely commanded "Stop!" I did not cry out, nor speak, nor ask God to save me. I simply inwardly silently said "Stop!" with every aspect of my free-will and being, knowing the next landing would otherwise be on the rocks far below. I knew that landing would be the end of this particular life on Earth. Almost instantaneously, it was as though an unseen force or hand grasped me by the back of my head and neck and very rapidly, almost instantly, in contrast with the slow-seeming motions previously, jerked me abruptly several meters backwards in midair. The force jerked me backwards and downwards with incredible speed and power, yet somehow inexplicably causing me to land relatively lightly upon the rounded boulder, as if I was sitting comfortably upon a horse's back. I was unaware of any pain whatsoever in the brief moment that I landed gently on the boulder. What was most astounding and incomprehensible of all in retrospect was that I was momentarily transfixed by the incredible beauty of the mountain scenery. I sat serenely upon the boulder, relaxed and quite happily looking outwards at the distant valleys and the other surrounding mountains, seeing the clear blue sky, feeling the warm breeze and a powerful sense of peace and well-being for a few seconds, as I blissfully viewed that gorgeous panorama. During those few seconds I was unbelievably, inexplicably completely unaware and did not at all consciously recall my very recent serious fall off the mountain rock wall.

Suddenly, a flood of intense memories along with the full realisation of what had just happened mentally 'hit me' with far greater force than the fall itself or the final landing. Instantly, I was gripped by a very intense fear that is difficult to describe, so there will be no attempt to do so here. Suffice to say that immediately my mind virtually froze with some form of stark terror, so severe that no thoughts occurred at all. In that instant of realisation of what had just happened to me, my body began immediately to violently shake or convulse to such an extent that I was understandably worried that I would lose my precarious perch on the boulder and continue my fall again. Shaking uncontrollably, I eased myself backwards along the boulder, away from the sheer 200 meter drop about a meter in front of me, holding on for dear life. I sat terrified out of my wits and unable to think, with my back to the vertical wall on the dirt ledge, still trembling violently throughout my entire body for at least five minutes, as I reflected upon the events of fall by re-playing them in my mind, which did nothing to ease my fright.

After what felt like about ten minutes, I gradually somewhat calmed myself down and began to assess my various injuries. Several fingernails were broken and bleeding, my right knee was very swollen and sore, but not broken as I had thought. I also had a couple of bloody gouges, with one to the bone on my right forearm and a couple others on the small of my back where I landed on the dirt ledge, but oddly not even a bruised feeling between my legs where I had softly landed, straddled on the large boulder. I gingerly tried to move my right knee and managed to stand up slowly to determine if it may be able to support my weight. Then I heard my brother Scot, with some concern in his voice, call out from a safe ledge from well above me, "Jim, are you all right?" I called out, as bravely as anyone scared out of their wits could, "I had little fall, but I think I'm okay". He was silent a few moments, since he and the other guys knew there was nowhere on that sheer rock wall to "have a little fall" from the height I had reached. Then he asked if I could get down to the trail by myself. When I partially tested my weight upon the injured right leg, I realised from my many years playing basketball that it was not too seriously damaged, just very swollen and quite sore when my full weight was on it. I said "Yes, I think so". I then very slowly and carefully somehow managed to crawl, hobble and work my way down toward the more gradually sloping area, adjoining the ledge on the rock wall and then back downwards to the easier path the other guys had taken.

Once we were all back together on the trail, we all silently looked up to where the fall had happened. Someone asked, "So where did you fall from because there is no place to fall there and live?" I couldn't speak to explain, so I just pointed to the rubble pile at the point where my foot and hand holds had given away and then to the boulder upon which I finally landed. They all laughed loudly like it was a big joke because there was obviously no way to survive such a fall and then I too began laughing for my own reasons, totally humbled and confused about how I had avoided death. They took turns helping to support my weight on my injured knee, as I carefully limped my way down the more gradual mountain trails. They looked at the minor cuts and swollen knee, not much further being said by any of us, all realising that I was very fortunate to still be alive. As we drove home, not much was said either, as we all reflected upon our own thoughts about the day's events and possible explanations about what may have actually happened.

Anyone who has miraculously survived a serious vehicle accident or other life-threatening emergency where they had to rely upon their full set of human capabilities or some form of divine intervention may relate and empathise with some of what was experienced in this event. Another aspect to consider is one's mental responses and a host of other factors occurring in such an instance. It was difficult to evaluate the situation when the accepted physical laws of gravitation regarding objects in motion are definitely violated in a fundamental, inexplicable, seemingly impossible manner. It was challenging to accept the self-evident facts of what happened to me at the time, as well as upon careful reflection and contemplation over the days, weeks and years after the event. It was equally interesting to see the reactions of people with me, as they sought to rationally and logically analyse what happened to understand how I had not died or at least been severely injured in such a long fall. It would have been easier for us all to convince ourselves the event had not occurred; however, the injuries and my vivid recall of these events, even 40 years later, preclude that option. We sometimes experience and acknowledge aspects of life that defy normal understanding and confound our ability to explain or truly know exactly what happened. Our primary intellectual tool to interact within existence is our conscious awareness, which we can use to reassure ourselves that something amazing really did happen to us or others we know. In such realistic circumstances, an analytical, reasonable, definitive explanation for the exact nature of these events is not really necessary, regardless of how much we seek rational conclusions through the abilities of our logical, deductive mind. One factor is absolutely certain in my consciousness regarding that fall. If I had simply mentally accepted the apparent reality of those events and had not so intensely said "Stop!" with every aspect of my being, then almost certainly I would have continued on my fall to the rocks 200 meters below and on that particular day, my physical life on this Earth would have ended in that event.

You can be sure I have endeavoured to avoid such situations since that time, as I have no desire or intent to willingly re-test myself with such an experience again. The exact processes that somehow enabled me to alter the effects of gravity, momentum and force remain unknown. Perhaps it occurred by some inner expression of will-power, through the unrecognised assistance of aspects of my "higher self", and/or even more astoundingly, perhaps by the unseen assistance of other external life forms existing beyond my awareness that I am not aware of at this time. There are no easy definitely conclusive answers to explain these events, so that is not what we seek to understand here now. Rather, we want to simply be consciously aware and fully appreciative of the factual nature of the experience in my life. We must accept the 'impossible' did occur in this case, at least from my perspective; someone who actually vividly experienced the fall and the abnormal, remarkable, mystifying, paradoxical, unintelligible, undeniable subsequent events resulting in the relatively fortuitous final landing. The consequence of the entire event and its multitudinous subsequent influences upon the development of my conscious is among the most important preliminary realisations to acknowledge.

That single event conclusively demonstrated to me that we, as individual self-willed beings that temporarily are inhabiting our physical body in this lifetime on Earth, do in a sense determine and create our own reality to a significant degree throughout our lives. By our choices and state of consciousness, each and every one of us, individually and collectively, help to create and sustain our reality, in countless ways over passing time, throughout our eternal existence. Conversely, some aspects of life and reality are apparently beyond our ability to influence them sufficiently enough to control and manifest anything we seek in this life through the simple force of our own will-power and physical efforts.

It is said that some aspects of physical life are much like a dream; whereas the nature of our eternal consciousness or Soul, is actually what we truly are as creative eternal beings, made in God's image. Each human being's true nature and form is essentially an eternal energetic consciousness that we know as Soul, which is a purely immortal form of consciousness that periodically inhabits physical forms, such as our present body. The process of living life in a physical body enables our eternal consciousness to develop, evolve and unfold into greater levels of awareness and capability. This cyclic process allows us the opportunity to learn through our experiences, interactions, realisations and creative activities on this Earth. This eternal process thereby enables us all, as Soul, to become integral aspects of the creative energetic processes in various systems of reality that we, as human beings now existing upon Earth, currently perceive as the Universe. Once we evolve beyond this present level of physical existence as we now experience it to be on Earth, then greater levels of reality will reveal themselves to our eternal consciousness. Soul is ultimately our true nature of conscious awareness and eternal existence. Soul already actually exists at an eternal level of existence that far exceeds our human level of intellect and perceptions to such an extent that we are presently unable to comprehend with the human mind the comprehensive systems of reality within which we exist.

Many aspects of our consciousness and physical form are not fully recognised by the vast majority of human beings because it is so natural for us to exist in this physical state of being. It's often primarily by a real trauma of some type, such as a near-death experience, or possibly the difficult loss of a loved one, or some other form of dramatic, relatively unusual event, that momentarily "awakens" our daily normal level of perception and awareness to higher levels of awareness. Each of us is quite fortunate to periodically experience various types of events that prompt our level of conscious awareness to function at a higher, more inclusive, perceptive and capable state of being. Generally, after the emergency, unusual event or emotional situation passes, then the human tendency is for our less attentive daily level of normal consciousness to fairly quickly revert to its standard level of functionality. Very importantly; however, the vivid memory of the experience, the emotions, the realisations and one's responses remain available for your continued consideration. Therefore, we can and do continue to learn from and be greatly benefited by such events throughout our entire lives.

The following example is included because it seems so normal for us to have all types of dreams when we sleep at night. Most dreams are often basically ignored by most of us as curiosities that have relatively little significance in our lives. This is surely not always the case since often our dreams provide us with information that could be helpful to us.

I was driving on a long trip to see my family and stopped overnight. In the early morning I had a vivid dream in which I was standing at an accident scene at night, observing events there. The policeman and the ambulance driver were attending to an overturned car in a ditch. I heard the police officer say that it appeared the driver must have fallen asleep at the wheel. In the vivid dream I was standing quite close to the officer, so I then tried to explain to him that there had been another vehicle that had caused the accident. In the dream, the officer could not hear me and took no notice of me at all, as though I was not even there. The accident seemed to be a fatality because of the unhurried manner and relatively calm resigned attitude of the emergency personnel attending the scene.

I awoke quite startled and concerned at the intensely real seeming dream. I could not return to sleep for about 30 minutes, being unable to get those clear crash scene images out of my mind. I decided to get up, since it was almost 4:30 a.m. and a good time for an early start, even though it was a dark, cold winter's morning. A more perceptive person may have realised the dream could have been pre-cognitive in some way and gone back to sleep or avoided getting out on the road immediately. Being me, there was a date with destiny to keep, so I was on the road within 15 minutes. No sooner had I gotten on to the four-lane divided interstate highway located near the motel, than the frightening dream was forgotten, as my thoughts turned to other issues. Momentarily I became somewhat distracted by doing things inside the car as I drove along a curved section of divided interstate highway. There were no other vehicles in sight at the time. When I briefly looked up from my coffee and breakfast, I noticed a set of vehicle lights coming toward me on the curve, but incorrectly assumed they were on the other side of the wide, well-marked, divided four lane highway. A couple more moments went by as I was still foolishly distracted inside my car and when I glanced up I noticed the lights were moving very quickly; perhaps well in excess of 100 mph. But in West Texas on a clear almost deserted highway, at that time of early morning it was not uncommon to travel at that speed and I was going about 75 mph. I was still ignorantly focused on my activities inside the car, preparing a snack as I drove. When I glanced up again I suddenly realised the approaching car was going well over 100 mph and that it seemed to be on my side of the divided four-lane highway, which was two lanes wide. At the time I was in the inside lane on the curve and by the time I realised the oncoming car was speeding directly at me in my lane I only had a couple seconds to act before a violent head-on collision would occur on that course. The rapidly approaching, large dark-coloured car was not slowing down at all, nor was it moving out of the lane it was in, my lane! In that instant my first impulse was to quickly pull off the nearest roadside shoulder to my left to get completely off of the highway and out of this car's way. In the split-second of final choice to avert the oncoming accident, the dream instantly flashed through my mind. I knew the car in my recent dream that had crashed was on the left-hand side of the highway and it was likely to be my car, if I went off the road to the left side. Immediately, I steered sharply toward the further away, right side of the highway, just as the large black car hurtled past me, only a couple feet away from a head on crash, never slowing down or veering and quite likely a drunk driver at the steering wheel. I felt the force of the wind buffet my car strongly as the vehicle went past me, so I knew how close I've been to a fatal head-on accident. I was quite shaken, with the dream and the actual event so frighteningly fresh in my mind. I sat in my car on the right hand shoulder of the quiet highway, out of the traffic lanes for a couple minutes to recover somewhat and to gratefully appreciate that I had not been killed in a head-on collision. I was chastising myself for not paying full attention to my driving, especially after such a vivid dream of a car accident. Since there were no other cars on the dark road and I felt too shaken to walk properly in the freezing dark early morning air, I (again foolishly) drove back across to the left-hand side of the road where I would have instinctively pulled off the highway to escape the oncoming vehicle if my first reactive impulse had been followed, before instantly recalling my dream when the critical moment to act arrived. You know I was not at all surprised to see in the dim light that, unusually, there was no shoulder on the left side of the highway. There were only a couple feet of pavement, then a very steep embankment that looked exactly as it had appeared in the dream. The only difference, much to my huge relief and gratitude, was that my car was not crashed at the bottom of the embankment, as it had been in my nightmare, nor was I injured or deceased. The realisation of how close I had come to death in the head on crash and the process by which the vivid dream helped me to avoid a single car accident, if I had taken the closer left hand shoulder to avoid the oncoming vehicle, powerfully asserted itself into my conscious mind in that moment and subsequently, from time to time.

This curious event that involved this vivid dream is quite relevant because it demonstrates several key principles: First, that the sequence of linear time flowing from what we know as our future, becoming our continual present moment of experience, and then becoming an aspect of our past experiences is definitely not occurring exactly as our normal conscious mind would define or understand the matter. Second, the dream revealed that one's future has several alternative possible probabilities available in each action. I could have simply rolled over and gone back to sleep and never had another thought about that odd dream again. Life was enabling me to see into the nature of possible probable realities in a way I could clearly recognise, fully appreciate and even remember; by threatening my life! Third, that we are benefited by making our life's choices with as much access to all the available information as possible for us at the time of our decisions to act and that we can constantly update our thoughts and actions with new information and improved experiences in a progressive way. Later in our discussion, this issue of obtaining and utilising greater access to information to apply in one's life will be given further attention, since it is an important concept and capability that we are all continually in the process of developing. Fourth, it reminded me that aspects of life beyond my normal levels of perceptive comprehension are constantly involved in creating our various experiences and state of being. Fifth, this event encouraged me to be a more alert, careful, responsible driver, regardless of apparently safe road conditions. Sixth, to more fully appreciate aspects of life and its positive influences upon us all that help to keep one safe, healthy, happy and increasingly aware of the greater reality within which we all exist. Seventh, that the actual comprehensive nature of what we define as being "dreams" vastly surpasses our current level of normal human understanding in relation to the greater levels of reality within which we exist. Various other lessons and realisations also resulted from that event, too numerous or inappropriate to mention here. There are a multitude of lessons and realisations to be gained in our eventful lives every day; if we are attentive, receptive and gratefully eager to acknowledge and embrace them, as we share our own bits of wisdom, kindness and love with others.

Various other implications that such unusual experiences indicate to us, as they integrate with one another, along with those similar or related ones you have had personally or are aware of through other's experiences, will serve to better reveal the wider nature of reality. These will be progressively addressed as we proceed with our discussions here. Many more events from my life will be presented for your consideration to stimulate the recall of similar events and realisations in your own life or in the lives of others that are important to you. Some of these example events from my life will seem somewhat mundane, others quite unbelievable, or perhaps simply debatable, unlikely, or simply may seem somewhat meaningless to you at this time in your life. However, when these and your own life experiences are considered as a whole through the extensive, inclusive scope of our discussion, you will obtain far greater cohesive meaning than any one event could demonstrate by itself, independent of all other important life experiences.

There is no hurry on our endless journey of discovery through eternal life, nor in our discussion here. Please make time to continuously examine and reflect upon the events, thoughts, emotions and realisations that have continuously occurred in your own life. This patient perceptive type of approach and attitude toward life's circumstances helps greatly to make one's earthly and eternal journey far more enjoyable and more mutually beneficial to you, your loved ones and us all.

Chapter 4

Social Situations

Let's more closely examine the process by which most of us are to some extent prone to accept at face value the information provided to us. This is especially true when it is presented by those considered by society to be experts that are extremely experienced, well-trained and knowledgeable in their particular field of endeavour. We must acknowledge that such proficient, well-informed, intelligent people in our modern, technologically specialised civilisation would encompass every profession. However, regarding any one subject, there undoubtedly exist various perspectives, opinions, methods and solutions for any circumstance known to humanity. There appears to be some significant social pressure to conform one's viewpoint within what are deemed to be appropriate, commonly accepted parameters which serve to establish the 'norm'.

Historically speaking, one could consider various social practices such as: government and legislation; warfare; religions; politics; labour; ownership of property; male and female interactions; ecological and environmental issues; child rearing; forms of slavery; interactions with the natural environment; agriculture; industrialisation; innovation; business development; banking and finance; numerous fields of scientific research and application; urbanisation; construction and infrastructure development; international global relationships; medicine; education; communication, mass media sources; transportation; population growth and birth control factors; humanitarian aid; sports; interactions between nations, states, cultures, religions, ethnic groups, inter-racial relations, differing age groups; economic and environmental sustainability; and various other substantial human activities that affect us all greatly as individuals, as cultural groups of people, as nations and as a global civilisation.

As the complexity of life has increased, there has been an enormous, exponential expansion of specialisation in almost every field of human activity. Since the gradual decline of our human ancestors' nomadic, 'hunter gather' lifestyle at least five thousand years ago, our present global civilisation has evolved and flourished with amazing increases in knowledge, population, production and interrelated social systems. However, as one closely scrutinises the present civilisation's patterns and processes of thinking, behaviour, and the resulting societies, cultures and environments we are now creating, there are some serious reasons for concern for this civilisation's future well-being and continued progressive development.

The numerous factors now challenging our earthly civilisation are well-known and conclusively proven to any perceptive, aware, thinking person in this age of global communication. It is now becoming a self-evident fact that an increasingly chronic, unstable international situation exists whereby unless fundamental beneficial adjustments are made to our civilisation's social, economic, agricultural systems, and natural environmental protection processes, then seriously adverse consequences will undoubtedly occur, as we currently see in various so-called 'trouble spots' around the world. This deteriorating situation will surely intensify dramatically within the next two decades and unless considerable adjustment and improvement rapidly occurs, then these results will detrimentally alter our world civilisation as it now exists. Fortunately, these dangerous imminent circumstances have already become well-recognised among various circles. Unfortunately, at the present time internationally only relatively feeble, ineffective rates of positive, constructive change are yet occurring; therefore, unless this situation is drastically altered for the better, then it is most likely to be 'too little action, too late', to avert a multifaceted social disaster from occurring within our global civilisation. Not nearly enough wise, innovative solutions are currently being applied to resolve the full scope of the problematic issues requiring rapid implementation for the necessary remedial improvements around this planet.

Some examples of the countless documented dire issues that require prompt attention internationally include: the massively increasing CO_2 emissions and the reduction of Earth's protective atmospheric ozone layer are contributing to potentially catastrophic global warming and/or cooling; centuries of rapid deforestation is now resulting in global climate disturbances and increasing desertification that could cripple the international economy abruptly; a swiftly increasing population in some of the most undeveloped, poorest and already over-populated areas of the world; global economic and political systems that are failing to adequately address and resolve many serious issues of every type; increasing over-fishing of the world's oceans; various forms of pollution and land degradation including the damage to much of the western world's best agricultural land; reduced fresh water reserves as the continents dry out and weather patterns become more extreme and unpredictable; increasingly serious global social, cultural, religious conflicts; an increasing tendency to resort to military solutions in the past century, resulting in very damaging, counter-productive world wars; renewed efforts to internationally expand nuclear proliferation for energy production and weapons systems creating many related dangers such as accidents, costly complex waste disposal issues and further environmental devastation from radioactive materials; serious threats of disease and famine increasing exponentially; the distinct probability that poverty stricken populations in all societies globally will become more violent, making civilisation as we now know it to be unsustainable in its present form; expanding terrorism and religious extremism currently demonstrating these tendencies to destabilise global society; international corporate greed and corruption destroying equitable economic opportunity for the majority of the world's people; ineffective governmental policy and corruption within most nations including so-called democracies; rampant addictive behaviours in most nations; violence in society not being resolved by governments or social policies, as well as excessive graphic violence portrayed in mass media internationally; and a great many others such serious, volatile, escalating problems of major proportions. Therefore, it appears obvious to any well-informed, sane, rational, perceptive, thinking human being that the complacent, relatively non-effective, 'business as usual' type attitude of the international business and governmental community's policies is making grossly inadequate real progress to avert or alter this increasingly complex, interrelated set of profound challenges facing our civilisation. The clearly proven, genuine warning indicators are readily apparent in undeniable profusion to demonstrate that our civilisation is currently upon an impending collision course with massive economic, political, environmental and socio-economic disaster, characterised by significantly more widespread warfare. Unfortunately the political and business leaders now in the key roles with unlimited access to the full set of information seem unable or unwilling to establish a long term, fundamental solutions-based approach to implement the necessary actions while opportunities exist to improve matters, before further synergistic cumulative problems intensify. These governmental, bureaucratic and business authorities have knowingly chosen not to make the comprehensive facts available to the public, in spite of their responsible role to do so for the good of our civilisation and environments.

Our global civilisation is a complex integrated system that relies upon numerous interrelated economic factors to establish and sustain its present levels of productivity and profitability. Warfare has been utilised for thousands of years in a primitive, unproductive feeble-minded attempt to solve a range of social, economic and environmental issues. Warfare is rapidly losing its appeal to most aware, intelligent civilised people that have a true capacity to analyse global conditions and develop viable solutions to the circumstances that confront and confound our world leaders. Malevolent, counter-productive plans and processes intended to create future global conflicts are now being implemented by various pro-war interest groups that are quite small in terms of actual numbers, when viewed as a proportion of the world's over-all population. Their apparent goal is to eliminate the truly democratic and free-enterprise principals and replace them with more autocratic forms of government, with more tightly controlled and less competitive international industrial, economic and agricultural productivity. We can now very clearly see the indicators developing toward renewed international military warfare by the majority of the world's governments, to some degree or other. This fact is exposed by examining governmental military budgets, as well as funds being dishonestly applied to military expenditures that are supposed to be used for social or other programs. Industrial policy in some nations is designed so that its economy is dependent upon the production of military equipment and maintaining a large number of military personnel as an alternative to commercially viable and much-needed peaceful productivity. The nations that are currently involved in these practices are well-known, numerous and these militaristic alliances are well-established, although constantly shifting in today's uncertain world circumstances. The devastatingly lethal nature of modern weapons systems is being developed at great financial cost to the global economies. Likewise, the cost in lost productivity by those people serving in the armed forces instead of productive civilian occupations is substantial.

Therefore, as our civilisation and earth's environments decline and deteriorate, our so-called leaders ignore countless available solutions as they knowingly prepare to repeat the same old foolish, unnecessary, militaristic mistakes of the past few thousand years of human history, apparently blind to constructive, positive alternatives available to us all. What they do not realise is there would be no 'winners' in such a world war. It would appear that the beginning of World War Three is already proceeding in a step-by-step progressive fashion, with Earth's people and environments being the intended primary losers once again.

So what does this set of daunting, disturbing, undeniable facts regarding current world events have to do with us, we asked ourselves? The answer is to simply be aware, since this is the likely devastated world we will leave to future generations if we simply watch and wait as the current international policies are allowed to follow the present course unopposed with complicity by us all.

Please allow me to make a few statements perfectly clearly so there is no confusion. When one carefully reviews the present global civilisation's policies and actions of the past century, from the first and second world wars and other military conflicts, culminating in the events surrounding the World Trade Center destruction, now known as 9/11, in relation to the long-lasting war in the Middle East over oil supplies and prices, it becomes painfully obvious that highly placed (to use the terminology of our human era) terrorist organisations have been active for a lengthy time period. Various types of terrorist organisations now adversely influence all activities in this current global civilisation. Militaristic powers seem to historically be in control of most governments, as evidenced by the widespread state-sponsored acts of economic deprivation and warfare upon civilian populations around the world in both nations that are purported to be democratic as well as those government systems that are openly totalitarian in design and function. Militaristic corporations sponsor political organisations that appear to control the establishment of international governmental policy and legislation to create an unstable political and economic climate in order to completely destroy all vestiges of true democracy, free trade, and sustainable productivity. These modern national and international laws are intended to eliminate what was once known under the Magna Carta as being the basic human rights guaranteed by any truly civilised society. Militaristic forces intend to blame the entire process of global destabilisation and militant violence on some very elusive, well-protected, and very well-financed much smaller so-called "terrorist" organisations to rally world public opinion to begin World War Three.

Their apparent intention is to fundamentally alter civilisation as it now exists and replace it with forms of autocratic government characterised by genocide, economic deprivation, warfare and outright murder that Adolf Hitler and Joseph Stalin would've been proud of, if they had lived to see these events unfolding in today's world. This purported situation may seem to you to be an unlikely, nonsensical paranoid speculation, unless one is willing to fully examine the extensive obvious facts over the past two thousand years that this current civilisation has endured its countless despots, dictators, and religious madmen. The current policy of the proliferation of nuclear arms, biological weapons and massive build-ups of conventional weapons systems are clearly becoming instruments of nationally sponsored, taxpayer-funded, international forms of militaristic terrorist-type blackmail by various well-entrenched business and bureaucratic organisations. The historic examples of policies that create the prerequisite conditions that promote and institutionalise the reality of international warfare now exist for all to perceive. These policies have also formulated the circumstances by which internationally funded terrorist organisations have for decades been knowingly sponsored and financed through the complicity of various national governments, intelligence services and business interests.

These vile, dishonest, disingenuous acts conducted against Earth's people are not something to doubt or debate, since these facts are clearly now being revealed in modern history through the events surrounding the 9/11 World Trade Center so-called 'terrorist' attacks. The terrorists who were responsible for destroying the World Trade Centers' Twin Towers along with other buildings including a fabricated attack upon the Pentagon in Washington DC have been obviously designed and conducted to further their agenda of global totalitarianism and conflict. The sequences of events surrounding 9/11 now disclose that these murderous attacks were intentionally premeditated, highly secretive processes that were carefully planned and implemented by primarily highly placed United States Government officials to contrive a series of destructive, inhumane actions and falsely blame them on Arab terrorists to begin the current so-called 'war on terrorism'. This fact has now been dramatically proven by massive amounts of circumstantially conclusive evidence that confirms direct US Government involvement, responsibility and undeniable guilt in an overwhelming clear manner for the entire world's people to see. It now seems to be a well-proven fact that those involved in international terrorism are not primarily the Arabs that were well-financed by mostly western intelligence agencies and their associates, then inaccurately accused and 'set up' as the instigators and perpetrators of the 9/11 related events by US governmental authorities and business interest groups. These Middle Eastern terrorist organisations, such as al-Qaeda, were blamed and apparently untruthfully accepted responsibility as being the perpetrators of 9/11 to further their own militaristic and financial agendas. Many of those people purportedly involved in international terrorism have subsequently been protected from capture, such as Osama Bin Laden. Those well-protected governmental officials and their secretive operatives who were primarily responsible for the events surrounding 9/11 now seem impervious to mainstream media exposure or any truly genuine governmental investigations of the actual facts of this case. This includes the feeble and ineffectual investigations into 9/11 related events and the limited set of evidence examined by the investigative committees in the Congress of the USA and other governmental investigative services, such as the US Federal Bureau of Investigation (FBI). Many highly placed organisations and people have knowingly or intentionally unknowingly served as compliant puppets or employees to refuse to allow the full set of facts surrounding 9/11 related events and the subsequent war on terrorism to become more widely known to the American and international public. By studying the developmental history of so-called 'terrorism' globally, it now seems clear that most of the already self-professed instigators and protagonists for international warfare, whether in the current form of intentionally sponsoring and funding covert acts of terrorism, civil unrest or openly militaristic wars, such as in the Middle East in Afghanistan and Iraq; are well-established insidious self-interest groups that are now firmly entrenched within the top levels of some of the world's major governments and business sectors within our world civilisation.

These surprising and sickening 9/11 related circumstances are now widely recognised and well-known by genuine researchers and normal intelligent people that are willing to invest time and make the effort to properly investigate and consider all the evidence. Therefore, one may or may not be at all surprised that so few international mass media outlets reported in the public news services address these specifically mentioned 9/11 or international terrorism related issues, nor the resulting contrived oil price increases, nor the resulting global loss of basic human rights by legislative means, and other such matters of social and economic relevance. In a later chapter we will address several of the key facts that relate to the premeditated covert 9/11 plot and subsequent cover-up within the highest levels of the US government. This conclusive scientific and circumstantial proof is likely to become widely available to the global public in the very near future, ideally before the publication of this book. (Author's note: These comments were written in about 2004, so much progress has occurred and more will occur.)

Again, we must ask ourselves, "What do any of these seemingly outrageous, seemingly dubious sounding assertions, that are now conclusively proven by historic and modern events, have to do with me?" It is simply our responsibility as citizens who are living in a purportedly democratic, 'free', civilised world to be within our basic human rights to ask a simple question, "Why?" and then to obtain an honest, accurate, satisfactory answer for ourselves. We do not need to accept any news agency report of the nature of these circumstances when the facts are clear and self-evident. We definitely do not seek to overthrow our elected leaders, since other equally corrupt and violent people would inevitably then seek to replace them, as has been proven to be the situation in our earthly history over thousands of years, as cycles of pointless violence endlessly repeat themselves. People that are proven responsible for acts of violence against Earth's people must be removed from their current positions of social and financial responsibility and their powers to enslave and deprive us all of our freedoms and hope to create a peaceful civilisation need to be held legally and civilly responsible for their crimes against humanity. They will need to be properly investigated, charged according the laws of our national and international justice system, held accountable for their crimes and prosecuted to the fullest extent of these laws for their unlawful violent acts that are intentionally designed and conducted to destroy our current civilisation and replace it with a fanatical, despotic, chaotic, extremist regime of terror, militarism, poverty and misery that will only benefit a relative few madmen, their allies and related business interests around this world. We simply want to be aware what is happening in our world's civilisation so we can calmly and reasonably offer viable alternative solutions to prevent the inevitable end of the earthly civilisation as we now know it. It is also possible, although highly unlikely, that our (free, intelligent, perceptive people of the world) assistance may be requested by 'the powers that be' before it is too late to make these important necessary changes. Historically speaking, very few governmental or economic systems have willingly and peacefully made the needed social and economic changes primarily because they were the proper course of action to improve matters. Therefore, we must adjust to the world the way it actually is now.

Some of our forefathers literally sacrificed their lives so we could now live in a world where some 'common people' have a real chance to experience a degree of true freedom and financial opportunity. We will simply document and observe the actions of the modern despots, tyrants, dictators and pretenders of our era, who actually are the world's most foremost terrorists, responsible for financing, equipping and training various minor terrorist organizations around the world. The military establishment is the largest industry in the world, followed by the energy industry, supported by the banking industry and governments. Why do most of us say and do almost nothing publicly, as we are living through this historical era when a few brave, intelligent, honest, committed individuals could possibly alter the flow of events and literally 'save the world' in that process? Alternatively, we world citizens can simply observe the facts as these well-entrenched insidious terrorist forces within the highest levels of earthly government and business foolishly destroy the very civilisation they seek to control and manipulate for their own selfish greedy gains. Obviously terrorists receive weapons and funding from those in powerful positions to supply these tools of war and destruction. Obviously the common folk of earthly societies are neither in a financial or logistical position, nor state of mind to fund and equip or protect terrorist organisations internationally, so who is doing this? Why have so few actual terrorists that have planned and conducted these attacks been found guilty internationally? Is this escalating violence a situation the people of Earth can allow to continue according to the present flow of world events? These are a few of our distinctly delineated choices, as individuals and as a global society.

I asked myself most of these same questions almost thirty years ago in relation to our overly militarised global civilisation and choose to make no public comments. Instead I thought, "No, let's see what they have in mind for Earth's people before I comment on the situation." A backward look across the global history of this past century is self-evident to any rational observer about the militaristic nature of our current civilisation. We now (2007) can easily see the Russians and Americans, according to the respective Presidents Putin and Bush, not so long ago professed to be 'allies' and 'kindred spirits', openly demonstrate and rejoice that the self-evident false versions of so-called 'democracy' and rampant so-called 'capitalism' is by far the preferred method for modern earthly governmental systems to make willing brainwashed economic slaves of people, who imagine themselves as being 'free'. It may actually seem to be 'freedom', only when compared to Stalin or Mao's brand of communism, where outright murder of opponents and widespread economic deprivation finally became a State sponsored 'art form'. The oppression and suppression of true freedom and limiting economic opportunity to create genuine prosperity is now widespread internationally and is being intentionally exacerbated by the refusal of governments and industry to seriously seek to conserve energy or seriously innovate with new sustainable and less costly environmentally friendly energy technologies that are readily available.

Now it would appear increasingly obvious that most of the world's governments and business leaders are knowingly ignoring real solutions to the multitude of challenges to increase the likelihood of increasing problems for our global civilisation into the next century. It is obvious to anyone willing to view the ample evidence that global warfare, disease and starvation is the probable reality 'unconsciously' planned to directly or indirectly exterminate countless hundreds of millions of people in the first phase of operations, followed by a few billion more deaths in the successive phases of their not-so-clever plan. We could debate the issues involved, yet it is preferable to observe some of the primary indicators of a society slowly going insane and progressively becoming prone to self-destruction. First, we can witness the massive military expenditures internationally; the establishment of huge corporate owned and privately operated prisons internationally; the attempts by mass media programming to stimulate widespread violence and desensitise people; while arming and training millions of soldiers and police, while methodically disarming law abiding people so they have no means of protection against heavily armed, well-equipped criminals, privately controlled death squads, religiously directed militias, gangs, and mercenary armies; making poverty endemic in innumerable locations globally, including within so-called developed nations, whose slums are sprawling rapidly into communities where once there were thriving middle classes with good incomes. We could list many more situations: such as declining educational and medical systems; widespread drug and alcohol abuse and gambling addictions with the resulting crime, disease, social chaos, family disruption and loss of productivity; rampant increases in mental illness in the forms of depression, psychosis, schizophrenia, neuroses, psychopathologies; onset of obesity and chronic disease among developed nations' populations through institutionalised and corporate policies; such as selling unhealthy so-called 'fast food' even in school cafeterias; in so-called 'developing' nations we see periodic starvation, epidemics of widespread disease and dispossession from native lands and well-armed violent gangs of religious zealots, criminals and private armies creating mayhem, genocide and destruction with little or no governmental protection, even with the United Nations troops' sporadic interventions and aid efforts that often are ineffective. These are increasingly becoming realities for huge percentages of the world's populations. These detrimental situations are made worse by the creation of unsustainable economic and agricultural systems, often using corporate hybrid seeds that will not produce viable seeds from the crops grown with them, and so on and on and on, pathetically so. We see countless examples of so-called humanitarian aid agencies, currently being well-financed by governments and public donations, that are truly doing great work which is being incessantly counteracted, undermined and corrupted by insidious forces opposing real progress and genuinely improved conditions internationally to these numerous problematic circumstances.

We could say to ourselves, when we are willing to examine the evidence of these and other similar such self-destructive activities that are now pervasively manifesting in our societies internationally, "Why are you being so negative, since I have a job and my family is being fed? Is this critical assessment correct or necessary?" One could easily falsely believe this particular perspective seems to be overly pessimistic and is erroneously misperceiving the global situation in too biased a manner. My words and perceptions following here will respond to those rhetorical questions, since as a social scientist my role in society is to observe what is now occurring and to comment upon the conclusive evidence.

Those German civilians living under the rule of the Nazis were often later surprised to learn of the horrible actions of their government led by Hitler, yet the early warning signs were obvious for anyone willing to view the mounting evidence. Some self-blinded, ignorant people continue today to falsely deny the holocaust of millions of Jews by the Nazis. Therefore, to naively remain oblivious of chronically deplorable events now unfolding when so much international evidence exists is unwise and irresponsible. However, just like in Germany under the dictatorship of Hitler, in modern global society we are being systematically brainwashed and covertly 'trained' not to ask ourselves such questions, nor to pose them to our elected governmental or bureaucratic officials for fear of being condemned as unpatriotic, deluded, or falsely accused of being terrorists. Are we therefore supposed to just pretend to be shocked and surprised when future wars are declared without any necessary public support and subsequently martial law is ordered to clear our nations of the so-called terrorist threats, as we willingly and blindly allow our children to be sent off to die in pointless wars to simply reduce the population and make a few wealthy people even richer from the spilled blood and misery of us all?

Aren't we intelligent enough in a purportedly 'free society', under the protection of the United Nations Code of Human Rights, to ask that our leaders consider alternatives to massive genocide, economic desolation, intellectual depravity, and the ruin of our civilization? Or does asking such questions or revealing volumes of historical and modern evidence of these events occurring somehow potentially classify us in modern times to be inaccurately defined as being so-called 'terrorists'?

You may ask yourself, as I have asked myself and the higher life forms beyond the human form, "Why is this world we dearly love no longer our primary concern and responsibility in this life, as the powerful institutionalised governmental and corporate terrorists wreak havoc, misery, devastation, suffering, famine, disease, warfare, dehumanisation, alienation from one another and introduce various forms of slavery and mind control upon us all?" The various probable answers may surprise you, as they did me initially. However, we will begin to more fully realise and accept various realities beyond this normal earthly one we experience in daily life, which are vastly more important to our eternal Soul, which is our true nature. Then earthly events begin to make much more sense. There is nothing that says the people of Earth must silently or willingly accept the destruction of our civilisation by evil forces. In fact, the converse is true in that as perceptive, free-thinking, democratic citizens of Earth our spiritual and governmental right and responsibility for ourselves and all future generations is to rise up together against the evil force of greed, militarism, corruption and environmental devastation to simply say, "No more!" We must work constructively together to solve problems peacefully, utilise our resources and capabilities far more wisely and productively to create a more sustainable equitable world where all cultures and religions have the opportunity to exist in relative harmony.

Thankfully, we now leave these interesting, challenging, somewhat frightening realisations and questions to one another for our own individual answers. If one is unconcerned by modern world events, then that is a definitive indicator of the mass social hypnosis that pervades much of modern society to 'blind and gag' it from witnessing the truth and speaking out against these vile circumstances. Now that we recognise to some extent that our very lives and those of our children and future generations are being seriously threatened with annihilation or an existence characterised by depravation, violence and suffering through the overt rule by totalitarian despotic governments controlled by the wealthy minority, then we can respond accordingly, in due course. We now will begin to focus upon other more important issues that will provide us with our own unique personal solutions, regardless of the destiny or fate of this world's current civilisation.

We know from history that civilisations develop, then over passing time these civilisations pass into ruins, and new ones arise to replace the rubble, time after time on this Earth and upon other such planets in this physical universe. Therefore, we are not to be overly concerned, frightened or despondent about this continual process. Rather, we simply observe, do whatever we think is right and appropriate for us as individuals in various changing circumstances, as we focus our inner attention upon our growth and evolution as eternally conscious, aware human beings. We are not to be distracted, nor dissuaded from our higher goals by the perverse ways of this or any other such world civilisation, nor our place or destiny in its progression. We simply needed to acknowledge the state of existence here on Earth now in order to better define our true, real journey of discovery. Let's now consider some other more enjoyable, worthy realities and have some fun !!!

Chapter 5

The Meaning of Life

We all seek at some times in our lives to question ourselves, others or God, "What is the meaning of life?" You may phrase the question differently to personalise it such as, "What is the purpose of my life?" or in times of difficulty and frustration simply ask, "Why me Lord?" Some of us are exceedingly sincere and committed to obtaining one or many more definitive answers to such questions as our lives progress, depending on our attitudes and circumstances.

    Life has made some aspects of reality very clear to me in a multitude of interesting and undeniable ways. This may be due to the fact experience has proven many times that I tend to be a slow learner, sometimes thinking and acting like a complete idiot and often being somewhat less perceptive than would be ideal in the development of my understanding of life's mysteries. Too often, each and all of us seek to demand that life and others meet our wants, expectations and needs; not fully understanding or appreciating that Life already has a good plan in store for us. All that is required is that we do our best with the opportunities available to each of us, learn from our actions, treat other people as we wish to be treated, and truthfully do whatever we say we will, to the best of our ability.

As a young man in my mid-twenties, I reached a state of mind where a few of my capabilities began to impress me quite a bit. In other words, I developed what one could quite rightly term "a few attitude problems". Among these was the tendency for me to want my own way, in spite of any suggestions to the contrary from others, and would try my best in almost any circumstance to achieve my goals, which primarily involved my own self-interest. Upon sincere reflection now, perhaps not that much has changed in the past thirty years! So, let's just say this next event helped me to be more careful about asking questions and demanding immediate answers about situations that I was unable to understand fully or cope with at the time.

Occasionally I was able to perceive and communicate on an inner mental channel with aspects of life's reality that I did not and still do not fully understand. By the time I reached my late twenties, these abilities resulted in my becoming, shall we say, a little 'overly proud' of myself and quite honestly 'too full of myself' or somewhat egotistical than was ideal for my own good, or anyone else for that matter. Some people who know me well might say that little has changed for the better since that time. While such an issue regarding my current attitude is still open to debate, what happened to me in the following experience shook me to the very core of my being in a split-second, when I glimpsed deeper and higher levels of reality in an unusual manner that I will never ever forget.

During this time I was taught to consciously access a mental state or brainwave pattern known as an 'alpha' state of mind. This is a fancy way of saying I was able to relax my mind sufficiently to 'meditate'. In other words, I could silence my internal mental chatter sufficiently to mentally visualise or 'see' the inner 'blue light' that we learned to associate with our ability to become somewhat aware of various aspects of life beyond one's normal five senses. The vast majority of people possess this capability, consciously or unconsciously, that enables them to access information that ordinarily is not available to their basic five senses.

In this relaxed, yet alert meditative state of mind, a small group of people would interact on a non-physical, psychic, spiritual, mental level with various people located elsewhere who had quite poor health. These ill people would request that we visualise 'sending them' healing energy and our prayers that they would improve, which we did to the best of our ability. After attending a few months of these weekly two-hour sessions, this activity began to really intrigue me because those of us who were in the group meditating were unaware of the individual's doctor diagnosed illnesses. We simply went into a mentally quiet, meditative alpha state and then were given a person's name, age and city of residence. Then, after about five minutes of silent meditative assessment, we as a group were asked to comment upon what health condition we each perceived in that person. Then each person would, in turn, offer any intuitive perceptions or impressions that they may have received about the ill person. Initially I thought the entire process was quite an unlikely way to assess anyone's illnesses or to heal anyone in that manner. I seriously doubted that I could somehow know what illness any unknown person located far from me might have or that any healing would occur because they had requested that we act as a channel to send them divine healing energy, along with our best wishes and prayers for a full recovery, while also visualising them being fully healthy. I was quietly very sceptical about the entire process because the concept was completely unfamiliar to me at the time. I could not believe that on such minimal information that we could possibly mentally locate the unknown person, or connect with them mentally to determine somehow what their illness was, nor that we could somehow channel healing energy to them or visualise them in a state of total health in a way that would be of any real benefit to them. The real reason I first attended these sessions was primarily to learn how to meditate and silence my mind from constantly talking to itself about anything and everything, incessantly. By that stage of my life, I had begun to become quite annoyed about my mind's endless internal chatter, especially since some of the topical matter was unwanted, boringly repetitive and all too often relatively imbecilic in nature, even from my own perspective.

Imagine my complete surprise when after only a few weeks, I would occasionally seem to "connect" with the presumed ill person whose name, age and city location that we were given. In such rare cases, I would basically "feel" within myself whatever that person themselves apparently felt inside themselves, in mind, body and spirit, which was especially noticeable when they were in a lot of physical or emotional pain. At first I thought that surely I was imagining things. Over the first few months of these weekly sessions, I usually remained quiet when the group leader, who was previously informed of the doctor diagnosed illness or physical symptoms, would ask for the group's feedback. Generally, I saw nothing with my mind's eye, except for a few changing coloured lights. However, what was quite noticeable for me were the distinct, unusual feelings of physical and emotional pain or unhappiness that seemed to be felt within my own body and mind and were apparently somehow emanating from them to me. I was not comfortable in saying what I intensely perceived and felt inside myself, since to inwardly perceive the intense emotions of a person who was crying, or felt afraid, or angry, were begging for help to save them, or simply screaming almost continuously in agony, loneliness or grief was most unusual for me to experience in this empathetic manner.

On the back of the page with the person's name was recorded their doctor diagnosed illness. After about fifteen to thirty minutes had passed and most of the experienced people had said whatever it was that they saw in their meditation regarding the sick person's health status, then we would be told exactly what the doctor's diagnosis or physical symptoms actually were. Then we all would be told that person had asked that we send them healing energy, which we understood came from a divine source outside of ourselves, through us, directly to the person seeking healing energy. We were also instructed to visualise that person as being healthy and healed. To me, it seemed very odd that we had almost no one being diagnosed with any form of mental illness; and that all these people seeking to be healed had simply been diagnosed as having various physical symptoms or diseases. It soon became obvious to me when I empathetically connected with most of the ill people that their inner state of being seemed to be characterised by unhappy, resentful or angry emotions; and in many cases, a mixture of many combined negative emotions and feelings. These chronically unhappy, suffering people were not that enjoyable to share one's state of mind and energy with, I assure you! After a couple months of saying very little, I gradually became more confident in my inner perceptions regarding the ill people, since I often felt in my own body some of the specific pains and physical symptoms that had been listed in the doctor's diagnosis.

I began to consider it possible and then increasingly likely that in some cases I had developed the ability to actually somehow mentally and physically connect an aspect of my conscious mind with theirs'. From the outset I was somewhat uncomfortable with the entire situation in various ways, yet I was rapidly becoming increasingly curious and truly amazed about my steadily improving capability to accurately predict to myself what part of their body would be the exact area or organs that were diagnosed as being diseased by their doctors. Over the next few months, I gradually became very capable at determining within my own body exactly what locations that their primary physical pain was being generated by their illness's symptoms.

When the group was asked, "What do you see?" I initially began to respond by reporting such things as, "Nothing, but I feel the person is very sad and crying" or in other cases, I would report my impression "That they were very angry" or were screaming over and over, "Why me?" or whatever other emotions that I felt within myself from that person at the time. Some people were at peace and relatively calm, yet they were far fewer in number to the others that apparently possessed primarily negative emotional states of being. Then I would report the exact location in my own body that I felt that the ill person's physical pain existed. For example, I would feel within myself that their heart seemed to be constricted, pained and weak, in which case they usually had been diagnosed with some form of heart condition. Sometimes they could scarcely breathe or their chest and lungs hurt severely, which tended to be lung cancer or other such lung diseases. Some people seemed to hurt all over, while others had only lower back pain, or quite severe headaches, and various other bodily and emotional pains, which I felt to a far lesser degree within myself than they apparently experienced in their own body and mind.

Obviously I found this experience to be perplexing and inexplicable, especially when I began to be about eighty percent accurate on the doctor diagnosed area of pain and illness in their body. We often had good information regarding the exact areas of bodily pain, usually obtained directly from the individual requesting our help to heal themselves, often with the knowledge being given to their doctor that they were "being prayed for".

There were some very capable, kind, good, loving people in this group who were far more talented than I in visualising the current physical condition of these ill people. As a group we spent about five or ten minutes subsequently visualising each of the ill people as being healthy again, while 'channelling' healing energies from sources outside ourselves, through us, to the person requesting this type of assistance and prayer. I became aware that sometimes there was a quite distinctly intense, incredibly vibrant type of energy, flowing into and through me, to that ill person. Very often I could actually feel the recipient relaxing, their pain reducing and some degree of peace of mind developing through my inner senses. In a few memorable cases, the people completely recovered their health, in spite of being medically assessed in a hopelessly terminal diseased condition. There were also a couple of truly miraculous cures, such as someone with a very large stomach tumour, scheduled for surgery the following day after our evening healing session with them. The following morning when the doctor prepared the patient, there was no external sign of the obvious swollen area where the tumour had been located, so the operation was postponed so further x-rays could be taken. Those x-rays showed the tumour was completely gone and the person was inexplicably healthy and well again.

However, the cases of healing in dramatic fashion were seemingly between five to ten percent and a great many of the severe cases were beyond anyone's help and those ill people died anyway, sometimes with lengthy periods of great suffering. Quite a few of these people were given to us for assistance week after week and others were only referred to us periodically over several months for this treatment. What amazed me most was that at least a third of these people seemed to significantly improve in their overall state of mental and emotional health, regardless of what their illness's condition, prognosis for survival was or their relative level of physical pain. About half of these people seemed to become at least somewhat better emotionally after our efforts with them from our remote locations. Although we never met any of those ill people in person, many of us in the group felt and shared with one another that in a deeper, quite personal sense, we indeed grew to know them quite well.

These experiences were interesting, intriguing, challenging, often emotional, sometimes frightening, inexplicable, occasionally joyous and generally somewhat frustrating because of our inability to help them recover full health in the vast majority of cases. It was very educational for me to experience such intimate mental, emotional interactions, characterised by such distinctive sensations and perceptions, where I would clearly empathetically sense inside my own self, aspects of their overall states of being. In the second year, I began to realise such an activity was not really ideal for my own state of being. Early in the process I began to 'evaluate' these mostly unhappy, suffering people's state of mind and spirit who had repeatedly requested our attention and assistance. It became clear to me that the vast majority of these ill people had mental, emotional and physical tendencies and attitudes that contributed significantly to their developing these terminal illnesses that were often characterised by physical and emotional suffering.

For example, a highly stressed, anxious, angry, somewhat self-abusive type of overweight person, who smoked cigarettes and drank alcohol heavily should not have been surprised or upset to get lung cancer, develop a weak heart or kidney, liver and internal problems. Nor should someone possessing negative thoughts about most other people and who invested a lifetime trying to control and dictate other people's behaviour be at all confused about the source of their intense migraine headaches, heart conditions, cancers or emotional turmoil. In the end, I began to clearly realise that the state of our mind and spirit will eventually manifest throughout our physical body in various ways. Some people felt lonely, sad, unloved, insecure or self-righteously omnipotent, so they ate, drank, smoked or otherwise abused themselves far too much throughout their lives and illness was a resulting physical symptom of their inner mental and spiritual condition. Others apparently felt no joy unless they could make other people take an interest in them and conform to their wishes, or they sought to make other people become upset or suffer in various ways, so they grew very unhappy when no one liked them or wanted to share their company, except others like themselves. We all perceived so much of this type of reality in the process of literally being "invited" so very deeply into these ill people's most intimate mental and emotional states of being that one normally associates with only their closest friends and family members. I had been privileged to learn and perceive things that I would never have otherwise known. Seldom in life have I delved so deeply into other people's essence of character, that it was sometimes a very uncomfortable, somewhat frightening and sobering set of experiences.

Therefore, I finally decided to focus my efforts upon adjusting my own ample quantity of personal flaws and my tendency to be overly critical of others and our world's situation. Obviously I'm still working on most of these same issues, as well as others, yet some real improvements have been made in those four decades.

My less than ideal personal tendencies and attitudes lead directly to the situation that I wish to share with you because it was another of the life changing experiences that may have relevance to your own life in some unexpected ways. I had always inwardly professed an attitude to 'help other people' and 'to help make the world a better place'. However, when I had the actual opportunity to help people in a real way, even those ill people that really needed some human compassion and empathy, even from a distance with complete anonymity, I chose to decline to do so after just over one year. I comforted myself with the rationalisation that they were mostly unhappy, anxious, somewhat angry, overly emotional ill people that generally deserved what life had given them for such attitudes and actions. I felt vindicated knowing that a few people had been helped. I learned to meditate and stop my internal mental chatter at will for up to several minutes at a time; that I could somehow receive information from other people that I did not even know over great distances; that energies could enter my body from somewhere else and go through me to other people that wanted healing; that other life forms exist beyond the human form and physical body, as we now know it; and that some of these non-physical life forms seem to take an active interest and involvement in the earthly human condition, among many other types of realisations and abilities.

These thoughts and perceptions encouraged a reflective, contemplative, fairly confident mood and attitude within me. I reflected mentally on what these experiences meant to me and how they would influence my life in the future.

I was well-aware of my own copious quantity of basically negative emotional and mental states of being. These included the usual young person's naïve resentments toward my parent's attitudes and conduct, who simply did the best job they possibly could to raise me under the circumstances. I felt considerable animosity toward the then President Nixon-lead US Government, who came within a few months of drafting me for a tour of military duty in Viet Nam in 1972 when I graduated from high school to make a "real American" out of me. Thankfully and fortunately for me and many other young American men, the mandatory draft ended and military service became voluntary in the USA. Most of all I resented and was displeased by a global civilisation that ignored so many important realities while it developed dangerous technologies and military capabilities at the cost of so much in lost opportunity for Earth's people. Over the next ten years I even eventually became somewhat resentful and angry toward my Creator, the God who allowed this world to become so unjust, unpleasant and difficult for so many people, including myself over the 'lost' love of my life that I had inadvertently 'driven away' by my inappropriate, foolish attitudes and actions.

As a youngster of twelve years old, I vividly recall my father 'Doc' Wonders, then a Major in the United States Air Force (USAF), saying goodbye to us when he volunteered to serve a year tour in Viet Nam to Command the AWAC's in 1967. Dad left my brother and me with the words, "I am going to do my service to my country in Viet Nam and hopefully I will serve you boy's tour there as well." My Dad had served as the Aide to a four star General in the USAF for twenty years when he chose to volunteer for Viet Nam, against our family's wishes. Dad's 'boss' in the USAF was the General who was in Command of the Strategic Air Command (SAC), which was in control of the B-52 aircraft, among other such military hardware. The squadrons of B-52's were the large bombers that carried the nuclear weapons toward the former Soviet Union 24 hours a day, until they reached the Soviet

Union's territorial air space over a flight path across the Arctic, at which time the squadron of nuclear bomb loaded B-52's would return to the USA, as the next wave of aircraft were leaving toward the Soviet Union for over thirty years that the 'Cold War' lasted. My father returned from Viet Nam, technically a highly decorated "hero" for all the Allied soldier's lives he helped to save especially during the 1968 Tet Offensive, yet by then Dad was a relatively disillusioned, unhappy and disturbed man who never fully recovered from what he saw in Viet Nam and the fact that the American government refused to 'win' that war for reasons never disclosed to the American people. Lt. Col 'Doc Wonders soon retired from the USAF and joined his former Commander in civilian life as his Aide in other duties with improving the Louisiana State Police as an Administrative Assistant. Like my father, there are some subjects that I have no intention to discuss publicly, yet suffice to say the governments and military industries of this civilisation are largely responsible for much misery and unnecessary suffering, as has been the case for thousands of years in our history on this Earth. Things must change, if we Earthlings are to ever become truly civilised, from the wider perspective of universal life forms.

    I grew to deeply distrust a world where, as young children born in the 1950's, we feared that the Soviet Union would attack the USA with nuclear weapons without reason or warning. We grew up in an insecure world where we were taught to run to nuclear bomb fallout shelters at school when the warning sirens sounded, to hide in those underground bunkers, under our school desks, or to just lie on the ground in a ditch if we were unable to get to a shelter. It greatly upset me that history was so full of tyrants, evil rulers and cruel dictators; that Hitler was allowed to rise to power even after the events of World War I; that Hitler and Stalin killed so many millions of innocent people in World War II; that my own life's contemporary heroes, President John F. Kennedy and Martin Luther King were murdered by fascist forces existing within the so-called democratic United States of America; just as were so many other previous Saints and noble, loving people in the past, such as Joan of Arc, Socrates, Martin Luther, Jesus, Gandhi and countless other martyred people in heinous immoral events like the Spanish Inquisition and the Middle Ages' witch burnings. I resented so much of human history and was appalled by the horrible things done in God's name by various so-called religions, such as during the Crusades. I absolutely did not accept a version of professed Christian reality where all humans were born of original sin, tainting forever our state of being in God's eyes, nor that because someone was born in a place that they were unaware of the Bible, or they had not been baptised in the name the Jesus Christ, or had not repented for their earthly sins to a priest before death, that such a person would spend all eternity roasting in Hell, worse than any earthly torture chamber. My awareness of aspects of the injustice and inequality of earthly life in the course of human history and the modern times in which I lived all served to inspire me to probe deeper into the nature of our civilisation on Earth and life's other realities.

This was the prevalent global 'climate' and the emotional personal environment and basic thought process that led to my introspective, intensive examination and assessment of the world around me, leading inevitably to asking myself the eternally relevant question, "What is the meaning of life?" In a brilliant flash of self-assertive, brash, naïve, youthful, vigorous wisdom that was based upon my newfound psychic abilities, I decided to meditate and contemplate on the issue. I then decided that I would ask the higher life forms that had kindly helped us to send healing energies through ourselves to the ill people, to tell me in clear terms that I could understand the answer to my question, "What is the meaning of life?" I thought my own individual life had limited meaning in this world, so I focused on the biggest, most basic question I could visualise: the very nature, purpose and meaning of existence, life and Creation, God and everything in the eternal universes. Surely Life Itself had some meaning. I was absolutely determined to ask the question to the highest Universal power that I, as a sincere human being, could contact for a definitive, realistic, basic response to this ultimately fundamental question of our life's existence.

Needless to say, by now I was really quite impressed with my state of being and confident of my ability to receive a definitive answer. First, I prepared myself with a half-hour of meditation, lying comfortably in my bed, clearing my mind of all other thoughts. I attained a relative peaceful, aware alpha brain wave pattern for about fifteen minutes, continuously seeing in my inward mind's eye the blue light which I associated with being in mental contact with a vastly higher form of consciousness than the normal human state of being. Then mentally, inwardly, calmly I asked this higher aspect of consciousness, "What is the meaning of life?" Within seconds, the inward mental reply was "Please rephrase the question." I repeated the exact same question and again was asked to "Please rephrase the question." This response was unexpected and I replied with thoughts to the effect that "It is a basic question that has a simple answer, so there is no need to rephrase the question." This mental communication went back and forth in a very repetitive manner for about fifteen minutes, with me becoming more and more adamant and insistent. I became rather frustrated and agitated while trying to remain relaxed in an alpha state of mind and in communication with 'the information source'. I began to think that I was playing mental games with myself or that I was experiencing a hallucination regarding these repetitive simplistic responses from the inward information source.

Then quite unexpectedly 'they', the information source, requested that "I make the question more specific." I very firmly restated that it was a simple, basic question that was clear and easily understood in exactly that form. To my surprise, instead of another repetitive response, I was instructed "Please wait." Then after about thirty seconds of total mental silence on my part and their part, I was asked again, "Are you sure that you did not want to rephrase that question?"

Momentarily I lost my temper and mentally shouted, "No, it is a simple question in that form!" A couple of moments of silence, then clearly in my mind came to words, I'll never forget, "Prepare yourself!" I had enough good sense remaining to suddenly realise this was definitely not a mental game with myself. Then for a few seconds I immediately silenced my somewhat fretful, restless state of mind, with the question posed in a nonverbal way in the core of my being, seeking simply to know the meaning of life.

Instantly, in a split-second lasting no longer than an eye-blink, a massive internal mental visual explosion of inwardly blinding brilliant white light impacted my receptive consciousness with such a magnitude of force, power and momentum that I truly thought I would die on the spot. There was no time or ability to think or realise anything, nor to scream for help. It was as though one were to have the volume of the ocean compressed instantly into one's head in the form of light and energy within a split second. Then, almost instantly, before my mind and body could burst into pieces, the experience was gone! The incredible intensity and sheer volume of the vividly white light and awesome energy, with its explosive, all encompassing nature in my relatively tiny consciousness is totally indescribable and incomprehensible. To say that I was immediately completely stunned is grossly insufficient to describe my feeling and mental response. I was unable to even mentally ask myself, "What was that?" I was unsure if I was still alive, as it was momentarily unclear to me whether or not I had died instantly due the violent force of the event because I was unable to feel my body or move from the shock of the event. In total mental silence, I lie motionless in my bed with eyes closed, not breathing for some relatively short length of time, unable to think a single thought, nor able to see anything on my internal field of vision.

Then, a few minutes later as I began to compose myself mentally and realised I was still alive and able to move my body somewhat, the same inner voice said to me, "Now do you know why you have to ask specific questions?" I was even unable to do so much as mentally respond "Yes" to the information source. This affirmative understanding was clearly evident to me that the events were certainly, then and even now, far beyond my verbal description or mental comprehension. I simply continued to lie motionless in dazed, stunned, shocked total silence for quite a while, unable to think a single thought. Finally, after many minutes passed in total inner and outer silence with eyes closed the entire time, I internally mentally posed the question to myself with some serious difficulty and considerable effort, "What was that?" There was no inner mental response from within me in that moment, only the realisation and thankfulness that I was still alive and safely in my bed, completely in shock at the incredibly powerful, unexpected experience. It was about another seven years before I asked 'the information source of eternal life' another significant question about anything.

The basic answer to the question, "What is the meaning of life?" is that earthly life, and Life in its entirety, is far beyond present human comprehension. There is so much unknown, unseen reality formulating eternal existence that no existing level of human awareness can fully perceive, be aware of, or comprehend the nature and comprehensive extent of total reality. The answer to my question was simply to provide my human consciousness with a relatively small sample dose of the actual reality that exists beyond one's normal five senses. There was absolutely no doubt at all in my mind or body that if the experience had been continued for any longer or at any more intense a level, then my human consciousness would not have survived the experience. At that time the experience and information related to me by that event was inexplicable in human language and relatively incomprehensible to one's human thought and realisation processes. What I was able to understand then was the realistic nature of the awesome event and also a vague sense of awareness that some type of important information about the meaning of life was conveyed to me through the memorable experience. Over the passing years, aspects of ongoing increasing awareness manifest in definite, observable, realistic and applicable ways. Some of these subsequent experiences; mostly far more subtle in the nature of their expression upon my consciousness (thankfully!), seem to be accomplished with greater ease. These experiences are usually accepted by me with less apprehension, confusion and resistance than may have been the situation if such a dramatic event had not occurred in that manner, at my own request.

The actual meaning of life as it now appears to me is a process by which all life forms evolve into ever greater and more inclusive levels of awareness, regarding the eternal system of reality within which we all exist. This process is not a type of competitive race. It is 'measured' beyond time and space as we now know it in our present human form on this Earth. Yet in infinite ways in this earthly life, we are all provided every day with a multitude of examples, indicators and factual proofs of life's incredible range of realities through our daily experiences. Later in this discussion we will focus more attention upon some of the higher realities that compose our eternal state of being. Initially, we are seeking to compile and to some degree assess a variety of events that specify various aspects of reality and human nature issues that serve to help reveal some of life's immutable principles that we each and all must deal with in order to survive and thrive.

Chapter 6

The Nature of Our Eternal Existence

A primary characteristic of all life forms is that they are forms of conscious awareness that are capable of independent perception, choice and action. We shall focus our attention mostly upon human consciousness, yet we will also consider that other so-called 'lower' life forms also possess a type of conscious independent perception and action, as well as some manner of communication among others of their own species. Some forms of communication also occur between various different species as well.

As a child observing nature very closely, it was easy to observe that even ants had enough room in their tiny little heads for a brain that allowed them to possess the ability to think and communicate with one another. They were able to perceive their environment, somehow communicate rapidly with one another, follow paths, obtain food, carry massive weights for their relative size, as well as to build and repair complex structures to house and protect themselves from other species of ants, predators and the weather. By observing bees, birds, fish, dogs and other domesticated animals, and other larger mammals such as apes, elephants, whales and dolphins it became obvious that these creatures possess and demonstrate high levels of conscious awareness, knowledge, learning, emotions, as well as complex forms of communication and interaction.

It is astounding that some feeble-minded people can still dispute the fact that animals such as dogs, elephants and primates like monkeys, chimpanzees and gorillas, as well as sea mammals like whales and dolphins possess such basic emotions as happiness, playfulness, fear, sadness and pain. Therefore, while we focus primarily upon the human state of consciousness here, we do hereby clearly acknowledge the fact that most conscious life forms on Earth possess a relatively higher level of perceptive awareness than is normally currently recognised or comprehended by most people. It even became obvious to me that dogs have a form of conscience and can experience highly refined emotions, such as guilt, which even some human beings seem incapable of experiencing.

We also wish to acknowledge the existence of a multitude of largely unknown and little understood life forms that presently inhabit Earth and live elsewhere in our solar system. Life of incredible diversity also exists on some other planets within our Milky Way galaxy and the larger universe within which we exist. The key point here is to consider the absolute fact that earthly human 'Homo sapiens' life forms are surely not; and I repeat, definitely are not the most highly evolved species of life in the universe, regardless of some people's chosen belief on the issue. In subsequent chapters, this matter will be further examined in more detail.

Now we seek to address the most basic functional nature of how consciousness exists in eternal, energetic, individual states of being within the larger reality systems within which we live and evolve. For people and religions that prefer to ignore the ample evidence that constant change and evolution occurs, or that life exists elsewhere in our solar system or the universe, we welcome them to discuss and debate this issue along with all evidence they seek to present to support their position with facts. Some people believe that life elsewhere aside from Earth does not exist, so they are highly encouraged to supply the factual evidence required to prove their assumptions and opinions. The evidence to support all statements in our discussion here is already available in the public domain in various forms, for those people who wish to seek it themselves. What is written here is based strictly upon my own opinions, experiences and my copious research of historical and scientific records regarding these issues. Therefore, little effort will be made here to present such scientific documentation on these issues, as we have vastly more important matters to address. However, if anyone that can logically refute and conclusively prove false any of the statements and opinions made here with widely available mainstream scientific evidence, they are most welcome and encouraged to do so. Much of what is written here is due to the fact that relatively little is publicly stated about a wider scope of realities that are so clearly evident all around us. We encourage debate and discussion regarding the issues addressed here because it is time for humanity to move forward into a better future, rather than repeating the same old patterns, myths and mistakes of the past.

All physical matter as we know it is composed of various states of energy. These vibrant energies manifest as material objects that appear totally solid to our five senses, yet the use of powerful electron microscopes prove conclusively that material objects are composed of countless billions of much smaller energetic frequencies of 'matter', which are created from aggregates of even smaller types of energetic 'matter' in the trillions of energy 'units', These include diverse energetic 'wave' forms that occasionally act as though they are 'particles' and other times not. This energetic apparent 'matter' maintains its patterns of existence through the interactions of unified fields of energy composed of mostly unknown structures and qualities. Humans have learned an enormous amount of verified information, yet much of this knowledge remains as relatively theoretical intellectualisations that make analogous assumptions and visualise situations that in some ways do not reflect or describe actual true reality. However, much progress in understanding the nature of existence is being made by human inquiry over passing time.

Therefore, most of what our five senses perceive as being solid material objects is compiled mostly of very tiny vibrating energetic 'elements' in rapid motion with mostly empty space being stabilised by electromagnetic fields to sustain external appearances. To make a feeble analogy, these energetic tiny 'forms' are held in 'orbit', in a similar manner that is analogous to the way the planets circle the Sun and maintain these motions by the function of electromagnetic fields interacting with one another. This implies that solid objects are primarily composed, on an ultimately finer and vastly smaller level, of mostly empty space and numerous energetic fields interacting with one another. Modern physics is continually expanding the frontiers of human understanding regarding the astounding, fantastically incredible, mysterious, intricately designed and created system of reality that seems to indescribably surpass the most unlimited form of consciousness that human imagination can currently conceive as being possible. Obviously, universal reality exists and the level of intelligence, wisdom and capability evident within this universal creation is so exceedingly far beyond present human comprehension that it almost surely implies, if not definitively proves, a supremely gifted super-consciousness is responsible for creating this seemingly infinite reality system. Modern quantum physics seems to be approaching the point whereby it appears close to scientifically proving the extremely high probability that some form of super-consciousness; that religious and spiritual people would define as being God, somehow created the entire universal reality system. The reason for making such a monumental deductive conclusion results from scientifically observing the perplexing creative symmetry, the unbelievably complex, interrelated, interdependent, harmonious function of a multitude of energetic, physical, gravitational, time and space, inter-dimensional, interstellar, galactic, and seemingly infinite universal processes and realising that there is always the clear indication of a super-conscious vastly intelligent creative force being manifested throughout this entire perpetual, dynamic reality system. In other words, statistical probabilities calculated by physicists have virtually negated the remote possibility that the universal reality system could have happened by statistical probability or chance, or by random natural evolutionary progression, or by any other possible means than through the involvement of some incomprehensible form of enormously creative super-consciousness.

The physics contained in our discussion will intentionally remain almost embarrassingly overly simplistic and fundamental. If you wish to determine the impressive current level of modern scientific perception upon these issues, then an analysis of basic quantum physics and research into the unified field theory, otherwise known as 'the string theory', will illuminate these issues significantly for you. Here, our generalised conclusions are based upon the factual evidence that composes our system of reality and will progressively become more inclusive and complex. This entire process of life illustrates a creative consciousness vastly superseding anything the human mind can possibly comprehend. Specifically, the creative force that designed this universal reality had to develop a system that could exist on a physical material level whose foundation in existence is based upon an energetic nature. This 'system of reality' was designed, created and functions in such a way that is intended to contain conscious life forms of many types, at various levels of existence; as well as the inclusion within the system of an animate, omnipotent, omnipresent, omniscient, immanent vastly higher form of conscious awareness existing throughout the entire creation. Additionally, movement, perpetual change, evolution and the continuity of unfolding reality systems within time and space complete this masterpiece of creative genius. This entire existence would not be an easy or quick task, even for the creative force that we humans commonly define simplistically as God. To complicate the design of existence, the consciousness of all life forms seems to be individualised to some considerable extent. This unique process of individualisation enables life forms to exist within a system of reality containing passing time in infinite space to unfold, evolve and develop through eternity. Now that is really special and amazing to even attempt to intellectually contemplate, much less to design and create!

To consider the size and volume of the Milky Way galaxy is difficult to imagine in human terms, yet the Hubble telescope in orbit around the Earth looked billions of light-years out into deep space. This marvellous telescope recorded images of millions of distant huge galaxies, like our own, that existed untold billions of years ago when the light from those galaxies began its long billion-year journey to reach Earth. It is quite likely that those distant galaxies still exist today. Life in our universe is not the exception; it is the foremost principle. So, on a macro scale of relative assessment and universal terms, we human beings are much smaller in relative universal terms than an ant or even a microbe on a microscope would appear to us from our perspective of life now.

Consciousness in the universe and far beyond into the unknown greater cosmic reality systems that are composed of the accumulated countless billions of stellar galaxies and other dimensions defies our human ability to witness or comprehend the creative forces functioning throughout eternal existence.

Consciousness is that aspect within one's being that can perceive reality and ask the question "Why?" Consciousness is that force within our self that can seek to discover answers to life's mysteries and plan how to accomplish any goal that can be conceived. Our quest is to better understand ourselves as human beings and our roles in this eternal, evolving, expanding, growing system of reality we know as 'existence'. We will intently examine the nature of consciousness itself for clues to our own eternal existence being a definitive fact of life, rather than to inaccurately consider one's eternal existence as being an interesting possibility, or as debatable fiction for one's wishful mind.

What defines life, as opposed to death, in this world or upon any level of reality? Life, as well know it on Earth, is simply the presence of consciousness existing within the physical body. Consciousness is the initiating force that sustains one's energetic, biological and mental functions. When the mysterious energetic consciousness finally leaves a physical body permanently, then immediately that physical form cools and begins to decay. It is the electromagnetic form which contains eternal consciousness that departs the physical form which causes death, as we know it on the physical plane of existence. While much of this is quite obvious, these basic facts need to be presented now since our discussion will later proceed into numerous more complex areas of consideration. This simplistic progression of information is necessary to prove in a conclusive, logical manner that consciousness exists independently of the physical body on the earthly level of existence. These preliminary basic facts are not open to serious debate due to the existence of conclusive scientific proof of these concepts. However, some of our subsequent assertions and conclusions may eventually encourage considerable debate among philosophers, scientists and all types of people from many cultures. In this discussion we have little concern about a wide range of eternal issues that are presently beyond human comprehension at this point in time. Instead, we simply seek to establish our basic facts, opinions and assertions so that the progression of our ideas creates a clear understanding of our fundamental concepts. Then, as we reach our various conclusions, there will be relatively few missing elements in the logical progressive sequence involved in our mutual discoveries here. A variety of examples will periodically be presented to identify key foundation principles, so that we can conceptualise aspects of reality that surpass the relatively limited perceptive ability of our normal five physical senses; sight, hearing, smell, taste, and touch.

One such example that science has conclusively revealed is the energetic nature that is contained within human beings and all life forms as we know them. As a normal functioning live human being your physical body temperature is about as hot as a summer's daytime temperature. This body temperature is approximately almost half as hot as necessary to boil water, so there are considerable heat and biological processes functioning in the human body at all times. If one's body temperature fluctuates too low or high, then serious injury or death results. Other life forms exist at various temperature ranges, as evidenced by some amphibians like frogs and toads being able to freeze in winter and remain alive to thaw in the warmer seasons. Other creatures can thrive in almost boiling water and at enormous pressures under the ocean depths. Life and aware consciousness can exist in an incredibly diverse range of environmental conditions.

A key scientific development in the past one hundred years has been the invention and refinement of what is known as Kirlian photography. This is a process by which a photograph is made of the otherwise invisible energy fields that permeate and surround all live physical beings, as we now know them on Earth. Such photographs reveal that a definite electromagnetic energy pattern exists that extends outward past one's skin. The energy pattern can vary somewhat in the distance it extends outside one's body. The energy can also vary in form and intensity, even due to one's health status or emotional and mental condition. Some people who have developed their higher perception of vision can actually physically 'see' aspects of these energy patterns and the various colours, shape, density and nature of other person's aura (energy field). I do not profess to see auras myself. However, I have seen Kirlian photographs of my own aura or electromagnetic energy field and over a period of time while doing this research I did witness a variety of changes or fluctuations in my own aura under various physical, mental and emotional conditions. When we acknowledge someone has a "good vibration" or a "negative vibration", we are often able to sense and intuitively perceive the quality and nature of their aura, their energy field, which in some ways is associated directly with their attitudes, state of mind and spiritual level of 'being'. People with the capability to see auras describe that various colours such as gold, violet and white radiating from any person's aura often indicate a positive spiritual quality in character; whereas black spots, dark areas or uneven auras tend to indicate that such a person is a relatively imbalanced, unhealthy, or an emotionally and/or mentally disturbed person. Kirlian equipment is now being developed for public use that can reveal the entire body's energetic auric fields for use in health diagnosis, as well as various other very useful applications. Our focus here is to knowledge the abundant existing scientific proof that electromagnetic fields exist within the human body and all known physical life forms, such as plants and animals. Upon death of the physical body, the energy field or aura within the body is no longer visible through Kirlian photography. This scientific fact proves conclusively that the energy field containing human consciousness departs the human body, and other physical life forms, upon what we define as being the 'death' of the physical body.

Contained within the energetic form within the physical body exists one's consciousness that utilises the brain in physical processes to interact with the earthly reality. Our core assertion here is that one's consciousness exists within the physical and energy bodies, which usually operate together in a coordinated manner throughout our earthly life.

Some of our subsequent assertions and perspectives may seem to be improbable to some people, or even seem impossible to others, yet this is why we discuss a range of revealing events, human nature issues and scientific discoveries which serve to clarify and support our observations here. Most people reading this book will already be aware of much that is being discussed here, so please be patient as we build our foundation of basic information.

To better analyse some of the ways that consciousness functions in the physical body, let us consider a person who is in a coma from a severe head injury. They may or may not show indications of brainwave activity. We assume that as long as life support is provided, their body will survive for extended period of time, as their health condition will allow. Obviously some muscular deterioration is almost sure to occur over the months or years that a person remains in such a condition. To an external observer such as a nurse, doctor or loved one, the person in a coma appears to be sleeping very soundly. The primary observable difference to normal sleep is they fail to awaken. By wake up, we mean to open their eyes, move their limbs, acknowledge others in the room, make conversation, etc. However, consciousness is an unusual aspect of existence in that some people who recover from a coma report various differing conditions. One individual may report no recall events from the time the accident occurred, only that they had seemingly awakened after a long apparent sleep experience. Another person when awakening from a coma may report a conscious recall of unusually vivid dream-like events where they were active on another level of consciousness aside from the physical reality here on Earth. Often such reports mention the location of these dreamlike events appearing to them to be much like earthly environments in a physical sense. Generally, they report possessing a similar type of physical body to the one they have on Earth, except sometimes with a few interesting differences, such as for examples: they could fly through the air without assistance of mechanical methods or swim under fields of ice without any scuba equipment, walk through apparently solid objects such as walls, were young and healthy again, or other seemingly impossible physical activities that sound similar to events occurring sometimes in our nightly dreams. Others may report that they could actually hear the people in their hospital room discussing their condition as though they were awake, yet they were unable to move or communicate with anyone. Some of these latter people may even be conscious enough to hear loved ones speaking with them and be able to apply enough willpower to gently squeeze a family member's hand when asked to do so, such as in response to "If you can hear me, please squeeze my hand." The ability to accomplish such subtle body signals provides an observer some basis for confidence that the coma sufferer is still consciously aware on some level and may recover. Some loved ones of a coma victim have been known to develop an intuitive inner communication, either in a waking or sleeping state, with the loved one who remains in the coma. Some people make full recoveries even in coma cases where no brain wave activity occurred for lengthy time periods. These people often report their consciousness was elsewhere, sometimes retaining vivid recall of experiencing events in another type of physical system of reality while in the coma state physically in our earthly reality.

The key issue here is that consciousness clearly seems to exist independently of the state of one's physical body, regardless of the state of physical health of someone who is experiencing a coma. The time spent unconscious physically varies from only a few moments or minutes, which we usually term "being knocked out" or "passing out" or "fainting", depending upon the circumstances; to a much longer period of physical unconsciousness that we define as being a coma, which can last for hours, days, months or even many years in some unusual cases, with full recovery. Others in a coma never become physically conscious again, yet it is virtually certain their eternally aware aspect of their consciousness continues to exist in other non-earthly realities. Even when medically induced life support systems are removed from a coma victim, allowing them to "pass away" or physically die, then their consciousness continues to exist at some other, more permanent level of existence. The critical aspect to consider here in relation to a coma is that our consciousness can exist, seemingly outside the body, when little or no brain wave activity occurs and the person seems to be clinically, mentally "dead", yet in many cases the coma victim later fully recovers their mental and physical abilities.

Sleep is a period of physical unconsciousness that is a normal necessary aspect of life for human beings that allows their physical body to rest and recuperate while the eternal aspects of their conscious awareness are freed to some extent from the physical body to experience various other systems of reality. There is more we will say about sleep later, yet for now suffice to say that sleep is grossly misunderstood within our current western civilisation, which does not adequately treasure the circumstances existing within this critically essential state of mind and being. We can remain alive physically as a conscious life form in a coma without being awake if we have medical assistance; however, after a relatively short duration of time of sleep deprivation, most people rapidly lose the ability to retain a sane, comprehensible attitude or behaviour pattern. Eventually, people who are continually sleep deprived for extensive periods of time will either fall asleep under any circumstances or simply die. That explains a lot about dimensional levels of reality, for those willing to consider this revealingly interesting fact. Likewise, it is equally illuminating that people can survive without food for a much longer time than they can survive without sleep, which is required to replenish their various energy fields and multidimensional levels of consciousness awareness.

Another similar circumstance related to coma suffers is revealed by people experiencing what is known as a 'near death experience' (NDE). Such events generally occur when one becomes very ill, has a severe trauma such as an accident, medical emergency requiring anaesthesia, or whose heart and breathing stops, such as in the case of electrocution or drowning and they must be resuscitated in some manner. These 'clinically dead', unconscious people often later report that they could see their own physical body nearby, which they observed in a detached way and later they were able to describe various events occurring around them which they could not otherwise have possibly observed in a normal physical sense, as people acted to save their life while they were still unconscious. This fact alone definitively proves the existence of an inner human consciousness that inhabits the physical body, which possesses independent perceptive senses by which it can interact upon the physical plane of existence as an observer of events here while their physical body is unable to do so through the normal five senses, due to inactive brain function. This is a vitally important factor to carefully consider and recall in our later discussions regarding the subject of consciousness existing upon higher levels, planes, or dimensions of existence.

Some people experiencing near death experiences (NDE's) have no recall of such a scene where they can view the events surrounding their unconscious body as it is being resuscitated. Instead, they sometimes report being vividly able to recall unrelated activities while being somewhere else while they were clinically dead, with no pulse, no breathing or brainwave activity. Many of these NDE people describe an incredibly real seeming 'dream' while they were unconscious of earthly events. They may report seeing deceased loved ones, or other people who communicate with them on all manner of possible subjects, depending upon the particular case, in a location that often seems heavenly and beautiful in nature to them. They often have recalled having the opportunity to choose whether to return to their earthly physical body or not. Obviously those people that report such events have generally made the choice for their consciousness to continue their earthly existence for various reasons. Many such people report going through a tunnel toward a bright light source as they leave their body, while upon the return journey they apparently simply wish to be back in their body and they usually report almost instantly awakening in their physical body, as if from a deep sleep. These people report having a body in their dreamlike NDE experience and sometimes they are much younger in appearance, as is the case with meeting deceased loved ones who often appear as they did in their youth or middle-age.

Thankfully I have not personally had any such coma or near death experiences. Instead, a couple of examples of somewhat interesting phenomena have occurred that enabled me to better appreciate that my consciousness is housed within my body in ways that surpass normal human understanding. A few years before the experience of requesting to know the meaning of life and receiving the explosion of white light which dramatically illustrated in unforgettable terms that the meaning of life was far beyond ordinary human comprehension, in my mid-twenties I had begun testing life's boundaries like an impetuous young fool, eager for adventure. For five years, I've been aware of the concept of 'astral projection' and already was quite an active 'traveller' in my nightly dream events. I was not fully satisfied with unconscious traditional forms of dream travelling when my consciousness would exit the physical body, as often occurs while we sleep and dream. I purchased a few books on astral projection and set out to learn to willingly enable myself to leave my physical body in a fully conscious state in my astral body. Big mistake! However, I only seem to know one way to learn about life's realities and often it appears to be 'the hard way'. The real benefit is that I seldom forget those lessons or experiences, although being quite prone to repeat some of my similar mistakes and errors in judgement in various different ways.

Over the months that I practiced this astral projection technique, I would invariably 'fall sleep' before I could watch and feel my consciousness exiting my physical body. At times I had some minor success, but quite rightly, fear regarding the process of what was happening would occur and then I'd instantly snap right back into my physical body with a bit of a jolt. I was unknowingly dabbling with potentially very dangerous practices. However, some of my nightly dream travel events were quite amazing, very vivid and extremely interesting to me, so I was persistent in my efforts to exit the physical body, in my astral body, with full conscious awareness. It was a very naïve, somewhat foolish thing to do in the immature manner I intended, because basically I was seeking to go 'joy riding' on the astral plane in my astral body, which would have left my physical body relatively open to all manner of unpleasant issues, as well as increasing the incidence of various other types of problems that were unknown to me at that time. Please allow me to strongly suggest that the appropriate natural way to travel in one's astral body is in one's nightly sleeping dreams and definitely not to stupidly attempt what I did in this case, which is a serious violation of spiritual principles.

One memorable night my self-assertive, somewhat arrogant personal will-power encouraged me to naïvely do a foolish inappropriate act that caught me completely unaware and taught me another very valuable lesson that I should have already known by then. I was absolutely determined to consciously exit my body and go upon an astral travelling adventure. Fully rested and very alert, I was fully prepared and totally committed not to fall asleep that time before experiencing the conscious moment when my astral body left my still awake, conscious physical body!

After the normal astral projection techniques failed, as they (thankfully) always did, I stupidly began to 'will myself' out of my physical body using the same ineffectual techniques. The more I willed myself out of my physical body, the more tightly my normal mental consciousness adhered itself to the physical body in real concern and sheer fright at this inept act of sheer idiocy. I was absolutely determined to exit my body consciously. After having begun the experience in a very relaxed, peaceful, meditative, alpha wave state of being, after about one hour of continual effort, I gradually had unwittingly become almost frantic in my efforts to consciously exit my body by the improper astral projection method I was using at the time. I realised I seemed getting hotter and hotter, as well as becoming progressively more and more uncomfortable, as I lie in bed seeking to 'eject' my conscious awareness out of my physical body by sheer inane, naïve willpower. An aspect of my higher consciousness, aside from my normal reason and common sense, which I had ignored from the outset, began to tell me to stop my efforts immediately. So, here we have my normal logical part of my daily conscious mind thinking thoughts to the effect that it never wanted to astral project anyway, along with the subtle, quiet, inner voice of my 'higher', more spiritual, eternally aware consciousness encouraging me to stop the effort immediately. But I persisted anyway, manifesting the spoiled child, self-righteous, egoistic, greedy, demanding type of mentality that often exerts itself in human character when we are known to act at our worst. This analysis of the three primary discordant interpersonal aspects within my overall character that were expressing themselves is also very relevant to identify and remember as our discussion progresses.

Suddenly, I became aware that I felt as though I was quite literally about to 'catch on fire', or burst into spontaneous combustion. I had previously read of various apparently very definitive, proven historical cases of spontaneous human combustion and that immediate realisation, along with the feeling that I was actually beginning to 'burn' myself took over and I immediately stopped the futile effort to leave my physical body by my conscious will-power. I was perspiring profusely, felt extremely nauseous and extremely uncomfortable throughout my entire body and it took me quite a while to cool down as I lay in my bed. I felt quite weak, out of sorts, physically ill and mentally disoriented for a few days following that event. By seeking to exit the physical body in my energy body through the inappropriate application of my will-power, I was taught in clearly understandable ways that to do so was against the laws of life and if I had succeeded in that manner, then it is quite likely that unfortunately I would have been permanently injured mentally, as well as physically, although a more likely result is to have simply died a horribly painful, indescribably traumatic death. To violate the spiritual laws of life, either knowingly or unintentionally, usually results in serious adverse repercussions, sometimes in disease, mental depression, insanity, physical incapacitation, or the creation of the circumstances that directly or indirectly cause the death of one's physical body. The intensity of the memorable experience left little doubt of that fact that death was a distinct probability if I had continued my foolish efforts, since the searing, burning pain sensations made quite obvious to me what is so difficult to describe in literal terms here for your understanding.

Subsequently, I read and researched everything available to me on known cases of spontaneous human combustion from around the world. It became obvious that such events do indeed occur, yet are quite rare. Realising how close I may have come to seriously injuring myself, as I read some of the cases, this quite rightly frightened and concerned me. Most recorded cases of spontaneous human combustion were usually chronically unhappy lonely people, almost all of who were reported to have either serious painful illnesses or were addicted to alcohol or had drug dependencies. Investigators of these events concluded in virtually every case that these were people who desperately wanted to end their lives. In most cases of inexplicable spontaneous human combustion, while even the bones were burned to ashes, which requires a very high combustion temperature, often the bed or chair in which they sat did not catch fire nor burn their house down. I can recall seeing a gruesome photo of an old woman's dusty remains on her chair, charred to the extent that almost nothing remained, yet the chair where she had sat was only partly burned and both her shoes were still intact, although the feet inside them were completely incinerated. There were numerous similar grisly photographs taken by police crime scene investigators who confirmed the existence of spontaneous human combustion in some cases.

While this is quite an unusual and somewhat inappropriate seeming event and topic to mention here, it is very relevant to our discussion. If one does not fully understand the immutable principles that govern life here on Earth and this universe, and one seeks to use any form of self-imposed, arbitrary will-power in any way that contradicts these unwritten laws, then problems will soon develop. My silly actions violated several spiritual laws and fortunately in my case I only became moderately physically ill as the direct result. To research the issue and see about ten photographs of fully or partially incinerated corpses, taken mostly in the early 1900s, when such information was more available to the public, dramatically showed me what my fate may have been, if I persisted in such an inappropriate activity for a longer length of time. Consciousness is not something one forces to do anything, if one seeks to avoid serious repercussions in this life.

It would possibly be helpful to digress briefly to address various meditative techniques, yet this is not an issue we will consider in any real detail for reasons that your mental, emotional and spiritual state of being will be the best evaluator of what techniques are best for you personally. What I will say is that for me now, much of my so-called 'mediative' activities are much more 'contemplative' in nature. Meditation for me implies a silencing of internal mental chatter and allowing one's consciousness to harmonise with 'the silence' within higher levels of reality, which can be and is enormously restful, beneficial and recuperative in nature for most people. My current ability to 'move' my conscious awareness is in no way associated with my astral level of consciousness in my spiritual 'travels' aside from normal unconscious nightly dream travel events. I am very deliberate and discerning when it comes to applying my higher abilities to any goal or desire these days, generally speaking. As Soul, one can shift their focal point of conscious awareness to other locations in physical time and space, as well as other levels of reality without having to physically, astrally, mentally or emotionally travel anywhere. This simple methodological procedure of shifting the location and vibrational focal point of one's awareness can be accomplished once one is able to attain and maintain a proper state of consciousness. This process of expanded conscious awareness occurs through the development and utilisation of aspects of one's higher levels of consciousness functioning through the 'third eye' located just above the eyebrows and between one's physical eyes. Basically one's 'third eye' is a higher type of spiritual sensory capacity akin to one's physical eyesight or the ability to intellectually perceive reality. It is challenging to explain how these higher capabilities functions in ordinary human terms and is therefore best understood by experiencing this through years of progressive developmental activity utilising a wide variety of functional mediation and contemplation techniques. This process is a key spiritual capability for those genuinely seeking to explore various higher levels of reality through their earthly and higher levels of immortal conscious awareness.

A few years earlier in my mid-twenties I clearly recall an interesting event that occurred late one evening as I sat alone on the sofa. I had been seriously considering the comprehensive nature of the idea that I was actually a conscious energy form that existed within or inhabited my physical body temporarily while living upon Earth. At that time, such a concept was still somewhat new and unusual for my normal conscious analytical mind to contemplate, intellectually understand and completely accept. I began to curiously wonder whimsically if my energy body could, for example, turn around within my physical body, as I sat motionless on the sofa. With thoughts and activities like this to 'entertain' myself, you can easily determine why I was living alone and did not have a girl friend at that time.

There was absolutely no conscious intention or effort on my part to turn my energy body around within my physical body. However, without warning, quite slowly that is exactly what I felt happening within me, with my eyes wide open. I felt 'aspects' inside me rotate very slowly, first one way, then stopping for a few seconds, then reversing the direction of rotation. It was taking about five or ten seconds to make one full rotation, as one would slowly turn their body clockwise and then counter-clockwise while standing. This occurred upon such a subtle level that while being amazed by the odd and inexplicable sensations of turning around within my body while sitting motionless on the couch, it was not at all alarming. Over several minutes, the rotations went from simple slow-motion horizontal turns left and right, to include forward and backward rolls. I sat motionless on the couch with my eyes open, since the unusual sensations of motion affected my equilibrium somewhat and I had not been drinking alcohol at the time. After a few minutes, I began to relax and enjoy the unpredictable sensations of inner movement while my physical body remained sitting motionless. Then a part of my inner energy body would rotate one way and another part would begin to simultaneously rotate in the opposite direction, so different aspects of my inner energy body were rotating slowly in various directions at the same time in a very precise, almost mechanical way. When the inner motion would stop one way, there was a definite moment of inner motionlessness in that aspect of my inner body, yet simultaneously I was able to quite distinctly feel that another part of my inner body was still in motion. Periodically, all inner motion stopped completely simultaneously, before continuing in another different series of directions. In the end, there were several parts of my inner body going in complicated slow rotations in various unpredictable directions, some rotating at a faster or slower rate than another part of me. After ten or fifteen minutes, I mentally thought the experience should stop since it was becoming quite an odd sensation. All inner motion then immediately stopped and such an experience has never repeated itself again for me, although I have never tried to encourage the repetition of such inner movements again. One should consider the fall off the mountain event to consider whether one's energy bodies have the capacity, in some special cases, to influence physical matter. I suggest that they do, yet will not seek to provide proof of such here now.

Admittedly, neither of these two personal example events in this chapter serve in a direct manner to explain or truly prove that consciousness exists independent of the physical body. These two events refer to the processes by which we can determine an inner energetic aspect exists within our physical body. A wide range of other events assure me that our consciousness exists within multifunctional, inter-related, multidimensional levels of reality forming the actual basis for existence, as we know it and upon levels we earthly human beings are quite unaware and completely oblivious of now. I choose not to share a variety of more private experiences here, mostly related to my spiritual unfoldment or research into higher life forms than those we perceive as being of earthly origins, or originating within this physical universe. Those issues will be addressed to a minor extent later, without going into much of my own experience for various reasons I will not discuss now.

Encouraging your own 'higher level' types of experiences is what we seek to illicit, recall and consider in relation to what you find here. These types of extraordinary personal events for you could include, for example, events that saved your life or significantly improved your state of mind in some way, or perhaps enabled you to communicate intuitively or telepathically with a loved one, or provided important information that assisted you greatly to achieve some personal goal, or any other of life's infinite individual daily miracles that grace humanity. Even out of apparent tragedies such as illness, addiction, suffering, personal loss or conflict there often develop realisations that significantly benefit and improve one's and society's conscious awareness to reach higher, more appropriate, more effectual and responsible mature levels of thought and action. This is what the evolution and development of conscious awareness is all about in terms of eternal existence.

Therefore, the reason these two previous events from my earlier series of life experiences have been included is that they both demonstrate various principles specifically related to the existence of the independent energetic nature of generally unrecognised aspects or characteristics within the human physical body. In the event where I foolishly attempted by sheer will-power to eject my consciousness from the physical body by using unwise, inappropriate techniques associated with an ineffectual and dangerous process sometimes referred to as 'astral projection', I unknowingly violated various laws of physical existence and temporarily injured myself by doing so. Upon later further researching cases of proven spontaneous human combustion an interesting, yet disconcerting set of additional information became available to me. That awareness enabled me to integrate and better understand a vast amount of other knowledge and experience, much of which had no obvious relationship with the basic facts that humans beings can in some rare cases become so upset and unhappy that they can literally set themselves on fire internally through the malfunction of their own intellect and other capabilities, thereby causing their own death in a very unpleasant and painful manner. I strongly suspect that a significant portion of insanity cases are the direct result of inappropriate mental and emotional activities by human beings, in one form or another.

Various life events taught me that there are clearly defined limits to the correct and appropriate application of one's will-power in relation to accomplishing various goals in earthly life. Countless other types of examples of our human consciousness's tendency to act inappropriately and unwisely could be included here, such as one cannot excessively consume alcohol, food, drugs or even water without damaging one's body and ultimately one's mind by such actions and attitudes. Any excessive and inappropriate application of one's will-power can have devastating results, especially upon a societal scale where the effects are greatly magnified; such as inappropriate unwise use of nuclear energy, deforestation, excessive consumption of fossil fuels, pollution of the environment, the manufacture of harmful biological and conventional weapons of war, various forms of drug abuse, wide scale over-population, endemic poverty, unjust forms of political and economic control, misuse of corporate and financial power, along with other similar examples. Therefore, examples of inappropriate use of one's will-power, whether involving life's immutable laws of existence in a personally self-damaging manner by excessive attitudes and behaviour or upon an all-inclusive, globally affected level of activity; the cumulative results eventually will be damaging. Ultimately the effects will become increasingly detrimental to the point where one's survival and sanity will be threatened, and then finally one's earthly existence will be terminated by one's own inappropriate or excessive actions. These are what eternal Life defines as Its 'boundaries' within which we are all privileged to exist and evolve into higher and higher levels of awareness. It is difficult for those of us at relatively lower levels of awareness to perceive, acknowledge and comprehend information and levels of conscious awareness and capabilities far above and beyond those we ourselves currently possess. The results of our attitudes and actions are quite obvious when earthly realities like warfare, starvation, economic and technological capabilities are concerned because these creations are easily and vividly clarified for all to see and understand. However, in the less obvious areas of human intellect, awareness, inner creativity, spiritual capabilities, moral conduct and the higher attributes, such physical earthly assessments are often not nearly as clearly identifiable or appreciated as being relevant and essential to our existence. This entire issue of integrating earthly reality systems with the nature of conscious awareness in relation to eternal existence of that consciousness is a key focal point in our entire discussion here. Therefore, for us to address the full scope of issues involved through many types of examples allows and enables us to better perceive aspects of life, our intellect, as well as our innate higher levels of consciousness, to better comprehend the entirety of the processes involved in eternal existence. This comprehensive process of discovery and evolutionary increasing awareness is really what each of us is here on Earth doing, whether we realise and appreciate that fact or not at this time in our personal, societal and spiritual development.

The totality of evidence, to me and anyone willing to research the issues included here, conclusively prove the existence of an energetic field or 'energy body' which exists within the human physical body of all of us. Furthermore, that immortal energetic body, existing within the physical body, contains and houses what we each and all experience as our human consciousness. What is most amazing is that the extensive totality of human conscious is actually composed of many unseen, unrecognised and unappreciated multidimensional and eternally aware aspects of being that relatively few earthly humans publicly or privately acknowledge at this stage in our evolutionary progression. Many of these issues are now becoming more widely accepted realities of life by modern aware thinking people, as proven by science, experience and various medical, religious and spiritual records available to all who care to sincerely consider them from unbiased perspectives.

The seemingly separate, yet closely related issue regarding whether or not one's consciousness is functional as an eternally aware life form of some type after it leaves the physical body upon the death of the physical body is something we will need to examine in more detail in various ways as our discussion progresses. Most of us are interested in discovering the reality of eternal existence while still living upon Earth. We are intrigued by thoughts and feelings associated with knowing we each continue the evolution of our conscious awareness into higher and more inclusive, creative, expressive levels of expression and other dimensions of reality after our physical death on Earth. This discussion will ideally be an encouraging, insightful personal endorsement in some ways of what you already believe and have experienced for great lengths of time already. It is essential that we seek to express and define various aspects of our continual ongoing development, unfoldment and evolution of the eternally aware aspects of our consciousness that continues to exist after the death of our present human mind, character and personality that is housed in one's physical brain and body. There are 'lesser' aspects of myself, my less than ideal attitudes and the more selfish, grasping, needy, aggressive, controlling aspects my present personality that I would dearly like to leave behind, at the time of the death of my physical body. Yet, unless I identify, address and resolve them here on Earth, then they will continue to be issues that will limit and diminish my growth, potential and the creative expression of my eternal states of being. In this discussion, we may be 'getting ahead' of ourselves somewhat. To discuss the actual nature of what we are truly doing here on Earth, what the actual true meaning of life on Earth is for us here and now; is surely a most relevant topic to mention. In earthly life it is important to keep our minds and attention focused upon the reasons for our existence here and not simply to be distracted by the lovely scenery, interesting events and the many unique lovable people that we meet and share this journey of discovery with as we progress along this eternal path we know as life.

    While you read and consider these various ideas you will note we often use lengthy, somewhat complex sentence structures and paragraphs to address these issues. This is necessary because much of this is not simplistic or readily available to those of whose intellect balks at intellectual and situational challenges. Please feel highly encouraged to stop often to reflect upon your own thoughts, feelings and experiences or take a nap to allow and enable higher aspects of your mind to integrate this material into areas of your normal consciousness. It is also helpful to meditate or contemplate, go for a walk, a swim or anything that you like to do that refreshes, relaxes and enlivens your mind and spirit. In this way you will become increasingly capable of progressing through what will often be some relatively tedious subject matter here. Feel free to laugh about what a self-important, seemingly melodramatic character I tend to be in presenting some of this information. Eternal life is a lengthy journey so above all, be kind to yourself, laugh often and enjoy life at no one else's expense so that you fully experience and know intimately the humour and joys in earthly life and the great beyond.

Let us briefly reconsider the basic aspects of our discussion regarding our physical nature. What is defined as 'death' is simply when one's energetic eternal consciousness permanently leaves that physical body. Various symptoms of physical death occur, such as a lack of brainwave activity associated with thought and autonomic body functions, the heart stops beating, and breathing ceases. When one's eternal consciousness permanently leaves the physical body there is a discernible loss of several ounces in weight and the body rapidly begins to cool and become rigid as rigor mortis occurs.

There are many cases recorded where people and animals have apparently died of various peculiar, inexplicable causes that did not seem to result from serious injuries to their physical body. These cases would include people who appeared to die of a 'broken heart' as a direct result of the loss or death of a loved one, whereas others are reported to have died of fright, in fits of outrageous anger, or simply willed themselves to die due to old age or illness.

Our focus here is to consider conscious awareness, as it relates to the life and death of the physical body and specifically to understand and accept that our eternal consciousness is contained within an energetic body of some description that supersedes and continues to exist beyond the physical death process. Now we do not seek to address the issues regarding the nature of one's energy body that houses our eternal consciousness, nor the origin of one's consciousness, nor where that consciousness goes after the death of the physical body. Our repetitive discussion here is expressing a key foundation principle that must be distinctly specified and clearly understood, so there is absolutely no confusion that our philosophy completely disputes and disagrees with the erroneous, mistaken concept expressed by some scientists that our consciousness has its origin in the human body's physical brain. Our eternal form of conscious awareness exists independent of the human physical body and brain, in spite of the fact for the duration of one's life, our consciousness apparently resides within that same body for one human lifetime. The extent to which this issue is being excessively clarified here is necessary to remove any and all possible uncertainty regarding this issue, even for people who may not yet firmly believe that they will continue to consciously exist after the death of their physical body.

The other personal example where my energy body rotated in a convincing, complex manner in various directions within my stationary physical body helped to conclusively prove to me that within my physical body exists an independent energy body, capable of its own distinct motions. Now we may interrelate here, for hypothetical purposes only; that these two events seem to demonstrate principles that we normally would not consider when assessing the full range of human capabilities. Please recall that in my fall off the mountain, some unseen, unknown 'force' pulled me backwards, in midair, to prevent me from falling to my certain death, partly due to my inner demand to "Stop!" There is no debate of that fact in my mind or life experience. What we can hypothetically consider, with no intent to reach any unprovable speculative conclusion, is that it is possible that my own energy body could have applied some unknown force to pull my physical body backwards and prevent my death by doing so. Alternatively, we could speculate that perhaps the 'hand of God' or a 'guardian angel' or some type of other unseen life form somehow acted to save me.

Or an even more unlikely possibility is that somehow a powerful, mysterious updraft of wind blew my body backwards onto the life saving ledge. What could the real answer be? Perhaps you have a speculative idea on what may have happened in such an event, yet for me it remains a completely inexplicable mystery to this day about what actually happened in that fall or exactly why I survived.

Our intent here in discussing and integrating various types of events with their possible causes and processes is to gain additional clarity regarding the nature of those events, as well as to further characterise and acknowledge our innate human and eternal states of being. Please consider the following set of logical deductions based upon my experiences. My energy bodies can rotate at will within my motionless physical body. Apparently one's consciousness is the motive force that initiates thoughts within one's physical brain, thus enabling the physical and energetic bodies to function either in unison with synchronized movement and/or at other times, these bodies can perform multiple differing functions that may defy our normal human understanding. Events in these two situations could possibly indicate that one's consciousness; whether on an unconscious or conscious level of one's normal thought process, could act in a way that enables presently unknown and little understood conscious processes to occur. This basic concept is a factor worthy of our most sincere, thorough consideration and research by examining the evidence within our own lives. Also this example of relating various seemingly unrelated events is to encourage our mental, intuitive and perceptive processes to analyse, compare, contrast and fully consider disparate aspects of reality that defy our basic level of human awareness and comprehension. As our discussion proceeds; the concept of perceiving and integrating various seemingly disparate unique aspects of our consciousness, knowledge and capabilities within our overall total human and eternal states of being will become increasingly important in our purposes here.

Therefore, to include two personal example events that are seemingly not directly relevant or conclusively provable regarding the topic of the nature of our eternal consciousness is specifically to encourage the processes of the integration of apparently unrelated and incompatible information. By involving wider, more inclusive sets of events, perceptions and speculations into our discussion, we are better able to understand the various conclusions we will reach through this increasingly complex process of life assessment and self-discovery.

The actual nature of our eternal existence as consciousness is ultimately based upon laws of nature that are beyond the present scope of normal human perception and understanding. Basically, we are not yet fully aware of all of the processes involved with creation in this physical universe, nor in the other levels of reality that exist beyond the physical universe. However, that's OK. We do know a lot and are learning more all of the time about the actual nature of reality, which is a reason for our journeys through the physical universe; to evolve into higher, greater levels of consciousness, awareness, capability and love.

One of the most fundamental scientific discoveries made by humanity regarding the principles of the physical universe is known as the Conservation of Energy Law. This law of physics basically states that energy cannot cease to exist. Energy can and does change levels of vibratory nature. These changes make energy seem to alter the forms of its appearance and the interactions of various forms of energy can and usually do affect other energy forms in diverse ways.

For our discussion here, the most important concept is that our consciousness is composed of pure, aware energy, existing at a relatively high state of vibratory being. This form of conscious energy composes the self-aware aspect of our individual consciousness. Our consciousness enables us to perceive ourselves as independent human beings, unique among other people and life forms living and interacting upon this Earth. We each gradually develop a sense of self as we mature from early childhood, so that we recognise ourselves as being distinctly different in some ways to everyone and everything around us. This conscious energy composes the essence of what we each and all truly are as human beings. This conscious energy serves the crucial role that enables each of us to independently perceive reality, think, imagine, create, plan, communicate, possess emotions, and respond to internal realisations as well as external circumstances and many other aspects of our existence that serve to sustain life as we know it. We seek to better understand and appreciate this internal state of conscious energy in such a manner that we come to recognise that our consciousness continues to exist on various levels of reality in what we would define as an eternal state of being, continually unfolding, developing, and evolving over passing time, as we presently perceive time to exist on Earth. Our consciousness, which forms the thinking, perceiving, emotional, active aspects of our character, is housed within our own unique and amazingly capable 'energy body', which is simultaneously contained within the physical body for as long as we live on Earth in this lifetime. Actually, what appears in Kirlian photography to only be one 'energy body' is composed of numerous co-existent energy bodies that are concurrently existing simultaneously superimposed within the same space, thus forming the overall comprehensive energy body. The divine essence of our immortal consciousness is contained within Soul, which is a magnificent energetic form or 'conscious vehicle' that will continue to exist and evolve into higher levels of spiritual awareness and capability for eternity. Soul exists both independently and in conjunction within these 'lower level energy bodies' that inhabit the human physical body. We will address this complex issue in further detail later in another chapter. Soul is the initiating, sustaining, pre-existing 'higher' consciousness that enables all other 'lower' forms of consciousness, including our human physical level of conscious awareness, to occur. The Conservation of Energy Law basically states and confirms that once energy exists, then that energy will continue to permanently exist, in one form or another, for eternity, as humans now comprehend that challenging mental concept of endless timeless existence. This is especially relevant when that energy is contained within and characterises the essence of an immortal form of consciousness, such as Soul.

The discussion of the nature of eternity is an area of consideration that also defies and confounds simplistic levels of present human understanding. But that's okay too! What we do understand is that there is a past, the time we existed "before", and that we seem to continue to exist at every passing moment is a state of existence we perceive on Earth as being the "now", the current present moment. The unusual challenging aspect for us to mentally consider is that the present moment, our "now", it is continuous throughout our lives. The 'now' that existed when you decided to begin reading this book is apparently the same 'now' as when you read this sentence, just as it will become the same 'now' that will exist when you have finished reading this book. The only difference will be that your mind, daily circumstantial events and attitudes will have ideally evolved somewhat throughout this progressive process. The evolution of your spirit and intellect will be an increasingly consciously recognised, accepted fact, hopefully to a more significant applicable degree than when you began to consider this information with me. Your unfolding developing awareness of Soul existing immanent within you will serve to clarify many of these concepts within the privacy of your own mind and conscious spirit over passing time and in ways one could not anticipate. We must acknowledge our ability to recall our past or imagine our future, yet primarily be aware that we continually live in 'the eternal now'.

Over passing time we each learn to use our minds to plan the utilisation of our 'now time' to improve our future lives in all manner of ways; materially, intellectually, physically, financially, and by developing more wisdom, love, joy, peace of mind and so on. This developmental process of increasing awareness and capability, like so many other aspects of life, is something we tend to take for granted as simply being the way things are and we seldom give the nature of 'passing time' too much serious consideration. The process of aging and advancing maturity does interest us considerably, yet this is generally related primarily to the physical body in most of us. What we are actually considering here is the aging or evolution, growth and progressive development of our eternal state of being, our eternal consciousness.

Much of our mental activity is related to what we recall as already having happened in our past and planning what we will do or want to accomplish in the future. Therefore, we are constantly creating 'the eternal now' through the thoughts and actions of our ongoing present moments of conscious awareness. Only our conscious minds seem able to travel through time, from the present into the past, forward into various probable futures and then rapidly back again into the present moments, continually and instantaneously throughout our lives.

This timeless, almost instantaneous 'movement' of our thoughts in assessing the events and realisations of our past, in the context of our possible imagined future options, thereby creates our lives today and every day, throughout eternity. In order to more fully evaluate the nature of one's own eternally aware state of consciousness in order to better comprehend this process, please consider the following two significant questions: What is the importance of silencing one's normally occurring internal dialogue in gaining a better perspective of the actual nature of 'eternity'? What is the role of one's 'higher', eternal consciousness, which exists within one's normal state of human consciousness? When we refer to one's internal dialogue here, it is the process by which we continuously think an almost endless, incessant series of thoughts and images in an inner dialogue communication with ourselves about everything happening in our lives. Many of these thoughts prompt a series of emotions, that prompt other subsequent thoughts and emotions, just like water flowing down a mountain stream is followed by more and more water, endlessly flowing past a given spot, which is the focal point of our conscious attention. Our ordinary conscious mind is somewhat analogous to a certain location beside the stream of water where the flow thoughts and the related feelings are relatively continuously flowing past us. Our normal conscious mind serves both as the observer of these thoughts, images and feelings as well as the participant in most cases. The flow is incessant when allowed to follow its natural course in a sequential manner. This is one reason why it is essential to be able to occasionally associate one's perceptions with one's eternal consciousness, rather than primarily to identify one's self strictly upon the human level of consciousness.

The methods to apply one's eternal perspective are numerous, yet share basic factors. Most of us are familiar on some level with various forms of what is known quite loosely as meditation, reflection, and contemplation. Any activity that enables one to observe life, one's self, or nature is a form of meditation, especially if one can temporarily remove their conscious attention away from the creation of the this seemingly endless stream of thoughts and emotions. One could also quietly observe one's thoughts and emotions like mental traffic, analogous to watching cars, trucks and buses passing by on the street outside one's home. Sometimes the mental and emotional traffic is heavy and at other times one's thoughts and emotions are not so busy, but there will generally be a variety of conscious awareness activity inside one's self. This explanation begins to address some of the issues related the first of our closely associated questions posed at the start of the previous paragraph.

What relevance does being able to objectively observe one's flow of thoughts, images and emotions, or to even turn off the flow to enjoy 'the silence', or contemplate one's focused attention upon only one specific issue, have upon better understanding the nature of one's eternal existence? This is a very important consideration within the context of our entire discussion and it demands a straightforward answer. We ideally will learn to earnestly more consciously identify with Soul, the immortal observer of the flow of thoughts, images and emotions; and begin to identify ourselves far less intensely with our temporal conscious mind, which serves as the purveyor of these habitual, somewhat automated, often mundane and inordinately externally influenced thoughts, images and emotions. We can do this by observing ourselves carefully from a higher, internal level of awareness than our normal level of daily human consciousness. "Why do that?" you might wonder. Most of us here are already abundantly aware of this practice of self observation, along with the reasons why we do so. The majority of us interested in such issues probably meditate or contemplate on a regular daily basis, so little of this information is new to us. Our purpose in this discussion is often to state the obvious, yet in the final analysis in this ongoing process here, we will be ultimately discovering new territory and stimulating creative ideas 'in the same old places'.

Standard meditation practices can simply be a reliable beginning point to learn how to simply slow, then periodically stop the continual formation of thoughts, images and emotions. This enables one to gain a significant degree of 'higher' Self (Soul) control over one's mental and emotional processes. This basic type of meditation in silencing one's internal dialogue is wonderful to give the mind and emotional state a much-needed rest for a while. However, for we who are living in modern civilization, this form of meditation is more of a challenge than for those who were able retreat to one's cave or monastery in the mountains or one's local silent flotation chamber, as the case may be for some of us in our modern cities. We will be able to go beyond meditation into higher aspects of contemplation, illumination and revelation on intellectual, spiritual and ideally even physical levels of existence. To identify more with the eternal higher aspects of our comprehensive character is possible, regardless of what life circumstances one may find themselves. This is among our preliminary quests.

We are discussing transposing or shifting our conscious awareness far beyond the levels of perception normally associated with basic meditation where one's goal is to silence one's thoughts and emotions for some length of time. Instead, we are seeking to identify our primary state of conscious awareness with our eternal, higher, more inclusive, state of conscious awareness, as Soul. One of the ways we do this is to observe our thoughts and emotions with a sense of relatively unemotional mental detachment, with respect to consideration to our perceptions and inputs from conscience and higher information sources. Basic meditation to silence the inner dialogue is definitely not our ultimate goal, so please realise that fact immediately. We will not become too preoccupied in watching ourselves think, nor will we be focusing upon feeling our past emotions, as some form of entertainment when we tire of watching television.

The initial preliminary goal we seek is to cease to be so firmly and almost hypnotically spellbound and entrenched in the perceptions, thoughts and feelings of our normal human state of consciousness that we are unable or unwilling to perceive life, events, thoughts and emotions in a more objective, detached way through our eternal level of consciousness. There is an old saying among some spiritual circles that "God must be re-won every day", regardless of the level of development one attains in life. What we are seeking here is to become much more accomplished and comfortable in experiencing, acknowledging and being 'at one' with our eternal aspects of consciousness while being simultaneously aware and functional in our human state of consciousness in the human physical body. In other words, we seek to better integrate the eternally aware and temporal human aspects of our various levels of consciousness so that we progressively develop greater inner harmony within our existing sense of self-identity. This process may seem a bit unclear and the reasons for attaining such a state of being somewhat vague and uncertain. Please allow me to assure you there are many benefits including: improved peace of mind, additional clarity regarding what is truly important in one's life, increased happiness, the achievement of goals that are personally meaningful in various areas of one's life, as well as more nebulous advantages that you will discover yourself or those to be mentioned later.

We are in the process of making conscious what we unconsciously often take for granted in life in a manner that increases the functional level and manifested capabilities of our perceptions and consciousness. The reason we strive to accomplish this development is there are significant benefits in expanding awareness for us as individuals and as a species that is currently in danger of destroying life as we now know it to be on this planet. Plus, it is quite a pleasant experience to perceive one's attitudes, talents, wisdom and compassion developing in ways that improve one's life and that of others around themselves.

Existing as a 'unit' of conscious, creative, evolving, divinely inherent, immortal energy as Soul, we each are eternal beings, whether or not we inhabit a human body or not. Our human state of existence enables each of us to experience physical reality to accomplish things, learn lessons in life and develop as an eternal being within the physical 'fabric' of space and time. Various forms of consciousness evolve, develop and progress at differing rates. Eternal evolution is not a 'race to be won'; rather it is a fantastic endless journey of discovery characterised by expanding awareness and capability. However, like an earthly school, we ideally will choose not to repeat 'first grade' too many more times before, as a species and world civilisation, we progress sufficiently to finally begin the 'second grade' in the primary school of eternal existence.

What is so ideal about individualised existence, is that you can travel through eternal existence at your own chosen pace of development, regardless of the rates of progression, stagnation or even de-evolution experienced by other individuals or our civilisation as a whole. Obviously some of us living on Earth have other agendas than simply seeing how much power we can exert over others, or how many material possessions we can acquire, or how many resources we can greedily consume or squander in our relatively brief earthly lives. Our goals here are focused upon developing ourselves in exponentially expanding ways that express and manifest the eternal wisdom, capabilities, awareness, inner joy and peace, love and true wealth of spirit that will remain in our truly timeless possessions throughout eternity. In this progressive unfoldment of eternal character, we learn in countless ways through life's unlimited sets of experiences to do our best in all circumstances to retain our higher values, ethics, purpose and vision of why we truly exist. One's reason to exist is a very personal and private aspect of one's life. We do not presume to know or judge what choice individuals or civilisations make in their unique decisions, yet we do have the right and obligation to select our own destiny, one way or another. When we realise we have made mistakes, then we need to take the appropriate actions to correct them; first in our attitudes and then subsequently through all of our responsible behaviours.

As a youngster, I really carefully considered the wisdom in the old expression in relation to material and monetary wealth that "You can't take it with you when you leave this Earth". This important realisation at such an early age in my life served me well in making key decisions upon where to invest my efforts and private allegiances when choosing to focus upon either the development of my overall character or my material and professional status in society. Because I have sought to live a life characterised by freedom and independent lifestyle to pursue my own goals and dreams, my material and professional life has suffered to some extent because of this choice. However, the various realisations resulting from my chosen path through life have served me well and now ideally they will provide some 'food for thought' and also serve you well too, in your own unique ways. We can now choose to create an abundance of character development along with responsible, sustainable material achievement. We can decide now to focus on developing and integrating our various levels of capability relating to our eternal, evolving consciousness. This is the real true wealth of spirit that has no boundaries, no limits, no taxes, no external controls, no failures, nor any liabilities in the eternal scheme of reality.

Why would we seek to intellectually differentiate our unified consciousness into the human consciousness and eternal consciousness when it actually forms one integrated consciousness? For most of us, our human state of consciousness, which we associate with normal daily thinking and emotional processes, is overly predominant. Conversely, our more subtle, less overtly expressive, eternal state of consciousness' level of function is often comparatively diminished in most of us, to the extent that its role is somewhat limited to that of an observer of our human behaviour. Our normal, more temporal, logical, socially-oriented human consciousness tends to dominate our daily mental and emotional processes to a large extent; thereby, reducing the influences or even preventing the more perceptive, all inclusive, creative, eternal aspects of our consciousness from mental and emotional expression in much of our daily experience or in making key life choices. This lack of integration between these two aspects of our consciousness results in most of us generally failing to fully utilise the vastly more astute, proficient, well-informed, eternally aware aspects of our overall consciousness, thus allowing our less aware, less brilliant, normal human level of consciousness to freely act as the primary determiner of our thoughts and actions. We can clearly see the unfortunate results of this human tendency portrayed through illuminating degeneracy now existing within our global civilisation today in 2016.

Our conscience is an aspect to some extent of this 'higher mind' we all possess, yet often fail to utilise fully in earthly society. We vividly can determine the less than ideal choices made by people who possess little conscience when it comes to their negative, overly competitive, often adversarial, confrontational, attitudes characterised mostly by exclusive self-interest in regard to their treatment of other people or what they consider to be lower life forms, for example. Such people apparently can rationalise, justify or condone almost any cruel, greedy, inappropriate attitude or behaviour that they possess, so long as such attitudes and actions are not directed at them. Such earthly conditions are a lucid insightful indication that their thinking and emotional processes are dominated virtually entirely by what we would define as the 'lower' aspects of the human state of consciousness that has no consideration for the 'higher' concept of treating others as one wishes to be treated, which is "the golden rule" in any truly civilised society or culture. We can see the obvious results of this predominate type of thinking that is becoming more prevalent and accepted in our global civilisation among certain groups of people and institutions. Therefore, we will seek to address these issues in the scope of our discussion here. We will examine various perspectives that enable us to create an improved state of mind and set of capabilities for ourselves and to ideally instil these within our children so we will begin to interact more honestly, responsibly and productively with other like-minded people who demonstrate the 'higher' values and morals that we all aspire to manifest through our lives in diverse ways.

Addressing this disparate, separated division of our total state of consciousness is a key focal point and primary issue at the center of our discussion. To use one's own mind to observe, consider, contemplate and reach conclusions about the nature and purpose of consciousness requires us to make some artificial distinctions of logic to help differentiate and define various aspects of our consciousness in this challenging process of self-analysis. In other words, to use our mind to examine itself within the comprehensive nature of our consciousness is a complex and inherently difficult process. As our discussion continues into considering the eternal nature of our existence, this is exactly what we shall do.

Chapter 7

Integrating Our Consciousness

Increased awareness of every kind is a distinct advantage to human beings. Integrating one's human level of consciousness with one's eternal level of consciousness is among the most beneficial activities in life that any of us can accomplish. This is a complicated issue to intellectually visualise or achieve for most of us because one's mind is the instrument of assessment and the primary means by which we comprehend life's realities. Even more challenging is the reality that higher levels of spiritual development generally surpass to some extent our existing normal mental understanding and perceptions. Additionally, the depth, scope and subtle nature of the subject matter tends to make one's mind want to 'switch off', due to information overload. No doubt you have long ago discovered that fact. If you think this subject matter is tedious and difficult to read and comprehend, then you should try writing about these topics coherently.

Therefore, this subject is one we must address in a fairly basic, step-by-step manner. For some of us the entire concept of integrating one's human state of awareness with their higher, eternal levels awareness is a somewhat odd and unusual situation to mentally conceptualise, much less accomplish. That's OK. Others of us are already well-along this path, even if the process of integration has been occurring upon a primarily unconscious or subconscious basis for lengthy time periods, as I suspect is the situation for most of us. This entire process, like many others in this book, may seem to be a bit peculiar or somewhat alien to our prevalent ways of thinking and out of context with our daily activities in life. This is quite understandable. Others of us will be more familiar with this process of unification of the various aspects of one's consciousness and be pleased to know they are not alone in their evocative challenging quest of self-discovery in unifying and integrating their various levels of conscious awareness.

For most of us, many of these ideas and unusual experiences at times will seem to be some type of inexplicable, real-life science fiction story. The diversity of events that life organises for each of us serves to continuously expand our perceptions and realisations in a multitude of ways. Many of life's experiences test, strengthen and develop us on multiple levels. Regardless of the way the events we each experience in this life occur and whatever the nature of our resulting individual responses, the most basic reassuring fact is we each are progressing at the pace that is right and best for us individually. Collectively, as a global civilisation, this progressive evolutionary development and maturation process is also occurring. As individuals, we simultaneously exist within our local communities which are formed by a myriad of unique interactive cultures and groups that blend together to compose our national identities, which perform their roles in the international global arena. Our individual influences within this larger process generally depend upon one's circumstances, abilities and life goals.

This is the basic 'big picture' in how we each and all fit together into earthly life, and the old saying "It takes all kinds to make the world go around" is quite an accurate portrayal of circumstances here on Earth. What a dull, boring, virtually pointless existence it would be if all human beings, cultures and environments were clones and basically identical to one another. When we speak of integrating diverse aspects of our overall consciousness, on the human level, these increases in awareness continue to interrelate well in applicable beneficial areas within the system of reality we experience here on Earth. Additionally, on the eternal level of consciousness, each of us is more focused upon various systems of reality operating at a level of awareness and capability that often surpasses our physical senses of perception and normal conscious understanding. We accept this entire subject matter is a bit vague and uncomfortable for most of us to consider, yet the positive results of this process of self-discovery and integration can be fantastic! Even relatively small incremental advances in this area of one's life can enable one to attain exponential achievements through the expansion of one's overall awareness which can create countless favourable influences on daily life. An essential component in this developmental integration process is to remain 'balanced', in the sense that both aspects of one's human and eternal levels of conscious awareness harmonise and begin to resonate in concordance together, which is a delightful realisation and feeling.

First, let's examine what we call ourselves for clues to our true nature as life forms on this Earth. We call ourselves, very aptly and intelligently, 'human beings'. The descriptive word 'human' refers to our physical body, mind and active state of being in this earthly existence. The other integral aspect of our self-chosen descriptive assessment of our nature is the word 'beings', which expresses the energetic, eternally aware components of our overall state of conscious existence in the ever-present moment that we term 'now'. These two dynamically integrated aspects of human existence are essential in our ability to function within the physical universe, which exists within the vastly larger and unknown context of what we define as being 'eternal reality'. The nature of eternal reality, referring to the apparently infinite levels or dimensions of energetic reality systems existing throughout and beyond the seemingly limitless physical universe, is entirely beyond the perceptions of five normal human physical senses. Therefore the magnitude of this entire system of cosmic reality can only be fully experienced through the perceptions and higher abilities associated with our energetic, spiritually aware, eternal levels of divine consciousness. The term 'human being' is a distinctive, descriptive, overt acknowledgment made by the self-aware people who first experienced and consciously realised the actual nature of the human physical and energetic forms of consciousness in their assessment of reality. This innate and astounding wisdom attained over countless eons of time by humanity's ancient ancestors gradually developed into spoken and written language. Human beings, a species of highly aware, self-conscious life forms capable of existing simultaneously within both the temporal physical universe and upon various higher energetic levels of reality, established a self-descriptive identification for ourselves as a Species of life that acknowledged and celebrated our impressive dual nature!

Generally speaking, in modern times human consciousness for the majority of human beings on the planet has tended to develop more toward the greater use of the logical, linear, analytical aspects of our minds to create and sustain the technologically advanced civilisation that many of us in the world now experience as our daily reality. Actually, all aspects of our overall conscious awareness are utilised to some extent, since creativity and intuitive abilities are largely functions of higher levels of consciousness. However, in most of our daily thought processes in modern societies we predominantly seem to utilise the more 'down to earth' aspects of our human level of conscious awareness. This is could be a misapprehension upon my part, yet this seems to be the case from examining human social and psychological thought processes. This fact is surely not to ignore or minimise the important role that religious and spiritual beliefs and activities have in the vast majority of people's lives throughout the developed and developing nations of the Earth. Instead, we are acknowledging that the foremost aspects of our daily conscious awareness generally relate to logical, logistic, materialistic, analytical types of thought processes, where one's perception and level of awareness appears focused primarily through the human levels of our overall consciousness. This pragmatic organisation of our perceptive, active consciousness is a necessity for the vast majority of people on Earth due to the technologically active 'western' type of culture within which most of us currently live. This assessment from my perspective is surely not intended to inaccurately seek to create artificial, overly exaggerated distinctions regarding the structuring and utilisation of human consciousness, rather to observe what seems to be the situation based upon human attitudes and activities as self-evident realities.

Some cultures and societies on Earth tend to focus more upon the 'being' aspects of their consciousness upon a daily basis. For example, people sincerely practicing religious faiths such as Islam, some forms of Christianity and Judaism, Hinduism and other less well-known religions, periodically throughout the day focus their attention upon creating an inner awareness and connection with their Creator, known as simply God to some. God is also known by many other names, such as The Great Spirit, Allah, Jehovah, the Lord, the Father, Christ, Sugmad, The Almighty, The Creator, It, The Life Force, The Force, 'the power that be', etc, depending upon one's personal religious, spiritual or other beliefs. One of the fundamental unifying, outstanding characteristics of the vast majority of human beings of virtually every culture, nation, race or tribal group; regardless of how remotely they may be located or in what period of history, is that they almost always believe in and in some way worship a higher Creative Force or God. This common belief in God or some form of highly intelligent life that created our universe and life as we now know it is surely one of the most focal, defining similarities between most peoples of Earth. The vast majority of human beings periodically consciously or unconsciously seek to share some form of inner or verbal form of communication, acknowledgment, respect, thanks, appreciation, commitment, and allegiance to their Creator, God, or Saviour, or simply to commune with nature in some form of unifying practice of prayer, worship, meditation, contemplation, chanting or other such activity. For the vast majority of human beings this relationship is certainly an integral, extremely significant part of our lives, although many of us are quite private regarding the depth of meaning this relationship with God, or our chosen Prophet, or Saviour, or Messenger of God, has for us personally. Some people have no definitive beliefs or opinions about their relationship with, or the existence of, some unseen Creator or God, so they may tend to simply relax and feel at one with life or nature, while still other people may feel quite uncomfortable in life and challenged by these earthly circumstances, regardless of their belief systems.

Whatever the form or manner of practice our prayer, meditation, contemplation, or acknowledgment of a divinity within and/or beyond ourselves may be that enables us to affiliate ourselves with higher, more intuitive, creative, energetic, divine, eternal, immortal aspects of our consciousness; this is a core aspect of our existence. The vast majority of people on Earth possess some socially accepted religious teachings in written form, such as the Bible, Koran, Torah, etc, which formulate and record a human experience-based interpretation of humanity's beliefs in regard to God's existence and Its aspirations for human beings. Throughout recorded history various mostly self-proclaimed prophets and messengers have expressed to humanity various concepts about the reality of God's existence as the Creative Force in the universe, which created human beings and enabled us to exist in an eternally aware state of being. The creative essence of our immortal higher consciousness is thought to be composed of a spark of the omnipotent, omnipresent, eternally-aware God Consciousness, which most religions define as being Soul, the Holy Spirit or some other similar concept. If there is one primary defining characteristic of all human culture on Earth, it would be the belief in some form of Creative Intelligent Force or God having created the physical universe, human beings, and everything in life. It seems clear that this set of shared beliefs in some form of divine Creator, based upon the countless diverse experiences of human beings since we developed a form of self-conscious awareness of the world and universe; is acknowledged and proclaimed by human beings of all historical ages, of all cultures and races on Earth. This fact is revealed by the way all people identify our selves foremost as human beings, then in a secondary way as being members of a given culture, state, nation, religion, tribe or race. Some cultures define themselves in their native languages as "the children" or "creations of God". The modern theory of evolution does not in any way scientifically explain the existence of Soul which is the animate energetic conscious 'force' that inhabits all physical bodies, regardless of the species. This omission does not undermine the theory of evolution; rather it simply indicates it is only intended to explain a perspective on the development of physical life on our planet, of which various other theories are also applicable and are strongly supported by those who adhere to those beliefs.

We must also acknowledge a distinctive minority of people have taken a personal viewpoint that there is no visible indication of God's existence from their perspective, so therefore they have chosen to refuse to accept the idea that such a creative force exists, which is their prerogative as free-thinking, perceptive human beings. Such people are a significant portion of the population. However, we all have the opportunity to contemplate upon the nature of our spirit and intellect that inhabits the human body and the origin of that consciousness in ways that suit our beliefs and lifestyles. Some people think that no divine creative force or God could exist because they believe It would not allow all of the suffering, devastation, wars, and ills to exist in this earthly life. This too is an understandable, reasonable, valid viewpoint expressed by mostly logical, intelligent, analytical, good-hearted people that would generally describe themselves as agnostics, or as atheists, or simply as people that are unable to accept that a compassionate, divine Creator or God could allow such misery to occur on Earth without taking action to improve the situation. Why so much suffering, depravity, greed, inequality, injustice and violent death exists on our beautiful planet is indeed among the most complex, challenging and difficult issues for us to comprehend in the course of our earthly lives. All thinking, feeling, perceptive people throughout the ages have sought answers from within themselves, from their community and religious leaders, and especially from the God that created all life for the reasons why so many aspects of earthly life and human interactions seem inherently challenging, unpleasant and even odious to our ideal visions of how we would prefer this reality to be on Earth.

    My simplistic response to this issue is that the nature of life on this planet Earth is currently designed to serve as a 'schoolhouse' for quite a large group of Souls and many of these could be classified as 'beginners' or even 'slow learners' who are now experiencing the mortal physical form as live human beings to better learn the many lessons that will assist and enable us to become more compassionate, understanding, empathetic, creative, loving, kind, eternally aware beings, who will possess and express a progressive level of divinity that could not be achieved in any other non-physical way. We are indeed fortunate that there are also some highly advanced Souls serving on Earth that are directly involved in our evolution and spiritual development. Some people prefer to believe there are no 'higher' or more evolved life forms in existence than themselves, and they may also deny the possibility that there is any 'higher' or true purpose to earthly life. Such people may choose to believe that life on Earth is a 'once only' visit where all here should simply seek to have a good time and do whatever they wish; all too often without empathy or consideration to the rights, thoughts, feelings or desires of others. Such people often justify and rationalise what most of us would define as unsocial, inappropriate or immoral attitudes and behaviours. Other people have no need for a moral or religious code, nor to possess a belief in a Creator or God in order to innately live their lives by the "golden rule", which is to treat all other life forms as we ourselves wish to be treated, with mutual respect, kindness, in an ethical, moral manner simply because it seems the right and best way to think and act based upon the influences of their conscience. These complex issues will be given significant further consideration as our discussion progresses here.

We must accept that some people do not believe in or admit the possible existence of an eternally aware, immortal Creative Intelligence or God that enlivened our eternal consciousness. These people are also likely to strongly dispute and deny that the primary purpose for our earthly lives is to educate our immortal consciousness, Soul, through a lengthy progression of earthly and also other temporal lives where we exist upon 'higher' planes of reality that some would perceive as being 'Heaven' or other less delightful alternative non-physical destinations upon other 'planes' or dimensions of existence. All these physical states of eternally ongoing existence are apparently sequential in nature when located within time and space. In the more comprehensive infinitely expanding cosmic reality systems, there exist various 'levels', or 'planes', or dimensions that we, as human beings, would now perceive as being 'locations' in different times and places. These are apparently not ordinarily directly perceptible from normal physical earthly viewpoints. Upon the level of Soul or Spirit, we each exist as an eternally aware life form, possessing an indestructible energy body that houses this immortal divine consciousness that exists 'outside' or 'beyond' time and space as we know and understand it to be on Earth in this physical universe. It is via Soul that human beings seeking to perceive deeply into the actual nature of cosmic reality systems are able to utilise their more divinely orientated attributes and miraculous capabilities to access all manner of illuminating, transcendental experiences, astounding information and intuitive perceptions.

We definitely must acknowledge the rights of people to believe whatever makes reasonable sense to them based upon their own experiences and reasoning abilities, so long as their beliefs are not arbitrarily or detrimentally imposed upon other people who choose to believe otherwise. We welcome other people to express their opinions that contradict anything stated here. For example, anyone who disputes or denies the existence or the possible existence of a Creative Intelligence or God is most welcome to assert their perspectives philosophically, scientifically or otherwise. Some theories that explain existence do not directly address this issue, such as the Big Bang Theory, which is intended primarily to explain the physical creation of the Milky Way Galaxy. Likewise, some Christians have a belief in 'creationism' as explained in the Bible. Other cultures have various explanations for how reality came into existence. All people possess their own beliefs, logical rational assertions, their personal experiences and are fully entitled to their own opinions. It would be difficult to attempt to conclusively disprove or prove the existence of a Creator of the physical universe or God that is the creative force of life and conscious awareness. Thankfully that is not our goal here. From my perspective, the existence of the highly ordered, functional universal reality system seemingly implies and vividly reveals in a self-evident manner that an awesome Creative Force is functioning within and throughout reality. However, this is only my personal opinion from my life experiences and you have every right to your own unique attitudes and belief systems. These debateable cosmic issues regarding the nature of existence are not directly relevant to our discussion of relating one's personal experiences with those of other inquisitive people that are seeking to obtain greater understanding of life's mysteries and to discover new, exciting, uplifting information about the nature of our eternal existence and how these eternal aspects of ourselves integrate within our human level of existence. Therefore, we will largely evade the controversial issue of discussing how people possessing widely differing perspectives consider God, a Creator, or nature's role in existence or whatever personal theory one may have to explain the comprehensive system of reality. It is impossible to adequately address, fully consider or even partially explain all people's attitudes and perspectives and this is simply not our purpose here. We must acknowledge people are exceedingly unique in their experiences and beliefs and possess rights to whatever system of ideas and attitudes that make sense to them. Hereafter, we will leave it to each individual to express their own beliefs and opinions themselves elsewhere about their attitudes, which will in some cases fundamentally differ in many significant ways from what is being expressed here, as evidenced by people's complex interactions in our world today.

One's own individual conscious beliefs and experiences contribute significantly to the development and evolution of one's awareness in the realm of both the physical and eternal levels of existence. This path of self discovery, ongoing personal development, with continually increasing perceptive awareness and capability is a completely individualistic activity. It is essential that we realise and accept that one's progressive development in the realms of eternal existence is definitively not a 'race'. One should never 'rush' or force this developmental process of natural unfoldment and accomplishment. There appears to be no 'finish line' in the infinite scheme of Life, where one finally stops developing, learning, evolving, unfolding and achieving creative positive goals, attributes and realisations. We gain a better appreciation and comprehension of immortal Life's most important realities through our unlimited unique personal life experiences; such as understanding the countless aspects of love and its related positive states of being, as opposed to its converses, which are so often unpleasant in various ways. Most of us have experienced the loss of human love in our life, which can be an intensely painful experience that can close our hearts in some cases for a while, yet we learn that divine love and unconditional love are never withdrawn from us, in either our temporal earthly or immortal eternal lifetimes.

We seek to view our human state of consciousness that exists in this earthly life as being a temporal level of existence, concurrently co-existing with one's immortal state of consciousness upon an eternal level of Life. As one achieves various levels of progression on the human earthly levels of awareness, then one proceeds to the next level of consciously aware eternal existence where new and different types of realities, lessons and achievements are accomplished. We here on Earth have all lived a huge number of earthly human lives throughout history among different races, cultures and religions; living lives in both male and female bodies, often travelling into the greater realities surrounding us, almost every time we sleep and dream. The actual fact is that our immortal eternal aspect which we term Soul or Spirit, exists beyond time and space as we now understand it; upon a vastly higher, more all-inclusive and creative level of reality that co-exists with physical reality. This ability for our eternal immortal Soul consciousness to exist simultaneously upon earthly and also upon other higher systems of reality that do not experience time and space, nor physical laws as they exist on Earth, is a complex topic to consider intellectually and we will address it in further detail as we progress here. It helps in one's comprehension to allow intuition and one's higher aspects of conscious awareness to present impressions and a sense of direct innate 'knowingness' that surpasses normal thoughts and feelings. In this manner these challenging concepts do not seem so foreign or difficult to consider or accept for our human consciousness, which is conditioned by a far less inclusive perspective and comprehension of reality than Soul possesses.

As one particular earthly lifetime ends for each of us with the death of our physical body, then some aspects of that human state of consciousness that are no longer applicable to our progressing evolving state of consciousness in a sense die along with that temporal physical vehicle. In between the time when another lifetime on Earth or elsewhere in the universe begins; our existence is 'punctuated' by 'visits' or 'lifetimes' upon other levels of reality, lasting varying amounts of earthly time from only months, to a few years, or for hundreds or even thousands of years of earthly time. The purpose of these lifetimes in other systems of reality that actually co-exist simultaneously with the physical level of reality is to rest, learn from our previous earthly experiences by putting them into the context of our eternal lessons and realisations, and to prepare ourselves for future lives in various systems of reality. This includes living additional earthly type lives in the physical universe, including in some cases living lives upon other physical level planets, aside from Earth. These 'higher' level locations could be describe as somewhat like what we would imagine to be living in upon a more refined civilised planet or if we are especially fortunate, then akin to our vision of Heaven. These other lifetimes may be spent in locations within various vast regions within the Astral Plane, the Mental Plane, or even upon the Soul Plane, or upon other such immense and unimaginably extensive Planes of existence, beyond the physical universe that we currently exist within while on Earth.

There are, of course, also other non-earthly, 'higher', non-physical dimensional locations where the lessons are far more harsh and intense, much like we see here on Earth today in the more 'troubled' areas of this world. This sort of vivid, dramatic and quite often painful realisation process is usually required by people possessing extremely negative human attitudes, characteristics or behaviour patterns. These types of non-earthly locations would seem to be more like the traditional concept of Hell and these types of destinations have been established for those people and life forms that have wilfully chosen to create great destruction and misery for others in their time upon Earth or elsewhere in physical reality systems. We all would recognise that in earthly life there are a significant variety of states of existence here now, as well as an amazing diversity of types and levels of consciousness possessed by the life forms that we recognise as human beings. Some entities that inhabit human body forms may in some cases actually be rather unpleasant forms of life that are not actually real human beings, at least not in the same sense that you or I, who are truly interested in our spiritual evolutionary growth. A revealing situation is that some of these earthly entities do not possess any morals, ethics, or any functional conscience, such as we understand or experience this aspect of our 'higher' self or Soul. Seriously consider the possibility that we should not be fooled that just because someone appears physically to be a human being, that the entity or spirit that resides within that human physical form is what they appear to be externally. We do not seek to be alarmists here, only to be aware that not everyone or everything on Earth is exactly what it appears to be at all times, in all ways. Attitudes and actions reveal the self-evident truths in most situations, so remain perceptive and aware in this earthly life at all times.

By considering the lives of people around us globally, we are all acutely aware that some people's lives are somewhat like they are now existing in a Heaven on Earth, while other people seem to be living much less fortunate lives where their existence is truly like a living Hell on Earth. Very often these vastly different states of being, so-called 'heaven' and 'hell', here on Earth are found to be located in relatively close proximity to one another. The fact remains clear to be seen that one's attitudes, perceptions, state of mind, actions, and responses to life's circumstances have a massive direct influence upon how one perceives one's circumstances upon Earth. Some people endure suffering, oppression, depravation, illness, misfortune and adversity of all types, while maintaining a noble, stoic, positive state of mind and affirmative response to life's challenging circumstances and utilise them to improve their character through the realisations they receive in that difficult set of life processes. Other people may experience a life of wealth and leisure, yet have all manner of mostly self-inflicted maladies, addictions, tend to unceasingly complain about various aspects of life, and exhibit uncivil, unkind and inappropriate behaviours, with few resulting beneficial lessons or realisations being derived from such a life. The state an individual's life and one's responses to these diverse situations vary greatly; depending to a huge extent upon their unique perceptions and self-created choices throughout the progressions of one's various earthly lives. In the boundless realms of infinite eternal existence, the processes of eternal 'higher' justice and self-responsibility for one's thoughts and actions continuously form an integral aspect of eternal Life. Therefore, we are destined to continue this procession of lifetimes on various levels of reality, which periodically include earthly lives, until we can permanently 'graduate' from this earthly 'schoolhouse' and proceed progressively onwards into higher and higher levels of eternal existence.

Various earthly religions would dispute what is being mentioned here, yet most of these religions were established by fallible people, who primarily sought to establish institutional hierarchies intended to develop reliable ways to better control and 'educate' the general population. History is full of gruesome examples where religion or fanatical ideologies have been misapplied to promote disharmony, discord, chaos and violence among various groups of people; often under the false hypocritical guise of seeking peace, order and the common good. These situations have historically often resulted in civil conflict, religious and cultural wars where each side generally views themselves as God's chosen people, with anyone who thinks differently being demonised and perceived unjustly as the vile enemy of these self-proclaimed so-called 'chosen' people. Religions are usually created by people that espouse the best possible intentions, yet unfortunately we clearly can see some of the self-evident results littering the pages of our sanitised history books' perspectives of the actual events involved. Religions often contain ample human inspired doctrines that seem to have little or no apparent relation to what could possibly be defined as being creative, uplifting, positive, constructive, beneficial or spiritually responsible attitudes or behaviours inspired by God or the Creator. Instead, much of religious scripture is apparently written and enforced by humans who primarily seek power over one another as their primary goal. All too often historically, religions have periodically served primarily to establish, breed and espouse beliefs and attitudes that supplant freedom, equality, opportunity and justice with false divisions and contrived separations among people who generally actually share many of the same basic belief systems, goals, life styles and aspirations.

A modern example of religion losing its higher purpose and direction is the development of so-called 'fundamentalism', whether it is a Christian, or Jewish, or Islamic, or any other version of religious or philosophic extremism of the worst kind. Such examples have continually plagued humanity throughout history in various forms. Extremism in its many unpleasant, divisive, amoral, chaotic forms is surely not limited to so-called 'religious' people and institutions, nor to philosophic ideals such as extreme versions of capitalism, socialism or fascism. These extreme life perspectives that deny the rights of people who disagree with their modes of thinking and actions serve to historically exemplify and characterise the most negative, evil, counter-productive human traits that create and sustain much of what desperately needs to be improved in our earthly civilisation today. We address this issue briefly here now to better clarify what we define as being truly 'spiritual' in nature, as opposed to what we would define as being 'religious' in its human applications. Spiritual values cherish and uphold the rights to freedom, equality and justice for all people; whereas conversely, many so-called religions or extremist philosophies profess hypocritical beliefs that sound ideal, yet in actual practice they are proven through action to be committed to fanaticism, gender bias, inequality, slavery, genocide, brutality, hatred, and institutionalised conflict.

Just as surely as the sun radiates light and unseen forms of solar radiations, such as ultraviolet (UV) light, continuously twenty four hours per day onto the Earth, the sun's radiant light is not actually limited to shining only about half of the day, as our physical senses incorrectly tell us. Likewise, various self-proclaimed religious zealots will express their opinions that what is recorded here is inaccurate and an affront to their dogmatic, unproven, self-styled, version of what they believe to be reality because this book does not conform to their beliefs or physical sense impressions. To make an historical analogy, a self-proclaimed autocratic authority figure may deem it 'heresy' to say the sun radiates light continuously, punishable by death by being burned alive to say otherwise; just as they may also deem that one can not criticise their religion or form of totalitarian government, punishable by death or a life in jail. Is this form of earthly authority based upon true justice and is actually sanctioned by God as some religions tend to attribute their self-righteous use of power over humanity, including those unfortunate people who possess other beliefs, or it is it based primarily upon corrupted evil applications of despotic power for these religion's institutional self-interests? People are entitled to believe what makes sense to them, so long as they do not seek to dictate their belief systems onto other people who choose to believe differently in a peaceful manner. Conflict develops when any set of beliefs is forced upon others, or when one group seeks to control, inflict injury or deprive others by force of will, militarily, or by the use of economic controls, or other forms of human power.

We are simply seeking to unify various aspects of our overall consciousness in this process here. Therefore, it is important to identify what belongs in the realm of our chosen reality system, according to our own unique personal opinions, be it rightly or wrongly believed from other people's perspectives. It is for this reason we will address various issues related to a few of the major organised earthly religions to clarify some of the ways we may choose to develop our own set of individual beliefs that differ in some significant ways by examining these beliefs in more detail to determine whether these ideas are something we wish to accept or perhaps reconsider from another perspective.

It is supposed to be acceptable to openly express one's own opinions in purportedly democratic nations in the so-called modern 'free world'. Let's consider a few ideas along these same lines of thought, as we digress briefly to compare a few of the current religious opinions that have been recorded in modern religious texts that are currently being inappropriately used to create and sustain much adversity and misery in today's world, in my opinion. We hereby seek to analyse and compare what is being stated here in our discussion about the actual nature of eternal reality, according to my own personal opinions, observations, and thorough research of history that is based upon eons of accumulated experience and evidence that is clearly before humanity now. This is an important process for those of us who are willing to seriously consider and debate such issues from an objective perspective. We do so in a way that is likely to be objectionable to some people possessing viewpoints that seek to promote and sustain the prevalent hypocritical rhetoric mentioned previously. These multitudes of mutually supportive characteristically dictatorial, authoritarian philosophies of life inaccurately and untruthfully profess to be derived from the 'word of God', as recorded by men centuries ago, who were purportedly simply documenting the teachings of purportedly self-proclaimed 'prophets of God'.

I surely do not, not, not proclaim to be a prophet of God; nor do I seek to create a new religion; nor copy any existing religious teachings in this book; nor do I seek to criticise any religion; nor assess or assert whether or not any purported Prophet in history was 'a' or 'the' Messenger of God; nor am I expressing my opinion regarding whether or not a particular religious text is indeed the literal, factual Word of God;

nor am I implying or stating that anyone who believes differently than I do is incorrectly informed, from their perspective, regarding life's system of reality. Rather, I am just someone who seeks to express their personal opinions, perspectives and experiences that are related to the existence of a more all-inclusive, comprehensive nature of reality. In this manner, anyone who is curious about or interested in these issues can consider them in the privacy of their own mind, heart and Soul. If you wish, you are encouraged to then discuss some of these ideas, along with your own unique experiences and opinions among other people. We simply seek to gain an improved vision and comprehension of reality than what is currently being publicly acknowledged when all the evidence of human experience is properly accumulated, analysed and discussed among thinking people of all faiths, races, cultures, sexes, ages, and nations of Earth.

Since religion is such a sensitive issue in today's global civilisation in 2016 when this book is being published, let's not identify any specific religions in the nature of our discussions here. Instead, we will to some extent generalise upon various religious belief systems, including a few specific examples of various unnamed religious teachings that seem to be open to debate. Additionally, we shall be contrasting and comparing other simular, although somewhat unique, beliefs that are recorded in various religious texts, as expressed by each religion's more fervent and fervid adherents, devotees, advocates, members, or followers. We seek to do so only to better understand how other people think and live their lives, so we can better comprehend ways to improve our own lives and interact with more empathy and compassion with people who believe differently to ourselves so that there can be more harmony, peace and forgiveness among the diverse peoples of Earth. To do otherwise would certainly not be according to the character of a mature, reasonable species of intelligent life forms, such as most human beings profess to be in our modern diverse global civilisation.

As we discussed previously, the majority of people on Earth believe in a form of God or creative force that somehow resulted in the existence of all of life upon this planet, which includes human beings. All around us in the physical universe we perceive the evidence of this incredible divine creativity in action. Life manifests creative genius in the manner in which these systems of reality are designed, through their constant states of endless change, development and evolution, while maintaining continuity of function in ways that encourage infinite varieties of life forms to exist and interact with one another harmoniously. These life forms all possess amazingly diverse of types of consciousnesses that form complex ecosystems that make physical life possible. The mystery and wonder of the entire system of reality we see around us in this solar system and within the known physical universe is astounding. The sun's solar energy that we perceive to be light and heat with our physical senses is actually a vastly more complex and active energetic substance that makes all physical life as we know it possible, including the existence of many other types of life forms that we human beings are not yet aware of at this time in our evolution of awareness. Therefore, to understand why we include so many seemingly unrelated issues into our discussion regarding the integration of our various types and levels of human beings' overall state of consciousness is that our higher nature, the source of our conscious awareness, Soul, which is actually aspects of God's Consciousness incarnate within us, has an affinity for certain preferred states of being and mental development. Soul chooses to dwell in all manner of life forms in which human beings are only a distinctly tiny minority in the overall scheme of life in this universe. For any human being to manifest improved awareness and expression of one's higher indwelling states of consciousness, it is preferable to establish fertile receptive states of being, spirit and mind that attract Soul's influences into our daily consciousness and life. So, to discuss the prevalent thinking, beliefs and activities that human beings presently manifest into action and literally express in today's religions, secular societies, various public institutions, modern technologies, and overall civilisation is necessary. This process enables us all to gain an improved perspective on what changes we each and all need to make to continue to develop and mature as a species of life that is about to enter the intergalactic community of life forms, as well as gaining a greater understanding and appreciation for the full magnitude of the nature of other higher levels of existence beyond the physical plane, where we all now exist in this present incarnation on Earth.

Before we consider a few of the belief systems of various earthly religions, we need to remind ourselves that certain negative emotions and types of thinking generally prevent Soul from expressing Itself to a considerable extent within the normal aspects of our conscious awareness and daily lives. It is for this reason we need to assess and carefully evaluate what types of thinking, beliefs, emotions, attitudes and actions we manifest inwardly and externally into the world and in our interactions with other people. Negative emotional and mental states of being such as anger, fear, hate, aversion, greed, lust, desire for power over others, complaint, gossip, contempt, derision and criticism of others, lying and all forms of intended deceit, including manipulation, rationalisation, and excuses for inappropriate treatment of others are all examples of the types of thinking, emotions and actions that are to some extent evident at various times within most of us. These unpleasant, problematic issues are now becoming rife within our various societies, institutions and global civilisation. These states of mind and being surely do not, not, not attract the expression of our higher, divine states of consciousness within us. Therefore, we subsequently are less able to benefit from these higher states of being in our daily lives, and our global civilisation is thereby limited and unable to achieve its true potential. As human beings, individually and collectively as a species of life forms, we would greatly benefit by creating receptive states of mind and positive emotional conditions to encourage the development and expression of the higher aspects of consciousness within us. Toward this result, we seek here to identify all manner of issues that are currently preventing our comprehensive levels of awareness from functioning, as could be the natural positive state of existence for us all.

To integrate one's levels of consciousness requires one to truly "know thy self". This is a complex and sometimes unpleasant process where most of us tend to blame others for many of our own problems and challenges, while we too often steadfastly refuse to accept complete personal responsibility for our own chosen thoughts, emotions, attitudes, perspectives, opinions, and deliberate actions in earthly life. We need to examine every aspect of our lives. What follows is intended to help all people more clearly consider, assess and fully evaluate our most treasured religious teachings for clues to some of the adjustments we can make to improve our societies and our global community to interact more humanely, more kindly, with greater justice and equality, among all groups of people on planet Earth. We all profess to respect, admire and seek to emulate history's greatest, most noble, saintly, kind, generous, good-hearted, truly spiritual people. These truly spiritual, divinely inspired, godly leaders throughout history were quite often persecuted and reviled by those authority figures in society that were threatened or incensed by their moralistic, devout beliefs whose teachings had unwanted influences upon public opinions. These spiritually aware and exemplary truly spiritual people sought to live lives characterised by the higher set of values, ethics and moral behaviours that have been recorded in various religious scriptures, which are now perceived by their devotees as being the literal 'word of God'. These ancient religious scriptures were compiled and refined by numerous human authors who recorded these spiritual teachings over a time spanning many thousands of years of human history. These sacred religious scriptures were inspired by the higher wisdom and purpose and now are intended to serve humanity as messages of hope for establishing a more harmonious vision for a better world civilisation. These prophet's ideals have been shared among the world's great civilisations since even before recorded history began and are among humanity's most noble, cherished, beneficial works of wisdom, hope and true value.

Now in many of our modern world religions some of these ancient religious scriptures are being re-interpreted and in some cases are obviously intentionally being misinterpreted and misapplied by people who clearly seem to have strayed somewhat from the original intention and actual teachings provided to us by these spiritually gifted prophets and teachers. These apparent misinterpretations of the original uplifting teachings are definitively proven by the self-evident fact that some aspects of modern religious interpretations are being inappropriately used to justify and condone all manner of ungodly beliefs and acts, such as the murder of innocent people, and even self-murder, purportedly in God's name for selfish, evil inhuman reasons.

Therefore, we are going to be discussing some of the ways that mankind may have misinterpreted, misapplied, convoluted, contorted, distorted, altered, undermined, and changed some of these saintly people's messages for humanity. Now, many centuries after the time when these spiritual leaders lived and inspired humanity, their teachings have been recorded and complied into religious texts. These religious documents have sometimes been translated from their original language and then re-interpreted by various unknown authors. In some cases these written scriptures have been significantly altered from the original teachings of these spiritual messengers who first presented their ideas to humanity. These prophet's mostly verbal teachings have subsequently been repeatedly re-interpreted, translated into various languages, and re-written again and again, often by men who in many cases clearly possessed relatively little true divinity, as expressed through their self-evident actions and attitudes. It is worthy to note the male gender usually dominated the compilation of these religious texts and sought to personify God in a masculine sense, in spite of no evidence to support such an idea. For example, we can perceive a religious tendency to resist portraying the female gender as equals to the male gender. Therefore, we must become aware of the prevalent male orientated bias we see manifested in most modern religions as something that is also not likely to be the result of true divine Godly origin; rather it is a human inclusion intentionally introduced by the men who recorded and interpreted these manuscripts.

We now would all be greatly benefited by once again taking self-responsibility to personally develop a reasonable set of spiritual and religious beliefs that will be truly divine and unconditionally loving in nature and intent, considering what is reasonably possible in our challenging world. Such attitudes, beliefs and actions need to be individually relevant to our daily lives as we increasingly integrate various aspects of our eternal immortal states of being in a balanced, realistic way. We seek to accomplish a transition away from a spiritual path or religion being a largely matter of 'faith' based primarily upon human religious scriptures, where we are encouraged to place our trust in proven fallible purportedly religious people who profess to serve as God's representatives in our lives; toward a set of spiritual beliefs based far more upon personal experience in truly realising our inner divinity through events that reveal the kindly, compassionate, peaceful, loving nature of our true Creator or God in our daily lives, hearts and minds. Most of us that are attracted to the topics being discussed here are already well-advanced along the journey of self-responsibility and self-discovery we refer to continually in this book. Yet, it is important to keep our goals clearly in mind at all times, especially when we ask ourselves "How did I arrive at this point in my life?" and "Where to from here?". It is quite helpful to examine various religious beliefs to determine whether or not they may be somewhat confusing or inappropriate for us. In some ways, some religious beliefs could even be serving to create fear, distract us, or may actually be leading us astray from actually realising and expressing our already existing true inner innate divinity. This endless progressive spiritual journey of discovery is a personal process whereby each of us learns to develop a much better personal relationship with our Creator, which we know as God. We accomplish this by first developing a vastly better, more integrated, vibrantly real, inner relationship with our innate divine aspect of our real self, Soul, which is our true source of conscious awareness, creativity, joy, love, and meaning in both our earthly and eternal immortal Life. The inner expression of our conscience is prompted by Soul, which prevents us from acting in evil, violent, controlling ways; except in rare cases of self-defence, when confronted by murderous oppressors.

We definitely do not seek to be critical of any specific religion, nor of religion in general. All religions perform a vital service in their members' lives that ultimately assist them to become better people, with a closer relationship with God. We will simply specify a number of beliefs and practices by various unnamed religions to consider whether or not those ideas recorded in many religious scriptures are actually likely to be established by God. Alternatively, it seems quite likely that many religious doctrines and these inappropriately termed, so-called 'religious laws' are concepts and actions that have been developed and recorded by mankind for its' own autocratic, corrupted, self-serving purposes. From an analysis of various major current religions, as well as those we know of throughout recorded human history, it often would seem to an impartial observer that these religious institutions' activities have not resulted in the creation of the ideal types of societies that were envisioned by the original prophet's spiritual and philosophical teachings. Prophets have spoken to the common people of God's divine love in the creation of human beings and all life forms, and taught us about aspects of our inner divinity and God's actual existence. Some of the essential, vital truths contained in the messages of these prophets seems to be relatively lost or confused, as evidenced by the manner in which most modern religions tend to apply these prophets' spiritual teachings now, many hundreds of years after these prophets provided humanity with what they truly believed to be God's messages of love, true justice, peace and goodwill to all life.

Again, we will not intentionally identify any specific religion when discussing these beliefs in a generic, unbiased, objective manner. It seems self-evident to most impartial, perceptive, well-informed observers of earthly life that the majority of major modern religions to some degree seem to share in their apparent misinterpretations in the actual applications of ancient prophets' messages to humanity who taught us about love, peace, justice, freedom, equality for all life in the eyes of God and other such spiritual values. We ask ourselves, do modern religions manifest in their actions the accurate earthly representation of a truly divine, loving, creative, nurturing Creator and God that created us from the essence of Its' own Being, as eternal immortal Soul? Or do these religions seem more focused upon materialistic, monetary, earthly institutional issues related to human nature issues? Your opinion is better than mine in making an unbiased answer to these questions. My attitude and opinions are going to become abundantly clear as our discussion progresses.

Religions certainly have helped enormously to establish an accepted common vision for a better world civilisation than we people currently have created. In some key ways it is obvious that these institutionalised religions seem incapable of making the necessary social and spiritual improvements through their present structures and activities, regardless of how sincerely committed their leadership may be. What follows in the next few paragraphs is intended to lead you to question whether these issues are likely to be of human design and intent as they were incorporated into our existing major religions; or whether or not God, the Creator of all life, whatever form that may be, has established these rules of life for us to believe and follow, as defined by mankind's religious scriptures.

Our personal goal here will be to develop an inner awareness and affinity with aspects of one's higher, more divine, eternal aspects and integrate those in a conscious manner within one's normal life so that the expression of our inner divinity in daily life is enlivened, revealed, welcomed, cherished and facilitated in a progressive manner over passing time. We are simply seeking a 'better way' in our lives by including all aspects of our entire immortal, eternally aware states of being, rather than relying primarily upon our more temporal, earthly, human, social aspects of knowledge, character and perception. Our ongoing thorough examination of our belief systems will sequentially include many other topics as well as our present religious beliefs, yet this will be a key consideration in this process of spiritual self-discovery.

Some religions profess to believe that each human being has one, and only one, opportunity to get this particular life 'right'; otherwise, we are told that our fate is to suffer eternal damnation in a timeless location of unimaginable torment, pain and misery. However, in some religions we are also given an option for eternal redemption to live eternally in some form of blissful heavenly state, if we are able to somehow repent and be forgiven for our earthly sins before we die, or if we help to do God's work by the nature of our death. What are defined as being 'sins' are quite numerous and diverse in all of the modern religions. One well-known religion includes a sin that we ourselves did not commit in our lifetime, which is termed the 'original sin', which was purportedly committed by our earliest ancestors, for which all people are guilty, and for which we all must be forgiven by the salvation of a Saviour, or suffer eternal damnation. If this were true, then it would surely seem to be the act of a stern, unforgiving and vengeful God. We have also heard that God is compassionate, kind, loving, patient, and forgiving; so where is the actual truth to be found? We shall see that your truth and wisdom in life is best discovered through developing one's own inner relationship with Divinity. You can encourage your inner spark of God, known as Soul or Spirit, to express and reveal Itself in your daily life in many ways. In this fashion you will increasingly experience a direct, personal, inner relationship with God, your Creator.

We have been taught by most modern religions that there is only one true religion that can provide one's eternal salvation and no other religion is acceptable or genuinely God's true, chosen religion. However, several different religions declare this is the case and state that other religions are not the real spiritual paths to eternal redemption and salvation to be with God for all eternity. These religions insist that any other spiritual path is doomed to eternal failure. This fate of eternal damnation even applies when the unfortunate Soul never had the opportunity to be 'saved' because they were unaware of this religion due to their remote location, or they were a member of another religion, or even simply because they lived at time in history when this path to eternal redemption and heavenly bliss was not yet available to them. Does this situation seem to be a manifestation of divine justice to you or does it sound as if it is a man-made religious rule?

Let's consider a few other ideas and practices that religions currently impose upon their members, either under the threat of eternal damnation, or simply to be considered a good member of that particular religion. There are few limits to the many rules and the so-called 'laws' that govern most religion's members. We will only address a relative few of these beliefs or so-called scriptural laws in our discussion here in order to better perceive the general idea that most religions do not specifically respond to or definitely answer individual people's spiritual needs or fully explain their individual spiritual experiences sufficiently. Rather, these mainstream major world religions have developed over centuries to become institutions that have been designed to govern people's thoughts, beliefs, attitudes, and to some extent their behaviours as well. Until one can differentiate what one truly believes, based upon one's own unique thoughts and experiences, then it will be quite difficult to fully become aware of one's inner divinity and integrate aspects of one's higher, more eternal set of abilities and innate wisdom into one's daily life and future progressive development. Some of us wish to be told what to believe in life, since this manner of blindly accepting all information provided to us is a simplistic way to live. However, for most of us reading this book, we have long ago ceased to live our lives by accepting everything we are told by so-called authority figures in earthly society. Instead, usually we seek to examine our own beliefs in respect to our own intuition and experiences, as well as to inquire into the beliefs and lifestyles of other people of differing cultures, religions, nations, and philosophies in life for clues that enable us to improve our lives and societies. After we consider all issues from both objective and subjective perspectives that include all possible information sources, only then are we truly better able to gain improved understanding of life's mysteries and our individual purpose in this universal system of reality. The following ideas are intended to contribute toward developing this broader, objective understanding, and are definitely not included to be critical of any one's chosen belief system, religion, or chosen set of religious laws they live by.

We are aware of a major religion that has a somewhat curious practice that seems to be relatively primitive from an objective modern perspective in that this religion regularly practices the ceremonial ritual act of symbolically eating a small wafer of food that is intended to represent 'the body' of their Saviour, as well as the drinking of a small amount of wine, which represents 'the blood' of their Saviour. This religious ceremony is currently practiced by hundreds of millions of civilised modern people and is intended to ritually instil the godly spirit of their Saviour into themselves, as well as to cleanse themselves of their sins through their Saviour's own redemption upon their behalf. This religion's uppermost clergy have for many centuries demanded that all their religion's members partake in this ritual ceremony; otherwise the priests declared the person would certainly suffer eternal damnation, as mentioned previously. In past centuries, historically termed the Middle Ages or Dark Ages, anyone who would not join this religion or those who refused to participate in this rite of 'communion' could be put to death for their beliefs. In fact, over the past two thousand years there have been countless millions of innocent people killed in various murderous ways upon the direct orders of this religion's leaders and their many international governmental representatives simply because these guiltless people believed differently or were members of another religion that had been deemed to be untrue to this religion is some way. This religion, over thousands of years of earthly history, has also declared many wars upon the people of other religious faiths, harmless people of different cultures, which included sovereign national governments and countless indigenous tribal people across the globe; by declaring them to be 'heathen savages' who apparently deserved to die, if they refused to convert to this religion. This very same ritualised ceremonial pattern of behaviour could seem to an impartial observer to be somewhat similar and akin to the beliefs and practices of indigenous tribal people in places like Papua New Guinea. There the practice of ritualised actual cannibalism has existed for thousands of years, where warriors would, in ceremonial cannibal fashion, literally eat various body parts of their deceased enemies or deceased relatives in order to gain from their strength and wisdom in a ritualised manner. Imagine the resulting confusion in these native people after they were 'converted' to this religion and told their own previous practices of actual cannibalism were sins that would result in eternal suffering and damnation. Then, later after they were 'converted', they would be then encouraged to ceremonially eat the ritual body and drink the ritual blood of their newly chosen, long deceased Saviour! This seems to be a minimal distinction between these two practices and neither ceremony is likely to be demanded by

God, the Creator of all life in the cosmos, in order to avoid being 'divinely' sentenced to an eternal damnation of suffering. Millions of people that have refused to participate in the act of 'communion' over thousands of years have been mercilessly slaughtered by this religion, which again seems more an act of barbarous inhumanity, rather than an act of divinity.

Another major religion has some extremist members who have now declared that members of other religions must convert to their religion of be murdered as infidels and that their God supports this attitude and action. This same religion denies women rights to all manner of freedoms, such as the right to choose the time of her sexual consent with her husband or to marry the person of her own choice, what types of clothing an adult female must wear in public, who women may associate with publicly and privately, as well as many other rules that govern these people's lives. These man-made religious rules have been deemed by these self-declared fundamentalist religious autocrats to also apply to and include people belonging to other religions and other cultural customs that differ from their own. In short, they seek to demand the entire world convert to their religion, or to suffer in what they define as a holy war until all others either willingly choose to convert to their religion, or are murdered, die, or commit suicide. Extremist zealots within this religion also profess that it is an act of religious eternal salvation to commit suicide by blowing one's own body apart with explosives, if one's intentional suicide kills innocent defenceless people from other tribes, nations and religions simply because they believe differently than the fanatical leaders of this particular religion. Again, is this type thinking and action a set of rules created by God for our betterment, to bring love, justice and peace to Earth; or is a set of man-made religious rules designed to control people and create continual disharmony and conflict? The answers are quite self-evident to any reasonable thinking perceptive human being when viewing current world events where modern religions are being inappropriately used by militaristic zealots to rationalise and falsely justify all manner of evil, ungodly, destructive, counter-productive inhuman activities. Some of these fanatical extremist so-called 'religious' leaders now have established a few national governments that legislate and mandate the adherence to only this one religion for all the people within their countries, and those who object can be punished by death, torture, beatings, imprisonment or other forms of harmful treatment. These tyrannical people seek through violence and intimidation to expand this barbaric form of religious control into many other nations across the planet; intending to install similar religiously dominated governments elsewhere globally through mass murder, totalitarian controls, warfare, and acts of terrorism against innocent civilians, including the accidental death and injury of countless members of their own religion in some of their indiscriminate acts of heinous, chaotic, evil violence. Again, does this sound like the acts representative of a God that is kind, compassionate, loving and seeking peace and joy for its creations, or are such attitudes and actions more likely to be the vile, inhumane, despotic acts of mankind being falsely conducted in God's name by evil people in self-professed positions of earthly authority? Your opinion is likely to be better than mine regarding these divisive issues, since my perceptions are somewhat prejudiced by such fanatical zealots' self-evident violent attitudes and actions.

Are we to seriously now continue to willingly believe that God created physical systems of reality for us to live upon, then to create human bodies, inhabited by eternal Souls composed of Its' own essence out of love and devotion to us, Its' children, for only one 'make or break' earthly lifetime? Why would such a supposedly loving God knowingly 'sentence' what are deemed to be 'sinners' to eternal suffering by forms of unholy, unloving, evil torture for all of eternity? Why would God knowingly establish various religions, then have its members fight among the differing religions, to murder one another, create misery and death and destruction? It is more likely that the 'negative force' that was created by God to help teach us, Souls, to cherish divine love, freedom, peace, creativity, wisdom, joy, and purpose in life is actually at the 'heart' of these modern man-made religions. We must examine the historical evidence by their actions over many centuries of continued ideological oppression, so-called 'religious' wars and unending chaotic social calamities. A careful examination of history reveals quite clearly that most intentional man-made earthly destruction in some way has involved religious and economic conflicts between people believing largely in the same one God that created all Life that is known by different names by different religions who now seem to be in conflict over man-made moot issues. Anyone that seeks to debate this perspective is welcome to do so. People who wish to differ with this perception of various religions' roles in earthly conflict should first carefully study history to fully comprehend the countless ways that earthly religions have evidently misapplied, confused, and contradicted the messages of love, justice, peace, harmony and inner divinity that the world's prophets that taught us in regard to God's vision for humanity collectively, and also for each of us individually, as Soul, a spark of evolving, developing God essence.

What are some of these supposedly horrible sins that would result in one's eternal damnation, you may wonder, as if we are not already abundantly aware of what they are purported to be from our own religious indoctrinations? Let's examine this issue of 'sin' to enable us to get a bit more clarity about who designed and organised modern religions, so we can begin to distance ourselves from some of the concepts that tend to keep us in a confused state of mind regarding becoming more self-responsible in our quest for our eternal salvation and spiritual development. These supposed, man-declared 'sins' are far too numerous to record them all here and since most of us know many of them already anyway, let's recall just a few of them for the record. There are, of course, the ten most well-known primary 'deadly sins', one of which deals with murder. Apparently by mankind's religious laws, if one kills a person in battle upon the orders of some earthly authority figure, be it a religious leader or a military leader, then that is OK and no eternal damnation will result, one would hope. If the unfortunate murdered casualties accidentally are non-combatant innocent women, children and other defenceless people, then it is still OK because God will understand since the murder can ask for forgiveness from God, with the assistance of one's religious authority and spend eternity in heaven anyway. However, the murdered innocent victim may not have had time to pray to God asking for forgiveness for their sins before their untimely death, or have been unable to receive absolution for their sins from a religious authority figure, so do they spend eternity in suffering for that sin or others that may have committed? Does this make sense to you? In other words, someone who goes to war, by the orders of someone they do not know or necessarily agree with, can kill others, even though murder is one of the ten major sins, yet not subsequently spend eternity in suffering, especially if they are provided with 'redemption' by their earthly religious authorities. However, will someone who is not a member of the 'right' religion go into endless eternal suffering, even if they have lived a good life and been kind, loving and respectful to their God and other people?

How about the sin of stealing to feed one's family, especially if they are starving to death because invading religious zealots burned their crops and stole their remaining food? These issues are likely to be written and enforced by mankind, rather than by God, in my personal opinion. A loving, kind God would want us to act in a noble, honest, productive, decent, kind and loving manner, granting others the same freedoms and opportunities that we humans are granted by God, in my opinion. Therefore, we do not require threats of eternal suffering in order to freely decide to do what is right and proper, if we are truly godly, spiritual, good people. People who act poorly and in an evil, destructive, ungodly manner can be seen for what they are by their thoughts and actions, even when they attempt to disguise themselves in hypocritical religious rhetoric and enforce their perverse version of self-created reality upon the majority of people, by force of religious so-called law, government, or by threat of death by knife, bomb, stick, stone or gunpoint, as the case may be.

Let's also consider a few less serious type sins that could also result in eternal damnation according to various religious authorities: One could experience what are deemed to be 'impure thoughts" and deeds, unless forgiven in the proper manner, then they would supposedly suffer endlessly in damnation. Who defines what is impure or pure, aside from mankind in these religions and where is their proof that the rules have come directly from God? Alternatively, in another religion according to their religious scriptures, a husband can freely commit wife 'abuse' of a physical or even sexual nature, while the wife is not allowed to complain or resist according to their religious beliefs. In some religions various types of eternal damnation is apparently waiting for those people who are not aware of the 'right' religion, or who refuse to 'convert' to the 'right' religion that God supposedly prefers as the 'true religion' on Earth. Would eternal damnation also truly apply to those sincere, God loving good people who practice their religion improperly, such as missing the required number of weekly church services (or daily prayer services in some other religions); or not taking part in the required ritualised cannibalism ceremonies known in some of these religions as 'communion'; or for failing to be able to be properly forgiven for one's sins and repenting for all of one's lifetime of sins through a priest to God before one dies, and so on? In other words, some religions say one can do anything that is defined as being a sin, yet if they properly ask God, through the correct earthly religious authority for forgiveness, salvation, and redemption, then they can spend eternity in heaven with God, while others who lead a good, kind, noble, hard-working life may be sent to eternal damnation for being unable to repent properly or be a member of the 'right' religion before their death. Is this so called 'sin' that is currently recorded in some religious scriptures actually sounding like the 'word of God' to you or do these issues seem to be more like the unreasonable, unfair, divisive, arbitrary rules of mankind to you? This intentional repetition here may be annoying, yet it is no different than the 'programming' most of us have received from numerous religious authorities throughout our earthly lives.

Currently some modern religions are justifying all manner of unloving, unsocial and despicable acts, purportedly encouraged by extremist interpretations of their scriptural texts, which were written by men hundreds and even thousands of years ago. While many of life's realities remain as they once were, modern culture has developed considerably over the ages since the religious texts were compiled by male religious scholars. Few ancient religious texts, which are currently being taught today, clearly acknowledge that females have just as much innate right to freedom, economic, political and religious expression and equality in the eyes of God and the human legal and social systems as does any male. If these religious texts are truly supposed to be 'the Word' of a just, loving, equitable and compassionate God, then why is this not more clearly stated in these religious scriptures? It would likely seem to most modern reasonable thinking people that God would love and protect both male and female equally. One could also observe that women, as the mothers of all human life born into this world, possess an intuitive wisdom and clearly demonstrate compassion for their children in their nurturing spirit that portrays an affinity with their creative role in earthly life that in some ways appears to surpass that of most males, who never experience bringing a new life through their own body into this world. Males clearly appear to be much more prone toward violence, sexual abuse and other such seemingly ungodly forms of behaviours than most women would exhibit. Therefore, to have various religious scriptures state that females must be subservient to and obey men; regardless of whatever they say to do, be it right, wrong, unfair, or obviously an inappropriate behaviour, is an indicator that some parts of religious scriptures were written by males, with the control and subjugation of women as their objective in writing such nonsense into these supposedly religious documents. The patriarchal male dominated cultural, gender and social bias which is involved in these dogmatic teachings and beliefs is quite self-evident and has nothing whatsoever to do with the actual Word or Will of God, the Creator of all life in the Universe, including humanity. Would any sane, reasonable woman honestly feel in her heart and deepest spirit that she is less worthy or loved in the eyes of God than any man, just because of the sexual gender of her body? I would surely hope and think not! However, such absurd, somewhat insane types of thinking and so-called religious 'law' are promoted by many of the major world religions today. How could any truly Godly modern religion state in its most holy scriptures that a man is somehow superior to women and that women must obey the men in their lives to remain true to religious scripture, as written and interpreted by patriarchal males over hundreds and thousands of years ago?

Equally absurd and nonsensical is the concept that all people today are born into life as sinners because of the supposed 'original sin' of our ancestors and that all people are destined to sin by our nature and that many of us will suffer eternal damnation for it, unless forgiven and properly absolved of these sins by the human self-declared and self-ordained so-called representatives of God. Well, that may sound great to some people who do not think too hard about things they are taught or told. Imagine the difficult situation for someone in ancient history as they faced the Spanish Inquisition and were asked to declare their allegiance to the 'right' religion, or die an inhuman death. The person held by the religious authorities during the Spanish Inquisition could be tortured endlessly until they died to obtain a 'confession' or to encourage them to name and testify against another person as a sinner, to free themselves.

Those accused as being sinners were tried in religious courts and sentenced to various inhuman deaths, such as being burned alive or torn apart limb from limb by horses, or crude machines. Is this God's way or mankind's way?

Or perhaps we could more easily imagine in modern times a person being held by some so-called 'fundamentalist' religious fanatical group of people using religion as their excuse to think and act like a murdering gang of thugs, as they have a knife to your throat, asking you to either convert to their religion or die because they deem you to be an infidel in the concept of their religious beliefs and as an enemy of their version of God. What would you do in such circumstances? Would you choose to convert in either situation to their version of religion, to save your life? If you were born as a female and educated into such a religious culture, would you also willingly marry any man selected for you by your family, even if there was no love for the chosen man, knowing if you refused that you could be stoned to death, killed in some other fashion, or just beaten severely or other such cruel harmful treatments? These are choices that one must ask one's self in helping you to decide whether one's purportedly 'religious' beliefs and behaviours are truly God inspired and directed; or whether they are actually the ways of mankind being implemented falsely in the name of God, that have brought humanity so much pain, violence, conflict and destruction over many thousands of years of our global civilisation's recorded history.

Today we again see religious lunacy running rampant in most parts of our world and creating all manner of unproductive, unnecessary, senseless hostility, misery, divisiveness and devastation. It is essential that perceptive, well-informed, clear thinking, free people seriously question and debate these peculiar, outmoded, man-made supposedly religious ideas and practices that seem absolutely absurd, insane, hypocritical and completely unacceptable in a modern civilised world. Surely we need ethical values and mutually agreed moral principles upon which we live life on Earth.

However, we people of Earth do not need life's higher principles to be autocratically deemed into existence in earthly life by men with self-serving unpleasant agendas that suppress freedom of thought, expression and life purpose by the inappropriate controls of various dogmatic, sterile, unloving, degenerate, conformist philosophies of life, which for many centuries have been continuously 'force fed' to us as purportedly religious thoughts and practices. Emancipation day from false religious teachings has arrived on Earth!

No untruthfully contrived so-called 'war on terrorism', nor some inappropriate, falsely declared, untruthful lie being inaccurately called a 'holy war' being unjustly declared by gangs of violent and fanatical people who are falsely calling themselves religious people who dishonestly profess to acting upon behalf of their self-established version of God will distract or dissuade us from this quest.

We clearly see numerous self-evident truths existing in our global civilisation and we will not fall victim to the same old propaganda and lies that we have been told for centuries by our religious, national, and tribal so-called political and economic 'leaders', especially when the direct result is the creation of more suffering, misery and depravation for Earth's people and our environments. We do perceive the facts that are currently so obvious in earthly life, as well as various aspects of our eternal Life. We must become more determined to carefully and thoroughly consider and analyse all aspects of our lives and the world within which we live to better define and clarify our thinking processes to formulate and declare our own personal better vision for our daily thoughts and actions. Then all Earth's people will be better able to work together toward a more just, equitable, productive future, with no one being perceived as being our 'enemies', not even those who will surely oppose us to maintain the status quo so that nothing changes or improves during our lifetimes or that of our children or their children. Those people that are truly ungodly or who represent the forces of evil are those who advocate violence, who create and apply the mechanisms of repression, depravation, slavery in its many forms and various types of warfare; be it militaristic, economic, cultural, racial, or environmentally combative behaviours, as well as those who knowingly create repressive legislation which is applied against peaceful, innocent, productive, law-abiding, hard-working people. Everything in this world today and its history is vividly revealed before us to see, feel and know in our minds and hearts, with modern communications and technology. We need not continue to choose to blindly accept and believe lies any longer or live lives based upon deception or fall prey to detrimental adversarial religious, social, political, nationalistic, or economic philosophies. A better today and tomorrow begins with one's choice to take self-responsibility in one's own thoughts, life and dreams in creating a better future for all people.

Soul's timeless wisdom, inner guidance and astute leadership serve the individual and society far better than do our temporal earthly personalities which are so often governed by our learned religious, cultural and political perspectives and our individual or group's vested interests. Therefore, to integrate one's daily human consciousness with Soul's unlimited, timeless wisdom and perception is one of the most productive activities that anyone can achieve in this lifetime. It is exceedingly relevant to our survival as a species that we, as individuals and collectively, begin to clearly differentiate between what we are being misleadingly and deceitfully told or taught is fact and the actual facts of life as they truly are, at least from our own perspective based upon all of the information available to us. This dramatically improved level of discernment regarding all aspects of our earthly and eternal lives is an essential component of our developmental process. Let's continue our assessment of a wide range of human attitudes and activities to better comprehend and learn to more accurately determine what it is truth, as opposed to what are obvious deceptions fabricated by mankind as manipulative lies that are currently being misused to undermine our entire global civilisation to serve the interests of a relative few truly evil, adversarial groups of people and their violent, destructive, militaristic, greed and power-focused, counter-productive organisations.

Until we begin to perceive the sometimes hidden, more subtle and insidious patterns of thought that we almost blindly accept or 'take for granted' in our education and socialisation processes, we will continue to be unable to truly acknowledge and respond to the positive encouraging uplifting influences of Soul and God within our lives. These issues become even more unclear, obscure and confused when our political, religious and other leaders falsely state opinions as facts that lead nations, cultures and religions into open warfare because of their knowingly inaccurate, misleading, self-serving agendas which are creating such destruction, poverty, depravation, injury, death and misery in our world today. Additionally, we will examine some of our more personal belief systems and daily actions in our individual lives that tend to inhibit, limit and prevent a more comprehensive expression of Soul's positive viewpoint and uplifting influences in our lives. It is usually easier to see problems, negative issues and inappropriate attitudes and activities in others and the world around us than to observe and constructively address and resolve them within ourselves personally. It is partly for this reason that we initially are focusing upon the more obvious problems and challenges existing in our global civilisation before taking a more sincere introspective look at our own negative personal attitudes and tendencies that primarily serve to constrain the functions of Soul within our daily consciousness. Our civilisation is an external manifestation of humanity's combined attitudes and actions, so this is why we must assess the full scope of issues that require solutions and begin to determine the steps necessary to radically improve these circumstances before the situation becomes irreparable.

For example, environmentally we now hear a lot about the serious issue of 'global warming' which is partly due to the rapid increase of excessive amounts of carbon dioxide and other pollutants into Earth's atmosphere. Global warming and severe adverse climate change is also being seriously exacerbated by the unprecedented global destruction of our forests by excessively damaging logging practices, the extensive clearing of natural land for agricultural and grazing for domesticated animals, and higher levels of captured and radiant heat from our roads, buildings and exposed land surface without adequate vegetative cover to the increasingly intense solar radiation reaching Earth's surface. Additionally, apparently scientific records indicate an increased level of solar radiation from the sun is currently occurring which is intensifying the situation. This entire issue of global warming; the other related environmental and ecological disasters and rampant devastation now occurring upon Earth, and countless other chronic problems are definitely not being honestly, thoroughly or appropriately addressed by our political, economic or social leaders. Instead, we see endless examples of their feeble, ineffective, theatrical, heartless, mindless, hypocritical 'lip service' responses to what we are globally experiencing today in 2016. There already is graphic, overwhelming proof of the undeniable existence of these potentially catastrophic problems that are already creating massive unrelenting exponentially increasing damage to our entire global environment and economic system occurring every day. The pathetic hypocritical dithering by ineffectual, inept, unmotivated, self-absorbed, greedy, corrupted political and economic so-called 'leaders' knows no limits in our current global civilisation. They unwittingly serve as the ultimate enablers of the destruction of our present civilisation on Earth and we, the thinking people of this planet, are foolishly allowing this to happen without much more than a whimper of uneasy discontent. What are we truly thinking and doing to fundamentally improve and solve this extremely detrimental and possibly devastating situation individually and collectively as Earthlings? Virtually nothing of any real substance or serious remedial change, aside from some inane discussions by various so-called political, economic and environmental 'authority figures' who are mostly theatrically playing to the media cameras egoistically like they are movie stars; receiving another great pay check from working people's toil and suffering, as our once beautiful planet literally 'burns up' around us. We people seldom do much more than to blithely ask ourselves, "Does it seem to be getting hotter, or colder, drier, or are there more extreme weather events now than in the past or is life on Earth becoming more and more intensely uncomfortable to endure physically, mentally and spiritually?" A genuine examination of the real condition of our rapidly decaying planetary and entire global social system should see us all out in the streets and active within the so-called 'corridors of power', absolutely demanding that we participate directly in immediately initiating every necessary positive, constructive, definitive, fundamental change and improvement required in the way earthly policy and activity occurs within our civilisation and upon our planet. We, the intelligent, perceptive, visionary, ethical, responsible, motivated, free-willed, genuinely committed, hard-working, experienced, aware people must actually directly and personally participate and lead these efforts into the creation of functional, sustainable, equitable, reliable, efficient public policy and then work within the resulting organisations to insure the necessary adjustments are successfully applied and completed for the short and long-term best interests of all life forms on planet Earth. Any other option is unacceptable. The reason for this particular solution through direct participation by 'the people' is that the vast majority of the falsely so-called 'leaders' in this global society are not leaders at all. Instead they are mostly the servile, simpering supplicants and slavish puppets of the powerful hidden actual 'rulers' of planet Earth who; through their politically elected officials, appointed bureaucratic servants and corporate soldiers, they allow and encourage this process of degeneration and mayhem to occur for their own evil, self-serving, short-sighted, idiotic reasons.

A different, yet somewhat similar global challenge to the very existence of our civilisation, as we now know it, is currently developing due to the cultural and religious warfare now manifesting itself due to events in the Middle East and elsewhere. Once again, this potentially catastrophic international situation is intentionally created and sustained by these same hidden, 'behind the scenes' despotic actual rulers of earthly civilisation, to promote future violent conflicts now developing over limited natural resources such as oil, clean water, productive farmland, timber, food, energy and so on, for diabolical reasons that no rational, sane, humane person could possibly understand.

We know by examining our world's history that various philosophies of government, commerce and religion exist and that in their ideal, philosophic forms that most systems of thought and action have constructive, mutually beneficial results intended as their earthly manifestation. Such philosophies include: freedom, capitalism, democracy, 'free trade', feudalism, socialism, communism, totalitarianism, fascism, dictatorship, and various major world religions. All these differing systems of human culture create various social models, possessing often complex economic processes that are then manifested into reality. Our global dilemma is that the numerous seemingly opposing and differing philosophies of thought and activity are increasingly coming into conflict with one another as each culture, nation, race and economic system competes with others to such an extent that obtaining functional integration with one another becomes more complex and more problematic. We can make all manner of value judgements and discuss these issues endlessly with no definitive conclusions that all people will agree upon completely, so let's attempt to agree that most forms of human thought and behaviour are intended to somehow improve the overall human condition, from someone's perspective. Therefore, what we are saying is that from various perspectives, depending upon one's point of view and the group's consensus of opinion, that each and all various perspectives can be validated as correct and functional in some ways, to those members that support and believe in whatever philosophy, religion, national identity or cultural group exists at any given time in history. It is often when internal problems begin to develop and become serious that leaders in these circumstances will seek a solution by condemning, then attacking members of other philosophies, cultures, races, religions, nations and their allies and so on, just as we see so prevalent in human history for countless thousands of years. This counter-productive behaviour does not represent or define the ideal character of a mature and responsible civilisation; to seek external scapegoats or to blame other societies, nations, religions, or races for our own internal problems, nor to knowingly and willingly seek to reduce the population by war, starvation, mass murder, disease and inhumane conditions.

Let's examine the problem of over-population, related to the notion that some religions and social conditions have encouraged people for many generations to have as many children as nature will allow. This reproductive success has resulted in the world's population growth becoming virtually unsustainable, especially in already impoverished, so-called 'developing' areas of the world. This escalating population growth has intensified and progressively worsened the debilitating conditions which have severely altered and are currently destroying much of the Earth's natural ecosystems. Population growth and the deteriorating environmental situation have contributed to increasing economic, social and philosophic competition for limited resources and opportunities, which is leading to an increased likelihood of more widespread intercultural and international conflict and potential for more widespread warfare globally. These basic factors and many other interdependent variables indicate the multitude of reasons we all must now be very clear in realising how humanity's thinking, beliefs and our resultant activities are creating the realities we all share on Earth.

If any religion, race, nation or culture encourages its people to have more and more children over countless generations that exponentially increase the population continually, then ultimately the land, resources and economic capabilities of the society will become unsustainable. Historically, this situation has been solved by various forms of warfare, genocide, selective murders and sacrifices, famine and disease, along with unpredictable natural disasters of many types, to reduce their growing populations. Often so-called 'enemies' will mutually agree, for various reasons they mutually rationalise, to fight and kill one another en masse to reduce the numbers of especially their breeding age men and boys, yet women are often included, as well as the elderly, children and all other life forms when the conflict becomes serious. Historically, we recognise that some societies may also kill young females for various reasons; to limit the available number of women who can bear children over many generations; as a cultural practice, while strictly controlling the reproductive rights of various segments of the male population according to their chosen criteria. Some modern societies prevent the birth of unwanted children in the womb by abortive medical procedures. Most societies have developed some natural, relatively safe form of birth control that women can use to avoid pregnancy, when they wish to do so. Some religions have deemed that any form of intentional birth control is a sin. All thinking people clearly recognise the need to avoid and limit unwanted or unplanned pregnancies, even if publicly this practice is not acknowledged or condoned among certain circles of influence.

Modern civilisation is already well-aware that over-population is now creating environmental degradation due to unchecked unsustainable industrial and agricultural expansion that is undermining and destroying the foundation of our social and economic systems. Additionally, the perversion of the system termed "capitalism" is now creating huge problems in the global economy by the fact that large multinational corporations, private companies and business entities greedily seek to continually increase their profits for the owners and top level employees of their businesses with little or no regard for the damaging effects of its' actions upon the people, governments, economies and environments of the world. This deteriorating situation is rapidly becoming a major plight that also has a massive detrimental influence on our global civilisation because so much of humanity's potential to make significant accomplishments to improve conditions for all people and the environment are currently being wasted, unused, or misapplied to such an extent that large segments of the global population have little opportunity to do truly productive work to earn a worthwhile level of income to support themselves and improve the global economy for all of Earth's citizens. So-called democratic nations now in most cases possess governmental representatives and bureaucratic officials that generally seek to placate, mollify and pander to the vested interests, political influences and economic controls exerted by these multinational business conglomerates and their super wealthy owners. Too little regard is given to the needs or opinions of the voting public, or the true best interests and good of the entire nation or the world in its entirety. This circumstance clearly reveals that a dysfunctional state exists where there is a corruption of justice, responsibility, equality and reason in many of the world's governments. This is also evidenced by the inappropriate ways much of taxpayer's hard-earned income is squandered by democratically elected public officials or dictatorial leaders, who are largely not fully accountable or under the controls of the voters in real terms. Various forms of corruption are becoming the norm in the functions of our global governments and economic systems, which is evident in the widespread various types of fraud in the electoral systems globally which serve to prevent the will and wisdom of the common people and pragmatic leaders from being implemented to benefit all of humanity.

    It is sheer stupidity to blindly continue these unreasonable, foolish, short-sighted policies because of greed and a lack of resolve to apply available solutions that require considerable investment to develop innovative alternatives that are more humane, equitable to all nations and cultural groups; that will be much more economically and environmentally sustainable. A crisis of true leadership now exists regarding the longer-term vision for what must be accomplished to improve our world's plight, since this challenging situation is rapidly intensifying and becoming more complex over passing time. Therefore, free-thinking people who possess a reasonably active inner relationship with the higher aspects of our eternal Self, Soul or Spirit, that is a true inner communication with the truly godly aspects of our innate nature; must begin to assert our perspectives and opinions through the ways we live our daily lives. We must learn to speak out regarding life's important issues and become personally exemplary in manifesting our attitudes through positive, mutually beneficial, productive forms of activity.

We continue our discussion regarding what we are herein defining as 'human nature issues', in relation to the influences that various philosophies of thought and their resultant actions have upon one's overall levels of consciousness.

How does one intentionally seek to smoothly and harmoniously integrate their daily conscious human character, which is an incredibly complex mixture of mental and emotional processes that are often influenced by temporal issues, self-interest and external social forces; with one's immortal, eternal, spiritual, intuitive, creative aspects of their nature as a human being? In other words, how do we more effectively integrate the 'human' aspects with the 'being' aspects within our total character and state of being? The first step is to intellectually acknowledge, understand and become comfortable with the fact that this integration process is something you already do to a significant degree upon a mostly unconscious level. If you have been doing this integration process consciously then you are to be congratulated and thank you for making these worthy efforts! The developmental challenge is to establish this integration process as a primary personally significant goal in one's life. This will require you to possess a receptive, 'seeking' mental condition that consciously inspires the more obvious expression and outward manifestation of your true inner eternal nature, Soul, into your daily life, through your normal mental and emotional processes. To a variable extent, this subtle process has already been naturally occurring in mostly unconscious ways for eons of time, so to make the process more conscious, it is necessary to seriously begin to examine one's entire life, including attitudes, beliefs and the resultant actions to better determine what achievements have already been accomplished and what adjustments could be made to facilitate this process of integration. Once this series of conscious realisations have occurred, then you must reconcile within your own conscious mind that this integration process is a desirable, natural, beneficial, spiritually progressive, evolutionary development that you want to achieve. Over passing time, one simply begins to consciously make the required alterations to manifest these personal developments in consciously observable, useful, beneficial ways that are applicable to all aspects of one's daily life. This progression is quite a unique individualistic unfoldment process where you will sequentially experience and perceive a range of minor seeming adjustments occurring within your mental, emotional and behavioural tendencies. Generally these subtle, almost imperceptible alterations in your normal responses to daily events and one's internal intellectual and emotional functions may appear so natural to your receptive mind that nothing will seem out of the ordinary, which is fine so long as your remain conscientious about observing what is happening.

For example, someone may do something that would normally upset you in various ways, such as be rude to you, intentionally attempt to hurt your feelings emotionally, be dishonest with you, or in some way try to threaten or harm you and so on. By consciously utilising the integration of higher mind into the processing of one's conscious response, instead of the other person inciting a hostile, emotional reactive response from within your character, there could simply be a more discerning observation upon your part of their attitude and intentions. Your observation of the entire circumstances enables you to remain in relative control of your own overall state of mind to deliberately select from all possible responses available to you instead of automatically reacting impulsively according to the type of response they may wish to elicit from you. In this way, an unwanted, unexpected, potentially negative event perpetrated by someone else could be resolved by you in a positive, self-controlled, emotionally and mentally beneficial manner. This method of interacting with others allows you to more carefully observe their state of mind and intentions as you determine the facts of the matter, as opposed to the external appearances involved, to more effectively choose your resultant behaviours. In this way daily life ceases to so readily or easily evoke reactions within us that seem unwanted and out of our normal preferred character traits. We can choose to limit how other people and daily events adversely influence us to experience undesirable, unproductive, reactive thoughts and emotions such as anger, sadness, fear or to act in unwanted ways such as rudely, aggressively, resentfully and so on. Rather than to basically 'mirror' other people's inappropriate attitudes and behaviours, we increasingly develop the capacity and proclivity to autonomously choose our own inner and external responses to life's multitudinous range of experiences and realisations. There are enormous benefits to your gaining total control over your exact mental, emotional and behavioural responses to all of your life's daily events. This does not imply that we will always choose to respond in any given way to a specific situation; instead, we simply carefully perceive events and attitudes around us to selectively determine what choices we will make in any circumstance. Obviously this status implies a considerably enhanced degree of astute perception and greatly expanded scope for spontaneous actions within all areas of one's life.

People with a huge desire and lifelong commitment to assist other people, like Mother Teresa; and others who seek to influence humanity to protect the environment, such as Jacques Cousteau; and those who promote more justice and equality for all people in the world, such as the civil rights leaders Martin Luther King and Nelson Mandela; are among the true leaders of humanity that most of us highly respect and admire. Most of us wish to somehow emulate in our daily lives the attitudes and actions of these wise, genuinely committed, inspirational people who work selflessly to heal illnesses in others, feed the starving or help the oppressed peoples of the world. We also quietly much appreciate and respect the perceptions, commitment and attitudes of people like the Australian conservationist, Steve Irwin, who recognise that all life forms, be they humans, whales, dolphins, and elephants, crocodiles or any of the multitudes of life forms that compose unique ecosystems, such as virgin old growth forests, our oceans, the atmosphere and even the Earth itself, do possess an inalienable right to life and freedom from destruction by any humans or other life forms that may seek to assert ownership or dominion over them. All of these types of people are actively manifesting aspects of their higher spiritual awareness through their daily lives, just as most of us are also doing in countless ways through our own daily lives. We seek to consciously make well-informed, highly motivated decisions about exactly how and why one chooses to apply their actions to improve their own life, that of their family, local community and world. These accumulating, accelerating, integral processes all coalesce to manifest enhanced harmony and higher purpose in one's character, personality and life.

At the extreme opposite end of life's scale of true justice and productivity are the types of humans who mostly functioning from their lower states of temporal being to the detriment of us all. These people have limited inputs from their higher nature, so there is little or no real inner voice of conscience and higher reason assessing, governing or limiting their thoughts, plans or inappropriate actions. Such people have little or no remorse as they seek to enslave others and all life forms in a comprehensive global fashion to achieve their self-serving goals; as they willingly and knowingly abuse, degrade and ultimately destroy the environment, one geographical location at a time, if allowed to do so. Such people overtly intend to undermine and eliminate true freedom and widespread prosperity in our global civilisation for the vast majority of people by various methods. They involve other people who are willing to participate in their plans in return for jobs, security, power, prestige and other such benefits. It is obvious to see that for countless thousands of years there have been almost endless attempts to intentionally destabilise and limit the productivity and sustainability of regional, cultural, religious, ethnic, racial and indigenous groups of people throughout all areas of Earth. Now these counter-productive global influences are functioning together in a self-evident fashion to promote international warfare, international corporate domination, supported by corrupted governmental institutions, espoused and controlled by the despotic super-wealthy minority, in order to intentionally and adversely limit human and environmental sustainability, thereby promoting attitudes and actions that seek to prevent future generations from enjoying a life worth living on this Earth. This is occurring primarily to retain total control over our earthly civilisation, to the considerable detriment of all life on Earth.

Therefore, at whatever the level, scale or nature of our earthly daily lives, each and every one of us is having a range of influences and actions upon our local community, environment and also upon global civilisation within which we exist. Our personal attitudes, beliefs, choices and actions as individuals and within the groups with which we identify ourselves, all serve to exert dramatic influences. We are either seeking to create a better world for ourselves, all people, and future generations of people in ways that actualise aspects of our spiritual, immortal, higher, better natures; or alternatively, some of us prefer to habitually choose to identify with whatever temporal conditions or desires we seek for ourselves, regardless of the damaging impact upon other people, the environment or future generations. The fact is we all have a variety of often conflicting and opposing influences upon our world, regardless of our conscious intentions. Therefore, we seek to become more aware of the inclusive, pervasive, interrelated nature of our own inner thoughts and actions, in our relationships with other people, and our global environment because this developmental process is essential to the well-being of our material physical earthly lives and the progression of our eternal, spiritual aspects of being.

While these issues are often so complex that much debate surrounds them, the contrasts in our earthly lives are clear for us all to perceive now, if we are willing to consider or examine them to reach some definitive conclusions. We are saying here, just as one of the ancient prophets once said, "By their fruits (actions), so shall ye (you/all of us) know them". We seek to first perceive, then to manifest 'right' appropriate thoughts, through 'right' necessary actions. This developmental process requires that many issues be considered and subsequently numerous solutions must be applied; in consideration with and not in opposition to, what are temporal issues, including people's self-interest, profitability and mutual benefits. We, each and all, must surely evaluate and to a reasonable extent continue to act upon what is best for our selves individually, our family, social group, community, and nation. However, we absolutely must cease to do so in relative isolation to considering all other perspectives and possible options. There must be much more widespread communication, genuine interaction and reasonable consensus reached between all people and groups before decisions or actions are taken by those people in positions of social authority and responsibility in our lives. People must regain more autonomous control of their own intellectual, emotional and daily actions, as well as within their families, communities, differing cultures, nations and religions, in all areas of the world.

Upon a strictly personal level, we each possess a valuable reliable inner process whereby Soul, the inner true eternal aspect that is the true consciousness we each actually are as human beings, can be encouraged to express and assert Itself within our consciousness in a multitude of positive ways. This enables one to much more clearly assess the nature of one's thinking, perceptions, attitudes, emotions, beliefs and the resultant actions so that Soul's viewpoint becomes vastly more 'enlivened' within our daily reality. This process tends to inspire the creation of a more truly meaningful, purposeful, productive, enjoyable life that is characterised by a fully vibrant state of conscious awareness that has a uplifting, positive, beneficial effect on one's own life, as well as that of others and even upon future generations of life on Earth. Each of us, as individuals, is Soul at some level of developmental unfoldment, possessing enormous innate wisdom, if we are willing and able to access and apply this aspect of our overall state of conscious being. Unfortunately, many of us are so mentally focused upon our present human level of material existence that we fail to listen to our heart's wisdom, which is also the soft, unassertive voice of Soul, which possesses unlimited grace, truth, peace, patience, and joy that composes our conscience. Now we seek to listen, better hear and apply Soul's wisdom into our daily lives.

All the religious prophets of olden days have taught us that God is readily and intimately available to each and all of us. This realisation is where we begin; each within our own heart, mind, Soul and body. We discover, reveal and encourage the expression of aspects of our inner immortal system of divine reality into our daily earthly lives, individually and collectively. One ancient prophet said words to the effect that, "As I am, so shall you become" in relation to his communication and true communion with God who he called his "Father" or as we are calling our 'Creator' or God. This same prophet, like many other prophets and saintly people throughout human history, accurately perceived his spiritually evolved state of mind and being as "the way" for those people who sought, through following his example, to search for and ultimately to find God within and through themselves. It is solely through experiencing one's inner innate divinity that we, each in our own unique ways and time frames, are able to learn to communicate and become 'as one' with the divinely conscious energetic essence, known by some as the Holy Spirit or the ECK. The challenge of existing within a temporal physical human body, living on this Earth for a relatively short lifetime, yet coming to discover and cherish one's inner divinely inspired relationship with one's Creator is among the most wonderful of life's experiences. It is through experiencing this sublime conscious realisation process that the prophets of many religions have lived exemplary inspirational lives that demonstrated their achievement of manifesting an inner harmony with God, their Creator. This has been accomplished for them, just as it can be for us; by experiencing one's inner divinity through expanding and enhancing our greater awareness and integration with what we define here as being Soul, or Spirit, or Higher Self.

It is essential to recognise, fully acknowledge and comprehend that it is our own unique personal responsibility to develop and manifest our inner divinity in the way we think, perceive reality and live our lives. I wish here to mention an important point. To my knowledge, no true earthly prophet that I am aware of has ever claimed to be God Itself, the Creator of all life on Earth, and of the infinite Universes. Through their teachings and life examples, these prophets or saviours seem to have professed to believe they were "the Son" or 'a creation' of God. They have only differed in what various names for God, their Creator, or their eternal 'Father', that they have used to describe this immanent divinity existing and expressing aspects of Its being within them. God is known to humanity by various names by various religions throughout recorded human history. It is apparent from my understanding of many religious scriptures that none of these prophets, not even one, ever wished, asked or demanded that people worship them as God, the Creator of all Life. To state otherwise seems to me to be a graphic untruth or even to be a type of actual heresy of some description. It is not for me to comment upon whether or not some people may choose to believe that their prophet or saviour was the actual Being, Creator, Life Force or God that created the entire universe and all life in it. We, as human beings in our present form, were not consciously 'there' when the universe was created; so to address such a debateable inconsequential issue while other more important urgent issues confront us seems inappropriate and foolish.

What we do know is various religious scholars have recorded what is purportedly thought to be the words, deeds and teachings of various prophets throughout recorded human history. These religious writings have been compiled from the work of numerous authors into lengthy scriptural volumes, which have subsequently been studied, interpreted, re-recorded, modified, re-interpreted, further edited and then been complied by other, more modern religious scholars and religious theologians. For most major world religions, these recorded events are reported to have occurred from between a few thousand years ago to about a thousand years ago, and these religions continue to dominate much of our global culture to some extent. Additionally, there have been numerous more recent modern self-proclaimed prophets who made similar claims and who have inspired their own groups of adherents, who have established other religions. The key point in our discussion is to realise and accept that these religions were created by people according to their interpretations of the people who actually experienced a direct inner relationship with some aspects of their innate divinity that enabled them to interact or communicate in some fashion with what and whom they believed to be God, their Creator, the Creator of all life in the Universes. Their experiences and teachings were then recorded as religious scriptures which form the basis of all current religions on this Earth and they indeed do influence all of our lives to some extent, wether we believe in any particular religion or not.

If we seek to do so, we each and all have the individual right and opportunity to discover our own inner direct personal relationship with God, the Creator of All Life, which includes the eternally conscious aspect of our own personal selves, that we term Soul. Whatever God's actual name may be, as defined by any specific man-created religion; is not the important issue here. Other people also have a right to believe there is no God or that they perceive no direct personal proof that a Creator exists in this Universe. We do not dispute or deny anyone's prerogative to such attitudes, yet they and we all must accept the self-evident fact that we each and all do possess a self-aware consciousness that enables each of us to perceive reality and to exist within this system of life as a live, sensate, free-willed human being that currently inhabits a physical body. Therefore, regardless of our personal beliefs or daily customs, we all share an independent, functional state of conscious awareness of some description that is capable of self-analysis, if we choose to exert this introspective ability to examine the nature of our own existence as an active, alive, conscious, thinking, perceptive physical life form.

Our purpose here is to personally develop an intimate heightened level of conscious awareness that enables one to attain an improved inner relationship and direct connection with the omniscient, omnipresent, omnipotent, immortal, infinite, all-knowing, unconditionally loving and timeless Creator of all life. Through our life's experience, we seek to progressively realise the fact that God's conscious energy is everywhere at once; throughout and also beyond all time and space as we know it on Earth. God's all-knowing conscious awareness is somehow connected to each of us, via Soul, and every other life form as well. We must accept that it is impossible to fully mentally comprehend God's state of being with our normal intellectual processes, nor to adequately explain linguistically this mysterious amazing situation that relates to God and our own inner eternal divine nature. We each, in our own unique special ways, do have the opportunity to become increasingly more and more receptive to becoming 'at one', at peace, in harmony and in resonance with God (via the Holy Spirit or ECK) through the expression of our divine nature that formulates a portion of our overall earthly consciousness. This Divinity that exists both within and beyond our earthly self is generally a subtle, almost magical, mysterious and incredibly fantastic aspect that serves as the creative cosmic force that initially enlivened our eternal consciousness and subsequently manifested Itself in our earthly existence. Therefore, there is little wonder that our best efforts with verbal and written language fail to fully define, adequately express and properly explain God or Its true relationship to all of life. The only thing we each can do is to seek to experience this to the best of our individual ability by being characterised with a receptive, relatively genuine, questing, searching, pure, peaceful, kindly, perceptive, loving state of being.

Again, how do we accomplish this state of being? For each it will be a unique, individual journey of discovery, of mystical receptivity that will find experience, expression, answers, solutions and unfoldment deep within one's private inner states of existence; within the comprehensive nature of our earthly, immortal, eternal, infinite levels of existence. To be inwardly at peace and receptive within myself may help me, yet for you or another person, the inner discoveries and experiences may come through intense questing with rigorous meditations and contemplations to commune with God or one's Prophet, Saviour, Saint or spiritual Master or Guide. To each individual, their own unique self-chosen path to the discovery of Divinity is ultimately always through and within one's inner self. Apparently there is no ultimate ending point to this eternal quest, since we are told that life itself is infinite in every respect, so enjoy the blessed journey!

Let us briefly continue to ask some questions regarding modern religions. Would a divinely loving, moral God or Creator truly ask or demand that anyone kill another human being, in the name of any man-made religion? How did we arrive at a situation where we now find that some modern religions which were established from the historical teachings of prophets seeking peace and love upon Earth, are being misused by advocating that people kill, torture, and deprive one other of liberty simply and falsely in the purported name of God, or because of our nationalistic philosophy, or our chosen cultural practices? Would our ancient or more modern prophets that once taught us about love, peace and seeking harmony among all kinds of people in this world now begin to suddenly condone and recommend the killing, torturing and enslavement of people of differing belief systems or those of other tribes, races or life styles than our own? The obvious answer is no, they would not. Since recorded history on this planet began, some depraved, degenerate humans have represented the lowest levels of consciousness and have continued to exert inappropriate influence and control in modern civilisation. There is absolutely nothing 'godly' about this current earthly situation. Nor has there ever been anything 'godly' in the historical abuse of God's name or higher values by the destructive, debased, evil, negative-minded, controlling humans who have consistently sought to misinterpret the intentions of the prophet's teachings to abuse, degrade and deprive humanity and earthly environments, as they knowingly sought to mislead the people regarding the divine eternal nature of existence and God's love for us all.

The key attribute and gift our Creator endowed within each of us is the ability to perceive reality and utilise our capacity to choose our thoughts, actions and express our free-will, once it is developed and recognised within each of us. Historically speaking in most cultures and nations, we the people, choose our spiritual prophets and true leaders because of their willingness and ability to openly speak the whole truth about what most of us recognise in our hearts, minds and Soul as being right for us all, even if at the time it meant they were confronted, attacked and possibly were killed for expressing their beliefs publicly. There are countless examples in human history where the best, most eloquent and most innocent and truly beautifully spirited of humanity were slaughtered for their beliefs by those humans who were not aligned with their higher natures.

In this materialistically dominated world, many of life's realities certainly tend to encourage predominately human levels of consciousness to exert themselves over those more humane, eternally meaningful levels of existence. As defined by the Oxford dictionary, 'materialism' is characterised by those people possessing: 1) an interest in or emphasis on physical rather than spiritual things, and 2) the theory that only physical matter is real. We easily recognise people professing to be religious in their belief system that act in a primarily materialistic manner which consistently reveals that in actuality they are motivated strictly according to their own personal, religious, economic or cultural forms of self-interest. This is definitely not a truly genuine spiritual attitude and those who behave in such a way while proclaiming themselves to be religious in spiritual matters are hypocrites of the worst variety. Generally such people and the organisations they establish think and behave in a way that makes them oblivious to other people's perspectives because they simply do not care what other opinions and lifestyle options exist, aside from their own personal self-interest. Psychology defines people with little or no conscience, empathy or concern for the feelings, well-being or rights of others as being sociopaths or psychopaths. We can easily see the woeful results in the history of humanity when these perverse types of maladjusted, deranged, imbalanced people assume positions of social, political and economic positions of authority and responsibility that enable them to apply their hateful, destructive, greedy, evil influences upon our civilisation.

Let's consider a range of descriptive conceptual words that can be used to define, acknowledge and more fully understand the lower aspects of malevolent, harmful, oppressive human nature that have continually plagued and attempted to dominate our earthly civilisations, as is currently occurring in 2016, especially in the USA, Israel, Great Britain, North Korea and in other locations internationally. Some of the indicative dysfunctional traits that express the full range of selfish, immoral, insidious, deceitful human value systems and behaviours that are becoming increasingly prevalent in positions of political and corporate leadership internationally are as follows: self-indulgent, predatory (in the sense of taking unfair advantage of other people), opportunistic (defined as someone that takes advantage of opportunities with little or no regard for values, principles or consequences), arrogant, superficial, disingenuous, capricious, tyrannical, dishonest, autocratic, acquisitive, violent, unscrupulous, perfidious, unjust, destabilising, destructive, haughty, disloyal, unwholesome, depraved, corrupt, hostile, venal, dishonourable, aggressive, decadent, manipulative, avaricious, vicious, greedy, impious, deceitful, brutal, debauched, atrocious, unethical, unreliable, hypocritical, cruel, lazy, quarrelsome, angry, irritable, vindictive, hateful, cowardly, xenophobic, fearful, pessimistic, bitter, self-destructive, resentful, callous, biased, spiteful, oppressive, prejudiced, antagonistic, and so on and on. These detrimental, lower types of human temperaments only continue to exist because we allow it to be so through the ways many of us think and live our lives. We now earnestly and genuinely seek to elicit the very best within ourselves as human beings. We must refuse to become intimidated, apathetic, debilitated, diminished, degraded, belittled, devalued, weakened, restricted, corrupted, debased, defiled or brutalised and not allow ourselves to be coerced into manifesting negative, inappropriate, amoral attitudes and actions; nor to fall victim to rationalising, condoning or accepting these evil characteristics within ourselves or those people and organisations with whom we associate ourselves, and certainly not from our civilisation's leaders.

To manifest one's innate higher nature of consciousness requires the inner unfoldment, development and external expression of various aspects of one's truly spiritual nature. Let's now shift our focus to consider a number of descriptive conceptual words that define and enable us to more fully comprehend and act upon this genuinely noble, generous, empathetic, magnanimous, compassionate, loving type of attitude that characterises our 'higher', eternal, more truly godly nature. We do so when we are exhibiting a peaceful, considerate, altruistic, respectful, benevolent, kind-hearted, good-willed, affectionate, humanitarian, warm-hearted, wise, joyous, giving, sharing, harmless, amiable, hard-working, diligent, patient, friendly, helpful, charitable, philanthropic, gracious, humane, accepting, loving, courteous, humble, grateful, happy, selfless, sociable, unenvious, tolerant, affable, decent, gentle, merciful, hospitable, civil, beneficial spirit of mind that serves to create an uplifting positive influence upon others and our selves by our constructive actions. We are indeed fortunate and blessed if we actively seek to realise, express and truly demonstrate these higher aspects and divine characteristics of our overall state of being, through this earthly life. In this process, we consciously intend, seek and commit ourselves to being increasingly aware of our entire, comprehensive state of consciousness in all of our activities. Initially this state of mind may seem to be an oddly vulnerable and unusually perceptive condition; to intentionally habitually become increasingly consciously attentive regarding various levels of one's mental, emotional and spiritual character, moment to moment. Basically, this process involves becoming more consciously aware of what one is currently thinking and doing about issues which previously you were likely to be relatively less conscious of in your daily life. Examples are unlimited, depending upon your current state of mind and being. If you were not already moving in this direction; toward far greater levels of self-awareness, then you would not be drawn to read this book, or you would have long ago set it aside until you were more receptive to these ideas and in applying them into your life in a serious manner. It is primarily by looking backwards over our lives' most significant events, lessons, mistakes, and major realisations that we are better able to perceive and understand the progress we are making, as well as how and why this process functions as it does.

In closing, it is imperative we now acknowledge the exceedingly encouraging fact that a relatively small number of highly intelligent, divinely motivated, quite wealthy, magnanimous, influential, internationally active, like-minded, extremely capable business people are now publicly and privately joining in cooperative allegiances to make significant improvements in our civilisation's vision for the future. They are by their own free-will deciding to make genuinely positive, constructive, remedial, innovative, effective, progressive changes to affect a beneficial shift in humanity's consciousness by their exemplary attitudes and generous activities. Their authentically humane motives and divinely inspired perceptions illuminate the enormous potential for humanity to swiftly rise above the current prevalent pathetic degradation, conflict, destruction and misery sought by greedy self-interest that serves to characterise the lowest factors expressing themselves at the highest materialistic echelons in our world civilisation today. Humanity has a great many truly high quality, well-motivated, exceedingly intelligent, capable true leaders available to us. We, the good, hard-working, kindly, compassionate, peaceful people of Earth must set our vision above that of the rabble seeking to ensnare us in endless cycles of contrived hostility against fabricated, illusionary, falsely created, non-existent 'enemies' and the continual seeking of materialistic accomplishments in preference to more important meaningful activities and personal qualities. Our only real enemies are those people, corporations and institutions that refuse to allow us to work together to engender peace, equitable productivity and prosperity, environmental sustainability, beneficial innovation, and good-will among all people, to ascend into a position where these goals and attributes serve to characterise our earthly civilisation. Let us all commit to supporting our truly wise, good, capable, intelligent leaders; who possess a better vision for earthly civilisation and will help us create it now.

Chapter 8

A Consciousness Integration Experience

Our goal will be to increasingly become conscientiously conscious regarding our entire states of mind and being in such a persistent way that our higher levels of awareness begin to function more effectively in all aspects of our daily earthly lives. This process of introspection will also involve our sleep states; becoming as aware as possible of events occurring in our dream states, including our waking 'day dreams'. To some of us this continual state of perceptive awareness whereby one is observing their own mind and emotions in direct relation to all the events around us, including the mental and emotional states of other people, may seem to be a curious, unusual and challenging situation to intellectualise upon, acknowledge or describe to one's self and others. We will hereby gain an improved insight into what types of experiences develop more acute, elevated levels of perceptive capability from this type of astute acuity. These increases in perceptive awareness occur from all forms of experience and comprehension, so it is difficult to innumerate the ways in which this attentive, inquisitive, percipient attitude will benefit us. As this enhanced sentient process progressively unfolds over passing time, you will be surprised, amazed and delighted by what occurs.

Let's consider a very basic event that helped to explain and demonstrate the meaning and application of this concept in my life over a decade ago. The event served to prompt me to share some of these experiences with you and has lead to much character development, resulting in an observable improvement in my personal capabilities, qualities and realisation processes. It is primarily by looking back retrospectively over our lives in a probing, analytical, meticulously scrutinising manner that we are most able to become cognitive of the prodigious extent of our greatest lessons, realisations and life's significant 'turning points'. By thoroughly considering these types of experiences proactively, we are able to ascertain a comprehension of the progressive evolutionary nature of eternal reality, as well as earthly reality. This following simple, somewhat mundane seeming example is one event that greatly assisted and inspired me in this process of self-discovery. In evaluating the experience, one can determine that key spiritual realisations and transformations sometimes do occur in quite normal circumstances, when we least expect such an increase in our overall level of awareness to manifest itself. God does indeed 'move in mysterious ways'.

In the thirty five years that have elapsed between the previously recorded events of my mid-twenties, many other inspirational, uplifting, interesting, informative events and realisations occurred that have not been mentioned here. This is partly due to the fact that many of them would not serve our topical matter in the sequential order that is most ideal to assist you to develop a more lucid full understanding of these issues, from my perspective. Suffice to say that between the ages of twenty five and sixty two years of age, numerous additional experiences akin to those already mentioned here have significantly helped to clarify and confirm various fundamental realities. Some of these have already been addressed in a limited manner and various others which will be included here later. Some additional major life improving experiences will not be included in this book at all because they are of a private or personal nature, or would not be especially relevant, and some such experiences would likely be even more difficult to describe, believe or fathom than some of what has already been addressed in our discussion. This is mentioned now so that you recognise and accept that some of your experiences should and always will be better off to remain private, or shared only with those people most likely to be understanding and supportive of your most precious life experiences. In this way, your inner journey of discovery remains your most precious, special, uniquely treasured personal possession that no one can ever take from you, impugn or tarnish. Such knowledge, wisdom, experience and awareness remains with you throughout eternity, as manifested by who and what you are as a human being and Soul.

We are focused upon simultaneously developing our transcendent immortal nature in harmony with our transitory mortal human character. Therefore, various aspects of your sublime inner spiritual nature will be unacceptable for public disclosure, especially as you ascend into loftier perpetual realms of existence that defy normal levels of human understanding and are not intended to be shared with other people for a variety of ineffable reasons. If I were not being encouraged by the ceaseless daily insistence of my own higher transcendental aspects of character to record in written form some of my experiences, along with my opinions and perceptions, then most of this information would have remained confidential. As you would recognise, much of what we discuss here is focused upon the types of experience that is generally beyond the realm of normal daily consciousness for the majority of human beings on Earth today in 2016. However, there is now a dramatic global shift in the advancement of positive consciousness occurring in a relatively significant proportion of humanity. You typify this encouraging transcendental progression, so thank you for being YOU!

This book is intended to be an open honest discussion whose probity and vision will ideally serve to assist you to connect directly with a higher omnipotent source of divine inspiration, through your own eternal character which is Soul, an evolving spark of God's essence. You are actually Soul, the self-aware inner Spirit that resides in your physical body in this lifetime on Earth. You are an energetic, everlasting, unfolding, creative, free-willed, divinely sentient conscious immortal being that continues to exist long after the death of your present earthly physical body. It is time for you, and each of us, to discover at your own pace and in your unique fashion, a closer intimate relationship with your divine immortal sublime state of existence that is 'the real you'.

In the process of reading this book and searching inquisitively through your own life's unique, special, mysterious and sacrosanct experiences, you likely will have already recalled and carefully considered numerous life improving events and realisations. If so, then now we have reached the point where you are capable of more effectively probing and acknowledging my relative state of perception and consciousness, within and through your own intuitive processes. For some people, this following experience will surely seem to be quite mundane, or falsely believe it to be some form of delusion on my part, or simply be another of these "so what?" type of events that are recorded here for your reflection and analysis. Whatever the nature of your response or perception of this event, for me it contains some significant vital clues to some of the preeminent reasons for human existence on Earth for us, as individuals and collectively as a species of life. Big realisations are occasionally derived from some rather ordinary seeming events and circumstances. No words can or necessarily should adequately express the full implications or resulting subsequent revelations which continue to arise from these humble beginnings when my normal level of human consciousness willingly agreed to integrate and unify itself with superior, transcendental, immortal aspects of my overall consciousness in a receptive manner that defies my current intellectual understanding in some ways. This relatively brief event resulted in a modest, definitive 'quantum leap' in my consciousness that remains difficult to fully assess, adequately describe, or to quantify in regard to conclusive advancements in my overall capabilities. I do know this following event was among the most beneficial in my life. This fact can be best understood by you personally experiencing something somewhat similar within your own consciousness; then explanations are unnecessary.

One afternoon I was lying on the beach after a swim, enjoying the warm sun, beautiful scenery, thinking of nothing in particular, as I watched nature move. I was apparently unintentionally doing an unconscious form of contemplation on the beauty around me. At the time I was thoroughly invigorated from body surfing for about an hour, then while resting on the sand, I became fully relaxed with a quiet, peaceful conscious mind, simply observing the azure waves rolling onto the golden sandy beach, the distant green hills bordering the seashore, the gulls effortlessly soaring above in the clear sunny sky. The situation was one where I was 'at one' with the delightful naturally enchanting panorama of the tropical beach located nearby where I live in Australia. Unexpectedly, almost as if I was being spoken to by someone else, yet clearly originating from within my own familiar mind came the simple question, "Would you like to have access to additional information?" Within my silent mind, the sudden internal question was startling to the passive, inactive state that my normal conscious mind was enjoying at the time, so the unusual question seemed to be from a somewhat external source although it definitely originated within my mind, just as would any normal thought one has in an inner verbal dialogue with one's self. Because my normal conscious mind was surprised and perplexed by this unanticipated question that presented itself within the private sanctuary of my non-existent thoughts at the time, I responded with thoughts to the effect, "Pardon me?" In other words, mentally I replied with thoughts meaning, "What was that?" or "What is being asked here?" Again, immediately the same exact question was communicated to me directly from a source seemingly within my quite attentive, curious mind, "Would you like to have access to additional information?" I instantly knew this was not something occurring within my own over-active imagination, since occasionally previous communications had occurred in this manner, although not too often with this clarity and with no obvious involvement on my part. In this event, I had evidently enabled my normal daily form of conscious awareness to be relatively silent, receptive and available to what then occurred, as follows.

I was immediately a little cautious and a bit apprehensive, quickly recalling my previous 'I want to know "What is the meaning of life?" event' which was somewhat of the same nature of communication. A few other similar such illuminating events of varying intensities also rapidly made themselves known to me, which reminded me to be careful and sincere about responding to such significant issues. I somewhat tentatively mentally responded, "Yes, that would be okay", then quickly thinking about it further, I added, "What kind of additional information are we referring to here?" The response was very low-key, pleasant, calm, and reassuring, "Just more access to various types of information". While this may seem to be relatively innocuous and non-threatening to most people, the access I already had to all manner of information to topics not yet mentioned here, primarily related to earthly issues, did not particularly fill me with enthusiasm or confidence. Acknowledging my suspicious, concerned state of mind, I was again gently reassured there was little danger involved with accessing the so-called "additional information". Since I was still relatively relaxed, yet attentive and very alert at this time, I responded with more enthusiasm, "Where or how would I access this additional information?" The response was thoughts to the effect "You will just know, or it will be provided to you in various ways". I then thought "That's sounds okay" and all was mentally silent as I contemplated upon what that would possibly mean in my life.

In that relaxed, alert, receptive, accepting, contemplative state of mind, suddenly I quite literally 'felt' an 'integration of mind' occur between whatever the source of the question was within my normal conscious mind.

In that instant, my own heightened normal conscious awareness and receptive acceptance enabled a process of integration to occur, whereby aspects of my higher, eternal levels of consciousness and my normal temporal daily level of consciousness mutually agreed to a more consciously unified existence. The mental feeling was really quite unusual since the nature of one's eternal consciousness is exceedingly powerful and pervasive, especially when compared to one's human state of consciousness. As my normal conscious mind silently and willingly observed the process of integration occur over a few seconds, the primary sensation was one of an intense feeling of unity, wholeness, completion, relaxation, comfort and an increase in my peace of mind. As the integration of these two aspects of my overall consciousness occurred I, the human conscious aspect, was immediately aware of the considerable influence, perceptive power, level of awareness and capability that had 'settled itself' quietly, yet distinctly within and throughout my entire conscious state of awareness. Mentally silent and physically very relaxed, with eyes closed, lying down in the warm sun, quite oblivious to my surroundings, I, the human consciousness, felt this pervasive, impressive level of awareness achieve a high degree of co-existence within my normal conscious mind. To say the quality of the inwardly manifesting consciousness was 'huge' and 'comprehensive' and 'compassionate' are relatively inconsequential, inadequate descriptions of the actual processes or characteristics of this integration experience. After a minute or so of this profound experience, my normal conscious mind became tentatively concerned by this unusually calm, peaceful, perceptive state of mind and asked the mental question, "What will be my role now?" implying "Who will be in control?". Instantly, the eternal aspect of myself reassuringly replied in thoughts to the effect "Nothing will change. You will simply have access to more information. Sometimes you will not know its origin or why it has come to your attention". This realisation was very comforting to my normal human aspect of mind, primarily in the sense that no changes would occur in the actual way that my mind would function. The obvious central concern to my daily normal level of consciousness was "Who is in control?" and the idea that 'it' would have access to more information was of far less significance or interest than the fact that my normal human consciousness would remain 'in control'. I refer to this relatively lower, temporal aspect of my overall consciousness as 'it' here because this description seems accurate in that 'it' seemed distinctly to be less 'me' than were other aspects of higher, immortal mind and being that I was aware of at that time.

What was so significant was that experience felt as though in the process of willingly accepting this mental integration, these two primary aspects of my consciousness were now in harmony after a lengthy period of relative discord. The event was a delightful, fantastic knowingness in unity that defies simplistic literal expression here. My ordinary conscious mind has often tended to reject, debate, or ignore all types of information presented to it for a significant number of reasons. This memorable event definitely seemed to heal, mend and unify diverse aspects of my consciousness that serve different roles within one's overall state of consciousness. In some senses, this experience was as though peace was finally being declared after a lengthy period of conflict within myself.

A number of analogies could be made to define, describe and better explain this process of the integration of various types of awareness that occurred, although none of these are exactly akin to the experience itself. Imagine that your heart would say to you that you love or like someone very much, yet your mind would innumerate many reasons that a relationship or friendship would be unsuccessful or unacceptable by criteria of assessment that were not relevant to one's heart-felt emotional feelings. Such conflicts between various aspects of one's self are common and are experienced by us all throughout our lives. Another analogy would be that one is considering a career change and aspects of one's mind say to stay in your current job since that is a sure way to assure yourself of financial security and maintain your current social status; however, another aspect of your consciousness seeks another type of work that allows for more freedom, creativity, self-expression and is less stressful in its lifestyle. On the one side of the equation, you must consider the advantages of staying with the uncomfortable, secure, well-known possible future; and on the other side of the debate you want to choose the possibility to create a better lifestyle for yourself and your family, unfortunately with less financial security, due to the uncertain demand for your desired future alternative occupation. These choices challenge us to make decisions that affect us in countless ways. Another analogy would be that in one's conscience one feels an act to be either right or wrong, yet other aspects of one's character can rationalise the situation to conduct one's self in a way that proves to be hurtful or not in the best interests of one's self or others, as well as being somewhat inconsistent with one's preferred values, beliefs and moral philosophy of life. Choices in favour of achieving self-satisfaction, pleasure, wealth and convenience can quite often powerfully influence one's perceptions, rationalisations and decision making processes in earthly society and be incongruous with our inner values and beliefs. Another related analogy would be if you had an addictive, self-abusive, counter-productive habit that you do not want to do in one part of your consciousness, yet another aspect of your character would seek to continue to indulge in the self-destructive behaviour. Basically, none of these brief analogies related directly to the actual nature or significance of my previously mentioned integration of consciousness event, but they do reveal that various aspects of one's consciousness can be and often are in conflict with one's values, information inputs, beliefs, desires, and best interests. The results of our actions can therefore become contradictory and opposed to the mental and physical choices that would be most desired by us in our lives.

The consequence of this situation whereby differing aspects of our overall consciousness possess differing and often contradictory viewpoints and attitudes and value systems means that we are sometimes likely to find ourselves doing things that we really do not want to do. We experience all manner of situations in life where we are uncomfortable, in conflict, or at odds within our overall character about our life choices, both in regard to major and less significant issues. We may stay in an unpleasant relationship or job for security and out of fear of the uncertainty that a change would create. Most of us are prone to continue to endure negative situations even though some aspects of our being are being suppressed and ignored to continue in the situation. Such circumstances often lead to inner and outer conflicts in our lives that eventually can prove to be counter-productive, debilitating, or prompt actions that are wrong from our conscience's perspective. Likewise, living through challenging life circumstances and resolving important issues that enable us to improve our character serves to strengthen us, in spite of these unwanted difficulties.

In this event various aspects of my conscious awareness knowingly integrated and unified themselves in some form of mutual agreement that resulted in additional harmony of conscious mind and purpose in life. The integration process benefited me in multitudinous ways, some being beyond my present levels of conscious awareness and comprehension. Prior to this event it had been quite common for me to consciously or unconsciously ignore, debate and reject a wide variety of internal impressions, impulses, thoughts and perceptions, especially when the information was from unknown sources or was inconsistent with or contradicted my personal preferences, plans or seemed to be unrelated to the logical assessment of my normal rational state of mind which is generally primarily focused upon earthly realities. Instead, I began to more sincerely consider, evaluate and include a significantly expanded, more diverse set of information. By more sincerely and conscientiously applying the inputs from the more harmonised, unified, integrated aspects of my overall consciousness, usually in a normal mental and emotional process, the result has been a series of progressive, beneficial life changes and realisations. These personal adjustments have included improvements in awareness, interpersonal interactions, occupational choices, lifestyle and peace of mind which have developed in a quite natural favourable manner in most situations. However, at times, especially when some information or an inner impulse is contrary to or discrepant with my logical and personal preferences, at times I balk like an unruly horse being lead into a new pasture, through an unfamiliar gateway. This integration event occurred before I considered writing this book, so the ongoing influences of that experience have altered my life in positive ways.

As individuals, groups and as a global civilisation, we quite often resist the unpredictable influences of our eternal aspects of consciousness because these promptings may seem to occur without a perceptible rational logical origin, or the inspiration may not apparently be in our personal best interests and preferences, or it may encourage unwanted change and irksome realisations in our lives, or may even be in direct opposition to some of our favoured mental and emotional conditions. Whatever the reasons that we tend to ignore, deny and thwart the illumination, wisdom and inexplicable source of our erudition being somehow supplied through innumerable sources by our 'higher self', which we are defining as being a perceptible, integral aspect of our eternal consciousness; the consequence is we too often fail to experience possible improvements in our lives. The result is that our existing, predominate normal daily state of mind tends to remain rigid, limited, inflexible, and opposed to making these types of beneficial evolutionary developments. Alternatively, it is possible to consciously learn to acknowledge when an unknown or inexplicable aspect of one's higher, more inclusive, aware states of being are originating intuitive information or impulses that express themselves through an inner knowingness. For most of us, these mental and emotional inputs seem to usually occur in such a natural manner that we hardly consciously notice them as we live our daily lives. However, at times these vital functions of our 'higher self' or eternal levels of consciousness can literally save our lives, or simply make essential knowledge available to us in a conclusive way that we otherwise would not possess.

Countless examples in my own life eagerly seek expression as we reach this fundamental juncture in our discussion here. Now is when you can greatly benefit by reflecting carefully upon your own life to perceive and recall such events that at the time may have seemed to be coincidence, pure chance, an odd twist of fate, or fortunate destiny that lead to experiences, enlightenment or opportunities that changed your life for the better. Sometimes an event or realisation may have been upsetting or even quite painful in various ways, yet the eventual outcome can be absolutely wonderful and life changing for the better. In an opposite manner, we all can recall events when aspects of our conscience continually beseeched us not to do a certain thing, or to give up a bad habit that damaged our health, state of mind or lifestyle, yet we steadfastly stubbornly refused and were eventually physically and emotionally hurt in the subsequent realisation processes. When we consciously or unconsciously ignore, deny and counteract the positive, uplifting inspirational influences of our eternal consciousness we are often choosing to learn the hard way instead of knowingly and willingly selecting the best possible path that life offers to us. Opportunity could indeed be around every corner, but it generally does not appear to present itself every day for most of us, especially in 'locations' where genuine character development occurs in this earthly life. This false misperception occurs because our minds, hearts and spirits are somewhat closed or impervious to perceiving much of the potential joy, achievement, meaning, true love and kindness that surrounds us all every day. We, as individuals and as an intelligent species of life on Earth, are continually being presented with countless opportunities to make marvellous, wise, splendid, magnificent, excellent, virtuous, valuable choices. Yet, if we fail to do so, then it could be longer than we expect or wish to be the case before another auspicious, pivotal, momentous, instant of choice presents itself, often when and how we least anticipate it occurring.

Various unexpected opportunities can occur in any area of one's life; in personal relationships, lifestyle choices, business, the location one chooses to live, selecting a partner, pet or a vehicle, taking a few moments to share a few kind thoughts with another person or even something as common as deciding what route to take to work and the exact moment of one's departure. Some of these situations are obviously quite mundane, yet other choices, such as mutually selecting one's spouse, or living according to one's own set of values are issues of foremost importance in the resultant effects upon our lives. Surely we all have been tempted and tested by an almost endless variety of experiences in life, depending upon our character, circumstances and the multitude of individual lessons and realisations we each are most in need of learning. For example, someone in a good financial position with excellent legal knowledge and capability may knowingly organise to utilise a legal loophole to intentionally steal from or unfairly take advantage of another person, such as a building contractor, whose knowledge of contracts is inadequate to protect himself or who has insufficient financial ability to seek and obtain restitution in the court system for unpaid accounts that he is legitimately owed. While the years go by, such an unscrupulous person who preys upon other people's trust or lack of business acumen could become vastly wealthier financially than would be the case if they adhered to a more kindly moralistic code of ethics. However, it could be equally possible that such a dishonest opportunistic person may attract to themselves a spouse or business partner that would be equally deceitful with them, in which circumstances the cheat could become the victim of another person with similar inappropriate ethics and attitudes, exactly like himself. In such a way, this person would be provided the opportunity to experience the full set of emotions that he had previously created for other people that he had disadvantaged by his actions, especially if he was bankrupted in the process and subsequently experienced a mental crisis over his perceived misfortune. Or, he may simply end up with a fear of other people, believing that due to his unprincipled conduct, other people were 'out to get him' in some ways for the loss and suffering he had created, which would likely detract from his level of contentment, happiness, security and as a result, he may develop stress and other health related problems as an indirect effect of his lifestyle and attitudes. The result could be that such a person would eventually learn from his poor choices and dubious values and willingly change his lifestyle accordingly, to improve his attitudes and behaviours.

In another unrelated such example, someone may abuse their power, trust and authority over other people; such as a child molester, or a corrupt democratically elected politician, or an oppressive violent dictator, who later in life suffers in all manner of ways partly due to the grief, trauma depravation and pain they inflicted upon others by their selfish, callous acts. We all hurt and deceive ourselves and others to some degree, in various ways, sometimes intentionally and in other ways unconsciously. For example, a man may idly sit watching television sports on the weekends instead of interacting with his family, to the potential detriment of relationships with one's spouse and his children due to his inattentiveness, reduced mutual interaction and perceived lack of affection. Alternatively, we may indulge in a bad habit that we know damages our health. Or, we may deprive ourselves and others of activities we would truly enjoy and that would benefit us, to instead do counter-productive, unenjoyable, costly things that ultimately serve little purpose in making our lives better, such as gambling. We could list numerous other such examples, with many being very specific and some being quite upsetting to us all. This is especially true when we consider the nature of warfare and violence in human history and the poor conditions currently being experienced by some unfortunate, unhappy, frightened people in various parts of the world due to such hostile circumstances.

In an eternal state of existence, which is the actual nature of reality in spite of all appearances to the contrary on Earth, one is privileged to endlessly experience all types of events in lifetime, after a lifetime, after lifetime. Throughout this progression of existence within various types of reality systems, one is quite likely to eventually encounter virtually every type of life situation, if not now in this lifetime, or in a past lifetime, then perhaps in a future lifetime. Please recall that Soul, the essential self-aware aspect of your immortal consciousness, originates and exists upon a higher level of timeless reality that co-exists with the material, physical plane of existence here on Earth. The less one is willing or able to integrate their eternal, more divine aspects of consciousness within and through the expression of their human character, the more life will pummel one into submission over the course of seemingly endless, increasingly challenging lifetimes upon physical levels of existence. Conversely, the more one is able to acknowledge, personify, integrate and express their divine 'higher' aspects of being and quality values in thought and action; then the better, easier, more productive and enjoyable life becomes for that individual and those around them. However, the challenges in life persist, regardless of one's relative level of achievement or spirituality.

This process in eternal life is open to considerable debate among those who believe we only live one life upon this Earth and then we are judged once by God for the remainder of eternity. So, some people profess to believe if we 'get it right' in our earthly lifetime then we are welcomed into Heaven to reside there with God, the Prophets, Saviours, Saints and Its chosen people for all eternity. Some people also believe that if we are able to repent for our sins, saying we are honestly sorry to God, or through the assistance of a human representative of God, such as a priest, minister, or other religious official; earnestly beseeching for forgiveness so that we are absolved of these earthly sins, then they too can live in Heaven for all eternity, even if those sins involved, for example, the responsibility for murdering civilian women, children and the elderly or other violent, immoral or anti-social acts against other people or God's Earth. Others that are less fortunate, not particularly clever, unlucky, or are unaware of these purported procedures invented by mankind's religions to "go to Heaven, in spite of your many sins" may believe they will be tortured in a horrible Hell for all eternity. Many other people find these systems of belief in any such afterlife too unlikely or upsetting to consider such a system of reality as being possible or rational, so they may choose to believe nothing exists after death of their physical earthly body. Such people would likely see earthly life here and now as being the only level of existence, as manifested by their human five senses. It is little wonder that such people generally seem to perceive relatively little true meaning in life, aside from their material wealth, social status and enjoyment in life. A portion of people who do not believe that aspects of their consciousness continue to exist after earthly life or that they can be absolved of their sins by some method are sometimes prone to possess a diminished degree of human compassion and empathy for others, or perhaps a feeble or even a non-functional conscience. If the latter is the case, then their relative lack of functional conscience may result in them demonstrating a relatively poor ethical value system that is generally based upon whatever their self-interests dictate, regardless of their deleterious, negative influences upon others in the manner in which they live their earthly lives. Such beliefs exist among a substantial portion of the human population, especially as evidenced by many of those people currently enjoying positions of enormous power and control over governments, religions, financial systems, international corporate affairs, etc. We clearly can perceive at the highest levels in human society an entrenched group of wealthy, influential people whose families and businesses have long dominated our civilisation to the point they now largely appear to control all governments, financial markets and industries on Earth. Many such people do indeed exhibit a tendency to mollify or publicly seek to negate the depravity of their adversarial, self-serving, greedy attitudes that continually inflict deliberate punitive actions upon our global civilisation. Such plutocratic people tend to conceal themselves within their 'ivory towers', gated mansions, protected by security guards, their apparent control of military and police forces, as they confidently flaunt their capabilities before humanity; seemingly gladly accepting or remaining unmoved, unmindful, unmerciful and unprincipled by the needless suffering and depravation that their attitudes, policies and activities intentionally create in order to retain and strengthen their financial, governmental and ideological positions in our increasingly totalitarian societies. It is ironic that many of these people publicly profess to be religious, to believe in God and yet their unconscionable attitudes and actions demonstrate disregard for truth, justice and many basic spiritual values.

However, this complex situation reveals the crux of the dilemma and true purpose of life on Earth: to enable each of us to act appropriately and learn at our own pace, in our own ways and with one another, responsible for our own thoughts and actions, endlessly through time as we now know it on this level of existence and beyond. We each and all are being held personally accountable by a far higher, vastly more capable, all-knowing, omnipotent, omnipresent Creator that we call God by many names. Those who falsely believe they will never be held accountable for their insidious, dishonest, malevolent thoughts and actions will eventually learn far more about suffering than they ever care to know. We who acknowledge and gratefully embrace our more civil, humane, noble, divine aspects of character are incredibly fortunate to now be observing, learning and evolving through the myriad of experiences and edifying realisations we perceive developing within our rapidly destabilising, volatile earthly civilisation.

It is impossible to adequately express everything here in such a manner, yet please attempt to understand the hidden implications of the phrase "time, as we now know it to be", as our discussion continues. We are developing a deeper, more inclusive type of communication as this interactive flow of ideas and experiences continues, as your eternally aware conscious aspects increasingly seek to reveal themselves in ways that are acceptable and beneficial to your overall character and life. These immortal aspects of your conscious nature obviously exist at a higher level of reality that is beyond time as it appears to flow upon Earth for us now. It is essential to allow yourself to become exceedingly comfortable with the inner-found certainty of your own personal experience or 'knowingness' that supersedes all logical, linear thought; acknowledging yourself foremost as a self-aware, conscious, evolving immortal being, Soul, which is currently acting in conjunction, harmony and shared purpose with and through your ordinary temporal human level of being. As Soul, you exist simultaneously beyond and outside of, yet also within earthly time as you understand it. However, your human character is usually only able to perceive itself and physical events in a temporal, sequential, logical, linear manner of thought and action. The greater one's awareness and commitment to consciously invite the immortal, omnipotent, omnipresent, omniscient divine nature within each of us to express Itself through our daily life, the more we expand our sentient state of being in multitudinous inexplicable, yet discernible, illuminating, enlightening, uplifting ways. Conversely, the more we suppress, deny and ignore the divine immortal consciousness within ourselves by instead focusing our attention and behaviours upon the more squalid, debauched, sensational, materialistic, transitory components of earthly life, then the greater our lower, less divine, instinctual, self-serving temporal human characteristics assert themselves to dominate our mind and daily actions. Consequently, when one is focused in this strictly humanistic state of being, where influences from one's more divine nature are largely limited to that of a patient observer, the result is often that ethically and morally repugnant thoughts and actions become dominant while such people foolishly seek to use, control, manipulate and undermine those people around themselves to the detriment of all people and life forms. This is a grossly oversimplified analysis of such a process because we all have a multitude of tendencies available for expression within each of us, depending upon the circumstances we find ourselves in at the time, along the inner discipline and nature of our overall character's integration.

Many of us know why we choose one thought or action, as opposed to a different one that may seem on a basic level to be preferable. One must learn to differentiate what aspects of one's comprehensive character are seeking expression in thought and deed. What may appear to be a motive of helping and being kind to others could easily become one of vested interests that is damaging to both participants, depending upon how the action is manifested and for what substantive reasons. The possible examples are endless regarding this tendency in life and please attempt to consider a variety of them from your own set of experiences and from the lives of those around you in your family or local community. We can indeed learn from the experiences and mistakes of others, only if we sincerely commit ourselves to doing so. Otherwise, we simply continue to 'learn the hard way', or because that process can be too painful, frustrating and upsetting, instead we may choose to make relatively meagre progress throughout our earthly lives. The vast majority of people now living upon Earth have been learning and advancing at a far slower, more convoluted, somewhat random, sporadic pace than is otherwise achievable for countless lifetimes here and in other realms of existence. Let's do our best to sincerely evaluate our past experiences with a determined intent to recognise our errors in judgement and make the necessary adjustments to select virtuous choices. This will enable us to create a better future individually and collectively, as human beings; increasingly aware of our immortal journey of discovery as being the preeminent focal point that characterises our present earthly lives.

As our discussion continues, various types of historical examples will be provided on a wide range of issues affecting humanity. None are intended to single out any particular nation, religion, race, culture group or individual for our critical observation. Rather, we will primarily seek to clearly express the variety of ways that one's thoughts, ethics, values, morals, attitudes and beliefs in life manifest themselves on this Earth. Our intent is to define and continue to differentiate some of the characteristic indicators that reveal and identify one's relative level of being, as it relates to manifested thought, belief and attitude through behaviours in our individual lives and our global civilisation as a whole.

Becoming acutely aware of the more divine levels of consciousness within each of us is an individualistic goal, to be accomplished at the rate of progress that best meets our temperament. This process is one of the most important achievements available to us in both earthly life and in the scheme of one's immortal existence. Likewise, as a global society composed of an infinite variety of unique Souls, it is our responsibility to recognise our inner divinity as well as our diverse variety of less auspicious, self-serving human characteristics, so we can all better perceive and comprehend our unified reality system that we are constantly creating by our attitudes and actions. This developmental process identifies that many modern human beings are rapidly becoming more aware, more mature, and more kindly toward one another, as well as protective of the earthly environment, which we share with countless other life forms. Humanity will become better aligned with the balanced aspects of both our human and our divine levels of existence that characterise our overall nature. We, like our ancestors, are still evolving, progressing, changing and growing in wisdom, capability, intellect, perception and spirit. Becoming more conscious of this ongoing process and seeking to accept and affiliate ourselves to a greater extent with our higher, eternal more divine omnipotent nature of our state of being has fantastic benefits available for each and all of us. To do otherwise is to ignore and negate our true purpose in this life, which is detrimental to us all.

Integrating one's overall consciousness is a challenging perpetual process, since we are all evolving continually, or intermittently devolving as the case may be for some us, before we surge forward in our developmental unfoldment again. One can learn to consciously recognise the manifestation of higher consciousness in numerous aspects of one's daily life. Usually the majority of people are blissfully unaware of the actions of Soul-directed levels of consciousness within their lives. It is beneficial to examine our lives and those around us to acknowledge some excellent examples that serve to reveal and characterise higher consciousness by uplifting, benevolent, noble, utilitarian, selfless, loving, kind, thoughtful, giving, sharing, helpful, joyous, happy, positive states of being and actions that are expressed and demonstrated in our daily lives. These inspirational events can and should prompt realisations that Soul and God are actually quite active in our earthly lives. This knowledge provides us with an abundance of personal and societal circumstantial evidence that can encourage us to rejoice and be grateful for the infinite blessings in our lives, many being so ingrained and subtle by their nature that they can often evade our conscious attention, remaining almost unnoticed, or taken for granted by us in our hurried modern lives. Our quest is to become more conscientious, inquisitive and aware of such uplifting attitudes, states of being and their illuminating actions in our lives so that we begin to more easily recognise and encourage the expression and manifestation of these aspects of our consciousness on a regular, habitual basis.

A fine positive example is that recently a relatively small, interconnected group of extremely financially wealthy, highly motivated, exceedingly intelligent people decided to contribute a significant portion of their personal fortunes to genuinely assist and help others that are less fortunate in our world. They had previously already established international humanitarian foundations for that purpose and been active for many years in these types of constructive, much needed activities. Instead of using most of their enormous financial wealth to further expand their business activities, or purchase more impressive material possessions, or to focus upon enjoying their lifestyle, or gain ever greater controls over governments and the global economic system as some other wealthy groups of self-serving people have chosen to apply their vast financial wealth, these magnanimous, kindly, astute people inwardly would have likely acknowledged being inspired by divine aspects of their higher character, Soul. The commendable personal qualities that these people demonstrate do reveal and exemplify their true nature as human beings. They knowingly act decisively according to their inner set of higher beliefs, goals and attributes in diverse, productive, humane ways that apply their personal and business capabilities toward sincere efforts devoted to improving our world and to help make life more equitable and prosperous for those people less fortunate than themselves. These inspirational people raise our vision to perceive loftier realisations of the many beneficial changes that are possible, as we each in our own ways do accomplish similar beneficial actions with those like-minded people with whom we associate. It is all about becoming receptive to recognising and then evoking the best within our characters to manifest its self. Over passing time, this realisation and behavioural development process becomes a normal part of our daily conscious minds to the extent that we recognise, embrace and integrate with the higher sources of our creative conscious abilities. This engenders the expression of our comprehensive immortal nature through our daily thoughts and actions to continually elicit the powerful, compassionate, sublime manifestation of our higher character in a multitude of beneficial ways.

Chapter 9

Human Nature Issues

We are all eternally aware, spiritual beings that currently inhabit a mortal physical body for the purpose of experiencing earthly material life to learn, develop, evolve, achieve and progress in a variety of ways. Some people believe they are here on Earth simply to have a good time and enjoy whatever they can in this life. Others prefer to devote their efforts here toward making as much money as possible and utilise their material wealth as they believe appropriate. Some other people seek to become famous, influential, powerful, admired, a benefit to society, or simply to be remembered by future generations for some reason, while some others seek to become all of the above and much more. When one considers the diversity of human attitudes, personalities, motivations, characteristics and actions then it becomes apparent how unique individual people actually are, as well as how incredibly diverse national, tribal, religious, cultural, and ethnic groups of people are when contrasted with one another. Equally relevant is the vast array of basic similarities that compose life's major realities which we all must address in living our daily lives, regardless of one's status, income, location, level of development, or state of mind.

Therefore, the topic we shall define as 'human nature issues' is so complex and all encompassing that it will be necessary to focus upon some of the most fundamental factors that affect us all, each in our own individual ways. Human nature issues generally occupy the attention and dominate the daily activities of the significant majority of people in this earthly life. It will be challenging to even superficially discuss many of the key aspects of human life here within the context of our overall theme and due to the length constraints that reasonably exist in a comprehensive discussion such as we are having in this book.

Our first critical realisation in this process is to acknowledge how intensely complicated and interrelated modern life has become upon a global scale in our present civilisation, which includes all environmental circumstances within the synergistic systems that serve to perpetuate our increasingly technologically focused society. As free-willed individuals, our role is to somehow fit ourselves into this earthly existence in some productive ways, while also attempting to create and sustain a life that is enjoyable, profitable, meaningful, as well as being conducive to raising our children with an opportunity for a quality future that enables us to achieve some of our goals in life. We must perceive the various elements required of us in our individual relationships with one another, as well as those inner requirements, that encourage us to unfold and develop the comprehensive levels of our overall being. There is a distinctive relationship between one's outer and inner lives and we are sincerely seeking to balance these aspects of ourselves in improved, self-directed, autonomous ways.

Many of the statements made here in our discussion are inclusive of numerous multi-dimensional ideas regarding interdependent reality systems and our individual perceptions of these often contrasting influences and emotional situations. Rather than to feebly attempt to relate numerous overly simplified concepts listed one after another, we must instead seek here to interrelate realities and concepts that challenge our intellect, stretch our spirit, test our character and serve to help define our evolving creative nature as human beings: eternally aware life forms that inhabit all manner of multi-dimensional reality systems throughout our immortal existence.

For some of us this style of addressing the controversial content of our subject matter is acceptable, if only marginally so, even from my own perspective. I found this part of our discussion here to be by far the most difficult, complex and odious to consider and express in this form. These human nature topics are essential to address in our overall subject matter, yet it was not particularly enjoyable to compile this information, rather it was extremely unpleasant from my perspective. It simply had to be written in this form, in my opinion. This information will certainly not be too pleasing for any of us to sincerely evaluate due to these excessively complex, challenging circumstances and lesser human tendencies. Most of us, myself included, will definitely find some of this information to be debatable, quite tedious, unpleasantly upsetting and very objectionable, boring, somewhat confusing, and sometimes just quite annoying to consider in the light of honest introspection and analysis.

The majority of us will discover that our minds can only consider a limited amount of this information and sincere reflection upon one's own life before some sort of distraction or sleep will be the preferred optional activity. The reason for this is that the human aspects of our comprehensive character are somewhat resistant to making certain realisations that identify areas of our lives, as individuals, as a species and as a developing civilisation, that now quite literally scream out to demand positive, constructive change, beneficial adaptation and progressive development.

Humanity was once composed of primarily nomadic hunter-gather type cultures that lived in small tribes with much simpler lives than we currently experience, so there is some residual tendency to resist innovative development, regardless of the reasons and benefits of making improvements in our personal and societal behaviours. So much of the positive change we could make in our personal lives is apparent to us and yet we often fail to make the necessary adjustments and instead wait until a crisis of some description shocks us into action or otherwise necessitates our remedial choices to save our lives, our marriage, our health, our financial circumstances, our ethical and moral values, or our spiritual condition. As a global society composed of diverse cultures and ethnic groups of people possessing a broad scope of attitudes and capabilities, our unique differences are attributes, talents, wisdom, strengths and experiences that exist as our civilisation's greatest accumulated asset that enables us as a developing species of life to accomplish incredible achievements. To continue our development as a global civilisation without experiencing a massive collapse of devastating proportions, it is necessary that we address and resolve a wide range of situational challenges, difficulties, counter-productive, wasteful attitudes and activities. We must do so while sufficient time remains to make the required changes to avert major disasters, just as we would try to do in our personal lives.

By reaching this point in our discussion, you have already considered a great many aspects of your life and levels of being that have not been recorded here as topics of consideration that are quite important to you in various ways. The most important aspects in this discussion are your responses to what occurs within the infinite possibilities of your own private thoughts and realisations. A significant portion of this inexplicable, mysterious introspection has had little direct relationship to what is written here and far more to do with improving and strengthening your inner relationship with the higher, vastly more aware, perceptive, capable inner aspects of your multi-dimensional immortal Soul, the real you existing within and through your present physical body. There is every reason to believe you will be able to evaluate the following concepts with the same clarity of mind, in spite of our natural tendency to wish to avoid thinking about the intensely pressing need to acknowledge and resolve these complex, multi-faceted, significant human nature issues in a large-scale societal manner; including each of us in our own individual ways.

Now we will begin to look more deeply at human life from a more objective, relatively alien seeming perspective. This perspective is unusual because it will in many ways not be congruent with the attitudes expressed by the mainstream international media, nor the prevalent political rhetoric, or religious dogma, or that of the education systems, or of the prevailing business community, yet much of what is stated here will make good sense and 'ring true' on many levels. We will examine what is presently occurring upon Earth, along with some basic history to remind ourselves of our habitual patterns of activity over the past few thousand years that recorded history serves to identify and characterise our actions so that we can learn and benefit from these events, if we wish to do so. Some aspects of our mind and character are challenged or stimulated by analysing situations that upset, or sometimes even anger or frighten us. Some of this information and opinions will be rather unpleasant to consider and will likely sometimes encourage you to assume an adversarial or contradictory viewpoint to what is being discussed, from your perspective. This is understandable and is actually a very good thing in this process of discovery for us all. I will initially be focusing exclusively upon some quite negative aspects of human nature while seeming to unfairly ignore and intentionally avoiding balancing these unfortunate realities with the positive, uplifting, noble, generous, charitable, saintly wisdom and true love that is also innate within our human nature. To consider these extremely distasteful, hideously malodorous aspects of our human nature is exceedingly offensive to us all and we need to recognise and accept this brutal fact. We would all prefer to gaze serenely and blithely upon the better aspects of our character as human beings, rather than to delve too deeply into the prevalent ideological ugliness that perverts our entire modern civilisation to its core, making a bitter hypocritical mockery of our noble spiritual intentions and aspirations.

This acknowledgement and evaluation process is intended to result in an increase in one's overall awareness regarding a broad scope of additional issues that will never even be mentioned here. By genuinely considering internally within one's comprehensive states of being what follows here, you will independently begin to expand your consciousness to include all manner of other events and attitudes that need to be discovered, considered, and resolved in various ways that you personally will be in a position to accomplish, through the unified efforts of your family, friends, business associates, religious members, cultural groups, school friends, governmental affiliates, and so on. We will encourage our minds and emotions to perceive earthly realities in somewhat new and unfamiliar ways, understanding that some of these realities and ideas are going to be upsetting and even diametrically opposed to the subtly programmed current state of human awareness that we now possess and accept as 'reality' here on Earth.

It is difficult to select topics and examples from the information available to us because much of it is so extremely unpleasant to consider in significant detail. In my own opinion, such hideously debauched human experience and factual information would be so unacceptable to most of us that it would quite naturally create a mental block within us to such an extent that our true purpose here would become incomprehensible. We seek to avoid challenging our present view of earthly reality in counter-productive ways. It is impossible to fully acknowledge the comprehensive perspective of life on Earth in our discussion here because to do so would be destabilising to our current world view, which is focused upon establishing an improved reality system here. To be too graphic in our following discussion regarding the depraved aspects of human nature's historical evolution on Earth to include vivid descriptions of human's lesser tendencies and proclivities would not readily assist in the overall purpose of accomplishing the necessary changes and adaptations in our attitudes and actions. Specifically, our minds are comfortable and secure when life's events proceed smoothly, in a relatively orderly, seemingly predicable manner. However, when things that we have long accepted as factual are revealed as being totally false or even partly incorrect, we tend to feel a bit uncomfortable and our world view is temporarily destabilised. The key word here is 'temporarily' because fairly soon, most of us are able to more fully consider the facts of any situation and make various mental adjustments, compensate, acknowledge, respond and then move forward with the new concepts acknowledged as being realities. This is a key evolutionary aspect involved in making progressive changes that are essential to our functional well-being as individuals and as a civilisation.

Let's now define our words more clearly and concisely since we have considered a variety of examples of what we term human nature issues. These are characteristics and tendencies within the human level of consciousness that generally speaking do not exemplify or reveal the better aspects of our moral, ethical, or spiritual states of being. These diminished qualities of attitude are expressed through all manner of what we can simply term to be 'small-minded' behaviours, as descriptive of their intent and application in life. Specific terminologies have been created within all languages to characterise, describe and define many of these woeful attitudes and their associated rancorous, unproductive, contentious behavioural characterisations. What follows is a limited list of words that help us to better characterise what we are defining as being the 'human nature issues' that we seek to overcome, improve and transform in beneficial positive ways. This is an essential developmental process as we mature; as individuals, as the human Species of life on Earth, and as eternally aware, spiritual beings that exist within the infinite multi-dimensional universes.

As we are defining them here, what we would include as negative human nature issues are: greed at the expense, misery and depravation of other people and life forms; jealousy and resentment of many types; seeking power, influence and control over other people and life forms exclusively for one's own or group's benefit to the knowing detriment of those being controlled and used; all types of unprovoked, unjustified, senseless aggression and violence toward others, especially those with relatively little ability to defend themselves. This would include economic attacks, as well as inappropriate, falsely critical, opinionated, judgemental statements and gossip about other people who harmlessly chose differing cultures, religion, opinions, beliefs and lifestyles to one's self or group.

Other negative human characteristics include: intentional lying, deceit, misleading, inaccurate and untruthful statements being presented as facts, and immorally acting upon such incorrect disinformation; and the establishment and implementation of unethical, immoral, amoral, corrupt behaviours for the exclusive benefit of one's own or group's self-interest. Likewise, the inappropriate use of legislative laws to legally condone behaviours that are morally and fundamentally criminal and harmful because they are opposed to the common good, justice, productivity and what benefits others in society. Those who falsely claim to be unaccountable or irresponsible for their own statements and actions due to rationalising, excuses, or pretences that are without factual basis, are knowingly false, or are based entirely upon misleading information. This would include the so-called 'insanity' or 'temporary insanity' plea in criminal or civil legal matters. Stealing all of its countless forms that include people that intentionally seek the protection of courts, lawyers as they knowingly and unjustly use the laws to legally rob or otherwise deprive people by using unfair and unethical contractual and business practices. Other times people are forced by circumstances beyond their control to steal to survive, such as when their crops & food have been plundered or destroyed by warfare or they are suffering from other forms of economic conflict and disparity. Often governments and bureaucracies inappropriately, unjustly and unsustainably tax its citizens excessively, then corruptly and inefficiently spend and squander public funds to enrich private interests that influence those in government office in all manner of unethical ways.

Murder in its countless forms, including the reprehensible indiscriminate use of various types of warfare that knowingly kill and injure civilians, as well as those serving in the armed forces on both sides of the conflict primarily to reduce the population and earn profits for vested interest groups who own companies that manufacture and finance the weapons and related supplies of war, as well as the medical facilities required to care for its injured victims. The intentional limitation of useful, beneficial, necessary work, industry, innovation, job skill education programs and construction projects to maintain a state of relative poverty and lack of opportunity among various social groups and regional areas globally, simply to maintain the status quo of existing corporate and financial controls on the economy. Incorrect or misleading information provided by government, industry, education, any type of research group or other such sources, especially the mass media outlets, such as the newspapers, magazines, radio, television and in the movies, including the improper glorification and sensationalism of all forms of violence, sexual exploitation, criminality and anti-social, self-destructive, unhealthy behaviours such as drug taking, alcohol abuse, cigarette smoking, suicide, etc.

All forms of abuse by wrongful acts committed by one or more persons against another; such as forced marriage, assault, rape, child molestation, intimidation, kidnap, and other such aggressive unwanted acts against any type of victim. Unnecessarily dangerous and health-harming work environments and inequitable economic conditions exist that abuse employees through excessive work schedules, extremely long hours, difficult tedious types of work without adequate rest periods, unjust fees and production quota fines being charged by employers to employees, unreasonably low or unfair wages, especially in locations of the world where poverty is high or the cost of living require higher wage than employers will pay, intentional forms of under-employment to keep workers desperate and other injurious, unrighteous workplace conditions. There exist debilitating standards of lowered education, health, transportation, sanitation, environmental protection, and decreased economic opportunity for some people which are perpetuated by governments, with the collusion of private and corporate well-protected interest groups who often avoid paying their fair share of taxes.

Some corporations knowingly operate businesses that do not serve the public good and only exist to further increase their owners' excessive profit margins through the harm, addiction and suffering of others. The tendency within one's self to primarily only apply one's best efforts to activities that do serve one's own personal self-interests in a direct manner, even if in some situations others are disadvantaged in that process. The ability to deceive one's self or others and to rationalise attitudes and behaviours that are inappropriate, unethical, immoral, and wrong primarily to benefit one's self or one's group. There is a counter-productive willingness to damage earthly environments without consideration to future generations or the other life forms that inhabit those areas. Intolerance and hatred toward others exists in all its forms. Many people are ungrateful for the assistance, generosity and love of others. There is an inaccurate belief among some of us that other people and life itself 'owes' one something that should require little or no efforts upon our part to achieve or obtain what we want. There are countless other similar examples of negative human nature issues that we could identify seemingly endlessly, which are socially, economically and spiritually damaging types of attitudes and behaviours that hurt and deprive us all in unfathomable ways.

These human nature issues usually contradict and ignore the philosophy age old wisdom of "do onto others as you would have them do onto you" or the more modern version, "treat others as you wish to be treated". Almost all of us will recall and acknowledge various times when we did not, in retrospect, be as honest, kind, thoughtful, understanding, patient, tolerant, loyal or loving with someone as we wish we would have been or as we definitely could have been. However, some people seem to have very little, if any, conscience or conscious concern or empathy or true sense of what is righteous behaviour when it comes to their attitudes and treatment of other people or life forms. It is these people who are almost always able in some way to justify and rationalise their behaviour, no matter how inappropriate, wrong, deceitful, harmful or painful to others that their actions may be. Such people rarely, if ever, apologise for any of their maladjusted actions because they seldom perceive they have made any errors in judgement, mistakes in life, or have treated others poorly or unfairly. If such people do at times apologise, then their apology may seem to be somewhat insincere and they may seem to believe that because they have made an apology, that it should eliminate the issue altogether from ever being considered to have occurred. Interestingly, such conscienceless people often tend to be very critical, judgemental, untrusting, fearful, and even angry or resentful toward others, as well as tending to blame others for any difficulties and problems they may encounter, even if they themselves are responsible for these situations. These people do not seem prone to examine their own attitudes, choices and behaviours by introspectively delving more comprehensively into life's situations in order to fully learn from their experiences the way to select better, more effective, appropriate forms of interaction from the discordant aspects of their own character and in their relationships with others. In other words, they do not comprehend many of life's more obvious lessons, so they tend to make few improvements in their attitudes and actions, and they become upset when life does not meet their expectations.

While it is tempting to first mention a few personal examples of human nature that we could all related to in our own lives, instead let's first consider a few simplistic basic ideas. In past ages, the world was once thought to be flat like a table and not round like a ball among most people. Another theory was that the Earth was the center of the entire Universe and everything else revolved around it. It may astound us to realise that there still exists a very small minority of people that continue to choose to believe in this 'flat earth' concept, as well as that the Earth is the center of the Universe and that no life exists anywhere else in the Universe. Thankfully, in the past four hundred years the number of these people has significantly reduced in proportion to the entire population. You will ideally recall the related fact that only a few hundred years ago that people, including scientists, astronomers and scholars, who were bold enough to publicly profess an opinion that the Earth was indeed round like a ball and that the Earth was not at the center of the Universe around which all other life revolved, were savagely tortured to encourage them to recant or renounce their opinion publicly. If they were unwilling to do so, they were then usually publicly burned alive or otherwise murdered by various inhuman methods by the so-called religious authorities of the day. These European religious authority figures, some of whom for many centuries had claimed to be infallible, divinely inspired, perfect human beings, ordained and religiously consecrated as God's representatives on Earth; had officially decreed that the accepted belief was that the world was flat and existed as the center of the Universe around which everything else in creation revolved. They had further decreed as immutable consecrated fact that the human life forms on Earth were the lone intelligent inhabitants of the Universe, and that God created the Earth in six days, with Adam and Eve being made in God's own image, and so on.

Today, in supposedly more 'modern' times the interesting theory that life on Earth did not evolve over billions of years, as current science seems to have conclusively proven in countless ways, is still under hot debate by millions of people who still adhere to the 'creationist' theory of the Universe, as espoused by a minority of Christian theologians. This is a simplistic example of how very slowly beliefs that have been taught in our societies over a long time period can be quite resistant to change, in spite of abundant volumes of indisputable evidence that contradicts and disproves one's preferred beliefs or attitudes. We must seriously consider our own mental outlook regarding any chosen belief we ourselves now hold, just as we would be ready to arbitrarily judge someone who in our example here, would continue to debate and contradict the theory of evolution. We may feel prone to rationally justify our human tendency to unfairly ridicule someone who honestly chooses to believe that God created the skeletons of countless trillions of ancient creatures within the strata of rocks in the purported time of Creation in six days. The point here is surely not to be critical and judgemental of people who wish to resist and deny the modern discoveries that challenge and finally disprove their preferred theories of how life was created on Earth, nor upon the legitimacy of the claims or accusations made by self-proclaimed religious or governmental authorities in earthly societies. Rather, we seek to address the manner in which all beliefs are developed, maintained and how throughout passing time that our thoughts and realisations are adjusted, refined and progressively developed by many people's accumulated experiences. This process facilitates human comprehension to more accurately attempt to describe, define and better approximate actual reality, so that our perceptions and beliefs are characterised by a significant degree of verifiable, quantifiable, recognisable, mutually acknowledgeable 'truth'.

The key points of consideration here are: First, over passing time our knowledge and awareness increase.

Second, that some people's thinking and realisation processes are clearly beyond the generally accepted norm of the age in which they reside historically and that these people pose new theories based upon their perceptions and experiences. Third, some people will always refuse to consider new information; and they will often without any verifiable proof aggressively debate, contradict, and vilify those people that seek to express any new ideas about the nature of reality. Fourth, it is very well-established historically that entrenched authority figures within the bureaucracies of religion, government and business will often be the most vehement in their attacks and denials of this new and different information.

This unreasonable resistance among entrenched authority to genuinely consider the merits of the evidence supporting or contradicting the situation, often continues to exist even long after the obvious facts are readily apparent to any sane, objective, rational, reasonable alternative perspective. In these situations no real consideration is publicly given to anyone who disagrees with the 'official' version of their selected purported 'facts', which are actually 'officially sanctioned' myths that serve vested interests in most cases. A prime current modern example of this situation would be the assertion sponsored by vested interest groups that nuclear energy is a safe, reasonable alternative to fossil fuels for our global civilisation and that nuclear waste can be safely stored under ground and not be harmful to future generations of life on Earth, as is still being parroted by some national governments in 2016.

Well, events since then confirm facts we will mention later here. Those people and organisations that disagree and rightly say, "Nuclear power in this current form is a toxic nightmare that must end." are often publicly ridiculed by the mass media, or pro-nuclear advocates in government and industry. Public mass media condemnation is increasingly the currently favoured method used to disparage new and inconvenient science, facts or alternative viewpoints to those being presented for public consideration by the so-called 'establishment' that owns and controls the mass media and holds a dominating influence globally on most governmental policy making processes. This fact is clearly and pervasively evident across a wide range of issues prevalent in our global society.

Fifth, and the last way we will identify that people with new ideas are dealt with in modern civilisation is that in many historical cases, the presenters of new and controversial information or ideas are threatened, attacked, jailed, and eventually are quite often killed for expressing their unique beliefs or evidence publicly. There is ample proof of this fact.

The belief in the 'flat earth' theory and the assertive autocratic manner in which it was rigorously defended for many centuries under the threat of death by those in religious and governmental authority for no obvious productive purposes is one simple clear example revealing countless human nature issues, many of which we will discuss in more detail here. It is exceedingly relevant to realise that an organisation professing to be religious and acting upon behalf of God would continuously over thousands of years knowingly, willing, and often with great enthusiasm chose to torture, jail and murder those people that believed differently than their version of man-written religious texts purporting to be God's law and reality system.

Now in early 2016, when this book is being edited for public access, a number of specific comments about world events will be deleted from the 2008 version. It is prudent to have these sections omitted about those people, governments, organisations, corporations and religions to avoid the potential for issues to be upsetting and providing provocation to the proven guilty parties for legal and other reasons because it distracts from our goal of achieving a more unified and peaceful human civilisation. The criminal actions and corrupted ethics of many of those people and institutions that hold trusted positions or social responsibility are well-documented by numerous researchers and 'whistle-blowers' who have proven these facts, for those with a curious mind to inquire into these issues, such as has been extensively done by this author.

Here, generally speaking, we do NOT feel the need or desire to name names, or point accusatory fingers of blame at the murders of millions of innocent people. Some few will be mentioned, as it is likely the way things are progressing on Earth, they will likely be held publicly and criminally liable for those heinous actions. These untold millions of victims do include those who feel so disheartened that they self-murder themselves by their own suicides. It is a revealing fact that so many people of all ages and cultures in modern civilisation, mostly due to the misery of their pitiful living conditions where they could endure no more, finally murder themselves; which is against spiritual law, as well as being a painful damaging reality that touches all of our lives in various ways.

The countless ways people are butchered or simply die of neglect or starvation, unnecessary diseases, manmade poisons, medical malpractice with harmful pharmaceutical drugs, and so on will NOT be fully addressed here, although these facts are not going to be ignored. Many acts of government and religious sponsored 'terrorism', militarism, sexism with the oppression of women and other forms of blatant slavery, which includes more modern forms of caste slavery, wage slavery and human trafficking. It is the prevalent war mongering that humanity has unwontedly inherited as an ongoing plague of misery over many thousands of years that is most revealing of the 'dark', violent, pestilent, parasitic, predatory influences who seek to perpetuate themselves to the suffering, detriment, and depravation of us all that must cease its vile activities.

Peace on Earth is already a reality for most people and life forms, who have found a degree of peace, hope and love in their hearts.

Those people, organisations, religions and institutions that promote warfare, human suffering, intentional scarcity, knowingly are responsible for allowing and actually encouraging the poisoning of food, water, air and soils; will be held criminally and civilly accountable for their crimes if the matters do not cease in the near future. The culprits are self-evident and brazen in their admitted responsibility and complicity with one another and can easily be identified in current times.

The key issue to start the 'recovery of honesty policy' is regarding 'official' US government admitting that many U.S. government agencies in cooperation with Israel enacted the government 'sponsored' concocted 'false flag' terrorist event known as "9/11" in New York City. They can also admit other similar attacks against Americans and all people of the world. Obviously that will involve also looking further back into history to Viet Nam, Nicaragua, Panama, and countless others … What a shocking embarrassing murderous painful expensive nonsense it has been and it is time to end it all once and for all, by the admission of guilt and making genuine apologies and efforts to improve things now and into the future.

We can easily see these same patterns repeated at Pearl Harbour where the USA government knew the Japanese attack was coming, yet did not serve the nation to protect its troops. Or, at 'Custer's Last Stand', to knowingly provoke conflict by sending 200 soldiers into a remote wilderness area where 20,000 Native Americans who were upset by their poor treatment by the European invaders were meeting at the time, and in many other such events. Humanity can identify untold thousands of events where innocent, non-combative civilians were massacred in relatively small numbers (Kent State shootings, or others by police upon unarmed individuals who were clearly not doing any criminal actions), or in the hundreds, thousands, or millions, such as in Cambodia, or by those supporting Stalin in Russia or Mao in China. Many pages of such examples could be provided. This bloody, murderous phase of human history simply must END NOW !!!!

In modern times in 2016, we can see clear examples of these attitudes and actions being perpetuated by various so-called 'leaders' in various nations while falsely purporting themselves to be 'people of peace' or 'leaders of the people' when they are actually serving the war and slavery machine, as we have seen endlessly throughout human written history. The truth is actually far worse than historians are allowed to reveal, as the established system chooses to hide behind lies and misinformation mixed with facts. We the people can and now do clearly discern the truth of matter. Greater awareness exists even among those who pretend to know nothing about it; by denial, blame, rationalisation, distractions, pointless debate, etc.

Therefore, in our discussion here, we will consider a variety of human life's inconsistencies and dichotomies to better develop an understanding of our own tendencies as a species and as individuals. Another example of inappropriate human nature issues would be that historically so many people professing to devote their entire lives to God, human decency, justice and godly values would knowingly and intentionally molest, or otherwise violently abuse innocent children under their care. The fact that some trusted modern religious authorities at the highest levels have sought to deny the conclusive evidence that some of their clergy have acted in unlawful, perverted, inappropriate, unwanted ways to manipulate, coerce or otherwise force themselves upon members of their religion in order to seek sexual gratification, seems to indicate an unwillingness to confront, admit or even apologise for some unacceptable circumstances in life. Another unfortunate, yet repeatedly proven example would be that any so called 'leader' of a nation or group of people would willingly disadvantage or even murder millions of its own loyal, hard-working citizens who had committed no crimes, such as Stalin, Mao and countless others in other nations in our long human history.

We must be aware, openly acknowledge and freely discuss the fact that quite evil aspects existing within human nature will often present one set of hypocritical beliefs outwardly to the public while another, diametrically opposed set of attitudes, motivations, intentions and premeditated actions are simultaneously functioning in direct opposition to those falsely stated, pretended attitudes and actions. In such situations false and misleading statements are intentionally made, often under the guise of righteous thought and activity, which actually are maliciously intended to deceive and distract people from the real facts and events being planned and enacted. The examples of this occurring in our world and private lives are virtually unlimited and are becoming increasingly pervasive due to the modern international media saturation to which most of us are continually exposed in our daily lives.

Before we address some of these 'larger' human nature issues, let us first begin to personalise the various ways we each and all participate to some extent through our thoughts and actions in both self-deceit and various ways that we seek to deceive others. We will identify and consider a few of our own personal attempts to falsely influence the attitudes and behaviours of others, as well as our selves, to better determine how these processes function within our private personal lives. In this way we will be less prone to assume an inappropriate attitude of pious, self-righteous indignation and condemnation in regard to the multitude of negative forces that so strenuously seek to adversely influence our lives within our global civilisation. The basic fact is that to varying degrees we all tend to lie to ourselves and others or rationalise our attitudes and behaviours in more ways than can be enumerated here.

Generally this variable state of mutual deception seems to have great merit in our earthly lives, as we must acknowledge to some extent. We may lie to avoid hurting other people's feelings, which is a feeble excuse more than a reason because relatively rarely will the truth hurt anyone more than lies will, in most situations. We can all think of innumerable examples to rationalise and justify various types of lies and this too is an indicator of how prevalent and condoned deceit is in our global civilisation now. The main deception we seek to focus upon ultimately is the often almost unconscious tendency in various circumstances to willingly deceive and intentionally lie to ourselves and others about many issues in our lives, as well as about aspects of our own character that we do not wish to acknowledge openly and honestly within our own minds.

Another excuse is that we lie to ourselves to improve and protect our self-image, which seldom works well in the longer term. Examples would be endless, but things such as "I will stop smoking when I see my health is being damaged", or "I will improve my eating habits when they begin to make me overweight", or 'I'll willingly allow my emotions and desires to control my mind and life choices because it makes me feel better about myself', or "This drinking of alcohol or taking of drugs is the only way I am able to cope with life and it makes me happier", or "It is OK if I am rude and unpleasant toward other people because they deserve it and it makes me feel better", or "I can steal or hurt others because they mean nothing to me" and so on and on, almost endlessly in our current society, as evidenced by our mutual actions.

As a society composed of like-minded individuals to a significant extent, this is a destructive, demented, unbalanced, diseased type of insane thinking that reveals a serious mental illness exists within our present culture. The fact that the insanity of our mass self-deceit is not even discussed openly is another sign of our denial, and further seeking to ignore the problem, individually and collectively. The extensive societal and personal damage that results from this type of unrealistic self-deceit is compounded dramatically because it is commonly accepted as normal simply because so many people participate in this maladjusted type of thinking process. This mental malady can only be corrected by improved, honest, more realistic perceptions, truthful thinking and positive, genuinely constructive actions. It is necessary to develop a functional personality to survive and thrive as a sane productive member of our clearly 'insane' society; so we must identify the ways and reasons we lie to ourselves and others to adjust and improve and correct our habitual thinking processes. It is essential to maintain a healthy, positive attitude toward one's self, yet we cannot do so by lying to ourselves because the actual truth is distasteful or seek to deceive others because we falsely believe that is acceptable behaviour that serves our interests.

How one affects others in society and our environment is a relevant factor in all of our lives today. Lying and deceit, like violence in any form, is rapidly becoming an antiquated, primitive, ineffectual, poor mode of thought and action in a progressive, modern truly civilised world society. Those people and interest groups who disagree with the above two statements are generally characterised by a diverse set of inappropriate attitudes, whose motivations originate strictly according to whatever achieves their own self-interests, and these types of people tend to rationalise, justify and condone any immoral, ill-advised, or otherwise counter-productive act as being acceptable, if they benefit and are allowed to continue doing so.

Therefore, whether we are speaking on a personal or societal level, we all have an influence on other people and our environments by our thoughts and actions. It is time that concerned people begin to sincerely strive to establish within modern society a higher set of internal moral values that dictate our actions other than those that modern legislation and religions would create for us. Negative forces within our civilisation are currently seeking to promote and produce a philosophy of thought that clearly tends to diminish truthful interaction within our societies. These loathsome tyrannical forces which are largely dominated by their own self-interested motives intend to redefine and debase our interpersonal relationships and limit the opportunity of economic sufficiency for the majority of people on Earth. They are knowingly and intentionally attempting to thwart our noble aspirations to create a civilisation characterised by higher human values, real freedom and opportunity to create a truly just, productive, peaceful, happy global society with acceptance of cultural and ethnic diversity.

The fact is that these demonically demented people are few in number and now are being greatly diminished in their ability of control the flow of events than they previously were in years gone by. This is increasingly self-evident. If those seeking to perpetuate war, scarcity and misery on Earth do not cease those vile, unwanted and predatorial actions, then they and their allies will be held personally accountable. One would not want to foolishly be devoted to thwarting the Will of God, or murdering Its' Children and other creatures, truly. Really, these are interesting times and we will discuss these things further.

Instead of striving together to establish the conditions to create a better possible world civilisation than we now possess; we the thinking perceptive people of the world can now clearly perceive the existence and ongoing activities of the carefully fabricated, insidiously interrelated, vested activities of a well-entrenched, dictatorial, powerful minority of unethical, influential, wealthy people working in unison to establish a civilisation characterised by autocratic, militaristic domination, fanatical totalitarian government policies under the false facade of purported democratic values, touted by media propaganda and various forms of educational indoctrination to establish hypnotic acceptance within the 'dumbed down' people. Their concerted, combative, comprehensive misinformation campaign is based upon false, unprincipled and misleading logic that is designed to encourage, coerce or simply force the vast majority of people to accept their intended depraved, vile, unkind, unjust, corrupt, inefficient, pathetic social system that hypocritically enforces inequalities, servitude, lack of ethics/values, rampant poverty and generally a lack of true opportunity on the vast majority of the world's population. The primary method in this madness is to institute a dishonest, deceitful, manipulative, cunningly devious, inequitable social and adversarial cultural system through an endless series of attacks upon human decency, honesty, justice, freedom, truth, ethics, genuine productivity and culturally meaningful activities. The issue here is revealing, discussing and eliminating the ability of those greedy, controlling, vested 'self-interests' to continue to utilise deception, lies, misinformation, and fear mongering that constantly upon our society and within our individual lives. We must and are in the process of exposing the situation so that we can begin to seriously commit ourselves to creating viable equitable solutions.

How do we respond to deceit in our individual lives? Personally speaking for myself, I clearly recognise and realise that lies, misinformation, deception, manipulation, and the related force of one's self-interested will-power over others is a vital fundamental causative factor in most of the unresolved problems and negative circumstances that so acutely plague our current civilisation and many of our personal lives.

How about you? How do you view the effects that lies, deceit, manipulation for one's own self-interests have upon you, your life and our societies locally and globally? We could choose to accept that lies and deceit are an integral component of modern civilisation, yet we can already determine where that attitude eventually will take us, since we already see this pathetic miserable situation clearly being evidenced within our global civilisation now.

Let's consider an obvious personal example that typifies certain attitudes to better clarify the results of lies in our lives personally speaking before we examine some of the larger lies within our civilisation at this time in its history. Imagine the adverse affects upon a relationship between husband and wife or lovers who falsely professes to be fully committed within a mutually agreed, monogamous, loyal, faithful and truly loving relationship, yet one or both knowingly lies and misleads their partner over passing time for their own self-interest, pleasure or other reasons. In this process, the deceitful person(s) would be violating the other person's trust, emotional security and their innate right to receive honesty and decency in their interpersonal interactions. The fact is that every aspect of their relationship will be damaged, diminished, confused, and debased by such dishonest attitudes and actions. We each and all can usually easily point the finger of blame and self-righteous condemnation at others, yet we seldom are so eager to identify ourselves when we are lying to others, or ourselves, or are acting out of the lowest aspects of our own human character.

Have you ever intentionally lied to someone in a serious personal relationship to protect your self-interest to their detriment or withheld important information from another person about your feelings or intentions? Very likely the honest answer to that question would be to some degree to the affirmative: yes. We have all been confronted and challenged at times by our conflicting, discordant internal thoughts and feelings about another person or in our deliberations regarding a difficult decision in our lives. Life's complexities demand thorough evaluation of our thoughts and feelings to select responsible, reliable, just, kind actions from the available choices in a manner that our quality values and motives are applied to everyone's better interests, in an ideal world view. Life presents all manner of differing choices to us in our daily lives. Many of these options tend to challenge us to make the right and better decisions from a moralistic, ethical aspect of our higher character, while simultaneously conflicting aspects of our lower human tendencies lacking ethical restraints also seek expression. The focal problem here seems to be that modern society and culture seems to be pervasively suppressing, denying and undermining many aspects of our higher character in a multitude of ways, intentionally and unconsciously.

A key issue we must therefore address is developing methods and motives for limiting our tendencies toward fostering self-deception within our minds to the best of our ability as individuals and within all aspects of our communities, cultures, religions, businesses and governments. To accomplish this, it is helpful to establish a mutually agreeable comprehensive definition regarding the nature of a lie, deceit or deception. Basically a lie is an untrue statement made with an intention to deceive. This would include false or misleading beliefs and attitudes that we incorrectly think are truths within ourselves. We must acknowledge that there will always be some areas of differing perception and opinion, depending upon one's assessment of the facts. It is usually possible by analysing all of the evidence objectively to determine a relatively clear understanding of actual unbiased truth and accommodate various opinions as well. Intentional omission of pertinent comprehensive information, or telling 'half truths', is also a prevalent form of dishonesty. What we are truly seeking to reduce, limit, avoid and ideally eliminate is the use in any form of intentional lies, or overtly misleading information being used as a manipulation of the facts to knowingly be applied to disadvantage other people, or earthly environments and other sentient life forms.

We must publicly acknowledge that some inherent deceit exists within our current civilisation through its cunning, manipulative use of misinformation and blatant lies. The practice of lying in various ways has become a pervasive, commonly accepted behaviour and 'art form' among people and institutions that use this dishonest method of false communication to achieve their objectives. Lies in all their forms that are intended to mislead and manipulate others are applied by some people within every aspect of human interaction to some extent. On Earth today there exists willing, intentional, widely practiced misrepresentation of the real facts and the use of falsehood primarily motivated by greedy devotion to one's self interest, often at the expense or suffering of others. Other times people lie simply because they like the sound of the lies better than the truth, or they conveniently do not want to know the actual facts, or simply refuse to express the truth. Outright lies and misleading statements are a defining characteristic of our human nature at this time in our history as a species.

The key realisation here is that we all absolutely must begin to adjust our attitudes and behaviours in positive, beneficial ways to become more truthful, genuine and fair with ourselves and among our interpersonal relationships. This change toward honesty and accountability must occur without excessively focusing retrospectively upon apportioning blame, condemnation punishment, guilt, shame, self-degradation, and so on. This tendency toward deception developed for many reasons throughout mankind's evolutionary processes, so now our efforts must be directed upon honest, accurate communications and verifiable assessments of the truth in all manner of situations.

"How can and why do so many unkind, unjust, inappropriate, despicable events happen in our modern societies?" we must ask ourselves. Living within this physical system of reality necessitates an enormous amount of interaction among various powerful forces that utilise a vast array of circumstantial relationships in extremely subtle ways, some being to the detriment of our civilisation, its people and the earthly environment upon which we all depend. It is obvious that many of modern society's attitudes and activities are wasteful, counterproductive, destructive, inappropriate, unwise and critically flawed when analysed in regard to the best long-term interests of our civilisation. Unfortunately, a part of humanity's group conscience seeks to ignore, deny and rationalise these facts along with the vile events of our historical past that are extremely distasteful to acknowledge publicly. Therefore, our social pattern has been to cyclically repeat the errors of the past and continue to make poor choices in the ongoing present.

One such example is our global civilisation is now knowingly perpetuating a primitive, warlike, adversarial international social and economic system under the false guise of seeking to create peaceful cooperative relationships between all nations. The proof of this fact is the continual massive military expenditures among many nations internationally, which has persistently escalated over countless hundreds of years. Most government propaganda and diplomatic rhetoric consistently falsely professes to be genuinely committed to seeking peaceful relations among all nations, even while wars are already being aggressively waged in many cases.

Any person with even a feeble functional mind can easily determine by examining the abundant evidence that the vast majority of the more powerful and wealthy nations have been and now are endlessly 'preparing' for war. Every day massive amounts of taxpayer's hard-earned money and labour is being unwisely squandered upon excessive expenditures upon weapons of war, to train our young men and women to kill one another, and to pay the accruing financial interest payments for taxpayer's debts to banks and military equipment suppliers. Warfare is a devastating plague-like social and economic process that has been perpetuated on Earth for many centuries for a wide variety of reasons. An examination of modern nation's military budgets establishes their ongoing, decade after decade build-up and the development of increasingly destructive weapons systems that clearly identifies these governments are currently engaging in a warlike mentality. Large segments of industrial productivity are presently being devoted to preparing for the wars of the future, and basically dealing with the 'casualties' in a dismissive manner.

These planned wars that would destroy our civilisation as we now know it are intended to reduce the population, stimulate selected national economies and increase the wealth of weapons manufactures and their owners' family fortunes. Wars also are intended to subjugate and dispossess the vast majority of Earth's people, capture control over dwindling natural resources, and to insure that current distribution of material wealth and the subtle forms of despotic control of human populations remains firmly in the hands of the relative few people and organisations that now control these resources and decision making processes internationally. Such warmongering forces are dominated by their own self-interest to such an extent that they rationalise and widely promote their view that continued periodic wars have many benefits, and ignore that wars create socio-economic devastation, incredible destruction of humanity's accomplishments, untold depravation, misery and suffering for earth's people. Therefore, I know that modern government funded warfare and preparation for war is a gross and inappropriate misuse of human efforts and resources and is a very bad thing for our earthly civilisation, from my perspective. I am prepared to debate the topic succinctly.

Today these highly debatable concepts regarding the pitiful, nonsensical so-called 'benefits' of warfare are rapidly becoming publicly recognised as being inane, insane, inadvisable, exceedingly counter-productive, and unacceptable in a truly civilised world. Weapons of extensive mass destruction, such as nuclear, chemical and biological weapons systems, have been created at incalculable financial cost to human civilisation. This multiplicity of modern weapons systems can destroy the environment completely, making Earth uninhabitable to any human life forms for many thousands of years. In modern times, any warfare utilising such weapons systems that will so drastically ruin our earthly environments is an unacceptable policy internationally. Yes, of course there are weapons that kill only the life forms and do not destroy the environment, but this does not make that form of warfare any better or wiser.

People of Earth must demand positive reform immediately to avert this insane rush into another global war. It is absolutely nonsensical to argue that modern warfare in any of its many forms is a viable international policy for any nation and to profess otherwise is completely false and untenable. The advocacy and the overt and covert preparations for war among so many nations proves this idiocy and insanity that has become widely accepted internationally among those responsible for our peace, security, prosperity and sustainability in governmental and business sectors of our civilisation. The people must now demand a positive change in policy that is based strictly upon creating a sustainable, equitable, environmentally responsible civilisation that engenders meaningful productivity for the world's people.

So-called 'democracy' as it exists in 2016 has proven itself to be simply another form of autocracy, a totalitarianism that is dominated by wealthy individuals and international corporate businesses that largely control and influence party politics according to their self-interest, not the best interests of the people or humanity's future or that of earthly environments.

A quick trip down the 'memory lane' of human history will remind us of our primitive, war-like attitudes. This is included here just in case some people would choose to forget, ignore or debate these facts and instead focus upon the artistic window dressing and hypocritical moralistic rhetoric that our civilisation so dearly prefers to focus its attention upon as it prepares for the next war. Then when war begins again, society proceeds almost without conscience to knowingly slaughter innocent people by the millions and destroy the efforts of billions of people in building our civilisation, only to rebuild it again. We will not attempt to mention the full extent of the unpleasant truths regarding the violent, destructive, oppressive history which characterises aspects of our current civilisation. The awful truth of the extent of human sadism, evil and torture by oppressors knows no limits and it is not reasonable to specify the manners in which people are tortured and murdered here in this discussion.

Suffice to say that the abdominal, vile set of human indecencies committed upon one another by those few people holding violent power over one another are horrible beyond any description we could provide. However, these inhuman advocates and perpetuators of war always seek to somehow justify and rationalise these heinous acts of torture, depravation and senseless murder as being necessary, from their insane, distorted, perverted perspective. We must identify the mentally ill, deranged war mongers for what they obviously are: insane people and institutions that now urgently require unified social action to limit and ultimately remove their power to wage war. Modern weapons of mass destruction would kill and deprive humanity of our ultimate destiny as civilised life forms: to live peaceful, productive, happy, truly meaningful lives characterised by a sustainable predictable good future for our descendents.

History has been 'sanitised' (intentional omission and distortions of the facts) and is actually a work of fiction to a significant degree. What follows are a few basic reminders of these factual events in our history. We all will be aware of the millions murdered and enslaved by the Roman conquests beginning about two thousand years ago. The resulting Roman Empire served as a foundation for the current so-called 'western' culture in Europe. About five hundred years ago, about the time when Christopher Columbus discovered America, the oppressive feudal monarchical European governments began their earnest attempts to dominate the world militarily, ideologically, economically and religiously. Western cultural practices initially professed to be trade orientated, yet as soon as possible the military conquest of indigenous peoples throughout the world followed. These imperialistic murderous colonial policies were always sanctioned by a narrow-minded version of Christian religion which falsely deemed that all people who were not baptised, properly practicing Christians were heathen savages.

This pompous, arrogant, inappropriate and incorrect attitude viewed all indigenous people basically as lower life forms that could be exterminated as could any wild animal. The native peoples who were not murdered if they resisted the invaders of their ancestral lands were often forcibly enslaved to work in inhuman conditions for their self-appointed masters or were transported to work elsewhere as slaves, as was a centuries old practice. Additionally, many millions of native people were intentionally and unintentionally infected with diseases which they had no natural resistance and they were murdered in their millions in this manner. These indigenous people were indoctrinated with unfamiliar religious beliefs and practices that seemed cruel, vindictive, and oppressive to the native peoples of the world.

These native peoples were actually the legal resident owners for thousands of years before their violently conquered lands were unjustly claimed and taken by military force or unfair financial agreements or treaties by their oppressors. Leading up to and during this historical period, various so-called 'religious' wars were fought among differing cultures. One example is the Crusades which were between the Christian Europeans and the Muslims that mostly inhabited the Middle East and Northern Africa, which continues to some extent into the present time. There were also the Mongol wars, Chinese wars and countless other wars over thousands of years, occurring in cultures around the world and into pre-historic times. So, we must admit to ourselves that on Earth warfare has had a long, destructive, unholy life.

Many of these wars were fought in the name of religion. The fact that this practice of war in the name of God and to promote one's man-made religious beliefs continues today is an appalling reality that proves the modern human civilisation has learned very little from its bloody heinous past. Any religious leader that advocates war or violence against another differing race, nation, culture or religion is hypocritical and is not truly a man or woman of God, since we accept that God and our Prophets or saviours all profess God as being a loving, constructive, creative force that seeks the best for humanity and life on Earth. Warfare is clearly an unjust, violent, aggressive, evil and unproductive futile activity so it is heretical and hypocritical for anyone professing to be religious or spiritual to advocate war, except in clear cases of self-defence, especially in a role as a holy representative of their religion.

Likewise, any form of religious oppression such as the heretical, abdominal, unjust persecutions by the Catholic Church during the Spanish Inquisition upon anyone who was deemed to be a threat, or who held differing beliefs was persecuted, tried as criminal heretics, often tortured to confess what were deemed to be 'sins', or even to accuse other people of alleged crimes or so-called profane acts in the eyes of the church. These tortures and unfair trial-like prosecutions were usually sanctioned by national and regional government, as were the subsequent cases in which those found guilty were dispossessed of their wealth and property, imprisoned, excommunicated from the religion, or in many situations, the purported offenders were unjustly murdered. The manner in which these tortures and murders were perpetrated include; being burned alive, hung by the neck or otherwise crucified, decapitated by various means, drown, or simply physically torn apart by various horrible methods. These sadistic, often public executions were intended to create fear in the people so that they would not wish to resist their vile hypocritical oppressors in any way. Other similar events in other nations by other so-called religious authorities have occurred throughout human history. These at times included human sacrifices made falsely in the name of God, in which innocent people were killed by having their heads cut off, their beating hearts cut out of their bodies and removed while they were still conscious and such other acts of depravation and sheer evil, all in the name of some religious beliefs by men falsely professing to possess and represent godly virtues. The stoning to death of people for non-violent offences is a similar example of religiously sanctioned barbarism and savagery. The truth is self-evident in these horrendous evils in the name of religion.

    In more modern times, we have witnessed the 'western' government instituted and sanctioned massacres of indigenous peoples upon every continent in the world over hundreds of years: the Native Americans, the African natives, the Australian Aborigines, the Asian people and countless smaller groups and tribes of native people living freely and usually peacefully upon their own lands. Then we have in more recent history witnessed the mass murders of the Jews and other nationalities by the Nazis and Japanese, Stalin's mass murders of Russian citizens, the Chinese purges within China and Tibet, the religious and ethnic genocides in Yugoslavia, Ethiopia, Sudan, Congo, Northern Ireland, Cambodia, South Africa, Zimbabwe, and countless other places, tribal genocides in Rwanda, Viet Nam, Myanmar (Burma), South America and elsewhere across the world, on and on, almost endlessly.

Today we see much of the discord internationally has been focused upon events in the Middle East due to the wealth of oil and natural gas located in this region of the world. At the heart of this conflict is the fact that the Jews living in Israel have denied human rights and autonomy to the Palestinian people, both of whom have inhabited that area of land in the Middle East and whom are genetically inter-related from the same 'tribe' of people thousands of years ago. That conflict involves diverse groups of Christians, Muslims and Jews in a religious, territorial, political, cultural, and resource-driven state of ongoing warfare which is presently destabilising the entire global civilisation in various ways. The international dimensions of the ongoing war in the Middle East which has been a continual cycle of violence, retribution and revenge has been drastically incited, manipulated, and provoked by the widespread involvement of government sponsored and independently funded terrorism in this and other regions of the world. The Jews in Israel have every right to defend their homeland and faith from those nations and religions seeking to destroy them. However, apparently the Israelis have failed to learn the painful lessons that oppressors, such as the Nazis were to the Jews in the Second World War, are never truly justified in autocratically enslaving or denying other ethnic, racial or religious groups their innate human and political rights to existence with some semblance of autonomy and freedom from persecution. The entire world must learn a valuable lesson through this cycle of violence that can lead us through this self-inflicted quagmire of misery, oppression, revolt and suffering toward the creation of improved interpersonal, diplomatic, peaceful, equitable, genuine ways to resolve reasonable disputes and accommodate the needs of all people.

It is absolutely wrong and totally unacceptable to aggressively initiate violence, to attack another nation, group or person, simply to steal and illegally take by sheer military or physical capability, others' wealth, resources, land, or other possessions. Likewise, the practice of slavery reveals the very worst in humanity. In more modern times, the 'western', so-called 'developed' nations have refined and adjusted the practice of enslaving people significantly from the olden days when they unjustly subjugated the indigenous peoples of Earth by murderous militarised colonisation processes. The western nations' own native indigenous European populations had already been enslaved by various methods over thousands of years, so for its common people there was no hope or way to escape or avoid the powers of these so-called 'civilised' oppressors of true freedom. Slavery, in all of its many forms, was widely institutionalised within the so-called 'civilised' world by the ruling 'royal' families, governmental, religious and business systems that reveal the malevolent, harmful, deceitful, hypocritical nature of many of our current civilisation's activities. It is an undeniable fact that many of these noxious, uncivilised, inappropriate, oppressive, inequitable, wrongful attitudes and activities continue upon various levels within our modern day civilisation. Much propaganda is constantly being devoted in all nations to rationalising the reasons for maintaining these ill-advised, unacceptable, injurious, counter-productive workplace situations as dominating influences upon our current modern civilisation and its people, institutions and our economic systems.

We must acknowledge that it is a basic factual truth that our global civilisation for thousands of years has relied upon a horrible, violent, counter-productive, and oppressive war driven social and economic system. We definitely do NOT condone, nor accept the continuance of the current situation. To address such awful realities opens one up to the accusation, "Don't bring up that unpleasant past because all of that is over, so let's focus upon the present time and doing the right things now." Whenever someone is reasonable, perceptive and moral enough to point out the various negative characteristics of human nature in the past, the present or those that indicate problems for our future; then usually there is upset, denial, diversion, distractions, some feeble and ineffectual rebuttal and always lots and lots of lies, falsified documents and counter-accusations. Recall that Jesus Christ was crucified for publicly stating facts of daily life that offended the vested interests of both the Roman conquerors and the Jewish religious leaders. One example was removing the money changers from religious temples. So, in Jesus (or Martin Luther King Jr. or President J. F. Kennedy) we have a fine example of someone who was publicly 'put to death' for truthfully and openly expressing social realities, as well as spiritual realities. We are still fighting over these issues. Unfortunately, the basic realities remain exactly as they were two thousand years ago. This is why we must resolve these issues here and now, or continue to suffer the horrendous consequences that could end civilisation as we now know it and lead to environmental devastation on Earth.

When the full set of deleterious facts are presented to perceptive, aware, informed, intelligent thinking people who have already observed and commented upon as being unacceptable are conclusively proven by unfolding events, then it is often too late to take the necessary appropriate remedial actions to solve the problems, or hold the guilty parties personally accountable which does not really assist the victims. Such an example now is similar to the relatively few knowledgeable people who publicly warned that Germany was preparing militarily and culturally to start the Second World War. They correctly predicted that widespread war and genocide would subsequently occur, only if the Germans were allowed to continue their military build-up in contravention to existing international laws to prevent that from occurring based upon the experiences of the First World War. They were largely ignored or had their voices of concern suppressed by various methods. Had these people's warnings about the Germans been heeded and acted upon promptly to prevent the massive illegal weapons development program of the Germans and their allies leading up to the Second World War, then that catastrophic war would have not occurred. Then there would have been no need for the feeble excuses, rationalisation, excuses and apologies or meagre financial compensation to the victims. The innocent people that suffered in that war included those who fought in uniforms from every nation, just as well as the innocent civilians, who all gave their lives and suffered countless losses in their efforts, property and shattered dreams of their desires to live a better life characterised by peace and prosperity. Those who fought to protect us from the Nazis, the Japanese and their allies in the Second World War helped to avoid the creation of a vast international global fascist state, yet what was the result we see before us now? Here in early 2016, we see the morally, spiritually and economically bankrupt U.S. government continuing to foster, sponsor and promote warfare, social destruction, and religious and international conflict while hypocritically (lying) 'talking peace'. This same pattern can be seen repeating endlessly in our human civilisations' history. We clearly see the development and manifestations of a predominant militaristic attitude that reveals that a relatively small portion, of the otherwise mostly sane human population, is actively devoted constantly to maintaining and breeding a warfare mentality within our global civilisation in order to maintain the existing social and economic structure we see today globally.

At some point in time the violent human past of our current civilisation is arbitrarily, publicly, internationally deemed to "be in the past" and it becomes a taboo subject for perceptive, socially aware and ethically responsible people to point out similarities between previous perilous catastrophic historical events and those akin to our present time in history. Those brave people who do publicly acknowledge and proclaim the problems of the past are reoccurring in the ongoing present are usually ridiculed, persecuted, attacked and otherwise chastised for speaking of their perceptions, especially if it contradicts the socially accepted norms of the nation or culture within which they live. If one is to extrapolate upon current events as indicators of unpleasant, cataclysmic potential future events, then they are likely to be labelled as a scare monger, a lunatic, a disloyal fanatic, a terrorist or other such derisive classifications. In modern society, public attacks upon those people and organisations that seek social justice are often perpetrated by the media; the legal fraternity, business and financial interests; various government and related bureaucratic institutions, such as the tax department, regulatory authorities; or diverse religious authorities; or by covert intelligence organisations and their various operatives. In any case, there exist a variety of forms of control and oppression that are utilised by those people and institutions that protect the interests of those powerful few materialists who quietly control and direct our civilisation's policies and economic system from behind 'hidden closed doors'. These powerful rulers in our modern civilisation have their own best interests in mind currently, just as they have done for many centuries of our history. It is now time to clearly identify the types of thinking that formulate the governmental and economic policies that have created so much unnecessary suffering, deprivation and destruction on Earth for thousands of years. It is now time to alter in a positive, productive, non-violent manner, the ways in which our civilisation functions so that real, lasting peace and prosperity with opportunity, freedom and justice for all people and life forms on Earth is possible and is achievable in our present generational lifetime.

It is now time for the self-deceit and internal lies to end in our own personal lives by those of us who are willing and able to take this bold, beneficial step forward toward establishing a more positive state of being. In these ways we can then better assume roles that encourage this developmental process to occur within our wider social, governmental, institutional and international communities.

There are numerous examples of beneficial progressive social and cultural adaptations occurring within modern civilisation. We more easily recognise the technological and materialistic achievements, yet it is the attitudinal, philosophic and cultural developments that establish the basis for our true progress which is revealed by our civilisation's civility, discernment, justice, dignity and virtuosity in its human diplomatic and environmental interactions. One significant example of beneficial social change is observed within the institution of marriage among most modern nations and religions. In the past couple generations there has been some social, legal and religious adaptation to enable marital partners who no longer wish to remain as husband and wife, the opportunity to willingly separate temporarily or permanently. Systems of socially and legally recognised divorce have been designed to facilitate and regulate this vexing, problematic, emotionally painful, upsetting process. Generally and idealistically speaking, no longer is someone forced against their will to remain married to someone they do not like, love or wish to be with in modern society. This is a positive development that has improved our societies because it considers the happiness of marital partners and their children in acknowledging that some people no longer wish to remain together. Divorce can be a difficult and unpleasant experience for all involved due to the various emotionally painful and financially challenging situations; however, it is much better than the lesser alternatives, as existed in past ages.

To further develop this concept and relate it to interpersonal interaction we can consider some reasons for divorce. A few of the common reasons why people no longer wish to remain together may include the following: within a marriage one spouse may feel unappreciated, somewhat ignored or even is being abused to the point they believe their partner does not truly love them or is incapable of ever genuinely loving them; or that one or both partners believes the other is not doing their fair share of the work in the relationship in a way that contributes to the income of the family or the smooth functioning of the household; or that one or both partners are involved intimately with people outside of their marital partnership; or that one partner is spending too much time away from the family; or because the couple no longer enjoy spending time together; or believe their partner is preventing them from being themselves by their demands and attitudes, and so on. Often both partners have quite valid, reasonable, legitimate, observations and critical comments to make about one another, some of which are admitted or proven to be correct by both partners. In such situations where people decide that divorce offers hope of additional peace, sanity and security in their lives, we can usually identify and empathise with someone who has made such a decision. Perhaps it has happened to you personally in some way.

Surely my own divorce ten years ago was one of the best decisions of my entire life, regardless of how difficult and painful the experience proved to be at the time after ten years of arduous marriage. It is so unpleasant to be treated poorly, or be endlessly accused of something you did not do, or try to change one's character and activities to please another person, or accept another person doing things one believes are inappropriate, rude, and upsetting, or especially to know one's children are being damaged and upset by the unresolved disagreements. When other people close to us knowingly commit various types of acts to disadvantage, anger or hurt us, then we know they do not truly care about our personal well-being. Whether an aggressive, dishonest, vindictive, disloyal, or uncaring attitude motivates the conduct of a marital partner, a parent, a business partner, or even an unfair government toward its citizens; we recognise that malicious, mean-spirited acts of intentional disregard for our well-being, security, and peace of mind reveal a simple truth that such an attitude should not and must not assume control over our lives to our detriment, misery and depravation.

When we consider objectively how we are viewed by and treated by other people and institutions in life, we learn that we must establish a significant degree of autonomy in our lives if we are to be free to seek what is best for us as individuals. What is it like to be unjustly accused of something you did not do, especially by someone you know is being dishonest, disloyal or aggressive toward you? What is it like to realise that they do not care at all about any upset, inconvenience or emotional damage that such false accusations create for you? How do you feel if these personal attacks are intentionally designed to function as a distraction and an aggressive form of self-defence when they know they already are maliciously doing hurtful, inappropriate things to you and you begin to address the issues directly to seek resolution? Suppose you know definitively that something dishonest or illegal did occur and when you confront the person or instigator of the situation, instead of discussing the relevant issues, they prefer to ignore the issue, or deny any liability in spite of the conclusive evidence, or even verbally attack you with unrelated nonsensical issues, initiate legal court actions, make threats, or use physical violence. This process could include typical events like a theft, a breach of trust, an act of disloyalty, or through ongoing intentional deceit that was proven from clearly verified evidence or experience. Please carefully recognise that when someone is accused or confronted by the person with the distasteful undeniable facts, then quite often the deceitful perpetrator, instead of admitting their guilt, will subsequently express a series of vehement denials, perhaps some other forms of verbal abuse or threats and various other counter-accusations against one's self.

    A specific example of this type of situation would be if you caught your marital partner being involved in an intimate relationship with another person. Then when you addressed the deceit and lies involved in the experience, your partner would either deny the obvious facts or simply insist that your behaviour, attitudes and actions were the provocation for their actions. They would seek to falsely use your character or behaviour to justify or to somehow condone their actions, even though they may have never previously discussed their displeasure with you directly nor said they would seek intimacy elsewhere. In other words, you justly express a dissatisfaction that you have been deceived, robbed, offended, or deprived or hurt in some manner by another person and they then basically respond with either denials, or words to the effect that you deserved it, or even with threats and counter-accusations. Sometimes they would respond with a more plaintive response such as, "Please forgive me, I did not know what I was doing, it was a foolish mistake and I'll never do it again" and so on.

Most of us at some time or another in our lives, have been caught by others doing something inappropriate or sought to deceive others over something and been quite guilty. Likewise, we ourselves will have from time to time been the victims of such unkind, deceitful behaviour by other people. Therefore, we all at some time or another will have experienced emotionally upsetting situations of various types. In some of these circumstances the events are so extremely distressing and disappointing that you would never have believed your, or the other person's responses and reactions or state of mind, without having had that memorable experience. What is odd is people with a functional conscience can sometimes feel as hurt and humiliated by acting inappropriately as would those who have been victimised in such an event. It is important to consider in relation to all of these so-called human nature issues are that some people, corporations and social or religious institutions possess little or no active conscience. This trait is among the key criteria used by mental health professionals in evaluating someone as being sociopathic or psychopathic. Consequently, these people usually express no remorse because they do not perceive nor feel guilt or shame, regardless of the nature of their actions or attitudes. They may tend to 'play act' some empathy or compassion, yet the facts are proven by their premeditated actions; not their false forms of professed conscience, or requests for forgiveness when caught.

The key factor we will assess is everyone can be identified by their actions, far more than by their words, assurances and promises. In our society there exist countless people and groups that seek to hide their true thoughts and actions and those who covertly pursue unwholesome activities hidden from public view or even from their family, friends, work associates or others close to them for reasons they rationalise and justify from the perspectives of their own self-interest. We will come back to the issue of conscience in relation to human nature issues as this discussion progresses.

For now, let's generalise about a variety of concepts we all will be familiar with in our own lives. Please try to recall an event or any number of events in your own life that lead you to being in some ways seriously disadvantaged or even harmed to the extent that you considered yourself as having been betrayed or victimised by others' attitudes and actions. This could include imagining a previous situation in which you yourself have intentionally or unconsciously treated someone in a deceitful, inappropriate, uncivil, or possibly even in an unlawful or immoral manner. For many of us, it hurts 'enough' to known you wronged another person, yet being 'on the receiving end' of unkind or inappropriate treatment, as we all know, seem to hurt and upset us far worse.

Human nature issues know no boundaries. Some human activities are quite unpleasant, unkind, vile, malicious, villainous, and can be premeditated with careful planning, or in other situations may seem to develop virtually unconsciously with minimal overt conscious intent. Basic human character possesses an innate capability in certain circumstances to think and act inappropriately for an incredible diversity of reasons. The human saying, "the ends justify the means" is a perfect example of this type of amoral and immoral philosophy that has resulted in so much destruction, anguish, intentional injury, violent death and unhappiness in our lives and world civilisation.

This observation is definitely not to unjustly characterise human nature itself as being inherently bad, evil, negative, murderous, unloving, unjust or unkind by its actions. Rather, we need to address the entire scope of human behaviour here. We need not and must not pretend falsely about the entire scope of human attitudes and behaviour, nor ignore or deny any aspect of reality. What we will do is more thoughtfully examine many issues that relate directly to creating the lives and world that we now live in by every possible means of assessment. We will not allow ourselves to simplistically perceive human beings to be predisposed toward evil nor necessarily to be noble and good in character. Choice and the overall result of one's thinking and actions primarily determine whether or not something is right and proper or wrong for the particular circumstances. Few things are simplistic in earthly life, yet we will establish more clarity as this discussion process within our minds.

We seek to encourage considerable debate on various sensitive topics existing within our modern civilisation in 2008 when this book is being written. The realisation that some ideas here are a bit 'ahead of their time' necessitated that international publication be postponed until people were individually and collectively ready for these positive progressive changes. Now in early 2016 when this book is finally being made available to the public due to its timely nature; we can vividly perceive that it is even more important than ever before to make these necessary character and value improvements to one's own personality, as well as within our key interpersonal relationships and collectively as a species of human life on this lovely planet.

One of Earth's greatest philosophers once said words to the effect, "by their acts you shall know them" and "treat others as you wish to be treated". Therefore, along with human nature issues, we will begin a very sincere, in-depth consideration of how and why one's ethics, values and morals comprehensively affect our personal lives, as well as our global civilisation.

Our examination of human nature issues will serve as the balancing factor to assess, test and better describe aspects of our eternal, higher, more divine inner spiritual character that so often feels somewhat confused, vulnerable, detached, ignored and unappreciated by some events and emotions in this earthly life. We do not seek to escape, or to even confront our human nature; rather we are primarily learning to acknowledge countless factors that are concurrently functioning in this world. We must fully and accurately assess reality and our state of being in order to become the best possible human being that we as an individual in this time and place are able to do, with our present state of mind and level of being. Self-awareness is a useful powerful tool for you and for us as a species of life striving for continued survival and sustainable progress during these challenging times that test one's character.

The process of identifying the differing components within your overall state of being that formulate your character is an essential prerequisite to properly and thoroughly understand one's complex, eternally conscious nature. As unique individuals, we each must recognise that we have considerable diversity of thoughts, tendencies and behaviours within the entirety of our private inner personal states of being, as well as our outwardly manifested societal character. Depending upon the unpredictable, often discordant circumstances experienced in living our life, various personality traits clearly reveal themselves. For example, if we are unavoidably confronted by a hostile aggressive person who is attacking us verbally or physically, most of us will tend to instinctively defend ourselves in a similar manner. Experience has proven it best to avoid such situations, yet some people consciously or unconsciously create such events in their lives through their attitudes and behaviours that draw like-minded people to themselves so that ongoing periodic confrontation, self-defence and the related stimulation of mostly negative emotions and thoughts are prevalent within their daily lives.

Other people are able to somehow become virtually impervious to those who would seek to engage them into unwanted interpersonal conflicts of any type. Why is this situation so common? It is largely a matter of one's state of being, attitudes and responses to others that permits some of us to facilitate smooth, mostly pleasant interactions with all types of people, while others of us seem prone to somehow instigate disharmony and antagonism wherever we go, even among some people who are generally quite pleasant and non-aggressive. In general terms, it is fairly evident that the vast majority of human beings are peace loving people who seldom or never attack other people, unless we are first threatened or attacked to provoke such an aspect of our character to manifest itself into such an action. It is necessary to examine closely why and how some people's character is functioning in a way that they intentionally and unconsciously initiate unprovoked verbal and physical assaults upon others, so this tendency is one easily observable trait that can be assessed to better define their relative state of being.

We also hear of many cases in the public media documenting instances of defenceless people being violently attacked and calling for help to numerous bystanders witnessing the events, who choose to not become involved. Unfortunately, in some cases this unconscionable attitude also includes the police whose professional responsibility involves protecting people that are being illegally victimised in any ways. This single factor indicates insights into realising that many humans do not empathise with the suffering of others nor recognise their right to obtain assistance from those people nearby that are able to help them. People often refuse to assist others in need because they fear it may disadvantaged or endanger them personally or that it may involve unknown issues whereby previous conflict situations are being resolved to 'balance and settle old scores'.

However, those who do nothing when someone is obviously being victimised unjustly by others reveals the onlookers are either dominated by fear of injury or they seem to have little empathy or compassion for the situation of the hapless victim. Likewise, a small minority of people will not even choose to defend themselves when they are being unjustly assaulted and victimised by another person or persons. Relatively few of us would consider ourselves to be included in the latter category, whereby we would refuse to defend ourselves from an unjust, unlawful violent aggressive assault. However, when the assaults are of a more subtle, insidious, covert nature, the vast majority of people tend to allow all manner of inappropriate, harmful activities to occur with relatively little assertive protest or forceful remedial action being taken to resolve the issue. This is a fact that we will address in copious and tediously repetitive detail, until 'the reality' truly awakens within one's consciousness.

Numerous examples exist regarding humanity's self-destructive activities that are now prevalent in our society. A few of these include: the governmental health regulatory agencies approval of the manufacture and public use of proven disease causing food additives, such as some artificial sweeteners, toxic colouring agents and 'flavour enhancers' such as MSG; the widespread use of harmful cooking methods, such as by microwaves; the unhealthy processing of foods, such as the irradiation of a variety of foods to preserve them; and the addition of cancer and disease causing agents into all manner of building materials, fossil fuels for vehicles, home furnishings, cosmetic and body care products, factory emissions; nuclear and other types of toxic waste disposal; and so on and on almost endlessly, in our modern civilisation. Also, the widespread production and consumption of so-called 'fast foods' that are primarily composed of unhealthy sugars and fats, which is creating an obesity epidemic in most western nations where these generally toxic types of foods and beverages are consumed. These highly processed, adulterated foods contain unhealthy amounts of commonly accepted food products such as sugars, including glucose, sucrose, fructose, maltose dextrose, 'corn syrup' and various others; adulterated poisonous types of salt in many forms, and debilitating types of man-made so-called 'trans-fats' and a multitude of other types of harmful additives that are too vast in scope to mention here. When ingested over months and years, these poisonous foods damage health by making us: overweight; possessing lowered immune function with a lack of energy; overload the digestive tract with various ingredients that slow digestion; restrict blood circulation; create excessive bile and mucous in one's body; establish an acidic pH in the body that creates an internal physiological environment that is ideal for the development of cancer, the growth of parasites, viruses, yeasts, bacteria, pathogens of other types, and promotes disease states such as liver, kidney, heart, lung, and lymph illnesses; among countless other factors that simply kill us slowly and often quite painfully, at great social, emotional, and financial cost.

Additionally, modern so-called 'conventional' farming methods involve applying toxic chemicals, as well as unbalanced amounts of artificially created fertilisers to both soil and plants at huge cost to the farmers and consumers. These conventional farming practices have severely damaged soil structure and kill most naturally occurring microflora and earthworms that occur in their billions in a small amount of healthy natural soil, which symbiotically create the nutrients that makes foods nutritious and healthful to eat. Therefore, the foods we eat no longer contain sufficient amounts of vitamins, minerals or the additional nutrients that are necessary for good health. In many situations additional synthetic and processed nutrients are supplemented during the manufacturing process of modern foodstuffs, and added to bread, juices, wheat, rice, processed salt and innumerable other products. The vast majority of all types of 'processed' foods contain innumerable additives used to make the foods more appealing in taste and appearance, to increase shelf life and to unsuccessfully attempt to increase their nutritional value to approximate that of what we require for a healthy physical body.

The use of antibiotics in increasingly larger doses in all types of livestock to keep pathogens from killing many animals in their unnaturally crowded, confined, filthy, unnatural growing conditions creates antibiotic resistance in the pathogens and enters the human body when one consumes the animals. Humans also ingest these pathogens that die in the cooking process as well as some that manage to survive in improperly cooked and raw meats and fish. A serious problem is developing from the widespread use of artificial synthetically made growth hormones, as well as the use of natural growth hormones being extracted from live and dead animals to speed the growth rates of these cultivated domesticated animals in a way that they also contain larger, unnatural amounts of unhealthy 'trans' fats. These growth hormones have resulted in children showing abnormally earlier maturation, increasing obesity, mental and emotional 'issues', among many other health and behaviour problems. The feeding of animal products (meat, bone meal from dead animals, faecal waste, old and rotten grains, various toxic 'filler' materials, including known carcinogens) and unhealthy plant based proteins, and unsafe and unproven genetically modified plants, such as soy bean derivatives and others; to animals that historically have only eaten a basic natural vegetarian diet of grass; have all adversely affected the quality of our animal based food sources. Many of us are seriously questioning if animals of any types really need to be on the human menu because alternative, high protein quality food sources are identified and commercialised globally. The rhetorical question is "Do humans have the right to treat other life forms as though they have no rights to life, unless it serves humanity in some manner?"

More recently, science has begun to include genetically modified and genetically engineered foods into our diets. Originally this developmental process began through the creation of hybrid seed stock that produced larger, pest resistant, improved appearing produce, etc. as being their officially stated motives and benefits. Now we recognise that the seeds from these patented hybrids are in many cases unable to reproduce or grow properly so the corporations' monopolies on seed sources would be maintained using what has been aptly called the "terminator" gene. Now there has been some evidence that this practice is not a wise one from various perspectives that are too numerous to specify here. Suffice to observe that this situation is primarily about making money and protecting unfair corporate monopoly rights in agribusiness; not about protecting people's right to eat healthy foods.

One example is that large monopolistic international corporations with interrelated investments in patented seed and plant production, large scale agri-businesses, corporately owned farms, fertiliser and chemical companies, and food wholesale and retail distribution outlets are seeking to dominate these industries to gain control over the global food and agricultural business to the detriment of all people. These corporations are intentionally perverting and adversely altering the natural processes in their development of artificially engineered genetic lines of foods. We now see science and industry intentionally mixing the genes of unrelated plants species and even with the genes of creatures, such as jellyfish or other types of sea and land animals together in completely unnatural ways, purportedly to improve the qualities of these foodstuffs. Not only are these resultant hybrid and genetically modified species of plants often unable to reproduce naturally, it seems evident to researchers outside the agribusiness industry that such foods often contain components that are incompatible with normal human digestion processes. It appears certain that some real health damage and environmental devastation will result from these practices, which have not yet been fully recognised.

Additionally, it is well-documented that most of the man-made electrical fields (alternating currents or "AC electric power") and radiation sources (EMF) that are currently widely used in our civilisation are debilitating to health in various ways to the human body's own naturally occurring electromagnetic fields. The electromagnetic and radiation 'smog' within which we all live causes serious physical and mental diseases. Governments, industry and some medical experts who have long been aware of these problems still refuse to publicly acknowledge or resolve any of these situations. This situation is quite similar to the already proven case regarding the toxic effects of asbestos over many decades when people were knowingly exposed to this harmful man-made product used in homes and other places as insulation or toxic building materials that the asbestos industry and governments knew many decades ago would create the painful unnecessarily premature deaths of countless millions of innocent; mostly unwitting victims. Why does our so-called modern, civilised scientifically technological society generally continue to ignore these issues stated above and many other problematic issues like them, as illness rates skyrocket along with the medical costs of treating symptoms instead resolving of the causes of disease? Because huge amount of money is being made by interrelated, powerful vested corporate interests that are in a position to influence government and bureaucratic officials by various methods.

One clear example of fraud and deception at the highest levels of government, healthcare and the medical industry is the disease labelled cancer. It can affect many organs and areas of the body, and now even affects animals consuming man-made 'processed' and otherwise toxic foods are becoming cancerous in increasing percentages. Cancer was scientifically proven in 1925 by biochemist Otto Warburg MD, who won the Nobel Prize in 1931 for his conclusive research establishing that certain vitamins, minerals, now called "co-enzymes", are necessary to carry oxygen within cells. Otto Warburg later proved that cancer can only occur in oxygen deprived cells. It was conclusively validated that normal healthy human tissues will not and cannot develop cancer, if an optimum level of oxygen exists within cells. Therefore, we must ask ourselves, "Why has the incidence of cancer continued to rise so dramatically since this discovery has been made about eighty years ago?" Why have no mainstream universities, medical schools or cancer research institutes chosen to focus their attention and financial resources upon this simple, conclusive, long recognised cancer solution, to increase the oxygen content within human cells? Instead of funding quality research to determine how to best provide human cells with the optimum health producing nutrients to supply ideal amounts of oxygen to prevent cancer from occurring, the vast majority of cancer research funding has ineffectually and inefficiently been squandered upon research into the secondary causes of cancer, including research into genetically inherited predisposition to cancer and genetic cures for cancer. There has been an intentional refusal by mainstream science and medicine to adequately research the simple fact that the primary prerequisite cause for every type of cancer is the lack of adequate oxygen levels (hypoxia) in the cells that eventually become cancerous. In 1966 Dr. Otto Warburg again made this discovery publicly known in a speech to Nobel laureates in Landau, Germany.

Likewise, cancer is unable to grow within a human body possessing a relatively alkaline pH; whereas in an acidic pH within the body knowingly produces an ideal internal physiological environment for cancer causing pathogens to develop. It then seems to be a real mystery why most modern processed foods serve to create an acidic internal state in one's body, as if the responsible authorities have not had adequate access to the copious volumes of quality scientific and medical evidence proving these simple facts as realities. Still, science, medicine, government and food processors all seem quite united in their reluctance to address and resolve this obviously simplistic situation. Why is this? We know and it is time to say, "Enough now."

Does this one example prove a covert reluctance and pervasive reticence upon the part of health and medical authorities to effectively conduct research to reduce or eliminate cancer which one of the major plagues of our age? Perhaps the answer could be found in a similar historical event. Centuries ago, the then health and medical authorities refused to seriously consider the fact that disease was being caused by human faecal waste and raw untreated sewage, included rubbish and animal wastes, contaminating areas where drinking water was being obtained from local water wells in towns and cities across Europe. It took hundreds of years to publicly accept that this unhygienic practice resulted in a variety of diseases occurring in these areas from microscopic pathogens. One can relatively be sure that the wealthy ruling people of that era did not have faecal waste and sewage flowing directly into their water wells, or is that just another amazing coincidence?

We hear and see abundant amounts of rhetoric from the international media and medical health authorities about the great progress continually being made in their research. However, the statistics prove that the incidence and prevalence of cancer and many other diseases is dramatically increasing exponentially, as are many forms of recognised mental illness. We have identified a wide variety of human activities and serious issues that definitively indicate that in spite of all the misleading efforts and huge volumes of propaganda and 'official lip-service'; there is almost no genuine realistic consideration and effort being applied within these socially responsible government and medical agencies to identify and resolve the fundamental causes of disease and illness within our bodies, environments and societies.

Disease is not only a physical condition, for it has many underlying causes; some of whose root origins are in our attitudes and spiritual condition. Most of this aspect is being ignored or discounted by mainstream science, medicine and education. There are a great many genuine people who are very sincere in their efforts to truly improve humanity's health and well-being physically, mentally, and spiritually; however, at this time they are in the distinct minority, at least as far as receiving government financial grants are concerned.

A thorough analysis of the attitudes, actions and motivations being publicly expressed by some of the major interrelated industries and corporations involved in health related fields, such as the pharmaceutical, cosmetic and medical industries, decisively proves they currently are focused strictly upon profitability with little regard or respect for the best interests of the public. How many times in our lives have we seen or heard words or seen acts that seek to falsely validate, condone or rationalise a wide variety of inappropriate activities according to the woeful philosophy that wrongfully says "the ends justify the means"? This despicable attitude is an obvious, real life manifestation of the 'hidden' existence of a philosophic and practical pathological disease state within the moral character of the current unconscionable 'corporate' and government institutional mentality. We must carefully consider that corporations and entire industries, such as the militaristic weapons industries, the chemical and petrochemical industries, the aviation industry and so on, are all heavily supported, endorsed, licensed and protected by interrelated political, governmental and bureaucratic governmental institutions, financial institutions, and various other vested self-interest groups clearly act in ways that demonstrate their minimal regard for the public's overall best interests, historically speaking.

For example, the aviation industry has long recognised that the large number of passengers using their services carry various contagious diseases, such as colds, flues, tuberculosis and other such conditions, which can be and are often transmitted by airborne inhalation. In spite of existing technology to greatly minimise the circulation of these airborne pathogens by the use of high quality air filtration systems being installed in planes and airport terminals, this does not occur. This is such an obvious, simple and inexpensive solution. We must ask ourselves again, "Why is air purification not occurring to prevent the spread of diseases in all forms of public transportation systems?" We could be asking the same thing about impurities in our global water supplies, including the chlorine and fluoride and other toxic compounds that are intentionally added to our water supplies in many so-called 'developed' nations when other safer, proven effective solutions (such as adding tiny doses of colloidal silver or vastly improved filtration, with added ozone) being far more healthful.

A focal issue here is to realise that modern foods have a drastically reduced nutritional content than foods produced only a hundred years ago by more traditional farming techniques. Eating nutrient deficient, overly processed, poisoned foods results in people being far more susceptible to disease due to lowered immune function and a lack in the necessary body-building nutritional components needed to nourish their bodies. Countless quality medical studies by the world's most capable and prestigious institutions have conclusively proven that good sanitation practices, clean water, and proper nutrition are the best ways to prevent disease. However, the vast majority of global health funding is not being devoted to the prevention of disease through well-known health sustaining activities. Instead, these financial resources are inefficiently applied, squandered and basically stolen or misapplied in many cases by the development and use of all manner of pharmaceutical drugs and medical procedures that primarily seek to suppress or eliminate the symptoms of disease, and not to heal the disease itself; only after the disease has already occurred. Why not prevent these diseases from ever occurring when the solutions are readily available and are relatively easy and inexpensive to implement? We know the likely answers already and they are all related to profits and control over human populations.

The massive web of interrelated medical and pharmaceutical industries, the major medical schools, and their governmental and financial collaborators are clearly not now willing to focus their efforts upon applying the available proven solutions to many of humanity's greatest health problems. Instead there seems to be significant evidence that these institutions have covertly been guilty of instigating and perpetuating many known health problems for centuries before public pressure forced a change in improving matters. An overwhelming volume of quality scientific and medical research exists to conclusively prove that good, balanced nutrition, containing less man-made toxins, with less unhealthy processing of foods and improved soil health will synergistically function to better nutrient people to improve their immune systems and thereby prevent disease and stimulate better health in people. The modern corporate agribusiness interests are primarily focused upon producing the largest possible profits, expanding their production and distribution monopolies, and artificially maintaining the pleasing appearance of foods at the expense of their naturally ripened delicious taste and nutritional value, by producing food with a longer shelf life, rather than to willingly produce the most nutritious, healthful quality food products possible.

The core human nature issue we seek to acknowledge here is that the majority of humans tend to focus upon our own individual perspective. The businessman and farmer's major priorities are their profitability, while many consumers often are simply seeking the cheapest, best appearing and tasting food choices available to them. The following wisdom expresses some of the problems our civilisation must confront in regard to most of these complex detrimental circumstances. *"It is difficult to get a man to understand something when his salary depends on his NOT understanding it." – Upton Sinclair.*

These types of people generally disregard the food's nutritional health value as being a less important factor. Most people are relatively inattentive to the primary reason that we eat food is to provide sustainable nutrition and energy to build and maintain our bodies in a healthy state; not simply to feel 'full', or to have our hunger satiated, or toxic 'tasty' processed foods, or those that lasts longer in storage, or does not require refrigeration, and so on. The direct result of this pervasive state of disinterest and lack of awareness is that our agricultural soils are being depleted and destroyed and our health suffers as most of us eat poor quality, nutritionally 'empty' foods. Medical costs, disease and suffering all increase dramatically, as those who eat in this manner become increasingly obese and malnourished in spite of the large volumes of food many people consume daily. One can recognise now that diseases begin prematurely in the young, as well as the middle aged, and certainly long before the elderly, who are generally experiencing a number of simultaneous chronic painful diseases; such as debilities, high blood pressure, poor circulation, chronic pain due to inflammation, premature bone and tooth decay, Alzheimer's disease, and many others.

There is little real public or government outcry about this chronically deteriorating situation, nor about the epidemic of escalating suicide rates. There is almost no genuine mainstream attempt to alter or truly improve these damaging, dangerous and expensive trends in modern civilisation. This entire complex circumstance has become a serious, life disabling, murderous assault on human health and its progress over a long time period has been subtle, insidious, invasive and carefully calculated. The evidence is undeniable that this assault upon human health has been intentionally devised by various vested interests whose avarice reveals an immoral willingness to deliberately disadvantage, injure and deprive people of health at enormous financial cost to society to further their corporate profitability and control over humanity. Because the symptoms of moderate forms of malnutrition are not so readily noticeable as are cases of severe malnutrition or starvation; there is less of an indication that this entire situation is actually a deliberate act of institutionalised corporate and government condoned covert aggression in our societies today that also serves to foster an increasing supply of medical patients requiring urgent assistance. Expensive medical procedures, costly hospital visits, increasing insurance and health coverage premiums, early onset of disabling health conditions and diseases, avoidable premature death for people that never reach an age to collect their old age financial benefits and many such reasons exist for these deliberate circumstances in our civilisation.

Whether one is being violently attacked by a callous murderer that uses a gun to deprive us of our right to freedom from aggression, or one is attacked by a self-interested murderous group of corporations that knowingly poisons their trusting victims by slowly providing imperceptible doses of disease and obesity causing toxins into their diet, or starves them by removing the nutrition from their food so they gradually sicken and die from preventable illnesses and malnutrition; the result is the same: an unnecessary, unjust, painful, premature death with much needless suffering. If an individual is intentionally poisoned by unknowingly ingesting toxic substances in their foods that very slowly kill the non-aggressive, hapless victim by establishing the physical and mental conditions where disease and eventual death is inevitable, then by definition this constitutes first degree premeditated, intentional murder in any court of law in the western nations. In due course, this matter will be heard by the International Court of Settlements in the Hague and the certain victory by the class action 'plaintiffs' will bankrupt these offending corporations and their closely related government 'sponsored' and protected co-conspirators.

While we are likely to assertively resist an aggressive act of violence, it is seldom the case when conditions seem to pose no sense of immediate threat or obvious imminent injury. When will the governments and courts begin to view this situation as intentional genocide? Examine the motives of corporate greed and whenever people are intentionally killed quickly or slowly, it is still murder and the hapless victim still ends up dead in the final analysis. Again we must seriously re-consider the prime example of many widely used, known poisonous and toxic substances, like our previous example of asbestos. How can asbestos continue to be used even after the asbestos industry and governments knew about its catastrophic health damaging effects on those breathing its particles into their lungs? What about the use of pesticides such as DDT and other poisons which have been· banned in some progressive countries that are aware of their extremely toxic effects on humans, while other countries still knowingly use poisons that are severely damaging people and the environment? We can begin to perceive an integrated campaign to injure and kill people in many ways, simply to pursue the 'profit motive'.

Another closely related situation that damages public health and costs our global civilisation trillions of dollars annually is the plague of addictive drugs, alcohol, cigarettes and other such counter-productive substances. Gambling in its quite numerous forms is another serious problem which our societies encourage that limits genuine productivity and robs people due to their poor choices and habitual actions. We will not address it in detail here now because it is more of a mental and emotional health issue, in my opinion, than a physical health issue. Suffice to observe that gambling generates untold billions annually for vested business interests with this 'license to steal money' by pretending people may win a large sum of money when actually the vast majority of participants are consistent 'losers' by intentional design. Taxes on gambling and various harmful addictive substances 'earns' government huge taxation revenues and 'insider' corporations with obscenely large profits with no productive result, at a massive 'cost' to our civilisation in personal misery and financial depravation.

A careful analysis of international drug production and trafficking reveals this complex, long established global industry is another major method that is widely used to distract, control, use, abuse and ultimately to kill and disrupt the lives of huge numbers of people. This would include many so-called 'legal' prescription drugs, although obviously not all these would be harmful or toxic. It is estimated that over half of violent crime and theft is somehow related to seeking funds to acquire drugs. Therefore, well over half of all people involved in crime that are now in jail in 'western' nations are imprisoned either directly due to drug crimes or for thefts, assaults and murders to acquire money to buy drugs and other addictive substances.

We clearly see that neither government nor industry prevents nor solves these serious problems of drug production or addiction in our current civilisation. In the few modern "war against drugs" publicly undertaken by some western governments, notably by the USA which is the world's largest illegal (and legal) drug consumer, the result was that the supply of addictive dangerous illegal drugs available to the public dramatically increased rather than decreased, in spite of the expenditure of billions of dollars to address the issues involved. The international illegal drug industry is conclusively proven to be a modern day plague upon humanity. The putrid corruption involved in the entire situation is revealed when some of the governmental agencies that are directly responsible for law enforcement and national security are intimately intentionally involved in the international illegal drug industries.

These facts are revealed repeatedly over many decades, even back into history when prominent European governments began the importation of drugs from Asia, South America and elsewhere. Ample, well-documented, conclusive proven evidence exists that well-established criminal organisations often received various types of covert and direct assistance from a relatively small number of wealthy and influential people possessing good working relationships with those associates positioned in top levels in governmental, as well as national and international law enforcement agencies.

It would also appear certain that much of the actual law enforcement activity over the years has been primarily intended to politically gain public support. The truth behind these costly purported law enforcement activities were primarily designed to remove so-called "independent operators" from this ruthlessly evil business, gather intelligence, and ultimately to further improve the production volumes and expand the covert distribution networks of these illegal drugs, such as by collaborators with the CIA, which often includes other organised crime syndicates of various types. This ongoing process assisted the larger criminal organisations to gain monopoly control over most international drug production and distribution networks. This entire situation is being authorised and directed by a secretive group of people who are well-established at the top levels of legitimate and organised criminal international business, who falsely believe that both legal and illegal drugs are a necessary evil in our civilisation. Those responsible for perpetuating this hideous devastating plague upon humanity at all levels of the complexly interrelated addictive drugs industries are profiting from human suffering by their refusal to truly resolve and seek to eliminate the production and sale of addictive and harmful substances of many types internationally.

For brevity, we will combine the production, distribution and consumption of all types of legal, government approved, regulated, addictive drugs. This includes all forms of consumable alcohol; all types of tobacco products, whether smoked, chewed or used as 'snuff' up one's nostrils; various addictive pharmaceutical and illegal drugs that do not serve to heal the body and are primarily taken to alter one's moods in various ways, and also includes addictive and otherwise harmful food additives, such as artificial sweeteners, flavours and preservatives that are currently being internationally marketed under many brand names and identifying numerical codes.

Let's begin by acknowledging that ample conclusively proven evidence exists that these highly addictive products are damaging to human health, yet they are approved for consumption by legislative enactments and health authority regulators. Also, the public already knows these substances are toxic to health, especially in excessive dosages over lengthy periods of time and yet they willingly continue to consume them in massive quantities. This would include using antibiotics and vaccines to treat diseases of a viral or energetic nature which are ineffective for those specific applications. Most political organisations and politicians receive huge campaign donations from the various corporate lobbyists that represent these industries, apparently to encourage them to be receptive to ignoring these health issues in their roles as representatives of the people's best interests. Additionally, governments receive an enormous amount of taxation revenue every year from the public sale of these products, as well as intellectual property protection fees, such as Patents, Trademarks, etc. Not even five percent of the government's total taxation revenue from the production and sale of these many harmful legal addictive substances is applied to the rehabilitation of these afflicted people, nor in helping their disadvantaged families.

Much taxation expenditure seems to be primarily invested upon expensive hypocritical public awareness propagandising in the mass media about the deleterious health effects of primarily smoking, with less attention to the many deleterious effects of alcohol on one's health or the social damage alcohol creates internationally. Actually, relatively little is now actually being done to substantially remedy these serious problems of addictive behaviours in society. In the vast majority of non-animated theatrical movies produced in this historical time period in the USA, the leading actors are very often seen to be smoking cigarettes almost continuously and periodically many are seen to periodically drink 'brand name' alcohol or poisonous 'soft drinks' throughout the film. This is indicative of this prevalent social malignancy and serves as intentional, unavoidable free advertising for these health damaging products.

Far more people die every year from excessive alcohol and tobacco consumption, prescription drugs and the related substance-abuse diseases than from all illegal drugs and vehicle accidents combined. Nevertheless, we do not hear a public outcry or any political rhetoric to make excessive consumption of alcohol or tobacco products illegal. So long as you do not drink alcohol and then drive a vehicle or become a public nuisance, it is legal for one to literally drink themselves to death and many people do exactly that every year. The same thing could be said of smoking cigarettes or taking pharmaceutical drugs. If you can obtain them, then nothing legally prevents one from consuming as much as humanly possible to the point where death occurs directly or indirectly from that substance abuse. We see plenty of people that are 'freely' self-destroying themselves in exactly this manner.

The volume of various pharmaceutical drugs such as anti-depressants, sedatives and pain killers that are misused in our western civilisation is unbelievably common and is a very serious problem that these many millions of addicted people are unknown to wider society since most of them attempt to hide their addiction to the best of their ability. These addictions to legal substances and the resulting devastating health-related issues are never addressed by the government or public in a similar way to illegal drugs, which currently are demonised at every opportunity. In other words, one can legally ingest government approved toxic addictive substances literally until an afflicted person kills themselves or dies of illness, without fear of prosecution or unwanted mandatory social intervention. However, to use or sell a wide list of illegal addictive substances can result in a criminal prosecution, and if convicted receive a lengthy jail term, and in some countries the death penalty. I do not advocate the use of legal or illegal addictive harmful drugs or toxic substances of any kind and this would include caffeine artificially added to many beverages humans consume such as 'soft' and so-called 'energy' drinks which also contain absurd amounts of artificial and man-made toxic sugar-like substances as additives, along with addictive poisonous substances as artificial flavourings or preservative agents. Again, sugar and most man-made artificial sweeteners are excellent examples of other known harmful addictive substances, especially when ingested in the excessive quantities that are now freely allowed by government regulators, directly against the public's best interests, in favour of corporate profitability.

From my perspective tobacco (and excessive alcohol) consumption is among the worst of the self-inflicted poisons ingested by many billions of people within our global civilisation. There are absolutely no redeeming social or health benefits for smoking such an intensely harmful addictive substance. It is an indicator that some people in society are intent upon knowingly self-abusing their bodies and mental state, irrespective of the damage it does to them, others around them or the enormous financial cost to people on low incomes and to society in health care costs resulting from the subsequent diseases this awful habit usually creates over extended time periods. This is an example of the types of behaviours humans must learn to stop doing by making the necessary personal choices, which ultimately is likely to also involve the political and legislative process. We can improve our world by committing our attention and resources to fostering productive fun activities and more beneficial forms of recreation than watching others play sports, or hypnotically consuming the nightly ongoing 'doses' of mostly unpleasant and fear provoking TV news 'gossip', or watching an endless stream of fictionalised idealised movies for one's entertainment. Instead, we can 'freely' choose truly enjoyable, productive, meaningful activities with one another so that addictive attitudes and behaviours are much less prevalent in our families, communities and civilisation as a whole.

The numerous positive medical benefits of cannabis is only more recently being made public after almost a century of prohibition and suppression by the industries that would lose profits if it were legalised for medical use, such as in the relief from acute pain, in various cancer treatments, and ideally at the least, being 'de-criminalised' for 'recreational' or 'mind expansion' uses.

The high and unsustainable cost to tax payers for applying such 'curiously motivated', cleverly designed and selectively enforced drug legislation for the police to find, arrest marijuana 'users' and then for the Court system to incarcerate the convicted marijuana 'criminals' is absurd, divisive, unpopular, and must end with a more enlightened perspectives. This entire charade is an intentionally designed situation to criminalise and marginalise a significant percentage of the population. We can easily identify the inter-related groups of corporate 'vested interests' that seek to promote the addictive, unproductive so-called 'legal' recreational activities (like gambling and the vast array of 'sports' events, which are often designed specifically with gambling and marginally beneficial forms of employment being the focal point of the income generating process. The toxic products mentioned previously are definitive examples that are well-proven facts now.

It is 'vested corporate interests' that are active within government that created the current prohibition of cannabis in the early 20th century. There was an intentional decision to aggressively suppress 'pot', which is proven to diminish aggression in any culture/nation when compared with alcohol or most mind-altering 'legal' pharmaceutical drugs that are prescribed by doctors for many mental and emotional maladies. Relatively little effort or professional expense or expertise is applied to creating viable solutions. Instead, those vested interests decided to control the production, distribution and of promotion 'legal' addictive drugs like alcohol, tobacco, acidifying 'stimulant drinks' containing caffeine, toxic compounds and sugars and many others that have a far more adverse and damaging influence on human behaviours and health, with no proven health of disease curing benefits. This is only one minor example among the countless areas requiring adjustment and remedial action to create solutions in the next few years.

Instead, for just for a moment, let's briefly consider the amount of people who are daily involved in self-murder/suicide, which is a statistic that is suppressed publically in most nations. In 2015, among U.S. military veterans apparently about 22 of these people kill themselves EVERY DAY in the USA due to depression and other reasons related to their combat experiences or inability to 'fit into' society. In addition to this huge number of daily self-murders; how many bankrupted farmers/ranchers or business people kill themselves when they have lost everything financially and face foreclosure or bankruptcy and decide to choose self-murder instead of continuing to endure life's hardships and inequalities any more? The same could be said of young people that have lost the will to live, or the elderly no longer wanting to live in an uncaring seeming society, or those with chronic debilitating physical or emotional pain.

People are 'quietly' killing themselves in greater numbers than ever before in known human history. There is little public media hype to address or solve the situation. There is no ongoing pervasive 'scare campaigns' to limit self-murder as we see regarding terrorism, with no governmental outcry in Congress or the United Nations to solve the related causative factors involved. The fact more people kill themselves, or are killed by so-called 'legal' prescription drugs than die in all automobile accidents and by terrorism or crime within society is ignored by both the 'mass media' and governments of the world because this transparent, self-evident attitude serves their own 'vested' (self) interests. This terrible situation is no longer acceptable in a civilised society.

One does not have to possess a powerful intellect, nor be particularly perceptive to witness and understand the conclusive evidence that numerous ways have been developed throughout history to exert considerable control over the vast majority of common people by a ruthless small minority of power seeking people that desire to callously and selfishly 'rule over' all life on Mother Earth, including the planet itself. Those despotic people and institutions in human society who intentionally create autocratic, totalitarian type governmental, economic and social systems that serve only a minority of the population's best interests are revealed throughout history. We will briefly review the developmental progression of various forms of governmental control over people through recorded history to provide a better perspective of what is occurring today from the origins of government in our civilisation.

Beginning in ancient times, into the present in some places in the world, indigenous peoples have been somewhat nomadic, occupying the land according to their needs, and moving freely within their mutually agreed territorial areas. In most locations, they developed agriculture, domesticated animals and began to permanently remain in one location, especially as population and environmental pressures forced them to be relatively confined onto a defensible designated area of land. In maintaining possession of one's ancestral lands, one would understandably assume that it was usually a matter of "might makes right", which is a relatively primitive concept that we are still quite familiar with in our modern civilisation. Thousands of years ago, society progressively organised itself into more complex interactive groups of people occupying larger areas of land under one ruler and tribal war lords oppressed and conquered peoples by genocide, slavery and depravation. Most of these war-like leaders and their supporters attained and maintained their power over conquered territory and people by ruthless, violent, evil forms of oppression that are still seen today in our world in some places. Some leaders in times of relative peace and prosperity developed societies that were responsive to the needs and wishes of the majority of their people. However, for people who had become enslaved by being conquered in these wars, any true freedom or justice existed to a far lesser extent than was experienced by the ruling people or their citizens.

Over passing time, a multitude of forms of feudalism developed around the world, which was always dominated by a relative few powerful people whose control was usually maintained through violence, oppression and intermittent internal warfare focused upon various groups within its own population, as well as upon other tribes, cultural or religious groups, or other nations. A primary characteristic of feudalism was to unjustly claim all lands conquered in warfare as being the absolute, legal possession of the monarch, who by force of military power declared themselves as sovereign or supreme ruler, with the title of king, queen, emperor or empress. Feudalism was usually closely associated with some form of officially institutionalised religious beliefs. These religious forms of governance were used to institutionalise various forms of theological control over the common people's beliefs and activities.

The history of the Roman Empire is especially revealing in its barbarism when conquering vast areas of land through carefully planned and conducted acts of great violence and subsequent repression over many hundreds of years. Roman Emperors were generally focused upon maintaining and increasing their power and that of the Roman Empire; regardless of the destruction, depravation, misery and death resulting from their actions. We can recall the Romans persecuted numerous religions, cultural groups and later developed their own heavily edited version of Christianity; the Roman Catholic Church, to better control the citizens and slaves of the Roman Empire. The Romans encouraged the development of an early form of feudalism, which owed its allegiance to the Roman Emperor. In most forms of European feudal monarchy there also developed an intimate, direct, interdependent relationship with the Roman Catholic theocracy located at the Vatican in Rome. This pervasive theocratic international form of government evolved over two thousand years, beginning in the earliest times of the Roman Empire and in some ways this system remains functional into the present time.

Theocracy is defined as a form of government by god or through a priestly order, who claim to be acting upon god's direction or authority, just as we see in various fundamentalist religions around the world today. Over the centuries, the power of the Roman Empire diminished militarily. During this time, along with misdeeds and eventual demise of the Roman Emperors, there were also the widespread scandalous behaviours by a succession of Roman Catholic Popes who were often quite openly vile, depraved, murderous heathens of the worst types. These cruel, destructive ancient Popes unjustly declared themselves to be the perfect, infallible absolute earthly representatives of God on Earth. This was clearly not the situation, based upon their despicable attitudes and morally corrupted deeds; unless they represented the forces of evil upon Earth, which is exactly what they were doing at the time. Many of these ancient Roman Catholic Popes personified and represented the forces of evil on this planet at that time in history, along with others like them of that age. These Popes had declared themselves to be incapable of error and as being God's representatives on Earth to further augment and institutionalise their power over all people, including all the monarchs of Europe.

Over hundreds of years of passing time; widespread public displeasure and disillusionment arose under such an inhuman, brutal, heinously corrupted papal religious leadership, which demonstrated that a system of theomania had become a reality. Theomania is defined as 'religious insanity' or the 'false belief that one is God'. Numerous medieval Popes were obviously heretical, given their scurrilous, villainous attitudes and behaviours, over the centuries their sequential misdeeds occurred. These vile, corrupted and murderous acts indicated to the public that theomania definitely characterised these depraved Roman Catholic Popes, whose self-professed claims of infallibility were quite absurd, as they continually committed acts of unconscionable evil, rampant greed for power and limitless efforts to attain material wealth.

The result was that Protestant and other 'sects' of the Christian religion developed with their own versions of theocratic government, which also allied itself with various European monarchies. Almost all nations in Europe at this time in history were operating under a system of feudalism of some type. These monarchs were expected to be subservient in various ways to the Christian theocracy with whom they usually shared absolute supreme power over the common people in every aspect of their daily lives, including to dictate their system of beliefs through religious indoctrination and monarchical authority; both being preserved and enforced by military power.

It is illuminating to 'refresh' our mind with specifically how the predominate forms of government have evolved, along with some of the defining characteristics of these forms of government. We will consider the specific definitions that describe the concepts, roles and relationships existing within various types of government and philosophic thought that distinguish various aspects of modern governmental systems. This historical analysis is helpful to re-discover the progression of development resulting in our current governmental systems internationally. Most people have only received some basic history in school about the key events that shaped our national identity in regard to its international role in the world. Much of this information contains considerable 'sanitisation' that involves carefully 'adjusting' or creating the purported relevant historical records to present a rational sounding, although somewhat fictitious and publicly acceptable accounting of historical events. Therefore, through mainstream educational processes, most of us have come to readily accept our modern governmental systems without fully consciously recognising the intricate, pervasive ways in which our present social systems have progressively developed from exceedingly brutal despotic beginnings.

Humanity now must become successful in effectuating more responsible, sane, efficiently functional systems of government that are capable of fostering the survival of the human species within a truly civilised international community. This process requires additional freedom, opportunity and capability for all people to become involved in the development and implementation of all the necessary integrated synergistic solutions to the many challenges humanity now faces.

More forms of oppression, warfare, cultural violence, disease, starvation, misery and environmental destruction are simply unacceptable in a truly civilised world culture. Drastic improvements in all areas of human endeavour are essential prerequisites toward the development of a truly civilised world culture, so it is quite helpful to determine how we arrived at this vital juncture in human history. We must comprehend the various forces that are so powerfully active in the establishment and maintenance of our present world civilisation to better enable perceptive thinking people everywhere to promote, facilitate and manifest the beneficial positive changes that will improve our overall civilisation. Our generation must be the one to provide true hope in the form of beneficial deliberate action to create a better future.

We all can see the ample evidence before us now that numerous complex issues are threatening the survival of our current civilisation's well-being in many ways. It would be most unfortunate if we, who can perceive reality so clearly before us now, were to foolishly and irresponsibly allow a minority of controlling self-interest groups to pervasively misuse social, religious and governmental institutions; unchecked, unabated, with impunity, often in a blatantly criminal, evil manner to completely disregard humanity's and the Earth's overall best interests. Let's now resume examining exactly how our present forms of government evolved over the past couple thousand years.

Feudalism was the favoured medieval European system of government which was based upon the relationship between the 'vassal' and 'superior', arising from holdings of land on condition of homage and service. In other words; the vassal is a person or family group that is allowed to occupy land by feudal tenure on conditions of providing homage and allegiance to the king, queen or their local representative (prince, lord, duke, noble, etc). A vassal is defined as being a "humble dependent" or 'slave'. A slave is defined as being a person who is the legal property of another or others, and is bound to absolute obedience, and is a "human chattel". Chattel is defined as being "moveable property". The vassal was legally defined as being chattel, the human equivalent of what we today would define as being our own livestock such as cattle, chickens, goats, horses, etc. This relationship clearly defines the vassal's legal status; whereby, if and whenever the king or an authorised representative of the monarch orders one to vacate the land, or go to war, or pay more taxes, then that was what happened or one could be legally prosecuted accordingly. The legal penalties for criminal offences against the crown or church were often quite severe by modern standards, even for what we would view as minor offences today. This would include lengthy jail time, or indentured personal servitude to nobility, or being physically sent overseas to penal colonies such as Australia for crimes such as minor as stealing a loaf of bread to feed one's family to avoid starvation, or the financial inability to pay one's designated taxes to 'the Crown'. I imagine there would have been some form of leverage' to 'encouragement' or to 'enforce payment of the 'deemed' religious 'tithings' to church officials, or their representatives.

In medieval history, the sometimes oppressive living conditions under which most common people lived became so severe and unbearable that periodically small and larger scale revolts and revolutions occurred. Most of these rebellions were quelled with enthusiastic military vehemence upon the orders of the monarchy or local nobility. However, occasionally the peasants had sufficient support from within the entire community or nation to succeed in ousting the monarch or invading occupier. In such relatively rare situations when the people violently overthrew the ruling forces, then various improvements in the legal rights of the people to better treatment by their governmental and religious institutions did occasionally occur.

Most notable of these successful revolutions in establishing a legal basis for human rights being protected by governmental legislation that could not be repealed was the signing of the Magna Carta by King John in England in the year 1215 AD. That unique 'great charter' was the first document of its kind to be signed by any feudal monarchy, which legally conveyed a diverse group of personal and political liberties to the English people. The Magna Carta was and still is the most important legal precedent that enabled the progressive establishment of more democratic systems of government characterised by clearly defined legal rights, possessing a more just and equitable system of governmental obligations to its citizens, working in conjunction with a traditional monarchy. The Magna Carta espoused and defined a set of basic human rights that has for centuries served as a model for justice, liberty from brutal forms of arbitrary oppression, and served as the advent of increasingly truer forms of democracy to later develop in countries such as the United States of America.

Today we see over especially the past few decades that the USA is consistently enacting legislation to reduce, modify and certainly to eliminate some of these human liberties and inalienable rights that were once guaranteed in the U.S. Constitution. For a couple hundred years the USA has been the best hope for true freedom and democracy in the world. Now in 2016, we see that role is being shared by primarily China and Russia. The US global leadership role is exclusively devoted to the narrow perspective of enforcing what a few 'elitists' believe to be in their own best vested self-interests internationally than what is truly best for US citizens, Earth's people, our natural environment, or future generations.

This fact is clearly revealed in the grossly flawed Middle East policy decisions over many decades by the US government. Now in early 2016, when this book is being edited a final time for the public to consider, we see the militaristic policies of the USA in the Middle East are historically focused on creating war and disaster; not peace and prosperity. This is self-evident fact that is obvious to any student of history, in spite of any rhetoric to the contrary.

It is worthy to note that the CIA and various other departments of the USA government and specific individuals working within those organisations have recently (during 2015) been 'tracked' sending/receiving emails to known ISIS contacts and apparently also directly communicating with one of more 'studios' making gruesome purported 'beheading' videos for terrorist purposes. I am unable to confirm at this time that this link to the funding of these terrorists will be publicly revealed, or not. Events in Syria will demonstrate new ways to bring peace through the effective Russian and Chinese military intervention to 'root out' and destroy most of the ISIS fighters and to thereby begin to clearly 'signal' the end the U.S. military's domination of the world; as well as end the financial tyranny of the Wall Street banks, the FED, and other such 'vested' interests that promote disharmony, warfare, needless suffering, and economic deprivation globally.

Now we shall focus upon some of the key ways that all forms of non-autocratic government share a positive, beneficial sounding ideology that professes to be intended for the best overall interests of all people by design. Unfortunately, in most cases the best designed governmental systems over passing time develop a variety of problematic situations. Historically, locations like the ancient Greek City States characterised early attempts to achieve a wonderful vision for a governmental system that sought to provide regional identity, security, equality of opportunity, along with a degree of harmony among all occupations and classes of people that shared a mutual purpose to attain social cohesion and economic prosperity. The evolution of efficient idealistic functional types of governmental systems has continued into modern times.

The key problem facing all governmental models is the overwhelming fact that behind the facade of external appearances, the vested majority of governmental systems are actually forms of a plutocracy. A plutocracy is defined as a system of government which is ruled by the wealthy. Another closely related concept and term in our present society is the reluctance to publicly acknowledge that some people's lives are revealed to be functioning primarily in a plutocratic manner. Plutolatry is defined as being the worship of wealth. One would surely think we would hear this descriptive word used more commonly and widely in our current materialistic, technology-driven world culture, yet this is not the case. The self-evident, undeniable, proven fact is that for countless centuries earthly governments have been devised by and controlled by the wealthy and powerful people, whether they are self-professed nobility, religious leaders, military generals, despotic dictators or simply successful business people.

These wealthy people have continually established numerous institutional systems that perpetuate their dominance and control over all entire earthly cultures and monetary systems. The direct result is that governmental and economic systems tend to serve the narrow self-interest of these groups of people, rather than the best interests of all people and earthly environments. Their general attitude is characterised by a sterile desire to accumulate more wealth, profit and power, regardless of the adverse, debilitating socially destructive effects of their attitudes and actions upon global culture or any group of people that do not directly and willingly serve their interests.

The history of slavery on Earth is another 'window' into seeing the motivations and character of those wealthy and powerful people existing mostly 'behind the scenes' of public life. These 'hidden' despots arbitrarily deem that everyone that can be subjugated by weapons, ideology, depravation, disease, religion, poverty or any other means available; exists only to serve their own self-interests, whatever they may be, rightly or wrongly. As we continue to evaluate various forms of government, a valid perspective to consider is that all forms of government ultimately seem prone to eventually serve the vested interests of the wealthy and powerful elements in our societies rather than what is actually best for the vast majority of Earth's people and the other life forms that co-habit this beautiful planet with us. If one thinks the history of slavery is unpleasantly revealing, then consider the fates and position of any other life forms existing on this planet; be they fish, bees, trees, wild animals, whales, elephants, birds, domesticated animals or any other thinking feeling creature that exists here. They are all perceived as "chattel" or the possession of those able to claim, utilise, destroy, or even eat them as people wish, if they are able. Not a particularly pretty picture, yet these situations and attitudes are simply another defining aspect of historically verified human nature.

Let's resume our brief consideration of some of the more commonly recognised forms of government ideologies as well as few that we may not be so readily aware of in modern society. We believe we know all about democracy, communism, socialism, republicanism, and federalism, yet these governmental systems seldom, if ever, approximate their ideal version in functional reality. These basic types of government were originally composed to manifest the most noble, best intentions in the people who contributed their wisdom, vision and dreams in the creation of these attempts to improve existing forms of government for all people. Humanity has experienced the results of these forms of government in more recent historical times.

We recognise the serious problems that plague autocratic, totalitarian, fascist dictatorships and other similar types of despotic government, which usually result in warfare for neighbouring nations and chronic misery for the people unfortunate to live under such brutal oppressive systems of governmental or religious control. A few related systems of government that are less well-known are quite common in the history of humanity. These include: oligarchy, aristocracy, elitism, gerontocracy, and hierocracy. Hierocracy is a term to describe a government by priestly rule, while gerontocracy describes a government dominated by old men. Many of these forms of government are also characterised by militarism, which is defined as being a form of government with undue prevalence upon military ideals, tendencies and spirit. All these forms of autocratic government tend to be intolerant, inflexible, uncompromising, callous, persecutory, authoritarian, merciless, tyrannical, punitive, arrogant, coercive, dictatorial, exploitive, suppressive and Draconian. Ultimately, they all become an unsustainable, miserable, painful, costly failure.

It is interesting to note that Draco was a legislator in Athens in about 620BC, so not all aspects of the previously mentioned ancient Greek City States were as representative and noble as intended in actual practice with regard to human well-being of all citizens. In a similar though unrelated way, it is most unlikely that a government dominated by peasant farmers would ever be able to develop a complex technological society within a short length of time.

However, we see China has become the world's most dominant manufacturing superpower within only a few decades of being a primarily agrarian dominated society under the authoritarian communist rule of Mao Zedong. Mao had a 'higher' vision for the Chinese people to be a great nation again and we see this is now a distinctively obvious reality; thereby creating better conditions globally for us all. Another famous dictator, Fidel Castro, has been widely appreciated by most Cubans for his social and cultural accomplishments, in spite of the austerity practiced out of necessity under that regime for almost half a century, which has resulted in a more equitable society than was possible under the former capitalistic economic system. Criticism is easy, yet it is the viable solutions we must focus our attention upon now. There are lessons to be learned from every type of life experience.

The point here is many quite different types of government share many similar goals and methods in promoting the efficient, productive management of their national societies and economies. The problems arise under any governmental systems when there is no peace, prosperity, meaning, joy, freedom, nor sufficient free time to enjoy with one's family and friends. Any system of economics or government that reduces or seeks to eliminate most legal forms of real opportunity for the vast majority of people is doomed to fail. Likewise; a social leadership that exemplifies poor ethical behaviour and ignores the needs of the people and planet is doomed to a catastrophic failure, which we now seek to avoid. It is the working people everywhere that sustain every society on this planet and feed, clothe and care for all people; rich, poor, powerful and otherwise. It is now time to truly realise we are all in this life together and all should enjoy the benefits of our labour because justice, freedom and a more equitable economic system is achievable.

One of lesser known types of governmental systems is egalitarianism. Egalitarianism is a form of government characterised by genuine adherence to the principle of equal rights and justice to all persons. Contrast this with oligarchy, which is government by a small group of persons; or elitism, which is government by a select group of wealthy, powerful or religious people; or aristocracy where a privileged group of self-professed 'outstanding citizens' or a 'class of nobility' arbitrarily dictate policy to the masses of people.

Another lesser known type of government in our modern world is meritocracy; a form of government by persons selected according to merit in competition, with regard to their experience, ability, thoroughness and positive character. A meritocracy would be a government run by people who are the most intelligent and capable, truly noble in character, and proven by experience to be genuinely committed to accomplishing the public's best interests.

A novel, amazing, refreshing idea would be the combination of egalitarianism and meritocracy in establishing a much better, more efficient, equitable, harmonious, polite, relevant, ethical, functional governmental system! Within such a new governmental system, the wealthy would still retain their wonderful lifestyles and enormous financial capabilities, yet the positive difference would be that they would cease to be directly involved in controlling these governmental systems to the complete disregard and detriment to the remainder of humanity and the planetary environments, The wealthy could then focus more upon enjoying the fruits of other people's labours, which has always been their greatest talent and desire and we would not wish to deprive them of that joy.

The problem is that regardless of how fantastic any governmental or economic ideology or model appears or seems to be in its idealistic design and intent; reality has countless methods in distorting, confounding and obstructing the desired final result, usually due primarily to the adverse, negative, pervasive set of human nature issues that we are identifying and discussing here.

The essential relevant reality of modern times is that 'the powers that be', in early 2016, these 'cabal' (Illuminati, Satanists, 'high level' criminals, or whatever term you prefer to describe the relatively small group of evil 'controllers' here on Earth and their 'minders') are rapidly becoming "the powers that were" here on Earth, for many valid reasons that we will not discuss in any detail here now. These unloving, unkind, greedy, power-crazed, arrogant, unconscionable, self-absorbed, predatorial, parasitic, aggressive, psychotically counter-productive people have managed to usurp (seize or assume control of wrongly) almost total control over all forms of government; including pseudo-democratic, pseudo-communist, pseudo-socialist, pseudo-republican types of government, and enthusiastically support the establishment and continuance of fascist, plutocratic, and militaristic dictatorships to accomplish their selfish goals.

Their self-evident intention is to institutionalise various detrimental mass-population control systems; such as through creating endless cycles of international warfare; social disintegration, with poverty, scarcity, misery, uncertainty and fear being the daily, ongoing life experience for most people. The relative few ultra-wealthy have a (now failed) plan to continue this autocratic despotic unsustainable system globally, with a continuation to rule ruthlessly over the entire population and planet as they see fit. The goal is to persistently, permanently maintain the status quo (keep relatively things as they now are) in regard to their overt, subtle and pervasive influences and control of our communities, nations, cultures, religions, economies and the entire world civilisation. These self-interested, extremely greedy, malevolent people form only a tiny minority of Earth's total human population and they definitely do not care enough about the best interests of humanity, as proven by their self-evident attitudes and destructive actions. Therefore, if they seek to continue to rule our civilisation and to continue to act as our business, religious and governmental leaders; then they will need to conduct themselves, our societies and economic development in more sane, responsible, sustainable, ethical, equitable, just and trustworthy ways.

It should be carefully noted here that when we say these ultra-wealthy people are 'powerful'; we definitely do not intend to imply that they are powerful in terms of their physical, intellectual, or spiritual abilities. They are exceedingly powerful in deceiving and manipulating people; who they perceive as 'chattel', or any other type of domesticated creature they own and control as they wish. This is challenging for 'normal people' to understand or believe, until one clearly examines all aspects of their life and that of the civilisation existing today globally. The so-called 'power elite' that have historically been among the 'public faces' of nobility are generally 'lower level' servants of these 'behind the scenes' super-wealthy families, who are cunning strategists, business-minded profiteers, and those who have historically been adept at getting others to work for them in various ways. Those willing and less willing 'servant workers' learn to serve their 'minders' interests, as well as to protect them from harm as those controllers seek to dominate others from their 'hidden' positions of financial, genetic lineage and circumstantial power. The current group of 'cabal' thugs are clearly not obeying the wishes of their 'minders', so big world changes are occurring right now and it is for the best for ALL people.

Their true talent has been their ability to entice and manipulate other more truly powerful and capable people into acting upon their behalf to oppress and control others, through their governmental and religious despots, dictators or elected officials. These historically controlling types of people often can be characterised as being primarily 'profiteers' or 'parasites', depending upon your perspective; in the sense they often rely upon intentionally creating scarcity, slavery, desperation, conflict, misery, and destruction to more effectively accomplish their goals to control and subjugate the vast majority of people in our civilisations, past and present. The self-evident fact they do not (yet) fully utilise their intellectual and financial abilities in their roles as the true, actual responsible leaders of our world to greatly improve conditions here indicates they are not nearly as intelligent or noble as they may assume themselves to be. This is not a pleasant situation to consider, yet these are the self-evident realities that are clearly and obviously before us now.

Thankfully, there are positive exceptions to this generalisation in that some of the world's most wealthy 'public face' types of people now clearly do have a degree of sincere consideration for the best interests of others and earthly environments. There is no doubt that truly productive, innovative, hard working people with higher vision still do exist within the wealthiest elite class of humans, yet they and their organisations are among the distinct minority of those ruling our civilisation now. However, these truly noble, kind, loving, compassionate, truly spiritual people among these ruling 'behind the scenes power-elites' are now beginning to assert their genuine desires to create a more prosperous, productive, peaceful, equitable, just and sustainable 'golden civilisation' here on Mother Earth. Apparently there have been clear 'signs' from Divinity/God/Creator that this mission is now 'in process' for us all.

Again, we see the 'dated' nature of some comments and realities here, as thankfully the entire world, including the planet Mother Earth Itself, is transforming for the better. This is occurring on many levels and in countless beneficial ways, so we shall see the end of the current forms of violent and oppressive civilisation and the replacement of a far better social, economic, environmental and spiritual civilisation which is now happening, with visibly accelerating speed and unstoppable momentum of ideas whose 'time has arrived' on Earth.

Unfortunately in modern times we see that there are no sane, reasonable socially imposed limits or constraints upon the expansion of some people's self-interest, quite often being achieved at the expense and suffering of others. Those seeking to maintain and increasingly strengthen their control over our civilisation are generally characterised by their greed and depravity. This is resulting in an observable, definitive international culture characterised by more widespread insanity, as evidenced by what we see around us in the world every day. Others within humanity have a far better plan 'in process'.

One example that indicates insanity is being encouraged intentionally by various malevolent, evil forces on Earth is the extremely high levels of graphic obscene violence in all entertainment medias, such as on television, the movies, video games and in publishing. This violence is now being manifested in public culture globally, with rampant acts of insane violence occurring in our daily lives upon a much more commonplace basis than it once was in western society. Why are the innumerable sources of unconscionable, unproductive, detrimental illustrations of excessive, unrealistic, insane cycles of violence and retribution not being more widely censored and made illegal by our purportedly protective, well-meaning governments? Why the ongoing celebrations related to wars and the damaged warriors and so few memorials for the millions of innocent, defenceless, non-combatant victims like the children, women and elderly? Because there is an intention and desire by those controlling our world to promote, instigate and conduct acts of violence in order to create chaos, instability, fear, insecurity and destruction in our civilisation because that is what these sorts of people and their organisations thrive upon emotionally, financially and ideologically. They seek to set one group, religion, race, or nation against the others endlessly. There are already many forms of unnecessary and inadvisable censorship existing that is actually counter-productive for society. Again, so why not censor the graphic, obscene, pointless, gratuitous excessive violence we see daily pervasively in the media? Because governments and the ruling powers are more focused upon censoring information they believe to be potentially far more threatening and dangerous to them, as follows.

One such example of inexplicable censorship involves the unwillingness of most governments to freely make full public disclosure of all government expenditure of taxpayer's funds. If government can censor, hide, or lie about governmental policy decisions and expenditures then why not censor senseless violence which is potentially so damaging to human psychology? Would publicising government expenditures and the profits being made from tax revenues, the sale of publicly owed national assets to private companies, or the financial cost of operating our political processes damage our societies as much as these copious volumes of senseless, unproductive, sensational daily violence that humanity is now being subjected? Would publicising the honest actual full financial accounts of big business's true levels of profitability or their actual taxation rates per dollar earned be beneficial for society or is there a genuine need for such information to be kept confidential for business security reasons? Why the reluctance to publicly publish the true environmental records of industry; or the true income of wealthy people, corporations and institutions that are the major shareholders in a diverse, interrelated groups of international companies that knowingly pursue corporate policies of environmental destruction, unnecessary pollution and often mistreat their third world employees by forcing them to work very long hours, at low pay or no pay in some cases, in often dangerous and unhealthy working conditions? Why is such information not readily available in the public domain, without great efforts being necessary to acquire these types of information? It is an odd situation that information regarding many important issues are not generally available or even accessible to the public, who should have a right to know these basic facts in our purportedly 'free' and 'democratic' western societies. Why would records on the murders of the Kennedy's, or the suicide rates, not be available to the public immediately?

No, there are regulations that closely govern the release of all manner of information unjustly categorised as being private and confidential in our society. Another such example is that the local community is not notified if a child molester, thief, drug dealer or convicted murder is released from prison on parole into one's community either. Nor are they generally confined to a location where there moments can be easily monitored or even controlled for the safety of society. We could list countless similar examples of information that we should have that is publicly unavailable or censored with no explanation, as well as document innumerable examples of potentially destructive, disruptive, or deleterious information that is freely available and not censored, such as information on bomb making with chemicals or explosives. Weapons of every description are freely available throughout the world at varying prices, so what source is enabling, allowing, supplying and perpetuating this volatile situation? Why is there so little public consultation in our purportedly free and democratic societies about issues of importance in enacting key legislation affecting our families, workplaces, environment, human rights, the legal system, governmental budgets, and so on? Why use legislation to mandate vaccinations in many western nations? Why?

Because controlling people and institutions have determined that THEIR own self-interested needs, desires and opinions are vastly more significant than those of the citizens. Nor do these oppressive, self-serving interest groups wish to receive any of the inputs, research findings or conclusive facts that could be presented by any independent experts who are knowledgeable and unbiased in matters of public consequence and are known to be acting upon the public's best interests.

Therefore, we must again ask ourselves, "Why are we being inundated and continually bombarded with images and thoughts of violence, fear, anger, poverty, discord and emotional turmoil in our global community?" To me, the well-researched undeniable facts indicate this situation is a carefully orchestrated, long term strategic plan to encourage all forms of violence; promote social and economic motives for violent revolution within the mostly peaceful human population; to increase anti-social, insane and pathological attitudes and behaviours; to gradually desensitise us to accept violence and insanity as a normal part of life; to devalue human life; create optimum conditions for ongoing world wars, and so on.

If you disagree, and you honestly believe the (unlikely) answer to the previous question is, "No, this current situation is not occurring through intentional design by hidden, insidious, evil forces that seek to incubate, stimulate and create conditions of chaos, violence, disharmony, injustice and insanity within humanity."; then, what is the actual reason that we see so much artificially contrived theatrical and real, live, vivid violence on all forms of mass media?

Recall that all major international mass media is now owned or controlled by a relatively very small, very wealthy, very powerful group of people who seemingly possess no conscience and who have vested interests in every aspect of our global economy. It appears conclusive to any reasonable, perceptive, well-informed thinking person that this excessive violence constantly inundating us is intentionally being 'fed' to humanity in order to program, promote and instil within us an unnatural proclivity toward violence, aggression, conflict, discord, cultural and religious disharmony. It is apparent that an increase in violence, fear, anger, depravation, destruction and the resulting suffering would somehow serve the self-interests of those who control our world now. Do you believe this situation is quite probable or even likely to be possible? No? Perhaps? Definitely! What is your explanation, especially as you reflect upon the history of mankind over the past few thousand years?

Another example of the undeniable insanity characterising many of the people in control of our civilisation is the renewed propaganda campaign internationally to more widely utilise nuclear energy to generate electricity. This is truly insane, given all the factors involved in how potentially devastating the widespread use and misuse of nuclear technologies could become if accidents, wars, waste disposal problems and terrorist acts become more predominant in the future. However, the extensive use of nuclear technology is now what the autocrats plan to generate electricity in the near future. Please carefully consider the lack of any functional effective 'clean-up' of the massive radiation source at the nuclear disaster in Fukushima, Japan. The current civilisation has no solution to its' own waste creation and this too is not a debateable issue, so a dangerous poisonous technology is being used with no concern for its longer term environmental damaging effects.

There is no real discussion about conservation of energy, or why our cities all need to be so well-lit at night as to appear to be like football fields of massive proportions when viewed from outer space, or is so brightly lit that one can easily read a book on most city streets at night. Could it be a fear of the dark by those in power and that those nasty big 'boogie men' may come out and tear down their despotic civilisation while they are sleeping behind their secured perimeters? Civilisation wastes more energy than is possible to calculate, so why does our civilisation need to consider nuclear power when it is toxic to all physical life forms? The answer is it is unnecessary and will make more profits for those profiteers already wealthy beyond measure.

Why is the 'fracking' to release natural gas allowed environmentally when that activity destroys and poisons fresh water aquifers globally by this insane practice? The answer is that it is all about the money and the intentional destruction of earthly environments for greedy self-interest by people that obviously do NOT care about the damage or suffering of people, other life, or the Earth. Two other self-evident self-destructive mass poisoning of people by design activities are 'chemtrails' and intentionally adding toxic fluoride and chlorine into the drinking water supplies in many nations.

The many solutions for Humanity are available and this includes access to non-polluting natural energy sources with amazing new innovations and these will soon be coming to us all for a reasonable cost. It is exciting to be aware of how much positive beneficial change is NOW happening on Earth in early 2016 and will continue to exponentially expand in the coming years, as we all will much enjoy. In future this will be my focus; applying solutions.

The unrestrained expression of amoral, immoral and psychotic attitudes that some people now in positions of social power and responsibility possess and wish to impose upon us all is of huge concern to us and future generations. It is easy to observe a wide range of unwholesome realities exist within our modern world. We must realise that if these problems are allowed to develop according to present trends, that this process will destroy our current civilisation and likely result in a social and environmental situation that is vastly worse than the serious challenges now facing humanity. The vast majority of 'our' so-called 'western' political, businesses, religious and social leaders are definitely not adequately committed at this time to addressing and resolving the escalating problems we are creating for ourselves as we see in the Middle East and the economic hardship globally due to these flawed policies. The proof of this is undeniable.

However, thankfully and most encouraging is that in September of 2015 President Putin of Russia and China's President Xi Jinping, now do both agree publicly at the United Nations and militarily, as evidenced in Syria, to bring ISIS under control. It is clear that the days of US military conquest globally are now 'officially' over.

The recent unexpected and unexplained 'resignation' of some key US military staff and Congress people will also serve to confirm this fact though no reasonable explanations are available. The same can be said in regard to all of the recent bankers that suddenly became suicidal, went oddly missing as in the past scientists researching 'free energy' tended to do. It was a similar unexpected 'case' when the former Pope quickly found a 'reason' to resign (over the weekend) before he was 'served' with an arrest warrant by the Italian Police for war crimes and the paedophile activities of the Catholic Church for centuries and into modern times. Oddly, that same arrest warrant has not been 'executed' upon the new Pope (yet). Again, we the people do not hear the full true facts in whatever is actually happening globally.

Therefore, let's continue to examine a few related issues, to better comprehend the parameters of the situation, considering we will need to take some calculated actions to improve matters in our own lives and by working together with all types of people to solve these conditions while the opportunity is available to us. It will also be of significant relevance to carefully record, analyse and directly confront those people, groups and institutions that will surely oppose a sane, responsible solution based approach to the challenges and problems that now exist within our civilisation.

Let's shift our focus to address a variety of other related human nature issues, beginning with the loss and erosion of fundamental constitutionally guaranteed human rights in the United States of America (USA) in recent decades. We use the USA as an example here because that nation has for two centuries been the best available exemplary model for functional democracy and true economic opportunity existing in the modern world. Or perhaps this is what Americans have been told (within the USA and internationally by the US propaganda services) and they simply were gullible and stupid enough to believe the lies. One must question this purported 'fact'.

Of enormous significance is to closely and thoroughly examine the sequence of events that lead to the legislated diminution of these basic human rights. There has been a protracted assault upon Americans' civil rights to privacy, economic opportunity for all citizens, and freedom of public expression of one's opinions. The US Constitution and Bill of Rights guaranteed and protected these civil liberties and structural safeguards, which have been diminished and undermined by endless series of executive, legislative and judicial changes. One of the most notable that stripped Americans of equitable economic opportunity was the right for wage-earning citizens not to be taxed upon one's income, rather only taxed by governmental levies upon goods, services and trade. An unlawful and incorrectly enacted Amendment was included to the US Constitution that overturned and removed that protection, so the entire amount of financial earnings of working people would be taxed at whatever rate 'the government' and their controllers decided was appropriate. American wage earners have suffered financially thereafter because the prevalent wages paid to the majority of citizens have not increased nearly as rapidly as have the costs of living.

The result has been dramatically increased levels of debt being accumulated by these people, for those 'fortunate' enough to be qualified to receive loans from banks or to obtain credit cards. The total number of homeless, bankrupt, destitute, unemployed, and incarcerated people living in America has skyrocketed in recent decades, with many jobs being exported into developing nations by international corporations that originated in the USA or overseas. Meanwhile, the U.S. government has continued to spend taxpayers' money without any functional public restraint or true checks and balances since that time. Political party politics is primarily controlled by international 'big business', who now controls the U.S. government, so democracy is an illusionary concept in the United States of America.

Former US President General Dwight Eisenhower publicly warned the US nation against the eminent dangers posed by the military-industrial complex existing within the USA government and bureaucracy before he left the Presidency and his warnings are proving correct. We can also recall that the 'founding fathers' of the United States of

America, after the 1776 victory in the War for Independence from Britain, who were the authors of the United States Constitution and the Bill of Rights, were well-aware of the dangers posed from the internationally active 'power elite' existing within and outside of America. They made significant efforts to establish the foundation to create an equitable true representative democracy by enacting laws to protect the rights of the American people from these determined autocrats and plutocrats. They warned the citizens of America to be continually vigilant against the invasive, insidious erosion and removal of their inalienable rights guaranteed and legally enforced in these monumental documents; thereby seeking to install and maintain a true form of democracy in the USA. Now we see this threat has become a pervasive, self-evident, pathetic reality in the USA. Indications are that the American people are now awakening from this terrible nightmare.

Freedom of speech as evidenced by the right and ability to express one's viewpoint without being persecuted in any way has deteriorated since the 1950's with the anti-communist campaigns. Martin Luther King, US President John Kennedy and his brother Robert Kennedy and countless others were murdered in public execution fashion for implementing their civil right to honestly, freely and open express themselves publicly and encourage positive change in American society. We have seen a wide variety of attention-seeking distractions occurring over passing time; such as the so-called 'war against drugs', the so-called 'war against terrorism' and many other such costly, futile, deceitful, public display types of insincere actions whose covert real intent was to limit the constitutionally guaranteed rights of American citizens. In both of these cases, both the availability of illegal, highly addictive expensive drugs and the numbers of acts of international terrorism skyrocketed because covert government policies and actions actually helped to create these problems.

Another such assault on American freedoms, justice, ethical conduct and transparency in governmental decision making has been conducted within the entire American judicial system. The US Court system has long been the domain of the relatively privileged elite in US society, yet this too is escalating out of reasonable limits regarding the Supreme Court's questionable interpretations of the US Constitution. This would include their 'quick' convenient 'ruling' against the Florida election recount of ballots in the 2000 Presidential election in which George W. Bush was defeated by the then Democratic Vice President Al Gore, who won the popular election vote count. It was proven that in the critical state of Florida, where George W. Bush's brother, Jeb Bush, was then serving as Governor, that there were innumerable obvious proven cases of vote irregularities, vote fraud and misconduct by state officials. All of that evidence was disregarded and basically ignored in the Supreme Court's decision to illegally, unconstitutionally and immorally to declare the actual loser of that election, George W. Bush as being the 'winner' and ruling that he become the President of the USA. We now know many years later what that fiasco has meant not only to US citizens, but also the entire world. My personal opinion or perception is that George W. Bush is among the most despotic, corrupted, imbecilic, hypocritical, evil, and damaging Presidents that the USA has ever had the misfortune to endure. Now this is a matter for history and perhaps in due course for the International Court of Justice in The Hague to determine.

We are getting 'ahead' of ourselves here, so let's resume our cursory examination of these exemplary situations. The Supreme Court has seemingly misinterpreted the US Constitution in its recent review of other legislative decisions, such as the so-called Patriot Act. The US Patriot Act is invasive, totalitarian style, draconian legislation which quite clearly contravenes the US Constitution in many ways, yet the Court approved it to pass into law in the USA. The independence and viability of the decisions of the US Supreme Court is no longer unfettered by external self-interests, including those adverse influences from the executive branch of government and powerful financial and business interests. Some of the dubious decisions of the US Supreme Court are self-evident to be witnessed over an extended period of time, going back over a hundred years.

There is a distinctive tendency for the US Congress to enact some legislation that is clearly not in the best interests of taxpaying US citizens, nor the long term best interests of the United States of America. In this regard we must ask ourselves whether or not such actions indicate that the USA intends to continue to remain the world's most successful democracy that genuinely seeks to inspire the development of a freer, more equitable, prosperous and peaceful world in the future. We have experienced two major world wars being fought in the past century due to the divisive militaristic forces we currently see at work to create ongoing conflict around the world. We can perceive that the USA is now being prepared by the world's controlling forces of despotism to lead the way forward with an increasingly militaristic and confrontational global foreign policy. It would surely appear to be the undeniable case and thankfully as 2015 came to a close; both China and Russia are simply asserting that this is now over, without using overt military force to make their decision clear to President Obama and his 'minders'. Furthermore, soon the Chinese RMB currency will become the 'official' Reserve Currency of the world, thereby replacing the debt-based U.S. Dollar, probably before you read these words.

Consider the Middle Eastern war that the USA is now intentionally escalating which is focused within two nations that were originally financed and supported militarily by the USA, Afghanistan and Iraq. There is now also increasing attention upon initiating conflict with Iran supposedly due to its development of nuclear capabilities. The current Iranian fundamentalist Islamic government seized power in 1979 from the US sponsored former dictator in Iran, Shah Pahlavi, whose brutal oppressive dictatorship was supported by the USA in every way possible, often through the covert activities of the CIA. The Iranian fundamentalist Islamic government has evolved into a protagonist for the USA largely due to

Iranian public opposition to the despotic, violent policies and activities of the deposed Iranian dictator, whose violence and western capitalistic extremism engendered the unfortunate social and economic conditions for revolution in Iran.

There are direct analogous similar parallels to the dictator of Iraq, Saddam Hussein, who was also extensively supported financially and militarily by the USA for many decades, just as the Shah of Iran once had been. We could also clearly recall and consider the similar cases of US installed and supported brutal dictators, General Suharto of Indonesia and General Pinochet of Chile, among other locations such as Nigeria, Burma, Argentina, Venezuela, Nicaragua, and on and on. Additionally, we must not forget that the Taliban was initially also financed, supplied with weapons and trained by the intelligence agencies (CIA, NSA and others) within the USA, which makes one quite curious about al-Qaeda, as well as various other terrorist organisations internationally such as ISIS which seems to be especially well-funded in a time of extensive poverty and deprivation for most people living within this war torn region, such as Syria. ISIS has plenty of new trucks and weapons that are rapidly being destroyed by the Russian and Chinese armies with the U.S. naval fleet having recently left the Middle East permanently. The closure of many U.S. bases globally will follow in the months and years to come.

The undeniable proof is increasingly self-evident to anyone seeking to consider the facts about the once clandestine funding of international terrorist groups like ISIS and others mentioned here by the CIA and NSA, as we can now finally see more clearly. This review of past events can be done historically as well. Many U.S. crimes against humanity are now being mentioned publicly and proven internationally. This includes President Putin's recent inspirational speech given to United Nations, so these facts will become common knowledge globally. As we saw when the Berlin Wall 'came down' unexpectedly, dramatically and swiftly; the rapid demise of the current forms of corrupted, militaristic, autocratic, treasonous U.S. government and the vile, subservient political leadership in the USA are very likely to come to a swift and unexpected ending. This will occur when U.S. Citizens recover the right to rule the nation by the U.S. Constitution and Bill of Rights again. This may occur with the assistance of high ranking officers within the U.S. military, who help restore true democracy within America. Passing time and improving circumstances will reveal it all to us in its miraculous ways.

Interests within the US government have consistently been proven to provide financial and military support and meddle in the internal domestic political and cultural affairs of many nations internationally to elect, or otherwise install through covert or open revolution; 'leaders' or 'subordinate stooges' as the case may be, that favour the self-interests of big business and who actively promote a modern version of American colonialism. If anyone doubts these facts, then they may wish to review the conclusive evidence and examine the social and political results of America's intimate involvement with many of the world's most corrupt, tyrannical, murderous dictators. Is there any real justification in the rationalised reasons professed to be substantiating the need and validity for these overt and covert policies and actions by forces of oppression and domination within the U.S. government? In Afghanistan, the U.S. military seems to be primarily now involved in 'protecting' the opium production and 'insuring' the reliability of the subsequent heroine production and distribution systems, with the assistance of the CIA.

In the minds of those whose self-interests have been served in these despotic and disingenuous activities, they would likely falsely and knowingly contend that these actions were justified, from their own perspective; because like any psychopath, the only perspective that matters to them in any way is their own self-interested viewpoint. They feel no one else's misery, depravation or death because their conscience is non-functional in relation to others. Therefore, they do not conduct themselves as human beings possessing a truly active spirit in relationship with higher aspects spiritual existence that we define as being aspects of Godliness.

There could be a very strong case made that the United States of America no longer functions in a truly democratic manner, nor according to the U.S. Constitution, as was originally intended by the founding fathers who authored the US Constitution. Additionally, a good case could be made that the USA no longer conducts its activities as a nation living by the motto of "In God we trust", if its actions are considered instead of the meaningless rhetoric, constant misinformation and blatant lies. The obvious fact is that the legislators elected to represent the opinions and will of the American people have been demonstrated to provide their allegiance to political party principles and to serving the favoured big business lobby interests, rather than the ordinary citizen's best interests. Examining the legislation that the U.S. Congress enacts is an excellent indicator of this fact.

What events lead to George W. Bush being in office for the curious events of Sept 11, 2001 to occur? By far and 'almost never discussed' is the previously mentioned election for President in the 2000 year when the Democratic Party candidate Al Gore won the majority of national votes in the Presidential elections. Proven voting 'irregularities' (fraud and corruption) occurred in Florida where Al Gore actually won the majority of votes in that State, where George W Bush's brother, Jeb Bush was Governor, which implies the so-called 'irregularities' were intentional in many cases, especially when thousands of eligible registered voters that would likely support Gore were unfairly removed from the Florida state voter registration records for various reasons. The Florida electoral commission declared George W Bush the winner in Florida in that 2000 election, which provided Bush with the key 'Electoral College' votes to enable him to become the next President of the USA. This is mentioned again because it demonstrates one way true democracy is intentionally sabotaged by design to favour the intentions of those people and interest groups that are currently controlling our governmental and economic systems from behind hidden closed doors primarily for accomplishing their own agendas. The fact that the U.S. Supreme Court ruled against allowing a more honest review and re-count of all votes in the State of Florida demonstrates how the collusion within high levels within the U.S. government occurs on various issues of importance.

The Electoral College is a system in USA where each state has a specified number of state voter 'representatives' appointed according to the population size of that state. These appointed representatives are supposed to cast their votes according to the public's votes in their states of origin in Presidential elections. In other words, this system is an 'indirect, representative' form of so-called democracy. All the Electoral College votes in every individual state are normally cast in favour of the candidate that wins the popular vote in that particular state, making the more populous states far more important to win in Presidential elections. Florida proved to be what is called a 'swing state' in that who won that state's Electoral College votes would win the U.S. Presidential election in 2000. In the 2000 Florida elections, it was later proven that the thousands of proven cases of so-called 'voter irregularities' had unfairly and incorrectly indicated Bush as the winner of the totals Florida vote count. Actually, the popular vote in Florida, if fairly conducted and tallied properly would have resulted in Al Gore winning the popular vote count in Florida, thus making him, not Bush the President of the USA in 2000.

Since no criminal charges were ever laid in Florida regarding this clear case of injustice and the inappropriate and possibly illegal actions of various Florida electoral officials, one must decide for themselves whether or not this is a situation of one well-placed brother choosing to protect his other brother on his way to the Presidency of the USA. This is clearly a matter of the historical record, yet for some this issue is open to debate. It may simply remain as an inexplicable 'irregularity' that will be hidden from the American people in much the same way as the actual findings of the investigations into the JFK or RFK murders, or the 9/11 governmental investigations being withheld or coming to a dubious final assessment. However, it is an interesting 'possibilities' that these matters will be proven over passing time and with further investigation.

There was an appeal by Al Gore to the Supreme Court when Florida declared Bush the winner in that state due to the massive conclusive evidence of the widespread vote fraud in Florida. The evidence was being prepared for review and a recount of the Florida was being undertaken when the U.S. Supreme Court interceded and declared George Bush to be the duly elected President. The valid fact is that the Supreme Court of the United States of America, the highest Court in the USA, made such an unjust, poor decision without even considering the full evidence that Al Gore had actually conclusively won the Presidential election in both popular vote and by the electoral representative vote count. Why did this happen and how could it happen in a truly democratic nation, against the Constitutional guarantees to prevent such events from occurring? The answer is it could not, if the process had been equitable and according to true justice which obviously no longer exists to any significant extent within America.

How did this happen? The highest level of the judicial branch of government, the U.S. Supreme Court, had previously been 'compromised' by numerous controversial judicial appointments made that espoused a conservative, Republican Party ideological perspective by previous Republican Party Presidents. These conservative judicial appointments were made over several decades under the administrations of former Republican Party Presidents George Bush (the elder), Ronald Regan, Gerald Ford and Richard Nixon. Again, this is merely my own opinion and perception based on a thorough assessment of the facts that have come to my attention. However, it is not adequately or thoroughly investigated by those whose legal governmental responsibility it is to do such things; so what does this tell us about those that should investigate the issue honestly?

Throughout this entire process, we see a definitive 'vehicle' for institutionalising the control of party politics through corporate and other vested interests that financially support political parties that enables these politicians to be elected into public office. They then appoint their like-minded friends, business associates and family members into roles of authority in government and bureaucratic institutions and the 'fix is on'. The inbuilt 'checks and balances' that serve as ethical control features no longer function effectively within all levels of government due to the adverse influences over centuries of passing time by the wealthy 'power elite' to drastically pervert and control all aspects within the Legislative branch (enact the laws), Executive branch (presidential leader) and Judicial branch (courts that review and rule upon the legality of the laws and the application of those laws, according to their interpretations of US Constitution) of government.

The ultimate result is that these extraordinary influences and control mechanisms establish a governmental system that intentionally serve primarily the vested interests that support them financially and that weld massive power globally, yet we can clearly see this power is diminishing rapidly, as 2016 begins with positive changes sweeping the Earth now. American Citizens and the entire global population are increasingly recognising the overall set of complex reasons why so few aspects of the U.S. government or the U.S. bureaucratic institutions serve the best interests of Americans or the world in modern times. The American government openly states it has no real commitment to do anything except protect the nation's best international interests under the leadership of the despot George W Bush and the powerful people who placed him in the role as President and subsequently have kept him in that role in spite of the evidence that he and some of his closest governmental associates are actually international war criminals, in regard to events surrounding 9/11 and the Middle East, which we will soon address in further detail. President Obama is a curious man that seemingly 'came from nowhere' to eloquently speak exactly whatever the American people wanted to hear just to be elected; then he followed the destructive, flawed, draconian domestic and international policies, just as the most recent 5 Republican Presidents have done.

America now is conducting foreign policy that is diametrically opposed to the best long term interests of world peace and prosperity. This is a lamentable, deplorable, unacceptable situation, especially considering the democratic will of the American people was unjustly and inappropriately contravened by the judicial branch for apparently political reasons, as recent history has proven to be the case in the 2000 US Presidential elections. Our world would be far better if the will of the American people had been accepted and instituted with Al Gore becoming the President of the USA in 2000. However, the corrupt rulers of our world knew that George W. Bush would strive to promote conflict, destruction and suffering that would increase their family wealth and control, just as did his father the first President George Bush, so we see the results clearly before us now.

Please fully consider the destabilising subsequent affects of George W. Bush being elected in 2000 to the most powerful public office in the world today. We will consider a few issues in that respect next, as we gain better insight into the hidden agenda and methods of operations by those lawless, corrupted, immoral global power brokers who seek to instigate conflict, discord, and chaos around the world for their own greedy, self-serving reasons.

The well-verified information originating from thousands of independent unbiased scientists, engineers and professional independent researchers has accumulated into a vast volume of undeniable evidence regarding inconsistencies, irregularities and outright 'impossibilities' in relation to the events of September 11, 2001 in New York City, otherwise known as 9/11.

What will be presented here is only a small fraction of the information now in the public domain and will be further verified that hidden agendas exist to destabilise international peace. The present deplorable situation in the Middle East serves to distract global attention and financial resources from addressing other serious issues. It is not at all surprising to realise that none of the major news media outlets have yet chosen to publicly present any of the overwhelming evidence that 9/11 was a not at all the type of Arab inspired terrorist attack that the world was incorrectly led to believe initially. The following information is a matter of public record on the internet and many videos and books have been produced on this subject so there is no longer any doubt on the majority of facts involved in the 9/11 event.

In the early days after the events of 9/11 in New York City when the World Trade Center complex was completely destroyed it was immediately falsely blamed on the purportedly fundamentalist Islamic terrorist organisation al-Qaeda. Since that time, over 10 years of extensive research has conclusively proven the entire event was staged by covert elements within the United States of America with the prior knowledge, consent and some assistance by a number of highly placed officials in the U.S. intelligence services, to falsely appear to be a terrorist attack. There is also ample conclusive evidence to prove some direct involvement by elements within the British and Zionist intelligence agencies, yet we will focus upon American involvement because it is so much easier to address here.

When the full set of facts eventually becomes public knowledge, there will be an excellent criminal court case to prosecute the responsible people; including top level people like the former U.S. President George W Bush, and some key U.S. government personnel known to be within the 'need to know' Bush team of 'insiders' for knowingly planning and later intentionally committing mass murder, numerous acts of treason according to the U.S. Constitution and Bill of Rights by promoting the Patriot Act legislation under false contrived criminally murderous circumstances, and subsequently for making endless numbers of intentional false and misleading statements to wrongly seek to justify the wars in Afghanistan and Iraq, among many other recent events, such as in the Ukraine, Libya and Syria, to name a few.

Understandably, to some people this bold, exceedingly well-documented and scientifically proven assertion seems to be absolutely preposterous, yet they will be those who have not thoroughly considered the evidence to support these facts. Initially, before my investigations began, I wrongly believed it would be impossible for the U.S. government, U.S. military and various international intelligence agencies to be so foolish, corrupted and evil as to intentionally conduct such an insane operation in murdering thousands of innocent people in the 9/11 event in New York. The high quality of my first key sources of information were 2 men connected to the intelligence services of 2 nations outside of the USA whose information soon changed that perspective, as did reflecting upon my own personal experience in knowing about certain top level military procedures from my father, Lt. Col. 'Doc' Wonders (USAF) who was Aide to a 4 star General (David Wade) who was in Command of Strategic Air Command (SAC) for many years.

One example such 'proof' of U.S. military 'collusion' or even participation is that all airplanes of a civilian or registered military type have a transponder on board to track and record their location at all times. No plane is allowed to fly off course according the flight plan they nominate or fly into populated areas without being 'intercepted' by U.S. military armed fighter jets who have orders to get the plane on course, or order it to land, or if ignored then the offending airplane will be shot down with a guided heat seeking missile. Such a situation is generally resolved within 5 minutes of the plane leaving course; however, in the 9/11 event, the first jet flew 'off course' for about one hour and finally into the building without any attempted military intervention apparently.

Observing this is a gross violation of military procedure and terming the event as being 'curious' does not even begin to address the facts involved here. No one was prosecuted or Court martialled for dereliction of duty or any other such charges related to the failure of the U.S. military to protect the innocent people of many nations that were murdered or the gold in storage under the World Trade Center, much of which had mysteriously 'gone missing' before the event. Another revealing fact is that a few armoured vehicles and some that were already mostly loaded with gold bars from the World Trade Center were discovered abandoned under those buildings yet had to be left as events unfolded there.

The thorough research into the full set of evidence available to me over several years proved to be so definitive, so comprehensive and so extensive that one could only conclude that the clear indication was and still is that no group of Arab terrorists could implement such an elaborate, well-designed, well-coordinated series of actions. There were explosive charges set within the building to detonate and destroy the supportive steel structures and these terrorists simply did not have unfettered access to the buildings for the months required to set all of those explosive charges, which included thermite which melts steel, within the many levels that are visible being detonated in the slow motion films of the towers collapsing. These videos include Tower #7 which was never hit by any plane, nor was it damaged by any significant amount of falling debris from the other Twin Towers. Tower # 7 is where the records of key corporate fraud records were being stored for the court cases being prepared or in process by the U.S. government.

The evidence of the 9/11 related events conclusively demonstrated the direct instigation and control of that entire covert operation by the U.S. intelligence services, with some lesser involvement and duplicity by numerous personnel within various branches of the U.S. military. Only President Bush (and his 'superiors') had sufficient Executive power and the abilities required to order and conduct that state sponsored act of international terrorism to further its' own insane world domination agendas by illegally creating and financing terrorist groups to justify its desire to eliminate freedom.

A number of key facts will be repeated to make abundantly clear and revealing that the entire subsequent U.S. purported investigatory process was a strictly controlled 'cover-up' operation designed to avoid truly considering any of the contentious facts that would uncover the actual implementation of the 'attack' was done by 'inside forces' who were connected intimately with a carefully select, loyal, neo-conservative or fascist minded group of top U.S. government 'officials'. These people were in a position to plan, order and accomplish this dastardly homicidal act and then blame it falsely upon so-called 'terrorist enemies' that these same 'forces' had previously created and financed. This demonstrates ongoing historical connections between agencies of the U.S. government, which as the CIA and NSA and international terrorist organisations that seemingly 'appeared out of nowhere' and were very well financed and supplied with weapons and vehicles while being located in poverty stricken areas of the world. We can also determine that extensive 'inside' control of the international news media services was applied to prevent the major media outlets from making public many of the dubious or absurdly ridiculous findings that were presented or mention the key ones that were omitted from any assessment by governmental investigators or were 'explained away' with no scientific basis in fact, or were total fiction. One such example is that jet fuel could burn through the steel supports of the Twin Towers of Tower #7, which had no jet contact at all. Countless aspects of the copious volumes of definitive evidence that proves the direct intentional premeditated involvement or knowledge of some top level US government officials, very likely including the President of the USA, George W Bush and some of his closest associates and advisors was simply not considered in the official investigation, nor in the final report on 9/11.

Here there will only be a brief list of the more obvious facts in the case, because it is simply our intention to use this devastating event as an example of the types of contrived false events that are deviously concocted and implemented by war mongers and chaos makers. These vested interests presently feel they are entitled to be in control of our current global civilisation, yet this is now unacceptable due to their unscrupulous greedy violent behaviours over many generations. Some mindful repetition will be included to make clear a few key relevant facts from time to time here.

The 9/11 event is simply another of countless thousands of such terrorist attacks by the so-called 'power elite' upon the people of Earth over the centuries. We document the basic primary aspects of the 9/11 case here because it is the ultimate ideal example that definitively reveals the trademark insane mentality and demonic capabilities of these well-insulated, self-serving chaos and misery producing elements and groups of evil people within the highest levels of our governmental and business communities within our present earthly civilisation. Their days 'in power' are rapidly drawing to a close here in early 2016, as we shall see with unfolding events to come soon.

The 9/11 was a carefully planned, poorly executed, foolish, naïve direct attack on freedom and security, as well as upon religious and cultural harmony upon a global scale. The fact that 9/11 was premeditated and carried out with top level U.S. involvement is proven by several key factors that will be identified here, which are all now well-known among all 9/11 investigators. These facts are undeniable when the footage of the event is viewed, especially in relation to various statements made by President George W. Bush at the time and subsequently as comprehensive attempts to cover-up the publication of the categorical evidence that conclusively proved top-level US prior knowledge, planning and direct intentional involvement in orchestrating the entire 9/11 events. The key facts from my perspective may to some seem to be relatively insignificant parts of the overall set of available evidence, yet they are vitally important in proving direct top level U.S. prior knowledge and premeditated involvement.

Regardless of the inhuman, insane, perverse rationale of those U.S. governmental employees and contractors who conducted this covert operation to falsely, inaccurately and dishonestly blame Middle Eastern based terrorists; what these facts will reveal is the entire 9/11 event represents a clear cut unequivocal case of the intentional mass murder of thousands of innocent civilians by entrenched forces of evil and militarism within the U.S. and Israeli governments. The very existence of these people occupying top levels of responsibility within the U.S. and Israeli governments reveals and proves the obvious presence of a well-established, insidious, long-existing 'government within a government' that operates as a controlling entity within the highest levels of the US government, that supersedes even the authority of the President of the United States of America.

Perhaps when the former President George W. Bush is finally publicly tried in an international Court of law for war crimes against humanity, and for treason against the American citizens, he will gladly and eagerly seek to spare his own life by identifying how he acted merely as a puppet for evil forces that installed him into power, just as occurred with his father who became the first President George Bush, Senior. Perhaps George W. Bush, the 'not so bright' son, will continue to lie and completely deny his and the USA's involvement in orchestrating the various 9/11 events and the failed attempted 'cover-up', yet ideally he will admit his guilt, sincerely apologise and ask genuinely for forgiveness. People of the world are not holding our breath waiting for this amazing event to occur, yet justice will be done in this case. Many of us can recall former President Richard Nixon admitting his complicity and subsequent attempted cover-up of the Watergate burglary as a edifying event in American political history. President Nixon wisely resigned office before being impeached for his proven crimes. No such admissions were forthcoming with the self-evident 'curious' murders of the Kennedys or Martin Luther King or while George Bush Senior was

Director of the CIA. Let's view some evidence that proves these issues in regard to 9/11.

The World Trade Center towers were not brought down from the airplanes that struck the buildings nor from fires; rather by explosive charges that were placed throughout the buildings prior to the planes hitting these buildings. These explosive charges were detonated intentionally long after the planes had impacted the buildings, including Tower Number Seven that was never actually hit by anything except perhaps a cruise missile, which was caught incoming on film. The three World Trade Center buildings were intentionally destroyed by internal controlled explosive detonation while innocent people were still in the process of exiting the buildings, along with New York City the brave firemen and policemen. Tower Number Seven was never hit by any aircraft, yet it was completely destroyed, although no rubble from either of the tall Twin Towers fell upon it, or should I say into the crater where it once stood fifty stories tall.

Again, it is quite interesting and very revealing synchronicity that Tower Number Seven had contained vast volumes of criminal and civil investigative evidence being accumulated against numerous international and U.S. based corporations that would be used in Court proceedings against these corporations, trusts, and individuals. The same was true of the areas within the Pentagon where officers from Naval Intelligence were compiling similar types of sensitive information intended to identify and prosecute various 'insiders' within the U. S. government and related agencies. Vitally important investigative information was destroyed completely and thereby 'lost' in the 9/11 destruction of Tower Number Seven. Is this a simple unusual coincidence or not? You can be the judge.

The evidence that the Twin Towers were detonated long after the planes struck the Towers is vividly recorded in seismic (earthquake) equipment, which clearly revealed a massive simultaneous explosion within the World Trade Center Buildings immediately before they began collapsing upon themselves. The buildings all fell within the footprint of the building exactly as any professionally detonated building does, rather than to topple over from the location where the planes had struck the building. The heat of the fires was insufficient to melt the steel either at the crash locations. The destruction of these buildings occurred initially at the base of the destroyed World Trade Center Towers, and then moved rapidly upwards as various floors were detonated sequentially as the slow motion film evidence shows with relatively small sized particles of debris being ejected from the building as these detonations occurred.

The Trade Center Towers' foundations were detonated along with a material called 'thermite', which melted the steel at extremely high temperatures. For those who are not familiar with thermite, it is defined by the Oxford dictionary as follows: "a mixture of finely powdered aluminium and oxide of iron that produces a very high temperature on combustion, used in welding and incendiary bombs".

Therefore, did these so-called Middle Eastern terrorists gain unlimited access to one of the most secure buildings in New York City to plant explosive charges upon every floor, as well as to set thermite laden explosive charges in the basement sections of the three World Trade Center Towers that were levelled to the ground in the 9/11 event? If so, then how would they gain this access to these buildings for the lengthy time required to prepare such an extensive number of explosive charges? Some New York City firemen and policemen on the scene who were fortunate enough to survive these explosions and who were already quite experienced in attending other previous building demolitions for safety reasons, clearly recognised and commented upon the fact the Towers were "pulled" (a professional term used to denote a controlled demolition of a building) by the actions of a professionally controlled demolition sequencing of the explosions within the World Trade Center Towers. Why was this evidence not presented publicly or considered in the subsequent so-called independent 9/11 investigations?

The steel at the base of these towers remained in a molten state long after the 9/11 event due to the excessively high temperatures involved with the use of thermite to melt and destabilise the foundations of these Towers that killed thousands of innocent people from many nations around the world.

Crime of the century, you may wonder? Well, compared to some of the previous mass genocides of innocent civilians by the evil forces at work and play in earthly civilisation, it would hardly appear to rate a mention, unless one views what this event has created internationally since then. There have been numerous historical cases where tens of millions of civilians were massacred by a single government, such as by the Nazis and the Russians under Stalin, as well as many other relatively recent situations where many millions of defenceless Souls were viciously slaughtered by their own people rather than invaders or avowed enemies.

What differentiates this 9/11 event from other genocides is the calculated way it has been carefully contrived to falsely accuse another culture and religion to rationalise and attempt to unfairly justify a series of sequentially planned massacres of blameless victims who unfortunately happen to reside in strategically significant, oil and gas rich nations in the Middle East and elsewhere around the globe. People of the world were lead to believe that Russia has also conducted similar state sponsored terrorist attacks upon its' civilian populations and attempted to falsely contrive fabricated so-called 'evidence' to untruthfully implicate other groups as being responsible, such as the people of Chechnya. Now we see Russia is actually serving as a model in promoting and 'insuring' international peace, along with the Chinese and others in regional areas; which demonstrates great hope for world peace to manifest itself on our war ravaged planet. International terrorism is predominantly now conducted by various national and international intelligence services, or their 'independent contractors' at this time in history.

The Americans have knowingly openly and covertly financed and well-armed murderous dictators like Saddam

Hussein with weapons of mass destruction, along with stockpiles of biological and chemical weapons, including a host of other conventional modern weapons, and provided the technological capability to manufacture such advanced weapons systems, in order to retain power in Iraq and to fight the Iranians. Osama Bin Laden was also trained and financed by the American intelligence community over a lengthy period of time and the Bin Laden family is still business partners with the Bush family and their associates. Therefore, it is not an imaginary idle observation to identify the hypocritical attitudes of the US administration to suddenly declare those two individuals as 'enemies' of the United States of America and to name them both as being directly responsible for the 9/11 events. Now we can perceive the results of the calculated plan developed to incite warfare in the Middle East that has involved the USA and some of its allies into a quagmire in the Middle East, which is exactly the intention of those policy makers who are apparently seeking to instigate and promote long-term regional conflicts and eventual full scale warfare throughout the world for reasons they justify to further their own rapacious avarice. We repeat various facts because they require repetition, since decades of state sponsored terrorism seems to have largely gone unnoticed or is not yet believed to be valid information by the majority of the American public. This too is rapidly changing as people awaken to the ongoing examples of proven historical evils that have intentionally and wrongly perpetrated by U. S. government and its closest allies since the end of World War 2.

So what other 9/11 evidence serves to establish the facts in this case? I have accumulated at least thirty major indicative factors in this matter, yet only a relative few of these will be required to further provide the conclusive circumstantial proof of the definite U.S. governmental direction and implementation of the 9/11 destruction.

It would appear from my scrutiny and careful reflection upon this entire 9/11 situation that the operation was so poorly organised and ineptly conducted that it is extremely likely that there were numerous 'insiders' directly involved who intentionally and knowingly left a series of circumstantial 'footprints' to be readily found within the execution of the covert operations to reveal the full extent of the U.S. and Israeli governmental involvement from the outset. In this manner, they made it relatively easy to establish an obvious, conclusive, visible recorded record of verifiable evidence to enable investigators and researchers to detect and publicly reveal the actual sequences of 9/11 events to the world.

This possible deliberate sabotage of operational secrecy by some well-placed military and contractual 'insiders' may seem to be an unlikely situation. However, having grown up within the highest levels of the US Air Force, and the fact that I also have access to a large amount of confidential information on various subjects, it has come to my attention on numerous occasions that there are countless true Americans whose first and only real patriotic allegiance is to the U.S. Constitution and their inner conscience. These true patriots may have their lives threatened, their families held to ransom, and even be callously eliminated through public assassinations, deliberate 'accidents', inexplicable poisonings, unlikely or impossible 'suicides', mysterious 'disappearances' and other such heinous crimes of murder; yet they ultimately remain faithful to their higher values and spiritual allegiances in the final analysis. Therefore, in spite of their required involvement in the execution of the 9/11 sequencing of events, in all probability on a conscious or unconscious level there were individuals involved in key strategic and operational areas that chose to express vestiges what they believed to be their remaining patriotic duty, as true American citizens, to disclose the 9/11 event for what it clearly and definitely is; another concocted, fabricated, deceitful, insidiously evil event in American history. One could add the intentional, violent mass exterminations of the Native Americans an example of American governmental conducting murderous policies historically.

The two aircraft that collided with the Twin Towers both were videotaped from various angles that distinctly revealed the shape of a mounted missile launcher under the right wing fuselage. Prior to the entry of the plane into either building the video footage plainly illustrates the launch of a missile from the plane's fuselage into the building at very close range, which then resulted in an almost immediate explosion emanating from within the building, travelling in an outward direction, well-before the plane even fully entered either building. This proves better than any other single piece of evidence that these planes were not those passenger carrying aircraft that were purportedly high-jacked by terrorists. When could supposed Middle Eastern terrorists armed only with box cutters have the opportunity and capability to mount military-style missile launchers onto these passenger jets prior to guiding them through heavily restricted airspace into the World Trade Center Twin Towers, about one hour after they were reported to be commandeered? If you can actually 'explain away' or otherwise discount this undeniable fact, then perhaps you will be able to assist these guilty parties with their legal defence when their trail occurs in the not so distant future.

We must very seriously consider the exact sequence of events surrounding the time when the 9/11 attack began officially and prior to it in specific detail. We need to thoroughly analyse President Bush's public admission on two different occasions that he first witnessed the video footage of the first plane crashing into the World Trade Center's North Tower before he entered the Florida school. Since that footage of the first plane's impact into the North Tower was NOT shown publicly, then we must assume and wonder how President Bush was privileged to witness this crash on his own personal closed circuit television video footage, which miraculously was stationed with an ideal view of the exact moment and location of impact when the first plane struck the building. Far more damning is President Bush's admission he simply believed upon seeing video footage of the first plane crashing into the World trade Center that it was simply a case of a very bad pilot error.

People are encouraged to genuinely believe that President Bush then went blithely into the Florida school and calmly was reading to school children 'upside down' books (please see still photos of President Bush purportedly 'reading' the school children a story from a book he is holding in an inverted, upside down position) while he already knew that "America was at war". Are these the appropriate patriotic attitudes and actions being demonstrated by a self-proclaimed "wartime President"? Or are these the actions of a man 'playing to the cameras' while the covert plans are being implemented?

Subsequently, President Bush has freely and foolishly admitted to media reporters that he made no immediate visible response to the news when his aide quietly informed him that the second plane has hit the South Tower and informs him with words to the effect that 'America is now at war'. For about eleven minutes which have been publicly shown on television footage, President Bush is distinctly seen to simply nod his head in the affirmative to his aide, acknowledging that 'America is now at war'. President Bush then continues pretending to be reading a story to the children in the prearranged, staged photo opportunity. We must ask ourselves the question, are these genuinely reasonable reactions of the President, the Commander in Chief, of the most militarily powerful nation on Earth? Odd response to say the least, especially when considered in relation to numerous other factors related to the similarly bland, ineffective and nonsensical responses by those in positions of military Command at the time in NORAD and other military services. I was born and raised into the US Air Force upper levels of command, since my father served as an Aide to a four star General for almost twenty years and so I know various military security procedures were knowingly being violated in many 9/11 related events. Again I repeat this information because I know what should have happened, yet did not happen in any of these 9/11 related events.

We must consider what type of object impacted the Pentagon. It was definitely not a passenger jet as we were foolishly initially led to believe by government officials. The photos of the crash site almost immediately after impact very distinctly illustrated the relatively small sized hole about ten to twelve feet in diameter in the front facing base of the Pentagon in an area under renovation at the time. The point of impact shows no signs of aircraft debris, very little resulting fire or external damage to the surrounding areas of the building which are still largely intact, aside from the near round hole in the ground story of the Pentagon. Light and power poles standing within the flight path of the object that impacted the Pentagon were not damaged as would have naturally occurred if a large passenger jet's wings had truly travelled upon such a low angle flight path into the front of the then mostly unoccupied area of the Pentagon. Therefore, very serious questions pose themselves regarding: exactly what type of object struck the Pentagon; why was there no aircraft wreckage at the crash site; and why was there no resulting fire from the purported crash of a fuel laden passenger jet?

What unknown principles of physics allow for a passenger jet to apparently impact a thick concrete building with sufficient force to literally vaporise all traces of its passengers, their belongings, the plane itself and its load of jet fuel? What sort of idiots are we supposed to be to believe such a ridiculous fabrication and obvious outright lie of the most ludicrous type? People may seem quite dumb or perhaps appear to be moronic imbeciles to some casual observers of society, yet exactly how inane and completely stupid and gullible are average common people and the more astute, aware, and well-informed individuals among us supposed to be, to even consider accepting such a blatantly irrational, impossible, inexplicable scenario?

Surely the international mass media news reporters are intelligent enough to figure the official explanation was preposterous, yet they seem to have nothing to say publicly on the issue. Why is this, as if we did not already know all too well? If people were officially told that a cruise missile impacted the Pentagon, are we supposed to gullible enough to accept that those pesky clever Middle Eastern terrorists from caves located in Afghanistan managed to obtain and launch a cruise missile or drone jet airplane from within the USA and guide it knowingly into a mostly vacant section of the Pentagon containing mostly Naval intelligence personnel who were responsible for investigating U.S. government and corporate corruption? Virtually impossible is the answer.

My opinion has become that a variety of factors, including some mentioned here, logically indicate that many 'acts of patriotic and humane conscience' occurred within some of the higher level covert 9/11 strategists, who managed to introduce a diverse set of unlikely and impossible scenarios, along with a multitude of verifiable circumstantial 'proofs' of the actual events into the 9/11 covert operations in a calculated, deliberate manner. Otherwise, we must consider the even more unlikely possibility that U.S. military and intelligence officers are 'dumber than dirt', which we definitely know not to be the situation.

It seems increasingly likely that in the not too distant future that we will experience the (former) US President George W. Bush and various others among his closest group of advisors being publicly charged in an international criminal Court for mass murder in relation to the 9/11 events. This case can and ideally will be convincingly proven utilising the voluminous verified evidence now already in the public domain, as well as that to be made available by various 'insiders' who survive the likely murderous assassinations, purges of likely 'weak links', probable informants and witnesses, many of whom will have recorded their testimony in written and video form for release to private and public investigators in the case of their unexpected or untimely demise, or natural death when their oath of secrecy will expire from their perspectives. The American people and legislators may seek to avoid this international embarrassment by first charging these same seemingly guilty people with treason, premeditated murder and many other high crimes; some of which result in the imposition of the death penalty if found guilty "in times of war", just as President Bush often stated now exists.

The fact that that the wars in Afghanistan and Iraq wars, and then the wars in Libya to oust President Kaddafi and President Assad in Syria have been predicated upon these fabricated U.S. and Israeli organised and instituted 9/11 autocracies will likely also lead to international criminal charges for war crimes and other heinous offences against humanity, as a direct result of this evidence becoming widespread public knowledge. Surely the intentional, premeditated murder of so many international citizens in the Twin Towers on 9/11 will insure that international murder charges must be filed in this case, when the evidence is placed before an international war crimes Court.

It is also likely that by convicting the former President George W. Bush and sentencing him to life in prison or even death, just as would be any other convicted war criminal, that it would be a great progressive step toward peace in the Middle East and the world in seeing true justice finally being done. Ideally it would also serve as a distinct message to despots and power brokers globally that a new and better, more just and peace loving global society has arrived on planet Earth.

Another possible scenario could be that the unfortunate President W. George Bush, along with a great many of his closest implicated associates, numerous perpetrators and related 'independent contractors' that conducted and participated in these vile murderous acts will inexplicably 'not survive' to reach an American trial upon treason charges. Therefore, those people would not be available for international criminal war crime trials in Europe.

It would be interesting to see if the seemingly guilty participants from the top down, not so mysteriously begin to have an incredible series of untimely 'accidents', or terminal 'health' issues; just as have many other people with knowledge and capability that upsets or somehow threatens 'the powers that be'. This would be true of bankers, scientists, doctors, military and governmental people, as well as countless others. Passing time will reveal exactly how the actual scenario unfolds. The seeds of truth are now being publicly revealed and conclusively demonstrated regarding the awful lies, deception, injury and murder of thousands of innocent people in 9/11 related events and the subsequent additional millions of innocent people that were murdered in the resulting wars mentioned here. We cans see that for many years the nation of Iran has been targeted to be next 'in the firing line' for U.S. forces and their rapidly diminishing number of purported international allies. Thankfully, we see the international community has prevented the USA from attacking Iran directly, so instead the US attacked Libya and Syria instead with virtually no legitimate reasons for doing so and they will definitely be held accountable, as we could state in relation to the nation of Viet Nam also.

The real fundamental source and cause originating numerous acts of terrorist types of violence conducted against thousands of innocent civilians in almost every nation in the world at some time or another are those people and organisations who are directly or indirectly responsible for the financing, supplying, training, and protection of the nationally sponsored 'state' terrorism networks and their related multitudinous 'civilian' and the wrongly so-called 'religiously' motivated terrorist organisations. The entire system is established and operated through 'rogue' elements within various national intelligence agencies, covert organisations, and privately controlled 'security' forces, along with their mercenaries; who are all ultimately taking orders from well-insulated, hidden, entrenched, seemingly powerful groups of wealthy international elitist forces, characterised by unrelenting evil, greed, corruption, depravity, and violence. My attitude has always naively been that even these despicable types of people can admit their crimes and ask for forgiveness and genuinely seek to change their ways for the better. However, unfortunately history shows us that it is far more likely that another course of action will be required to resolve these issues to bring some degree of real peace, true justice and equitable prosperity to Earth's people.

Let's make a quick observation regarding intimate intentional relationship existing between diverse forms of 'state' sponsored terrorism (terrorism sanctioned by 'rogue' elements existing within most national intelligence agencies and their associated 'private' terrorist organisations) and the current so-called fundamentalist religious forms of terrorism. The ultimate source of all well-financed purported terrorism on Earth today seemingly originates from the earthly autocrats directing these awful activities upon all nations upon Earth. These hidden, well-insulated, so-called 'power elite' that rule our civilisation ruthlessly, despotically, for their own self-interests are now being revealed here on Earth at this time. They are historically responsible for centuries of fostering and initiating war by manufacturing and distributing the weapons of war; encouraging oppressive social and economic conditions that would promote civilian terrorism; by directly financing and controlling the terroristic and militaristic operations globally; by owning and controlling the mass media to prevent the truth being known publicly; intentionally creating chaotic poverty conditions to promote social and economic desperation that is fertile breeding ground for discontent, social unrest and finally their not so clever plan is to establish open hostility between the Earth's mostly peace loving people.

This entire process is counter-productive, unnecessary, and quite ineffective and must change for the better in the near future. Otherwise, civilisation as we know it will end. There are insane elements within these contentious groups of so-called 'power elite' that do plan to instigate global conflict and catastrophic destruction as their goal, based upon crazy motives that no reasonable sane person would believe possible or understand, so we will not address those issues here. Suffice to say their plan is NOT going to be successfully implemented and those responsible will be held accountable in the Courts.

Now let's briefly consider some of the insane, probable strategic 'reasons' why the 9/11 events were instigated, so we can begin the healing process through increased awareness and improved understanding of these people's perverse mindset. When the Soviet Union and its potential allies, including especially China, were falsely perceived to no longer be an immediate military threat to the USA and its allies, a tacit agreement to quietly join forces in a covert manner to dominate the world economically and militarily seems to have occurred. Therefore, the elitist people sought to destabilise world security in a sustainable, relatively controllable manner to consistently promote their agenda of ongoing relentless militarism. Terrorism was selected as the best method for accomplishing a perpetual state of militaristic activity that would seem outwardly to be publicly justifiable and become the rationale to massively reduce the global human population by selective mass genocide.

This relatively recent advent of apparent widespread international terrorism required some adjustments of governmental and economic policies, as well as the pressing need to instigate a series of expedient, contrived cultural, national, religious, economic and regional terrorist based conflicts to create the means to engender an ongoing environment conducive to breeding seething hostility among disadvantaged, disempowered, poverty-stricken and unwanted elements within the human community on a global scale. When these unfortunate bereft people were at first unwilling and refused to initiate terrorist activities of their own volition, which was usually the case since most simple people seek peace and prosperity with a degree of freedom; then the corrupted powers utilised various national intelligence agencies to establish, finance, equip and train their own terrorist organisations by various means.

How does one believe these terrorist organisations have been able to receive such large volumes of weapons, bomb making materials, training, and covert funding to pay people to participate in terrorist activities? Weapons and countless billions of dollars do not simply appear from nowhere to finance international wars. Highly placed, wealthy people; acting through their numerous subservient controlled organisations that were already in possession of a large variety of weapons and massive amounts of superfluous money, that supply these materials and funding to terrorist organisations they have established covertly and also directly. As mentioned previously, in the earlier stages, many of the international so-called 'terrorist acts' were actually 'state sponsored' acts of terrorism by forces within the intelligence community, in association with field operatives (agents), their related international organisations, and in some cases with their local dupes and stooges. The evidence is now conclusive that 9/11 was exactly such a staged, contrived act of 'state sponsored' and conducted terrorism intended to falsely appear to be the premeditated act of Middle Eastern terrorists. 9/11 was inappropriately utilised to justify and condone the resulting wars in Afghanistan Iraq and elsewhere as mentioned previously.

The evidence we have briefly outlined here in relation to 9/11 events is far less than ten percent of the available major facts involved in substantiating and proving the origination, complicity and the final execution of the 9/11 event was intentionally conducted by U.S. and Israeli based government employed terrorists and their 'independent contractors'.

It is treason to use one's own government personnel and national military equipment to intentionally plan and intentionally murder attack one's own defenceless citizens, as happened in the 9/11 events. 9/11 became an international war crime when victims from nations other than the USA were knowingly violently slaughtered in the destruction of the World Trade Center, simply to further the spurious cause for initiating the wars in Afghanistan, Iraq, and to promote the spreading plague of terrorism and war globally.

It was also an international war crime by the indiscriminate manner in which some of these resulting military operations in Afghanistan and Iraq were conducted that killed, injured and disadvantaged millions of innocent, uninvolved, peaceful civilians and adversely influenced the lives of billions of people globally and within these war ravaged nations for generations to come.

The international cost in emotional fear, grief, frustration, anger, resentment and pain, as well as the financial cost, and loss of productivity must be calculated. America as of the middle of 2007 has had over 70,000 combat troops killed in the Middle East and over 1 million permanently injured according to the Veterans Affairs official statistics that are not openly acknowledged by U.S. Government sources. This is 'dated' information and these numbers are far higher now in 2016, yet for the Iraqi people the damage has been incalculable and horrendously terrible with many millions dead and injured over these awful decades of relentless warfare and deprivation.

There has been an environmental radioactive contamination disaster created by the widespread use of 'depleted' nuclear weapons in that area of the world. We must seriously consider that instead of financing these terrorist acts and the resulting wars, that these enormous financial resources could have been devoted toward accomplishing beneficial activities for humanity, such as developing alternate energy sources to fossil fuels. By realising the futility and contrived nature of terrorism and warfare, then we will readily understand how completely unacceptable, inappropriate, contemptible, vile and counter-productive these acts have been for all Earthlings. We as a civilisation are finally becoming increasingly determined to avoid future acts of warfare within our civilisation. The immoral instigators and perpetrators of international terrorism and warfare, includes all those people and corporations who are responsible for every aspect in the sequence of these types of events. They are knowingly creating these situations; from the planners, to the weapons manufactures, to the distributors of the weapons and funding sources to fight these wars, and the political puppets that sanction and endorse sending our people into these horrible situations falsely in the name of their national pride and honour to defend their nation. People must simply refuse to fight these wars and refuse to conduct these terrorist acts, regardless of the financial incentives and overt rewards being offered within our poverty prone nations.

Those who advocate and instigate terrorism and warfare need to be brought into the public's scrutiny and held legally, civilly and criminally accountable for their crimes against humanity. If and when these so-called 'power elite' people and their international organisations, including their inter-related corporations, Trusts, Foundations, etc; are forced to pay terrorism and war reparations and financial damages for the countless conflicts they have been directly responsible for creating, then they would not be nearly so wealthy or powerful anymore. Then they could be tried, convicted by a jury according to the overwhelming evidence against them and either executed for their crimes or they could spend the remainder of their lives in one of the many prisons they and their associates have been responsible for constructing to house mostly uneducated poverty stricken social 'misfits' and various types of people they consider to be undesirables.

The 9/11 fiasco will remain permanently in earthly history, along with the heinous misdeeds of the Nazis in Europe and the Japanese in Asia during the Second World War, as being among the most deplorable examples of humanity's lowest possible character. 9/11 will remain in human memory as a prime example of how people entrusted with social and moral responsibility in their governmental leadership roles did knowingly, in a premeditated calculating manner, function as conscienceless megalomaniacs, with irresponsibility, deceit, abuse of authority, and hideous depravity to achieve their destructive agendas through vile acts of sheer madness. The long historical list of such state sponsored murder of innocent civilians is far too extensive to mention even 1% of such cases here.

What is NOT mentioned is the real/actual First World War was when the 'western' European nations exported their version of militaristic predatory 'civilisation' to the entire world over many centuries, starting with the Crusades into the Middle East and expanding into every continent on Earth, killing, starving, exploiting, enslaving, 'colonising and industrialising' all areas of the world and disadvantaging Indigenous Peoples everywhere. In total, well over 200 million Indigenous People have been massacred globally in about 500 years, considering when the Europeans first came to North America, there were apparently 50 million Native Americans on that continent alone.

We could assume that the fundamental reason for such actions are to establish a continual, evolving global mental, emotional and physical condition on Earth to perpetuate a climate of fear, depravation, uncertainty, intercultural hostility and to internationally legislate increasingly oppressive limitations upon various human rights, especially the public freedoms of expression and interpersonal association. Likewise, the plan has been understandably to create a industrialised modern civilisation that serves the desires of those that consider themselves to be 'the rulers' of humanity and all life on Mother Earth.

Basically, this evil strategy has been to continue the age-old "us versus them" attitude in opposition to the innate desire and commitment of the vast majority of Earth's people to attain lasting peace, with some real degree of prosperity and freedom. As 2015 came to a tumultuous close; the vast majority of governments that are not allied with the USA are now revealed as being the true military and economic 'superpowers'. These BRICS nations are working fairly effectively in cooperation with one another on most issues of mutual importance as never seen before in modern history. There is indeed much hope for creating a vastly better, more peaceful and prosperous future for our civilisation, after we resolve some of the unpleasant counter-productive issues that have continued to plague humanity for countless ages.

Human nature issues existing within our overall character can often be in relative disharmony; vacillating between higher, more divine, loving, perceptive, inclusive, refined, noble eternal aspects of one's multi-dimensional character in some situations, and alternatively in other circumstances reveal the lower, less ethical, immoral, strictly self-absorbed, temporal, materialistic, aggressive, hedonistic human aspects of our human nature. Comprehending this aspect and tendency of your comprehensive character can significantly benefit you in numerous ways. This potential for discord within the human consciousness resides within one's own self, yet also can be found existing between members of one's own family, within any social or cultural group, between members of differing cultures, economic strata, religious affiliations or philosophic perspectives. Disharmony created and sustained by exclusionist, separatist, divisive, confrontational states of being is the primary scourge of humanity at this vital crux point in our civilisation's history.

We must now stand together, each and all of us uniquely special and independent in our individual natures, to oppose the doctrine of the "us versus them" mentality that is now seeking to impose itself upon the Earth's people and its environments. This stance may seem quite hypocritical upon my part, considering the opinions, perceptions and evidence presented here about the adversely detrimental effects of the so-called 'power elite' upon our civilisation. These facts need to be presented, and resolved; not ignored.

We do not need to concern ourselves with endless accusations, or to present mountains of valid proof that substantiates the self-evident evils being perpetrated against earthly citizens by those entities and people who seek to control our civilisation. The global population is composed mostly of "have nots" that are dominated now by brutish terror, military force, disease, the threat of starvation, lack of fresh water, persecution of ethnic, religious and economic classes of people, contrived civil wars, various forms of 'wage slavery', human trafficking and all types of poverty, among many other such realities in our contemporary civilisation.

Why do we not need to devote our greatest efforts in expressing the facts about the adverse reality system that exists here on Earth now? Because it is all so clearly, vividly self-evident and pervasive for any thinking, feeling, perceptive, independent minded human being who is even mildly willing to examine the current and historical state of this civilisation's activities and global policies. One world government has long been a factual policy among the international wealthy 'power elite' segments of society, with national governments serving in the purported role of semi-independent states, whose main economic and military structures alternatively 'take turns' playing the "good guy" and the "bad guy" roles. In all cases, it is generally the average, normal, simple, 'common' people who have historically suffered under this set of circumstances, with occasional respites from these acute stresses. We are documenting the fact that our overall civilisation is the primary loser with these types of ineffectual, antiquated, minority-serving policies. This civilisation oscillates between cycles of relatively intense productivity and debilitating catastrophic, cannibalistic forms of self-destruction. Now it is time to uplift, transform, enhance, improve and beneficially, progressively, fundamentally alter our overly-materialistic, militaristic, violent, abusive, counter-productive, unstable state of existence, through our daily choices as individuals in all aspects of our lives, as a unified peaceful global civilisation.

We acknowledge it is a struggle to harmoniously integrate the disparate aspects of one's overall character; create a pleasant loving family life; establish a productive, profitable, secure work environment, while seeking to find one's ideal place in the world and true meaning in earthly existence. These fundamental factors are interrelated with one another upon a deep basis. In other words, the basic elements in life are similar in one's self, within one's interpersonal relationships, as well as upon a comprehensive global societal level. Our efforts to identify and improve these variables will result in huge ongoing progressive accomplishments.

More relevant to the overall theme of our entire discussion in this book, we Earthlings, as a maturing civilisation composed of eternally conscious energetic life forms that periodically inhabit physically material form in what we see here on Earth as being human bodies, must now more seriously begin to develop our civilisation's social conscience as a self-aware species of life in this universe, if we are to progress into more spiritually evolved states of existence. As Earthlings, we must truly begin to very astutely, actively, perceptively become vastly more conscious of how and why our attitudes and conduct are manifesting this shared system of reality. We all are well-aware that serious problems exist and are continually developing in an increasingly complex and debilitating manner through the situations we perceive around us individually and comprehensively as an entire civilisation. We are all in this challenging situation together, so we must work peacefully, productively, in good mutual spirit together to manifest viable solutions to the adverse issues.

Some of us are quite able to ignore and even aggressively deny that these malevolent threats endanger our present civilisation because in western nations for most of us our daily lives are actually relatively comfortable and everything seems fairly good when superficially viewed from a strictly materialistic, fictitious, deluded, self-absorbed, 'exclusive' perspective.

We, in the so-called developed nations, are not like the seven of every ten people in the total world population who are now being trapped within lives that are characterised by wretched poverty, cycles of violence, disease and starvation; goaded relentlessly by unattainable images of a vastly more affluent and technologically progressive world racing wildly toward some fictitious hypothetical goal of unimaginable riches. Most perceptive people realise high levels of monetary accomplishment exist only for the relative few and their achievements are generally based firmly upon 'cheaply' utilising the endless laborious efforts of the quietly suffering vast majority of Earthlings.

To some well-to-do people that would have been unlikely to ever consider the content of this book, this opinionated assessment here may seem absurdly negative, biased and wrong. However, we have the education to read and understand the vocabulary used to delineate issues here that less fortunate people quite literally confront every day with the price of their lives at stake, by struggling to survive, to feed themselves, and to avoid death. The majority of earthly people who do not themselves experience the bounties of modern civilisation are the exceedingly challenged, because they do not live "the good life" as many of us are fortunate enough to do now. These troubled people valiantly rise every day with determination to work at some activity that will earn them enough, grow sufficient food, or find enough resources that will enable them to survive in whatever situation they find themselves in at the time. Most experience some degree of futility because, in spite of their best efforts, they seldom seem to do anything more than barely meet their most minimal actual needs for the time being, with no real certainty about what tomorrow may bring or deny them. On an individual basis, most people in western society tend to perpetually seek to possess or attain more of life's bounty, better homes, cars and appliances, etc. Once this state of existence is attained, then most people habitually seek to progressively acquire even more material possessions and better living circumstances. When this state of improved circumstances is achieved, then generally such acquisitive people seek even more, and then even better again and again, in a cyclic manner. This also includes desires for improvement for ourselves, our families, and our social and cultural group's various alliances.

For most materialistic people, there is seldom ever 'enough' to cease their expansion of desires, to stop and begin to earnestly begin to focus upon the real life-threatening needs of others less fortunate than ourselves. For some, our desire to improve conditions for ourselves and others includes forms of humanitarian activity and donations of money to worthy causes. It may be decided to send them some surplus grain or flour to keep them alive or to drill them a water well to stave off death from lack of fresh water; often mostly to make our consciences feel better about ourselves. Now we can see increasing genuine global desire and commitment to truly make real progress by fully applying ourselves morally, financially, strategically, logistically and loving in good spirit to help us who are capable to help them to resolve the fundamental causes of their deprived conditions permanently.

The self-serving minimalist human characteristic that prefers to rationalise, procrastinate, and ultimately to basically deny other powerless people access to real justice and the opportunity to improve their life's conditions has lead to the destruction or failure of most previous earthly civilisations. Before our current civilisation further self-destructs in an ongoing series of massively inane, foolishly inept acts of sheer idiocy by our political and economic so-called 'leaders'; we the so-called 'thinking people', must strongly and courageously voice our united perspectives, along with providing and applying innumerable solutions. We must begin to sincerely devote our very lives to tirelessly working in every way possible to achieve the productive accomplishments necessary to improve and thereby save our civilisation. We can not afford to simply wait for this civilisation to collapse or self-destruct due to its leader's avarice and seemingly boundless appetite for war, revolution, corruption, despotism, fear, misery, devastation and self-annihilation.

Every failed tribe, like every failed civilisation, has had a relative few brave individuals and groups of people that have sincerely attempted by various methods to address the numerous challenges and difficulties in order to provide functional solutions. This originally began with issues such as shelter, food, security, reproduction, health, reliable access to drinking water and so on. We can note that not much has really changed substantially in this regard, although we are far more technologically adept and knowledgeable than our less evolved seeming ancient hunter-gather humanoid ancestors. Historically, as one challenge to reliable survival was resolved, then sequentially other survival factors became more important priorities, in a continually ongoing, progressive fashion. Change in the past ages was necessitated by major problems such as: over-population that could not be sustained by increasing the available food resources; outbreaks of disease that occurred from poor sanitation practices; resisting unwanted violent physical attacks by invading aggressive people from other locations necessitated strengthened defensive capabilities, or unwise, ineffectual leadership was being demonstrated by the leaders in key positions of authority and responsibility in the society who were unable or unwilling to solve the problems, etc. These unresolved problematic issues eminently threatened to overwhelm the society's ability to survive these difficult circumstances; so only then did some less pragmatic, less reasonable, more unpleasant options become considered as likely solutions.

To resolve over-population issues, priests may have declared the people sacrifice one or more of their children to appease the gods. Creating a caste system of male children who were born to become warriors that protected their lands and attacked other unaffiliated nearby groups of people were developed. Likewise, religious priestly, marital, economic, racial/ethnic or other types of genetic or family caste systems were developed to better control and prevent some people from breeding 'freely' as they wished to do.

Societies that were unable to solve their challenges peacefully with wisdom and effort eventually tended to use warfare to obtain food, slaves, enlarge their own territories, and specifically to reduce their population of strong young opinionated men or unwanted and uncooperative females to reduce population growth. Generally, the older 'favoured' men in these societies, who over passing time had been promoted or had advanced themselves somehow to attain their leadership roles, realised that young men who did not periodically go away to war tended to reproduce frequently which increased the population and also consumed large amounts of limited resources. In larger numbers, young men bored with hard work in the fields, quarries, and hunting could potentially threaten the status quo when disenchanted. Alternatively, these single men could become bored or wanting the elusive female companionship that was often unavailable to them for various reasons, so these excessive numbers of 'lower caste' young men were far more potentially threatening and unwelcome by the older men who led the society than were the younger, more peaceful women, who were more easily controlled when they already had 'acceptable' children to raise and protect. Basically, through the millions of years that humanoids have occupied Earth, it was by this crude evolutionary process that most major earthly civilisations historically have eventually relied upon periodic warfare, selective murder of their own people, and various forms of genocide to solve some of their difficult social, economic and environmental challenges. The remaining vestiges of these social, religious and economic caste systems can still be seen globally.

Now humanity is very much like the ancient cave-people who discovered how to create shelter, fire and tools. Our modern technological achievements and improved comprehension of nature's processes have enabled our current civilisation to develop a relatively high standard of living for many of Earth's people. Now it is essential that our inner spiritual character awakens to assert aspects of our higher eternal nature, if this civilisation is to survive as we now know it to be and improve to achieve our higher, readily available true potential. There are various insidiously wicked forces and other villainous human self-interest groups at work to hold back the evolution of human beings.

Interestingly, this also includes various non-physical dimensional types of life forms that are apparently NOT indigenous to Mother Earth being active upon the Earth at this time, as well as a number of extra-terrestrial (ET) species of life that do not want peace on Earth to ever occur here. These evil allied forces are constantly striving to encourage degenerate proclivities to manifest themselves to such an extent that our civilisation can be encouraged to revert to even more depraved, brutish, immoral, feeble-minded attitudes and activities than we see in evidence on Earth today, if that is believable. These misguided Souls constantly seek to promote and reveal the lowest aspects of the human consciousness. Such people and unwholesome life forms seek to instil and institutionalise fear, hate, discord, warfare, terrorism, alienation, poverty, disease, anger, depravation, totalitarianism, fanaticism, chaos and devastation upon the Earth's people to maintain their centuries-old grip on power and control here on this planet.

Many people and multi-dimensional being here on Earth now are well-aware of what is happening and are communicating amongst themselves and in books like this one about developing a range of solutions to prevent an unnecessary, counter-productive series of cataclysmic events here on Earth. Some of us have a great level of awareness about things occurring here that are generally are not too obvious to the majority of people until matters deteriorate to a seriously undeniable degree. For many people globally, these untenable, unacceptable, miserable conditions now already exist in war ravaged nations and those who are trapped in endless cycles of poverty, scarcity, illiteracy, and who have been physically, emotionally and spiritually damaged by their ongoing generational and cultural experiences over many earthly lifetimes. Those whose heinous attitudes and actions vainly attempt to thwart humanity's evolution are now seen quite clearly in their positions of despicable responsibility. Humanity now seeks to become progressively transformed from the overt and covert insidious evil pressures currently being applied by a lower, callous, barbarous, amoral level of human consciousness, into becoming truly characterised by superior magnanimous virtues that demonstrate a more caring, noble, loving, joyous, productive, grateful, peaceful state of human consciousness that is our true eternal nature as Soul.

The idea that a so-called 'new world order' is seeking to establish itself on Earth is another feeble, nonsensical half-truth used to confuse, fool and distract people. The so-called 'new world order' is actually the same 'old' ugly self-serving, corrupted, despotic world order that has tightly controlled our present civilisation for many thousands of years. The 'old' and 'new' world order is one and the same awful evil beast. The monster of so-called 'world order' or the so-called 'power elite' is now blithely attempting to disguise and re-invent itself to hide the obvious fact that it is characterised by odious, hideous, despicable attitudes that intentionally instigate and fuel unnecessary conflict and chaos in order to cannibalise itself upon humanity. These demonic forces personalised in human form and their disincarnate 'minders' are now greedily 'feeding' themselves upon an ample diet of induced fear, hate, anger, sadness, misery, despair and depravation here on Mother Earth. They appear to grow fatter and stronger by literally nourishing themselves upon the blood, sweat, tears and energies of this planet's people and other suffering and exterminated life forms. The existing new and old world order are in actuality the earthly physical representations of one 'evil entity' that we can recognise when it so adeptly reveals itself through a demonic physical incarnate form within pathological, murderous types of humans. Vicious conscienceless pathological humans often possess a form of spirit that is governed by the disincarnate forms of this evil consciousness that has been mentioned in various religious texts, including the Bible. This seemingly evil force does indeed exist here on Earth, which is so vividly revealed by the attitudes and actions of the present "world dis-order".

Thankfully, there are many indications that global events are indeed changing rapidly for the better here as 2016 rapidly approaches and these processes to achieve solutions in every area of human activity are most encouraging !!!

It is clear to see the failures by that awful aggregated 'entity' (evil cabal) and its associates are sincerely hoping and planning that modern people will not recognise its disguise or distractions, nor become determined to take swift, decisive remedial action against this unbridled wickedness that has been occurring for thousands of years. To protect itself from justice, truth and freedom, just exactly like any autocratic fanatical dictatorship does when people refuse to accept the tyranny any longer; the present "world dis-order" now seeks desperately by any and all means possible to maintain its power, authority, material wealth and leadership status over our civilisation.

To avert the possibility of humanity freeing itself from this situational stranglehold by evil forces, it (the evil 'cabal') has for countless ages been using warfare, violence and fear to retain its dominating position over humanity. We, the people of Earth, do now clearly perceive reality by genuinely examining the ample historical and modern evidence that the current world dis-order is using its vast array of weapons systems to destabilise our civilisation. Consider how many millions of potential combatants are employed in the world's vast militaries, largely because these particular people wanted to be patriotic or could find no other more productive work elsewhere. Aside from the limited options of unemployment, or accepting work as a lowly paid 'wage slave', or participating in illegal activities, or suicide; then they seemingly have few viable alternatives to joining the military in their nation, or travel to a country at war as a paid fighter or escape as a refugee from economically deprived, 'war torn' areas of the world to survive.

The evil world dis-order now openly threatens large segments of humanity with annihilation, if we seek to dislodge it from its position of control in favour of a more equitable, compassionate, productive, harmonious type of civilisation that no longer is willing to use war, violence and fear to characterise its spirit and life choices. These wicked forces have for almost fifty years threatened to end life as we now know it on Earth; through nuclear warfare in the days of the 'cold war'. Now this threat is again being made more openly as it relates to terrorism and international warfare. Additionally, we now often hear news in the mass media and see frightening theatrical movies about the existence of massive amounts of biological and chemical weapons; secretive new weapons systems, such as laser technologies, neutron bombs, weather destabilising and earthquake producing technologies; electronic, sound and microwave weapons systems; orbiting space-based weapons systems; with the countless forms of conventional weapons systems; that are all ready to devastate civilisation if the 'power elite' are removed from their powerful positions of purportedly 'protecting us from ourselves' or some nebulous 'unknown' ET enemies from elsewhere.

Does this sound as crazy and counter-productive to you as it does to me? The people and entities that create hundreds of times more weapons systems than would be required to kill all forms of life on planet earth, are supposed to be protecting us from one another and ourselves? That does NOT make rational good sense to me. What is your opinion?

All of these weapons systems are being developed, manufactured and deployed at a massive cost to taxpaying citizens. We citizens, even in the world's most open and free so-called democracies, presently have little or no real authority, even through our governmentally elected so-called 'representatives'. There is no serious debate regarding these vitally important issues publicly. There is no process made available in democracies to disagree by majority consensus in a public referendum vote on such key issues that would genuinely enable citizens to influence politicians or business leaders to some degree control and prevent the excessively onerous decisions that are being made by governmental policy whose actions could deprive and damage us all.

So where is the real democracy we keep hearing so much about? The honest, painful, unfortunate truth is democracy does not exist in modern civilisation. It is a fictional figment of the mass propaganda media that is intent upon keeping people quietly struggling in subservient poverty, and living in relative ignorance and inescapable social and governmental systems. Myths and false information are being continually perpetuated by the governmental and mass media personnel about the purported existence of a free and open democratic system as being factual. There are no functional true democracies existing in any nation on Earth as 2016 begins on this planet. All legal forms of activity and opportunity are in some ways being controlled by political party and governmental structures, and their actions are being directed and controlled by well-concealed, entrenched, elitist financial 'power' structures. The 'power elite' who have heavily influenced the current 'world dis-order' for thousands of years are committed to preventing any real positive, beneficial, progressive, rational, innovative, efficient, harmonious, constructive true change toward the development of any equitable, unlimited prosperity on this Earth now. They are not going to be successful, as Divinity has another plan for Mother Earth.

These days of conflict and intentional misery are now numbered in increasingly smaller numbers. As a wise and aware commentator recently commented in regard to many of those evil people mentioned herein; he recently said "Soon they will be running for their lives."

Truth be known; there is NO escape, as Mother Earth is now a 'quarantined planet' which is being enforced by a host of galactic, multi-dimensional and other forms of ET (extra-terrestrial) Beings, as well as by 'higher' eternal life forms of incomprehensible ability and wisdom. This may seem stranger than any science fiction to some people, yet is happening now, as can be determined by world events and by people with an inner connection with God.

Can you genuinely look around yourself to perceive the deplorable, deteriorating conditions that led us into this set of troubling circumstances sufficiently to become determined to assertively seek positive changes that will establish ability for us to work together as Earthlings to build a better future for ourselves and future generations? I sincerely and genuinely hope so. Writing and then after an intentional wait of almost 10 years for the right social and economic conditions to manifest for me 'to make public' a book such as this in early 2016 could cause me to receive some unpleasant, unwanted 'attention' from those whose attitudes and behaviours I have been so critical for obvious reasons we have discussed. Do you think that really matters to me now? No, 'the cabal' is unlikely to 'bother with' me, as they have larger and more immediate real concerns now.

What truly matters now is that we are aware, willing, and able to speak and share our own version of 'truth' with other perceptive, receptive human beings; as well as those people who would strongly dispute and disagree with much of what is stated here. We each and all must do this according to what we each experience, see and know exists around and within us; individually and collectively, as Earthlings. Those with love, compassion, kindness and peace in their hearts, minds and Souls always have been and always will be the only true power in the universes of God. Now it is time for love, kindness, true justice, peace and mutual respect to rule on Earth, in my opinion.

For all the genuine religious people who may be interested in this goal too, in my opinion we will not need to wait for the physical 'second coming' of Jesus Christ to achieve a more peaceful loving civilisation upon this Earth, as some sincerely believe. The so-called 'second coming' of Christ is actually a process by which Soul and God Consciousness begins to awaken and express Itself within and through one's own usual consciousness. It is usually evidenced by one's attitudes and actions manifesting in divinely motivated, positive, kind, loving actions that originate from one's higher, better aspects of character and immortal consciousness as Soul.

This transformative, illuminating spiritual experience is not an external physical event where Christ returns to Earth in physical form to save us all, remove the bad people and create Heaven here on Earth, as some fundamentalist Christian people so strenuously believe. It may happen that way, yet it seems more likely to be an internal spiritual event where the God inspired Spirit ('Christ Consciousness') becomes enlivened within one's Soul to be manifested individually within people of all religions, each in their own manner and time. This transcendental process will then begin to reveal its expression within humanity as a whole in due course; thereby physically manifesting the personification of Divine Spirit through physical form, within and through those people for whom such an experience is possible.

Jesus Christ promised to 'return again' and he likewise also said words to the effect that, "As I am, so too shall ye become". This clearly referred to the possibility for our own individual spiritual evolution to grow in spiritual awareness, to recognise the innate divinity existing within each of us. The divine Christ (God) Spirit existing within Jesus enabled humanity to recognise that some aspects of God's Consciousness can in some situations be revealed and expressed through our human incarnate physical vehicle and mind, as occurred with Jesus Christ and other divine Prophets.

Humanity is now poised with all the capabilities necessary to create a civilisation able to: feed itself, even with its growing populations; safely and humanely control excessive population growth by utilising various forms of birth control, education, as well as through scientific and medical methods without the need to resort to warfare; to eliminate the occurrence of most common diseases primarily by improving the body's natural defences that function with a quality diet of foods with ample nutrition obtained from healthy natural soils; end chronic poverty and unemployment; further extend the average life expectancy in good full health with an improved quality of life; to peacefully solve cultural, religious, regional and international disputes by discussion, mediation, conflict resolution and honest forms of diplomacy, rather than by resorting to mutually destructive, inefficient, costly wars; to apply technological innovation to resolve energy shortages, desalination of seawater for human uses; reduce or eliminate people's insurmountable debt repayments to banking and governmental institutions, and other such positive solution-based behaviours.

Does humanity really need to allow the same old forces of evil domination to threaten us with self-destruction of a type that would cause our civilisation to revert back into something akin to the Dark Ages again? Some of these despotic forces plan to survive such a war by protecting themselves in large underground bunkers akin to underground miniature cities with what they believe to be adequate food, water and other resources, yet in spite of those preparations modern warfare could also likely make the planet completely uninhabitable for thousands of years due to radio-active nuclear, biological and chemical contamination. Must humanity blindly and fearfully accept these overt insane threats to destroy earthly environments and nations with the devastating mechanisms and vile emotions of warfare that would provide a type of woeful existence that would be much worse than any previous wars?

The simple definitive answer is "No, humanity does not need to accept such a situation", where war will again characterise our civilisation, especially at this opportune time historically when we have so much real potential for success to establish a more peaceful, noble, productive future on 'our' Mother Earth.

These negative powers and vested interest groups aligned around interrelated policies and businesses focused upon warfare, sustaining poverty, environmental and ecological devastation, rampant addictive and violent behaviours acting as a plague among people, implementing unfair governmental and taxation legislation that burdens us all, the judicial protection of violent offenders that victimise other innocent people with impunity and countless other forms of anti-social activities all join together to serve adversely to plunge our civilisation into a self-defeating "us versus them" warlike mentality. There exist on Earth right now truly evil, hopelessly corrupted people. Seriously consider the revealing godforsaken attitude of President W. George Bush, who publicly stated, "Either you are with us or you are with the terrorists", which basically says words to the effect that 'to dissent is treason'. Some pro-war politicians within the Republican Party made comments about those that their political opponents that opposed the war in Middle East with words to the effect that 'liberals are seditious traitors'. This was publicly stated by one of the key people responsible for helping to plan and then placidly allowing 9/11 to occur to further the "us vs. them" attitudes and the intentional creation of global warfare that we can clearly see in 2016.

President Bush's comment that "Either you are with us or your are with the terrorists" represents the epitome of absurd hypocrisy and blatant treason; considering the direct knowing involvement of malevolent forces within the U.S. government, along with various operatives within some U.S. intelligence services that did intentionally initiate and carry out the genocide and volitional destruction of the World Trade Center complex in New York City in the 9/11, as well as a string of related dastardly events. This was followed by an ongoing massive series of 'cover-up' of the entire operations, which are simply no longer any secret to aware knowledgeable people around the world.

These heinously depraved, insanely unconscionable people seek to promote the "us versus them" mentality to maintain their autocratic, evil, counter-productive, malevolent grip of control through fear, violence and depravation upon this current world civilisation. It has now been distinctly revealed to the world that they themselves, the so-called 'power elite', the 'old/new world order', 'the powers that be', the 'government within all governments' or whatever identifying name one wishes to use for those that ruthlessly rule our earthly civilisation, these people are actually proving themselves to be the 'corrupted elite' or the 'warmonger elite'.

They are the very source that is intentionally instigating, financing, promoting and perpetuating the international, religious and intercultural conflict, chaos, violence, poverty and suffering. There is ample evidence many other so-called "terrorist attacks" globally, such as some bombings in Russia that have been planned and conducted by the Russian intelligence services or the U.S. intelligence services and falsely blamed upon various terrorist groups to create social conditions that favour international conflict and genocide because in some hideous ways these policies serve to promote the war-like adversarial interests of some powerful well-placed individuals and groups within various governmental and corporate organisations.

The self-evident proof of these damning and unpleasant facts, repeated endlessly over thousands of years, should and must serve as the ultimate persuasive culminating factor that ends their totalitarian rule over humanity. How long is humanity supposed to remain quietly compliant in relation to these ongoing heinous insane acts by those in control of our social and financial systems that are intentionally and maliciously directed against the harmonious intercultural and religious relationships in order to destabilise and undermine the productive nature of our civilisation to further reduce freedom, eliminate financial sustainability for most people and impose unwanted fascist forms of autocratic militaristic governmental rule upon people of this world?

Once again, this is not the institution of a 'new world order'; rather it is the last few desperate acts of the 'last dying' attempts of the same old evil, greedy, murderous world order, seeking by all of the same old historical methods to maintain and strengthen its weakening dominance on power and control over the world's people and environments.

In both the USA and in Russia, as well as in many other modern nations, the former Directors of their secret police agencies (CIA in the USA and the KGB in Russia) have risen to the position of President in those nations. The current President George Bush's father, the first President George Bush, was the Director of the CIA under the administration of President Regan. In Russia, President Vladimir Putin was once Head of the KGB Russian intelligence service. What does this self-evident fact reveal about the processes occurring in our national societies and current governmental political situations when in both a major former totalitarian communist nation and in the largest of the modern so-called democratic and openly militaristic draconian of nations, the USA; we citizens purportedly 'freely' elect individuals who were administering governmental agencies employing spies and all manner of amoral people to do immoral, unethical illegal and violently predatorial activities, supposedly upon the best interests of their nations and their citizens? This reveals that political processes and political parties as they now exist in the world are truly corrupted.

Now in 2016, who could have anticipated 20 years ago that both of the leaders of Russia and China are truly the 'hope of the world' in applying governmental policies and actions that finally manifest a real goal and plan for peace on Earth? Unexpected blessed gifts of hope and new beginnings are self-evident everywhere one cares to look now, so be encouraged and take wise action to help these cherished positive beneficial world changes to occur in an ongoing manner until world peace becomes our new reality system here on Earth. It is up to people of every nation, culture, and attitude to join together in cooperation to create the better world and life we all desire.

Many creative inventive people have developed innovations that provide inexpensive, sustainable, non-polluting and abundant energy sources, or vehicles that run on water, or who seek to make cures for diseases available to humanity are very often suppressed, threatened, jailed or even murdered. What does this fact reveal about the real attitudes of the 'power elite' or those facilitating governmental suppression of these much needed technologies? Governments are clearly NOT now serving people's best interests or those of the planet. The entire political and functional civilisation 'systems' should be transformed in beneficial, responsible, transparent, utilitarian, pragmatic ways to eliminate these unacceptable situations from every level of government in this world. Is this likely to happen, we wonder? Each of us can become a positive force for beneficial change in our own unique ways as we learn to better cooperate with one another to accomplish worthy goals.

Did anyone anticipate Dr. Keshe (www.keshefoundation.org) would become the modern version of Nikola Tesla? Not likely, but watch what happens when his technology becomes more widely known and utilised in many ways!

Relatively few people really expected the Berlin Wall to come down in their lifetime, or for the former USSR to grant independence to many of those former USSR Nation States. Therefore, if and when we see the former U.S. President George W. Bush and the key co-conspirators who orchestrated and committed the 9/11 massacre in Court on trial for international war crimes, high treason and mass murder, then 'we the people' globally will be more likely to believe and KNOW that real change is occurring. Until then we will simply continue to observe reality, as it reveals itself to us through daily our life experiences. The facts already have been clearly and repeatedly proven that the USA (and others) have for decades conducted brutal acts of state (and 'religious') sponsored national and international terrorism through their national intelligence agencies and their 'independent contractors', as have many other nations too numerous to mention here.

None of the responsible 'top level' or 'behind the scenes' people that ordered these terrorist attacks have ever been publicly charged, tried in Court or convicted civilly or criminally for these despicable acts of terrorism against one's own citizens. There is no real patriotism among these war mongers; only greed for power, wealth, controlling influences and other forms of avarice. We must work toward creating changed circumstances where those responsible for planning and ordering acts of state sponsored terrorism such as has occurred in the USA and elsewhere are brought to justice, charged with war crimes, publicly tried with all the relevant evidence being presented, found guilty criminally and civilly and sentenced to life in prison for their war crimes, or perhaps receive the death penalty.

For some people, this 'surprise' result may seem unlikely to occur in the near future, yet to others this increasingly seems to be a virtual certainty considering the unwillingness of those perpetrating these countless crimes against humanity and the Earth to 'cease and desist' war mongering and immediately 'remit' (pay their financial debts) and surrender their evil intentions and ask 'the people' genuinely for forgiveness for those crimes.

This new development where the key national leaders of Russia and China clearly advocate and strongly support the implementation of real positive change and global peace is indicative of the new beneficial attitudes and the equitable application of justified righteous noble power and an end/termination of the various forms of 'protection' being provided to the evil, war-like, adversarial predatorial people within civilisation at this time.

The fact that President Putin has in recent years been a primary advocate and real 'force' of global peace is among the clear indications that major positive changes are happening in our world right NOW!!! Who would have predicted this self-evident 2016 fact 20 years ago, except perhaps Mr. Putin himself?

The simple fact is political parties, government institutions and the legislative processes in democratic nations are not controlled by aware, free-thinking people who truly represent the will and best interests of the vast majority of the voting public. The present government and laws primarily are dictated by the relative few people who control: big business interests; the banks; the weapons manufactures and distributors; energy, oil and natural resources corporations; pharmaceutical, medical and chemical manufactures; large scale agribusiness corporations; transportation manufacturers and the major airlines; corporations controlling the mass media, entities responsible for the production and distribution of addictive substances, both legal and illegal; and many more interrelated groups, organisations and their associates. All of these and many other interrelated vested interest groups are committed to maintaining the old world order by any means necessary. Those influencing the mass media intend to falsely assert that this new process of globalisation is the advent or beginning of the 'new world order' simply to confuse the issue and play mind and propaganda games with people's lives, the world economy, world security and virtually every major type of activity that is important in the functioning of our civilisation. Most people are not so stupid, gullible, hypnotised, weak or forgetful that they will be permanently fooled by events in the 9/11 event, or in the Middle East, that are almost identical modern day duplications of the Crusades against the Jews and Muslims many centuries ago.

The leaders in the Middle East and elsewhere are tired of being identified as the convenient enemy of the so-called western nations around the world and used as a battle ground for global power plays. The people of the Middle East are weary of fighting and killing one another. Because of events being forced upon them, they now are becoming eager to seek vindication on an external enemy that is meddling in their internal affairs once too often, from their perspective of historical events. The western world is running out of self-created false enemies and underdeveloped nations to colonise and plunder economically. They now see the abundant supplies of accessible, high quality oil and gas located in the strategic Middle East as the ideal location to focus their militaristic and financial power in order to gain control of this vital region of the world. The Arab nations, their national allies, their business associate nations, which include China and Russia, have large incomes derived from oil and gas revenues. They also have huge gold and other precious reserves and productive activity that is not based upon violence or any form of economic predation.

The western nations and their few remaining loyal international allies have very unwisely chosen to wage a mutually self-destructive Middle East war with virtually no genuine provocation. We must recall that the 'western' or European world has been in conflict with the Middle East as a colonial aggressor for thousands of years already. In the latter part of the twentieth century, the USA was primarily responsible for interfering in many of these countries' political circumstances, such as providing large amounts of weapons to the nation of Iran when the Shah of Iran was the U.S. supported dictator there, and to Iraq under Saddam Hussein to fight the Iranians and in Afghanistan to fight the Russians through Osama bin Laden. Also, we must not forget that the USA supplies Israel the most financial and military support being provided to any other nation on the planet for many decades. Now these nations seem to be the key participants in this entire unstable, contentious situation. This is especially true when one considers exactly how the massive financial and military aid being provided to Israel by the USA has been used for the past few decades. Israel now feels powerful enough to refuse to sincerely seek to promote genuine, lasting peace in the entire region of the Middle East. This must change.

It is obvious in this continuing rant, that 'we' are seemingly needlessly continuing to (using an American saying) "beat this dead horse" here, as the existing self-decreed so-called 'power elite' are now the 'power depleted' or the 'powers that were' now in 2016 and into the future. This self-evident fact is NOT apparently yet clear to those 'cabalist', evil seeking aspects of the war-like groups known by various names such as the Illuminati or others. We hear endless media stories that are designed to instil fear and a sense of hopelessness among people, so for us to repeat a number of our key perspectives and opinions is simply an attempt to balance the scales here. If you find it annoying to read all of this repetition, as I do while writing and editing it in some ways, then please carefully consider the enormous volumes of falsified and hyped-up "be afraid" or "life is a dangerous painful event" types of images, messages and attitudes constantly being programmed into those who watch TV, 'mainstream' movies and other forms of mass media. We are in the process here of 'de-programming and re-educating our attitudes to focus on creating the ideal better realities that we all seek to share together.

This book and countless millions of ongoing daily and major other transformative, truly illuminating and enlightening world and individual events and obvious miracles are occurring now. These are serving us all to identify the facts for those that do not wish to willingly 'awaken from the nightmare' that has been earthly reality for far too long. We will gently assist them, yet for others who feel entitled to continue to abuse, assault, deprive and murder earthly life forms; they may indeed be in for a very abrupt, seemingly rude and quite an effective 'wake up call' in ways they would not anticipate even today in this 'monumental year of change' in 2016.

What obviously needs to be done is to genuinely work together in honest good relations of mutual respect to consider all international perspectives in the Middle East to resolve the key issues that are related to Israel. There must be a commitment to take swift, decisive action to establish a new internationally recognised homeland and nation for the Palestinian people. It is an urgent necessity to directly address and resolve other important issues in the Middle East to peacefully develop a workable consensus agreement and apply the mutually required solutions consistently and reliably with full international approval and participation. The USA and Israel will certainly need to cease being intentionally problematic in their fruitless, predatorial, counter-productive activities in seeking to prevent global peace and harmony from occurring between all nations and peoples of the world.

It is clearly self-evident that those two militaristic pariah nations are quite foolishly seeking to perpetuate the ongoing cycles of lower human nature that are characterised by greed, violence, 'power' politics, conflict, and historical and religious vendettas. We can observe the escalating cycles of insane, devastating violence and retribution. There still exist some unnecessary civil wars and inter-cultural conflicts between some Middle Eastern tribes and religions that have been adversaries for thousands of years. This too must end soon.

Through the entire inter-related cycles of increasingly complex violence, the war mongers and their financiers gleefully dance with joy because this unfortunate situation for the world simply makes them richer, more powerful and fuels the fires of hatred, fear and slaughter, which is their favourite activity. Meanwhile, the nations of the Middle East squander their fortunes on weapons of genocide, destruction and misery for all people, just as the old world order so predictably plans as its goal.

Likewise, the U.S. taxpayers are bankrupted, the U.S. economy is devastated and the actual instigators distract the world's attention away from those who have intentionally created these vile circumstances and blamed it falsely on nebulous hidden terrorist groups that were financed and organised in most cases by the intelligence agencies of major world governments; primarily the USA. Where is the governmental responsibility to the citizens it is purported to represent when such actions are taken that so pervasively undermine the prosperity and security of all our nations through the treasonous actions of recent leaders within the U.S. government and its agencies and allies? The U.S. government has for many decades been repeatedly conclusively proven to abnegate its' responsibilities to the United States of America's Citizens; therefore, these political and bureaucratic institutions are irrelevant and must cease operations in the current form of non-representational, illegal activity.

China, along with Russia, India and Brazil among the major BRICS nations, has established and is progressing very well with their wise strategic plan to become the world's foremost economic 'super-power' through manufacturing much needed goods to the world and providing quality reliable ethical leadership globally. China is now accomplishing these beneficial goals within a relatively short period of time, in historical terms. This rapid development has occurred with much assistance from western nations that have moved their manufacturing operations to Asia and by their desires for inexpensive manufactured goods. These positive encouraging activities are expanding the influence and abilities of the BRICS nations to transform our entire civilisation for the best in the near future, especially as further ongoing progress occurs.

Another global conflict is the desired result that the USA and Israel currently sponsor. Fortunately, this possible scenario is now looking very unlikely at this point in time in spite of the mass media propaganda attempting to promote warfare and conflict internationally. Humanity is always the biggest loser in warfare. If a major world war does occur, then our entire global civilisation could rapidly be reduced into polluted piles of rubble. Global warfare may seem to be an unlikely event considering the lessons humanity should have learned from the two world wars in the past century. Negative human nature issues enable nations to justify or rationalise their insane, self-serving policies and unreasonable, unworkable, false ideals in order to condone attacking their neighbours through immorally and illegally seeking to create territorial empires through violent military conquest. This is simply unacceptable now and will continue to be so in the future, as earthly civilisation matures.

The exceedingly high military expenditures in many nations clearly is indicative that these nations are preparing for war. Otherwise, they would not be so heavily investing essential financial resources desperately needed to revitalise the national infrastructure; for more efficient transportation systems; water resource development; environmental rehabilitation; education; economic development; innovation development; better living conditions and employment opportunities; improved health through the prevention of disease; development of alternative safe, renewable, emission-free energy production and conservation programs; more representative and innovative political processes to improve the functionality of governmental systems; assisting smaller size businesses to be competitive in the local, national and global markets, and other such constructive pragmatic development programs.

In 2015, the formation of the BRICS nations sets of alliances and the development of an 'alternate' and parallel banking system to insure a more stable, reliable, equitable, functional, 'asset backed' (gold, silver, precious resources of value) financial system is currently happening. Hooray!!! This monumental positive step is a reason for great celebration within humanity; as the cabal's evil financial tyranny over global finances is first neutered and then to be replaced by a far better system for the benefit of all life forms on Earth.

Instead of focusing genuine serious committed efforts and financial resources into such productive activities and policies, most 'western' governments and the financial sectors are taking a 'business as usual' type of attitude; seemingly preferring to remain intentionally 'oblivious' to the massive set of challenges and problematic issues that are now confronting our civilisation.

Leading up to 2008, those in positions of responsibility could be justified from their own perspectives in saying words to the effect, "Well, everything is just fine in my life and my business is profitable, so what is all the fuss about?" Now in 2016, in considering the bankruptcy of the USA government and many others, to declare such an attitude is absolute insanity and total denial of actual reality.

We can look back into history and see that often the ultra-wealthy, along with their political and religious supplicants, are the last people to realise when serious, potentially devastating conditions exist within their societies and environments because they are stuck in their magnificent 'ivory towers', living in an artificial world with a limited perspective on what is really happening in the 'real world' outside of their vision or experience.

Therefore, what do you think the likelihood might be of a social scientist (such as myself) being hired by the 'power elite' who are rapidly becoming the 'power deplete' to advise government and industry on these issues and being paid like a Council gardener or perhaps a corporate executive for providing viable solutions? No, there is no need for alternate perspectives within the mainstream of this civilisation's decision and planning processes, until it is far too late to make the necessary remedial actions.

Now, interestingly in 2016, we see major changes happening globally, so my involvement with a world peace movement, Global Mission of Peace (GMOP) is a positive factual indicator that the actual functional, staffed, funded 'structures' to implement these much needed remedial transformative social and economic improvements are already in existence. Many quality people and organisations globally are in the relatively 'early stages' of working in cooperation with others similar groups to create a prosperous global peace for humanity with shared values, great vision, enormous experience, vast financial and integrated logistical capabilities to establish a better world for us all.

This process is NOT about 'throwing money' at problem areas and simply hoping things improve. It is about careful strategic assessment and planning to implement to readily available solutions in a comprehensive manner that benefits all people and earthly life forms.

Actions by the relatively few governments possessing the massive military budgets that have historically demonstrated a proclivity toward aggressively using war and economic predation to further their national interests now continues to openly threaten to thwart prospects to create and maintain global peace and to manifest financially and environmentally sustainable technological and societal accomplishment that will insure the enhanced equitable prosperity. They seek to perpetuate misery, fear, deprivation, greedy control by a few over the many through all manner of hurtful attitudes and activities. That is enough of that attitude now.

Love and peace that is achieved through meaningful sustainable prosperity and creative beneficial diverse forms of true productivity assures us all that a better life will be enjoyed by future generations within our newly developing global civilisation.

It is a certainty that the 'old world order' as it now exists in its current form, is a self-evidently evil force on Earth, which is now being clearly revealed by their unsuccessful attempts to escalate the warfare mentality through its contrived and totally deceptive so-called 'war on terrorism'. Their clear intention is to intentionally promote more intensive, larger scale wars, involving other nations whose interests and allegiances will become directly threatened. We must remain vigilant that these wars are simply intended to create destruction, chaos, fear and upset among people and make profits and retain control by those benefitting from war, needless diseases and poverty. It is now obvious to some people that not all of these wars are intentionally designed to acquire resources and territory. This level of intentional violence being conducted by insidious forces working through the USA and Israel is now being clearly seen and publicly acknowledged by other governments such as Russia and China.

It must be openly and genuinely acknowledged globally that it is wrong and illegal to blatantly steal other people's possessions and kill and injure many millions of people in the process, simply because of the military ability to do so in order to make more 'misery money' for a few insane psychopathic individuals, through their corporations, trusts and foundations. No one or group of people has a legitimate right to adversely control and deprive others of their ability to enjoy a decent, secure life here on Mother Earth.

Wars today are more about maintaining international fanatical totalitarian control over the world populations by aggressively preventing the rise of true freedom, the expression of independent thought, more equitable widespread prosperity and abundance for all people. Warfare is the awful historically proven preferred method that the old world order utilises to crush all real hope of our societies to transcend what we now experience in our lives in order to attempt to work together to improve and transform our social and economic systems for the better of all people. Most of the world's population actually live under relatively dour, stifling, somewhat oppressive, uncertain and potentially threatening social and economic conditions. Some people would doubt and debate that from their perspectives. Part of the ample self-evident evidence is that the wealthy are concerned about protecting their material abundance from those who would legally and illegally earn profits in abundance and even those profoundly poor and disadvantaged who may become prone to try to steal enough to survive. The vast majority of people are not dishonest, lazy or particularly greedy. We simply seek productive reliable work to earn a reasonably good living so they can enjoy a lifestyle that is not excessively dominated by endless toil and excessive forms of taxation and unreasonably high costs of living that are unaffordable on fixed wage systems. Doing work we enjoy and that benefits society and the environment is the goal for us now.

While one aspect of the mass media propaganda inundates us with false images to "be very afraid", another message that mass media is constantly portraying are nonsensical insignificant platitudes that everything for some 'lucky' wealthy fortunate people is wonderful and glamorous. They present this false 'dream' as though a bigger television set, nicer vehicle, new stylish clothing or more grandiose home will actually satiate our inner desire to live truly meaningful lives. The majority of the world's populations have little opportunity to attain such an idealistic material lifestyle.

Most people living in developed nations inaccurately believe material wealth is a primary prerequisite for attaining happiness and fulfilment. The truth is that a certain level of materialistic security is necessary to be comfortable in life. However; real peace of mind, true meaning and the ability to deeply enjoy more fulfilling, loving, joyful relationships with our families, friends and business associates are the most important types of experiences in the creation of a wonderful life. In western societies we now live under conditions dominated by crass materialism for the 'fortunate few' who are financially able to afford that elusive 'lifestyle of the rich and famous' that we constantly hear about and see continually portrayed the mass media outlets, such as in the Hollywood movie industry. They do not show what it would be like to have tourist helicopters flying overhead most of the day to view the mansion or having desperate people interfering with them in various ways. Seeking material wealth in the form of money and political influence to some people and organisations has become their actual 'religion' or primary purpose in life.

The majority of people in the world simply seek a lasting type of peace, characterised by freedom to be unique, without harming others, and productive in their own beneficial ways. We people want, need and deserve to experience a life worth living joyfully and fully; not an empty shell or façade of a life that promises us grand things and happy times, but only delivers most citizens mostly hard work, sacrifice, disappointment disillusionment, false promises, shattered relationships, inevitable chronic illnesses, huge levels of endless debt and despair because we did not achieve the ideal 'dream life' that so few people ever actually attain, regardless of their accumulated wealth or fame, in our materialistic dominated, glitzy western societies. We seek true meaning through lively, genuine, lovingly peaceful, enjoyable interactions with others. We all desire the ability to have sufficient time with adequate financial resources and freedom to thoroughly enjoy one's family and friends.

True productivity, in the form of personal profit for one's labour in the normal economic environment most of us exist within, is currently being 'misappropriated', or literally stolen and then mostly squandered by those controlling the 'old world order'. This is especially evident in the attitudes and actions of their corporate henchmen's commitment to obtaining excessive profits regardless of the costs to others or the resulting environmental destruction. They lobby for domination of governmental policies that serve their exclusive self-interests through legislation that also arbitrarily imposes unfair levels of taxation upon the working public in relation to their actual profitability after their excessively high costs of living are calculated and deducted from their modest incomes. Corporations and businesses are able to deduct all of their costs of operations, materials, overheads, lawyer's fees, donations to political parties and various forms of bribes, etc as being 'tax deductions'. Therefore, such costs of conducting business are not calculated into assessing their taxable income to the government, especially when they locate their corporate offices in low tax or no tax international jurisdictions known as 'tax havens'. Corporations and wealthy individuals do not pay their fair share of taxes at this time.

It is certain that within a more equitable, fair taxation system that fixed-wage earning working people should be allowed to deduct from their taxable income the modest reasonable amount of their income that is required to pay their most basic costs of living for items such as: food, rent, mortgage payments, transportation, health care, education, utility expenses and so. This is the equivalent of corporations calculating their expenses of running their businesses and deducting these costs before declaring a profit upon which they then pay income tax. For wage earning people these costs of operating their lives are governed by external forces because their fixed wages are so low that after these basic living expenses are paid to others, then most of these workers would have no profit to report, or to put into their depleted bank accounts. In such a case, then they would have no taxes payable to the government, aside from those massive levels of taxation already hidden within the costs of everything they and we all purchase. This system for wage earners and self-employed people would be the equivalent of personal tax deductions, similar in every way to those any business or corporation would enjoy under current taxation laws internationally.

Additionally, a fair and equitable taxation system on corporations and the rich and poor alike would be a small 1% to 2% tax on all funds move into and out of any bank account, which would generate more than sufficient taxation revenues to replace all taxation systems currently in place. The present taxation system is grossly unfair in many ways because the majority of taxpayers proportionately to the total volume of taxation revenues are relatively low paid workers who have no taxation deductions and have relatively high living costs compared to their overall income. The simple fact is there have been endless ways designed/legislated to 'legally' and immorally cheat, deprive and to even 'eliminate' superfluous people by various cruel and unnecessary methods by those relative few privileged people that are currently dominating the old world order within our modern civilisation.

The conclusion to this relatively 'polite' tirade of discontent and frustration about the adverse human nature issues that are now plaguing humanity is that 'we', the good hard working peaceful decent loving people of Earth, do not want, nor can or will we again allow the warfare mentality to assert control over our world in such a way that another world war is initiated by the old world order. If this ongoing unwanted hostile attack upon humanity and Mother Earth continues, then those directly responsible will, as one very well-informed unnamed observer commented recently, "They will be swinging from the light poles." This is clearly NOT what we want for the criminal psychopaths attempting to create chaos and misery upon Earth. These people urgently and desperately need to wake up very soon from their self-induced nightmare of violence and promoting discord before they are personally and collectively 'held responsible' and accountable by the people. There are obvious concerted attempts now being made internationally to inaccurately blame global conflicts upon elusive, shadowy, hidden groups of oddly well-financed and heavily armed, so-called 'terrorists". The financial and military aid being covertly provided to these so-called 'terrorist groups' such as ISIS have been traced back to the intelligence agencies of the same few rouge nations mentioned previously. It is both interesting and quite curious that with all the sophisticated intelligence gathering capability possessed by the western governments that these terrorists, such as Osama bin Laden or others, are able to avoid capture for such lengthy periods of time. Who are really the 'terrorists' in this world and who is really funding and protecting them?

For example, any total idiot could see the unfortunate man in Iraq that was arrested in a bunker, wrongly identified as being Saddam Hussein, then charged, tried, convicted in Court and executed was NOT actually the real Saddam Hussein. Observing only the incredibly poor dental condition of that man certainly revealed him as being a poor quality 'body double' of Saddam, when photos are compared to the actual former U.S. sponsored Iraqi dictator, who had immaculate white teeth.

The same could be said of the almost farcical, purported 'death' of Osama bin Laden and many other such fictitious events. Are we to willingly and compliantly be endlessly lied to, robbed, disenfranchised of our democratic and civil human rights, subjected to poisons intentionally in our environment and diet, sent off to die in pointless economically motivated unnecessary international wars and even openly murdered by these so-called 'power elite' through their governmental, religious and mercenaries without so much as a right to protest or seek through peaceful means to improve these circumstances or this maltreatment? No. This is more than 'enough' now.

In an international forum on the terrorism issue (about 10+ years ago, and not too long after the 9/11 events), the U.S. government representatives could not even agree with other international participants about establishing a mutually acceptable definition of a 'terrorist' or 'terrorism' for the purposes of addressing the related problems. According to the dictionary, terrorism is basically defined as being "one who favours or uses terror inspiring methods of governing or of coercing government or community." Depending upon one's perspective, one can easily understand the many reasons why this reasonable, commonly held, logical definition of terrorism would not be well-accepted by the Americans. According to the previously defined, simplistic, concise, all-inclusive assessment of terrorism, the USA would obviously qualify as being a terrorist nation, as would Israel, from the perspective of many of the world's more truly civilised nations.

Inexplicably, no clearly defined, mutually agreed internationally accepted definition of terrorism currently exists, although we are told by various western governments that there is now an international war against terrorism being waged militarily. Does this mean that soon a so-called 'terrorist' could be inappropriately and unjustly defined to include simple, defenceless, peaceful, starving, jobless people who are seeking to feed, clothe and shelter their families in a world that has dispossessed them of their land and opportunities for employment? If you think this is impossible or unlikely then look again closely at the barbaric history of the old world order.

At one point in time, the Japanese government publicly and quite falsely sought to identify the environmental protection organisation Greenpeace as being a terrorist organisation in response to the peaceful efforts that Greenpeace is making to disrupt and bring to the public's attention the Japanese illegal whaling activities in the Antarctic Ocean.

The fact the Japanese are illegally hunting, killing and processing for commercial sale internationally protected whale species, supposedly for scientific research, is not perceived by themselves as genocide and terrorism against intelligent whale species located within Australian territorial waters and international waters. Interesting to perceive examples of how those 'vested interests' who are seeking to violate international law are seeking to vilify an organisation that is protecting these whales by incorrectly and falsely mis-identifying or 'deeming' them as terrorists. Is there any real justice in such government sponsored statements or activities? If such things continue, then please do not be at all surprised when, at some point in time, that these 'responsible' people within government, politics, some corporations and bureaucracies will be re-identified as treasonous liars, immoral criminals, the sponsors and actual perpetrators of most terrorist acts globally and then they will be directly held personally responsible for these crimes.

To people seeking to kill intelligent life forms such as whales, apes, elephants or any other may ask themselves, "Is this righteous ethical loving behaviour?"

Around the world we see endless examples where the same abominable forces of self-interest, oppression and aggression are seeking to re-invent themselves to become known as the so-called 'new world order', which I choose to define as being the same old 'world dis-order' or the 'chaos elite'. The simple fact is as Jesus said, "By their acts, ye shall know them."

Thankfully, those few war and terror mongering zealots are being more clearly perceived by 'thinking', working, good people as the lying, stealing, evil predators and slave masters. The evil cabal seek to be our 'rulers' in the future, yet this is simply NOT going to happen. A new time has arrived here on our Mother Earth in 2016, and beyond, into a much better future for us all.

Peaceful, hard working, innocent people throughout human history have constantly been periodically ritually slaughtered by the same evil forces that are seeking to label themselves as the 'new world order' that is now seeking to establish a totalitarian style one world government and falsely pretend it is a democracy. The history of human civilisations globally reveals that this powerful controlling minority of people have periodically cannibalised humanity, as well as enforced all types of slavery and declared an endless series of mostly senseless unnecessary warfare. These malevolent, greedy, power hungry people represent the evil forces that currently seek to exert total control over our world. They always seek to deflect and deny any problems that are publicly presented, focusing untruthfully upon the myriad of superficial comforts characterising modern civilisation to negate and ignore the real truth that for most people this earthly existence is surely less enjoyable and meaningful than it could be if people were allowed and enabled to improve various situational difficulties.

Now we must examine a somewhat unusual and more meaningful question that each and every one of us must ask ourselves, "What can I do about the world's situation?" Honestly, we are best able to improve various aspects within our own individual lives in ways that exemplify our higher personal attributes and demonstrate our positive, peaceful, constructive solutions. Most of us simply want our lives to be as pleasant as possible. There is nothing inherently wrong with that attitude; at least not from my current perspective. The problem with this desire is only when it is achieved through the needless depravation, suffering, slavery and death of other people.

To gain a better perspective, please imagine that you personally were in absolute total autocratic control of the entire world, just as I have done to gain a comprehension of the people whose self-declared responsibility it is to lead our civilisation. One then becomes much more aware of their very difficult, complex and challenging global leadership role. It is quite challenging to consciously imagine the enormous diverse set of responsibilities involved in maintaining the reliable, functional operations of a global civilisation today on

Earth. This massively complex type of situation is precisely what each of us, as individuals, must be willing to consider; not so much for the world as a whole, rather to assess our own individual modest, relatively small, yet essential unique role within the efficient operations of the larger social and economic systems within which we all live.

This realisation impressed itself upon me when I realised the basic fact that many of our civilisation's leaders do not possess the necessary knowledge, skills, moral attributes, intelligence and capability to function successfully within the limited old social and economic systems that were developed in past ages. Therefore, they are now seemingly unable to adequately resolve the current problematic circumstances that are intensifying within our complex, highly technological, heavily populated, chronically inefficient socio-economic systems. Thankfully, there are major public actions being implemented to improve matters in China, Russia and most other BRICS nations internationally; starting with avoiding another unnecessary world war.

In short, the old world order requires new solutions to age old problems and their own group of well-educated sycophants, dim-witted servants and militaristic 'yes men' are unable to provide these adaptations quickly enough to prevent social and economic disaster. All they can do is maintain a pathetic, feeble-minded non-functional reaction to retain power and save 'face' by relying upon the proven ineffectual, primitive methods of the past, which we have discussed to the point of absurdity here already.

New ways of doing things to create real solutions to our challenges is in the early stages of occurring. As the years rapidly roll by past the upcoming year of 2016, then this part of our discussion here will be increasingly irrelevant and wrong; as the upcoming great progress happens for all people and life forms on Earth to witness, experience, benefit by and truly enjoy.

How do the people controlling our world's civilisation acquire the much needed inputs from free-thinking, perceptive, creative, innovative, highly intelligent and talented people when such people have periodically been aggressively persecuted so extensively throughout human history? The majority of people have for many centuries been brainwashed into blindly adhering to the same thought and behaviour patterns of those who educated them. Creativity requires a more refined, heightened level of awareness and a truly all-inclusive, comprehensive perspective of life. Some aspects of eternal life will always seem mysterious to some of us and this is a key aspect that defines our physical earthly reality system.

Creativity illustrates one's higher vision and among the vast majority of people this quality is a characteristic that often struggles to be expressed consciously within one's self. Truly productive, constructive, artistic, philosophical and spiritual creativity can be daunting to demonstrate publicly within one's personal life in most earthly societies because there is often a severe price that one 'pays' in various ways for manifesting beneficial creativity. This is predominantly not true of creatively producing innovative products and services; provided one is working for a major business group, one's products do not conflict with existing vested interests, or one is willing to sell or give away one's ideas and capabilities to international corporations when the ideas are accepted by mainstream society. New ideas regarding improved patterns of human behaviour are not manifested easily, reliably or swiftly; yet they definitely do exist within the minds, hearts and spirits of people like us. We must apply our individual creativity to assist our civilisation's progress.

Please allow me to assure you and then to further reassure you that if you have reached this point in this book, then you are assuredly a great hope to humanity. You are indeed one in a million Souls in this earthly life. Only a relative few people care enough about these issues of personal and social self-development to persist through topical material that is as mentally arduous and emotionally testing as we have been repetitively discussing here.

You can know and feel sure in your heart that when you join in cooperation with others of 'great spirit' like you; together, we can, will and are making the necessary adaptations, adjustments and changes that will enable humanity to avoid potential self-created disasters in order to transcend the difficulties that will allow us to transform our civilisation for the better world we seek to create. In so doing, we Earthlings will join the truly civilised universal inter-planetary community, with whom Earth already has a strong, developing relationship. We will address a variety of those future related issues as our discussion progresses. For now, let's continue to determine what we each can and ideally will do to improve our roles in enabling these beneficial positive adjustments in our civilisation to occur in a peaceful, efficient, loving manner.

Individuals must be willing and able to examine, assess, evaluate, analyse, define, perceive, understand and finally act decisively and consistently upon our human nature issues, first and foremost within the confines of our own individual states of consciousness. We each must learn to acknowledge our own human tendencies, frailties, faults, habits, unconscious programming and lesser proclivities so that we can moderate, adjust or eliminate those negative, unproductive personal characteristics to the best of our ability. We are most able to uplift our own lives first, then to subsequently serve as useful, productive, free-willed, exemplary citizens. We seek to characterise and reliably personify whatever is good within us so that we justly possess and openly demonstrate the right, responsibility and obligation to help establish the best possible society and world for ourselves, our families, and all people globally and for future generations. This ongoing process begins within one's own heart, mind and spirit and grows outward from there.

It is not about 'saving' other people by converting them to your ways of thinking, living or praying. It is about being true to virtuous higher inner values, ethics, morals and goals so that you personally exemplify the superlative qualities you aspire to as a human being. You treat yourself, others and all life with the kindness, decency and respect you would like to enjoy yourself from others. We each and all have many opposing tendencies and personality traits that reveal themselves through various circumstances.

For example, the truth is I can sometimes be 'unpleasant' when people wrongly act inappropriately or violently with me. Fortunately and thankfully for us all, this sometimes quite outspoken part of my USA born 'character' seldom reveals itself these days, since I became a Naturalised Australian in 1990, where the national culture is more relaxed and generally is more 'easy-going' and accepting of others. This is among the reasons I waited almost 8 years to publish this book, so humanity is truly ready and able to apply this transformation into peaceful times of prosperity and relative equality on Earth.

Our challenge and opportunity is to affiliate our state of consciousness with the most admirable attributes and characteristics within ourselves; to be and become personified expressions of the very best aspects within ourselves in each and every life experience. We seek to conduct our attitudes and behaviours in a positive uplifting manner, even while life is often so adept at confronting us with situational provocations to express the lower aspects of our overall character.

In some cases, surprisingly enough, this will mean that we do NOT any longer simply 'turn the other cheek' when someone has 'slapped us' or has knowingly transgressed against us for the tenth or even the second time. Likewise, if the old world order seeks to violently impose a fascist style of 'new world' government with few human rights; minimal real economic opportunity for the masses who are intentionally restrained in various slavery-like living conditions; characterised by mostly poverty, violence, disease and premature death being our likely fate; then they will create a serious revolution that will destroy this civilisation entirely. If this occurs, a new civilisation will arise from the ashes to replace our present civilisation and they will no longer be in control of our destiny.

Fortunately, we are seeing some very encouraging new positive and potentially very beneficial developments around the world and within many of us as 2016 begins as being a very good time that is clearly signalling humanity's definitive positive 'transition phase'. It is very likely that this uplifting trend of improved attitudes and behaviours will continue to flourish and that peace on Earth will become a reality for the vast majority of people and life living here in the near future. Those few that seek to prevent this mutually beneficial progressive development will soon find themselves 'held personally accountable' and that is unlikely to be a pleasant or rewarding experience for them. Therefore, working together in cooperation peacefully, respectfully, and with genuine purpose to create and sustain our new and better world is going to be the only salvation available to us, in my opinion.

Our journey of self-discovery is to acknowledge who and what (values/beliefs and attitudes) one truly is as a human being. Then, with this awareness, it is each person's unique responsibility and opportunity to more appropriately assert what you truly believe and want to represent in life. The focal nature of your quest here in this sometimes arduous, yet often very enjoyable earthly life, is to simply 'be your best'. Ideally, this is a journey of becoming more alive, aware, volitional and sentient than ever before; thereby enabling your true, higher, more divine-like actual self more intelligibility, coherence and meaning in your life. Being true to yourself in life implies that you do not abnegate personal responsibility to make principled decisions in your life to enhance, advance, uplift and ultimately help to transform our civilisation, from your own uniquely relevant position in the scheme of life. We should not be content to quietly discover our true selves, and then wait passively hoping that our children and their children will have the strength and courage to fight the necessary battles that we were too afraid or weak-hearted to wage ourselves.

Some of our ancestors managed to win freedom and more representative forms of government from the old world order by devoting their very lives to their noble causes. Countless times throughout history, to seek even the most minimal freedoms has resulted in the streets, pastures, woods, rivers, prisons and churches running deep in the innocent, peaceful butchered people's blood for speaking or acting upon their cherished opinions. In such times, those brave people who sought some semblance of peace, justice and freedom had their severed heads impaled upon stakes, were burned at the stake, or had their tortured dying bodies hung in the trees for all others to see, or the more numerous slaughtered corpses were simply piled together and left to rot, or were burned and then buried in great numbers. If freedom has historically only been won at the enormous cost of human life, with innocent defenceless civilians being pitilessly massacred by the oppressors, whomever they may have been depending upon times and locations of the struggle; then I firmly know we must openly, honestly and loudly speak our minds and hearts when so few of us will be murdered for our courage in saying what we all know and feel in our hearts. This is a time of wise united peaceful action.

To be true to one's self as Soul means that each of us is humbly confident in knowing that divine inner conscience will always ultimately reveal truth to you, if you are willing to look for it. You must look within and through your 'higher' self to find real truth and eternal wisdom in this 'external' physical world.

We must stop depending upon the pervasive sources of mass media, or our schools, or church leaders, or the politicians, or even our parents to explain life's truths to us. Your conscience will reveal itself openly to you if your simply examine your innermost thoughts, beliefs and realisations. In this manner, you will not be as prone to rationalise or wrongly justify and condone inappropriate activities just because they do not appear to directly impact your life personally or because your own vested interests would be served in some way. Your conscience will inform you when people are being hurt, deprived or maliciously used in the processes of life, if you are willing to examine reality sincerely.

This eternal journey of self-discovery is all about reclaiming our own sense of values and morality primarily through the 'mirror' or 'window' of our ongoing personal experiences. This does not mean we consider other people's less noble attitudes and actions as being something that is being done directly personally 'against' us as individuals, in spite of the damning evidence that falsely appears to make it appear to be so. We are seeing the 'bigger picture'.

One solution is expanding the continually progressive development of our own set of personal convictions and abilities that are not reliant upon any external controlling person, authority figure, institution or religious leader being required to tell us what we should be thinking and doing with our lives for us to act righteously. Our path toward the re-discovery of the highest divine aspects of our comprehensive eternal state of being is found by being true to one's inner conscience. For most of us, this initially requires that we struggle to hear the soft impulses and quiet firm voice of our own conscience and divine intuition over the din and contentious babble of external inputs from our socially programmed ego-conscious mind and the outside world, with its perverse, outmoded, inaccurate systems of belief and activity. We must re-discover what we perceived and knew as young children; directly and innocently perceiving a world of self-evident experiences and realisations that will tell us exactly what we think, feel and know. It is through the proof and wisdom of our own set of personal experiences and through our conscience and higher values about what is right, proper and fair for us as individuals that we better find what is best for us as families, communities, societies, cultures, religions, nations and as a relatively united, productive, harmonious world civilisation.

The many valid observations made herein would surely appear to be unfair complaints and dubious criticisms from some other perspectives. However, in spite of these constructive observations, the good people of Earth clearly do not now hold any bitter resentment or animosity toward these oppressive controlling people, institutions, governments or business interests that seem so prone to exploit people and circumstances throughout human history. We shall not forget the past, yet we are now peacefully primarily focused upon achieving solutions to life's many challenges in the present and the future.

It is necessary that we have somewhat assertively defined in an openly biased and opinionated manner, a imperfect set of images of human attitudes and actions that have an apparent 'winner' and a 'loser', a 'master' and a 'servant', the 'evil' and the 'good', the 'just' and the 'unjust', the peaceful and the violent and so on. It is necessary that we examine the various contrasting values and tendencies that have served to establish our present technological civilisation, by our self-assessed earthly standards of assessment as honestly as humanly possible (for me).

We must introduce and demonstrate the necessity for a new, more refined, evolved and equitable sense of ethics, values, morals, freedom and justice than presently exists, as evidenced in the ways of the world that are so clearly and extensively illustrated around us. The governmental laws and religious texts of our times certainly do not serve everyone's best interests in a reasonable sustainable manner that will enable our civilisation to progressively develop into a more splendid, truly civilised global society.

It is NOT our intention to develop our own hypocritical, inadequate and adversarial version of the prevalent 'us and them' attitude that has so damaged, deprived and maligned our current civilisation. It is not pragmatic or prudent to silently ignore the terrible threats to freedom and peace by the self-serving forces that seek to stifle and suppress the monumental opportunities now available to create an economic and ideological system fostering more equitable, sustainable global prosperity and peaceful abundance upon Earth. The existing oppressive, adversarial, contentious self-interest groups around the world are asserting themselves with increasing self-righteous impunity, often against one another and against freedom and peace. This deteriorating situation requires that the vast majority of good, peace loving, productive, honest, tolerant people from every culture, nation and religion on Earth must express themselves and take remedial action to prevent the forces of negativity and self-annihilation from destroying our civilisation's hopes and plans to create a much better future in the short term, historically speaking.

There are those malignant malevolent forces that quite openly aggressively assert the primitive untruthful opinion that 'might makes right'. These so-called 'super powers' and those 'cabalists' of the 'old world order' do not wish any other nations or groups of people to possess any real means of self-defence against their many forms of military, economic, energetic and resonant or multi-dimensional sources of aggression and oppression. As we have already discussed at length, these pathologic types of people have proven to be the evil scourge and primary detrimental deleterious element within humanity. Unfortunately these people always seek to usurp power and control over other people in order to hide, disguise and deny their own weakness, fear, insecurity, unworthiness, laziness, or feeble-minded spiritual condition; regardless of the particular doctrine they espouse, or the time in history in which they live, or the nation in which they reside, nor due to their genetic heritage, nor their levels of affluence. Ultimately, nothing within physical reality can overcome the power of Divinity to manifest Its' Will within Creation

We can clearly recognise the existence of a number of wealthy elitist capitalistic families within the USA and internationally, who have consistently expressed an avowed autocratic, domineering, violent, greedy, power seeking, insidious propensity for promoting war and genocide. One such example is the USA Bush family. Observing their attitudes and actions over the past 100 years can assist our understanding of how 'well-placed' wealthy people can influence public, economic and governmental policy and thereby adversely alter the course of human history. We will briefly examine a few aspects of this American family to determine some of the ways that they attained their current positions in American society. This will be a most minimal historical assessment that ignores much additional information that is publicly available about this politically and economically active family. It also provides a glimpse into how interconnected elitist families and their corporations owned by these capitalistic businessmen and their associates have organised their activities to assist one another to earn fortunes and to a large extent control the international economy; a practice that is fundamentally pervasive and undeniable within today's global business culture.

We can begin our limited analysis of the Bush family tree with the patriarch George Herbert Walker, who was the father of Prescott Bush, who was the father of the first President George Bush (Senior), who is the father of the former U.S. President George W. Bush. In 1920, the business partners George Herbert Walker and Averell Harriman purchased from the US government the former German Hamberg-Amerika Line, which at the time was the world's largest shipping line, which was taken from the Germans at the end of World War One. Both Walker and Harriman perceived the situation in Germany as excellent business opportunities, including their financial and logistical support of the Nazi political party during the time that Hitler became its leader. In 1921 Prescott Bush married Walker's daughter Dorothy.

In 1926 Prescott Bush was named by Walker to become Vice President of W.A. Harriman and Co., a New York investment firm, and at that same time to become Director in the Union Banking Corporation, which was instrumental in obtaining and directing U.S. investment from various 'inside sources' into Germany after the end of World War One. Union Banking Corporation and W. A. Harriman were interrelated New York based investment firms that were focused upon obtaining and providing US financial investment to German industry and they developed a close business relationship with the German industrialist Fritz Thyssen. Prescott Bush was then given the responsibility to manage the financial accounts of Thyssen, especially his United Steel Works in Germany which during the course of World War Two supplied the following percentages of German industrial output of these war materials between the years 1932 to 1941: pig iron, 50%; universal plate, 41%; galvanised sheet, 38%; pipes and tubes, 45%; explosives, 35%; wire, 22%. By 1928 Thyssen was the primary financial benefactor and logistical supporter of the Nazi Party.

Another key American participant in this business alliance was Samuel Pryor, Chairman of Remington Arms and a Founding Director of Union Banking Corporation, as well as American Ship and Commerce Corporation, which was the company that controlled Hamberg-Amerika. Remington Arms entered into a Joint Venture Agreement with the notorious German weapons and chemical manufacturing company I.G. Farben regarding explosives manufacturing. At this time and over the next decade many well-known US corporations were active in Germany, among them were Standard Oil, General Motors, IBM, and notably Remington Arms and its associated groups of companies. Without the financial and logistical material support of these and other United States industrial capitalists Germany could not have waged World War Two. For example, between the years 1932 to 1934, Union Banking Corporation sold fifty million dollars worth of Bonds to US investors in support of German industry. Henry Ford supplied the Germans with the knowledge and capability to manufacture assembly line style production of all the war materials that Germany utilised so effectively in conducting that war.

In 1934, Col. William Taylor reported to the United States Senate investigative committee that the German political associations; like the Nazis, other fascist organisations and criminal gangs were being supplied with large volumes of U.S. manufactured guns and ammunition, such as Thompson submachine guns, revolvers and other such weapons. These activities included supplying other forms of logistic support to the fascists to facilitate widespread violence and Harriman is also known to have had major business dealings with Italy's fascist leader Benito Mussolini and similar financial connections with Spain's aspiring dictator, General Franco. In 1939, when Hitler ordered the German invasion of Poland, Hitler also nationalised all of Thyssen's industrial holdings including the Union Steel Works, so Thyssen fled Germany when Adolf Hitler the elected leader of Germany, his former subordinate, openly turned against him. Prescott Bush continued to manage the investments of Union Banking Corporation and W.A. Harriman and Co. throughout the Second World War. When in 1951 the assets of the Union Banking Corporation were unfrozen by U.S. authorities, Prescott Bush received one and a half million dollars for his one share in the company, which was a considerable amount of money in those days. Can you even begin to imagine the amounts of money and chronic misery that these 'vested interests' have 'created' by wars in Vietnam, Korea, the Middle East, Latin America, Africa, and in many other locations?

    This is a very superficial assessment of a few of the key participants that provided financial support for the establishment of the industrial capability developed by Germany in the years leading up to the beginning of the Second World War. These same capitalistic industrialists were primarily responsible for funding the Nazi Party in Germany and promoted its rise to governmental control through purportedly democratic elections in Germany. The Nazi Party selected Adolf Hitler as its leader to voice the elitist totalitarian attitudes possessed by relatively small, yet financially powerful international groups of autocratic, plutocratic zealots located within Germany, the USA, England, France, Italy, Switzerland, South America, Russian, Japan and in many other nations, who wished to remain out of the public's scrutiny before, during and after World War Two.

It should be carefully noted that the USA did not join in the war against Germany even after the Americans were made aware of the autocracies being committed against the nations they invaded, as well as the untold massacre of millions of innocent civilians. Why did the Americans not join the western allies early in the war? Because wealthy influential American corporate and private business interests were making huge fortunes from supplying weapons and loans to both the Allies who were fighting the Germans and the Germans, along with their Allies.

It could also be noted that a similar situation existed in Germany prior to World War One in regard to American investment and logistical support of Germany and its allies. A similar study could be done on how Japan was able to finance and develop the industrial capability to prepare for and wage World War Two. However, it is most important to carefully note that after World War One, international legislation was enacted to prevent Germany from again building its national war machinery to such an extent that it could again militarily threaten or attack other European nations. Many of these actions listed previously, in retrospect, were in obviously in direct illegal contravention of those American and international laws. We see the results of these people and corporate actions that were motivated by greed, power, extremely dubious political choices and unconscionable morals. These wealthy capitalistic internationally active industrialists and many others like them from all nations of this world have a proclivity for 'obliterating memory', ignoring 'inconvenient truths', developing 'convenient historical amnesia', supporting 'corporate friendly dictators' and justifying empowering totalitarian political forces, such as the Nazis and other international fascist dictators do, if it serves their needs and goals. They have repeatedly openly or covertly proven a willingness, to seek to illegally and legally evade national and international legislation that is intended to prevent such unjust activities from occurring.

It is important to scrutinise the Bush family history to determine the tawdry, corrupted, greedy, power seeking nature of their belief system and actions over almost a century of American politics. Prescott Bush seems initially to have been something of a pawn that was initiated and trained in the ways of skulduggery and conscienceless attitudes and virulent behaviours by those powerful wealthy industrialists with strong connections to international banking interests (such as J.P. Morgan) who placed him into his positions of responsibility. Over the passing generations, the segment of the U.S. Bush family that was fathered by Prescott Bush has resulted in the evolution and fundamental formative influences that created, raised and educated the first President George Bush (Senior), who became the father to the former President George W. Bush, the evil moronic imbecile that is the cumulative result of the Bush family's own eugenics breeding program.

President George W. Bush consistently appeared to be the ideal 'puppet' or 'pawn' for the 'behind the scenes' international capitalistic corporate industrialists because he genuinely seems to have no conscience, seems to possess little understanding or concern for the misery and destruction that his national and international policies create for our civilisation or the innocent people that die needless violent deaths because of these evil actions.

These 'cabalist' people, their allies and servants are happy when making money and have proven a willingness to literally 'do anything' they deem as being necessary to maintain their positions of financial power and social control. They seem oblivious to the fact that these falsely contrived and maintained ongoing devastating wars are primarily intended to further their own greedy corporate policies, which include the intentional murder and injury of millions of innocent people over centuries of their despotic rule. To hear that these unfortunate 'non-combatant' people and their property are now termed 'collateral damage' is a revealing insight into cabalist attitudes. They must feel very clever indeed, to see how well their obvious long and short term plans are working in today's world societies, much to all of our detriment.

This branch of the Bush family tree in this century has proven conclusively by the ample historical evidence to be entirely devoted to supporting evil attitudes and governmental policies of warfare, oppression, genocide as a means to increase their own wealth and influence, especially among corporate circles of influence. The Bush family, their advocates, business associates and financial sponsors strongly and consistently favour a governmental system based upon autocratic, fanatical elitism, and the establishment of so-called democratic form of plutocracy (government rule by the wealthy) that is financially 'sponsored' primarily by corporate donations and various (mostly) wealthy people who apparently endorse the policies of the Republican Party in the USA. This financially corrupted trend to gain the financial and political support of the large corporations who profited massively from both world wars has been well-documented. The Nazis obviously had many friends in very high business and political circles internationally, so the USA only became involved in World War Two when the American people basically demanded it after several American ships were attacked and sunk by the German U-boats and after Japan attacked America at Pearl Harbour in Hawaii. The American elitists only chose to enter the war because they could see that Hitler had ceased to adequately serve their interests and apparently had developed his own plans for world domination.

Thankfully, English under the genuine leadership of Winston Churchill, steadfastly refused to capitulate or surrender to the Germans, in spite of their indescribable losses of life and property. The fact that Hitler's orders for Germany to foolishly attack Russia; their former ally, was the only reason Germany and its other international allies lost the Second World War, in my opinion. Hitler unconsciously sowed the seeds of his own destruction. Perhaps he intentionally sabotaged the carefully conducted plans of the old world order to gain control of the entire world in his actions to attack the fascists controlling Russia; who had installed Stalin as their puppet leader there. We will never know the full story, yet the facts are clear enough to see for us all right now in our world today. After President Bush left office in the USA, then surprisingly arrived a mysterious, little-known cabalist Obama, who used exactly the words and images needed to arouse the hopes and dreams of the American people into electing him instead of another Republican with fascist type agendas. Over the past 7 years, President Obama has sought to lead America further down the 'misery road' of seeking to institute endless global wars. History will assess the Bush families' and Obama's actions better and more inclusively than I am able to do here now, thank goodness.

History has already well-documented the Nazi's and Hitler's inhuman policies. The heinous misdeeds of the Nazis have dramatically proven their intentions was to institutionalise various forms of slavery upon the common people of the world, while they sought to institutionalise a program of eugenics to breed a pure Germanic race composed of Arian people. Oddly enough, Hitler did not appear to be a pure Arian type German genetically, yet because of his convenient fascist attitudes, this obvious fact was seemingly ignored. The Germans also selected blond, blue eyed Jewish children and separated them from their parents in the concentration camps and then many Jewish children were adopted by German families because of their Arian appearance. The Nazi's policies were quite convenient, muddled and much was done primarily for propaganda purposes and to obscure the truth.

The Nazi's true agenda was to install an international murderous totalitarian imperialist regime, and with their allies to rule the world as a Nazi fascist empire. Why would anyone, such as the American Bush family and their business associates, knowingly support such a policy of insanity and genocide unless it served their personal and financial interests and they had no conscience whatsoever? The

Nazis espoused the belief system of a significant majority of these 'power elite' who currently rule our global civilisation from 'the government within the governments'.

Now in more modern times, we see first President Bush's lack of moral character exhibited while he served as the Director of the CIA under President Reagan. The illegal and immoral activities of the CIA in both South America and in the Middle East are historical fact, as were the covert dealings with the Iranians which was against U.S. law. As Director of the CIA, George Bush, along with Donald Rumsfeld, was instrumental in supplying money and weapons to Saddam Hussein's government in Iraq, a US policy that continued for decades. The list of crimes committed by this Bush family are available in the public domain, as are many of those committed by their close business and political party members and corporate contributors which are far too lengthy to record here. The Bush family's attitudes and actions are self-evident in roles of authority in Texas, in Florida, as Director of the CIA, as President of the USA in the 1991 first war in Iraq, and more recently by his son President George W. Bush's involvement in and response to the 9/11 related events that were immorally used as a knowingly false, fabricated pretext for war in Afghanistan and Iraq. The patriarchs of this Bush family over several generations have designed their own personal policies of militaristic aggression to acquire wealth and power and cunningly implemented them relentlessly, culminating with their successive ascensions to the highest political office in the western nations, the Presidency of the USA.

In the Presidency of the USA, both George Bush and his son George W. Bush have instigated and fought unnecessary, unjust, very expensive and counter-productive wars in various parts of the world. Their motives seem to be largely to further their own financial interests and those of their powerful, wealthy 'old world order' masters who remain hidden from public view through all manner of international disasters. We know the interests of the American nation have not been well-served by the inappropriate, illegal, horribly damaging, exceedingly costly militaristic activities of the Bush family, their close associates, business partners and their many allies in the violence business. Their 'old world order' masters sit quietly 'behind the scenes' directing the activities of their subordinates, such as the Bush's and many others like them internationally. These elite wealthy groups of international autocrats may inaccurately believe they are safely hidden from the view of the people and the mass media 'behind closed doors' and the avowed silence of their co-conspirators and stooges. Silence may be 'golden' for them now, yet their days of 'comfortable living' upon this war-torn planet are rapidly coming to an end, as their countless crimes are being exposed to the public who has quietly suffered in miserable conditions for far too long already. The only question that remains to be answered is, "What type of 'ending' will be experienced by 'we', the Indigenous Citizens of Earth?" Yes, the cabal and their 'minders' previously openly planned to instigate massive world wars and genocide, along with martial law and openly totalitarian style governments globally. See the information on the internet about the 'Georgia Guidestones', for those who are conveniently still unaware or oblivious of this overt, clear, ongoing plan for the extermination of most of the world's human population. This may continue to appear to be the case right now, but who knows what passing time will bring? Who could predict what may eventually be revealed about specific people that now comfortably reside behind the veils of secrecy that disguise the originators of mass murder upon planet Earth, such as the staged fake 9/11 events being wrongly blamed entirely upon Middle Eastern terrorists?

This entire current situation is so seemingly impossible and bizarre that it could not possibly occur in the truly free and democratic world that now purportedly exists. This 9/11 event and the subsequent attempted cover-up with the complicity of other nation's intelligence agencies, the mass media, the 9/11 participants, the falsely blamed al Qaeda terrorists who willingly accepted responsibility for something they clearly did not do, government investigators, U.S. Congress and countless others actually proves conclusively that we no longer live in anything resembling a free and democratic global civilisation. In fact the opposite is now the case. We live in a covert totalitarian, autocratic, industrial-military dominated, hedonistically inequitable; greed-dominated capitalistic system that disadvantages the vast majority of Earth's people and all other life forms residing upon this planet.

The circumstances seem to be amazingly akin to the much less offensive fictitious story about the much feared Wizard of Oz, who actually turned out to be a decrepit, insecure, mostly 'well-meaning' old man; who was finally found hiding behind his frightening illusions, possessing very little real power, who retained his position of authority from the use his extensive façade of false grandeur, with copious amounts of lying. The difference today is these crazy people have incalculable weapons of mass destruction at their disposal, as well as more monetary and logistic wealth than most people could ever comprehend. Many efforts to start another world war have been averted by the Russians and Chinese and so it is self-evident that President Obama is not the man of peace that he pretends to be publicly. "By their actions, so shall ye know them."

Therefore, can future potential generations of our children and their children afford for us here and now in 2016 and beyond; continue to permit madmen, murders, liars and proven criminals to remain in control of our civilisation? No is the simple answer. This is a very serious question requiring a quite serious solution. My opinion is that ideally these people must willingly 'give up' their positions of political and economic power over humanity and the planet and willingly admit their many crimes publicly through their own mass media outlets and ask humanity for forgiveness. This would be similar to when 'we' saw President Nixon do in his resignation speech, after he was 'caught' ordering the Watergate crimes and then seeking to 'cover-up' his involvement.

Everything was recorded on audio, so Nixon's guilt was self-admitted on those voice recordings, just as other evidence will prove to become in the 'upcoming' cases of the Bush family and others. These cabal leaders (like the Bush family and others); need to publicly ask for forgiveness for their self-evident treasonous crimes, such as 9/11 and many other so-called 'terrorist' events. While this seems almost impossible to conceive happening; it will definitely occur sooner than we can imagine. Otherwise, these responsible people will finally be publicly, criminally and civilly held accountable for their crimes and theft in International Courts of true Law. Then the price they pay will be with their own lives, along with being stripped of their accumulated financial fortunes and then perhaps they will wish that they had willingly 'surrendered' and remitted payments for their many accrued debts.

The only difference between Hitler, his henchmen, their ideological and financial backers and the modern day Bush family is that the Bush's have not yet been allowed to begin World War Three, in spite of appearances to the contrary. The same is true of the cabalist President Obama because Russia and China possess advanced weapons systems and the strategic ability to defeat the USA and its few remaining allies, if a world war were to occur now. The Bush's, Obama, their cohorts and their unprincipled masters have already made some ongoing catastrophic errors in judgement and action that is now firmly etched in their own minds and now this information and experience resides within the people's 'collective consciousness'. The negative 'powers that be' surely do realise this process is not going well, nor according to their careful plans, in spite of some of their intentional insane 'successes', such as the devastation and chaos in the Middle East that has been created by these wars. It seems that the criminal and civil prosecution of the 9/11 conspirators, including President George W. Bush who seems to be proven complicit in his prior knowledge of 9/11 events and the subsequent government cover-up will eventually occur, if he and his co-conspirators live long enough to face the International and American Court systems.

The attempted suppression and control of the international mass media in not publicising the actual facts involved will eventually cease to be practical or enforceable, considering the extensive information already in the public domain. Today there is increasingly conclusive, damning evidence becoming available to the public on a regular basis that absolutely, definitively proves that most 9/11 related events were primarily a U.S. government planned and conducted covert operation from start to finish. These 9/11 related events were clearly a carefully orchestrated, staged event where thousands of innocent people were massacred, intentionally and knowingly and in premeditated conscienceless cold-blood in order to incorrectly blame Middle Eastern terrorists and begin the current wars in the Middle East. The wars in Afghanistan, Iraq, Ukraine, Libya, Syria, along with many unsuccessful attempts to include Iran; are intended to increase oil and gas prices to make the wealthy even wealthier, to destabilise the world and distract people from the elimination of democratic government and human rights globally.

The only step toward a final solution to this complex nightmare is to thoroughly investigate the issues involved in a comprehensive truthful manner which is more likely than it may seem as 2015 came to a tumultuous yet positive ending and 2016 begins with great hope to create a better future by cooperating peacefully together globally; thanks primarily to the 'peace seeking' Chinese, Russians, and their BRICS ally nations. When the facts prove the guilt of those responsible for ordering the 9/11 event through offices in the U.S. and Israeli Governments, then only an international trial for war crimes against humanity and American prosecution for treason against the American people through the legally ordained Court systems would serve to pacify and placate humanity to some marginal extent. We see that in Iraq that prosecution process functioned slowly in regard to the capture and execution of the purported 'body double' of

Saddam Hussein took many years and was a farce for the public to watch as a TV show drama, while the real Saddam Hussein's location is currently unknown to most people.

Therefore, it may require a number of years to manifest the international trial in regard to President Bush's prosecution for treason and international war crimes in relation to 9/11 related events, yet time will tell all.

Russian President Putin has moved strongly in the direction of manifesting and insuring global peace, in spite of rhetoric from the USA about the excellent demobilisation of ISIS that Russia, China and their allies of Iraq and Iran are now doing in the Middle East, primarily starting in Syria. President Putin has distanced himself from adopting an aggressive war-like attitude in spite of war in the Ukraine and the other challenges to peace that currently exist globally.

Cabalists have sought to control (influence) and 'fix' the decisions being made in the International Court of Settlements by various methods. Recently, this proved unsuccessful when the United States "Federal Reserve" Bank (FED), which is a privately-owned cabal business, attempted to declare bankruptcy to avoid being held financially accountable for its massive international debt, which is related to all the other international "Reserve Banks". The owners of the FED were dismissed in seeking bankruptcy by the International Court of Settlements in mid-2015, so this event is of monumental significance. Therefore, it only seems to an uneducated, uninformed, naïve, biased observer that successful prosecutions for criminal offences will not occur there. Imagine the excitement and responses when the comprehensive true facts, U.S. military procedures and witnesses are able to be fairly and openly presented comprehensively. We can now clearly perceive, if such cases were to be honestly considered by these International Courts, and then finally justice will be served. Times are changing for the better.

If the two George Bush's, their affiliated knowledgeable relatives, government henchmen, and closest business associates; including some of the so-called terrorists that they and their organisations have been financing were to be publicly tried in American and/or International Courts for their decades of crime and misconduct, then Earth's people would learn what the German people learned about the Nazi's horrible death camps for Jews and other so-called 'undesirable people' after Hitler lost power. The Bush family history, in relation to that of their father and grandfather, desperately needs to be publicly exposed, not hidden by a knowing mass media that is owned and controlled by cabalists. Additionally, it is undeniable that copious volumes of undeniable evidence now exists to initiate and prove in an International Court of Justice that intentional war crimes have been committed in the 9/11 related events and subsequently in the Middle East wars.

Once officially charged in a truly 'fair and impartial' International or USA Court, and possibly facing certain execution for treason and/or war crimes; then perhaps the Bush family would begin to plea for mercy and be much more willing to provide statements regarding their involvement in various plots against humanity. Surely they would be far less jovial and self-assured than they once were when publicly knowingly falsely blaming the so-called terrorists for these horrific international crimes and the resulting chaos. After the evidence is presented that conclusively demonstrates and proves the U.S. government's participation in planning and carrying out the 9/11 related events, imagine what a surprise it would be for the Bush family and their co-conspirators. Ideally many of their co-conspirators would seek immunity from prosecution to publicly reveal to the entire world the full extent to which they are involved. Being involved in an international conspiracy to commit intentional war crimes against humanity in order to serve their own greedy purposes, such as to gain control of oil and gas supplies and to drive the price of these commodities upwards and further implement their totalitarian controls is unconscionable psychopathic behaviour.

When this happens, then finally the mass media would have something news worthy to publicise and discuss endlessly. In a similar manner to the Berlin Wall 'falling', or the USSR 'imploding', and just as the dishonourable Republican President Nixon left Oval Office rather than be impeached for his crimes; so too will the tarnished and corrupted Bush family and their co-conspirators finally be brought to international justice. They are presently unwilling to openly admit their obvious 9/11 crimes in early 2016. However, when these prosecutions occur; then one can expect most (but not all) of these murderous cabalists to be unwilling to openly confess and ask for forgiveness for these hideous crimes against all people. They are likely to remain full of pious denials, until such time the truth is proven conclusively for all to know. Then will come the piteous crying, screaming and begging for leniency when their undeniable guilt becomes proven in Court and they can clearly see an impending ultimate execution or life in prison with hard labour as being the final result for their intentional war crimes against humanity.

The people can then remind these murderous cabalists of the millions of Innocent civilians, or the 'collateral damage' that have perished in these acts of terrorist violence and widespread warfare that has been intentionally initiated without reasonable cause and then exuberantly administered by the Bush Administration, President Obama and their supporters for decades. We can then perhaps realise that to execute the unrepentant perpetrators for their crimes against humanity would be an act of true justice, in my opinion. For those proven guilty that refuse to ever willingly or openly admit their guilt for their crimes against humanity, or genuinely apologise, and seek true forgiveness from the victims, as we see before us in 2016, then this attitude will require other solutions, as we will see manifesting over passing time and improved international events.

Is the long-overdue criminal trial for the conspirators and perpetrators of the fake staged 9/11 events and the contrived Middle Eastern wars likely to happen in this civilisation today? We shall see what unfolds over passing time. What matters most is to acknowledge that 'we the people' are well-aware of what has and is happening, as we see here now. We are communicating these facts with other like-minded people, as well as to 'less receptive' types of people (as I myself once was in the 'early days' in regard to 9/11, until a number of 'inside' people I respected and trusted with access to high level intelligence connections referred me to specific information that is now widely available on the internet). In this process we are better able to determine exactly what we think, feel and believe for ourselves; independent of the many media sources of dis-information that inundate us now.

The Bush family members previously liked to say whenever a family member was seeking election or appointment to any public office in the USA that they "stand on their record". Now many situations that are a matter of the public record clearly prove the various instances where various members of that particular family are evidently hopelessly corrupted by their desires for power over others in various forms, seeking financial wealth at the cost of misery to the world's population, arrogance, immorality, deceit, and various other evil traits. Obviously this includes treason against the American people and mass murder against the international community, which the USA is supposed to be a leader and example of good democracy in action.

Ok, so let's now see true democracy in the will of the people being applied to manifest justice through action internationally, before it is 'too late' and the USA manages to foolishly attempt to begin another world war. There can be no doubt this is the objective of the current past and present U. S. administrations and is a key aspect of their covert plans, as the self-evident evidence demonstrates. The days of politicians speaking what the people want to hear until they are elected, then do nothing productive for anyone aside from those few 'vested interests' dictating financial and governmental policies, are over permanently.

Through this ongoing process of increasing self-awareness, we can begin to gain better perspective of our lives on Earth. In this way we can mentally and emotionally adjust to these facts of life here to take positive action where we are able as individuals and cooperative groups seeking similar solutions. We can observe reality and directly participate in creating the improved future course of human events from our own unique perspectives. This process engenders a precious 'untouchable' inner attitude characterised by a type of 'detachment' to world events so that we continue to identify with the highest, best, most noble, divine aspects of ourselves, regardless of what happens to us individually or as a civilisation. This does require a patient, persistent, humble, loving, accepting, grateful, compassionate and understanding attitude, regardless of circumstances; so that we each as individuals do our personal best to exemplify inner and outer peace, considering the various events we experience.

Many of our spiritual prophets throughout history have said to their oppressors and murderers words to the effect that 'you cannot hurt me anymore now, by your actions to kill my body because my words of truth and righteous loving wisdom live eternally'. Both Jesus Christ and the U.S. civil rights campaigner, Reverend Martin Luther King said words to that effect when they were about to be put to death for having the audacity and bravery to choose to inspire human spirit of freedom and justice by their words and deeds. Both of these brave, noble, truly spiritual, God loving men encouraged all people to peacefully resist and defy oppression and the overt forms of evil being intentionally imposed upon humanity by the leaders of their historical civilisations. Joan of Arc suffered a similar fate in France, so a love and devotion to freedom and justice is NOT limited to male heroes in our human history. The feminine, mothering, loving, building, creative energies are alive and well on and within Mother Earth now and for all time to come. We do not need or want to martyr ourselves now, as noble human beings have so many times done through the bloody and ugly course of our lengthy human history.

Mainly, we should recognise that these brave good men and women demonstrate the reality that the death of their physical human body only served to strengthen their ideals within society and enliven other's eternally living Spirit that exists within each and all of the people of this world; the good, the not-so-good, and the overtly evil, alike. Our personal goal is to be true to one's own inner self's conscience, to live life according to meaningful ethical principles, to peacefully work to earn a living for one's family and be of service to one's community, to worship God or life in your own manner, and be an inspirational loving example to your family, friends and others in daily life.

We will together save this world, one small place and way at a time; only by each one of us being true to our own conscience first and foremost. God (Divinity, Life, or by whatever name or concept that you may wish to use to identify one's Creator) is alive and well within each of us now, as has always been the situation, even if we are not yet fully aware of the facts consciously.

Ours' is an individual inner journey of discovery alone, within the solitude of our own Soul, that we are able to seek and ultimately to find God expressing Itself within and through each of us. The beauty and inspiration of earthly life is that we all are travelling this journey together at our own pace, in our own unique special ways, as being our 'gift' to God for having created and sustaining us on our eternal journey of discovery. Each one of us is in life to attain perfection within the realities of the Creator, so it is going to be an endless, infinitely expanding journey of love, joy, peace, abundance and gratitude; only when we begin to make it so within the realm of our minds' sublime attitudes and our daily improved actions.

It is helpful to possess a real sense of humility, appreciation and gratitude for the level of spiritual, material and technological development occurring in many parts of this world today. For many people in developed modern nations there is a relatively high standard of living. Our daily lifestyles are fairly pleasant, safe, seemingly secure and quite enjoyable when compared to the alternatives we see in less affluent and more violent areas of Earth. However, in many of the simpler cultures; the people are far happier, living in true community where people help one another and are more closely connected with nature. These fortunate, spiritually wealthy people also generally possess a heightened affinity with their own inner divinity as Soul, regardless of their religion, nationality, or their relatively austere living situations.

Some self-deluded (yet otherwise intelligent) people would profess with some apparent validity that an abundant materialistic lifestyle and its relative personal freedom has only been achieved because of the protection by the nation's military defensive capabilities. However, this type of attitude would be only a nonsensical half-truth, even from a militaristic, cabalistic perspective.

The actual truth is our civilisation has been created and sustained primarily by men, women and children with a creative, innovative, solution-focused state of being that is willing and eager to work diligently toward their goals with other like-minded people in a spirit of mutually beneficial productivity. This has nothing to do with killing or depriving others that believe or behave differently to themselves.

In a complex modern society such as our global civilisation, we all depend upon many roles being performed throughout the development processes. Much innovation has been accomplished through the creation of larger, more destructive weapons of mass destruction, but has this process genuinely led to a safer, better world for us all now? No. Have the countless trillions of dollars worth of international weapons systems really improved the security for future generations to live in an environment of peace and prosperity that is going to be free from the costly destabilising, counter-productive preparations for future possible devastating wars? No. Has this militaristic strategy really served to properly protect one's freedom and national security in the USA, which was once the ideal democracy on Earth? No. Can the USA truly justify its current governmental policy that seeks to apply overtly aggressive imperialistic militaristic actions in the Middle East and elsewhere globally? No. This process of military conquest by the USA is very similar in some ways to the policies and actions that Hitler and Stalin applied in their vile dictatorships.

Thankfully in 2015, Russia, China and their many allies internationally openly demonstrated they will no longer simply 'stand by' passively condone and allow the USA to attempt to dominate the world militarily. America's days of economic world dominance are well and truly over through the intentional treasonous actions of the power elite located within America (and elsewhere internationally) by their intentional dismantling and attempting to destroy the American economic 'powerhouse' by exporting those industrial capabilities, technical knowledge and jobs to other countries such as China, Russia, India and many other nations.

People of Earth do not seek to endlessly repeat any insane, destructive scenario akin to the death and devastation that resulted from the two world wars in this past century. War mongers always plan for better ways to wage wars, even now considering manufacturing non-human combatants, just as they have already developed countless types of mostly automated, remote controlled weapons systems. Their focus is to devise ways to kill and enslave people as the world's hard working people fund this activity through their taxes, their spending habits and in many other unseen ways. It goes on and on and on, in a seemingly endless cycle of inane, insane, madness that is characterised by a form of lunacy and perversity that knows no reasonable limits. The world's good people themselves need to set these limits in the very near future, if our civilisation is to survive the coming century.

China is another global 'super power' that is emerging through its rapidly expanding economy, wise business strategies and capable active work force. To a somewhat lesser extent, this is occurring in India as well. These two most populous nations on Earth have not in recent history militarily attacked any of their neighbouring countries, aside from China invading and occupying the free and independent country of Tibet for many decades. China believes Tibet to be part of its sovereign territory and seeing the ways the USA seeks to establish military bases anywhere in the world that it can, perhaps this was a premeditated strategic decision to prevent what we see occurring in the Ukraine in regard to the USA threatening Russia. Both China and India are quite concerned by the violent events in the world around them. Fortunately for world peace, thankfully, these two technologically developing nations are currently primarily focused upon their economic development, rather than upon rapidly building up their military capabilities or attacking their neighbours to acquire more territory from other nations. Both of these nations have demonstrated huge economic potential by radically increasing their national production of goods and services within the past few decades (and unfortunately increased their greenhouse emissions as well). At the same time they have massively increased their populations and still managed to feed the vast majority of their people an adequate diet, educate many of them and provide other key social services to maintain their social and economic growth.

What would the fate of this world civilisation be if the nations of China, Russia, India and other nations suddenly decided to join the militaristic expansionist national policies to acquire natural resources, territory and subjugate other sovereign countries to their nationalistic will through warfare, just such as the USA now seems to be demonstrating in the Middle East and elsewhere?

Thankfully we see economic and financial strategic alliances being formed with the potential military benefits being undeniable in encouraging the fundamental re-shaping of U.S. foreign policy globally. Strategically in troop numbers, financially speaking and even considering some of the amazing new advanced weapons systems possessed by various nations that are NOT allied with the USA, it is apparent to any well-informed military strategist that the USA is currently a 'paper tiger' with all sorts of weapons systems it would be wise NOT to attempt to utilise. How long will the entire world silently and compliantly suffer the malevolent destructive policies being promoted by President George Bush, Obama, or others like them before remedial action is taken to improve matters? I suggest we see this already clearly happening over a few years to prevent an unnecessary war in Iran by the USA and Israel. This process truly became more evident and very effective beginning in October 2015 with the Russians, Chinese getting United Nations approval to work with their allies in Iran and Iraq to basically 'clean up' (destroy them militarily, encourage them to surrender, or at least to 'cease and desist' their hostile activities) ISIS and various other 'terrorist' groups that the USA has seemed unable and or unwilling to eliminate in the Middle East.

World governments are aware that the USA already possesses more weapons of mass destruction than those of the entire world combined, especially when more secretive weapons systems are included in the statistics. However, does this somehow justify the age-old, primitive and wrongful 'might makes right' scenario in the case of the so-called democratic USA, and yet not be acceptable regarding the actions of other, so-called totalitarian, communistic, or socialist governments?

The resounding clear answer to all of these rhetorical questions is that the Earth's environments and its civilised people can no longer afford to wage war or use overly competitive, ruinous, counter-productive business and ecological practices on other nations or groups of people according to the methods and rationalised 'justifications' of the past ages. The massively destructive capabilities of modern weapons and industrial systems have become an exceedingly serious threat with potentially incredibly unfortunate consequence to humanity and all life forms on planet Earth. To place the fate and destiny of humanity and global environments in the insane control of people with the mentality of President George W. Bush, or those of President Obama which are much the same in various ways, and those who endorse, financially support and benefit from these insanely adversarial militaristic policies and basically seek to 'protect' these abysmal types of so-called 'leadership' is simply unwise beyond description and definitely not at all in the best interests of humanity.

The fact remains that the catastrophic event of 9/11 occurred because George W. Bush 'served' as the President of the USA. President Obama has been consistently speaking eloquently of the dreams of the American people, yet in the past seven years his 'track record' clearly proves the hypocritical nature of his campaign rhetoric as evidenced by the USA being directly involved in promoting and waging warfare in various parts of the world. We can lucidly perceive the dire results of having unintelligent, greedy, madmen serving as world leaders, or carefully selected cabalist 'pretenders' like Obama, who owe their allegiance to the self-serving 'slave masters' that seek to remain 'in control' of what was formerly the world's most economically and militarily powerful nation, the USA.

The woeful current global political situation has become a reality mostly because people possessing relatively little real humanitarian spirit to serve the public's best interests have assumed leadership roles in all levels of society, especially within the existing political and economic systems. The political party process has amply rewarded 'yes men' (and women) who do not actually represent the will of the people that have elected them. Instead, the vast majority of people voted into political office internationally serve their party and various vested business interests that finance their political party, usually multi-national corporations expecting political 'favours' in return for their support. Since the influential business, banking and industrial leaders are most able to financially support all major political parties within every democratic nation to some extent, depending upon their preferences at the time; these monetarily and logistically powerful forces have managed to apply exceedingly pervasive control over most nation's political, legislative and judicial processes. This is accomplished in close association with the near total dominance of big business over smaller businesses internationally, as well as by adversely influencing community, regional and national markets for their products and services. Government and their 'owners' have intentionally sought to make life difficult for 'the common man' and small businesses, which employs the vast majority of people and creates the true productivity of our international economy.

Why has democracy become the political governmental style of choice throughout most nations? It is the most efficient and effective way that has been yet devised to appear to provide the majority of citizens with direct representation by choosing their own leaders, when in actuality, now voters seldom elect representatives in modern democratic governments that truly represent the will of the majority of people, nor even the best interests of their region or nation.

If a truly visionary, sincere, capable leader manages to rise up among the people to make substantial improvements in this system or in the lives of normal working people, then quite often they are destined to have various types of trouble created for them by the powers that object to their responsible productive activities. The difficulties such committed, genuinely service-orientated people experience in the political and social arenas to dissuade them from actively accomplishing the full potential their beneficial work manifests in any of the following forms: various types of threats against one's self, family, associates, or employers, etc; threats to expel them from their political party if it is contrary to party political policy; intentionally damage their personal property, business or relationships; publicly slander them with false information to damage their reputation; use law enforcement officers to have them arrested and possibly criminally prosecuted on some criminal or civil offence whether they were actually guilty of not; find out sensitive private information about them or their family and blackmail them in various ways; have their personal and business financial records audited for possible tax evasion; to have someone injure them, family members or associates in some way; put them in jail for a wide variety of reasons, including false charges such as tax evasion; and sometimes these noble good people mysteriously permanently disappear without explanation; while others are violently murdered, or die suspiciously, with the cause of death often being made to appear incorrectly to be a suicide, or as an 'accidental' death in any number of impossible or highly unlikely scenarios that we have heard or read about to remind other people to 'be afraid' and 'do nothing about anything'.

These are only some of the numerous types of offensive, devious, immoral, unscrupulous and criminal activities that are used by 'the powers that were' to influence, silence, or eliminate outspoken, positive, effective people through the use of unpleasant and often violent criminal methods to 'encourage them' to cease their work and public activities.. These types of coercive efforts are used to intimidate people who only wish to devote their efforts to making a positive difference in our societies and economies. Creative, positive, well-motivated, intelligent, good-spirited, hard-working, kind, loving, generous and compassionate people are often treated in a shockingly poor manner within our civilisation. Thousands of years of human history proves this to be the situation globally, especially in modern 'western' societies.

Another glaring and pathetic example of unacceptable, unpleasant human behaviour is the intentional abuse and degradation of women (and even children) that is widely seen in the global sex industry, especially in the massive 'porn' industry. The violence against all people must end. This process has definitely been happening in late 2015, as Russia, China and its allies begin to seriously make real efforts to eliminate the U.S. sponsored and funded ISIS groups and other such covertly funded 'terrorists' located in the Middle East and elsewhere, by applying well-coordinated military force.

Looking back into history, we can examine the following is a brief list of some of the reprehensible types of vindictive people that apply malodorous external pressure upon those seeking to accomplish good, productive, creative developments in our societies: political leaders attack their opinions, policies and credibility; likewise, people in the business community which often includes their work peers, such as in university or scientific research activities that are contrary to the majority opinions; various legal, taxation and governmental authorities investigate them endlessly at great emotional and financial cost; private enforcement or muck-raking goons harass them in various ways and have been known to plant fabricated evidence to justify inappropriate criminal, civil or taxation investigations and prosecutions; religious leaders may condemn their actions or motives within the community; one's own family members may intentionally create problems for them; people from their past will make all manner of dubious, unsubstantiated accusations, gossip inappropriately; and much more than we could possibly list here.

These odious social forces are proven experts at doing detrimental, unkind, immoral and even illegal things to a 'do-gooder' primarily to maintain the existing social and economic conditions. Such 'knockers' are usually negative, entrenched, highly opinionated people seeking to keep life exactly as it is now without making any really substantial beneficial improvements, even when the situation drastically requires positive change. In places where democracy is not now in existence we often see numerous types of military, police, hired street thugs or intelligence operatives being used by dictatorships to retain power, supported by the 'powers that were', often including external overt military hardware being supplied by one or more of the so-called national 'superpowers'. An example would be ISIS suddenly and inexplicably obtaining surface to air missiles as soon as the Russians and Chinese became involved in

U.N. approved, sanctioned 'peace keeping' activities in the Middle East. This is the world we live in now, yet it is indeed much better than some of the alternatives that could exist, such as if the German Nazis and their international fascist allies had been victorious in the 2nd World War.

As we have discussed at length, the obvious indications from the USA for over 50 years are basically characterised by a militaristic international policy governed by short-sighted, narrow-minded, feeble logic that is mainly motivated and dominated by the policy maker's financial self-interests and desires for expanding military power within the USA and internationally. Both of the Bush administrations have proven definitely that these foreign policy makers have little apparent understanding of Middle Eastern culture, religion or perhaps they just do not care what horrible mistakes they make there, due to their power-mad arrogance. Obama has been no better and adheres to these same fatally flawed, inhuman, draconian, war-focused policies.

This is a very dangerous situation for the USA, as we see being resolved for the better by the Russians, Chinese and their Middle Eastern allies. We can know the world's major 'superpowers' are not at all pleased with the entire scenario. As we see now, these nations have officially 'lost patience' with what is happening in the Middle East. By the end of the Bush Presidencies, far fewer than half of all Americans supported the actions, policies or attitudes that characterised them both. President Obama's popularity is now very low, with talk of a possible impeachment as 2015 came to an eventful close.

The treasonous, murderous exploits regarding the clear undeniable proof of direct premeditated U.S. government involvement in 9/11 related events and the subsequent extensive 'cover-up' is becoming more widely known and accepted every day in the USA and internationally. Many of Bush's political party associates were removed from their elected or appointed governmental positions, some being proven to have acted illegally and immorally; some of Bush's closest corporate allies and Republican Party Members and financial supporters, such as some top executives in the failed energy corporation Enron, have been convicted of serious fraud and are now in jail, along with people accepting fraudulent campaign donations from corporations, and even openly bribing Congressmen, and too much more to begin to mention here. Yet, through it all George W. Bush remained the President of the USA, without so much of a murmur of impeachment in the mass media.

Compare this situation to the previous clamour of the Republican Party members to impeach former President Bill Clinton for rumours of a sexual affair with one of his office staff and you will see the absurd hypocrisy of those biased Republican Party politicians and the complicit American news media that is controlled mostly by people loyal to the goals of that political party's elitist agenda. Toward the end of his term in office, the former President George W. Bush wisely said as little as possible unless it was previously written for him to say. When asked difficult questions unexpectedly, Bush would perspire profusely, often stammer incoherently, and even be sometimes seen to grimace with apprehension, as he attempted to evade definitive answers on almost any subject that was not prepared for him to address by his speech writers. President Bush ended his term being not nearly as arrogant as he originally appeared to be since he realised that the international community and the American people were not easily fooled by his countless misrepresentations of the facts, outright lies, false assurances, or intentional distractions regarding addressing key issues. President Obama can be characterised by his clever mixture of broken and forgotten campaign promises, copious amounts of intentional misinformation, flawed policies, and by a proven commitment to ongoing militarism, promoting further conflict among nations and closely related international economic disruption while publicly pretending to be 'a man of peace'..

Do you remember hearing in the mass media about the anthrax terrorism ploy when the initial investigations about 9/11 events were at a fever pitch in seeking definitive answers to what occurred? Well, it was not too surprising that when they tested the particular strain of anthrax they found that it was a unique variety that had been developed in U.S. government funded laboratories. Amazingly, that rare and 'well-protected' unique type of anthrax somehow inexplicably managed to 'find its way' into the packages and envelopes that were delivered through the U.S. Postal Service. Several American people died from exposure to that anthrax and there have not yet been any convictions in regard to that event, to my knowledge.

It is curious that no so-called 'terrorist' has sought to assassinate President George W. Bush, or President Obama, as happened to President Kennedy and also to his brother Robert Kennedy, who was at the time campaigning for election to the Presidency of the USA about the same time in American history when Reverend Martin Luther King was assassinated. It seems that if the genuine global terrorists were really serious in attacking the USA, then they would make efforts to target President Bush, or later President Obama with whom they are supposedly 'at war' with and is purported to be their major so-called 'enemy'. President Regan was shot when he apparently planned to end the right of the FED to be in control of the U.S. money supply; just as occurred with regard to President Lincoln. How many times does history need to repeat itself before people recognise and stop these patterns from occurring again by arresting the hidden criminals that sponsor these events?

Are these international terrorists the very same ones that were supposedly able to completely level the World Trade Center armed only with a few 'box cutters' and completely destroyed Tower 7 which they did not even hit with an aircraft, as well as to hit the disused section of the Pentagon closed for renovations with a vaporising jet aircraft that was disguised as a cruise missile and whom have managed to evade capture in Afghanistan. These are the same so-called 'terrorists' that managed to plant powerful steel melting explosives on almost every floor of the two Twin Towers without being detected by security staff or security cameras in those buildings, which resulted in the total destruction of those two buildings and the deaths of thousands of people. Are these the same incredibly cunning terrorists that have still been unable to apparently even make one identifiable effort to 'target' the very public President Bush, who freely travelled to many dangerous places internationally with much advanced notice, including Indonesia where the Bali bombings occurred?

It is an interesting coincidence that within hours of the Bali bombing that numerous U.S. intelligence officers were on the scene, almost as if they were forewarned of the devastating events that occurred there. Numerous dubious so-called "terrorist attacks" have occurred in Russia over the years, and continuously in the Middle East, Europe, China and so on globally. Where are these terrorists obtaining their weapons and explosives? Isn't it odd that no one is tracking these weapons suppliers and financial supporters to determine the exact culprits involved at all levels in this complex interwoven scenario?

These very capable terrorists seem to be unable to even attempt to frighten the amazingly brave President Bush with a close call or even to make any threats against his life, nor upon those of his key policy advisors who are supposedly trying their best to hunt them down and exterminate them everywhere in the world. Was it President Bush who said publicly words to the effect that, "There is no place these terrorists can hide. We will hunt them down anywhere in the world and kill them." These so-called 'terrorists' seem very good at killing, injuring and frightening innocent people, yet fail to make ANY attempted attacks on the policy makers who purport to be 'at war' with them, so what are the likely set of true facts here? These terrorists seem to be well-armed and financed yet no one can seem to determine how and why this occurs, so do we see these patterns emerging to create a clear picture of who is actually in a position and financial capacity to fund these murders?

It is very interesting and quite curious that the proven terrorists who admitted to be guilty of planning and committing the Bali bombing terrorist attack only received very short or no jail sentences. The weak and impudent (former) Australian Prime Minister John Howard and former President George W. Bush's comments were words to the effect that "We can't interfere with the judicial system of another country". Where is the tough talk at this obvious travesty of international justice when the facts were clearly proven and admitted by the actual terrorists? Perhaps President Bush's safety and bold ability to travel anywhere in the world is due to Bush's exceptional anti-terrorism experts and security team who have prevented such events from occurring. Alternatively, the probability is that he knew most terrorism globally was ordered and enacted by his own governmental agencies.

It is a shame they were not nearly as successful in defending innocent people from terrorism in countless places around the world for many decades, where they have been far less successful in preventing terrorist attacks, as have many other governments. Again we must question why it is so odd that they cannot trace who is supplying the bomb making materials, since they usually originate from major international corporations. They have managed to catch a few so-called terrorists and it is strange none of them seem to have been sentenced to death in spite of all the people they are supposed to have been responsible for killing civilians internationally in a time of war. One exception is Saddam Hussein, who for years was supplied, financed, armed and protected by the USA, as were so many other evil violent dictators globally for many decades. This only confuses me if I attempt to believe the lies and misinformation we are being programmed with by all the cabal owned and controlled mass media sources. None of this makes any real intellectual, strategic or logistical sense, unless and until one 'sees it' from the perspective of the propagandists who seek to create and manipulate public opinions.

Later, when the US military forces finally captured the man that they accused of being Saddam Hussein and whom was later hung in the gallows was evidently from his very poor dental condition one of Saddam's many look-a-like 'body doubles'. Therefore, the real Saddam is likely to be hidden away somewhere (in an unmarked grave or 'far out to sea' somewhere) along with Osama Bin Laden, conducting their well-financed and protected wars with the covert knowledge of the forces purportedly opposing them.

We cannot ignore the fact that over the previous decades mostly people in the U.S. government allied with the current 'neo-conservative', militaristic policy agendas had initially enabled both of these two individuals (Bin Laden and Hussein) to attain their position, funded them lavishly, and openly provided billions of dollars worth of military equipment to conduct these wars. It is truly insane to now pretend that these so-called ISIS 'terrorists' have not been intentionally created, financially enabled and encouraged to do exactly what they have done previously. ISIS has become the willing 'scapegoats' to be blamed for what the global power elite plan to use an a feeble, nonsense excuse to continue to remove freedoms, prevent economic opportunity and institutionalise poverty for most people within our global civilisation.

This is treason, war crimes and corruption of the worst possible kind by some of the leaders purportedly elected to serve the best interests of humanity and their nations when the facts prove they are the real enemies of our civilisation. Imagine the countless trillions of taxpayer's dollars that have been squandered in Australia, the USA, Russia, China, Europe and elsewhere globally on militaristic equipment and anti-terrorist advertising campaigns in order to instil fear and mistrust into the global community. We are well aware that people who live in constant fear and economic hardship are more easily controlled. It is also convenient to consider the subtle anti-Muslim message that is involved in western propaganda, without the least mention of the Christian or Jewish culture's roles in promoting international militarism or terrorism in all of its insidious and overt forms. Likewise, a distinct minority of Muslim leaders create discord among their members against other religions which results in ongoing conflict that also serves the goals of the so-called 'power elite' who are morally and spiritually 'bankrupt'. Their 'god' is money and control over other people. In the longer term, their god will not protect them, even if it is the Dark Force that some call Satan, or by other names. Creator/Divinity will not permanently allow these crimes against all life forms to go unpunished, as we all learn valuable life lessons within this process. God has all of eternity to deal with each and every one of us, as nothing exists for any of us outside of God's countless 'realms of reality'.

Consider the past for a few moments more in deciding why it could be that no attempts to assassinate the leaders of the nations purporting to be hunting for these terrorists have occurred. Countless thousands of innocent civilian victims have been murdered globally in hundreds of so-called 'terrorist' attacks, yet not a single 'cabal' leader has been targeted or murdered. Do you honestly think a genuine fundamentalist international terrorists would not seek to make such an attack because they are too busy hiding or because they simply prefer to kill innocent people instead of targeting the arrogant aggressive leader of their enemy's nation or an opposing religious group? Perhaps these well-funded and elusive terrorists live permanently in caves so that even with the USA's incredible satellite technology, they are unable to locate or kill the famous Osama bin Laden who periodically only came out of his cave to do a quick video before going into hiding again? Recall the press stories about the demise of those two people that were supposed to be Osama bin Laden and Saddam Hussein. Is this a reasonable scenario or does it sound like an absurdly fictitious story to distract us from observing other issues of those particular times?

Seriously, why would these terrorists choose to foolishly to attack President Bush and his people, or later President Obama when it would appear to some unbiased observant people that President Regan, President George Bush (the elder) and now President George W. Bush have proven to be long-trusted allies, who have financially supported their terrorist training and activities for decades, who have been covertly building their arsenals of weapons, including ample amounts of bomb making materials, surface to air missiles to attack U.S. helicopters, electronic and communications equipment, and so on, endlessly. Why would these 'real terrorists' seek to remove someone who is so adept at making so many absurdly counter-productive decisions in the Middle East that are bringing you thousands of people willing to kill themselves in sacrifice to attack American interests, including innocent people they falsely perceive to be American collaborators? Why did Osama bin Laden happily and gratefully publicly accept responsibility for the 9/11 events when he knew they were conducted entirely by the USA, using him as the 'scapegoat'? Because it served Osama's purposes to deceive people internationally into the false perception that these so-called al Qaeda terrorists were far more capable and well-organised than was actually the case. All of these things and so much more conclusively verified information is being accumulated by independent investigators and intelligence operatives who want the truth to become more publicly available and widely known on many issues of importance.

Please keep in mind that your role in our discussion is to review and investigate your experience, your own wisdom and information, and examine your own conscience to determine what you believe and know as factual, and then to respond accordingly, as you believe appropriate within the laws.

What is abundantly and painfully evident are the suspicious, almost unbelievably idiotic actions surrounding the 9/11 events. Many were serious, unprecedented violations of military and investigative procedure and protocol, including the subsequent military actions in the Middle East, which violated international law such as was the case in the invasion and destruction of Iraq by U.S. led forces with their allies. Circumstances in the Middle East have been volatile for thousands of years and the western nation's latest version of the Crusades has unfortunately begun that cycle of violence over again; not that there has been much of a rest period due to western imperialism in that region for hundreds of years.

It is now time for perceptive thinking people that are aware of the full scope of the facts involved in global politics to publicly acknowledge these issues to the entire world, through the forum of their local communities, their nations of residence, within their circles of friends, family and associates and most importantly; honestly within our individual selves. It has been extremely upsetting and actually quite painful for me to write and endlessly repeat some of these key facts for your consideration, as well as for public exposure. This is especially true because I know about so many more factors and incidents that will not be included here, that it makes this entire pathetic, unnecessary militaristic circumstance in our global civilisation far more frustrating in its unequalled idiocy and outright, blatant, impeachable, treasonous criminality regarding some key people within the Reagan, Bush and Obama Administrations and their covert Israeli 9/11 accomplices.

What relationship do these frustrating examples of international politics have to do with what we are attempting to define as human nature issues? These international events express human nature issues in a manner where there is absolutely no confusion or mystery. The horrible facts on all sides are clear to be seen for any perceptive, well-informed person.

In the Middle East there is a population explosion in arid desert regions with high rates of unemployment, within a denuded degraded environment that is suffering from well-over fifty thousand years of intensive human habitation. Oil revenues are the primary source of income for this region, as well as agricultural crops and some illicit drug production. About ninety percent of the world's entire supply of heroin now originates from Afghanistan. Why and how is this happening? Many of these Middle Eastern people would prefer to focus their attentions upon an external enemy, such as the USA, its few remaining 'allies' and other western nations that are being vilified as infidels or heretics according to their religious beliefs, rather than addressing and resolving their own situational and environmental difficulties. Western civilisation has been historically quite willing to serve as that perceived external enemy of people in the Middle East, because the western nations throughout history have many times have previously declared militaristic and socio-economic war against Middle Eastern nations. To condone this aggressive, unprovoked military attack, they have consistently falsely blamed or demonised the people of the Middle East or other locations they wished to occupy upon lies and misinformation. This pattern of the west's unprincipled hostilities and desires for heathen military conquest upon illegitimate religious or politically contrived rationalisations of the worst types is now happening again in Syria, just as happened previously with 9/11 in relation to Iraq, Libya and Afghanistan. Add up these illegitimate wars in Vietnam, Nicaragua, Panama, Korea and other places and we see this pattern, unless one chooses to ignore reality as so many seem prone to do in relation to these subjects within the 'western world'. These cyclic patterns of violence, retribution and then more violence are always justified by past events and current excuses, within nations located in the west, as well as within the nations of the Middle East. Warfare between some Arab nations and ongoing inter-tribal warfare has existed for thousands of years in this region of the world and this is an accepted historical fact. Let us all focus on the meaning and lessons involved here.

First, neither the people of western nations nor those located in the Middle East have any real hatred of one another, aside from the fake impression generated by fanatical, so-called fundamentalist religious zealots or similar minded political zealots and 'mass media' propagandists, on both sides of the disharmonious social equation. Most people are loving and compassionate by nature, unless trained by society to be violent and materially acquisitive. Second, such a war is created for reasons that are never truly and fully disclosed to those asked to potentially sacrifice their lives in service to their nation or religion by their leaders. Third, there are never any winners in war except those who finance and supply the waring nations and thereby rob the taxpayers of their hard-earned efforts and needlessly squander these precious resources and sacrifice countless innocent lives on these unnecessary unproductive wars. The common people all end up as losers in this process. The taxpaying and martyred citizens are primarily the ones whose homes and lives are destroyed, who are terribly misinformed to intentionally encourage them to support the unjust, contrived wars planned by the wealthy powerful minority that control the politicians and religious leaders, who shamelessly appeal to national patriotism and religious devotion to finance and wage these terribly expensive, counter-productive, mutually destructive follies of human greed and power seeking.

The people of Earth have simply had enough and demand the contrived wars end immediately, with lasting peace and forgiveness among all people here.

This particular situation, the so-called 'war on terrorism', along with the intentionally instigated and incited violence against western capitalistic nations and against Middle Eastern nations, with Syria being the latest intentionally planned US 'target'; is definitely a symptom of a malignancy and serious socio-cultural dysfunction within our civilisation. It is unfortunately an excellent example of the ways human nature issues accumulate to breed major problems and unnecessary turmoil in our lives, individually and collectively.

What shall we do now to cure the disease of spirit and values that afflicts us? One human tendency is to ignore the problem and hope that it will go away. This attitude seldom works effectively. Our attitude here will not be to address the symptoms of the issues that so debilitate and cause us suffering, depravation and self-doubt. No, we definitely do NOT advocate noisy protests or revolution, or any such actions because this further promotes the awful "us versus them" type attitude and would provide those despots in control of our nations and civilisation another self-created so-called 'enemy' to attack while they continually distract public opinion away from addressing and resolving the real fundamental challenges now confronting humanity.

We could have just as easily used various other examples of issues that humanity needs to resolve, such as: unfair taxation practices internationally; the oppression of workers globally; environmental destruction; health issues; the myth of democracy in modern politics; human trafficking; wage slavery; child abuse and molestation; the role of crime in our civilisation; drugs; corruption in law enforcement; organised crime; various forms of religious fundamentalism throughout history that has damaged our societies; the problems of our superficial, materialistic, capitalistic western civilisation; cruel treatment and murder of animals, and many other such factors that help us to define, characterise, exemplify and better comprehend human nature issues.

We have briefly addressed most of these basic previous human nature issues that are hurting our civilisation in numerous ways, yet primarily we have focused upon the damaging effects of deceit, greed for power and money, and violence in our global societies. These issues are widely recognised situations that require immediate, often complex solutions. Instead of our political leaders trying to develop viable sustainable solutions to our global civilisation's present challenges, they inefficiently prefer to identify convenient scapegoats and innocent victims to blame these problems upon. As these issues worsen over passing time, then these so-called leaders blindly and foolishly demand the application of other equally ineffective policies and actions, further compounding these escalating difficulties. Basically, the deficiency with this manner of dealing with social and economic issues is that there is continual change in policy and roles in government amounting to a lot of pointless dithering and rhetoric within government and industry, providing the inaccurate appearance of progress being made. Actually, relatively little true improvement occurs, and then usually at great cost to taxpayers and society in lost opportunity, time and in misapplied taxation revenues which are exceedingly disadvantageous to us all.

The only real solution to the complex dilemma facing our civilisation is to directly and honestly involve all parts of society in the governmental policy making and implementation processes. Experienced, capable, unbiased, intelligent, innovative, independent people from all relevant professions and areas of expertise need to be directly involved throughout the entire process, from start to finish. Citizen's action group representatives must participate with government in establishing the strategies to create viable functional integrated solutions. This requires excellent communication to develop the plans, establish the foundation for action, define the functional procedures, and apply these creative, innovative, effective solutions to the many factors requiring society's full and prompt attention. Be assured that most politicians, government bureaucrats, big corporate business interests and the international banking community would initially resist such an essential, long-overdue structural change in the methods by which our social policies are developed and implemented. However, we all would acknowledge that substantial changes in the ways our civilisation functions are necessary, if humanity is to continue to prosper, flourish and progress in this century.

Humanity will not indefinitely accept the many forms of slavery, inequality and rampantly evil mass murder and deprivation that have been imposed historically without a strong, united, proportional response to the relative few materialistically powerful people and organisations. The vast majority of Earthlings are peace loving people. Therefore, we all certainly need to work together on the issues demanding our unified efforts to progressively make the necessary improvements to successfully resolve the situational and attitudinal challenges in a coherent, wise, peaceful, solution-based manner.

Pandering endlessly to vested interest groups by feeble minded, power hungry, greedy self-serving politicians and business people will definitely not serve to achieve the required solutions. Dictatorships generally are poverty stricken nations ultimately because their society's most talented, intelligent and experienced people are usually oppressed, driven away, imprisoned, tortured, murdered, or are otherwise made ineffectual in creating and applying the needed beneficial solutions. We can see this has occurred in the world historically and again today, where in many locations around the world those that are most capable and committed to making positive adjustments are not being welcomed into positions of responsibility to accomplish these progressive developments.

I saw an advertisement for a prestige automobile that said, "For those brave enough to step forward". This is an indicative 'sign of our times' if one is being considered 'brave' to buy a luxury vehicle that is not even among the highest priced brands on the international market. This is a farce in my opinion.

A creative productive company like Microsoft was fined one billion dollars by a U.S. Court for being judged as a monopoly. Governmental legislation can be enacted to force them to become less competitive in their industry, in spite of the company's efforts to maximise efficiency while continuing to provide consumers with a proven quality, unique product at a fair marketable price. They can be coerced into enabling competitors to be freely given opportunities to more easily compete with Microsoft products and software, under threats that if they refuse, the possibility exists to restructure the entire company, which would include selling off key aspects of its business to external competing business interests to comply with legislation.

Conversely, do we currently see the oil or banking industries fined for intentionally seeking to limit competition in the areas of fuel and energy production or 'capping' (sealing off) large discoveries of oil and natural gas to maintain a limited availability upon international markets to keep the prices high for these essential commodities? Do we see the same occurring with regard to international monopoly law suits being filed against the natural resources sector for unfair price fixing on other essential commodities? Do we see the oil and natural gas industry charged with collusion in price fixing or for intentionally escalating the prices of oil and gas by limiting existing production in functioning oil and natural gas fields? Or do we see banking financial resources becoming less costly for consumers or more widely available in the marketplace? No, obviously we do not see the oil production, fuel distribution or banking sectors of the economy being heavily fined for their global monopolies that now result in exceedingly massive profits for their overtly monopolistic international industries at a huge adverse socio-economic cost to humanity. Are these industries forced by governmental legislation to in any way genuinely assist competitors to provide alternative sources of energy or financial services? The answer is definitely not.

Therefore, can we determine any actual real difference between these two situational examples? Why is a computer and software related company deemed by governmental regulators to be unfairly monopolistic for various reasons, yet other entirely monopolistic industries, such as oil production and the banking industry that are clearly monopolistic and very aggressive in seeking to minimise any real competition and maximise profits at huge social and economic cost being largely ignored by these same regulators? Why should these extremely profitable monopolistic industries also continue to inexplicably receive various forms of tax payer funded 'subsidies' or tax concessions to expand their businesses? Where is the justice and logic in this situation, when both the oil and banking industries have been proven to conduct their business activities in an often inequitable, profit mongering, predatory manner that reveals the worst examples of rampant unchecked capitalism that is of considerable detriment to our entire civilisation? Could it be due to these industries long history of 'lobbying' politicians through campaign donations to their re-election efforts? What about the same situation with the military equipment industry, or the aviation industry, or the pharmaceutical industry, medical industry, chemical industry, the 'fast food' franchise industry, automobile and truck manufacturers, insurance companies, multi-media ownership, the weapons manufacturers, and so on?

Why does the news media seem uninterested in such news stories, when some of their primary owners and corporate shareholders have such openly conflicting, un-disclosed, personal 'vested' business interests? Because of this inappropriate situation, does a process exist whereby taxpayers can say to their governments that the regulators and legislators are no longer being properly responsible in representing the best interests of the nation and demand the necessary legislation to better protect tax payers be enacted and that a system of national fines be imposed upon these other unfairly profitable and predatory monopolistic industries, just as occurred to Microsoft? It does not appear likely at this moment in time, yet one never knows when true justice and real democracy begins to be manifested in international politics.

Such a hypothetical attempt to make these two example monopolistic industries become more socially responsible would certainly attract the swift response of oil industry and banking industry executives, shareholders, their lawyers, lobbyists, bureaucrats, and the politically elected representatives who receive large political donations from these industries to oppose such a reasonable development. If such a case were to reach the higher Courts, then would the final decision likely be similar to that judicial judgement against Microsoft? What would a billion dollar fine mean to an industry earning trillions of dollars annually? Not much, especially if such fines were deemed to be another tax deduction on their balance sheets. In a more equitable, socially responsible, morally ethical system of regulatory, legislative and judicial review, then it would be likely that these two monopolistic industries; of energy and banking, would be forced to adjust their corporate policies to better consider and serve the needs of the public by providing their commodities at a reasonably affordable price, with a reasonable, justifiably large profit, as well as to willingly open the market to various forms of competition, just as Microsoft has been leveraged and coerced into doing by the U.S. Courts and regulators.

It is pragmatic to design social and economic systems that serve both the public and corporate business interests so that both people and business are able to maintain a reasonable adequate level of profitability through the way prices, production and wages are allocated nationally and internationally. This would require that the powerful vested business interests be willing to participate and endorse this progressive developmental process for the betterment of humanity and the sustainability of our global civilisation. For big business internationally to continually seek to abuse and disregard the public good primarily to obtain increasingly larger profits and further market domination, year after year after year, decade after decade, century after century, often with reduced services and value to consumers, is quite counter-productive to the global economy and is an unjust, unnecessary circumstance. Why should most hard working people spend the vast majority of their waking hours labouring in order to be able to afford to pay their relatively high taxes and costs of living, then at the end of every year in doing their financial assessment, they unfortunately determine they have not actually achieved any profitability or monetary savings at all? How long would most businesses or corporations continue to operate without being at all profitable? Not long under most circumstances, yet this is exactly what the vast majority of normal working people around the world experience virtually every year, endlessly. These relatively lowly paid, diligent workers are expected to keep on working with very little or no profitability without complaint or political recourse. This is definitely a situation that requires substantial improvement by obtaining the consensus of business, government and the public on implementing solutions that serve all these various interest group's needs for justice and more equability.

On a much more positive issue, let's briefly digress to mention one of the most positive expressions of magnanimous spirit being expressed through one's human nature in relation to the founder and CEO of Microsoft Bill Gates who has amassed a considerable fortune due to his success with his company. After Microsoft was fined about one or more billion U.S. dollars, Bill and Belinda Gates, along with their close friend and business associate Warren Buffet; decided to donate about half of their personal financial fortunes to their own humanitarian aid foundations. These humanitarian aid foundations help internationally to feed starving people, educate those who do not have access to schools or are unable to afford them, build hospitals, employ doctors, help improve water resources, sanitation, along with many other such worthy, noble, much needed projects in developing nations, as well as in some western nations. These two generous families, the Gates' and Buffets' have already recently donated about eighty billion US dollars (as of 2008) to these humanitarian aid foundations from their own personal savings because they recognise they are serving as guardians of monetary wealth that is much needed by millions of economically and educationally challenged people. They decided to create and finance these foundations to insure the funds were properly allocated and that the recipients of the humanitarian aid were the people requiring assistance, not primarily to the administrators or corrupted officials, as so often happens with the vast majority of much so-called humanitarian aid funding through normal charitable donations channels and such government and internationally operated programs. Since that time, others, such as the Gambles, have followed this wonderful example.

Therefore, this unprecedentedly exceedingly generous gift to humanity's needy people is an ideal exemplary act of noble, irreproachable, transcendent spirit made by wealthy people that are demonstrating the very best of overall character within our civilisation. These people are virtuous inspirations to us all, in many ways. This highly principled, philanthropic event served as a resounding positive testament of what is achievable by caring, capable, well-intentioned wealthy people who are committed to improving our world through their businesses, taxes paid to government that benefit us all, as well as their magnanimous, utilitarian humanitarian activities for the people of Earth. I have recently within the past year become aware of another major wealthy group that intends to improve our global society by funding worthy humanitarian and economic development projects. This is 'aside' from the Chinese 'government' who have already 'earmarked' about 21 trillion U.S. Dollars to global investment to stimulate productivity and 'save' the global economy from its intentionally designed 'collapse' by the cabal, who planned to institute a range of terrible events for humanity and Mother earth, as we see revealed before us in limited detail here and elsewhere. One such example is the 'clearing' or elimination of the outstanding debt accumulated by many poor nations internationally, so this is just the beginning of much better things to follow, ideally very soon as we shall see in 2016 when massive changes begin to be more obvious to us all globally.

Why do we not see more of this considerate, humane type of selfless, proactive, utilitarian activity by other of the world's most monetarily wealthy people and corporations? Perhaps that is a question they would prefer to answer, in due course, through their own self-evident actions. Right now we, the very perceptive good people of this planet, can easily determine that much of the world's excess financial wealth is being squandered on military expenditures, obscenely lavish lifestyles, 'locked up' within the banking and financial system, and increasingly 'wasted' or misapplied by pervasive inefficiencies and external governmental control measures upon basic human rights; while simultaneously reducing opportunity for working people through countless forms of unproductive and dysfunctional economic and societal activity, unsustainable polluting methods of producing energy, transportation, and widespread disregard for earthly environments by deforestation and avoidable pollution, among other such adverse and deleterious situations.

What are the answers to resolving these challenging circumstances? Public protests generally only attract confrontations with law enforcement, provide a venue for counter-productive agitators to incite senseless violence, and allow the mass media to ignore the key issues being addressed. Mass media enjoys portraying demonstrators as being radical, anti-social elements within society that are actually creating most of these problems due to their unruly attitudes and conduct.

Violent revolution is definitely and absolutely NOT an ideal method to encourage productive social change because it establishes a cycle of retribution and facilitates many negative forms of human nature to be manifested needlessly and unproductively. Historically, after most revolutions the status quo seems to inevitably prevail with a new set of public faces that are seemingly unconsciously committed to implementing the standard patterns of inhuman policies that created the revolution originally.

Therefore, we must peacefully advocate a new way of doing things while retaining and improving upon the many advantageous, beneficial social institutions that are inherent in the democratic, socialist, communist and capitalistic processes. There must be a societal focus strictly upon what is best for all people living within a more just, fair, productive, sustainable civilisation. We can learn to embrace the good aspects of all forms of government and culture, to apply some useful socialistic and communistic principles in harmony with democratic and capitalistic processes, as well as egalitarian and merit-based governmental, educational and business systems.

There will always be some people who are more gifted intellectually, more hard-working, wiser in some ways and quite fortunate by 'right of birth' or by their own diligent efforts in life. Some of us are more blessed with some traits, abilities or circumstances than others; so this is a natural, acceptable aspect of life. We understand, acknowledge and celebrate that other people will differ from us in countless ways. Some may be better looking, and others may possess more wisdom on various issues or more financial capabilities, while others could be stronger, smarter, or more well-connected with opportunity to advance themselves due to their education, social status, ability, etc. The key is to establish an inclusive, equitable, fair, representative system of government, enterprise, labour management and policy planning that enables a significant degree of freedom, autonomy and opportunity to all individuals and businesses that are willing and able to make genuine efforts to be productive and peacefully interact in good spirit with all people within society.

Vastly more difficult is addressing the various human nature issues that have always been a central causative factor in all the problems encountered by humanity since recorded history began. The influences of human nature issues in one's life are so incredibly pervasive that is impossible to innumerate them specifically for us all, or to be consciously aware of them all, even within one's own character, nor within one's own personal life with family, friends and business associates, much less civilisation as a whole. This does not mean that we, as individuals or as a global civilisation, can afford to ignore or take human nature issues for granted as an unavoidable aspect of earthly life. We must strive in every possible way to improve upon our negative human nature issues through our unified sincere persistent efforts.

The interplay of human nature issues are among the predominant ways we learn lessons in life. We can easily experience the direct results of our own thoughts, feelings, attitudes, and behaviours as well as those of others interacting with us. Unfortunately, the majority of us tend to learn our lessons 'the hard way', by making our own mistakes repeatedly. Too often most of us keep on repeating these same foolish patterns and errors in judgement until we finally have had enough painful repetition to realise our errors in thinking are actually the main problem and to decide to truly alter our attitudes, beliefs and actions to achieve better results. Few of us are seemingly willing or able to learn the easier, more pleasant way; by gladly accepting the advice, experience and wisdom of respected people we trust, like our parents, grandparents, mentors or other worthy authority figures in our life.

Human life on Earth seems to be divinely designed to make an infinite variety of situations, attitudes, feelings, actions, thoughts and realisations possible for each and all of us. Most people seem to be extremely slow to learn from life's experiences. Alternatively, others seem to innately know what circumstances to avoid, including seldom interacting with other people that would disrupt and adversely influence their lives. Consequently, their lives tend to flow fairly smoothly in a relatively positive, constructive, enjoyable, accident-free manner, when compared to others of us who would definitely be in the 'slower to learn' category, such as myself. It is absolutely certain that at times I can be a total idiot, although thankfully there are many signs of improvement. Some human nature issues are unavoidable because they are literally everywhere that there are people and such issues exist inherently within us as human beings and throughout all of our social situations. Also, positive, proactive, aware people generally tend to respond and rapidly adjust better to difficult and unwanted circumstances than less well-developed, unperceptive people.

Therefore, we are going to need to better learn to be consciously aware of these types of challenging life issues, especially as they express themselves through our own personality. Let's consider a diversity of common personal human nature situations that most of us have experienced and examine a few of the resulting issues that occur to determine what sorts of realisations and life lessons will serve to significantly improve and uplift our character. Such advancements are generally permanent qualities that increase our wisdom and help to establish our own set of guidelines that facilitate our progress by enabling us to make wiser better choices in life's sometimes unexpected, complicated, unwanted, or baffling circumstances.

We have such seemingly unlimited options and opportunities to choose from in modern western society that at times it is a formidable task to select the right interpersonal relationships, career opportunities, or the best location to raise a family, the preferred lifestyle, the better school for your children and so on. Many of the most commonplace choices we make can ultimately have a profound influence and impact upon our daily lives and future possibilities in unforseen ways. By analysing the manner in which human character traits and tendencies manifest in diverse experiences, many of which drastically increase the complexity in our lives; we can better perceive and act upon human nature issues in learning to understand, predict and control our behaviours. This starts by being more honest with ourselves and one another, in order to create more meaningful, harmonious, enjoyable, exciting lives that involve higher levels of freedom, love, self-expression and spontaneity.

This process is all about raising our self-awareness, while enriching our mutually beneficial, honest, joyful interactions with others. We seek to develop attitudes and behaviours that enable us to become more creative, aware, vibrantly involved within our communities, motivated, exhilarated and happier with our purposeful, self-directed life choices. Ideally, each of us will uniquely discover and create mutually beneficial ways to do whatever we love, that somehow improves the lives of other people or life forms. We also intend to progressively encourage more honest, open, authentic, compassionate communications between all people; to reduce the human tendency to deceive, lie and unfairly manipulate one another. We wish to establish a system of values that honours mutual respect between all people and life forms. Appreciating true self-expression over the current human proclivity to attempt to create false and misleading external impressions to influence others inappropriately and untruthfully is another important quality to develop. Beginning within one's self, total honesty is quite a challenge, yet it reaps huge beneficial achievements engendering a more meaningful, peaceful, secure lifestyle that is far less stressful and uncomfortably complex.

Life's range of experiences often involve significant emotional feelings of numerous types and our extensive variety of situational choices and those others make in our close relationships influence us remarkably. Part of our journey of self-discovery is to fully take personal responsibility for our choices, which is a wonderful uplifting development in one's life. We also want to classify the unpredictable personal decisions and human foibles of others around us as being of less importance, of less concern, or angst to us personally. We do not wish to react so intensely to unwanted, unpleasant life circumstances where others say or do things that upset us. We intend to learn to not react impulsively, without unpleasant thoughts or feelings regarding the unwanted, inappropriate attitudes and actions of others and stop considering them to be a personal affront or an intentional attack upon us, even when others obviously seek to intentionally or unintentionally do things that upset, hurt, disadvantage or anger us.

We have accomplished an outstanding progressive development in our lives by adjusting our attitudes to recognise that others have an innate right to make their own choices, even if we do not agree with them, or vehemently disagree with their ways. In so doing, one can to some extent 'insulate' themselves from the frustrating, upsetting, seemingly horrendous decisions and actions that are sometimes chosen by others; from your perspective, by realising it is simply their poor choice, even if it impacts your life in some unwanted ways. Likewise, it is helpful to cease being so 'hard' or unforgiving upon our own selves when we as individuals make poor choices, as long as we are not attempting to intentionally disadvantage, or mislead, or emotionally hurt, or attack others in the process of making our preferred choices in life.

This type of perceptive, objective mental response is vastly superior to an unthinking impulsive emotional or physical reaction because usually one does not tend to experience such an intensely detrimental effect when others act unwisely, unfairly, deceitfully, immorally, dishonestly, or wrongly in their relationships with us. This is surely not, not, and absolutely NOT to say or in any way imply that we would condone or in any way willingly accept enduring 'endlessly' their poor choice or transgression from our perspective.

Rather, we simply seek to develop the capacity to emotionally remain somewhat 'detached' (meaning not to personally identify with) and to fully apply the perceptive powers of our intellect and overall consciousness into examining the entire situation; including their perspective, to best determine what our responses should be to their actions or attitudes. In this way we cease to be so intellectually and emotionally reactive and hence increasingly influenced or even controlled internally by the various external events happening constantly around us. Instead, we learn to gain maximum control over our own emotions, life decisions and cease to be as easily influenced, manipulated, deceived, hurt or angered by the inappropriate or foolish actions of others. We have focused upon the negative human behaviours and emotions here because those are the ones we seek to avoid or resolve mentally, since they are most upsetting and damaging to us personally.

Let's briefly consider a few common lifestyle choices to determine how human nature issues are structured into our lives so that the attitudes we possess, even unconsciously, continuously reveal themselves through diverse situations. For example, if one chooses to marry, then that relationship will usually involve interactions with other family members on both sides of the relationship, which often do affect aspects of one's marital circumstances in unexpected ways. Also, by being in a mutually committed marital relationship, then that situation in western society traditionally is supposed to preclude one from becoming involved in other intimate sexual relationships, unless mutually agreed to the contrary, because marriage vows usually include a mutual promise and 'best intention' to remain 'faithful' throughout the marriage.

Unfortunately for many marriages, infidelity sometimes (or periodically, or often) occurs. This situation often results in the marital relationship becoming far more complex and volatile than it otherwise would have been, if both marital partners remained monogamous or mutually agreed with open honest communications upon whatever decisions were being made by both partners. Infidelity usually subsequently creates considerable emotional feelings; such as jealousy, betrayal and animosity, especially in cases where deceit and lies characterised those events. However, if both marital partners previously agree that both can freely interact with other people intimately upon a mutually understood basis, then perhaps in some situations that lifestyle would function well for them both. The relevant matter in this example is that couples decide to communicate openly and honestly to gain clarity and consensus of opinion in relation to the issue of fidelity in their marriage. While one's marriage may begin with one's best intentions to remain faithfully monogamous, over passing time, changing circumstances, and differing attitudes between marital partners; other decisions among the marital partners may become necessary to maintain harmony and some acceptable degree of personal gratification.

To minimise the potential damage to their relationships unnecessarily through a variety of typical marital situations that plague modern marriages as society's values have shifted to a more liberal, self-satisfying, libertarian perspectives and functional lifestyles; it is necessary to honestly communicate about these issues, before 'the fact' rather than later. This process reduces the potential damage to one's relationships and emotional pain that may be inflicted upon one's partner, and consequently also upon one's self in the shorter and longer term. Discussing all issues of significance in a deliberate, transparent, truthful, sincere manner enables the mutual expression of the genuine opinions of both partners in a way that totally clarifies matters. Ideally this honest, open communication process promotes a mutually agreeable decision that avoids future conflict, deceit and betrayal.

The apparent fact is that many men are admittedly prone to be unfaithful if the opportunity arises, especially if they can rationalise that their wives are not meeting their sexual needs. Generally, women are more likely to have extramarital intimate relationships when their husbands are unresponsive, less caring, rude, abusive in various ways, or away from home working, as well as when they are confident their husbands are already committing acts of infidelity. Directly communicating about such issues can often bring marital partners much closer together with a sense of mutual freedom and acceptance; creating more fulfilling and enjoyable lives in all respects.

Conversely, a lack of honest communication about intimacy and other issues of importance can stifle vibrancy, romance, spontaneity, love, affection, intimacy and joy within the marriage, resulting in acts that may lead to the unnecessary unhappiness, conflict, resentments, jealousy and possibly the divorce of the couple. While many couples seem to divorce prematurely over issues that could be mutually resolved in our societies; they always have the opportunity to resume that relationship at a later date, if they are mutually willing to do so. It is basically a matter of being honest with one's self first and foremost, then talking through the entire scope of related issues to achieve a mutually agreed decision and to progressively discuss issues of intimacy, human interaction, and any factors or situations that the marriage partners feel like communicating about in a refreshingly, non-judgemental, objective, truthful, revealing process of mutual discovery. While this process would undoubtedly lead to some intensely 'heated' discussions and perhaps some assertive disagreements of opinion, there would be genuine communication on all the important issues to be considered. Compared with what alternatively happens when people knowingly deceive, lie and manipulate one another; anything that makes communication and life choices more open, veracious and mutually consensual, the better, in my carefully considered opinion.

Alternatively, one may (unwisely) choose for various reasons not to enter into intimate relationships that are intended to be permanent. In such an independent lifestyle where one's interpersonal relationships tend to be transient and spontaneous, their lives and emotions are affected by differing processes and situations that may prove to become quite complex in an entirely different manner than those of a monogamous married person possessing a reasonably good relationship with their in-laws. The issue primarily being considered is the relative level of complexity involved in one's intimate relationships. In this example, if someone acknowledges to themselves and others with whom they wish to be intimate that they are uncomfortable with the concept or reality of marital commitment, then they are benefiting themselves and those with whom they interact intimately, as opposed to lying to themselves or others regarding this important issue. To discuss such personal concerns or fears with a potential intimate partner before becoming personally involved with them sexually to any significant degree would provide the opportunity for both people to more deeply communicate on a wide variety of topics. Ideally, they could become closer in the process or then decide to go their separate directions while maintaining a degree of respect for the other person's honesty, genuine communication skill, integrity and appreciate being privileged to gain a better perspective of the other person's viewpoint about life that differs from their own. The key factor is efficient, truthful communication serves everyone's best interests, as uncomfortable and seemingly inconvenient as it obviously may be at times.

A healthy, well-balanced person would seek to establish and maintain interpersonal relationships that tend to create happiness, peace of mind, comfort, enjoyment, stability, security and mutual purpose; as opposed to dysfunctional, stressful relationships that are often volatile, rapidly changing and emotionally troubling. We want to learn to avoid or transform relationships that tend to upset, stress and imbalance us, as well as those in which we are to some extent being unfairly treated, hurt, or manipulated in some manner.

Experience has proven to me that generally most people are reluctant to change appreciably for the better due to the influence or encouragement of others, and this would include me too. Therefore, if serious character differences present major problems, then (unless one is already married) avoidance or platonic friendships are preferable to intimacy or any form of 'serious' relationships, such as a business partnership or marriage. This (avoidance) may seem an overly simplistic response, yet to seek peace, harmony and mutually agreed perception in life beats unnecessary, counter-productive complexity and discord almost every time, in my experience.

Let's hypothetically consider a situation where a diverse series of human nature issues and emotional situations occur to identify how one ineffectual or poor decision can result in innumerable less than ideal results over passing time. Imagine a happily married faithful husband (no jokes here!) who has a great relationship with his wife's mother, who lives ten thousand miles away in another country that he has known from his native village since his youth long before marrying his wife, who was his childhood sweetheart. Further imagine the following sequence of events: Because of old age infirmity, the widowed mother-in-law moves into the married couple's home far from her native country, making the elderly lady uncomfortably dependent and lonely. Increasingly complex interpersonal relationship and human nature issues could easily begin to exert much more strain upon the marriage. It could be likely that the mother-in-law, consciously or unconsciously, starts to incite and instigate marital disharmony in order to convince her beloved only daughter to divorce her husband and move back with her to their native country. Imagine the elderly lady is no longer being polite to her daughter's husband or their children due to age-related mental deterioration and loneliness. From the elderly lady's perspective, she feels alienated from her own personality because nothing is as she once knew it to be; her own much loved husband has been deceased for several years, she no longer can properly care for herself or do her favourite hobbies, nor see her usual village friends, so she becomes quite disenchanted with her new life.

We can visualise how problematic such a marital relationship could become, regardless of how much the couple love one another, or how much they communicate about methods to keep the peace in the home and make the wife's displaced mother happy and comfortable in her new home and country. Further imagine that the increasingly frustrated and agitated husband arbitrarily provides the ultimatum himself, without adequate consultation with his wife, that the elderly mother-in-law will be re-located into a local aged care respite center ('old folks home').

Further consider that in the culture of the wife, her first moral obligation is always to one's parents, then one's own children; so therefore she has an inflexible cultural mandate to follow her mother's 'last' wishes. Her husband is culturally determined as patriarch of the household that his decision must be adhered to and obeyed. He refuses to have his mother-in-law promoting disharmony in his home, so to allow her to stay there is no longer acceptable nor can he understand that his wife feels an undeniable obligation to her mother, in spite of their shared cultural origin. Since the daughter's mother insists she would rather return to her own native country than go into a retirement community against her will, the daughter faces the awful dilemma to either return to the village with her mother and leave her husband (and perhaps her children also) behind, or to abandon her cultural heritage and dismiss her mother's wishes for her last moments of relative contentment in this earthly life by returning home to live out her final days on Earth.

The daughter/wife will suffer incredible angst and guilt for either choice she makes for the remainder of her life. Loving her mother very dearly, the wife perceives no acceptable alternative except to following her wishes, especially because on her father's deathbed she had promised him to always care for her mother when she needed assistance until she died and the elderly couple could then reunite in the afterlife together. The stresses become too great for the uncertain situation to continue, so the husband attempts unwisely to place additional pressure upon his wife providing another ultimatum that if she returns to their native village to care for her mother until dies, then he will seek a divorce with custody of their children before he will provide sufficient funds to fly her mother and herself home to the village. Therefore, to remain true to her mother's last wishes as she promised her father to do, the distraught wife reluctantly accepts divorce as being her only remaining option. National child custody laws enable her husband to become the sole parental guardian, something the wife did not initially realise would occur in this series of events.

Now imagine how emotionally torn by grief and frustration the loving mother would feel as she was forced by circumstances seemingly beyond her control to leave her children behind with her ex-husband, or seemingly 'abandon' her infirmed mother's last wishes in her final years of earthly life to the unpleasant confined conditions of an aged care facility that does not have residents that speak her mother's language. A terrible decision for anyone to make, yet the daughter unhappily moves back to their native country and lovingly cares for her ailing mother, who only survives a few years. Her husband, because of stubborn, self-defeatist male principles, sadly refuses to allow her to communicate at all with her young children, falsely telling them their mother had abandoned the family, which was true from his narrow-minded perspective. Later after her mother's death, her husband still continues to refuse to communicate with her about seeking marital reconciliation, in spite of the fact they both still love one another and the lonely confused children miss their mother dearly. Through the passing years the two divorced partners were deeply hurt and emotionally damaged by that terribly devastating emotional event in their lives and subsequently were unable to find anyone they could trust or love as much again in that particular lifetime on Earth. Imagine how lonely and discontented they both would be and how disorientated and unhappy their children would be due to this situation, which could affect them to some extent for the remainder of their own lives.

Without intending to seem overly melodramatic, the previous hypothetical situation or others of similar nature with unwanted complicated choices and attitudes, is akin to many normal events that occur in quite real, unique, equally unnecessary and extremely upsetting stressful circumstances.

My own divorce was the most difficult exceedingly painful experience of my life, so I speak with some experience about the suffering that occurs when families separate, regardless of the reasons. My divorce represented my life's greatest failure because I disappointed myself, my wife, my children and it meant the loss of my life's dreams. For many years and to a far lesser extent even today, I was angry and resentful over various things that I will not share here, as it would simply be my own biased perspectives and would likely upset my former wife and my much loved grown children. Thankfully, I am now able to speak with my former wife in a civil, kind, thoughtful manner. There is no advantage or need to 'defend' or rationalise my attitudes or behaviours, as some were clearly unacceptable and inappropriate.

I will say truthfully (and amazingly) that I was faithfully monogamous. When no marital solutions occurred, finally I felt compelled to obtain professional 'therapy' and openly discussed my situation with a psychiatrist on two occasions and participated in 6 months of marriage counselling, which assisted me to improve numerous behaviours and attitudes before making my ultimate decisions to leave our home to enable family peace to occur.

Over the ten years of the marriage both of us had endured a lot, as anyone living within challenging relationships can attest from their own perspectives. There were a variety of things I either could have or should have done to attempt to save my marriage, yet at the time some of my choices seemed unacceptable for numerous reasons and rationalisations. Anyone who has gone through a divorce or has been rejected by someone they loved, or simply 'walked away' from someone they still loved for the betterment of both, especially where one's children are involved, will understand the intense emotions and circumstances that these types of events can create.

During three frustrating years of intermittent separation before the divorce, it was important that I willingly made every reasonable effort to save the marriage. I sincerely participated in marital counselling to improve my attitudes and behaviours; obtained by my own volition a psychiatric assessment and had two lengthy consultations to obtain quality unbiased professional advice on my situation; as well as making many other positive character adjustments. I will not share those here, as we have all suffered enough in this assessment of various adverse human nature issues with far too much repetition and trauma being intentionally included already.

If you have found yourself becoming exceedingly frustrated and annoyed by this repetition about the forces of evil existing upon this planet, then this is excellent. You have realised my key point in doing this as a learning experience for us all is, "Why have you been unlikely to experience consciously the same abhorrent, frustrated attitude about the 'doom and gloom' and "be afraid, the world is a dangerous and uncaring place to be" that the mass media endlessly programs all of us with every day? This is about personal character growth and social change for the better; not about making us more comfortable by coping with our current lives within this reality system.

In my final meeting with the psychiatrist, after about two years of separation, I complained that the inner joy within myself that I always possessed was slowly ebbing away and felt as though I was in danger of losing my sense of self; of gradually ceasing to be a happy, active, good-natured person with a life purpose. He wisely suggested, "Do whatever is required to save yourself, because if you lose your inner happiness and your sense of self, then you will be no good to anyone; not even yourself". I thought at the time and still do that it was some of the best advice I had ever received. I am pleased to be able to share it with you now.

Therefore, soon after that interaction, for the sake of the children's and my own mental well-being and peace of mind, I had to decide to leave the family permanently and obtained a mutual consent, amicable divorce to preserve some semblance of peace for the family. Life has not been easy for the family since then, yet we are adjusting and remain in communication mutually doing better than ever. I see the children when they wish to do so, including brief, enjoyable civil exchanges with my ex-wife periodically, since we live in the same community. The primary issue here is that we are truly improving our interpersonal attitudes to heal old wounds and avoid creating further stresses, discord, and unhappy emotions among one another, which we all appreciate.

Considering the previous hypothetical example of the married couple's complex dilemma regarding the wife's mother, as well as briefly alluding to some the challenging elements within my own failed marriage are intended to portray sample situations where we each could see all manner of possible solutions at various sequential steps in the overall process whereby there could have still been a relatively happy ending to our story. Once again, I share some aspects of my own personal experience because in this case you can see that it is not always a matter of infidelity, physical abuse, addiction, financial pressures, or in-law issues that destroy family unity and peaceful relationships. Some marriages can survive all manner of challenges and because their personalities are incompatible, while in other situations people can happily remain together with little compatibility or even minimal love or affection for others fail for very little obvious reason. In some cases people that love one another very deeply are unable to remain happily together one another.

In my case, the character growth and realisations that occurred within the difficult marriage was astounding, from my own perspective. Those upsetting, stressful, painful, frustrating, costly experiences encouraged me to develop a much more acute sense of empathy for other people's perspectives; and it enabled me to become much more patient, persistent, forgiving, self-controlled, humble, determined, loving, understanding and willing to make difficult unpleasant decisions for the best interests of the entire family and myself. The most important realisations we can achieve in life are those that are developed through living in relationships with others in ways that encourages us to also periodically dedicate ourselves to a sincere self-examination, introspection, meditation, and active contemplation and ongoing reflection/analysis processes. We also have the opportunity through these relationships to obtain important information and experiences about how others we know very well perceive events, think, feel and respond to all manner of circumstances. This continuous process enables us to discover the innumerable aspects of our own comprehensive character, in relation to how other people manifest their 'reality systems' within our lives.

These accumulated experiences assist each of us become increasingly 'at one' with our true self; both as a personality, the uniquely individual temporal physical ego consciousness, which ideally exists in a balanced state with one's true conscious essence, Soul, which is the infinite eternal Divine, and the more 'hidden' aspect of our overall Being.

This gradual unfoldment of heightened awareness improves and expands one's conscious connections with the indwelling Divine Spirit and greatly facilitates and enhances one's overall understanding of the actual nature of life. This process of ongoing, cyclical, yet unpredictable enlightenment within each of us occurs at our own individual pace. Progressively, this process creates for each individual an unlimited series of events that are divinely designed (for those that wish to do so) to become more intimately harmonised with nature, Mother Earth and the Source of Life Itself, which is also described as being the ultimate creative Super-Consciousness, by the somewhat vague descriptive terms such as God, Creator, Divinity, etc.

Divinity cannot be adequately fully described or defined within human language. Creator/God must be experienced in an infinite multitude of ways throughout the infinity of time and space in physical reality systems such as here on Earth, then and simultaneously also upon 'higher planes' of existence which are equally 'real' reality systems, although these do possess some differing characteristics than we are familiar with in our current life.

Your particular life is the only real story that truly matters to you right now. Your journey of discovery is all about you getting your attitudes and life right, according to what you want, wish, make and dream it to be. That is exactly what this entire discussion is about between you and me here and now. You will be most advantaged by making the best possible decisions in regard to a seemingly infinite number of possibilities existing in your individual life. Ideally these will mostly be great choices, yet experience often proves our mistakes and short-sighted decisions 'easy upon yourself', unless you keep repeating the same old errors in judgement. We are discussing issues that will definitely help you to more fully recognise who and what you truly are as an eternally conscious life form that now inhabits your human body in this particular earthly lifetime. Our mutual quest in earthly life is to more independently and astutely make positive beneficial choices that create an ideal life and future for you and the ones you love. By making positive mental adjustments to life's many types of lessons, we can significantly improve our character, behaviours, daily lives and relationships. Let's continue to examine a few related scenarios to elucidate a few more of these factors that will assist in your decision making processes.

Please imagine the lifestyle of an independent single or divorced person who enjoys meeting and sharing interactions with a wide variety of people. Some of these social interactions will complicate their life in a wide diversity of ways than would be true if they spent a great amount of time on their own in daily life. This hypothetical individual likes the interpersonal activity because it distracts from their endless series of inner thoughts and realisations, which sometimes become too overwhelming to consider. They find the unique mix of people to be very entertaining and enjoyable. Occasionally this person will feel somewhat lonely and seek greater meaning from their relationships, yet most of these relationships remain upon a somewhat superficial level because of their fear of commitment or being rejected ultimately by someone they love and they seek to avoid that potential emotional pain and loss. After a while, they may begin to want more internal purpose, peace, happiness, coherence and deeper true meaning in their lives that no other person can possibly supply, regardless of how pleasant, loving or accommodating they may be. Even in a crowded place they may at times feel lonely and distant from the other people, so they finally decide they must develop a closer relationship with the one and only person that always remains truly loyal and closest to them always; themselves.

Likewise, another hypothetical single or divorced person with relatively little social interaction may feel lonely and alienated from other people who seem so different, mysterious, inexplicable, and potentially emotionally threatening; so their inner journey to discover themselves would seem to appear to take a more introverted route, yet it is much the same as anyone else's. The primary difference to the first hypothetical example is they will generally be dealing directly with their own issues instead of finding their lives complicated by unexpected attitudes and situations by external influences of many types. Regardless of one's level of social interaction, our inner responses to life's events are uniquely individualised to ideally become more spontaneous, flexible, appropriate, and progressing nicely as one gradually develops a more self-assured, comfortable, peaceful state of being that is based upon their spiritual progression and increasingly expansive perception of reality.

Another hypothetical married person who sought and found the loving, satisfying marital relationship with another person, who experienced a joyous family life, may also reach this same natural, personally positive 'crisis point' where one's inner truly conscious self, Soul, subtly quests for recognition, inner manifestation and external expression in one's daily life. That inner special memorable experience of dramatic higher conscious awareness and realisation could happen in countless unique ways; depending upon our character, life choices, state of mind, culture, age, health status, or any other variable one could mention. It all begins to get really serious when one's logical mind, feeling heart and omnipotent Soul openly and honestly communicates freely within the sanctity of one's own inner divine space that we define here as our own overall state of consciousness.

To discover one's true self, as Soul, a Divine 'spark' of conscious God Essence is the most precious gift and valuable realisation process that one can possibly achieve within eternal and physical existence. That reality is directly available to you and all of us who seek it right now.

Consciousness is our true direct mental connection with what people call God; or by any other similar word concepts, such as Cosmic Consciousness, the universal mind, the Holy Spirit, the ECK, the Sacred Oneness, the unified or 'morphic' field, nature, life, reality or by any of the individual names that humans have given to God in various religions or the many scientific creeds. We are NOT referring to so-called prophets or 'saviours' here.

What we call God is a form of immortal infinite consciousness characterised by omnipresence, omniscience, omnipotence, and omnificence that is inexplicable, pervasive within the universe, and forms the basis of the unique human consciousness that exists within each of us. Therefore, through human nature issues we are generously provided with abundant illuminating 'windows' into eternal levels of reality that vividly illustrate life's most rewarding magnificent mysteries, if one is willing to sincerely seek revelation with patient anticipation and an unlimited eager persistence that is characterised by a humble loving heart that quests for 'the meaning to it all'.

In earthly reality, there is no alternative to dealing with human nature issues, so we must freely accept and gladly embrace this immutable fact of life here. Life's endlessly unpredictable situations often dramatically intensify the emotional complexity of the challenges we face, which sometimes seem to increase exponentially out of our control in spite of our best efforts. Trust that our Creator has Its' own 'better plans' and goals readily available for each and every one of us. However, a key criteria to access this personal spiritual progression is that we must be willingly, freely and truly receptive to God's Will and the various intuitions and forms of divine guidance that are always available to better apply that inner 'higher' direction and innate divine wisdom. There is no way to cease interpersonal interactions while on Earth, even while one is seemingly 'unconscious', as when in a coma or a 'near death' experience of some type. We must learn to better adapt, attune and compromise with others, as we intently examine the depth of our own character to elicit the superlatives within ourselves through all types of events.

As stated previously; inner honesty in joyfully freely accepting total personal responsibility for all aspects within one's life and mind is an essential prerequisite to manifesting appropriate action externally in the world through our daily lives. Within one's own private mind, can we be completely truthful with our selves about our true needs and desires? If so, then this is an excellent beginning point to extend this deep level of honesty to include one's spouse; for example, in regard to how we perceive that we are being treated by our intimate partner as an issue of mutual respect, or discussing marital fidelity, or other sensitive important issues.

How would they respond to an open forthright discussion on such a vitally significant issues as marital harmony or thoughts of seeking extramarital intimate relations after years of married life, or even before the marriage began? Could such discussions serve to create instant discord in a relationship or would the process of communicating on such a sensitive and emotionally volatile subject serve to bring the couple closer together in harmonious relations, regardless of their ultimate decisions? Do they freely discuss related issues with one another in a sane, civil, comprehensive manner, or do they immediately begin to become overly critical of one another, accusatory, defensive, belligerent, hostile and impulsive in making conclusive decisions that would impede or prevent open honest communication that would then further damage their relationship? Would they decide through such improved communication to initially recommit themselves to becoming more attentive, loving, caring and romantic with their spouse before attempting to find more, excitement and affection within intimate relationships outside of their marriage? To me, quality honest communication among all people is the best possible result when addressing and resolving any issue. Others may hold a differing opinion based upon their own experiences in making these efforts and then apparently being somehow disadvantaged or even 'attacked' in that process of honest disclosure.

If one's private discussions were not held in confidence by either marital partner, would the issue become a topic of discussion among one's in-laws or other family members, perhaps being used in a vindictive way to further destabilise the situation? Would the conversation be used to incite subsequent arguments, months and years after the event and serve to be a focal point for accumulating marital frustration, friction and fuel further disharmony, distrust and alienation between them? Could the entire hypothetical issue become a nightmare; or conversely, a marital point of mutual consensus that assisted better communication and appreciation for one another that stimulated a higher level of love, commitment and romance in their marriage that made the idea of extramarital affairs seem absurd and unnecessary? Alternatively, perhaps they could mutually agree to allow one another the freedom to make choices without all of the personal pressures, or much further consideration to the purported social stigma and condemnation that some people with other opinions make seek to apply, if they became aware of the facts and disagreed with their personal choices. It would really not matter much if the opinionated person was completely external to the relationship, such as a neighbour or distant relative. However, if it was a child or young adult living in the same home, or an intolerant so-called 'religious leader' who objected strenuously and sought to create further problems (such as having them literally stoned to death, as still occurs in some locations of this world), then this 'fact of life' would also need to be considered in the decision processes, ideally.

This one hypothetical scenario is used simply to illustrate that an act of intended honesty within one's self that a marriage is not adequately meeting one's needs for companionship, affection, romance, intimacy, sexual satisfaction and fulfilling communication could result in two entirely different outcomes, or anything in between these extremes.

Some of us never even consciously consider the possibility that (ideally) there may be another lovely partner somewhere out in the world with whom one could be happier, more loving, in harmony and 'at peace' in sharing our lives.

It is tempting to share more detail regarding my personal experiences in my own marriage or other personal relationships now. Instead, suffice to say that eventually, I knew it was far more likely to find happiness and peace of mind within myself and elsewhere than to arduously continue to attempt to save our marriage. In response to my unhappy situation, I clearly recall the observation made by accepting the innate wisdom offered by the psychiatrist saying to me, "If you do not save yourself, then you are not going to be good for anyone else." The clear realisation at that time was I no longer even loved myself, nor did I know what true (divine) love actually is (which I am still discovering, as are we all). I was deeply unhappy with my various life choices and vainly sought to blame my ex-wife, society, my parents, or anyone aside from myself for obviously creating these miserable conditions for my family. I had major difficult decisions to make at that time, so I considered everything very intensively over a few years.

In the final analysis, when my wife said words to the effect, "If you plan to stay with me until the children grow up and then leave me, I would prefer that you leave now, so that I have a chance to find someone else to love me and have a chance for a happy life together with them." The power of her honest wisdom made me instantly realise that unconsciously I had begun to unjustly, wrongly and deceitfully unconsciously plan exactly that within the privacy of my 'closed' mind. I immediately realised she was right, so soon after, and for the sake of the entire family's happiness, I agreed to the divorce by my own suggestion. Obtaining the actual divorce occurred over three unhappy years of intermittent separation.

Now about fifteen years have passed since my divorce, during which time I met and got to know some truly wonderful ladies with whom I have had four relationships lasting from two to three years each. I am still friends to some extent with three of these four lovely ladies, yet I only see one on a somewhat regular platonic basis, which we both much appreciate. Her 'new guy' and partner is not nearly as delighted with our ongoing true friendship, although he is kindly polite and understanding with us both. Obviously, I have continued to find it quite challenging to permanently commit myself with one partner when the naturally occurring interpersonal differences, occasional disagreements and life's minor frustrations; such as resolving my current financial challenges, tends to consume my attention, time and efforts. I have reluctantly had to admit to myself that I am acutely over-sensitive to criticism, even when it is accurate and justified. Additionally, I clearly do not wish to 'follow', nor 'adhere to' the prevailing social conventions and cultural standards, which in many cases I perceive as seriously flawed, and not applicable to the vast array of available solutions that are required to genuinely improve civilisation or build better sustainable enjoyable family or professional lives for me, or others like me that enjoy and demand freedom to be productive and compassionate with others in my own unique ways.

Therefore, it has been my experience that it becomes a real struggle to maintain consistently pleasant, peaceful, mutually enjoyable interpersonal relationships with a truly compatible lady, as I have never (knowingly) met her yet. Perhaps in writing this book and sharing some of my inner perceptions and experiences, I will ideally attract a suitable compatible lady partner. The ironic realisation was, when I actually met such a lovely nature loving lady in real life, she was far too unique for me to 'deal with', mostly due to my urgent desire to truly improve myself to be worthy of quality relationships and I also had no desire to raise more children at that particular time. That was another poignant, memorable, amazing life event to get to know exactly how challenging my own attitudes and lifestyle appears to be to others, so I then accepted this reality as being ok too. You would be well-served to accept your unique character traits and change for the better those that do not resonate with your 'higher' nature, as Soul, which is your true eternal essence.

On my own for more than two years, and living In my natural state upon my rugged rainforest land, 'off of the grid', and communing daily with inner divinity and nature amidst the beautiful mountainous rainforest, collecting stone and crystal artifacts, growing some organic food and sharing the forest with uncounted millions of trees and billions of other forms of life living there; I have gradually and willingly become even more openly committed to being a unique or unusual type of person. However, I am happy now and well-connected with inner divinity, with no steady intimate relationship in about two years, as I work intensively upon improving myself and my life circumstances. Finally, I have accepted in good spirit that I am becoming an even more increasingly distinctive character with some personality traits that make it a challenge to be around me for lengthy periods of time.

For example, I have not watched television in about 10 years, virtually never drink alcohol or coffee, and gladly possess many other such qualities that differentiate me from most potential lady partners in my community. I remain focused on inner peace as a personal journey to assist me with connecting better with inner divinity, nature and thereby ideally helping manifest world peace in my lifetime. This is a dream I share with countless millions of other people, as well as other species of life, including Mother Earth herself. We shall see what the future brings. I trust all is for the best and it certainly is looking that way now, all things considered for all of my family members and a few organisations with whom I interact on a regular basis to create and apply needed solutions in life.

To some extent, this amazing uniqueness is also the situation in some ways for every human being; because we all are exceedingly special and do possess our own mannerisms, needs, desires, beliefs and goals in life. The focal realisation I had in relation to my difficult failed marriage was that my character improved significantly through the entire experience, especially in learning to be more patient and understanding of other people's perspectives, even when I did not agree with them. I also finally was able to develop the courage to willingly walk away from my precious family relationship with hopes that a better life could be created for all of us than if I had stayed in the chronically upsetting situation without providing any viable solutions. It has proven to be among the best decisions of my life, yet definitely the most difficult and painful. I continue to feel some sense of remorse over what could have been, yet was not possible for us at the time.

Now I am simply very grateful to have three strong-minded, independent children who are grown into fine young adults in their early to mid twenties that know I love them very much. True acceptance and love for one's self and others in life is a valuable quality to develop; like many other personal characteristics that these human nature issues demonstrate to us through an infinite variety of events, emotions and realisations, such as deep gratitude for life's many blessings and gifts.

A fundamental human nature issue to resolve is the tendency to want or desire something, and then when it is achieved, the experience is not quite as fulfilling and satisfying as one anticipated it would be. In life it is a huge asset and capability if one can learn to become relatively satisfied when one's goals and dreams are achieved, even if new goals and desires arise to replace them to some extent. This would be the situation even if our objectives have not been accomplished and seem unlikely to ever be attained, so one learns to accept the reality and make the best of life as it is and to re-focus one's attention on the many good aspects existing in life. At some point in life, we each and all (as humanity) need to truly acquire the ability to be grateful and contented with what we have achieved and refine our further goals primarily to serve our higher spiritual needs and aspirations. My life now involves more 'listening' to the

Creator's ideas through intuition, then consistently making the necessary actions that are necessary to manifest these potential realities. This process has required adjustment away from being a highly ego-centric, self-directed, opinionated, somewhat stubborn individual with relatively little true empathy for others, although I would have previously disputed that fact.

Let's continue our hypothetical examples of the manifestation of various types of situations that occur in a stereotypic fashion which demonstrate important life realisations or even unwanted 'hard lessons'. We could imagine that one partner in an unromantic marriage secretly enters into an intensely enjoyable sexually intimate relationship with a subordinate co-worker, who sees them as an exciting successful authority figure. The other spouse suspects infidelity, feels lonely, complains about the apparent situation, further alienating the marital partners from one another. The younger spouse having the affair even feels somewhat guilty for the intentional lies and ongoing deceit and begins to avoid home life because her children are grown and it was her husband who first brought up the subject of possibly having extramarital affairs to improve their enjoyment of life since they seldom had mutually satisfying sexual relations anymore. He claimed this was due mostly to his feelings of inadequacy with his wife having becoming the primary income earner after his retirement, which affected his intimate abilities in a detrimental way. The basis for this insecurity unconsciously developed primarily due to his own infidelity over many years with multiple people, which he had consistently denied to his wife vehemently when questioned about it by her.

Consequently, after several months of increasingly enjoyable times with her new friends, the career mother honestly informs her increasingly estranged and agitated husband of the newly developing situation. He is both surprised and deeply offended by his wife's new found intimate liberties and sexual enjoyment, especially when he finds it began with another lady working for his wife and later also involved her enthusiastic, capable, younger, good looking, athletic husband. Shocked beyond belief, primarily because he had imagined the affair being with another man, the upset husband responds quite poorly and becomes acutely jealous, sullen, morose, rude, and resentful toward his increasingly cheerful, vivacious wife, who is quite successful in her international fashion design and marketing businesses.

He seeks to improve his self-image by belittling and condemning the actions of his wife to their grown children, who tend to strongly identify with their mother due to the many years they saw her being unappreciated and taken for granted by her somewhat critical, domineering husband. The end result could be that he becomes so unpleasant to be around that his wife demands a divorce or simply decides to spend far less time at home and prefers to travel internationally most of the year on business trips and social excursions.

As the husband mentally reflected upon his being the first person in their relationship to mention the issue of his own desire to have extramarital affairs, already aware he had been doing so with many different ladies for years while his wife was focused upon her work and raising their children; he likely decides that honesty was surely not the best policy for him according to the results he experienced unexpectedly. However, from his wife's current perspective his desire to openly involve himself in extramarital affairs, rather than to continue to hide the fact, was a godsend to their superficial, drab, boring, lifeless charade of a marriage, especially in their later years after the children had become teenagers. He may additionally complicate his unhappy position by beginning an intimate relationship with a much younger woman who primarily seeks material comforts and intends to leave him whenever it suits her purposes; thereby further compounding his relatively discontented state of mind. This basic scenario is unfortunately somewhat typical in our modern society, although the particular sexual roles and choices made by the participants are of negligible relevance to the human nature issues involved.

Now try to imagine another hypothetical situational perspective of an exceedingly attractive young lady that believes she would prefer an intimate relationship with her older, influential, successful boss to receive expensive gifts, enjoy an improved lifestyle and further her career. Instead of choosing an intimate relationship with an interested readily available handsome work colleague of about her own age that has a similar background to hers' educationally and culturally, with compatible shared interests, lifestyles, musical favourites, and mutually acquainted friends; she prefers her company's much older CEO. In this hypothetical typical scenario, the boss intensely desires having intimate relations with his much younger voluptuous beautiful secretary primarily because of the pleasurable self-gratification he would undoubtedly derive from the entire experience. He was well-aware that she was flirtatiously acknowledging her availability and knew that her interest in him was due to his affluence, glamorous lifestyle, corporate power, his eager availability, as well as his dominant authoritative role in the workplace. He may or may not realise that her unstated 'dream plan' would be for him to eventually divorce his wife of thirty years, marry his secretary and then due to her encouragement, to (reluctantly) have their own children with him, in spite of the fact he would be in his late fifties or early sixties. They may do exactly that and live quite happily together until he dies, leaving her financially secure, yet in early middle age raising children alone with far less hope of finding someone who truly loves her that would be willing to endure her self-absorbed preferences. We often do not consider the future possible ramifications and results of the actions we choose when motivated by 'lower mind' impulses.

We could consider the pained, rejected, frustrated feelings and perceptions of the fit, handsome male co-worker, who was the potential true love of her life; who was basically dismissed without a real chance to prove himself because he was unable to compete financially or in prestige with their boss. If the boss eventually divorces his trusting, faithful, lovingly affectionate wife, then she may believe her entire life has been devastated and experience inconsolable misery. Deep ongoing resentment may also result, knowing that she had worked to support her husband through university, given up her own possible educational and career options to birth, nurture, and raise their children and provide her 'up and coming' young executive husband with a comfortable home to entertain his business guests lavishly to promote his professional advancement. Realising she had been unceremoniously dumped aside with little empathy, apology or real consideration by him; she may become vindictive and create other problems for him, such as with the taxation department or in other ways, such as turning his own children against him with 'fair cause' from their perspectives. For many of us in western civilisation, these hypothetical situations approximate some aspects of our own lives in various ways, or other people we know. Therefore, we need to learn and grow from our various life choices; and by demonstrating worthy values that are compassionate toward others that interact with us, especially family members.

It is most important to scrutinise and fully consider that one's decisions often result in creating drastic alterations to one's life as events sequentially unfold over passing time. Therefore, to make impulsive, gratuitous, amoral, unprincipled choices intently for one's own selfish interests, with little or no respect or real consideration for other's perspectives, needs, feelings, thoughts or circumstances is a despicable, counter-productive way to conduct one's personal or business life, in my opinion.

Unfortunately, we can vividly perceive innumerable examples of these immoral, corrupted, manipulative, self-serving attitudes manifesting around us to a seemingly pervasive extent in many global societies today. While it seems most people generally attempt to maintain ethically responsible actions, there are others who obviously have intentionally chosen to do the opposite. It would appear there has been a negative shift in the world today toward some people attempting to do almost anything that they think they can 'get away with', regardless of the adverse effects on others. Some people with little or no operational conscience will often say or do anything to get whatever they want and will intentionally avoid or not do what they have agreed to do, knowingly in a premeditated manner without any guilt or remorse.

This detestable, noxious, loathsome, anti-social type of thinking and behaviour is harming our civilisation immeasurably. It is a vitally important issue which must be addressed and resolved for humanity to become more enlightened, evolved and transformed into less contemptible states of being than currently exists. High standards of mutually recognised and socially agreed values and principled ethics are essential prerequisites to establishing a truly civilised global society where one's status and social position of responsibility is defined and maintained largely by how well they appropriately interact and accomplish their roles with integrity, in an honest, reliable, civil, virtuous, trustworthy, straightforward manner.

People that choose otherwise, expressing through their inappropriate actions a proclivity for greedy self-interested choices characterised by dishonesty, duplicity, aggression, and a wide variety of unfair, unscrupulous behaviours that reveal a corrupted, manipulative, predatory attitude; need to become socially reprehended in some reasonable effective ways. For example, they could be ostracised, deprived of positions of social responsibility, required to attend mandatory counselling, or re-purposed to do less challenging roles within their scope of ethical ability. In severe cases where fraud has occurred, then if no admission of guilt or wrong-doing occurs, nor any sense of seeking to improve their attitudes or behaviour, then these people should and must be justly punished for their counter-productive or overtly fraudulent activities. Aggressive and violent people would be removed from society until their attitudes and actions improved, or if they were unwilling to seek improvements then that separation from society of the well-adjusted would be permanent and they would be limited to living among their own kinds of unethical and sometimes violent or predatory types of people. In severe cases they would be placed into various forms of solitary existence.

Now in society we see many proven guilty criminals entirely avoid prosecution, or if proven guilty in a court, then they do not receive jail sentences for serious crimes. Conversely, some other social misfits or 'petty' criminals are actually relieved and happy 'enough' to go to jail to avoid the gruelling challenges of their daily existence of living in poverty, criminal activities and possessing various types of addictions that they refuse to stop. However, if those convicted of crimes were mandated to attend intense counselling, along with periodic hard physical labour, in a completely drug and cigarette free environment, and mandated to have ongoing monitored civil interactive communications with victims or their nominated representatives, as well as providing some forms of financial or labour related restitution for their crimes, then this would be a more just and equitable system that would reduce crime and recidivism.

We desperately require an improved system of responsible accountability and socially enforced honesty to promote the uplifted culturally accepted norms that engender improved human interaction processes, a quality work ethic with equitable work practices, in conjunction with fair wages, a reasonable sustainable cost of living and an improved simple taxation system. Until these progressive developments occur, along with many others that would greatly benefit our civilisation, then humanity will increasingly suffer in countless ways due to the paucity of principled values that now obviously afflicts aspects of our social consciousness from the highest echelons of society, onwards throughout all aspects of our earthly societies. There must be a socially mandated system of commonly agreed and demanded ethical criteria that all people understand and practice in all aspects of their daily lives. This may seem to be a virtually impossible, unrealistically high standard of social and individual righteous responsibility in one's actions; yet the alternatives are becoming self-evident through increasingly chaotic, non-functional and unsustainable circumstances in many nations and locations.

Constructive positive alterations must occur within all areas of society; including business activities, government, religion, interpersonal relationships, and humanity's interaction with the earthly environment. If this reasonable progressive development seems too difficult to achieve, then carefully examine and extrapolate upon the continuing decline of basic human values; into the treacherous chaos of institutionalised and personified deceit; rampant aggression and violence; pervasive corruption; multitudinous addictive behaviours; socially condoned forms of the victimisation of innocent, peaceful, law-abiding people; overt political, economic and governmental malice against the public good; the rampant spread of organised crime with the complicity of both law enforcement, government and entrenched vested interested within society; and the wilful destruction of natural environments for short term profits. A few additional current examples are: using nuclear energy to produce electricity without adequate solutions to safely dispose (or make inert and harmless) of nuclear waste; 'fracking' to obtain natural gas while knowingly destroying the ground water resources; poisonous 'chemtrails'; chlorine, fluoride, benzene, MSG, artificial sweeteners, colours and flavours and other known poisonous substances being intentionally allowed into our water and food supplies by government regulations; health damaging EMF radiations and prescription drugs being approved without adequate unbiased scientific and medical research and unbiased testing procedures; HARP types of damaging toxic technologies; extensive covert 'mind control' programs that are operating through the media and educational systems; mandated poisonous vaccines; and so on. Add to these situations, the militarisation and economic deprivation of global society at the expense of real social and economic progress and we see an unacceptable, totally unsustainable, well-integrated, intentional, vile, insane governmental system now exists in many nations globally. This is truly 'enough' now.

As we reach some key conclusions, please allow us to briefly summarise a few common activities that reveal various detrimental human nature issues. We could have chosen to examine in depth why and how some modern business relationships intentionally function within immoral, dishonest, adversarial, intensely unfair, 'rigged', predatorial systems that are falsely described as being 'capitalistic' or 'free market' global economic practices that are incorrectly deemed to be 'competitive' issues. We could examine endless proven examples of instances where those in government agencies or political offices blatantly tell the people or government regulators overt lies and make intentionally misleading false statements, and where even contractual agreements and the Patent system are routinely used deceptively to gain unfair advantage for the sake of obtaining profits, as well as unfairly bankrupting others for 'vested' self-interest reasons. These ethical and moral crimes against righteous attitudes and actions mean nothing to some people.

To unethical people, corporations and institutions; there is every intention to unjustly utilise the legal, financial and governmental systems to knowingly wage premeditated economic, emotional and physically attacks that cannibalise and victimise others and our precious natural environments without any conscience, reasonable cause, nor any semblance of mercy or guilt by the wrong-doers. This is surely a situation that must be rectified in a more equitably functional, rationally efficient, truly evolved, consummate society. I am acutely aware of many issues related to these circumstances in society, just as would the majority of us have already experienced some aspect of these relatively fraudulent activities in our lives. We should pause to remind ourselves of a few of the times when others sought to financially defraud us or others we know through illegal or immoral actions and attitudes. Additionally, many of us will recall instances of unprovoked physical and emotional attacks upon us by others. Those lessons and realisations will serve us well to avoid interactions with others whose unethical or violent conduct is detrimental, unacceptable and incompatible with the functioning of a truly responsible, equitable, civilised society.

We have necessarily chosen to focus upon considering a range of mostly adverse detrimental situational factors that are directly related to basic human interpersonal relationships that affect our families; people's entire physical, mental and emotional well-being; financial status; perception of reality, and (directly or indirectly) consequently that greatly influence almost every aspect of our lives. When we deeply investigate and analyse how people and institutions act in their relationships with others, then we gain enormous insights into the inner workings of the human mind and character as it manifests in our daily lives, for better or worse.

This is a focal point for you to closely examine and thoroughly consider within your own innermost thoughts, wishes, dreams, fantasies and imaginings on a variety of topical issues. What would your ideal relationship be if you could achieve anything you wanted in relation to other people's responses to you? What lifestyle would you ideally wish to have? If it were to happen according to your wishes, then would you be an asset to society or primarily devoted to indulging in various forms of self-gratification and hedonism?

Not too many of us would be willing to publicly express the full scope of our private fantasies, yet a vital aspect of our quest for self-discovery and appropriate thought and action necessarily also involves serious consideration of these issues. We have already acknowledged that most of us would at some point be prone to fantasise about obtaining things and situations that would not really be good or necessary for us or others. Surely, many of these desires would not involve genuinely considering the best interests of others in that process of obtaining whatever it is that we ideally would want, if we could organise it somehow without creating too many problems or legal difficulties for ourselves. The problem with this attitude is that most so-called 'normal people' (whomever and wherever they may be) apparently indulge in some forms of fantasy life mentally, even though these types of thoughts generally remain unspoken and private thoughts that are never acted upon in daily life. However, they definitely do have some sort of minimal or more overt effect upon own our lives, as well as upon the overall social consciousness that all people and sentient life forms share. We, as individuals and a global civilisation, are and will continue to be advantaged by carefully selecting the thoughts, emotions, imaginings and feelings we possess and act upon.

We all can easily recognise and usually condemn excessive, horrendously anti-social, violent acts by sociopathic, psychopathic, insane people who are basically acting out the worst of these more extreme forms of offensive, aggressive acts that some of us may fantasise about to a far less hostile or harmful degree, in order to attain our imaginary or real life desires. In other words, if one intensely wanted material possessions, then an insane person or one with no social conscience, or a cultural disposition toward violence and anti-social behaviour would simply seek to steal or somehow villainously acquire the object of their desires. If we were to place ourselves in a similar circumstance to fantasise about acquiring abundant material possessions, we may design a plan to work hard for these funds, or a less scrupulous person may choose to try to marry someone who had the capability to earn the funds or more likely already possessed the objects of their desires. Likewise, in the intimate relationships we have been discussing, some people choose to develop interpersonal relationships for many reasons; some for social convenience and enjoyment; some due to mutual personal interests and character similarities;

some out of a desire to genuinely love, respect and share all aspects of their lives with another person as their foremost goal in life; others because they are lonely and want someone to communicate with them; some because the person is attractive in appearance and it boosts their ego to be seen with them, and so on.

The relevant point being made here is most people have established a fairly well-defined set of reasons why they interact with others. Some people can and do rationalise that to have intimate sexual relations with another person primarily to express human forms of (highly conditional) 'love', or to obtain money and social status is morally right, or wrong. One's subjective perspective is a relatively arbitrary analysis based upon what one personally seeks and believes in life. Some people have a relatively minimal conception of what true divine love is, or the nature of human conditional love is, or the meaning and feelings involved in sharing real affection, or of what mutual respect, or human decency, nor any sense of knowing and experiencing what 'grace' actually is. With these people, it is difficult to discuss or experience the reality that we know as being 'in love' because that set of mixed emotions is truly not a part of their emotional or mental reality system for various reasons.

Are we to insist that any form of intimacy that is not intending to be characterised by true love is inadequate, inferior and improper, simply because it does not meet our ideal standards of moral assessment? No. Or, are we to say that in another culture that an 'arranged marriage' is somehow less functional or less 'sanctified' than what we envision in normal 'western' culture, primarily because we do not understand or agree with the cultural practice ourselves within our culture? No.

These types of issues are not easy questions to answer definitively, at least not in a simplistic way that we can address here in copious detail from numerous perspectives, as would be necessary to thoroughly consider the many ramifications involved in such debateable philosophic issues. Actually, we are trying to realise that the full scope of human nature is something that is uniquely independent to each of us individually, depending upon our own character, circumstances, culture and attitudes at the time, as well as those of the people with whom we are interacting. This can become very complex.

Human nature seems to always be in something of a state of flux; changing potentials and possibilities in relation to the internal and external events and attitudes within and around us. In differing circumstances what is logically and somewhat inaccurately defined as being good, right, proper and appropriate for one person or in a particular set of circumstances may be quite wrong, bad, improper, and inappropriate for another person or even the same person, if they were in somewhat different circumstances or culture, or were happening at another time and place in their lives. This entire concept is challenging to intellectualise upon, as are so many other ideas and realities we have mentioned and will discuss here. Therefore, it is easier and more comprehensible to utilise overly simplistic hypothetical examples or ideally our own actual life experiences to better describe, typify and characterise these ideas so they are deeply meaningful and edifying for you and your loved ones.

Let's briefly return to our previous example of the hypothetical people in the previous imagined events Also, please be highly encouraged to consider any interpersonal relationships that you would care to visualise; ideally ones that actually did exist in your own life's experience in a related way or could potentially have occurred. Please recall the older executive choosing to leave his loving loyal wife of twenty five years to marry his attractive young secretary. Realise that such a relationship may seem to be quite inappropriate from some reasonable perspectives, while we would surely recognise this as being a type of relationship that has in more recent times become very common. In past ages, such an executive or official would have been far more likely to somehow obtain a mistress whom he would never marry, as is still very prevalent in our societies. Likewise, if he was openly involved in acts of infidelity and somewhat ignoring his wife and mother of his children, then she too may become intimately involved with a lover to satiate her physical desires and needs for love, affection, or enhanced social or financial status. Alternatively, she may simply attempt to 'take her half' of their financial assets in a divorce settlement, if she is able or feels justified in doing so. Other insane men or women may simply decide to kill an unfaithful or abusive partner and this is totally unacceptable and wrong, in my biased opinion now; yet some find valid reasons to do so, such as in severe cases of abuse.

There is no reason to limit the example to any particular social class of people, nor race or nation, nor age group, nor culture, nor religious affiliation or any other such categorical variable one may devise, because human nature is all-pervasive. The fact is that most people innately seek forms of pleasure, gratification, joy, love and peaceful contentment, as well as excitement, spontaneity, adventure, comfort and so forth. The ideal is to share that with other people who wish to enjoy the same experiences. Problems arise when some people do not respect the rights, feelings, emotions, choices and desires of others and fail to act appropriately in various ways. Some people enjoy what most of us would define as quite unpleasant experiences and emotions and these people often are prone to victimise others because of their unconscionable attitudes, perverse desires and debilitated spiritual status. We need to remain aware that our choices should and must always involve mutual consent and be committed toward honest, transparent actions. The Golden Rule of 'treat others as you wish to be treated' applies only if the treatment is of a kind and considerate nature and is not abusive in any ways.

In any human relationships that are assessed over passing time, it is likely for people to grow intellectually and habitually closer together or further apart in various ways. To remain truly involved in a harmoniously united, mutually beneficial relationship throughout an entire lifetime; they must actively cultivate quality communication, some shared interests and interact in some mutually meaningful ways to maintain and progressively develop their compatible relationships, especially when intimacy, love and mutual respect are necessarily interconnected qualities.

In earthly life we would all recognise that over passing time some of our relationships seem to progress into a situation where in spite of all the positive aspects involved, one periodically finds themselves asking the rhetorical or actual serious question, "What was I thinking when I began this relationship?" The unfortunate answer may often be, "not much" or perhaps one was motivated by their immediate sexual, or financial, or emotional needs, or one's unspoken, unconscious desires were dictating the flow of events, etc. Later, as the sequence of events develops quickly or more slowly out of one's control or contrary to one's preferences, then the results can often become exceedingly complicated and unwanted situations may likely develop. The issue could then become one of, "How do I get myself out of this unpleasant, inconvenient, unacceptable, ill-advised, or otherwise horrible situation?" We could realise that the situation was actually much akin to one of our inner thoughts, dreams or fantasies being enacted in real life, yet not nearly as we imagined in all its manifested outcomes.

Many times in life we find ourselves in interpersonal relationships of all types where we seemingly suddenly discover, as if awakening from some sort of unaware dreamlike state that we actually have very little in common with the other person anymore. If we retrospectively re-consider the initial mutual attraction that brought people together, we determine that it was often a form of physical, intellectual, emotional, financial, status, or sexual attraction in nature. Therefore, over passing time, changing circumstances and attitudes; the entire relationship can become less desirable and could seem, in retrospect, to have been somewhat of an illusion from the outset.

It is important to mentally return to the initial sequence of events to recall how and why things unfolded as they did. Try to visualise exactly what sorts of issues motivated us at the time, the nature of our thoughts, our specific words and actions to examine them for clues to important indicators regarding the progressive processes related to those and subsequent events. In accomplishing this introspection and reflection we may be able to discover the subtle wisdom contained within the experience that could be likened to discovering a hidden treasure within one's past that results in enhancing one's current levels of awareness and subsequently prompting many realisations. Then ideally one will make improvements to their attitudes and behaviours that benefit one's self and others in this developmental process.

Rather than continue to intellectualise upon these issues and the interplay of changing reality from one's perspective over passing time, circumstances and attitudes; please consider the fundamental fact that all behaviour is motivated by something in us individually. Before we act, we should give some consideration to determining the nature of our motivation or inspiration for that action. Otherwise, as we all know from our own life experiences in some situations, we could be establishing the circumstances where we inevitably will experience unwanted consequences for our 'less than ideal' choices and motives in the future.

If we are habitually motivated by the best, highest, most noble, virtuous, altruistic aspects of our overall character in relation to our interactions with others, then the consequential results would ideally be more positive, beneficial and rewarding for us and those with whom we involve ourselves intimately and otherwise. This statement of course assumes rather naively, idealistically and over-generously that others will act toward us in an equally magnanimous spirit in their character, which is unfortunately not generally the case in a significant portion of life experiences. But, those are their human nature issues to deal with and this is why we must so perceptively assess and accurately as possible discern the fundamental nature and characteristics of our chosen interactions with others in various respects. "By their acts you will know them." usually proves correct over passing time and in varying circumstances, as we each and all have discovered to some extent already.

The situational possibilities and resulting emotional manifestations existing in our hypothetical examples are unlimited. Our experiences in life all too often provide additional evidence of more of the same old problematic human patterns and tendencies that create difficulties for ourselves and others. These few examples, including those you have hopefully thought about from your own life and those circumstances you are aware of from the people that you know well only serve to illustrate 'the tip of the iceberg' in relation to the overall extent that such human nature issues affect us all.

We could have delved far more deeply into the intensely acute, painful emotions that one feels when they are intentionally, uncaringly, maliciously, violently abused, or are deceitfully manipulated, cheated, robbed, and lied to. This emotional suffering and intellectual anguish is especially intense when we receive poor treatment and a lack of respect from someone with whom we have an intimate relationship which is supposed to be based upon trust, open communication, honestly and from whom we expect and want to receive empathetic loving kindness and understanding in their treatment of us.

Most of us have also been on the 'other side' of this equation to some extent as well, although apparently not all of us. If you have not ever been responsible for hurting someone else's feelings or betraying their trust by being dishonest or unethical with others in some manner, then you surely have my most sincere congratulations and my highest esteem! Alternatively, there could be a distinct possibility that if you truly believe you have never emotionally hurt someone, deceived, manipulated or were unkind to another person then it is quite likely that you are not being completely honest with yourself in your assessment process, or that you have a 'convenient lapse' in your memory. While we each may be 'perfect' in expressing and revealing our imperfections by assisting one another to learn about life's complex realities; this life on Earth right now is not an 'easy path' to travel for most of us.

We, who do possess an active functional conscience, have all experienced some degree of emotional suffering in life. There has been no real attempt to provoke too many of those sorts of self-critical emotions, nor to stir up too much personal condemnation about our own imperfections here because most of us know the negative, unhappy side of human emotion and our various 'weaknesses and character flaws very well, if we are willing and able to examine them deeply. We seek to stimulate, inspire and create the more divine, joyful, peaceful expressions of the potential human nature that exists within each of us. We recognise through our life experiences that love, joy, bliss, peace of mind, harmony with another person or animal, and other such positive uplifting beneficial emotional states of being are intensely meaningful and enriching to one's sense of self.

Contrarily, unhappy emotions such as anger, fear, jealousy, resentment and depression are quite unpleasant and self-destructive to our character, especially over long periods of time in such a state of emotional suffering. Life is a circumstance in which we are given the wonderful opportunity to experience all types of earthly situations that stimulate an incredible diversity of emotional states of mind, heart and spirit; so that we are able to learn to choose the attitudes and behaviours that are most conducive to our spiritual and human progressive evolution. These realisations and interactions in all aspects of our lives are the primary manner in which we learn to make the mostly constructive developmental changes in our perceptive and thinking processes to improve our future experiences. The diverse mixture of emotions, realisations and personal life choices and their consequences formulate some of the key ingredients that enable our lives to be so interesting, unique, unpredictable, mysterious, revealing and educational.

Life is an astoundingly individual experience in its ultimate form, regardless of one's interpersonal relationships. You come into this particular earthly life, alone within the realm of your own individual eternally aware consciousness. That will be the way you will leave this Earth; alone with your infinitely abundant realisations and accumulated wisdom that is contained within your immortal character as Soul, which is ultimately your only true form of eternal wealth that we possess within our consciousness. As a form of energetic consciousness, inhabiting a physical body in this lifetime, we now perceive only a small part of the comprehensive reality system that envelops us.

On the deepest most all-inclusive pervasive level of existence, we are each and all an integral individualised aspect of the infinite unified omniscient consciousness. In other words, our personalised consciousness is an evolving aspect within the universal hologram, known as 'reality'. Our individualised consciousness, or eternal Soul, is contained within infinite, eternally omnipresent, omnipotent consciousness, that some of us would define as being God. This creative conscious energetic life force is now believed to be the ultimate Creator of the entire universal reality system that sustains all cosmic consciousness within an infinite super-conscious life matrix that we are aware of from our earthly perspective of this universe. Likewise, apparently that same infinite super-consciousness resides within each of us as Soul, an evolving 'spark' of God Consciousness. Human beings (and all life forms in existence) are the microcosm within which the macrocosm dwells. This reality is repeated here numerous times in various ways because it a focal concept that forms our existence and it is helpful to consciously realise, accept, embrace, appreciate and welcome this fact.

The combined experiences of our human nature and other spiritual issues here on Earth, as well as within other levels or dimensions of reality; is the mechanism or system that establishes the eternally unfolding, progressive life processes that develop true wisdom.

Through an endless series of lifetimes, each Soul will periodically manifest into various reality systems as countless individuated personalities that are located throughout time and space in order to directly experience all of life's truths. This entire process is God's clever plan for all of us, as individuals and collectively as interactive life forms, to learn and progress. Likewise, all infinite systems or dimensions are within existence for Creator/God to directly experience Its' Own Reality through an infinite sets of unique perspectives, from Its' quiet, subtle and non-demanding manner and perspectives within each life form. In this way, God better understands the nature of Life Itself.

Each and all can clearly perceive one's individual and collective progress revealed clearly through our evolving and improving overall character. Our inner truth, love, wisdom are the only really tangible 'possessions' that we will take with us within our consciousness when we leave our physical body and earthly possessions behind upon our death here.

Our state of consciousness is the sum total of what and who we each are at the time of our death in the physical body. This is a key reason why we are so focused upon utilising our human nature to learn and realise so much about the application of eternal values, principles, ethics and apply them now in our earthly lives while we have the opportunity to improve ourselves and be of benefit to others in that process of discovery. It is upon this earthly stage, amid the real life saga of interacting with unique characters in complex, challenging circumstances that we each and all are tested in seemingly innumerable variety of ways throughout time, as we know it to be now.

Each of us may have a significant amount of influence in this earthly life, or seemingly only a tiny bit of impact on the flow of life's events, depending upon the various situations.

None of us will ever actually change the basic fact that this material world is a place of learning; a huge real life 'schoolhouse' and 'melting pot' for all types of life forms. We human beings all share human appearing physical forms, yet on the deepest level we are individualised Soul, an evolving, eternally aware tiny spark of God Stuff, the creative energy that exists within all forms of consciousness in this universe.

All live physical life forms including those that do not possess human form are Soul on the deepest most pervasive eternal levels of existence. The disharmony or war between divine love and materialistic power is manifested clearly before us here on Earth now. On the side of true love are countless positive states of being such as gratitude, generosity, truth in all its forms, kindness, humility, freedom in all its forms, balance, creativity, compassion, empathy, forgiveness, joy, inner peace, abundance, other higher levels of awareness and divine states of being and other such life blessings that are characterised by the true power of righteous proper thought and behaviour upon all eternal and material levels of existence.

The prevailing characteristics of earthly physical, material and technological power ultimately reveal less pleasant realities that are often characterised primarily by various forms of struggle, suffering, life challenges that can result in extremes of fear, anger, external controls, hate, degradation, greed, jealousy, insecurity, insanity, scarcity, resentments, evil in all of its forms, conflict in all of its forms, poverty of ethics in all of their forms; as we can now see manifested in our world today. Again, please consider the age old wisdom, "By their 'fruits' (attitudes and resultant actions), ye will know them".

As human beings and as Soul, it is our divine right and responsibility to resist being abused, degraded, hurt, deprived and enslaved by all necessary means. When any one, family, culture, nation, race or group of 'life forms' seeks to limit or deny our God given freedoms and rights to experience a peaceful, productive, meaningful life characterised by quality values, security, equitable opportunity to create prosperity through our hard work and savings, decent comfortable sustainable social living conditions, and an ability to lovingly educate our children according to these basic beliefs and human rights; then it is our social responsibility and spiritual obligation to resist and overcome those untenable conditions and attitudes.

People of Mother Earth and the innumerable variety of intelligent species of self-aware life that exists everywhere throughout the infinite physical, material planes of existence and other unlimited dimensions of existence that are co-existing with physical levels of reality all share this divine gift and privilege.

Ultimately, each and all possess the right and responsibility to develop, refine and manifest their free-will in positive, loving, kind, uplifting, creative methods of expression in life that do not hurt or deprive others of their innate rights to do likewise. Any force or ruling power or group of life forms that seeks by any means to adversely control or prevent constructive, balanced, beneficial expressions and manifestations of Soul's free-will is revealed to function on the lower forms of power. If so, then they automatically also seek to limit or deny our inner divinity its rightful acknowledgement and manifestation in our lives. Therefore, such 'lower powers' must be opposed on numerous levels in peaceful, productive, mutually beneficial ways.

When living in a state of awareness upon the physical plane, we recognise that when violence, murder, slavery, intentional scarcity and deprivation, inequality and forced incarceration are misapplied in evil ways; then in such times it is our divine right and responsibility to resist despotic oppression in whatever means are necessary to defeat such an illegitimate, inappropriate and counter-productive force to establish more equitable, beneficial, positive forms of self-government that serves the best interests of all life forms.

We must harmonise with our inner divinity and recognise its lesser forms and expressions while we carefully choose our thoughts, attitudes, emotions and actions wisely and then be fully prepared to be accountable on all levels of existence, eternally and physically alike. True justice is not blind, nor temporal, nor ignorant, nor contemptuously arrogant in dismissing any realistic viewpoints; rather it is omnipotent and omnipresent everywhere throughout eternity. This is why we seek to choose carefully and wisely from the highest aspects of our being always and all ways. We are all fundamentally Soul, independent, self-aware creations of God and thereby we each are eternally responsible for our own actions.

As our discussion progresses, we will consider another series of real life examples that serve to expand the scope of issues we wish to include to better understand our purpose on Earth. It is imperative that we each carefully reflect over our past experiences to recall, assess, evaluate, analyse and reach a series of definitive conclusions about the entire range of our own personal, private human nature issues. It is essential that you are exceedingly honest in considering the variable nature of your own ethical values in life.

We do this by examining how one interacts with the various aspects and tendencies within your own state of being; specifically as they relate to all of your daily and past earthly activities and your creative future that is continuously unfolding with so many new and amazing possibilities. Your immortal, divinely created and inspired, evolving consciousness is where your inner beauty, true wealth of spirit, and strength of sublime character reside and are discovered through introspective processes of experiencing earthly life and further developed throughout our expansive eternal infinite existence.

Chapter 10

Evolved Life Forms and the Nature of Soul

Thus far we have addressed a range of complex human issues; some being unusual and challenging to intellectualise upon because they defy simplistic normal common sense logic and in some cases, even the prevalent scientific methods of analysis. Other evocative issues are quite familiar to all of us, yet this does not necessarily mean that we find those factors especially easy to resolve mentally, emotionally or by just changing our external circumstances. Now we will endeavour to inquire into boundless areas of universal and cosmic reality that surpass most standard forms of empirical human investigation. We have already devoted considerable attention to considering the intrinsic incomprehensibility of some of the more obscure aspects of human consciousness that basic logic and scientific analysis is presently unable to adequately reveal or fully explain. The intricately perplexing study of human forms of consciousness is comparable and analogous to delving comprehensively into the inscrutable mysteries regarding other forms of universal consciousness. To gain an improved understanding of humanity's pivotal role in the evolution of our civilisation's potential to be openly invited to join the galactic, universal and cosmic community; we must sincerely evaluate numerous factors that affect our overall perspective of life in relation to the extensive existence of multitudinous forms of consciousness within the universe and our solar system. In short, earthly human beings are definitely not the only intelligent, evolved, self-aware, highly technological species of life possessing a well-developed civilisation within this solar system. It is time to recognise the exceedingly pervasive existence of an incredible diversity of highly evolved consciousness that now exists within our solar system, the known physical universe, as well as in the vast, unseen, infinite cosmic dimensions that are relatively impenetrable to normal human physical senses.

We will begin this progressive assessment by initially considering that there are innumerable varieties of other intelligent life forms that manifest their consciousness upon this Earth that we do not yet fully comprehend. In other words, most human beings are not yet adequately aware that other earthly life forms possess a much higher level of consciousness than most people would likely recognise or readily accept. Humans have not yet been able to communicate effectively in a mutually understood linguistic manner with Earth's intelligent animal life forms, such as dolphins, whales, gorillas, chimpanzees, elephants or even dogs. However, recent scientific research is now beginning to prove that these intelligent species of animal life do possess some ascertainable form of self-aware consciousness, emotional feelings, as well as a functional system of auditory and visual communication with members of their own species. It is also obvious from observing nature that many earthly life forms have developed mutually acknowledged systems of auditory and visual communication between and among a wide variety of species. We do recognise some forms of the most fundamental level of communication where mankind has domesticated many species of life to serve our needs, although in most situations we do not seem to particularly care much about what the animals' perspective about this relationship may be. Animals and humans, through millions of years of mutual evolution, have become in many cases somewhat co-dependent with one another. The fact we take such inter-species communications somewhat for granted is a relevant aspect of our topical matter. Humans arbitrarily assume an autocratic rule over all other earthly life forms, such that as long as animals serve their intended purpose and do whatever humans want them to, then they are allowed to exist. For many domesticated animals, their existence is a relatively good one, yet for others who are destined to become our food, the convenient relationship is relatively one-sided in humans' favour. Unfortunately, wild animals and entire environmental systems are often treated with far less consideration, respect and appreciation by human beings, with some encouraging notable exceptions where we see humanity becoming more aware in preserving habitats and endangered species to a modest extent. Consider the fate of ancient extinct animals such as cave bears, sabre tooth tigers, dire wolves and countless less predatory species of life that were used by our ancient ancestors as food resources. Human predation and intentional environmental destruction has been a deliberate practice for millions of years that lead to the extinction of countless species of life on Earth, which continues unabated, with increasing intensity in today's world. The vast majority of modern humanity has largely chosen to intentionally remain in selective ignorance regarding the interconnectedness of all aspects of life.

There is a developing awareness and more widespread public recognition of the innate inalienable rights of all life forms to humane, fair treatment; yet in these so-called modern times, the rule of the jungle, 'the survival of the fittest and strongest' maintains its predominant grip upon human policy decisions globally. Most ancient and modern indigenous people have been acutely aware of their integral intimate relationship with the natural environment and sought to inhabit their territorial lands with respect for the sustainability of their lifestyles within their ecosystems. History records many examples where our ancient humanoid ancestors and the more recent types of human life forms appear to have lost an appreciative, respectful, harmonious awareness of this vital connective natural relationship between people and the natural environment. The direct result of humans gradually ceasing to live in a concordant, cooperative way with the natural environment is littered with numerous historical examples of failed ancient civilisations, kingdoms and tribes of people, as well as innumerable now extinct forms of humanoid life whose progressive evolution eventually resulted in the particular species we now are: Homo sapiens. If modern humanity on Earth continues to insensibly and ignorantly transgress the immutable laws of nature; and flagrantly disobey its' own moral, religious and legislative laws of justice, civility and decency; as well as the universal and cosmic principles espoused and evidenced by all truly civilised life forms existing throughout the universes, then our current civilisation may relatively soon cease to exist in its present form. Humanity absolutely must adjust our attitudes very quickly to begin to behave in a much more civilised fashion, or suffer the dire consequences.

Inattentive, oblivious, unaware, ignorant people will often assert the characteristic deceitful beguiling denials that there is anything drastically wrong now in our civilisation or earthly ecosystem, in spite of the overwhelming evidence to the contrary. To suggest that our civilisation is behaving in an uncivilised manner in many respects would likewise be met with rancorous howls of dissent, yet as always such people do not believe they should have to support their opinions with factual validation. To observe that it appears certain from the progressive destabilisation of key fundamental elements that are necessary for peace and prosperity to exist in any society or global civilisation, that humanity is very likely to eminently experience potentially catastrophic militaristic conflicts, resource shortages, social upheaval, and environmental disasters would also likely be aggressively contradicted by such idiotically biased, unobservant, ignorant people. The historical parallels and synchronous series of events are self-evident, as are the countless early warning signs that momentous disaster lies ahead, unless humanity substantially changes its attitudes and behaviours.

There are many subjects included here for your consideration that would not be readily accepted by the normally educated public. We will only address a relative few of these matters in a superficial, cursory fashion. We choose this restrained approach because each subject is so contentious among scientists, scholars, religionists and others, that we simply seek to state the basic situation from the relevant applicable perspectives that address our particular subject matter. Truth does indeed reveal itself to sincere, capable, receptive, inquiring, well-informed minds that possess the intellectual capacity to incorporate some components of unfamiliar information with their existing knowledge and experience in a cognisant, coherent manner. Therefore, if some of the information is too obtuse or irrelevant to your life perspective, or it makes you uncomfortable; then attempt to withhold any form of judgement as you read those specific concepts. Instead, just consider such unacceptable or debateable information as you would any other work of fiction or science fiction, so that you can more easily progress through those sections to deduce the aspects that are of more interest and relevance to you personally. I have spent a lifetime acquiring such information and often the evidence initially seems far too unbelievable to consider it as being remotely possible, much less likely to be factual. However, by accumulating high quality circumstantial, verifiable evidence over passing time, my personal opinions and perspectives on many such debateable issues have progressively been transformed. In such a process of ongoing discovery, in some cases it becomes necessary to periodically re-consider what initially seemed to be exceedingly unlikely, as subsequently becoming something quite probable, then even later, as being factual from a newly acquired perspective. In a similar manner, we periodically benefit by thoughtfully adjusting and deleting various types of outmoded beliefs, attitudes, opinions and activities from our evolving life and that would tend to include some people that we are not in harmony with.

Many of the more perceptive and intelligent people of Earth realise that these factors threaten our survival as a civilisation and perhaps as the species of dominant life on this planet, from our anthropocentric perspective. However, relatively few such people in the public currently realise that planet Earth is actually already inhabited by a variety of highly technologically advanced races and species of life forms, some being distinctly human in appearance, exactly like ourselves. Exactly what am I saying here, you may think? Earth, the moon, Mars and some of the other planetary bodies within our solar system are already inhabited by highly advanced, technologically superior life forms, some of which are identical in general external appearance to we human beings that now inhabit Earth. Some of these life forms are quite obviously alien in appearance, yet this definitely does not necessarily mean they would consider themselves in all cases as being 'alien' to Earth because in many cases they have already been here for many thousands and perhaps in some cases for even millions of years. Suffice to say that the vast majority of earthly human beings at this time in our evolutionary development process are not fully aware of all the forms of intelligent life that exist upon and 'within' our planet Earth, or that exist upon other planets and satellites within this solar system, or in other dimensions of existence beyond the physical plane, known as the third dimension.

Just as people that immigrate to new nations from their ancestral homeland to eventually adopt their newly chosen national identity over their traditional origins, a similar analogous experience occurs for extraterrestrial species of life that now think of Earth as their adopted home planet. For some alien species, Earth is simply a convenient location to periodically visit to obtain supplies such as; water, minerals or metals, genetic breeding stock, or for other such reasons. Some of these extraterrestrials are analogous to earthly humans that travel internationally as tourists, or for business reasons, or as galactic scientists studying the natural environment, including the various humanoid and animal species around our planet. They simply do so upon an interplanetary, interstellar, intergalactic and inter-dimensional basis, in some cases. The important situation to realise is that there have been many such extraterrestrial life forms visiting Earth throughout human history. It is a well-proven fact that some of these beings have long ago and more recently, established communities here on Earth and elsewhere in our solar system.

Abundant historical records exist of earthly activities by technologically advanced life forms. Such voluminous evidence includes the following: most of the world's religious scriptural texts mention these events in great detail; innumerable ancient drawings depict unusual looking beings as well as their aerial vehicles; anthropological and geologic discoveries prove that highly advanced civilisations have existed upon Earth in pre-historic times; the written historical records of ancient civilisations from around the world mentioning gods visiting Earth that possessed highly advanced technologies and capabilities; and the widespread existence of written records of such events occurring in more modern historical times from all geographical locations around the planet. The sheer volume and scope of the current modern information that has been compiled would absolutely astound and boggle the mind of those aware of the extensive evidence that modern civilisation has acquired about these extraterrestrials and other highly advanced life forms co-habiting Earth and existing elsewhere within our solar system. These diverse information sources all serve to conclusively document the historical validation that technologically advanced races of interstellar beings have frequented

Earth for countless millions of years, as we now know and understand the concept of passing time. Ample evidence exists that some of these highly advanced technological civilisations are able to travel through enormous distances of space, through historical time and also between various dimensions or planes of existence, which clearly surpasses the current levels of human scientific understanding, according to the limited information being presented scientifically for the public's consideration.

For many of Earth's more aware, perceptive, historically and scientifically educated people, this is not an especially new revelation. This information about Earthlings interacting with or observing highly developed technological life forms have been reported in the public domain over several thousand years of recent human history. Some of these unique, technologically superior types of life forms are humanoid, appearing exactly as we human Earthlings do now, while others appear to be quite unusual and are noticeably of distinctly alien origins. This undeniable fact is supported by extensive documentation that is available to any seriously dedicated, open-minded researcher. Also, ample evidence exists that not all people that appear to be human beings are in actuality human beings as you and I. Some entities of various non-human types sometimes are able to inhabit physical appearing human forms and are discernible in some cases only by their attitudes and actions.

We will not invest much effort in substantiating the copious circumstantial historical, anthropological and geologic evidence that abounds in relation to these complex and often debateable issues. Instead, we will address what these events could possibly mean for us living here on Earth. For those people who doubt or deny the reality of these facts, it must be noted that they are likely to habitually ignore or perhaps unconsciously suppress their own ability to access the relevant information that is freely available from many sources. It seems evident that anyone in our modern civilisation who professes to be uninformed on this subject is intentionally committed to maintaining this perspective in spite of the conclusive volumes of evidence available to them. Therefore, we validly assert the proven fact that many extraterrestrial life forms have visited Earth throughout human history and that some of these beings have established communities here on Earth and elsewhere within our solar system at this time in human history. Those who disagree are welcome to prove me wrong.

To summarise; a variety of highly technologically advanced physical life forms, which are not presently publicly acknowledged by earthly governments, now reside upon Earth, as well as upon various planets and their satellites within our solar system, as well as elsewhere throughout the universes. We will not specify the various stellar systems from which these technologically highly developed life forms originated, nor to specify the planets from which they reportedly originated before arriving upon Earth, nor when they first arrived here. Such issues are purely matters of unverifiable, irrelevant conjecture from our limited perspectives and we have no interest in such issues in this assessment of the information that we wish to address here. Let's just suffice to say that I have been in a fortunate position to access much quality information on this entire subject for over four decades. Some information that is relevant to our topical matter will be shared here with you and extensive additional quality information is readily available in the public domain regarding many related issues that may also be of significant interest and benefit to you.

There will be no descriptions here any of my personal experiences in accessing, analysing and correlating a massive amount of UFO related information because I do not wish for any of that to become a matter for the public record at this time or perhaps ever. What we will share here is of far more relevance than would be any hypothetical assumptions regarding the nature, prevalence and possible motives involved in those beings that pilot UFOs through Earth's skies, waters and interior. We do not want to become distracted with listing interesting case material, documenting significant UFO events, relaying informative messages from alien extraterrestrials to humanity, and so on, because all of this is already a matter of the public record from many credible, well-informed international and multi-dimensional sources. Basically, I have been quite privileged to witness, experience, communicate and comprehend much information in relation to UFO and other forms of extraordinary, remarkable, highly evolved, conscious life form's activities on Earth. Information has come to my attention from many sources that are of great benefit to me in compiling the diverse, relatively comprehensive subject matter of this book and for that fact I am indeed eternally grateful. My present overall perspective enables me to focus primarily on issues that are relevant to us as individuals and as a civilisation, in a prioritised manner. One factor that is especially relevant to carefully consider is that these UFO related issues are definitely not, not, not, among the most important issues we are discussing in this book. Also, it is wise to distinctly realise and remember that NOT all aspects of apparent so-called UFO phenomena are likely to be, in true reality, just exactly as they appear to the senses to be. In other words, some things are not always as they appear to be; especially when such experiences or information is related to extraordinary, astounding, inexplicable events beyond ordinary levels of human awareness and comprehension. Please remember this statement. A factor of human consciousness is that if something is not in our ancestral memory, or within our current level of comprehension, or within the wave length of energy to which we are receptive, then generally we cannot perceive it or understand it through our normal human perceptions or senses.

In recent decades, people of Earth have witnessed a significant public education campaign regarding the possible existence of extraterrestrial life forms. This public education process to increase humanity's awareness of these issues has occurred through the mass media; predominantly through science fiction stories, fictitious radio shows, such as Orson Wells' "War of the Worlds", innumerable fictional movies, such as the 1951 movie "The Day the Earth Stood Still" and many television shows, such as "Lost in Space", Doctor Who" and "Star Trek", that portray alien beings and their spaceships interacting with future Earthlings, in widely differing types of settings, themes and plots. It must be noted that there is a prevalence in the mass media outlets to quite falsely and unfairly portray most alien species as characterised by the worst uncivilised human attitudes and behaviours; such as being hostile, violent, warlike, immoral, ugly, devolved spiritually, robotic, devoid of compassionate emotions, and often intent upon either destroying Earthlings or enslaving us, as the recurrent themes and plots of these fictionalised events are theatrically presented. Alternatively, some of these are more intended for humour or to inspire us in various ways and some of these productions would include "ET", "Third Rock from the Sun", "Mork & Mindy", "My Favourite Martian", "Close Encounters of the Third Kind" and various others. The theatrical movie productions that most destabilise us in a detrimental cosmic awareness sense are those that are intended to create a reaction of fear, loathing, revulsion, hostility and mindless opposition within human beings toward unknown alien life forms that would include countless movies produced over many decades, such as "The Blob", "Alien", "Predator" and "Independence Day", which seek to dissuade human beings from considering developing reasonable, mutually beneficial interactions with extraterrestrials, aliens, highly evolved, and otherwise technologically and spiritually developed life forms. We will assess more information on this issue as our discussion progresses. This is another example of small-minded, inappropriate thinking by earthly civilisation which often falsely characterises other life forms according to its own species' biased perspectives, self-absorbed motivations, inaccurate beliefs, 'worst case' scenarios and absurdly limited value systems.

While it may seem that the phenomena of humans interacting with physical life forms that do not seemingly originate upon Earth are a new development, nothing could be further from the truth. Human beings have had extensive interaction with what we would define as extraterrestrial life forms for hundreds of thousands, and probably millions of years on Earth. There is a huge amount of quality evidence regarding ongoing interaction, including non-consensual genetic breeding programs, being conducted by so-called alien races on and with human beings, in some cases with the knowledge and covert complicit consent of some earthly governments. What does this mean for us here on Earth now? To begin answering this question, we must first examine the attitudes and responses of our earthly civilisation's governments, namely the real functional 'hidden government within the government' and the earthly 'power elite' group of people that autocratically rules our world civilisation currently, which is known by some as 'the cabal' and would include their unidentified alien and/or multi-dimensional 'masters'; who have falsely made illegitimate 'claims of ownership' upon Mother Earth and all life forms existing here.

We first need to seriously consider a few basic facts about humanity's interaction with so-called extraterrestrial civilisations that are now frequenting Earth on a continuous basis. Most modern national governments continue to be extremely secretive about the entire issue and consistently refuse to publicly make a definitive categorical admission that earthly civilisation has experienced ongoing observations, communications and human interactions with a wide variety of technologically evolved, extraterrestrial life forms of known and unknown origins. The news media has sometimes publicly reported some of the more conclusive instances when numerous people witnessed events that were characteristically typified by a visual display of highly advanced technologies that obviously surpassed those of modern earthly civilisation's current level of scientific development. These unknown activities are generally labelled as being 'anomalous phenomena' or 'unknown aerial phenomena' or the more popular classification of Unidentified Flying Objects (UFOs) because generally the objects are seen flying in a manner that is impossible for modern aircraft, such as: silently hovering; instantly appearing, disappearing and reappearing; making impossibly abrupt turns at various speeds; flying in a zigzag fashion; making unnatural size, shape and density changes; displaying unusual lights and amazing luminosity; flying too fast or slow to be an airborne object originating from our civilisation's current level of technology, or various other astounding visual and other observable, detectable effects. On Earth there have been countless millions of these confirmed conclusive inexplicable events occurring over thousands of years. In recent times, many hundreds of thousands of such UFO sightings have been recorded by photos, movies, video and infrared cameras, electro-magnetic field detectors and conclusive radar evidence; further proving the factual existence of these unusual flying objects being reported globally. This includes numerous instances of astronauts from many nations witnessing undeniable UFOs in outer space around Earth, as well as capturing much photographic and video evidence of these extraterrestrial spacecraft in outer space and within Earth's atmosphere. Now humanity has also obtained undeniable clear photographic evidence from our unmanned space missions and satellite images of Mars and Earth's Moon that dramatically reveal extensive evidence of technological constructions upon the surface of these planetary bodies, as well as some other locations within the solar system. Additionally, various governments have over many decades progressively acquired numerous crashed or otherwise 'gifted' UFOs, so humanity is now in possession of the definitive physical evidence as well. In spite of the massive volume of confirmed cases of UFO activity around the planet for thousands of years, many earthly governments steadfastly refuse to publicly discuss the issue in a genuinely meaningful conclusive way. Information now being held under top secret classifications is even withheld from duly elected political representatives and officials. This fact alone clearly reveals the existence of a higher level of international authority than that existing within our national governments and international organisations, such as the United Nations (UN) assembly of national representatives. This self-evident fact very clearly illustrates the tip of the iceberg of circumstantial evidence that proves the undeniable existence of a 'government with the governments' in most, if not all, of the world's major governments and the United Nations, whether elected or in power by some form of dictatorial or monarchical rule.

When prominent politically elected leaders, such as a President of the USA, or high level government officials that are responsible for national security, such as the Director of the CIA, are over decades being repeatedly denied free and unrestricted access to the vast majority of documents related to so-called UFO activities, one must curiously wonder why? We ask ourselves why this is the situation in several respects. First, we must ask ourselves, as well as those authorities within government bureaucracies; why the people placed into positions of social and governmental responsibility at the supposedly highest levels in our national governments are being consistently denied access to such vitally important information, in spite of their requests to receive the information that is available within top secret government files on these issues? Second, we must ask ourselves and the governments of the world, why is this government controlled information being continually and intentionally withheld from the public domain when it is common knowledge in every geographical area of the world that these inexplicable UFO events are occurring now and have been occurring as long as history is available to record human activity on this planet? Third, we, the free-willed and well-informed people of Earth, must ask ourselves, and the governments of the world, as well as 'the hidden government within all the governments', and the so-called 'power elite's' representatives 'which is increasingly being known as 'the cabal'; why they refuse to publicly address this issue in a reasonable, transparent, analytical, thorough, comprehensive manner over an extended length of time in order to fully assess, review, discuss and make publicly available the numerous definitive conclusions regarding these UFO related issues?

These types of questions have been posed to 'the earthly powers that be' for many decades, as well as over thousands of years, in earthly civilisations past and present, with very few publicly available comments being supplied to the people. Therefore, we must assume that number of situations exist as possible reasons for such a non-conclusive, long-standing, definitely evasive response. Some of our most basic possible and probable scenarios will inevitably lead us to a fairly interesting variety of general and more specific probable conclusions that arise through the observational and experiential processes of our own deductive thinking. In other words, we will make our own analytical assessment of the entire situation from our relatively limited perspective, according to the ample array of facts in our possession, to achieve a broad range of possible and probable conclusions that are consistent with the evidence. Extensive experience as a researcher of inexplicable events of various types and as an independent private UFO investigator for four decades has enabled me to conclude that anyone who is even remotely curious about this subject material will be well-informed enough to acknowledge the self-evident facts in some of these cases. Earthly civilisation is witnessing unknown, highly technologically advanced aircraft traversing our skies that are capable of interplanetary and interstellar space travel. Substantiative reports exist of technologically advanced spacecraft landing on Earth and being clearly seen by local people that are confirmed not to be of earthly technological origins due to the type of construction, the materials, the alien appearing occupants, the unusual flight characteristics, etc. Some of these UFO case files also include innumerable events where these spaceships were boarded by humans and in some cases they were reportedly given a journey into outer space or even to other planets that were distinctly different from Earth. These events have occurred in all areas of the world, and have been reported by all types of witnesses to these types of amazing, vividly memorable, undeniable experiences. There have been numerous documented cases of some of these crashed or disabled spacecraft being recovered by various earthly governmental agencies and taken to governmental laboratories for analysis, to determine the methods of their propulsion systems and other such important technological information. In some such cases, such as the Roswell event in the USA in 1947, it is well-known that humanoid life forms were recovered from these crashed spacecraft that were distinctly alien in appearance. In various such cases it is also reported that alien or human appearing life forms were captured alive, detained and questioned by military and government personnel over lengthy periods of time.

These types of evidential materials leave absolutely no doubt whatsoever regarding the true nature or origin of these phenomena, from any rationally sane person's perspective. We must conclude that responsible governmental officials refuse to publicly disclose the factual, undeniable, conclusive information confirming that some of these UFO related events and highly developed technologies are extraterrestrial in origin. Likewise, they refuse to disclose any forms of ongoing interaction that is now occurring, including any agreements or treaties that have been signed by national or international governments or organisations, or their knowledge regarding these life forms possessing 'bases' or hidden communities on or inside of the Earth. What authority governs the activities of these covertly institutionalised 'officials' that are evidently operating at a level of autonomy that is obviously beyond the duly recognised status of earthly authority possessed by our highest normally elected and appointed governmental representatives that enables them to arbitrarily, secretly control and to prevent the disclosure of this vitally significant information to the detriment of the public's best overall interests? If the answer is they are being responsible in withholding this information, then exactly what is their rationale and motivation in doing so? The full implications regarding this question will be left unanswered here, yet it is ideally significant for you to reach a few probable possible optional conclusions of your own in this regard.

Earthly powers that we have previously discussed to nauseating lengths here, that are now covertly governing the earthly national and international governments, are currently not-so-secretly rapidly developing these advanced technologies, innovative energy production systems, sophisticated destructive weapons systems, mind programming capabilities, surveillance equipment, and a broad range of other astoundingly incredible technologies that they do not wish to disclose to ordinary earthly people at this time. This secrecy is occurring for a variety of reasons; but primarily to progressively exert ever greater dictatorial, totalitarian style controls upon earthly civilisation that will inevitably lead to serious conflict, not only among earthly citizens, but also other highly technologically advanced extraterrestrial, terrestrial and alien life forms that frequent Earth now and will continue to do so into the future. This is all about the power-crazed interests currently ruling our civilisation vainly attempting to protect and further intensify their insidious dominion over our planet. Ample evidence exists that in some cases these earthly human beings have intentionally allied themselves with alien appearing beings of various types, including 'dark entities' from co-existent dimensions that possess similar power-based negative value systems and motives based primarily upon self-interest that will result in various levels of slavery for all living under their autocratic governmental systems.

It is not relevant for us to discuss the mountainous volumes of excellent verified case material here to validate our position on this issue. Anyone who is unaware of the UFO related evidence to which we refer herein or who freely chooses to question these facts is most welcome to research these issues themselves. Anyone who disputes the existence of so-called UFO phenomena should be prepared to conclusively prove scientifically that these UFO phenomena do not exist, which they would find is significantly more difficult than proving these phenomena do indeed exist now in Earth's skies, land and waters. We will carefully consider how and why these UFO related phenomena remain so secretive and are rarely publicly debated among various governmental agencies; as well as how and why the international mass media seems equally adept at disingenuously ignoring or discounting the huge amount of film and photo evidence as being inconclusive or fabricated when ample conclusive physical proof exists that proves these phenomena are genuine, real and undeniable. Can we imagine why these facts are not yet being made available to the public by the various governments around the world that have recovered intact, functioning spacecraft, that included both deceased and live occupants, thereby conclusively proving these spacecraft and life forms were not of our present earthly civilisation's origin? Government and military officials withholding this information should be encouraged publicly to validate their reasons for this policy. Stephen Greer is among those people strongly encouraging governments to do so.

It is vitally important that we not incorrectly generalise or falsely assume that all of these spacecraft are of alien, extraterrestrial origin, in my opinion. Based upon abundant quality evidence, it is my firm belief that many of the spacecraft we currently see in earth's skies are piloted by humanoids that appear almost identical to earthly Homo sapiens. One does not have to be a genius to comprehend it is a very interesting, thought provoking coincidence that the human appearing occupants of a large proportion of UFOs are virtually indistinguishable from earthly human beings. There may be some differences in intellectual capability, internal physiology and obviously their social and technological knowledge resources would differ from earthly humans in various respects. Therefore, it would not seem too presumptuous to consider there could very likely be a genetic interconnected affinity between some earthly humans and these technologically advanced human-appearing beings that pilot some of these spaceships in Earth's environments and elsewhere within the solar system. We also know that not all UFO occupants are humanoid in appearance and that some have an obviously alien, extraterrestrial appearance and unknown physiology, so we are unable to generalise upon what life forms occupy any UFO until we see and communicate with the occupants to determine these facts. A few earthly governments are now in the process of building their own functional, man-made versions of these spacecraft from the technologies acquired from crashed or disabled spacecraft, as well as communications with alien, extraterrestrial and human appearing pilots of these captured or otherwise 'gifted' UFOs. Earthly human pilots from our national governments' military services are also progressively learning to develop the capability to fly some of those spacecraft that have been 'acquired' from the human appearing so-called extraterrestrials, as well as other aliens; such as the 'greys', the small, slender aliens possessing large heads and dark eyes that we see depicted publicly. It must also be carefully noted that there are efforts being made by these covert earthly sources to artificially 'manufacture' functional appearing replica alien life forms to falsely imitate actual alien life forms. This is being done so that faked alien abduction events and other contrived theatrical staged events by earthly forces can utilise these circumstances for their own purposes, which as we have discovered previously, often are characterised by the lowest of human motives.

These basic facts should encourage humanity to further assess and analyse all the relevant issues to reach our basic conclusions regarding most UFO phenomena. There are far more important priority issues for earthly humans to address and resolve rather than to be overly distracted by publicly debating these extraterrestrial and alien related events. Unfortunately, most earthly governments are presently doing relatively little in the way of substantially improving conditions in earthly society, global environments or with utilising the many available innovative technologies to better human civilisation in urgently needed ways. It is a well-known fact that earthly civilisation is already in possession of hugely advanced innovative technologies that would replace the need for earthly reliance upon the predominant use of fossil fuels and nuclear sources to produce energy, yet these technologies are generally being kept a secret from the public to maintain the status quo for various obvious reasons.

We must acknowledge that Earth has very likely been an interstellar travel destination for a wide variety of extraterrestrial life forms for a very long time. This clearly implies that the ongoing process of extraterrestrial visitation to Earth has endured over millions of years, not merely hundreds of thousands of years. The determinant evidence proves these extraterrestrial visitations have vastly exceeded the period of recently recorded human history of several thousand years, which now represents only a tiny fraction of the complete historical record of advanced human habitation upon planet Earth. This fact is not a subject we wish to address, debate, nor validate here in this discussion, since the evidence is overwhelming that human history on Earth is traceable into the distant past of prehistory when long extinct life forms were then co-habiting with human beings. Specifically, the geological and anthropological evidence illustrates that human beings of an evolved state of physical and technological development that was much akin to what we see today on Earth, co-habited this planet with the ancient hominid and the so-called 'humanoid ancestors' that anthropologists now theorise that we modern Homo sapiens are descended from millions and hundreds of thousands of years ago. To us now it may seem to be an absurdly preposterous notion that modern-type Homo sapiens could have possibly co-existed with ancient hominid ape-like creatures, yet there is ample archaeological evidence that seems to indicate this occurred in spite of it intellectually appearing to be impossible. This implausibility is only due to our society's prevalent thinking processes being constrained and influenced by our religious and educational background in such a way that it precludes such events being considered as reasonable possibilities. Modern earthly Homo sapiens presently co-exist with many types of primates, such as gorillas, chimpanzees, monkeys; so what is the real difference in these modern primates when compared to other ancient hominids? The answer is very little difference exists, aside from some of our preconceptions that are established by religious and scientific theories regarding how modern human beings arrived in our present state of development upon planet Earth. Consider the evolutionary development of modern apes, akin to what was theorised in the movie "Planet of the Apes", where thousands of years of evolution allowed apes like gorillas and chimpanzees to develop basic technologies such as our modern civilisation developed at the turn of the century. Human life forms have been on planet Earth for millions of years already.

For example, how would a religious scholar or evolutionary scientist 'explain away' or disregard the anthropological evidence of a set fossilised modern type well-preserved human footprints being found walking along a muddy stream in geologic conjunction with fossilised sets of various types of dinosaur tracks that were previously thought to be long extinct before humans began to walk the face of the Earth in their present physical form? Or, how could one 'explain away' finding man-made objects such as intricately made metal jewellery, iron nails, cubes and other metallic objects being found by modern miners in geologic strata that pre-dates known human history, such as those apparently man-made objects being extracted from deep within coal deposits? Or, perhaps one has a reasonable explanation for how a fossilised dinosaur skull would be found to have a perfectly round hole in its' head of the same dimensions as would be created by the penetration of a modern 45 calibre bullet, including the identical resulting inner fragmentation of the skull as would occur from a high velocity bullet fired from a modern gun? We could ignore or dismiss such geological evidence as has been found by modern humans, yet the primary reason would be so that we do not have to alter our existing preferred theories that so conveniently explain our system of reality in comprehensible ways. Alternatively, we could perhaps theorise that time travellers left these records for us to be mystified by now, yet that real possibility would obviously present more additional questions than we could reasonably answer here. This is a mysterious possibility if you believe that time is linear. However, if you believe that all realities exist within the 'eternal now', then this is all quite feasible depending upon one's technological and spiritual levels of development and capability.

We can carefully examine some relevant issues in ancient historical and religious texts for clues to human history on this planet. A good place to begin is the original scriptures resulting in the compiled biblical texts where we can clearly find a reasonable perspective on how modern human beings developed on Earth. Some of the so-called modern Homo sapiens on Earth could have very likely quite literally been 'planted' here by what ancient native people believed incorrectly to be 'gods' who assumed the image of human beings. These so-called 'gods' who purportedly 'descended from the heavens' are reported to have assisted the more primitive native earthly inhabitants in various ways, provided them with a set of moral and ethical laws that these 'gods' encouraged them to live by, and in some cases, these so-called 'gods' made in the image of humans reportedly actually procreated hybrid children with earthly humans. These reported events strongly indicate genetic compatibility which is an especially relevant issue for us to consider now when contemplating humanity's possible or actual origins on Earth. There were also historical accounts when these 'gods' purportedly punished mankind for disregarding their moral and ethical laws and acting like heathen savages, such as at the devastation of Sodom and Gomorra. It has also been recorded that these 'gods' sometimes protected their 'chosen people', which could have been their genetic descendents, such as when the Egyptians sought to attack Moses and the Jews as they escaped enslavement in Egypt. Moses then was reported to have received the Ten Commandments which were the early form of laws provided to mankind to govern our developing societies. The Jews were on various occasions fed and protected over their generations of nomadic travel in the Arabian Desert in a most unusual manner, 'from above' and 'from the heavens' that could have been interpreted to be from more highly evolved and technologically developed physical life forms, yet not necessarily directly from what we now would define as being God, the ultimate Cosmic Consciousness or Creative Force that created the universes. For technologically primitive people, the highly advanced aerial exploits of UFOs and their occupants would have very likely appeared to be the acts of 'gods' because they were so incomprehensibly developed beyond those capabilities that were possible within the era in which these relatively unsophisticated Earthlings lived. Additionally, we see revealed in religious scripture, the entire range of normal human emotions being displayed by their 'gods'; through vengeful acts; other loving, protective, kindly, humanitarian acts; and the encouragement of justice, freedom, laws and moral values to live by that served to promote social liberties, security, equitable treatment, and other factors that assisted greatly in the processes of civilising ancient humanity.

In actual fact, the religious scriptures written over thousands of years by humanity makes innumerable references to all manner of apparently highly evolved life forms, some seemingly to be 'gods' or some appearing to act as angels, ghosts, phantoms, or even some unusual reptilian or demonic life forms, depending upon the circumstances. By examining such ancient religious documents that often served as the historical records of their era, it becomes far more likely that many such apparently super-natural, seemingly impossible events recorded there were the results of actions of highly evolved life forms of various types. These highly evolved beings could originate from countless possible sources, including origins beyond the physical, material level of normal existence, which we will address in some detail later here. This well-founded opinion has been developed by studying various religious texts, other documents, modern spiritual events, and modern UFO related events. My own experiences and numerous other information sources necessarily include the opinions and research of many other experienced knowledgeable people.

This opinion is absolutely not intended to be misinterpreted to inaccurately imply that God has not been active in the progress of humanity throughout existence. Nor is it intended to deny that at some inner level that the essence of our creative consciousness is directly related to whatever we consider to be God, which is apparently in some incomprehensible ways; omniscient and immanent within all conscious life forms. By interpreting ancient records of humans interacting with 'the gods', such as the ancient Greeks and many other ancient cultures; we modern humans can begin to perceive how these so-called 'UFO type events' and encounters with various relatively advanced extraterrestrial civilisations could be experienced and interpreted as they have been historically and in religious texts. Additionally, reports of interactions with angels and demons are evidence of diverse life forms existing upon other levels of reality than the strictly physical plane of reality that we earthly humans now inhabit. Even now, some UFO events are of such a highly developed nature technologically, socially and spiritually, that some Earthlings would continue to believe these physically material life forms are like the angels, demons and 'gods' of ancient human history. It is most reasonable to acknowledge there are innumerable possible and probable diversely unrelated sources and origins for all types of inexplicable, anomalous phenomena that have been experienced by earthly human beings over unimaginable lengths of time. The actual objective truth is 'somewhere in the middle', from my perspective.

However, you get the basic concepts of what a few of the less well-documented possibilities and probabilities are regarding the history of human existence.

Another issue to briefly consider is how modern day Homo sapiens became able to so comprehensively dominate our planet. Are we to seriously believe those Neanderthal humanoids and countless other species of humanoids throughout earthly evolutionary history simply became extinct without significant 'assistance' from Homo sapiens? No, humanity is quite proficient and experienced in the art of killing any life form that is in competition with us in such a way that over passing time humans have made extinct untold numbers of species of life on Earth. Additionally, mankind's history of slaughtering and exterminating those other human beings that it identifies as its 'enemies' is characterised by subsequent forms of enslavement, torture and pervasively manifesting suffering wherever it goes. Therefore, as Earthlings begin to enter the Space and Technology Age, we all must become immeasurably more humanely conscientious about our entire scope of attitudes and actions.

There is ample evidence to strongly suggest that present day modern human beings are the result of a lengthy genetic breeding program that involved millions of years to reach this point in evolution for Homo sapiens. We do not wish to address the opinions of those who hold differing beliefs and attitudes about the nature of how human beings came to exist on Earth because everyone has a right to their opinions and perspectives. However, it is important we acknowledge that religious fundamentalists cling strenuously to their literal, word for word interpretations of their various religious texts, in spite of the fact those religious and historical accounts were documented, complied, and edited over thousands of years by thousands of different authors. Existing religious scriptures have been written, then re-written and re-interpreted countless times throughout human history. So, for us to express our opinions here is not a critical attack on anyone else's belief systems or religious convictions. We simply choose to acknowledge how the modern day religious scriptures were recorded throughout past ages of human history, so that we gain a better appreciation of these issues in the wider, more all-inclusive context of modern experience, scientific research and the processes of intellectual scrutiny that we each and all can apply to these complex and emotive issues.

It is not scientifically acceptable or possible to reach reasonable logical conclusions without supplying at least the basic factual information upon which one establishes their perspectives. Unfortunately, in modern society we continually see exactly that scenario in which governmental, scientific, corporate, religious and other so-called 'experts' or 'authority figures' profess to validate their perspectives on the most flimsy, illegitimate, nonsensical, easily refutable, so-called 'evidence' and claim falsely that it is 'fact', when it is actually total fiction/unreality. Alternatively, they often just request or require that we "trust them", or that they have 'confidential sources' that cannot be disclosed that prove their assertions. Well, then OK, since that convenient process makes all this simplistically easier for me and us here too. To do otherwise would require a frustratingly lengthy and the tediously researched documentation of endless series of facts, many being seemingly inconclusive or negated from other people's perspectives anyway. For us to continually digress in attempting to scientifically, philosophically, or in other ways seek to validate the majority of information in our discussion would undoubtedly significantly detract and virtually nullify the comprehensibility of our topical matter in many instances. I will simply mention various types of information that my extensive research and experiences have confirmed as being factual, to the best of my ability to ascertain such knowledge. This imperfect, though functional methodology will enable you to consider the full range of information in a simplified way that engenders the opportunity for you to assess and make decisions for yourself on all of these issues over passing time, utilising your own accumulating experience and research in regard to these diverse, complexly intricate subjects.

These opinions, experiences and facts related here in this book will ideally assist you in the processes of validating a wide variety of your own opinions, experiences and knowledge. Living in a supposedly democratic western society that professes to have legislated the rights of all people to freely express their beliefs and perspectives, according to what they perceive in the world and their communities; we would expect one's opinions and experiences would not be too severely condemned by others who think differently or have had other types of experiences. We know many of the experiences, opinions, and social observations made here will likely be assertively contested or perhaps even savagely attacked in various ways, while other information will not be mentioned at all publicly. None of this matters to me because it is time for all people to begin to express their own perspectives and truth, as they perceive it to be. It seems we all have an obligation to express ourselves based upon the information in our possession, especially in times when powerful global forces seek to institutionalise inter-cultural and internationally conflict and fail to address other issues of massive significance. What really is of importance in the following information is to realise what is contained here is strongly supported by the countless experiences of truthful, wise, perceptive, well-informed, genuinely sincere, good people throughout human history and up to the present time today.

We can now begin to make some possible and probable conclusions regarding the basic facts we have discussed thus far in order to progressively mention some unique concepts that may be somewhat of a surprise to you. You may be thinking, "Please tell me something that I do not already know!" To address that issue, this entire book is all about identifying various things and experiences we already do admit to ourselves, and that we already do know about our lives and our world. This book is a process of assessment by which many of our mutually held inner beliefs, realisations and experiences are now hereby being assertively publicly stated in this written form. Much of what is stated here in clear language and precise literary meaning is distinctly in opposition to the constant streams of blithering drivel, fanatical prattle, meaningless gossip and the redundant pointless rhetoric that we generally so predominantly hear parroted and propagandised in the global societies within which we now live internationally. This process is helpful and necessary to initiate a more self-directed, autonomous, perceptive, and determined effort for each of us to make a positive beneficial impact upon our world, in our own unique ways. It is significant to be aware that what is recorded here originates from extensive access to a broad range of information on the issues affecting humanity and individuals. What is recorded here is often understated and somewhat 'watered down', in spite of any and all appearances to the contrary. If some of what is contained here is upsetting, annoying or even provocative to some, then please be encouraged by the realisation that much more could be said about these issues in a vastly more graphic, powerful and intensely evocative manner. I have conscientiously chosen to formulate this communication of ideas in a relatively subdued, yet clearly stated manner; hoping to somehow inspire a relative few 'thinking people' within our current civilisation to improve our perceptions and conduct in various essential ways. What matters most here are your personal responses to what you comprehend, experience and express through your personal actions in your relationships with others and earthly environments.

Let's consider a few issues in regard to the fact that so-called extraterrestrial civilisations have been visiting Earth and our solar system for millions of years in human historical time. The Milky Way Galaxy in which we now live is already many billions of years old; so highly evolved intelligent life forms possessing amazing, unimaginable technological and spiritually developed capabilities definitely do exist in their teeming multitudes throughout our galaxy and within the surrounding visible universe. Therefore, one of our deductive conclusions is that Earth will continue to experience the regular continuous occurrence of UFO activity and related phenomena. We must ask ourselves, if we were in the role of the extraterrestrials educating more primitive species of intelligent life, then how would we reveal our presence and stimulate inspirational leaps in earthly human awareness regarding the existence of more evolved, developed life forms located elsewhere in the solar system, galaxy and universe? We would likely dazzle Earthlings with magnificent UFO displays; take a few carefully selected human beings for rides in our spaceships; provide encouraging messages of hope for human civilisation's evolutionary development; reveal advanced technologies that could defy commonly accepted earthly principals of physics; display incredible personal powers such as telepathy or the ability to levitate one's self; by mysteriously creating astounding, inexplicable types of geometrically precise, intricate 'crop circles' right under the watchful eyes of researchers and military personnel without being seen or detected, unless the extraterrestrial wished to be seen, and many other such unusual and conclusive examples of ways their overall capabilities distinctly surpass those of normal earthly human beings.

Let's list a number of ascertainable factors that may be of some interest to you, to get a better perspective of what is happening on Earth and within our solar system today that is beyond our normal daily level of earthly awareness. If we consider the evidence that Mars was once a much more hospitable planet possessing more water, we can consider the possibility that Mars may have once been habitable in a similar manner to the Earth. Regardless of that possibility, I have seen numerous satellite photos taken by earthly spacecraft of the Martian surface that clearly reveals the present existence of what appear to be numerous types of intelligently constructed structures; cities made of various shaped dwellings including obvious domes, with connecting roads, bridges, excavations, canals, dams, lakes and rivers containing water, changing polar ice caps and other such items that one would think would be of significant interest to the public. This is definitely not to say that the Martian atmosphere is capable of sustaining life as we know it without adequate protection from the harsh environment, yet this is known by some already. The same can be said of Earth's Moon, based upon the copious volumes of satellite and telescopic photo evidence is equally conclusive that some areas of the Moon are inhabited by highly technologically developed civilised beings of unknown origin, living protected from the environment by domes and other such structures. Ancient and indigenous people from various parts of the world mention in their native stories about a historical time 'before the moon was in the sky'. This implies that in relatively recent earthly history, the Moon was somehow placed into a precise orbit around the Earth by a civilisation with sufficiently powerful technology to synchronise the Moon's orbital location and rotational speed to such an extent that one side of the continuously rotating Moon's surface permanently remains facing away from Earth's view. If you will carefully consider how challenging it would be to rotate an apple around your body, while slowly turning it to keep one side away from your view, then you will better comprehend the obvious mystery of why and how the Moon is so precisely positioned as to rotate on its axis, while rotating around the Earth, yet keep the so-called 'dark side' of the Moon hidden from Earth's viewpoint. Someone forgot to explain that one to us in school or do the mathematical calculations on the odds of that happening naturally in nature, if it is at all possible given the minute fluctuations in orbit over passing time, etc. There is additional evidence that the Moon is not the normal planetary body that it appears to be from Earth's surface. Much evidence exists to indicate that the Moon has many other secrets to reveal over passing time and that much additional information is already well-known among certain circles where this privileged information is being withheld from the public.

There is considerable, virtually irrefutable evidence that various extraterrestrial civilisations have established hidden bases and communities upon Earth. These are mostly located under the surface of the planet; in the oceans, or elsewhere within the Earth. There has also been communication between various earthly governmental representatives and numerous extraterrestrial races in regard to many issues of mutual concern. Unfortunately, we realise that the past history of earthly civilisations in maintaining their part in treaties, agreements and contractual obligations is generally woeful over passing time and changing circumstances. In other words, there is a massive verifiable volume of circumstantial evidence that earthly civilisation has been the willing beneficiary of extensive technology transfers of information and capability from various technologically advanced interstellar travellers in return for their access to Earth for their own reasons. It would be prudent for earthly people to be fully informed of the exact contents of these unpublicised mutual agreements between earthly civilisation and these extraterrestrial and alien races. If no such agreements exist, then who holds sovereignty over planet Earth, in terms of intergalactic law? A strong intergalactic case could be made for the fact that the vast majority of native citizens living on Earth are the rightful, legitimate 'owners' and 'çaretakers' of planet Earth.

There is also strong evidence that Mars may have been involved in horrific wars, perhaps akin to some form of nuclear war that likely resulted in the environmental devastation of that planet a very long time ago. However, physical life forms probably much like or in some cases exactly like earthly humans and the aliens and extra-terrestrials living here on Earth or visiting us regularly now live on Mars. Likewise, Earth has experienced a number of cataclysmic events, both natural and created by humanity and possibly also by extraterrestrial civilisations. Such disastrous calamities have apparently occurred periodically over the course of millions of years that technologically sophisticated humans and extraterrestrial have inhabited Earth, often with devastating results for human civilisations and earthly environments.

Many of these issues are relatively moot points for most of us in our daily lives, since they seem irrelevant to us and there are few reliable ways for ordinary earthly citizens to prove or substantiate any of these previously mentioned seemingly hypothetical circumstances. However, it is a matter of considerable mystery and intense curiosity regarding why the existing covert 'government within all governments' would fail to address this issue publicly when it so drastically undermines their credibility to avoid and ignore such an important matter in the minds of the public, if only upon a subconscious level for most of us. To realise the actual level of covert, hidden cooperation between the earthly ruling 'power elite' and the various technologically superior civilisations of space travelling beings, we only need to consider and thoroughly analyse the recent extremely rapid technological development of our earthly civilisation. In less than one hundred years of recent human history, our human civilisation has progressed from the days of primarily 'horse and wagon' forms of ground transportation to much more sophisticated mechanised transportation systems. Within the last one hundred years, we humans have witnessed the advent of numerous types of land, sea and air travel; the incredibly swift development of advanced computer technologies, a technological explosion of electronic developments, including electric lights, appliances, innovative propulsion and energy production systems; and relatively primitive forms of space travel such as rockets, the space shuttle and the orbiting space station. Now humanity is secretly developing the early versions of electromagnetic, gravitational and other innovative propulsion systems utilised by the far more technologically developed spaceships of those civilisations assisting earthly 'powers that be' to make this astoundingly rapid transition to a much more technologically progressive level of development. There can be little or no doubt that the earthly 'power elite' or 'çabal' are clearly misrepresenting themselves as the authorised 'leaders' of earthly society. Therefore, it is our sincere hope and wish that they will begin to invest more confidence in the so-called 'common people' of Earth so that a more open, honest disclosure of global policy will be made public knowledge because there are obvious indicators that to do otherwise will become unwise and counter-productive for earthly civilisation.

Sadly and unfortunately, there is some very strong evidence that in the not too distant future plans and preparations will be made by the earthly 'power elite' to insidiously replace the current so-called 'global war on terrorism' with a falsely contrived, staged, faked, earthly originated, so-called 'alien conducted' 9/11 type of disastrous event. Such a duplicitous false event would spuriously and pathologically be used to purportedly ally the world's people against a fabricated, dishonestly trumped up, imaginary extraterrestrial, non-existent alien 'enemy'. The direct result of such a preposterous, perfidious charade by the earthly 'powers that be' would further institutionalise an increasingly more corrupt, despotic, evil, costly earthly governmental system that is characterised by deceit, treachery, squandered opportunity, and proven greedy ineptitude. The present earthly 'old world dis-order' governmental system has already repeatedly proven its determination to attempt to justify and implement all manner of horrendously vile acts against humanity and earthly environments and other intelligent life forms throughout recorded human history. To even consider, much less plan to conduct such a pretended malicious event as to fake an 'alien' attack on humanity or act in cooperation with their alien appearing earthly counterparts to conduct such an event and then blame it on non-existent so-called 'alien' invaders is definitely no way to begin to introduce people to the reality that our galaxy and universe supports a plentiful profusion of highly evolved, intelligent, technologically advanced, predominantly peaceful, productive life forms. Many of these extraterrestrial life forms have already mastered the art of interstellar space travel, with some physical beings apparently even accomplishing various forms of inter-dimensional and even evidently some forms of 'time travel'. There is also some valid indication that the earthly 'powers that be' are deriving considerable support in maintaining their present autocratic ruling position in our civilisation through the complicity and concerted efforts of negative or 'demonic' forces within various so-called extraterrestrial races, whose self-interests are currently being well-served by the existing 'old world dis-order' that has established its' authoritarian system of 'hidden government within the governments' on Earth.

Does much of this sound like the raving rants of a deluded madman? That is definitely what I too once thought myself, especially when I initially heard about the confidential covert plans to falsely contrive a 9/11 type event somewhere in the western world by the earthly 'power elite' to further institutionalise and legitimate its totalitarian and plutocratic forms of control over earthly civilisation. However, the 9/11 related series of events in New York City, Washington DC and elsewhere in 2001 proved to be virtually exactly as we were informed would be a possibility several years before the 9/11 related events finally occurred. Initially, we were quite surprised and extremely, exceedingly disappointed to learn about the direct intentional involvement of the massacre of so many innocent civilians by the US government authorities, working in close association under the authorised orders of the highest ranking people in that nation and from Israel. Imagine what sort of demonic people are willing to sentence normal innocent working people to their inevitable deaths to promote totalitarian power, such as in 9/11 and Iraq. Their murderous agenda is to further inappropriately, illegally seek to legitimate and legislate their chosen policies of corruption, greed and international conflict; while knowingly falsely blaming others for their evil deeds in order to declare a global war against people they themselves financed and then labelled as being 'terrorists', just as an excuse to declare the contrived war 'against' the people and life of Earth.

We can all vividly recall the pitiful horrific images of some of those 9/11 victims that decided to leap to their deaths from the World Trade Center, knowingly choosing to splatter their bodies upon the pavement far below, rather than to slowly be roasted alive by the flames threatening to engulf them, or to consider those who were killed as the purportedly indestructible buildings were intentionally detonated. What sorts of vile people would intentionally plan to detonate buildings containing the remaining survivors and their rescuers; knowingly planning to viciously murder them all without warning as the exploding buildings collapsed around them, leaving their last conscious thoughts to be consumed in terror, with the mixed emotions about their loved ones they were leaving behind, as they slowly died in the crushing rubble? Likewise, we can seriously consider the degenerate types of people that intentionally create and sustain the following pathetic, unnecessary debilitating conditions in earthly civilisation: the contrived oil and resource shortages; ongoing series of increasingly suspicious virulent biological disease outbreaks; the rampant intentionally created epidemic of addictive drugs in society; the widespread saturation of the mass media with endless cycles of real and theatrical forms of violence; the institutionalised forms of deliberate international economic instability to make monetary policies that favour the wealthy minority to limit and better control opportunity; the purported so-called health crisis created over decades by feeding the world's population on poor quality and inappropriate toxic foods full of known disease and obesity creating additives while intentionally limiting exercise in society for the masses, especially school children; rampant international corporate psychopathic behaviours against humanity for the corrupt greed and domination by the plutocratic few, the violent and sexual abuse or women and children, and the sickening list goes on and on and on, almost endlessly. Awareness equates with self-empowerment, only if positive, constructive action is sincerely undertaken to remedy these predatory, unacceptable, self-defeatist, cannibalistic attitudes and actions espoused and conducted by the earthly 'power elite' and their ET associates.

One factor that the earthly 'powers that be' seem not to have calculated into their noxious, odious, malevolent plans for humanity is the reality that there are far higher powers of justice, truth and capability than those they simplistically are able to comprehend from their relatively restrictive threshold of 'lower' comprehension and awareness. They have unfortunately willingly and knowingly chosen to ally themselves with exceedingly virulent, materially powerful forces characterised by destruction and predation, seeking to create a climate of fear, hostility and genocide on Earth in the near future. Not a good idea, in my opinion; knowing that other vastly more powerful forces representing true justice, freedom and love are simply allowing these events to unfold in order to hold those responsible accountable in both a physically perceptible manner, as well as upon a higher level of reality that these beings have relatively little awareness of due to their deplorable belief systems and lack of higher perceptive abilities. Also, according to the Mayan calendar, 2007 is the year we Earthlings get to meet the "neighbours". There are many people here who look forward to 'putting out the welcome mat' and will not be convinced that they are the enemy, whereas others will adopt the characteristic fearful war-like attitude to anything they do not know or understand. An ancient prophet said words that ring true today and throughout all time eternally: "by their deeds ye shall know them". We repeat this theme because over passing time actions always speak louder, better and more conclusively than words alone. Evil actions abound in earthly societies now, so to ignore or be easily fooled by rhetoric is an ignorant, irresponsible and self-defeatist attitude and response. Humanity is choosing a better way forward now.

Technological proficiency certainly does not equate on universal or cosmic levels of reality with philosophic or spiritual capability. This earthly and universal material reality system is only a minor visible aspect of total reality. Earth presently functions as a real life 'schoolhouse' to educate and challenge all types of beings existing at various differing levels of evolutionary development within physical reality. This mutual experience is designed to conclusively prove that some obstinate types of life forms really need to learn 'the hard way' over very long periods of finite time, seemingly trapped in repetitive cycles of their own self-created suffering and oppression. Others of us here on Earth and in the physical universes have experienced sufficient arduously revealing experiences of this type and now seek to traverse a more joyous, mutually beneficial, truly loving path through eternal existence. My opinion is that the sooner we begin to intentionally travel the wiser, learned, joyful, giving, grateful, loving path through eternal existence, including our sojourn through physical levels of reality; the better. Life has established its own immutable possible sequences of events, so we simply participate according to our roles in this process and 'let the chips fall where they may'. Life (and God, the Creator of the Universes) has Its' own plans for each and all of us to learn our lessons within this system of earthly and eternally infinite reality, so who are we to complain about our incredibly enriching journey of discovery? There is much more we could address in regard to issues related to the visitation and habitation of Earth by numerous different technologically evolved terrestrial, extraterrestrial and inter-dimensional travellers. We will address some of these more complex issues as we develop additional common understanding about some interesting, perplexing ideas that will help us to reach our basic conclusions. What we will say is the factors we Earthlings, whether human or alien in appearance, must confront and resolve are universally faced by all intelligent, conscious, free-thinking, perceptive life forms.

Now we turn our attention to far more extraordinary matters of importance, so we can better comprehend our present position in this physical level of reality. We will need to include a few explanations about the manner in which various aspects of cosmic reality are structured. These explanations will be overly simplified to keep the descriptions as basic and brief as is reasonably possible.

Most people interested enough to read this book and finally manage to reach this chapter are likely to already be familiar with the concept that there are numerous levels or 'planes' of existence that compose in the overall cosmic reality system. We are using the term 'plane' as being defined here to mean an actual 'location' or 'reality system' that is co-existent with a multitude of other types of simultaneously co-existent reality systems. In some ways, there are some interconnected, interdependent physical, energetic and other relationships existing between these different 'planes' or systems of reality. However, each plane of existence also has aspects that make them appear from an 'internal perspective' to be autonomous, independently existent, cohesive types of reality systems, from the perspective of conscious life forms living within those 'planes' or 'reality systems'. To better visualise this challenging concept intellectually, we comprehend that upon Earth we live within the Physical Plane of existence and our normal physical senses to do not ordinarily allow or enable us to perceive beyond or outside of this Physical Plane of existence. We on Earth are normally unable to directly perceive with our normal physical senses (not including to watch television images of these events) what is happening in other locations around our planet, such as in other communities or other countries, yet those daily activities elsewhere on Earth are quite real for the participants living in those locations.

It seems to earthly observers who are applying only their physical perceptions that the Physical Plane contains all life in the universe, yet this only appears to be the case because our physical senses of perception are limited and unable to physically perceive other 'dimensions', or other 'levels or planes' of existence, or other 'systems of reality' that co-exist at various other vibrational frequencies of reality. Likewise, other 'levels' or 'planes' of reality may ordinarily not be aware of us or interact with us upon the physical plane. However, we do already know that under various circumstances there are interactions occurring between various planes of existence or differing reality systems and that will be addressed in some detail later. What is significant to understand here is that there are incalculable individualised 'reality systems' existing within the comprehensive totality of cosmic reality, which is infinite from a perspective of human consciousness. Each of these systems of reality are composed of vast expanses containing incredibly diverse manifestations of aware consciousness that interact to create systems of cosmic reality that far exceed our current relatively limited intellectual comprehension, from our earthly physical perspective of life.

Beginning from our current earthly material perspective upon the Physical Plane of gross matter, there are a great many additional other 'planes' or 'reality systems' that co-exist simultaneously with the physical plane of existence. Going 'upwards' in the refinement of energetic and spiritual nature; the next 'higher' plane is the Astral Plane. It is an incredibly vast, seemingly infinite series of planes, sub-planes and regions within regions that seem to the 'astral plane' inhabitants who reside there to compose the entirety of infinite eternal existence; composing 'heaven and hell' and all types of innumerable locations that are spoken about in most religious texts. Jesus reported to have said words to the effect, "there are many rooms in God's mansion". As this applies to the Astral Plane of existence, this is a massive understatement beyond all comprehension, because apparently the Astral Plane is significantly more expansive and populous with forms of conscious life than the Physical Plane's universal reality systems. Next, is the Causal or Etheric Plane; followed by the Mental Plane, and these are also reported to be equally vast and seemingly infinite, when compared with the apparent physical universes, as they seem to us here on Earth.

If the subject of what conscious life forms exist upon the various Planes of existence sincerely interests you, then be highly encouraged to read a most informative book titled "The Tiger's Fang", which was authored by Paul Twitchell, the modern day founder of Eckankar. This amazingly book vividly describes a lengthy journey through the various planes of reality and identities some of the Divinely conscious Beings that are located there. Those Divine Beings 'speak' their truths to Paul and the ECK Master that served as his 'guide' into these exotic reality systems. This book and many others of exceptional quality and clarity can be ordered from: www.eckankar.org . As you will be aware, there are NO other books recommended here. This uniquely informative inspirational book from this exceptional organisation, "Eckankar, the Religion of the Light and Sound"; is well-worth obtaining, if you are genuinely sincere in learning about the actual nature of comprehensive cosmic reality and seek to experience these amazing realities for yourself by direct personal ongoing experiences. I have been a member of Eckankar for about 20 years and will never leave this 'spiritual path' because it is the most important aspect of my life. This 'one of a kind' spiritual path 'connects' one with the ECK or Holy Spirit, which is synonymous with Divine levels of consciousness; in a progressive manner that is specifically designed for one's unique character and state of being. This is certainly the most relevant and important paragraph contained in this lengthy book. Please note that none of my countless uplifting transformative personal experiences that have occurred since becoming an 'Eckist' are described here for various reasons.

Each of us experience life and access information in unique ways, with some of it being 'watered down' or 'adjusted' in various ways to make it understandable and relevant to us individually (and collectively). Therefore, how one person experiences or describes these 'higher' planes of reality is likely to be different to someone else's experience. Each point of view is equally valid and therefore accepted as such, just as we recognise is the situation in earthly material levels of reality as well. If one lives in plush luxury within a European mansion as the owner or a servant, then one's description of Earth is a far different 'system of reality' than if one seeks to survive in the deserts of Ethiopia while being hunted by opposing tribes, or living within a garbage dump in one of India's larger cities, or working in an Australian coal mine. The point is various reality systems are co-existent with one another and can appear different to various perspectives, depending upon the observer's system of reality, qualities of character and perceptions.

'Above', beyond and interpenetrating all lower Planes mentioned previously, the Soul Plane, or fifth dimension exists. Below the level of the Soul Plane, time and space seem to be linear in the sense there appears to be a definitive past, a future and primarily an eternally existing, ever progressing 'present moment' or 'now' in which we are consciously aware. At the level of the Soul Plane, time and space cease to function as human consciousness comprehends these aspects of life. One of the most important fundamental challenging factors to intellectually realise in our discussion is that Soul is able to simultaneously exist in the eternal 'now' in a seemingly infinite number of 'places' that would to an earthly observer would appear to be at 'the same time', in spite of being in differing locations and across limitless historical periods in Physical Plane existence. Soul's nature of existence and capabilities are exceedingly difficult for one's human consciousness to understand or visualise. It something one ideally must experience to 'know', even upon a minimal level of perceptive awareness. However, we must begin by attempting to become cognisant regarding how and why this process of existence functions at higher levels of reality. We wonder how God's awareness can simultaneously be in all places; within all historical times, and immanent and omnipotent throughout all existent levels of infinite reality. These sublimely significant factors reveal the intellectually incomprehensible manner that God's super-conscious levels of awareness, creativity and manifestation vastly surpass ordinary human understanding. We will now further continue this line of thought regarding 'higher systems of reality', as our discussion progresses.

Explaining the nature and what happens within each of these Planes of existence and their vast and seemingly unlimited sub-planes is not particularly relevant to our topical matter because we are primarily outlining this information in summary form. It would be foolish to attempt to address it in an all-encompassing manner, since that approach would be quite unsuccessful and seemingly speculative and unable to be confirmed here considering the extensive scope of infinite existence. It is important to conceptualise that each of these 'lower' Planes 'below' the Soul Plane are seemingly infinite to the inhabitants located there, just as the physical universe appears limitless to earthly humans, even through the Hubble Telescope. The conscious life forms existing within those various Planes would all appear to have physical bodies similar to those we possess on Earth in many ways. Their bodies would not be as physically 'dense' as ours', yet they would appear to be every bit as 'solid' and 'real' as our physical bodies do to us on Earth. Most of the living conditions in these other Planes or regions of existence tend to be characterised by circumstances that are relatively enjoyable in most cases, with most residents being less prone to our predominate earthly levels of stress, disease and environmental discomfort, for the most part. Of course there are numerous exceptions to this simplistic over-generalisation. For those people and life forms that require strenuous, intensive education, then these types of locations do exist within these Planes and their sub-planes, just as they certainly do upon Earth.

Please note that on Earth, we can see all types of individuals, lifestyles, social and economic status and various environmental locations all co-existing within relatively close proximity to one another. We can easily see poverty of spirit and devolved character within some of the monetarily wealthiest of Earth's people, just as we can often see materialistic forms of excessive poverty located within short physical distances of the greatest earthly monetary affluence and conspicuous opulence. In eternal reality, the extremes of life's circumstances can often co-exist 'closely' with one another, yet generally in the 'lower' Planes of existence such as the Physical, Astral, Causal and Mental Planes one progressively earns the right to 'graduate' from one 'lower' system of reality into continually 'higher' or better seeming states of existence based upon one's qualities, energetic harmonic resonance, and spiritual states of being. An important spiritual principle is that 'heaven must be re-won every day', which indicates that spiritual progression or the potential for regression or degeneration is a distinct possibility for life forms existing within eternally infinite systems of reality; although once Soul consciousness becomes well-established within the Soul Plane and 'above', then (apparently) this is far less likely to occur.

The most important aspect of our entire discussion in this book is focused within the next fundamental explanation, which many of us will already understand very well. We each and all are an eternally aware, evolving, unfolding Soul; an individualised aspect of God Essence. You are Soul. I am Soul. We are Soul. God is Soul upon an unimaginably higher level of ultimate reality that is incomprehensible to us now. On a much deeper and more inclusive level, as Soul, we each are unified as evolving individualistic aspects of one ubiquitous, immanent, united, infinite, eternal, immortal, super-conscious reality that we know as being God, or the sum total of all existence. By God, I definitely do not mean some personified, humanistic, so-called 'deity' that judges us for all our 'sins' and if we are found guilty, then sentences us for all eternity to suffer in Hell or blissfully go to Heaven, if we are absolved of our 'sins' before death of the physical body. That is the 'god' of the religionists and we leave them to 'believe in' and experience their versions of God, as they so choose or are able.

Presently all of us here on Earth and in these Planes mentioned here are individualised, evolving Soul. We do not possess 'a Soul'; rather we are Soul; a tiny spark of evolving, self-aware, eternally immortal, conscious God energy and an aspect of that Soul is now having a physical experience here on Earth. As Soul, you 'inhabit' a physical body in what your human consciousness would perceive as a 'lifetime'; whereas Soul actually exists permanently throughout timeless eternity. Obviously some Souls are much further along the evolutionary spiritual path by the incalculable wise choices they have made in countless physical incarnations and other lives on various planes of existence. Eternal life is an individual journey of discovery whereby the progressive unfoldment of Soul develops into increasingly higher levels of vibrational harmony and affinity with God Energy, the Holy Spirit, the ECK, or Cosmic Consciousness. Whatever name you care to use to describe the omnipotent, omniscient energetic God Consciousness that pervades and sustains the entire cosmic system of reality; it is the all-pervading, loving super-consciousness that created and sustains all life in all the cosmic levels of total reality. As Soul, an infinitesimal self-aware part of God's omniscient immanent eternal consciousness; the 'real you', Soul, is far more than your normal human intellectual mind could ever possibly fully comprehend. The essential concept to attempt to comprehend and visualise is that as Soul; you always exist upon the Soul Plane, which supersedes, pervades and is immanent (conscious within) throughout all of the 'lower' planes of existence. Soul is 'above and beyond' all time and space, as we now intellectually perceive it upon these 'lower planes' of temporal, sequential existence. The idea that the 'real you', Soul exists both 'within' and 'outside and beyond' time and space, as we know them to exist on the Physical Plane, is initially quite a challenging concept to understand, but that's OK. This is the way eternal, infinite life is supposed to be for all of us; something of an endlessly mysterious ongoing journey of discovery; forever expanding our levels of awareness and exponentially developing our capabilities. In this eternally expansive process, each and all Souls are learning to become Co-Workers with God, or co-creators of reality.

By considering the nature of Soul in meditation, reflection and contemplation; you will develop higher qualities of perception, imagination and visualisation that will gradually and imperceptibly augment, heighten, stimulate, expand, intensify, and advance your levels of awareness regarding the inexpressible aspects that characterise Soul. This progressive, evolutionary realisation process will serve to help clarify the inexplicable, indescribable, perpetual, inclusive, superlative essence of Soul so that your ordinary conscious intellect will acquire an inkling of the immensely capable qualities possessed and exemplified by the comprehensive nature of immortal Soul, the perceptive super-consciousness which is actually 'you'.

We do not wish to begin to play with semantics or intellectualise upon incorrectly perceiving ourselves to be far more evolved or divine in our present manifested human nature than is actually the situation for most of us here and now. Each of us does NOT 'become one with God', rather we have the opportunity to become increasingly aware of being an integral aspect of the ECK or Holy Spirit, which is the super-conscious infinite 'energy' that composes all eternal existence. We, as humans using our normal rational logical thought's abilities, are unable to intellectually fully comprehend systems of reality that far exceed the mental processes and boundaries of the entire scope of our physical experience, which vastly surpass anything and everything that we can even begin to visualise regarding the unimaginable, indescribable, limitless aspects of eternal infinite existence. I will nevertheless attempt to describe various aspects of this system of reality, as well as humanly possible for me at this time in my 'unfoldment', to make some reasonable, common sense, intellectual deductions to satisfy one's logical mind. Therefore, you are highly encouraged to engage your 'higher mind' to utilise aspects of your intuitive mind and higher perceptions that will serve you well in better understanding the key concepts that follow. Now you will truly begin to vividly discover what this inner visualisation and integration process regarding enhancing your own internal levels of awareness is really ultimately intended to be applied toward accomplishing; the integration of your basic human levels of 'ego-mind' with Soul, the 'real you'.

Upon the Soul Plane, reality begins to completely supersede our logical common sense analysis by the human levels of mind and perception. Suffice to say that the normal immutable inflexible laws of the lower levels of reality or those 'lower' Planes simply do not apply in various ways upon the Soul Plane and 'above' that Plane. As one travels 'upwards' from the Soul Plane into ever-increasingly higher and finer rates of harmonious vibrational frequency into the energetic realms of divine reality, these higher levels of reality are significantly more infused and characterised by diverse manifestations of God's Conscious Energy.

Once one is 'located' upon the Soul Plane, one has 'dropped' their 'lower energetic bodies'; the physical body, the astral body, the 'etheric' or causal body and the mental body. It is difficult, yet necessary to understand logically, that as Soul, one always exists upon the Soul Plane because that Soul level is the original causative basis of conscious immortal reality for each one of us. Soul is the form of eternal conscious awareness that inhabits all the various physical forms that we animate upon all the 'lower' levels of reality, including the temporal Physical Plane of existence. Soul is the foremost reality that exists initially and all other 'lower' systems of reality are able to manifest from and as a result of that ultimate, fundamental basic source of divinely conscious reality. While physical bodies are born and die sequentially throughout various locations in time and space upon these 'lower' planes of universal and cosmic existence; Soul is actually immortal and existing continuously both within and beyond all forms of time and space as we understand them, evolving throughout this process. The really difficult aspect to comprehend is how Soul evolves progressively if it exists in a timeless, eternal reality system, and that is one of the intellectual mysteries we refer to here. Soul appears or would be 'seen' on the Soul Plane as being a brilliantly radiant energetic light of indescribable incandescent beautiful luminosity. The immortal evolving spark of God Energy exists within and manifests through this energetic form that is defined here as Soul. This is another key concept to attempt to comprehend; that Soul is both the immortal observer and simultaneously the temporal evolving participant within eternally progressing systems of reality. What is also quite relevant for us to attempt to visualise here is that Soul does not at all need to obey the physical, astral, etheric, or mental laws of existence that govern these 'lower' Planes of existence.

The key concept we absolutely must try to realise is that all of these Planes actually co-exist simultaneously. We must try to comprehend that all of these apparently 'lower' planes 'below' the Soul Plane all co-exist with one another at various frequencies of reality. Likewise, the various planes that exist 'above' the Soul Plane also are simultaneously co-existent on eternal, infinite levels of reality, pervaded by Cosmic Divine Consciousness, in Its' multitudinous forms.

We are attempting to describe in a very limited basic manner the full scope of cosmic reality systems, yet all you need to accept is whatever you can visualise from these explanations at the time they are being provided here. Again, if you do not fully understand some of these issues intellectually, which is quite reasonable (unless you are already at or well-beyond this level of experience in your own spiritual evolutionary development), then please be encouraged to read and re-read them until they are somewhat comfortable and familiar within your normal human consciousness.

Then later, over passing time, Soul will become directly involved within your own consciousness to make available to you comprehensible additional perceptions, images, feelings and experiences that will clarify matters significantly in unique ways that are ideal for your own personal evolutionary development. Genuinely inwardly 'ask' God/Creator/Life for illumination within the deepest private recesses of your loving, peaceful, grateful consciousness, while being patiently receptive to the 'answers' and you will certainly experience amazing undeniable experiences that reveal these mysteries, according to your developing levels of spiritual progression.

Regarding the manner in which the various levels of reality co-exist and are able to function simultaneously and also seemingly in a sequential linear fashion; please allow me to make the following explanation. An overly simplistic analogy is that just as different radio stations are all able to co-exist independently upon a given radio band frequency, such as an AM or FM channel, there are many coexistent frequencies manifesting themselves within various systems of reality. Likewise, another Plane of existence would be analogous to a television band frequency where many different 'channels' or reality systems would exist simultaneously within that 'band', level, or plane of existence in a manner that would enable each of them to be independent of one another. Likewise, we all are well-aware that different physical locations exist within our local area, the nation in which we live, upon Earth, upon other planets, and within differing solar systems, galaxies, and so forth. There are also many differing 'frequencies' within the physical level or 'plane' of reality upon which aware forms of conscious life exists. This is also true within the other 'lower' planes of reality, such as the Astral, Causal and Mental Planes.

We humans on the physical plane only 'see' within a relatively small width of the entire spectrum of known types of energy, which we define as being 'visible light'. We must consider that other life forms existing in other frequencies of physical reality could perceive reality through various other physical senses, perhaps utilising infrared or acoustical sense perceptions, somewhat analogous to the ultra-sonic sensory perceptions of dolphins, whales and bats on Earth. Likewise, there is every reasonable expectation that other life forms existing elsewhere in the physical universes could evolve and thrive in environmental conditions enormously different than those we experience upon Earth now. Just as physically we human beings are primarily a carbon-based life form living upon an oxygen, hydrogen, nitrogen and carbon-dioxide respiration system; other conscious life forms could be primarily composed of silicon, crystal, or metal based elements, as unlikely or impossible as that may seem to us now. Equally probable is that other life forms upon the physical plane of existence would be able to survive and evolve in vastly hotter or colder temperatures, with much higher or lower atmospheric pressures, evolving according to the prevalent environmental conditions available to them on their respective planetary systems. Such an example within our solar system would be the planet Venus, or we could mention various other such planets; where life as we know it seems impossible to exist, so far as our powers of perception, scientific misunderstandings and intellectual logic indicate as being possible. This limited earthly attitude does NOT mean that various forms of highly intelligent, conscious life do not exist on Venus, or Jupiter, or elsewhere within our solar system right now. It simply means that we Earthlings are now unable to detect or comprehend their forms of life according to our current five physical senses.

  A final analogy regarding this situation is that because one is unable to receive a radio frequency signal where a particular radio station or television channel is transmitting; either because the receiver is too far away or because one does not have the right equipment to receive the transmission signals, does not negate the fact that such a signal could or indeed does exist. The fact that human civilisation's governmental and religious leaders fail to recognise or publicly acknowledge the existence, or the 'signal', being 'sent' or existing from countless other forms of earthly intelligent life as well as from elsewhere within our solar system and physical universe should not be at all surprising when we consider their historical record. Humanity's current so-called 'leaders' simply prefer to pretend to be 'listening' for extraterrestrial signals from other intelligent life forms, when in fact our 'radio' receivers are intentionally 'turned off' and we have our 'heads down in the sand' to prevent Earth's people from comprehensively observing and acknowledging the self-evident facts. The reality is that multiple extraterrestrial species of highly technological (mostly) humanoid type life forms and a vast array of multidimensional conscious life forms are currently visiting Earth and many have hidden communities or 'bases' located here and elsewhere within our solar system, galaxy and universe.

Some humans are currently unable to detect, or more accurately, unwilling to publicly and scientifically acknowledge and appreciate the obvious levels of intelligence existing within earthly species such as whales, elephants, primates or even domesticated animals, including our pets. Therefore, it is little wonder that we humans are now unwilling to seriously consider or publicly admit the definitive absolute proven fact that conscious life in the physical and cosmic universe manifests itself in a countless variety of forms.

What follows is challenging to intellectually understand because some of these ideas are contradictory to a significant proportion of how most humans normally visualise the nature of earthly physical reality. We have already mentioned the need to realise that cosmic levels of reality supersede some aspects of basic physical reality. This situation does not in any way negate earthly physical experience; rather it is primarily a more all-inclusive comprehension of how the various Planes or levels of overall reality function in mutual harmony with one another, while retaining their individual defining characteristics that are perceived as being the natural physical laws of each reality system. Higher consciousness is the one 'vehicle' that is able to freely and almost instantaneously 'travel' or shift/alter/adjust one's state of conscious awareness among these various Planes of reality. If Soul has already developed the conscious capability and spiritual right to do so, then some aspects of our normal human individual consciousness can become more aware and integrated with Soul levels of conscious perception and abilities.

Soul, one's 'higher, true, immortal self' containing the inner immortal evolving divine spark of God Consciousness within, inhabits multidimensional bodies that co-exist simultaneously upon all planes or levels of reality. Time and space certainly exist on these 'lower' Planes; yet upon the Soul Plane and 'above and beyond' in the 'higher' planes beyond the Soul Plane, time and space do not exist in the same manner as we perceive them to be in our present material physical reality.

First, it is necessary to do your best to visualise that Soul is able to somehow ubiquitously, immanently, consciously inhabit countless physical life forms that are scattered throughout time and space, as we know them to be. This is a huge reality to truly even begin to comprehend, intellectually and intuitively; through Soul's assistance. Soul consciousness is the actual originator of all conscious existence. It is the originator and source of your inner feeling and perception of your seemingly unchanging sense of 'self'. You can be helped to realise this fact when you carefully and thoroughly reflect upon all of the changes made during your life. Become more enlightened by realising the truth that throughout all manner of life dramas, personality adjustments, changes in location and circumstances; your basic sense of 'self' generally remains intact and relatively seeming 'unchanged'. You will notice fluctuating cycles of personal and spiritual improvement, character growth and upliftment, yet always the sense of 'self' remains consistent in spite of external circumstances. Soul houses the divine spark of God Consciousness existing exceedingly well-hidden, deep within numerous 'layers' of energetic spiritual 'substance' and deep within you, as Soul. Your true identity is actually that of Soul.

However, once in the human body or any other physical appearing body upon any of the 'lower' planes of existence below the Soul Plane, such as in an astral body, or an etheric body, or a mental plane physical appearing bodily life form, then inevitably you associate the inner conscious 'self' with that particular temporal 'vehicle' or body. Soul is the energetic conscious life force that sustains one's physical body and other various bodily forms containing our consciousness on the various other planes of existence below the Soul Plane. The energy that sustains us on every plane of existence, both as Soul and as a physical body, is called the Holy Spirit, Life Energy, Prana, or simply the ECK. This vital energy flows outwards into the cosmic universal reality systems from the creative cosmic consciousness we call God, the ultimate Creator of all Life, ever travelling further throughout all systems of cosmic reality until it reaches the lowest levels of the Physical Planes to be progressively received by all forms of consciousness within every level existence. This divine all-pervasive energy then cycles back to God: the infinite Source of all Creation; the ultimate self-perpetuating, self-aware, immortal, omnipotent, omnipresent Super-Consciousness.

So, how do we truly define what God actually is? Well, that is indeed the ultimate unanswerable rhetorical question here, which we are gradually attempting to answer to a modest extent from a human perspective in various ways. Regardless of how evolved, capable or spiritually aware a certain conscious life form may become, if that conscious being is not itself the immortal Source of all energy, love, consciousness and creative manifestation in the infinite cosmic universes; then that entity, regardless of how super-conscious, creative, divine or loving it may be; is NOT actually God Itself. However, all life is divinely created and has the potential to eventually manifest progressively greater levels and qualities of God Consciousness through its various physical and higher Plane incarnated bodies and eternally existing Soul.

Second, we must realise that all of these Planes co-exist simultaneously as independent, yet united, interrelated, differing aspects of the total comprehensive cosmic reality system. We each do possess individualised aspects of our 'comprehensive self', Soul, that exist independently within unimaginable numbers of locations within space and time, with each 'self' existing within each of those uniquely unfolding, temporal, evolving, continuously developing systems of reality. From the perspective of Soul, all of the 'lower plane' physical incarnations within the infinitely numerous bodies occur 'outside or beyond' time as we in earthly material reality understand time and space to be. This true nature of ultimate Reality is definitely not something your normal physical conscious mind is comfortable or familiar with considering, much less visualising consciously to any significant degree. However, to begin to consider the nature or 'state of being' of 'higher' life forms that vastly surpass and supersede human material levels of understanding; we need to get a better idea about these 'higher' levels of reality so we can begin to truly comprehend the actual ways that true reality functions, beyond our nominal, limited, ordinary physical, mental and emotional processes.

Third, it is essential over passing time for one to further progressively expand, advance, develop, successively transcend and supersede one's current realisations that all levels of reality co-exist simultaneously within the systems of ultimate reality existing beyond time and space as we now know them to be. This continual progressive process of 'opening' ever greater, more inclusive 'doorways' into increasingly enhanced levels of Soul's perception and comprehension, does result in some definitive improvements in one's human intellectual understanding.

Upon the level of Soul, all reality exists in the eternal 'now' state of being. What we experience as a seemingly endless series of progressive, sequential 'now's' from the perspective of Soul is one continuous, co-existing 'now'. This concept is extremely challenging, if not actually impossible, to fully comprehend from an earthly perspective. This is true only while using our normal conscious mind and finite, logic based, mental facilities that are extensively constrained by our traditional, linear types of understanding regarding physical laws of time and space as we now experience them on Earth. The eternally functional 'now' co-exists simultaneously upon all Planes of existence, from the perspective of Soul, the real 'you'. This ongoing realisation over passing time will 'unfold' in a manner that enables subsequently new realisations and unimaginable possibilities to progressively occur.

Fourth, the illuminating, encouraging fact is that Soul has direct unlimited inner observational access to consciously perceive the individual status of ALL of your innumerable physical incarnations upon ALL planes of existence, and throughout all historical locations. This miraculous, mind-boggling concept is worthy of your greatest possible consideration, reflection, meditation and contemplation. This astoundingly incredible mysterious truth reveals that 'you', as Soul, are a vastly larger, more complex, omnipotent, omniscient, immanent entity than human awareness can possibly comprehend under normal mental conditions. Soul has unfettered comprehensive introspection and astute powers of sagacious, insightful observation within the innermost levels of consciousness that we humans possess, as well as vastly 'higher' systems of reality than we understand now.

This clearly implies that Soul is far more accurately aware of the entire range of our deepest, innermost thoughts, feelings, aspirations, weaknesses, abilities, fears, dislikes, dreams, secrets, and desires; also including every other relatively superficial or unconscious/subconscious aspect of our overall consciousness that one could experience. This profound extensive knowledge is part of the reason why Soul and Creator are able to organise so many divinely synchronous and often unexpected experiences that address and resolve key issues in our lives. In this manner we are better able to make progressive improvements and changes in our lives, often from life's more challenging or upsetting circumstances. Soul is not constrained by time and location, nor temporal human social, cultural or personality characteristics, so Soul is able to simultaneously perceive the entire scope of our countless lives from within the diverse range of individualised consciousnesses that are possessed by the multitudes of 'personalities' or tendencies/proclivities that we internally perceive as being our 'own' evolving character. Our personality and overall character that we believe ourselves to be is often much different than who others would see us as being from their various perspectives, depending upon our roles in their lives and vice versa. Soul perceives 'it all' quite clearly from its eternally vigilant, much 'larger', more inclusive perspective; regardless of how oblivious or relatively more aware we are in our present physical incarnate lives at our particular level of evolutionary conscious existence within the historical time and location where we 'now' exist.

Through our innumerable incarnated existences in a diverse set of variant reality systems and contrasting life circumstances; Soul assists each of us to become more aware on a physically conscious level of the existence of higher intrinsic values and spiritual principles. This process occurs for us, as individuals and collectively as humans, by actually living life in ways that necessitate that we experience the direct and indirect results of our combined attitudes and behaviours. There are other influences Soul has upon each of us and among these are to encourage the realisations within our human levels of consciousness regarding our more divine, eternally aware states of being. Initially, let's examine how we as individuals can better familiarise ourselves upon ordinary human conscious levels, with Soul, so that we learn to benefit from a vastly closer, more intimate, communicative inner relationship with Soul. The many advantages and blessings of harmonising and integrating one's earthly conscious mind with Soul, one's true eternal omniscient self, are beyond description or comprehension. We mention this subject again because to fully appreciate and perceive the probable nature of the highly evolved life forms that we will discuss in the near future, it is most helpful to enable Soul's awareness to illuminate one's mind with such images and realisations, in the way most meaningful to you individually at this (ongoing) 'now moment' in your spiritual progression.

Spiritual enlightenment (Self/Soul Realisation), or God Realisation, or even more all-inclusive 'higher' levels of Being can be a somewhat misleading verbal description for someone who has not experienced such a stupendously uplifting event(s) in their own lives. I have NOT personally consciously experienced these progressive 'zeniths' of illumination; rather only become vitally aware that such states of being are possible to ultimately achieve for those Beings manifesting the necessary spiritual qualities. What most people would understand to be an 'enlightenment' experience is very likely to somehow involve the conscious realisation of one's own higher 'true self', or Soul Realisation. The inner mystical enlightenment experience of Soul Realisation is usually mistaken by human beings as an experience of God Realisation or God Consciousness, due to the unimaginable intensity of the indescribable experience. God Realisation is a distinctly higher level enlightenment experience which relatively few earthly humans have experienced. Soul Realisation or 'Self' Realisation is usually reported to be a relatively fleeting super-conscious, spiritual enlightenment experience that one never forgets, yet is generally unable to consciously repeat at will, unless the individual is spiritually evolved to an extremely high level. Few such people would admit to it publicly, even if they were divinely harmonised to that degree. Just for the record, I most definitely am NOT evolved to such a 'higher' level at this particular time in my present earthly life. I often struggle to acknowledge and express the better aspects of my higher spiritual and human attributes, so I have no false illusions in this regard. I simply do my best at all times in all of life's varied and unpredictable circumstances and generally consciously consent to 'Thy (God's) Will Be Done'. In our earthly lives, this preliminary aspiration for Soul Realisation is what really matters to us here and now. This is why we focus upon being the best we can be now, where our consciousness exists, in the progressing present 'now' moment(s).

Soul or Self Realisation or Soul Enlightenment precedes God Realisation in evolutionary terms by a considerable amount of spiritual development. We will not discuss God Realisation much since relatively few humans have experienced this fantastically rare, indescribably momentous enlightenment experience. Apparently throughout eternal existence there have and do exist an incalculable number of god Conscious Beings within this and other reality systems. The honest truth is I do NOT really know that much about God Realisation currently, from my experiences or perspective. For most of us to aspire to Soul Realisation is the greatest dream and hope in the next stage in our eternal evolutionary journey. Anyone claiming to have experienced God Realisation should be evaluated with the utmost perceptive clarity to determine whether or not their overall character manifests that reality in a self-evident manner, which in the vast majority of cases it will definitely not. There are apparently a rare few people now living upon on Earth at this time who have likely attained that exalted state of spiritual unfoldment. The one fact these truly enlightened people have repeatedly confirmed is that "God must be re-won every day". In other words, regardless of the lofty spiritual heights attained in one's spiritual unfoldment processes, one must always seek to remain exclusively focused being in harmony with and manifesting these divinely superlative qualities of Soul and God Consciousness to maintain and continue to progress. In spiritual terms, one is either progressing or regressing and the further one progresses, apparently the greater are the realisations, challenges and necessity to remain in balanced resonant coherence with these higher aspects of Soul and God Consciousness. This entire issue is not really a focal portion of our subject matter because it is so far beyond where most of us now are in our progressive spiritual development. It does quite seem relevant and necessary to at least mention these factual qualities and capabilities as being attainable for us, at some future point in our spiritual development process. We can conclude this topic by observing that all of the prophets and saviours of humanity's past have already pointed 'the way' for us to follow. To repeat an earlier comment, Jesus Christ once reportedly said words to the effect that, "As I am, so too you can become." The few true modern Prophets have also provided spiritual leadership by example, so that we are well-aware of the possibilities available to us to follow their eternal path. In our quest here, we generally do not seek earthly gurus or other types of religious leaders to inform us of what we can best experience inside of our own comprehensive character. I believe Jesus also said words to the effect, 'Seek first within one's self to find the kingdom of God'; so this is what we intend to do, while examining every aspect of our lives and character.

We ideally encourage an aware, receptive, eager, patient, persistent, relaxed, expectant, humble, refined, purified, peaceful, joyous frame of mind; with a truly loving, grateful, expectant, open heart and 'being' that has surrendered itself to God's Grace in preparing ourselves for Soul Realisation within our present earthly lifetime. Let's again summarise a few key concepts to better visualise the nature of this mysterious inner relationship where our temporal human mind recognises various divine qualities possessed by Soul and desires that they be harmoniously integrated into one's earthly life in numerous ways for the benefit of all. We begin by acknowledging that it is impossible to intellectually discern how Soul can be aware within us now, experiencing some form of sequential time and location in space upon the 'lower' Planes, as well as Soul being 'above and beyond' time and space, as humans understand these concepts of the lower Planes of existence. As Soul, the real 'you' exists 'outside and beyond' concepts of time and space as we experience them on Earth and in the other 'lower' Planes of reality. The key initial concept is for you to realise, intuit and visualise to the best of your ability is that the 'real you' is 'above and beyond' the physical 'time line' of historical sequential passing time, as we know it on Earth. The situation is likewise with regard to space for Soul. We need to realise that Soul possesses the capability to instantly travel via conscious awareness to areas of eternal reality within which it is progressively authorised to travel, due to Its' evolutionary spiritual and energetic 'unfoldment'.

What matters to you, and each one of us as an earthly individual; is that you/I make this particular lifetime truly meaningful spiritually, as much as you/I are able according to 'our' wants, needs, desires and natural levels of spiritual progression. There is every reason to become more aware of Soul consciousness within your current life experiences because these illuminating realisations infuse your life and character with abundant true purpose, divine love and joy. Another key concept to visualise is that the essential nature of Soul, the true 'you', contains the eternally evolving spark of God Consciousness that exists deep within you. The Soul is actually analogous to a super-conscious, evolving 'energetic vehicle' that 'houses' the inner spark of God Consciousness existing within Soul. God Consciousness is the true Source of all consciousness. It animates, enlivens and vitalises Soul. This description provides a simple clear explanation of the relationship between Soul Realisation and God Realisation, for those seeking to better comprehend this situation. In a God Realisation experience; Soul would experience the dramatic transcendent realisation that the existing inner God Consciousness is the actual Source of Soul's Self-consciousness, along with other realisations of their comprehensive Conscious Unity at the foremost all-inclusive infinite levels of Reality.

Another very unusual concept to consider is that through the involvement of Soul, in some situations, there can be an interactive relationship between various incarnated bodies that exist on various 'lower' planes of existence. Although such probable interactions would seldom be experienced consciously, Soul can readily access, facilitate and organise the direct involvement of multidimensional and historical levels of one's 'self' that we here on Earth are completely unaware of existing as another aspect of Soul, our 'true self'. Specifically, some aspects of one's character, such as innate personal attributes, spiritual qualities, awareness, perspectives and basic attitudes can be integrated and transmitted among various incarnations living in disparate reality systems and historical eras. For hypothetical example, information and experience from one historical physical incarnation can be relayed via Soul to your present human consciousness in ways that assist your life and capabilities dramatically. Also, a co-existent life form of one's Soul, such as an incarnation located upon the Mental Plane of existence, could attain an illuminating realisation regarding the integration of mental functions or any other helpful information or capability. Then Soul could make this experience available by an inexplicable process of transference to one's human consciousness on a subconscious, unconscious or even conscious level here on Earth due to these inner relationships within one's Soul consciousness. We exist within a human experience that ordinarily utilises physically verifiable intellectual perceptions, so it is exceedingly difficult to adequately theorise upon the incomprehensibly fantastic capabilities of highly evolved Soul. Therefore, an experience of Soul awareness is by far the best teacher because even if one does not intellectually comprehend the comprehensive nature or reasons for the manifestation of an incredibly mysterious extraordinary event, then at least we are able to recognise that it did truly happen!!!

To theorise upon by what processes this amazing capability may occur is less important than to realise that if one is truly committed and receptive to the integration of their overall, comprehensive, eternal, infinite character, that such an attitude will produce unexpected, fantastically bountiful results over passing time. In the realms of Soul; loving consciousness, a grateful attitude and peaceful intent are essential components that enable various transformative uplifting activities to occur. Soul possesses direct unlimited access to all aspects of your entire life history upon the 'lower' planes of existence. This is a vastly extensive potentially enormously beneficial resource for your earthly self to develop as your spiritual unfoldment progresses. The talents, realisations, capabilities and timeless wisdom that you already possess and are currently developing among various other incarnations in the lower planes can be constructively applied within your present earthly life.

This process requires that one sincerely commit to doing and 'being in' this divinely harmonious state of existence in a receptive, patient manner, so that you make yourself spiritually 'worthy' of an uplifting integration experience. These integration events may only occur upon a subtle, almost unconscious level in most cases, yet if you are genuinely receptive to the availability of such information and capability being provided to you in unexpected, spontaneous ways, then it is likely to happen for you. Realise that Soul always exists within all aspects of your being, whether you are living in a physical body on Earth, as well as having other aspects of your infinite reality being simultaneously located in countless other locations. For example, you as Soul, also simultaneously inhabits other physical, energetic, conscious life forms within various astral bodies in that reality system, as well as other aspects of 'your higher self'/Soul that is concurrently living within the etheric level of reality and other parts of your comprehensive Self existing within the mental plane of reality, etc.

Soul, the 'real you' that is now consciously existing inside your physical mortal self that you see as a live body in the mirror, is literally now inhabiting many, many millions of separate individualised conscious incarnated existences. Each and all of these individual incarnations are located throughout time, space and within other dimensions of reality, such as upon other 'planes' of existence. 'You' as Soul, are an incomprehensibly huge super-conscious life form containing incredible volumes of energy, wisdom, awareness, experience and capability. The 'normal' human mind has no intellectual process by which it can possibly fully assess, recognise or visualise the magnitude of these circumstances. Therefore, one must rely in such perplexing, unfathomable areas for Soul awareness to present these realisations, feelings, images, analogies and experiences to our ordinary conscious minds in ways that we can somehow understand and accept as being relatively factual/real.

Please pause to re-read and fully consider the information and implications contained in the previous paragraph(s). Realise as Soul, you are an omnipotent, infinitely capable and creative super-conscious life form of immense proportions. Contemplate upon this astounding reality periodically and experience the results this heightened awareness manifests in your mind, heart and life.

Soul will always be the 'inner observer', or the 'true self' or what I have defined as being the 'higher self' that exists within each and every one of us. Soul is actually an indescribable energetic, super-conscious, evolving, immortal 'vehicle' that contains the 'real eternal self' that is actually an aspect of God Consciousness. Soul seems from a human perspective to concurrently co-exist independently of our human experience, which seems to truly be the actual situation. Soul also exists within all of our unseen multitudinous 'lower' bodies, that are now simultaneously co-existing in various incarnations, located within those 'lower' and 'higher' various Planes (systems of reality). All of this is really not too difficult to visualise, once you 'get it'. Actually experiencing the fact is an altogether more impressive and unforgettable event, as I sincerely hope you already have or will realise for yourself; 'up close' and very personally. In this process, faith becomes believing; which in turn becomes direct 'knowing' through one's own personal miraculous undeniable experiences.

It is essential to visualise and eventually to personally experience the reality that the real 'you' that inhabits your physical body, Soul, is the actual eternal true consciousness, 'the observer' that is contained within what appears to be your overall mind. From the human perspective initially, Soul will incorrectly appear to be the ultimate Source of all your conscious awareness, yet this is not actually the complete situation, according to what we are struggling to adequately describe here in human language. God Consciousness is immanent within Soul Consciousness. This distinction may seem to be an irrelevant semantic, theoretical issue from our ordinary human levels of consciousness, yet such a view would be inaccurate. I feel compelled to address this issue in some detail because there will be some people reading this book whose awareness, comprehension and capability far exceeds my own or who are intent upon accurately understanding these issues regardless of how complex they may appear to some observers. I do not wish to make unnecessarily overly-simplified, erroneous explanations here, in spite of the fact that these clarifications may further complicate one's basic understanding of these basic matters of significance. Also, for an accurate assessment and explanation of these complex concepts and realities, one is highly encouraged to study the full written texts published by Eckankar; ideally without preconception, prejudice or judgment.

Soul actually transcends all the 'lower' Planes because it is able to be 'in' all of these locations simultaneously due to the 'higher', more inclusive, indescribably comprehensive level of Its' eternal existence. As one progressively identifies and harmonises 'them selves' (this use of the plural 'selves' is a key concept to seriously consider) as being Soul on all levels of existence, then the God Consciousness immanent within, progressively selectively utilises Soul and Its' various functional 'vehicles' ('lower' bodies) for the spontaneous expression of 'higher' consciousness to manifest within and 'through' us, as individuals and as Soul. It is important to comprehend that Soul is able to observe all aspects of life through Its' incarnated aspects (from within Its' various bodies located on all Planes of existence throughout time and space). In the right circumstances Soul is able to simultaneously manifest Itself through some or even all of its related, receptive, harmonious, conductive life forms; wherever they may be in time and space. In other words, the more 'in harmony' we, as fully conscious human beings, are with/as Soul, and the immanent God Consciousness existing within Soul; the more we can and will be an open, receptive 'vehicle' for God's expression in the lower planes and various areas of reality in which we live 'at the time'.

Another key issue to acknowledge and ideally to attempt to realise within yourself is that Soul, in the vast majority of earthly people, is relatively 'asleep' or simply in 'observation mode' as far as their normal conscious minds are concerned. In such people, inner Soul communication and external real life manifestation is generally limited to subtle, unconscious interactions because Soul's influences are often not properly acknowledged within the individual's mind, conscience, or heart sufficiently to result in positively altered conscious behaviours. This entire book is all about assisting both you and me to awaken and enliven Soul within each of us within our normal human levels of conscious awareness. We seek to encourage the higher levels of divine awareness within to synergistically stimulate the inflow of harmonious energetic frequencies of love, wisdom, truth, willing service and gratitude within each of us. This creative process enables Soul to become far more active in its' manifestation within and through us in our various concurrent lives upon all 'lower' and 'higher' levels of existence.

We know these concepts do seem unusual and somewhat confusing to logically consider or attempt to 'figure out'; even from a 'higher' level of intuitive, 'direct knowing' comprehension; however, these realities will eventually express and reveal themselves to you in a diverse variety of wonderful methods. All that is required on your part is to be sincerely persistent, in a relaxed loving way; making 'effortless efforts' to be receptive to receiving this information for the good of all life forms. We are motivated to advance our own personal evolution to become a better 'vehicle' for the expression and manifestation of some aspects of 'higher' consciousness throughout life's boundless reality systems. When one's character is sincerely committed in this magnanimous fashion, then Soul will progressively and spontaneously tend to 'awaken'. The direct observable response within your mind will subsequently be increasingly more able to express and reveal Soul's inspiring impulses, influences and assistance in unimaginable, unexpected, pleasantly beneficial, lovingly delightful ways.

There will be more to discuss on this complex subject later, yet for now let's finally address one of the more interesting realisations we can make in this journey of discovery in our earthly and eternally aware lives. Various highly evolved life forms beyond normal human levels of awareness and understanding exist on Earth, as well as throughout the universes. We will hypothetically assume that as Soul, an immortal, eternally self-conscious energetic life form that is currently inhabiting your human physical body here and now; 'you' have been continuously evolving for perhaps between about one to three billion years to attain this level of physical and spiritual unfoldment. This length of time is purely unsubstantiated speculation upon my part since I have absolutely no verifiable information or personal knowledge regarding the time frames involved in the evolution of Soul or human consciousness, so this estimate could be quite inaccurate. However, for the sake of our consideration here, this will be a relative assessment to compare the interval of time from the inception of conscious awareness inhabiting an advanced life form upon some 'lower' plane of existence in order to progressively evolve into increasingly higher levels of conscious awareness. This duration of time, from one to three billion years, may seem to be a very long time in human earthly terms, especially when related to an ordinary human earthly life span that now seldom reaches one hundred years.

Please now do your best to sincerely consider the state of probable or possible conscious awareness possessed by an evolving conscious life form that has existed in an endlessly developing state, just as human beings have, for an additional ten, twenty or even one hundred billion years. Let us consider as an analogy, the relatively rapid evolutionary advancements in the earlier ape-like hominid species over several million years that are supposedly the direct ancestors of modern day Homo sapiens. Would you seriously believe that after an additional five billion to twenty billion years or even one hundred billion earthly years of cosmic development that such highly evolved life forms would appear as human beings do today? From my present perspective, it seems extremely improbable to the point of being a negligible possibility, that after twenty to one hundred billion years of evolution that life forms would resemble anything we would recognise as being a normal physical life form, such as modern day human being, whale or another physical life form.

Regardless of their external appearances, surely if such a life form did continue to inhabit physical bodies like our human bodies, then they would be vastly more civilised and harmonised with their environments and other life forms than are modern day human beings. From my perspective it seems quite unlikely that we could even reasonably theorise upon what such an evolved life form may look like, if they remained upon the physical plane of reality for that length of universal time. Considering the relatively swift evolutionary development that anthropologists assert has occurred within humanoid life forms over a few million years, can we even begin to really imagine what human beings would look like in another one billion years, much less another twenty billion years?

Geologists and anthropologists have extensively examined the geological and anthropological information from the earliest stages of earthly evolution onwards to relatively recent times. Their scientific evidence indicates that over the last several million years of observable primate evolution, that our ancient humanoid ancestors progressed rapidly from a quite primitive primate somewhat like upright walking modern chimpanzee-like hominids to become far more human-like life forms possessing a nomadic hunter-gather life style. These ancient ancestors over a lengthy period of time began using fire, living in caves and primitive skin and stick shelters, and using stone and wooden tools. Apparently, within the last twenty to fifty thousand years, ancient European Neanderthal cave people were rapidly superseded by modern Homo sapiens, with little anthropological evidence to support the exact reasons for the extinction of the Neanderthal species of humanoids. Personally, I believe we know that Homo sapiens were somehow responsible for the rapid decline and disappearance of the Neanderthals, just as humans have exterminated many other extinct animal life forms over the course of human evolution. Anthropologists report that Homo sapiens have progressed relatively quickly in the last ten or twenty thousand years, to acquire agricultural skills, domesticate animals, learned metal smelting, and to build impressive stone buildings, towns and roads in the last several thousand years.

The Stone Age and Iron Ages were then followed by the Industrial Age, primarily beginning in the last five hundred years of human history. Within a few hundred years since that time, we modern day Homo sapiens are now entering the Space and Technology Age. This represents a fairly impressive progressive time line for human beings' earthy technological development, if this basic theoretical anthropological description is relatively accurate as it seems to be from our current perspective of recorded western civilisation's history. For the sake of modern theories of human development, or evolution, creationism, or whatever description one may give to how human beings arrived at this point in history; we will ignore and disregard the abundant undeniable evidence that much earlier highly advanced technological civilisations have previously occurred upon Earth, such as Atlantis, Lemuria and Mu. Those highly developed civilisations were virtually completely destroyed in previous global catastrophes of various types over lengthy periods of human 'pre-history'. What information has been lost in earthly pre-history is not relevant to this particular part of our discussion, so we will basically disregard it to maintain a meagre semblance of coherent continuity.

Therefore, if you genuinely deliberate upon what form modern human beings might theoretically possess if this species were to survive and further evolve another one million years, or ten million years, or one billion years upon the physical plane of existence, then you may develop a modest inkling about the probable life forms that have already been evolving an additional five billion, twenty billion, even one hundred billion or more years within cosmic reality systems. Please consider there are approximately four hundred billion known observable stars in our Milky Way Galaxy. By looking through various telescopes from Earth, astronomers have estimated they can now see about fifty billion other similar size galaxies to our own Milky Way Galaxy, located within about ten billion light-years in distance from Earth within the known visible universe. My mathematic calculations may be quite dubious, yet if we assume that only about one in every one million solar systems in the Milky Way Galaxy possess highly evolved, technologically advanced civilisations that can traverse interstellar space, then in the Milky Way Galaxy alone there would be about four hundred thousand stars with such highly technologically developed inhabited planets. Then, let's also do a similar calculation to include the approximate additional fifty billion galaxies that astronomers can see now from Earth within a ten billion light-year distance that are approximately the same size as our Milky Way Galaxy, give or take a few hundred billion solar systems. Four hundred thousand inhabited star systems within each of the fifty billion visible Galaxies; roughly estimated, would equate to about two thousand trillion stars being telescopically visible from Earth that are likely to contain life equally evolved to that upon Earth. My math could be wrong by a significant figure, so let's simply say it is a very large number since whatever figure calculated here is in reality quite likely to be a gross underestimate. Actually, it is probable that most of these highly evolved intelligent life forms would be far more evolved than present life upon Earth, considering that many less intelligent species would become extinct, due to their own self-defeating tendencies, or perhaps an inability to survive rapid changes in their solar and planetary systems, or for other reasons. That is really an incredibly large, almost inconceivable number of potential planetary bodies that could possess both intelligent and super-intelligent technologically evolved life forms within the physical third dimension universe. Add to this figure the apparent fact that a minimum of 12 additional unseen 'higher' planes or dimensions exist within the currently known over-all Reality System and you will find your consciousness expanding exponentially, if you wish to do so.

Earth is estimated to be about four to five billion years old, so we begin to see such hypothetical lengths of time are not as absurd to visualise as one may first imagine. Some may say that these extremely long periods of time, such as twenty billion or even one hundred billion years, would be exceedingly older than the age of our Milky Way Galaxy, which surely would be a valid observation from such a scientific perspective. However, in universal terms, within the relatively 'young' Milky Way Galaxy we see stars being born and dying continuously, so it remains debateable about how long an average galaxy may continue to exist. We do recognise that some visible galaxies seen and photographed in the further distances of intergalactic space by the Hubble Telescope form what appear to be limitless numbers of clusters of galaxies existing at the periphery of our present human powers of observation. The light from these furthermost galaxies that are visible to earthly observers requires from between one billion to ten billion light-years to travel these vast distances to reach Earth's view. There is no reason to believe that simply because we have reached the present limits of astronomers to perceive ever more deeply into intergalactic universal space, that there is likely to be a finite point in space where such galaxies cease to exist. Are we to foolishly assume that the profusion of galaxies we can now see will cease to exist at some point that is just beyond our ability to perceive with our increasingly more powerful telescopes? It seems more likely that infinite numbers of galaxies and universal systems of reality do exist beyond our ability to see them currently; meaning there is even more conscious life out there than human beings can hope to ever comprehend.

Consequently, to seriously theorise and assert that human beings could possibly be the only form of conscious, technologically developed, intelligent life in the entire universe is surely among the stupidest, most self-absorbed and small-minded assertions ever made by any supposedly intelligent conscious creature on any planet, in any galaxy, in any universe. Such inconceivably ridiculous, unimaginative, imbecilic beliefs do serve very well to exemplify the current moronic level of thinking that is still prevalent in some religious and scientific circles on Earth, as we enter the Space and Technology Age. It is important to assess the quality of our beliefs in relation to the existence of other types of intelligent life forms because such perceptions reveal so much about us as human beings. To analyse and theorise upon the exact length of time that human beings have been evolving upon the physical plane in this universe to reach our present level of development as a self-conscious species of life that is capable of creating advanced technologies is a relatively moot point because it has been a very long time indeed. Yet in relative universal time frames, evolution upon Earth has occurred for human life forms within a mere 'moment' in universal time. Human beings' technological achievements, such as the astronomical ability to look far out into distant space to help us determine the nature of our physical universe, is a massively huge step forward in some ways, yet our current global civilisation remains grossly primitive and immature in terms of its overall nobility, spiritual development and divinely manifested attributes. However, existing among us are highly evolved spiritual Masters, who personify and manifest Divinity and provide an example of the future that is achievable for us all, eventually.

We definitely acknowledge here that elsewhere in the Milky Way Galaxy and within this inconceivably infinite universe, there are innumerable types of highly intelligent life forms inhabiting physical bodies that have evolved at least double, or ten times, or even one hundred times longer than whatever length of time that human beings have been evolving on the physical plane of existence. These beings will usually not be stagnating in their spiritual development, if they are able to survive past the present stage in which our civilisation threatens to implode upon itself in a miserable, purposeless act of insane self-annihilation. There is also ample evidence to indicate that in some situations evolution can and often does progress in incremental 'leaps' and rapid mutations. Therefore, evolution can and does sometimes occur at a much faster rate of adaptation than a slower evolutionary process may normally occur, especially when evolution becomes consciously and intentionally influenced in positive, beneficial ways. We are speaking strictly about physical, genetic evolutionary development here, which has virtually nothing at all to do with technological, socio-cultural evolution, and the latter subject will be addressed separately later. Spiritual evolution or 'unfoldment' occurs in another entirely unique progressive manner, so these various developmental processes do function upon many variable rates. Some humans now seek to unwisely genetically modify our species' own evolution negatively in a de-evolutionary manner, under the guise of intending to improve human genetic structure. This is a natural divinely gifted process and it is my opinion that humanity should limit its involvement such activities until Earthlings have sufficient maturity and ethical values before seeking to scientifically alter any form of life's genetics, which are currently being done on Earth for primarily economic or egoistic motives. We currently see science altering the genetic structures of plants and animals in unnatural ways at a time in history when some parts of humanity are unable and unwilling to more simplistically and patiently work with nature to improve these species, rather than contrary to nature's immutable laws of life. Most modern human civilisation shows complete distain and little desire to learn about or obey nature's laws. Unless positive changes occur, then we will see the adverse results of this arrogant inane behaviour continuously magnifying various problems over passing time, as we clearly see this process now occurring globally within our collapsing civilisation and deteriorating communities.

It is an essential prerequisite that we earnestly analyse the approximate known size of the physical universe, which is apparently infinite to earthly astronomical observers now. The old story goes, if one could possibly travel far enough to reach the galactic 'edge' of our universe, if such a place exists, then what would exist beyond there, 'on the other side'? We pose this rhetorical question to represent an example of the limitations of human consciousness when attempting to comprehend issues that defy and confound our normal mental patterns of logical rational assessment. To understand how Soul can exist 'within' time and space, and yet also exist 'outside and beyond' all physical time and space is exactly such an inexplicable mental conundrum. Earthlings must now do much more than to theorise that intelligent, highly advanced conscious life may exist elsewhere in this universe. The facts seem to clearly indicate that the entire universe is teeming with an astounding diversity of intelligent, highly evolved life forms, many being beyond the ability of present human beings to acknowledge, perceive and understand, largely due to our own relatively 'modest' level of evolutionary development. Assuming that earthly humanity survives this critically dangerous period in our history and we further assume that the human species will survive another billion years within the physical universe in some form of habitable physical body, then what would the physical body of those vastly more evolved humans look like after that extraordinary amount of time? The hypothetical appearance of a resulting highly evolved human body after another billion years of ongoing evolutionary developmental is of less relevance than acknowledging the likelihood that significant physiological, technological and spiritual alterations would occur over that extensive period of time.

To address the question of species evolution over billions of years, let's consider one of the more interesting UFO cases ever reported, from my perspective. Whether this case actually occurred as reported is of lesser concern to me than the relevant issues that were purportedly discussed by the aliens and the Earthling. I had thousands of quality UFO cases to select from, so this is intended to be typical in various ways, as well as addressing the perspective I seek to discuss about the physiological evolution occurring over a billion years of physical plane evolution. Also this case will be included here because it relates to interesting concepts presented for consideration by evolved space travelling alien life forms that express the pertinent attitudes that are relevant to physical plane perceptions involving a range of relevant issues in our discussion here.

A man was driving along a highway in Central America when he saw an obvious disk shaped UFO land a few hundred meters away. He had always hoped to see a UFO, so curiously he pulled his car off of the road and walked over behind a hill where the UFO was located out of sight of the road. The man was surprised to see three alien beings about the size of normal human beings emerge from the craft, with one being somewhat larger than the others, although they were all absolutely identical in appearance. He became somewhat frightened, thinking perhaps he should run back to his automobile and was telepathically told to remain calm, that he was in no danger and they wished to communicate with him. The larger alien was the leader and seemed to be the one communicating with him. They were very unusual humanoids in appearance, with relatively thin features and tight fitting one piece clothing. When asked if the man wished to go for a ride in their space craft, his concern for his safety made him decline their offer. He stood outside the UFO, communicating with the three beings telepathically, since they told him they could understand his thoughts quite clearly, just as he understood them as though they were speaking his language fluently. Quickly, he began to feel much more at ease with these beings, in spite of their distinctly alien appearance. They discussed a range of subjects and then they volunteered some information about themselves when he asked where they came from. The larger alien indicated that they were highly technologically advanced beings that had long ago left their home planet, which became unable to support life.

For an extremely long time they had become primarily space travellers whose chosen activity was exploring the universe and they had even developed the capability to travel between distant galaxies in relatively short time periods. The alien stated his race had been evolving for a much longer time than could be comprehensible to the Earthling and said eons of time spent in space travel had 'hardened' their physical bodies through ongoing evolution to endure the rigours of these inner stellar and intergalactic journeys. The alien asked him to touch one of them, which he did and reported their body's surface felt as though it was solid and very smooth, somewhat like the shell-like exterior of a large beetle and yet they moved in a smooth normal flexible manner. Their eyes appeared unlike human eyes and were more insect-like in appearance, yet not frightening to look at, primarily due to their pleasant seeming demeanour and kindly thoughts. They stated they had evolved to such a point where they no longer experienced the death of their physical bodies, except in the case of accidents or other forms of inflicted death. They reproduced themselves on very rare occasions by inner division whereby one individual was somehow able to divide themselves into two individual beings over a number of hours. Each of the two individual beings would then be an exact replica of the other, with each possessing all the memories, knowledge and physiology of the original being. They realised the man seemed quite dubious about the explanation regarding how they replicated, or that they were basically immortal within their existing physical bodies, unless they were somehow killed.

The Earthling was then asked if he believed in God, which he replied in the affirmative. They said that their technology enabled them to create planets, life forms, stars and to live forever in their physical body without ageing. The alien leader then asked if from the man's perspective they were God, based upon their creative abilities and physical immortality. He replied by asking the aliens, "Did you create the universe?" The leader replied, "No, it was here already". The man replied, "Then you are not God as It exists in my mind." The alien leader became quite intent and told the man words to the effect that, "We have travelled through many galaxies across the universe, looking everywhere for God and have not found It anywhere, yet almost everywhere we go, all of you primitive mortal physical beings strongly believe in God, a creator of the universe and all reality. Surely, if God exists, then with all of our capabilities we would have found definitive proof of Its' existence somewhere in the universe." The man was stunned by their attitude and found it difficult to explain why he believed so confidently in the existence of God in spite of the seeming doubts expressed by the alien leader.

To distract from their difference of opinion, again the leader asked the man if he wished to go for a ride in their spaceship and told him they would only be gone a short while. They took him for a short ride during which time he saw the planet Earth grow small and disappear as they travelled out into the solar system. He stated that the stars in space were incredibly vivid and oddly did not 'twinkle' (change colours slightly when viewed) as they do on Earth. They quickly returned him as promised to the Earth and landed smoothly, asking him if he could return the following day for a short while because there was something else they wished to show him. He agreed, left and then returned at the appointed time the following day. This time four aliens emerged from the craft and the two slightly smaller ones indicated that the other even smaller two humanoid aliens were their leader, who had replicated itself to demonstrate their genuine ability to reproduce themselves, as they had stated previously. The smallest two aliens again spoke telepathically to the man and he sensed they seemed to him to be the same commanding being(s) that he had communicated with previously. The man remained somewhat uncertain, since it seemed to be impossible for him to consider that any life forms could reproduce themselves in such a manner.

The leader again spoke of God and asked why relatively primitive mortal life forms throughout the universe were so completely convinced of God's existence, when these vastly more aware, capable beings had so much more ability, time and determination to find God and had been unable to do so. The man felt great pity and empathy for these incredibly evolved, technologically developed beings. He could only try to telepathically explain that God was everywhere to be seen around them and also within Its' creations. He encouraged them to look within themselves to find God, as that is the only place they could look to find God now. He explained there was something about being born and knowing death was inevitable that helped one to understand and believe that God exists. He told the aliens that human beings are born and die over and over again, a great many, many times through their sequential earthly lives. He postulated that perhaps because the aliens remained permanently living one seemingly endless physical lifetime and observed that they did not get the 'rest periods' away from physical life that served to help remind humans about the existence of God. His explanation seemed to satisfy them. They volunteered some advice on human civilisation managing to survive this challenging period in our history as being something every civilisation must resolve, if it is to finally progress into a more civilised future within the universal community. They shared affectionate, appreciative emotions with one another and bid farewell. As he watched them fly away, he felt very good about the state of humanity, in spite of our problems.

What is especially relevant about these reported communications with highly developed alien beings, which can be taken as being fiction if you wish, should be self-evident. Some humans, like these aliens, are not able to intellectually or scientifically validate or verify the existence of God, so they withhold judgement or develop various other belief systems. We should carefully and appreciatively consider that because a species of life is able to evolve physiologically into a form of life that is virtually immortal within the physical body is no guarantee that it will automatically at some point in evolutionary time become God Realised, or even Soul Realised. The remarks made by the alien leader indicated some thoughts and realisations had occurred that lead them to conclude they were or could be God. However, the man's definition for God was the life force that created the universe, which precluded them from that role because they assuredly did not create the universe in spite of possessing some of what could appear to be divine-like capabilities. The aliens had indeed seemingly discovered the inner divinity that was the true Source of their consciousness, yet apparently they did not fully understand the inner workings of life beyond the physical plane of existence to the extent that we are discussing it here in this book as we seek to discover our inner divinity within our individual evolving being. Human beings are so fortunate because we do have the opportunity to experience so many aspects of reality through the nature of our physical and other dimensional levels of existence. Now let's consider a few reasons why we are able to comprehend reality, once we are able to become increasingly aware of a number of our inappropriate and outmoded preconceptions and lesser tendencies. After we further examine some of these issues, then we will sincerely delve into the nature of vastly more highly evolved life forms than the aliens mentioned previously, who were apparently to some degree trapped within the physical universal reality system, in evolutionary terms.

Human beings are physical creatures that are in many ways similar to other types of earthly animals, given that all animals have uniquely individualised species characteristics. Some people prefer to short-sightedly believe that for some inexplicable reason, the human form is the only one that can contain a highly developed form of intelligent consciousness. The result is that we humans have intentionally differentiated ourselves from all other known life forms on this planet, primarily justified logically because of our preference to utilise tools and technological innovation to alter earthly environments for our own benefit. We arrogantly fail to even consider it possible that any earthly creature possesses a highly evolved level of conscious awareness simply because those other species have not chosen to use electric tools, build huge cities, construct millions of miles of roads, make a billion vehicles, detonate numerous nuclear weapons, or wantonly massacre all other earthly life forms, including its own species by the countless millions, time after time historically without social conscience or viable alternatives being developed to prevent this needless self-destruction from re-occurring.

We blithely and happily ignore the fact that highly aware consciousness could exist within physical life forms that over many millions or billions of years have evolved to adapt their physical form to such an extent that they do not require or want clothing, tools or vehicles, nor to domesticate other creatures to serve their needs or assist them in the fulfilment of their niche roles within the environment. As stated previously, the debate still rages on what level of intelligence and type of consciousness exists within earthly creatures and many people would deny the fact that any animals have feelings and emotions. From what sort of oblivious, blind, self-imposed insanity is such a notion derived? Anyone who sees a dog wagging its tail furiously, smiling literally from ear to ear and quite literally jumping for joy when their 'owner' returns home or is preparing to take them for a walk should permanently end this foolish debate. Seeing whales and porpoise playing with one another, or an elephant gently and lovingly caressing the bleached bones of its deceased relatives with its trunk should clarify that a great many earthly creatures posses what we would define as some form of higher self-aware, conscious intellect and demonstrate various intense human-like emotions. Many primates existing in nature relate with one another in such human ways that it is almost frightening, especially when we can see the many similarities to our own less sophisticated behaviours, emotions and attitudes. Many animals use rudimentary tools, build elaborate shelters or nests to raise their young, communicate with one another in considerable detail, and comprehend the complex elements in nature and their integral relationship with their environment. Many species of life, including social insects like bees and ants, illustrate in diverse ways that they, even as individuals, are quite likely to be much more intelligent than most humans understand. Creatures in nature are extremely intelligent in the ways of survival, as proven when they survive unaided by others of their species and considering that they are generally quite able to adapt to their world in sustainable ways.

Anyone who intently observes an ant nest, or a hive of bees, much less a pod of dolphins, or a herd of elephants, or a group of gorillas interacting with one another should be ready to seriously reconsider what we humans define as being evolved intelligence. We will soon be considering evolved life forms that significantly surpass the entire scale of human evolutionary comprehension. It is wise to carefully consider life forms that are seemingly insignificant, just as a starting point in better realising something such as an ant, which is so small, apparently almost brainless and supposedly motivated purely by instinct; can communicate effectively with one another on many issues. Consciousness is far more complex and pervasive throughout universal and cosmic reality than modern day humans can possibly comprehend or visualise.

We must briefly revisit this basic concept now because it definitively illustrates so much about what humans in an overall social and scientific level still fail to realise, understand or publicly acknowledge. There exists on Earth a diverse array of intelligent, perceptive, evolved, beneficial, interrelated species of physical life forms possessing higher levels of conscious awareness than most humans are now able to perceive or comprehend. Humanity is painfully and frustratingly slow to assess, analyse, and conclude, for example, exactly how exceedingly intelligent mammals are; such as elephants, horses, dogs, pigs, cows sheep, goats, giraffe, hippopotamus, crocodiles, gorillas, chimpanzees, bears, tigers lions, birds, reptiles, or even the mice and rats already used in scientific studies. This analysis should also include sea mammals; such as seals, whales, dolphins, otter, etc; who could be scientifically studied by thoroughly analysing their audible and visual forms of communication with one another and by doing other types of intelligence tests. The unpleasant truth is the distinct majority of people actually really do not care to know how intelligent, consciously aware and emotionally active these creatures are in relation to human beings. In this way, by avoiding considering the issue of other creature's intelligence and emotional awareness levels, we humans can easily continue to inappropriately maintain this oblivious attitude out of self-sustained, intentional ignorance and arrogance. This allows our marginal level of conscience to remain non-functional, so we do not feel at all remorseful or guilty; as we slaughter them for food, destroy their homes and environmental systems, treat them in an abysmal fashion in scientific and medical experiments, and deprive them of all rights to life, unless we legislate otherwise, and so on. We recognise that usually communication with domestic animals is primarily 'one way traffic' in that they are taught from an early age to understand and obey our wants and requirements, yet relatively little thought is given to the state of these animals by most humans, aside from basic food and shelter. Some people would, for example, clear every tree in a pasture because it looks neater that way; not thinking at all that the animals may enjoy resting in the shade sometimes, rather than baking continuously in the hot sunshine.

As a young boy, I realised through observing my dogs closely that all dogs communicated with one another in numerous ways. This encouraged me to learn to detect the signals my dogs gave me, especially when we were hunting, which lead me to develop a much better level of communication with all dogs. Unfortunately, at the time I did not seriously consider the emotions of the unfortunate animals that we killed for food or their furs, yet by the time I graduated from university and had enough money to buy food, I never hunted again. At about six years of age, I once found some sadistically cruel older boys roasting alive upon a barbeque grill some baby birds they had taken from their nest. I can still vividly recall the horror I felt upon seeing such a despicable act and my screaming loudly at them in anger about their inappropriate barbaric behaviour. They simply laughed at me and told me that I had better go away before they beat me up and threw me on their barbeque too. That was my first memorable encounter with human cruelty. In over forty years, while I have not hunted animals for any reason, occasionally I still consider the fate of the billions of helpless animals humans consume for food, including myself, since I am not (yet) a vegetarian/vegan. It is very unpleasant to consider the actual nature and intensity of those condemned animals' feelings that became so evident to me during the summer that I worked in a 'slaughter house' for cattle and sheep to earn money for university. The pitiful cries of those fearful, trapped and struggling animals is not something many of us would care to visualise or recall as we sit down to our meals containing animal flesh upon an almost daily basis. Life upon the physical plane can be quite brutal, depending upon one's circumstances.

Humanity has steadfastly refused to devote genuinely dedicated, well-funded scientific efforts to learn two-way communication with the other intelligent species of life upon our own planet. This again reveals the egocentric, self-restricted nature of our social inquiry as it relates to other life forms co-habiting this Earth with us for the entire length of our evolutionary history. No exciting public announcements proclaim that humanity can now communicate intelligently with whales, dolphins, gorillas, elephants, or dogs with the assistance of any type of machine that reveals their brain waves or applies any other methods to record and translate their audible or visual communications into human language. Most humans remain largely ignorant of the actual level of intelligence possessed by creatures upon our own Earth. How can this be, if we are truly so intelligent ourselves? An emperor penguin can locate its spouse after months away at sea among many thousands of other penguins, simply by calling to them amid the din of other calling penguins, as can many other bird or bat species, yet we do not credit them with higher forms of intelligence. We mostly fail to learn anything of substance from these creatures' various forms of wisdom. Unless they serve humanity in some ways, then they are most likely to be themselves served as a food source to humans or largely ignored. Humans also impassively murder them without mercy for their fur, organs, simply for sport, or callously imprison and torture intelligent animals under the guise of scientific and medical experimentation, or perhaps just kill them to mount their heads upon a wall to decorate their homes or to make their human murders feel brave and dominantly powerful over these relatively defenceless creatures. In more recent history there have been increasingly numerous dedicated efforts to protect wildlife, especially rare and endangered species, since humanity has been the primary cause for the extermination of so many earthly species of life in the past. This is a very positive development, thankfully.

We can recall a relatively recent time in history when native indigenous people were classified by the invading imperialistic national governments as being no different than any wild creature. So, the colonists could freely and 'legally' slaughter these native indigenous people to deprive them of their ancestral territorial lands, or any other 'reason' they may have for killing them, including for 'sport'. What sort of bloodthirsty sanguinary attitude once legally and legislatively condoned the brutal slaughter of innocent intelligent native indigenous human beings without conscience or legal protection by an overwhelmingly superior, supposedly civilised conquering force? There was little or no compassion demonstrated for these native peoples globally by the forces of colonial imperialism as they stole these people's lands, defined them as lower life forms hardly any different than animals with no civil or human rights to justice or protection under the laws of the 'western' white men who conquered, and then oppressed them. Those native people who were captured and used as slaves, just like domesticated beasts of burden; were legally owned by their so-called 'masters' and treated no differently than any other animal possessed by their captors; able to be bought and sold like any other commodity. Could these unconscionable murderers and slavers not hear the anguished crying and the screams of desperation of these victimised indigenous people as they begged for mercy before being heartlessly butchered or sold into slavery? No, sadly the sadistic conquerors were quite intentionally unable to understand the terror filled screams in native dialects and managed to ignore the victims' tears that openly expressed the painful emotions experienced by any suffering human beings. There was no mercy for these unfortunate oppressed native people whose ancestral lands were stolen and they were treated just like any other animal, ready for the slaughter or sale yard by those so-called civilised people that were characterised by their cruel, obliviously evil perspectives. It is relevant to accurately portray the attitudes of our civilisation toward these native indigenous human beings that western civilisation, not so long ago, arbitrarily and untruthfully identified as having no rights, no real intelligence, nor emotional feelings, even though those indigenous life forms were and are Homo sapiens; human beings, just like ourselves.

Human beings have already proven to be unwilling to make sincere efforts to learn to communicate with obviously intelligent, aware earthly animals. Humanity has consistently and comprehensively denied that these conscious, emotionally aware life forms possess any true level of intelligence by conscientiously ignoring any evidence proving the considerable intelligence that these creatures obviously do possess. Now we will apply this same human tendency of denial and obstruction to genuinely considering the available evidence that intelligent life exists elsewhere in our solar system, galaxy and universe. As we have already discussed, it has been well-documented that most governmental authorities and scientists publicly tend to dispute the possible existence of any other more intelligent, unknown life forms. They do so by ignoring, hiding, suppressing and covertly hording all the copious amounts of verifiable valid evidence proving definitively that these technologically advanced beings are now visiting Earth, that some of them are permanently living here on Earth, and also living elsewhere within our solar system. Privately, some of the earthly rulers of civilisation and their employees are covertly in possession of numerous types of technologically highly advanced spacecraft and other innovative processes, and there have been ongoing communications and collusions with various purportedly extraterrestrial life forms. This has been conclusively documented by reliable witnesses' testimony under the threat of death for disclosing the secret information to a public with an inalienable right to know these facts, and is also clearly evidenced by human civilisation's unnaturally rapid technological development in the past century. In some cases, there can be no doubt that some of these earthly 'visitors' are extraterrestrial and alien to Earth in origin.

We must conclude that the majority of earthly humans are unable or unwilling to properly analyse and deduce the actual level of intelligence within the obviously consciously aware earthly creatures that have co-existed with us for millions of years of mutual evolution. Therefore, it seems unlikely that we would fully acknowledge, appreciate or comprehend the intrinsic, tangible qualities of any extraterrestrial life forms that we may encounter; unless perhaps they were eating us for dinner, or slaughtering humanity with highly technological weapon systems for the sheer fun of it, or to acquire ownership of the planet, as is actually currently the factual case. Demonic 'lower' types of alien and multidimensional life forms are now clearly preying upon humanity, just as we have described in relation to 'our' domesticated and Mother Earth's wild creatures. This is the fact that the 'hidden government' within all governments seeks to hide from humanity at this time in our global history.

These types of debased motives are things humans could personally identify and relate with, based upon our own attitudes and behaviours in our current civilisation. It is ironic how we human beings would feel unjustly mistreated if our civilisation were to be arbitrarily exterminated or enslaved by hordes of invading extraterrestrials civilisations, yet we willingly do such things ourselves to other intelligent earthly creatures, entire environmental ecosystems, and groups of defenceless people without much conscience at all, in spite of the lessons of modern history.

Now we will finally begin to directly discuss the certain fact that some exceedingly evolved life forms exist within the physical universe, as well as upon other planes and dimensions of existence. Most people on Earth choose not to recognise that these realities exist due to the limitations of our senses and comprehension of nature's infinite forms of diversity. It is time to broaden and enrich the scope of our vision in universal and cosmic terms on Earth, or suffer the enormous dire consequences for our idiocy and arrogance. We have already mentioned the probability that if earthly humans were to evolve physically and spiritually for another billion years, then it is a virtual certainty that our physiological structures would change somewhat, just as they have in the past ten million years, according to the available archaeological data. We would undoubtedly experience influences that alter the processes of our genetic selection, as well as developments within our social and spiritual characters as a civilisation, to adapt to differing circumstances. For example, human preferences could become more prone toward selectively breeding for genetic, social and spiritual traits that express more intelligence, divine values and higher intuitive perception than those requiring physical strength or manipulative cunning to be successful in the future. Another physical genetic quality could be a desirable appearance, such as more refined, slender, more petite physiological features, or a larger brain capacity (due to the lengthy historical use of medical birthing procedures that could produce descendents with a significantly larger head size than could naturally pass through the woman's womb), or whatever physical, mental, emotional and spiritual attributes are perceived to be more attractive or preferential over passing time, and so on. The idea here is for us to acknowledge that some type of ongoing human physical and spiritual evolutionary development is almost certain to occur over tens or even hundreds of millions of years and surely will occur over billions of years of passing time. Subsequently, we can likewise theorise that it is equally likely that other conscious, intelligent life forms would also evolve according to numerous factors in their environment and within their social and spiritual circumstances.

Now let's turn our attention to briefly consider the accumulation of human knowledge, as it applies to control of the physical environment. Advances in human awareness have lead to a series of social, cultural and technological adaptations that are also somewhat evolutionary in nature and application. The ability to utilise fire; make weapons to kill animals and defend one's self; build secure shelters to protect against predators, human enemies, and the elements; domesticate animals; the development of written and spoken language including systems of education; the progressive development of agriculture and industrial capabilities; the advent of a system of mutually agreed currency; improved transportation systems and various other essential developments have all greatly assisted and enabled humanity to achieve our present level of civilisation. The simple improvements in hygiene so that we can easily and inexpensively wash our bodies in hot water with quality products that prevent us from having foul body odours and being vermin ridden is a huge physical and cultural development for human beings, as has been improved sewage treatment systems. It required many millions of years to progress through these earlier stages for early humanoid life forms to transform themselves into modern Homo sapiens. Now we clearly realise the rate of progressive technological adaptation has apparently significantly surpassed human spiritual and socio-cultural levels of progression. However, along with the physical evolution have definitely come parallel increases in human intelligence, when compared to our earlier hominid ancestors. Gradually more ingenious forms of transportation, energy production, metallurgy, manufacturing, construction, scientific research, health, government and enterprise were developed. Through this entire process, the evolution of the spoken and written language became significantly more important as the primary way to communicate ideas and transform them into realities. The key point to recognise here is the extremely swift, exponentially increasing, progressive development of human technological capabilities have definitely NOT been equalled by a parallel progression of our social, intellectual or spiritual status.

To again digress momentarily; so what would a whale, elephant, gorilla, dog or dolphin be able to communicate to us about their perspective of life and innate level of wisdom that would assist us in our societies, if we were able to develop the willingness and ability to understand their thinking and emotional state of being? We would obtain momentous fundamental meaning from other completely unique perspectives of intelligent, self-conscious, highly experienced life forms that would inevitably assist humanity by providing additional wisdom and experience from other intelligent species that have shared our evolutionary path upon Earth for many millions of years. Where such hypothetical interspecies communications would lead humanity and these other species over millions of years is anyone's guess, yet it would likely be a quite positive development, when compared to continuing to ignore and deny the knowledge and experience possessed by such other intelligent species living on Earth with us. Obviously, just as some people are smarter, more perceptive, more eloquent in expressing themselves, or formulating ideas for others to consider; the same would be likely be true for various animal species, as well as for talented individuals within those species. Just as we recognise creative gifted minds and intellectual genius in the human population, animal species over passing time in their communications with human beings would present startlingly evocative information and philosophical perspectives, as representatives of their species contributed to the sum total of earthly wisdom. The issue here is to become aware that we human beings, through our governments and corporations, are presently not at all actively interested or seeking to acquire an ability to communicate upon any sincere level with any of the intelligent life forms already living upon Earth. This is an exceedingly relevant conclusion in our entire discussion here, so please sincerely reflect and consider the following important question because it reveals so much about our potential future. Likewise, would humans have so soon imagined that they could fly if they had never seen a bird flying? Therefore, why do we Earthlings now naively somehow believe that if we were approached by highly developed extraterrestrial life forms that we would genuinely evaluate and accept their wisdom and apply their suggestions to benefit our civilisation and other earthly life forms? It seems unlikely that humanity, in its woefully degenerate present state of social and spiritual being, would do anything more than deceitfully and disingenuously 'pay lip service' to those more evolved life forms, while remaining entirely focused upon obtaining such knowledge, information and capabilities strictly to further our civilisation's own self-interest with continuing disregard and contempt for all other life forms.

If this assessment seems unduly harsh and biased, then who among us is willing to sacrifice their own lives, if necessary, to protect the rights and lives of whales, gorillas, tigers, trees, the environment, and the starving or oppressed people for no personal gains? We all know that very few humans indeed would possess that level of commitment to protect other conscious, feeling life forms. However, we are asked by our governments or some by their religious leaders to violently kill and injure one another in our millions for greed and evil opportunism, relentlessly throughout recorded human history and this is also clearly evidenced in the archaeology of human pre-history. Can we each and all clearly perceive a significant problem with this convenient, self-interested, unconscionable human attitude?

Another important concept to recognise now is that human individuals range drastically in intelligence, traits and capability, just as would be the situation with other species of life forms. We have dabbled with this complex issue periodically throughout our entire discussion. It is especially relevant to acknowledge that some individuals and groups of people defiantly refuse to learn, are unwilling or unable, or just very slow to adjust their attitudes in a positive, beneficial manner based upon their experiences or the educational promptings of others. This tendency is unfortunately one of the defining, obvious, significant characteristics of our present human civilisation at this historical point in time in 2016.

Earthlings need to acknowledge that other highly intelligent, vastly experienced, technologically advanced, more perceptive, and spiritually evolved life forms possessing extraordinary talents and capabilities do exist in this solar system, in the Milky Way Galaxy, elsewhere in the infinite universes, and upon other innumerable 'higher' planes and differing dimensions of existence. Countless superbly evolved, astoundingly perceptive, wise and exceptionally proficient life forms possessing incomprehensible intelligence and spiritual attributes may have long ago decided intentionally to NOT devote their attention toward excelling in technological achievements. Instead, they may have preferred to occupy a niche in universal reality whereby they chose to accomplish purposeful activities that modern earthly humans would not easily recognise due to our existing relatively limited level of understanding and perceptions of life. We will discuss various life forms that have developed a wide range of exceptional technologies and abilities, with many of these apparently being able to transcend various physical laws as our earthly science now knows them to exist. Most humans are usually much more impressed by technological miracles, mysterious paranormal abilities, and unseen powers of influence than by divine levels of wisdom, truth and meaning. To make an analogy, most humans would prefer to watch a theatrical 'magic act' or other form of entertainment than to personally experience a spiritually illuminating, uplifting transformation or discuss the issue with someone who has experienced such an event themselves.

The focus of our attention in this book has been directed primarily toward enhancing one's inner perceptive capabilities and awareness that you, as Soul, are already vastly more spiritually evolved than the human mind can ordinarily comprehend. Soul assists one's earthly state of consciousness in the development of personal skills and attributes that encourage the manifestation of our higher nature in observable, beneficial, meaningful ways within one's daily and inner life. Analysing the amazing abilities possessed by other highly evolved, exceedingly intelligent, fantastically resourceful life forms of unknown origins that are now interacting with Earthlings better enables human beings to perceive what further qualities humanity can become capable of in our future, after we adjust and improve some of our ineffectual, relatively primitive, unwise attitudes and actions, as individuals and as a civilisation. We can easily recognise that some particular human beings innately manifest a distinctly higher resonance of divinity; as is expressed through their illuminating intelligence, extraordinary perceptions, uniquely brilliant capabilities, impressive creativity, kindly character, and an ability to share true love and magnanimous service to others through their noble spirit and characters. We are going to briefly consider the positive influences and examples provided by some of the extraterrestrial civilisations that have visited Earth, as well as examining the probability that other inter-dimensional travellers and inter-planetary humanoid species frequent Earth and in some cases, already co-inhabit this planet with us.

It is vitally important that we establish a series of distinctions to characterise or classify various life forms according to their motives, influences, philosophies, attitudes and especially their actions. Not all highly technologically advanced species of life are actually civilised, in the true sense of this concept. We have invested much time and effort here in revealing that modern day earthly humanity is an excellent example of a technologically developing, relatively primitive global society that is now characterised at the uppermost levels of leadership in our civilisation by hypocrisy, brutality, deceit, greed, corruption, sadism, arrogance, despotism, tyranny, aggression and subterfuge. Screams of dissent, howls of denial and rants of displeasure will certainly arise from various influential people in positions of earthly authority upon hearing such observations and accusations about human earthly civilisation, many of whom have knowingly closely allied themselves with extremely negative, quite powerful, dark forces of evil oppression, in association with evil alien and multidimensional invaders that now plague humanity at this critical time in our history. These are the same attitudes that were historically responsible for the extermination of large numbers of indigenous populations around the world and enslaved millions in chains, promoted countless wars, social suffering and economic chaos over thousands of years and up to the present time, as we can all so clearly see revealed. Because a life form has highly advanced technological capability and enormous persuasive powers of control over other life forms and the environment is absolutely no guarantee that they are truly civilised, divinely motivated or actually evolved in the real sense of the concept.

Thankfully, earthly life forms are very fortunate to have been significantly benefited by interactions with truly civilised, divinely inspired, benevolent, highly evolved life forms from numerous origins over inestimable periods of time. Often we Earthlings, including all other species of life existing here, have received the compassionate assistance, protection, support, intervention, and inspirational guidance from these various marvellously adapted, highly evolved life forms that are in harmonious concordance with divine levels of consciousness. Earth and all life forms existing upon and within this beautiful planet have progressively developed through the magnanimous, lenient, committed attitudes and efforts of many types of profoundly evolved life forms. Most humans would be blissfully unaware of the existence of these unique conscious beings because of their inconspicuous, subtle, ingenious, artful augmentation of environmental and other natural processes that are generally occurring beyond the range of normal human senses of perception or logical understanding. In other words, life on Earth has continuously been assisted by highly evolved, divinely motivated life forms; many of whom surpass the current abilities of human levels of awareness to comprehend their true nature, altruistic intentions, phenomenal capabilities, or their complex roles within the infinite design of life processes. Information and reality that remains beyond our current levels of awareness and comprehension does indeed influence humanity and other earthly life forms, whether or not we are able or willing to recognise these facts. It is significant to note that many indigenous native tribal cultures such as the Native Americans and the Indigenous Australians had and to some degree still possess an excellent, innate, highly evolved awareness regarding their integral harmonious relationships within nature characterised by great respect and appreciation for the Earth and higher types of various life forms that western cultures do not even acknowledge or understand in many cases.

Human beings must begin to acknowledge that we are definitely not yet even remotely aware of the full extent of life and consciousness that exists upon our own planet, within other dimensions of reality, or is located elsewhere within the Milky Way Galaxy, or within and beyond the observable physical universe. While such issues may incorrectly seem unrelated and irrelevant to us now on Earth, this is far from the truth, since all life is interrelated through consciousness. We seek to identify ourselves as Earthlings and as responsible, civilised galactic citizens that demonstrate our innate divine aspects of consciousness. Earthlings no longer wish to be unnecessarily and inappropriately characterised by the predominant lower forms of malevolent, selfish, temporal consciousness that profusely inhabit various locations within the lower planes of infinite existence, as is now being experienced upon Earth. Reality functions exactly as it has been divinely designed to do, so we simply need to better understand the overall nature of existence, especially as it relates to our own roles and responsibilities.

My personal interest has long been to preferably research and interact with 'advanced' life forms that have already evolved beyond the physical plane of existence and that now inhabit the 'higher' planes of reality, yet still choose to maintain a commitment to assist, inspire, interact and uplift earthly life forms in various ways. This quest for understanding the nature of higher consciousness than was exhibited by most human beings began in this particular life as a young boy, as was mentioned previously in this book.

The fact that I was privileged to experience what at the time I believed to be an 'image' of God in the clouds above my house while playing outside by myself is a memorable transcendent event that has positively influenced my entire life to the present time, more than fifty years later. Whether that event was indeed an interaction with what some would define as being an 'image of God', or was instead another highly evolved conscious life form of unknown nature; I will not be able to make a definitive conclusion in my earthly lifetime. What I do know about the wonderful experience is that I will never forget the feelings of awesome divine love, pure empathic joy, inner peace, innate purpose, conscious harmonious cohesion and the sense of secure belonging felt in those few interactive moments of incomprehensible, inexplicable, undeniable bliss. The timeless revelations that occurred within those fleeting seconds were perpetual in nature and have endured deeply integrated within my consciousness, although admittedly to a relatively subconscious degree, throughout my life on this Earth. This definitely real, illuminating, transformative experience at such a young age, was followed periodically by a wide variety of other mysteriously vitalising events that exhibited various other impressive qualities which have served to enliven, intrigue, inspire, and greatly benefit me in countless ways. This progression of revealing experiences and increasing access to all types of relevant information has drastically prompted my own character development and spiritual unfoldment, thus encouraging me to share some of these experiences and opinions with you and humanity now. It is these types of uplifting issues and beneficial experiences that we primarily seek to explore and progressively arouse within your life and our progressive civilisation.

Our quest is to interact with those human beings that are receptive and prepared to make this monumental evolutionary step forward and upward, into the conscious awareness and appreciation of higher aspects of ourselves, to join with other such highly evolved and divinely inspired life forms existing throughout the universal and cosmic systems of reality.

Most of us reading this book already recognise that a wide variety of non-physical entities exist that interact with earthly human beings. Some of these non-physical entities inhabit astral bodies upon the Astral Plane, just as we inhabit physical bodies upon the Physical Plane on Earth. The relationship between the Physical Plane and the lower levels of the Astral Plane have many similarities, especially since beings on both of these levels of reality can influence each other in some circumstances. This would be especially observable for those of us who can recall our nightly dreams while sleeping when most of us interact to a considerable extent upon the astral plane of reality. We are able to go places and do things that encompass a diverse set of variables that would often seem unlikely or impossible upon the physical plane in our daily earthly lives. Possible dream activities upon the astral plane could include the ability to: fly; change our size and shape; disappear from one scene and enter another dream location, sometimes by our choices seemingly controlling the activities occurring within the dream; see long deceased relatives, friends or even famous people currently living or from history; successfully defend one's self against huge ugly monsters or vicious wild animals; see our deceased or live pets or other life forms that behave in various ways that may be unexpected; meet unusual or alien beings; work through earthly issues in optional ways that assist us in our daily life; release emotions and take actions that may be considered inappropriate in normal earthly life; gain access to information and experience that surpasses earthly understanding and bring it back into one's waking consciousness in beneficial ways, and so on, and on. These examples of one's capabilities within the astral or other 'lower' planes while one is sleeping and 'dreaming' are only relatively minor examples of the much greater paranormal, super-conscious, 'higher' abilities and qualities that each one of us potentially possesses within the scope of their overall spiritual, immortal, omniscient, omnipotent levels of being.

When normal earthly humans experience interactions with life forms, physical or otherwise, that can function upon the physical plane in powerful and inexplicable ways; for example, just as we earthly humans can easily do upon the astral plane at night in our dreams, then we are readily astounded, perplexed and sometimes quite rightly frightened by these unusual experiences. It is helpful to do one's best to consider the possible sources of various amazing or unusual events, intuitive feelings and powerful emotions before immediately and instinctively responding to them unconsciously or consciously. The truth is I do not personally know definitively about many of the 'higher' planes and dimensions of existence, although some experiences and other reliable information have provided some revealing 'windows of perception' into these systems of reality. It would be overly speculative and too presumptuous to assume the motives and life patterns of a diverse range of life forms that surpass what we experience here on Earth on the physical plane. However, we will quickly list a few that most of us will have some prior knowledge of having heard about previously. We all are already well-aware of what seem to us on Earth to be disincarnate entities or other ghostly life forms, such as deceased human beings' disincarnate 'spirits' who have not left the earthly physical plane after the death of their physical body. Anyone who has had interactions with such 'lower level' types of life forms would realise that they do possess a form of conscious perception, yet they are existing upon the lower end of the scale of life, regardless of the nature of their existence. When we refer to highly evolved life forms that are beyond the physical realm of existence, these are more akin to what we may consider to be; angels, spirit guides, natural entities or 'devas' serving various functions within the natural environment, and numerous types of energetic, super-conscious hierarchal beings that some would define as angels and ascended 'masters'. Far 'above and beyond' that level of evolutionary unfoldment in the cosmic scheme of eternal infinite reality exist much more highly spiritually evolved life forms of incredible diversity and capability that are completely beyond normal human levels of comprehension, such as were briefly mentioned in our basic discussion regarding the nature of Soul.

The significant realisation we wish to make here is that innumerable self-aware, free-willed, energetically immortal, evolving forms of consciousness co-exist upon all levels of infinite cosmic systems of reality. These compose complex, interactive, universal and cosmic ecosystems that together create a fantastically abundant matrix of super-conscious, creative, loving, compassionate life forces. We humans, as Soul, help to formulate an integral aspect of this cosmic life cycle. It is possible for humans now living upon Earth to 'step up' our level of self-conscious awareness to include the more active participation of the 'higher' parts of our overall comprehensive self, Soul, into our daily earthly lives.

Developing a constantly aware, interactive, cognitively objective and subjective, perceptive attitude can be quite elusive, especially at the rapid pace of spontaneous earthly activity. The key is to keep one's conscious attention 'in the moment', consciously aware of events continually happening in the eternally progressing 'now', so that we are much more alert to all types of events occurring around and within us throughout every aspect of our lives. Periodically, when spontaneous, surprising, fascinating, baffling, marvellous, remarkable, enigmatic, inconceivable, awe-inspiring, miraculous, notable, unexpected anomalous phenomena occur then we must learn to take special care to observe the detail involved and our own instantaneous mental and emotional responses. This habitual attitude of enhanced awareness in one's daily life reaps multitudinous rewards and is an excellent consciousness training procedure that will enable one to increase their perceptive capabilities enormously in numerous, sometimes amazing ways. It is helpful to open one's mind and belief system to realise, accept and encourage our potential interactions with highly evolved life forms as a prerequisite to expanding our awareness and perceptions through our own conscious efforts. It is necessary to specify that we definitely do NOT want or need to interact with disincarnate 'lower level' life forms originating from the astral plane of existence, since in some cases they are exceedingly odious, spiritually devolved, quite negative types of life forms. Depending upon our attitudes and circumstances, we can better prepare ourselves to become more aware of a significantly expanded, magnified conscious perceptive awareness that enables us to more easily and accurately recognise positive, spontaneous, uplifting occurrences. By gradually learning to acknowledge them as they occur, rather than to instantly dismiss or ignore them, as is so often our instant reaction to such inexplicable or unusual experiences; over passing time you and all of humanity will benefit from the entire process in numerous unimaginable ways.

It is unlikely that unusual or uplifting experiences will immediately occur in our daily lives just because we are interested in experiencing such things, so initially examine and mentally define what you are truly seeking in this earthly life. We first will benefit most by improving our ordinary daily lives in subtle, easy to accomplish ways. Making an effort to have a brief pleasant conversation with a kindly stranger at some point in one's daily life; or a loving, encouraging communication with one's spouse or play with your child, even if they are older; help someone struggling with a heavy load or emotional crisis; slow down one's frantic pace to more perceptively observe what is happening around you; listen to the sounds around you; set aside some relaxing time to contemplate upon one's life and plans for a better future; consciously invite Soul to enter your daily conscious awareness in some manner that you will recognise and so on. These are all simple conscious patterns of thought and action that awaken your higher mind to act through your normal consciousness. This process develops and accelerates your various levels of awareness, cyclically in a fashion that is comfortable for you. You may detest the thought of speaking with strangers for no apparent reason, or it may be quite a normal positive experience for you already. You may feel or be somewhat estranged from your spouse or children and not know how or why to initiate such a communication, yet you will find a way if you just try. You may have no motivation to assist others in need of help or human compassion in troubled times, but perhaps you may find circumstances when your efforts synergistically help numerous others in spontaneous unseen and unanticipated ways. Take an interest in participating in local community events in ways that express your full character and personality, even with people you do not yet know as though they are already friends of yours. These normal events seem mundane, yet they are essential stepping stones intellectually and spiritually for us to gain improved interaction with one another, within ourselves and enable Soul to begin more fully expressing its higher levels of reality through our unfolding lives.

Another productive method is to take private time to delve into one's past, to intentionally recall and in some ways to relive our fondest memories of enriching, stupendously wonderful, potentially life-altering, positive experiences. Likewise, we can also choose to remember and analyse our unpleasant, unwanted experiences to glean significant realisations that enable us to release old painful emotions or to commit ourselves to making the necessary improvements to our habits, attitudes, life-style, choices and beliefs. Whatever the nature of one's examination of past events, it is possible to gain an increased level of awareness that can be applied within your daily life today and in an ongoing manner to improve one's future. As a civilisation of more highly motivated people seeking to manifest Soul consciousness through the experiences of our daily lives, we each can contribute to the betterment of our entire civilisation, if we choose to do so.

Earth is akin to a schoolhouse for Soul. Unfortunately this beautiful planet is now predominantly occupied by those beings and entities who have demonstrated a recurrent proclivity to resist making positive constructive choices that benefit their spiritual evolution, yet it is also cohabited with an exponentially increasing number of quite wonderful, highly evolved, genuinely loving, compassionate and spiritually aware beings. Many earthly humans and the negative entities that adversely influence them now maliciously seek to intentionally impede, control, thwart and prevent the spiritual and daily progress of other Souls. This is a situation that occurs commonly within physical and astral planes of existence. In other words, on Earth, this difficult situation is 'par for our course', so this is nothing personal 'against' you. Life here on Earth is meant to be extremely challenging in numerous ways in order to promote our conscious spiritual development, while some others find this to be a relatively lovely pleasant existence on Earth. These types of locations within universal reality are divinely designed and created to exist specifically so that evolving self-aware forms of consciousness can manifest within a system that engenders progressive development, increasing levels of awareness, and self-responsible patterns of thought and action. So, we may as well make the very best of our opportunities because life is generally whatever you make of it, regardless of the location where you reside within infinite eternity.

It is tempting to distract our discussion into areas where we speculate about and theorise upon the nature of other more highly technological and non-physical superbly developed life forms that visit or live upon Earth and those who exist elsewhere in universal and cosmic reality systems. After serious consideration, it seems advisable to focus more upon the issues and facts that are more directly relevant to us as individuals at this particular time in earthly history. What is important to acknowledge is these more highly evolved life forms definitely do not all share our similar materialistic, technological, status orientated perspective of life to define their roles and to provide meaning in their existences. The consciousness inhabiting a life form that is primarily energetic in nature, which vastly supersedes human levels of awareness and perception, could be responsible for maintaining ecological and environmental relationships that human beings do not even know exist. The power and knowledge contained in various forms of crystals, gemstones, and other such elements are far beyond most human beings level of awareness, so it is pointless to address these issues in a discussion such as this when so many other more relevant issues must, in my opinion, take precedence over matters that would seem so improbable or impossible to most human beings at this level of awareness and perception.

Suffice to say, there are unlimited aspects of consciousness immanent within many things within nature; the Earth itself, the planets, the stars, galaxies and the universes and infinite cosmological reality system that would absolutely and completely defy current prevalent human comprehension. To spend considerable amounts of time discussing these issues further is counter-productive to our journey of discovery here. The best way to investigate and confirm these realities in a manner that meets the present evolutionary status of one's life, is to directly experience and contemplate these issues for one's self, over the remainder of your earthly life. This process of perpetually exponentially developing conscious awareness and personal capability will continue after earthly life, when your consciousness is focused upon the higher planes of reality, since you, as Soul, exist as an immortal, omniscient life force of incredible capability beyond your wildest dreams, hopes, or imagination. Your challenge now is to begin to interact more harmoniously with the highest aspects of yourself, Soul and the inner divine super-consciousness we know as God Consciousness. By doing so, one will automatically resonate at higher and more refined energetic frequencies that will attract interactions with other highly evolved life forms of many types. You will recognise the magnificent diversity of astounding consciousness existing around you in your daily life, including other people who will reveal their higher aspects; other creatures will enable you to recognise their true levels of intelligence and innate divinity, as will various other uplifting life forms begin to communicate with you in harmony with the best aspects within your character. Likewise, we can sometimes recognise the lesser aspects of our own character and far more readily perceive the less than ideal attitudes and behaviours of others as well.

About twenty years ago, as a well-informed UFO researcher, I possessed a strong desire to personally meet with these more divinely inspired extraterrestrial and alien life forms and many interesting experiences resulted during those years. Finally, it was implied to me through a series of dramatic events that my phase as a UFO researcher could take two divergent directions. It soon became increasingly evident that once I began overt interpersonal direct face to face communication and interaction with these life forms, then my life would cease to remain 'mine'. That process would have resulted in me losing control of my life events and ending any semblance of 'normality' that I had previously enjoyed. On one very memorable occasion late at night in the New Mexico desert I had the long-awaited opportunity to board the spacecraft or to simply walk away. After some serious rapid deliberation and inner 'encouragement', I chose the latter option with knowing confidence. The simple powerful message I telepathically received after making that decision and began walking away from the direction of the landed spacecraft was the wise friendly suggestion to, "Go away and make something out of your life". That was over thirty years ago and although my highly evolved friends and their various associates still periodically 'check in' to determine how I am doing, they have generally 'left me alone' to discover many wonderful and significantly more important things. My life fortunately took a better direction that enabled me to learn alternative information and have other experiences than would have occurred if I had chosen to board that landed spacecraft in that remote private location, as I had 'requested' occur at that time in my life.

It is not appropriate or relevant for me to speculate with you about the actual nature and motives of the life forms that I am aware exist, nor those that I am informed by reliable sources as existing because what is most important is that you are able to consider such information from your own perspectives. It is not for me to define what level of consciousness and astounding capabilities that higher life forms possess, or even that of your own pets, or the wild animals around your home. What is vital is that you know these facts exist and are readily available to you, if you wish to experience them for yourself. We do not intend to share our most special life experiences, realisation, revelations and inexplicable transformations with others in a melodramatic, sensationalistic manner; as some people would remain informed by tabloids about the lives of famous people, or watch some television 'soap opera', nor as a type of interpersonal 'bragging contest'. No, this mentality has no relation to our quest for spiritual and intellectual enlightenment.

It has been challenging for me to deliberately omit an extensive variety of indisputable personal experiences that allowed me to determine the reality of some things. For example, I have experienced the reality of the disincarnate, powerful 'negative force' that some would call Satan, the Devil, or by other names, which currently exerts so much adverse influence within the Physical and Astral Planes of existence. It was a most unpleasant, extremely frightening experience in which I felt as though I was literally forced to fight for my life, which I did successfully with true love as my greatest attribute. However, even this negative force is an aspect of divine creation whose role and responsibility is to imprison Soul within the lower planes of existence until such time as Soul willingly evolves into Self-awareness and frees itself from the endless cycles of birth, death and re-birth in these lower planes of reality. This powerful entity has an immense non-physical energetic consciousness that influences and to some extent inhabits countless physical life forms, many that manifest all manner of evil and inappropriate states of mind and being on those within earthly, physical and astral levels of reality. One can unwisely choose to ally themselves with this pervasively available negative force and outwardly they may seem to gain quite an impressive array of earthly material rewards including great power, monetary wealth and control over other people and earthly ecosystems, etc. However, in this universe, nothing is really 'for free', so the resulting 'price' one pays for allegiance to the negative force that presently appears to heavily influence the physical and astral planes is much akin to what the religious and fictional stories have so often told us in regard to 'selling one's soul to the devil'. This is not a state of being that any reasonable, sane human being would knowingly wish to exist within by choice, so those that do so will have the opportunity to learn 'the hard way' over countless physical incarnations of the most challenging circumstances. They are also likely to encounter earthly forms of justice in the not so distant future.

We unwittingly 'sentence' ourselves to untold numbers of earthly life times in various relatively unpleasant physical locations, often living quite difficult lives that are often characterised by witnessing, inflicting or experiencing suffering, depravation and interpersonal conflict until we learn from these unhappy experiences and honestly seek a 'higher' better path through eternal existence. The only real perpetual salvation that is available at any time for one is to sincerely with all our heart, mind and being; genuinely decide to identify our self predominantly with God/Creator as Soul, the highest, best, most divinely loving and perceptively wise aspect of our comprehensive state of being. When we begin to consciously identify ourselves as actually being Soul; rather than the lower aspects of our overall nature, then we truly begin our transcendental increasingly bliss-filled journey of discovery 'home' to God, our Creator.

This is the entire point of this discussion in a 'nutshell'. At some point in our seemingly endless journeys through physical reality and the various 'lower' planes of existence; as Soul, our true eternal self, we each begin to again seek to unify our conscious awareness with God, the inner ultimate Source of all consciousness, our Creator. Then, over the infinite eons of expanding time and space, as Soul, we progressively evolve, develop and unfold into greater and higher states of conscious awareness and commitment to serve as a 'vehicle' for the expression and demonstration of God's manifestation in these various cosmic reality systems, regardless of where and who we may be at the time.

Alternatively, the negative force that apparently rules our planetary system of reality always finds plenty of debauched characters who are happily oblivious to the existence of conscience within themselves, denying consistently the realism or expression of their higher nature, as Soul, through their physical vehicles while in earthly life. Upon their death, when again facing the self-evident, mostly awful realities they created while on Earth or the other lower astral planes; then they usually plead for the mercy they failed to show to others during their lives. They may instead plead ignorance and profess to have been unable to hear their intentionally forgotten 'voice' of conscience, Soul, speaking internally or even externally through others, to heed the divine principles of love, justice and the rights of others to decent, fair treatment. Life in the lower planes is all about making the best possible choices according to what in our deepest true self, Soul, knows to be right and true; when contrarily there appears to exist so much opportunity for earthly material gain and hedonistic enjoyment available to those choosing self-interest and various types of counter-productive, unkind thoughts and deeds. So, in establishing this unlimited realm of possible choices for us, the negative force is simply doing its job in providing all the options for human beings and other life forms existing upon these lower planes. We each and all have the opportunity to freely, willingly, kindly, compassionately and lovingly to choose the best thoughts and actions in our daily lives, or the converses. In this life process on Earth and in eternity we indeed will reap whatever we sow, both literally and metaphorically.

Until one's body is dead upon the physical plane in earthly life, there is always the opportunity for redemption and divine liberation from the lower planes of existence. Many people in history that knowingly and deliberately lead lives characterised by unspeakable evil actions, have shortly before their death sought to purchase religious absolution for their horrible sins, or vainly confessed their sins in hopes of divine forgiveness through their pandering servile religious authorities. Sorry, this is not the way our eternal reality system actually functions, although many on Earth prefer to believe otherwise.

We have the wonderful opportunity to clearly see and understand the vivid unfoldment of earthly, astral and much higher levels of reality revealing their existence to us. We can simply examine this system of reality and look deeply and honestly into our own hearts, minds and character, ideally to become sincerely and devotedly committed to being the very best individual that is possible for us at this time in our evolutionary development. If we do so, then the infinite divine realities await our exploration and enjoyment. Otherwise, we will have the dubious opportunity to experience every possible optional event in earthly and astral levels of existence many countless times over again. This process of endless cycles of earthly and other 'lower' level lifetimes will continue to occur until we decide once and for all time to identify ourselves; freely, contently, and happily thinking, being, and acting according to the influences of Soul in our various incarnated lives on the infinite planes of cosmic existence. The choice is ours' to make, always and all ways.

On the other extreme end of the scale within eternal existence are the more divinely characterised life forms and entities that are much more divinely infused and inspired. The creative, omniscient, immanent God Consciousness existing within Soul is the ultimate Source of all consciousness within Soul. Conscious life is the preeminent cosmic reality. God Consciousness is the highest level of consciousness known to human beings, although reports of another higher level of Consciousness have been mentioned beyond that indescribable sublime state of Being. God Consciousness is pervasive throughout every plane and level of universal and cosmic reality. This means that in spite of the divinely sanctioned role and authority that the so-called 'negative force' performs in the lower planes to keep evolving Souls trapped and permanently incarcerated within these lower planes of existence until they learn enough to freely seek the development and manifestation of Soul within their normal minds and lives; there is always God's Consciousness, via Soul, available to each and every one of us. In this respect it matters not to us in our own eternal journey of discovery, whether any earthly plutocratic despotic minority of evil doers rules our lovely planet with totalitarian brutality, or whether someday some powerful alien race were to temporarily seek to dominate or attempt to conquer Earth, or whether the entity known as Satan and by many other names, actually rules the lower planes with its subservient evil earthly and astral incarnates doing its vile works for material and other temporal rewards.

The reality that really matters most is our individual choice to earnestly undertake our inner journey of discovery of Soul in this particular earthly lifetime. We do not need or want to wait until we die to attempt to discover a religious version of Heaven, nor find that our 'sins' have created a hell of our own making through our life choices. Heaven is a state of eternal consciousness and being where Soul discovers and consciously manifests the inspirational immanent God Consciousness within during our present earthly sojourn. The challenges presented by the negative influences with the lower planes are merely to serve as impediments and protagonists to slow our spiritual evolutionary progress, if we willingly allow that to occur. Life's many challenges and difficulties build spiritual strength and resilience, if we respond to them in a positive manner, with noble spirit, higher conscience, divine purpose, true love and compassionate kindness for our fellow spiritual travellers. There is nothing in divine law that says anyone should willingly consent to being victimised by evil people. In fact the contrary is true, and in spite of everything we hear in our society about 'turning the other cheek', there is nothing religious, spiritual, noble or brave about allowing one's self or family or nation to be abused, degraded, attacked or deprived by the ruthless, conscienceless attitudes and actions of despotic, evil people or institutions.

While it was surely my personal intention to relay much more information upon the probable nature of highly evolved, divinely motivated life forms and their interactions with Earthlings and other life forms, this has not proven to be the case here in our discussion. I had intended to share a few meaningful examples of incredible and mind expanding events that I have been blessed to experience, yet this is not proving to be directly relevant to the message required in this chapter, much to my surprise. The manner in which this has seemingly 'worked out' has in some ways been a little disappointing for me because I had planned to tell you a few more good stories, from my perspective. However, as you may be somewhat aware, this book is quite substantially a spontaneous communication of Soul, through my unique personality, with 'your' inner Soul. This discussion is not about personalities seeking to impress one another and to dazzle ourselves with fantastic, miraculous stories that sound like science fiction to the immature, unaware conscienceless minds and cold unfeeling hearts that are blinded by illusionary 'lower' aspects of existence.

The 'ripples' that God Consciousness is now 'sending' throughout time, space and all eternal infinite existence knows no boundaries. Those of us who are able to inwardly 'hear' and otherwise sense this innate divine consciousness expressing and manifesting Itself are in full understanding that "the times; they are a' changing", even in physical material levels of reality within this universe. We are most fortunate to be participating in this momentous transformation at a time and location in the physical universe where so many incredibly diverse life forms have arrived upon Mother Earth now to be directly involved in this transcendent moment in planetary, galactic, universal and cosmic history. Very nice to be travelling with YOU all; my friends, teachers and even the 'çabal' and other 'dark' protagonists alike!

May love, peace, gratitude, joy, grace and forgiveness awaken within us all.

Chapter 11

Life Continues After Earthly Life

We have cyclically repeated and progressively expanded many concepts and realities within this discussion. This has served to enable your conscious mind to gradually or intermittently make 'leaps' in intellectual and intuitive perception and understanding that surpass normal ordinary mental processes. This evolutionary process facilitates the development of direct perception by the higher aspects of one's overall state of consciousness, which continues throughout one's immortal existence, as Soul. By enhancing one's ability to integrate the ordinary conscious aspects of temporal logical human intellectual function with the vastly more perceptive, inconceivably wise, brilliantly enlightened, incomprehensibly capable qualities and attributes of eternally aware Soul consciousness, one is in some ways able to transcend the mortal physical conditions of the human body while still living upon this Earth. We do not need to wait until our earthly physical vehicle dies to learn to acquire the capability to enable higher aspects of our comprehensive integrated consciousness to explore cosmic systems of reality and improve our individual and collective reality systems by our wise perceptive mutual choices.

An earlier story mentioned an experience when as a young man I foolishly attempted to consciously astral project out of my body while in a fully awakened state, which is definitely not the process I am discussing here now, nor should that method ever be used for many reasons. What I am describing now is the capability developed under the right circumstances to learn to focus one's conscious attention, such as while at a deep level of concentration, in meditation, or in contemplation and then shift one's 'point' of conscious attention to other locations to perceive various things that ideally are beneficial to one's life and spiritual development. This may seem in some ways to be similar to what is termed 'remote viewing', or the previously recorded experience where we 'remotely' perceived people's health condition and then 'channelled' healing energies to them from Divine sources. While the processes are quite alike in some key ways, the application of higher levels of consciousness characterise this type of perception. The goal here is for one to be able to learn to 'move' or 'shift' an aspect of conscious attention to higher planes of existence while awake in meditation or contemplation, somewhat as we already naturally do at times when sleeping at night, mostly upon the astral levels of reality for many people, yet also upon the higher planes or dimensions as well. In this procedure we will basically enable Soul's conscious awareness to almost instantly 'travel' to the destination to experience various thoughts, feelings, perceptions, access information or illuminate our human consciousness in some manner. This uplifting contemplative process allows aspects of one's conscious awareness, through the application of various qualities of Soul consciousness, to consciously 'shift focus' to other locations, historical periods, higher planes of reality and various other cosmic reality systems, if one is 'authorised' to do so according to the level of spiritual unfoldment they have attained. Most human beings are generally limited or confined to the physical plane and while dreaming to the lower levels of the Astral Plane, yet as Soul, one has no such limitations.

We will nominally address only the basics in modest detail here because it surpasses what is appropriate for me to attempt to describe here due to the nature of such a relatively limited mode of interaction. However, once again, Soul has no such limitations. Soul exists within you and would be delighted to make information and experience available to you directly, as and when you are able to become receptive in your ability to acquire and utilise such capabilities in a reasonable, responsible, beneficial, positive, kindly', loving and peaceful manner. The focal issue we wish to elucidate is that you possess immensely magnificent potential, as Soul, to exponentially expand your conscious awareness capabilities while existing within the earthly physical body. This ongoing process involves your becoming progressively more conscious of Soul's existence within aspects of your overall state of being. As you begin to realise this reality and are able to sincerely identify yourself in a balanced sane manner as being an aspect of Soul, resulting in an enhanced inner conscious integration with Soul, there will be a sequence of ascertainable inner accomplishments that serve to characterise this developmental process. These would usually occur while in meditation or contemplation, yet they could occur unexpectedly at almost any time one is in a relaxed, positive, receptive state of mind. For each individual, this unfoldment process will likely vary in unique ways.

A few of the key indicators that one is making considerable spiritual progress are a heightened sense of inner peace, wholeness, comfort, joy, deep gratitude for life's many blessings, challenges, realisations, sense of connectedness and 'belonging' within life and enhanced inner self-acceptance that is derived significantly from the integration processes. It is important to realise this ideal state of mind exemplifies and reveals the occurrence of a 'shift' in consciousness that we have previously described. It is essential to recognise that one's mental status transforms from a relatively 'ordinary' state of being such as one experiences in everyday life, full of activities that keep one's mind jumping around to deal with everything that is happening within and around you, to this enormously more tranquil, perceptive, alert and spiritually functional state of being. By possessing an attitude characterised by a receptive, alert, lovingly positive, patient, consistent, persistent, relaxed state of being, then this shift in consciousness can occur. Once one is familiar in attaining these enhanced levels of consciousness, the transition can easily occur from one's normal levels of awareness to a significantly expanded type of conscious awareness within seconds or minutes. Ideally one seeks to increasingly manifest this enhanced type of conscious awareness continually as much as possible in all circumstances, including within one's dreams while sleeping.

Many of us reading this book will already have progressed well beyond this relatively preliminary level of heightened awareness, whether it has been accomplished through ongoing conscious practice or more unconsciously as a natural personal development or attribute. This capability is something for which we are all most grateful, because around us we can see many people that are really suffering in life and would dearly love to experience some peace of mind, joy, true love, higher levels of meaning and inner comfort. We realise we must continually develop to remain in harmony with this form of higher consciousness, forever progressively unfolding into more refined and more capable states of being. In other words, if one ceases to consciously attain these quality states of mind and being on a regular basis; then over passing time, these desirable states of mind will relatively quickly become more elusive and more challenging to experience 'at will'.

Let's mention a few other basic preliminary important characteristic indicators that one is making good spiritual progress. These would be the ability to inwardly, within one's 'spiritual eye'; the 'third eye' spoken of in metaphysical literature which is located just above and between one's eyebrows, 'see' the 'blue light' or other lovely colours after a brief period of relaxation, meditation or contemplation. This can be experienced by closing your eyes, relaxing by letting go of stresses, fears or other troubling unpleasant emotions and thoughts, and silencing one's internal dialogue and stream of thoughts; then 'look' within one's spiritual consciousness 'outwards' or 'inwards' as the case may be, to see the radiant vividly blue round light upon one's field of 'inner vision'. If you are able to accomplish this already or can do so after some practice, then this is a good indicator that one is progressing well. In some religious scriptures this ability has been related as 'seeing the light', although there are other ways one can 'see the light' both literally and figuratively speaking, such as during an illumination experience of which there are numerous varieties.

If one is having considerable difficulty in relaxing and settling one's thoughts and emotions into a tranquil, yet alert state of conscious awareness, then the following form of contemplation will be of great assistance. We use the term contemplation here, rather than meditation because this process is designed to be far more active. In traditional meditation one primarily seeks to establish silence within one's mind and establish one's consciousness upon the 'higher' dimensional planes. The following contemplation can be used for many purposes, including the preparation of our consciousness to progressively develop the unique qualities we seek to engender over passing time and ongoing cyclical spiritual unfoldment. One sits or lies down comfortably, relaxes the body, mind and emotions, letting go of all thoughts and emotions to the best of one's ability. Then with eyes gently closed, one summons an inner sense of peace, love, kindness and compassion to the best of your ability and 'looks' from a point about two finger's width above and between one's eyebrows in vertical line with one's nose, 'outwards' or 'inwards' with relaxed, receptive anticipation to see this intensely beautiful blue coloured light on the inner field of one's vision. Other coloured lights may appear, yet the vivid blue colour is one that indicates attaining the state of being that we are seeking in this contemplation process, generally speaking. It will be very helpful for anyone seeking to attempt this contemplation to either aloud or silently to softly sing the word 'Hu' (pronounced like the word 'hue' or the name 'Hugh'), in a long drawn out manner for between several seconds to as long as ten or twenty seconds upon the outgoing breath. Singing 'Hhhhhuuuuuuuu' in this manner can be repeated as many times as one wishes; for up to ten, twenty or more minutes, if necessary or desirable to achieve the results one wishes to attain, or it can be sung periodically if one finds that method more helpful, or even silently inwardly.

The word Hu is an ancient name for God and singing it, whether inwardly or in an auditory manner in this longer drawn out fashion, will definitely assist one to make considerable progress in harmonising one's consciousness with Soul levels of awareness over passing time. If one does not obtain results after twenty or thirty minutes, then simply stop the efforts and relax and enjoy the relaxation, then go about one's normal daily life. It may also help to invite Soul and Divinity to reveal or express Itself within one's normal consciousness at the beginning or during this contemplation experience. One may also significantly benefit by focusing their attention upon an overall attitude of gratitude for all of the gifts and blessings they experience in life in a humble, appreciative, loving manner, characterised by surrender to one's conception of Divine Spirit or God. This will often serve to calm and quiet an over-active mind if one is unable to readily silence one's internal dialogue.

A less well-known, further positive indicator that one is making good spiritual progress is to hear relatively subtle 'sounds' through inner perceptive processes that seem to be audible noises. These inwardly auditory 'sounds' vary for different people, yet commonly this pleasant 'sound' can often be akin to the noise a distant swarm of bees would make, like a high pitched humming noise, or somewhat of a pleasing humming sound like a highly pitched, energetic, electrical frequency type noise, although this sound is much more melodious and natural. Alternatively, one may hear the very soft subtle sounds of beautiful musical instruments playing, or a flute quietly playing a captivating score, or an unusually beautiful bird song that may fascinate you and inspire a wonderful feeling of peace, love and joy within you. Some hear singing or orchestral sounding music or even melodious chanting. Usually these experiences of hearing these inwardly audible 'sounds' occur while one is in a relaxed, peaceful, kindly disposition. This experience could occur at almost any time; perhaps while resting, mediating, contemplating, observing nature, or while watching one's children playing calmly and nicely together, or while watching a beautiful sunrise or sunset, or walking in the forest, lying on the beach, or even while playing golf, or almost anything that you enjoy doing that encourages a tranquil state of mind and being within you. This 'sound' in not an external auditory noise, rather it is a sense of inner spiritual hearing that one acquires and it is most beneficial and purifying in inexplicable ways. You may hear 'the sound' occasionally, or as one progresses spiritually, you may hear it far more often, or even all of the time and 'the sound' in no way affects or distracts one's normal physical hearing abilities. This is not at all related to the medical condition known as "tinnitus", although undoubtedly countless people have gone to their doctors thinking they may have this medical condition with ringing or other noise in their ears, when really it is 'the sound', an aspect of divine reality opening one's inner senses of perception. Just as we hear religious people say, "I've seen the Light"; well, we can someday also say, "I have heard the Sound." When I first heard about the Sound, I was somewhat dubious, yet please allow me to reassure you this is a reality that at some point definitely accompanies increased Soul awareness.

By consciously enhancing the acuity of one's perceptive awareness through integrating Soul consciousness within one's ordinary conscious mind, the flow of the 'light' and 'sound' increasingly intensifies as one is progressively enabled to cope with these beneficial effects. Basically, what we are describing is a process by which one receptively seeks 'with effortless effort' to establish and maintain the appropriate spiritual conditions within themselves to attract the inflow of divine energetic frequencies that uplift, enlighten and illuminate one's state of being to an extent that one is better able to serve God through various aspects manifested in one's life. These divine energies that we can visualise as being 'light and sound' are actually physically existing qualities composed of the essence of God's substance, known as the Holy Spirit or ECK. These energetic aspects of divinely conscious reality are available to us in direct proportion to our capacity to enliven and manifest true love, peace, joy, freedom, gratitude, humility, wisdom, truth and other such divine attributes in our earthly life and beyond.

Through the positive preparation of one's comprehensive state of consciousness and energetic bodies, the influx of these transformative light and sound energies progressively augment, in variable cycles of growth and resting, one's spiritual unfoldment or evolutionary ascendency in ways that considerably surpass human understanding. The goal is to welcome these divine energies into one's overall being; to cleanse, purify, regenerate, ameliorate, uplift and transform one's state of being by engendering the immanent example, expression and manifestation of various divine qualities and attributes through one's human characteristics and personality. This is a natural process where some simple adjustments to one's overall consciousness will inevitably result in these wonderfully invigorating incremental transformative qualities becoming exemplary characteristics within one's daily life in innumerably diverse and often internally unrecognised ways. The reasons we seek to alter our normal state of consciousness to become more attractive and receptive to these divine energies is because they are actually the energetic essence of divinity, which ultimately will openly express the higher levels of consciousness that are naturally manifesting through our physical bodies and mind. This process better enables us to realise the preeminent meaning and purpose for our immortal existence at each apparently successive, although actually co-existing, level of our eternal development. By receptively inspiring the influx of divinely conscious energies we perceive as being 'the light and sound'; our spiritual nature is nourished upon divine essence, just as our physical bodies are nourished by food, water and the air we breathe.

We can examine the resulting lives, bodies, minds and levels of consciousness exemplified by people who do not truly seek to receive or manifest the highest aspects of their overall states of being. An excellent example of this unfortunate situation can be observed in people that are addicted to self-abusive patterns of thought and behaviour; such as to drugs, alcohol, cigarettes, gambling, sexual depravity, greed, violence or other human vices. While some such people may appear outwardly to avoid paying a severe price for their attitudes and actions that establish various forms of self-abnegation of the divine qualities within themselves; inwardly they are existing in an energetically deficient state of being where they are unable to adequately replenish their expended divine essence because it is not being obtained as rapidly as it is being exhausted. In other words, most self-abusive, negative people diminish their reserves of divine energy much faster than it is being replaced, largely due to their attitudes, beliefs and actions. One can recall many examples of people we have known or observed in our lives who, as they aged, become increasingly depleted of their innate energetic essence. As a result, they subsequently began to deteriorate quite noticeably in a variety of indicative ways, such as through physical and mental illnesses, uncontrollable addictive behaviours, the loss of mental function and so on. Many of these types of people have little affinity with the divine spirit concealed within themselves, nor do they generally respect truth, justice, or true love externally, so they generally choose instead to energetically 'feed' upon other people's energies in various ways and also seek sustenance upon what we may overly-simplistically define as negative energies. These quite unwholesome, debilitating tendencies cause them to gradually acquire a vibrational status or 'vibe' that can be readily detected by perceptive people. It is very wise to **be exceedingly selective with whom we share our energies**, especially where intimacy issues are involved, because unpleasant life lessons are often affiliated with interactions with such deleterious people.

We seek to develop the capability to remain acutely perceptive in a relaxed, non-judgmental manner of the overall nature of people with whom we interact. One manner in which we do this is by observing the relative 'level' that various people function upon. Specifically, we would prefer to interact with those openly exhibiting sincerity, genuineness, higher values, truthfulness, reliability, a productive sharing nature, and inner happiness within their character. Conversely, people that habitually express negative emotional states such as anger, excessive complaining, jealously, or unreasonable fears and aggression, who possess various addictive behaviours, and who tend to be manipulative or seem to be overly guarded, unreliable, prone to flattery, deceit, with undue attention given to external appearances, and so on; would be ideal types of people to avoid or limit one's interactions with as much as possible, especially where intimate relationships are concerned. We all will recognise that some people present an external façade that is consciously or unconsciously deceptive to varying degrees, yet generally over passing time we will obtain an excellent perceptive awareness of the true qualities of people in our lives. If people prove themselves unworthy of our trust, treat us poorly in various ways or indulge in inappropriate behaviours that are unacceptable to us, then we need to adjust our relationships so that these people are no longer able to be a detrimental influence upon our lives. Admittedly we all have varying degrees of imperfections so understanding and acceptance of our own human nature issues, as well as those of others is important. However, if we knowingly remain in relationships that are damaging to our emotional, mental, physical and spiritual well-being, then we urgently need to examine all the relevant issues to determine the reasons for the continuance of such unpleasant circumstances. Then, with clear perception about the entire situation, we ideally will make a plan to improve matters and follow it through in a positive, responsible, kindly manner.

An essential aspect of our spiritual development is perceptively, very selectively choosing our preferred life experiences; and then accepting these events as being methods to reach realisations that increase our wisdom, ability to love and enjoy life. We do not need to knowingly involve ourselves with others that are upon a path of self-destruction due to their counter-productive attitudes and activities. In my opinion, all people have a right and inner duty to live according to their own choices, so an integral aspect of one's journey of discovery is to intentionally choose to predominantly associate with people who recognise their inner divinity, cherish life's blessings and seek to manifest the superlatives within themselves in daily life. This is not to suggest that we would ordinarily ostracise or go to ridiculous lengths of avoid people with lifestyles and attitudes that significantly differ from our own because part of our life path is to interact with all types of people here on Earth. We simply seek to make our own choices about all of our thoughts and actions according to the astute observational powers we possess so that our lives steadily progress, not regress and as much as possible are characterised by a sense of inner peace, joy and true love.

One of the issues that enable the problems and stressful conditions of our world to remain so prevalent is that the good, compassionate, hard working people are often quite prone to be coerced or manipulated into enduring negative situations. Or in more crude words, these kindly, well-meaning, somewhat naïve people 'willingly put up with other people's crap'. We have all experienced circumstances when others acted poorly, perhaps over long periods of time. As good, considerate, forgiving people, we are expected to continue to remain polite, supportive, patient and pleasant; in spite of the fact we are being intentionally abused, mistreated deceived, manipulated and damaged in various ways by such people who often proclaim themselves to be the ones that are being victimised in some manner or another. Well, my friend, we do **NOT** need or want to accept or 'go along quietly' with those deleterious modes of thinking and acting anymore. From my perspective, the time of self-responsibility for one's thoughts and actions has now arrived, as being the ideal way to achieve what is best for us, as individuals and as a civilisation. We seek to enjoy a relatively peaceful, happy, productive, simple, enjoyable life; not to knowingly involve ourselves in the detrimental, distasteful, misapplied, abusive lifestyles that some in our society indulge themselves upon. We are truly able to learn from all people, so we focus our attentions upon perceptively observing life's diverse realities upon every level of our existence.

This process of choosing and creating one's reality to the best of our ability is an essential attribute that we seek to engender throughout our immortal existence, beginning here on Earth right now, in earnest. To carefully select the various choices we make in our lives is the consummate preparation for the subsequent levels of reality where thought or consciousness composes the ultimate basis for those systems of reality. As one thinks, so they will become over passing time. On the higher planes of existence well-beyond the Astral Plane, thought is instantaneously applied into action. Also, one's thoughts and state of being are completely transparent and self-apparent to other life forms existing there, so there is no possibility to be as deceptive or manipulative with others as so often occurs here upon Earth. Therefore, by becoming more deliberate and self-aware of our thinking processes and the resulting actions, we are preparing ourselves for our lives upon these higher levels of reality that will be so much more equitable and enjoyable than life is upon the lower planes of existence for most of us.

As we have discussed previously, life on Earth is intentionally divinely designed to offer all life forms unlimited opportunity to make free-willed choices and then experience the results of those decisions manifested in our physical reality. The enormous challenge for us here in this earthly life is to freely aspire to personify an impeccable state of mind that is characterised by divinely inspired value systems and behaviour patterns that enable us to be a positive, uplifting, kindly influence upon those around us in earthly life. We also seek to benefit the earthly environments within which we exist, surrounded by other conscious life forms of enormous variety. Every thought, action and word has an effect on the present moment and future in some ways. We can make a conscious decision to make quality actions that can even help transform the past for the better, as inexplicable as that may seem to one's normal mind.

We need to be increasingly proficient in our ability to analyse and select the best available options by freely and deliberately choosing our thoughts and actions from the impetus of internal motive force; from within one's own consciousness. Most people are motivated in our earthly lives by many external sources, many of which seem virtually out of one's control or influence. For example, most of us need to work to earn a living. Far fewer of us truly love our chosen occupation or really enjoy the company of all the particular people with whom we share our working days, aside from some positive exceptions that we all would readily acknowledge. This situation can be a conscious or unconscious choice one makes, whereby one is willingly 'giving up' or resigning one's inner ability to decide exactly what we want to do to be productive in society to earn an income to sustain our lifestyle, which also influences the types of people we invest our time with upon a daily basis. Some of us are fortunate enough to have made internally motivated choices that gradually have created an ideal lifestyle with their chosen life companions. Often this process involves a complex series of sequential realisations, challenging decisions and the need to resolve onerous circumstances in order to accomplish this pleasant living situation, which is well-worth the efforts. This can be a lengthy process of self-assessment, preparation, ongoing persistent efforts, continual observation, complicated interactions, detailed external assessments, incremental improvements, reassessment, adjustment, further realisations; followed by more efforts, enhanced realisations and additional adjustments that are unified and integrated within progressive cyclic patterns of advancing circumstances; whereby one seeks and ultimately finds their rightful, relatively comfortable productive 'place' in the world. The prerequisite secret in accomplishing this process is to initially realise and commit one's self to the fact that to be successful we must first develop the 'right' mental attitudes, visualise and identify with the best aspects of our character and then harmonise with the sublime spiritual states of being within ourselves; which helps to create the external manifestations of our dreams, needs, desires and hopes.

We are now preparing ourselves for eternal life in our temporal earthly lives and this complex process is composed of an endless sequence of discoveries, progressive developments, ongoing refinements, applying increased awareness and capabilities. Because your immortal existence is an eternal journey; it is indeed a 'very long road'; so this is a focal reason that we must learn to 'relax into' the processes of life so that we are relatively happy, comfortable and 'at peace' within the various aspects of our own overall character. One key talent we must acquire is to become able to realise exactly what we truly believe and know as being truth for us as individuals; then being able to assert our own self-will to establish and maintain lives that are in harmony with our values, needs, standards, attitudes and preferred lifestyle.

For example, one may desire a relatively lavish lifestyle, yet to achieve such an idyllic earthly status we may believe that we must compromise our belief systems to become successful in this extremely challenging and competitive world. In some senses, this may be true from one's current perspective; however, by adjusting one's attitudes and perceptions, we can determine a wide variety of methods to attain a great lifestyle that meets all of one's other 'higher' needs and desires as well. Rather than to compromise one's values to do a type of work that one would find objectionable in various ways; we could instead decide that we do not really need to be as materially wealthy as we would ideally prefer to be, especially considering how much we would likely have to sacrifice in other areas of our life that would be far more important to our true happiness, security, peace of mind and joyous interactions with others. Our premeditated decision to pursue a less glamorous lifestyle in a lower paying occupation that we enjoy may inaccurately seem to disadvantage us in some ways. Actually, by deciding to focus upon what we like doing, or want to try to do even if we are unsuccessful; then it is likely that we will achieve a far better life and state of mind than if we had chosen other lesser alternatives that appeared superior, yet would have become detrimental to our overall character development. We are seeking to create immortal spiritual wealth and truly loving, generous, wise, strength of character in our earthly choices; not simply to acquire temporal material abundance and public recognition for our accomplishments here that will not really serve our eternal best interests. The ideal scenario is to accomplish everything we seek, want and need in earthly life and remain true to our higher values and aspirations as well. We are very fortunate to have some quality people in life to mentor, guide and inspire us. Also, it is important to understand that there is nothing inherently negative, evil or wrong with financial and material wealth, if one utilises these gifts of life in positive, uplifting beneficial ways to the betterment of one's self and others. There is nothing innately inappropriate or non-spiritual about living an earthly life characterised by an abundant lifestyle, rather the effects and influences this has upon one's own development and others is a key defining quality to consider.

All around us in earthly life today in 2016, we vividly see the deleterious effects of rampant greed and self-interest literally tearing our civilisation apart 'at the seams' by intentionally undermining and destroying the essential fundamental adhesive, integrative, necessary social structures. Family cohesion is under continual pressure, influences to disrupt inter-cultural harmony abound, the environment is being absolutely devastated, over-population is becoming a tragic epidemic in some parts of the world, our political leaders are inept, often corrupted, ineffectual and subservient to the forces of greed and oppression, the intelligent perceptive people of Earth have been subdued and estranged from positions of social responsibility to function mainly as observers and critics, and internally many individuals are gradually losing 'touch' with our innermost sense of true self. There also exist countless other subtle and overt confrontational alterations to disrupt and prevent the expression of the potentially positive attributes that should ideally serve to characterise our individual characters and global civilisation.

We can very clearly see that there are malevolent dark forces at work upon this Earth that have no consideration whatsoever for the status or plight of future earthly generations or other life forms living here. Imagine the horrible world we would already now live in if all people consented willingly to the plans and goals of these short-sighted, narrow-minded, extremely ignorant, greedy, corrupted, autocratic, arrogant, self-absorbed, moronic imbeciles? It is insanity to destroy our civilisation for the short-term capitalistic prosperity for the minority of those controlling most of the world's surplus wealth at the expense of earthly environments and the vast majority of the world's people. We can identify a large number of so-called political and business 'leaders' around the world that proudly epitomise this unmistakeably degenerate, pathetic, feeble-minded, conflict-prone, deluded, conscienceless mentality. These people clearly and openly hubristically represent the abysmal, rotten, putrefied, predatory, unsustainable ideologies of the ruling class and gladly inflict these debased, unsustainable, insane policies upon this Earth today, with all the unfounded over-confidence and self-destructive nature of any madman. These haughty deranged people obviously do not care about the innate wisdom or the 'will of the people' of this Earth, nor the fate of life forms living here. We can easily determine the probable disastrous destiny of our world if the current situation is not radically improved in the very near future through the commonsense, sane, productive combined effort of thinking people being exerted in all areas of social concern. This process begins within you and me, ideally today and every day thereafter. We have already seen the awful results of allowing the corrupted despots to control our civilisation and we will now more sincerely begin to choose another much better alternative: the rule of wise and good people. The ultra-wealthy will undoubtedly remain incredibly wealthy, yet ideally they too will recognise and accept the urgent need and benefits of enabling and allowing well-motivated, intelligent capable people to avert sure disaster by providing solutions through all working cooperatively together, without animosity or jealousy, with understanding that greedy and corrupt people will likely remain in that state of being for eons to come unless encouraged by sane, productive, loving compassionate, empathetic people to do otherwise. The unfortunate karmic justice that will surely be dealt out to degenerate, evil, psychopathic people throughout countless future successive earthly lifetimes that will be characterised by abject poverty, chaotic, violent and fear-ridden living conditions will provide them with a much better understanding of the results of their current inappropriate attitudes and actions.

It may seem strange to so thoroughly continue to mix our discussion here with so many different issues that seem to be beyond one's immediate influence or control. The key concept is the words 'seem to be' since we are usually able to accomplish anything we truly choose to do. This discussion is all about 'choice' here and we have seen the choices being made by those people now ruling our world every day of our lives and this simply is not 'good enough' anymore. As individuals, we can see the results of allowing our normal human consciousness to completely dominate our higher aspects of immortal Soul consciousness and this too is no longer acceptable for some of us that desire more in our lives than 'the lowest common denominator', or whatever type of meagre oppressed lifestyle that is offered to us by global society, traditional religions and our mainstream education and employment systems. Admittedly, many of us have wonderful lives and life itself is quite delightful, yet we see proportionately for the vast majority of people in this world, life presents far more onerous, unnecessary, unjust and inappropriate challenges than should ideally occur in a so-called 'civilised' global society.

Our innate wisdom surpasses everything we now see around us in earthly societies and it is time for us to join together with all like-minded aware people to stand up for what we believe in and know to be right and say "Enough is enough and we are not going to travel down the horrible road toward foolish unnecessary self-destruction any longer." Of course there will be some resistance to people expressing themselves in such a way, yet what are the alternatives? Do you want your children to die in meaningless wars, or do you want to die unnecessarily of painful diseases that could have been prevented by an adequate diet of nutritious foods or that could be cured with the available natural remedies widely known to various people, or do you perhaps suffer depression, insomnia, mental and emotional turmoil over your life's experiences, and so on? Why do we continue to allow the forces controlling our world to dictate so many unjust, counter-productive, inequitable rules and regulations for us to blindly follow toward our certain doom? As the millions of Jews in World War Two were marched toward their deaths; they were hoping for some mercy, some sanity, some justice and exactly what they received is clearly before us on photographs, on films and in the history books, as well as still being quite painfully etched in some people's lives permanently. Why should so many people in today's world and future generations willingly follow in the same footsteps toward a similar impending murderous fate as have history's other countless millions of innocent victims of genocide, war, intentionally inflicted disease and starvation at the vile hands of these inhuman culprits? No, not this time, my friends; this time we will not allow this to happen. For we who ask, "What can be done?" all that is required is to look inside your spirit and the answers will be readily available to you, to me, and to all of us. We do not seek violence, we do not seek confrontation, we do not seek unnecessary adversity, we are definitely not terrorists who seek to inflict harm upon defenceless people or anyone; however, we will not willingly 'lie down' to be slaughtered and further enslaved this time.

With these somewhat morbid, yet accurate inspirational thoughts and feelings being firmly secured within our minds and hearts to help motivate us; let's focus upon what positive actions we will do to improve our lives and our civilisation. First, we must examine our lives, our minds and those of our family to determine what we will do to improve our relationships. We can accomplish this best by initially stimulating an enhanced sense of self-respect by doing what we know to be right and necessary in our lives. It would be good to start with doing some things you enjoy doing or feel need to be done, which includes better honest communications and mutually respectful actions among all people. It may start with cleaning out one's garage, meditating, taking the family for a picnic, volunteering at an aged care facility, getting more exercise in moderation, planting some trees, working with your child on their homework, becoming a more relaxed and happier person, coming out of 'retirement' to become active in your community and world to better utilise your skills, knowledge and financial abilities, driving your vehicle in a way that conserves more fuel, be more conscious of your influences upon others, stop wasting water and other resources, express yourself more truthfully with others, be more loving with your family and be kinder to other people including strangers, be more forgiving with yourself and do your best to improve your character in various ways, or whatever you feel like doing that is beneficial, productive and enjoyable. Ideally that will not include travelling the world as an idle tourist in order to escape boredom and see that things need similar types of remedial attention just about everywhere you could go. Start at home, start within yourself, start within your own family and community and go from there; where your true heart, mind and spirit is located, where your real commitment and inner strength exists. Enjoyment will soon follow with your efforts and others of like-spirit. Say hello to a stranger in the street, attend a religious service of another religion to create more community harmony and mutual respect and understanding, or whatever you wish to do that creates love and enjoyment within your life, at no one else's expense. We do these productive, inspirational, uplifting activities because they serve to bring us closer to the 'higher' immortal aspects of ourselves, more in harmony with one another; thus providing us with greater purpose and joy in our earthly lives, which helps prepare one and all for our future lives within higher levels of eternal reality.

For each of us, the choices will be unique, yet our vision and ultimate purpose is united in perceiving what needs to be accomplished to genuinely improve our world civilisation and save our deteriorating earthly environmental systems. Most urgently we need to begin to develop and implement genuinely effective, efficient energy conservation programs globally, especially in all developed and heavily populated nations. For example, there is no sane reason to burn so many electric lights at night to light our cities while most of us are sleeping. Many people are somewhat afraid of the dark mostly because they are not 'illuminated' from within themselves. It is time we ceased to worry so much about requiring street lights in our cities so unknown strangers walking in the streets could be seen, if they were there and we were by chance to look out of our shuttered, curtained windows to see them walk by. We can now have sensor lights in our homes that detect movement and turn on if someone enters our property at night, which is far more energy and security efficient. It is now the time to delight in the opportunity to marvel in wonder at the millions of stars shining in the luminous skies at night and gather our inner most thoughts and feelings, instead of mindlessly watching so much inane television. We need to renovate and redevelop vast areas of degraded housing, closed factories and our damaged natural environmental areas within our cities and towns to provide better housing and employment for those in need of improved lifestyles, more fulfilling and truly productive work, enhanced self-respect, greater pride in our local communities, better communication with one another and to know they are making a positive difference to our world in the process. As we rehabilitate our inner cities and towns, there exists the urgent need to establish more tree filled parks, community food gardens, clean deep lakes connected by flowing natural water courses and revitalise the businesses that the local communities require and desire.

Our vehicles absolutely must become more fuel efficient and we must create a society so less travel is required, especially in the large cities, with adjusted work schedules to prevent traffic congestion that also include better designed roads with synchronized traffic signals for more efficient traffic flows. There are many alternative fuel sources such as water, solar electrical (photovoltaic) sources, hydrogen, geothermal and many others, such as healthful healing 'plasma' energy from Mother Earth; that are cleaner and cheaper than fossil fuels. We need to begin utilising them urgently and widely. Traffic control systems must be developed to more efficiently enable the flow of vehicles to avoid unnecessary stops. People must begin to drive with less urgency to save a few meaningless seconds of travel time, especially in our communities, so that they are not accelerating so rapidly, braking sharply and then accelerating rapidly again, which burns much more fuel than a more gradual, steady driving pattern would use. Being more considerate and friendly in our styles of driving would also become more enjoyable and relaxing for us all.

We need to conserve water resources and install water saving devices throughout all water utilisation systems; especially in industry, agriculture and home use. We can take less baths, turn off the water in the shower while we wash ourselves, and learn to not waste water and conserve that most precious resource in countless ways that will serve us all. Rain water and runoff must be captured with home and commercial building water tanks; developing improved community water catchment and recycling schemes; increased industrial recycling of water and acquiring additional water from sewage treatment plants to use in industries where human food consumption or sanitation is not directly affected; more efficient desalination plants must be designed and constructed, with the extracted valuable nutrients from sewage and the sea, with salt water being used in industrial and agricultural applications to rehabilitate degraded farm land; and more effective agricultural irrigation methods and crop selections for various areas must be implemented. There is no need to subsidise the agri-business sector to grow crops that use too much water, especially in low rainfall areas, or are in abundant supply in the international markets, or are used primarily as animal feeds or fabric, such as cotton, corn, soybeans, and sugar cane that are an inefficient crops in many drier areas of the world, since these are now being grown using excessive irrigation and chemicals. More food needs to be grown locally in smaller farms and within urban areas with improved organic growing methods so the nutritious quality, availability and so the cost is more affordable and agriculture becomes more economically sustainable with less transportation and storage being required to moderate and reverse the continually increasing retail prices of food that is charged to consumers. The 'middlemen' and retailers profit far more than those who actually produce our foods and that is an inequitable situation that must be improved as well.

There must be a method used to capture various forms of natural gas that are currently being expelled into the atmosphere and 'burned off' in massive quantities around the world, which is also creating enormous amounts of greenhouse gases in that exceedingly wasteful process. The 'fracking' of the earth to obtain these gases must end permanently. The reliance upon animal protein as human food must be reduced because animals like cattle, sheep and goats produce an enormous amount of greenhouse gas (primarily methane) in their metabolic processes and land clearing to provide ever more pasture is counter-productive and inappropriately uses inordinate amounts of valuable farm land to raise huge volumes of animal feeds or relatively nutrient deficient monoculture crops such as sugar, soybeans, corn, wheat, and cotton when better, more nutritious alternative crops exist. There must be rapid utilisation of all manner of available technologies to reduce pollution and reduce the manufacture and utilisation of toxic materials that are unnecessary or could be made from less toxic or more easily biodegradable safe natural components. Obviously, this would include most weapons of war and these manufacturing operations should be redesigned to manufacture useful, utilitarian items required to improve human civilisation, rather than to destroy it. If the owners of these unsafe, counter-productive, costly industries do not wish to participate in restructuring their corporate industrial operations to become helpful assets to humanity, then alternatively they can be encouraged to sell them to interested buyers or to simply close these businesses permanently, or be taxed out of existence" as being unacceptable, unprofitable and counter-productive enterprises. Taxpayers should demand reasonable spending limits and full accountability upon all military related expenditures in national and international budgets. In recent years, for example, in the USA there have been about three trillion dollars in unexplained expenses or 'lost' funds, which represents about one third of the US budget deficit. Subsequently, governments and people could utilise these manufacturing operations to construct the required industrial products our civilisation will require to rebuild and revitalise itself. We clearly can see that war is used to destroy what is needed by people to improve our lives, so we simply must refuse to participate in such a system of intentional, inefficient self-annihilation that destabilises our civilisation and ruins so many lives and our global environments. Taxation must become more equitable and simple, such as a 1% tax fee on ALL money moving into and out of EVERY bank account globally, including governments, religions and these rapidly accumulating funds would be closely monitored and not squandered by political and economic opportunists. All other forms of taxation would be abolished when that new fair tax system was mandated and then closely managed in a transparent ethical manner.

Beginning immediately, our global civilisation urgently MUST plant many billions of trees to re-balance our global weather patterns, to consume the excessive greenhouse gases, to cool the Earth's land surfaces by shading them from such excessively intense scorching exposure to the sunlight, especially since science has proven the sun's solar radiation has been increasing at this time in history. It is absolutely essential that humans become devoted to planting billions and ultimately many trillions of trees within every possible environmental niche upon planet Earth until this calamity is averted. Planting trees is quite enjoyable, good exercise, and is critically important activity that we all can be involved in; whether through financing the planting through our donations, hiring others to do it for us, or by our own tree planting and conservation efforts. We can all begin by intentionally boycotting timber products that do not come from timber plantations or sustainable, relatively 'environmentally friendly' timber operations that do not involve clear-cutting or the destruction of the largest old-growth forest timbers. We must sincerely manage governments globally to require that legislation be enacted and enforced to genuinely protect the existing forests, implement the widespread use of sustainable forestry methods in existing timber operations and to budget for the costs involved in earnestly planting the required billions and trillions of trees internationally that will help save our natural environments upon Earth for ourselves. These plant nursery and the subsequent tree planting and conservation projects will provide much needed employment to hundreds of millions of people at a time when various unproductive, counter-productive sectors of the economy are being redesigned to become more responsible and genuinely productive for our civilisation's best interests rather than the self-interests of a relative few already exceedingly wealthy groups of people. We must restructure the global economy in many ways and now is the ideal time to accomplish this, before massive social and economic chaos becomes far more pervasive than it is today in our world.

Algae, the small microscopic size water-dwelling creatures living in the oceans and fresh water and other such plant-like microflora, now account for a massive three quarters of all oxygen produced within earthly environments. This is another reason why we must improve and better protect the purity of the oceans, lakes, and our existing man-made water system because these tiny creatures provide the vast majority of the oxygen required in earthly environments, as well as being the foundation of the food chain for all higher animals, including fish, birds, insects, and ultimately we human beings. Protecting these algae, plankton and other microbial life forms that produce oxygen and food resources is especially important and not well recognised currently by many people. This is especially true now that humanity has for many thousands of years excessively cut down the Earth's once vast forests, making the rapidly dwindling number of trees far more important to retain while we replace those trees lost through 'slash and burn' agricultural methods, excessive logging and naturally occurring and man-made forest and grassland fires. While greenhouse gases are an influence on global warming, just as could be increased solar radiation, it is absolutely conclusive that the huge reduction in the forested areas of the planet have increased the radiant heat generated by sunlight reaching denuded, unprotected, under-nourished, depleted soils. One only has to observe the thermal differences in daytime temperatures upon land masses dominated by desert or forest to determine that this factor also has an influence upon global warming.

Fire is the major cause of CO_2 emissions; whether it is from the combustion of carbon based fuels in vehicles; or from fossil-fuelled electrical power generation; such as inefficient, dirty-burning coal and diesel generators, or the burning of natural gas; or fires used in the agricultural process such as sugar cane production, or to enrich the soil, or to clear forested land for pasture or crops, or fires started by people from carelessly discarded cigarettes, arsonists; and naturally occurring lightening. Consider this following simple example: The Launceston City Council in Tasmania, Australia says its wood heater buyback scheme is having a significant impact on the city's air quality. About 2,000 older wood heaters have been replaced under the scheme. The Council is hoping to remove another 8,000 heaters but that is dependent on funding from the Federal Government. The Council's General Manager, Frank Dixon, says winter is always a concern when it comes to air quality in Launceston, but this year the city is yet to exceed national air quality standards. "Since 2001 which is effectively when wood heater buyback schemes started we had 26 days of very high pollution levels in Launceston, last year we had six of those days, we've had none reported to council thus far this year," Mr Dixon said.

We must realise there are many other additional sources of naturally emitted 'greenhouse gases'. Many of these cannot be easily controlled by humans, such as methane gas produced from naturally rotting vegetation, an enormous amount of methane gas is produced by animals in their digestion processes, escaping earthly natural gas, and large amounts of greenhouse gases originating from volcanos and others forms of volcanism. We all must devote our lives to eagerly and intelligently assisting in the improvement of earthly environments, because as the environmentalist Al Gore recently wisely reminded us with words to the effect, "Human commitment to make the necessary improvements in our societies and world is a renewable resource."

We must sincerely develop the many safe, non-toxic, non-polluting sources of energy that are readily available and well-known now and nuclear energy is NOT among these now with our primitive nuclear technologies. There is an ulterior motive among many of those wealthy forces now heavily invested in fossil fuel technologies to greatly increase the widespread use of nuclear energy to power electric generators and this is a very bad idea from numerous perspectives. Nuclear energy proponents are now attempting to insidiously conduct an extensive public disinformation campaign in the global mass media by knowingly falsely stating the untruthful, purported so-called 'benefits' of nuclear energy used to produce electricity. One key aspect of the deliberate plan of calculated deceit now in progress by the nuclear lobby is to have energy production sources over-simplistically defined either greenhouse gas producing or not greenhouse gas producing. The current nuclear technologies are far too expensive and create dangerous radioactive contaminants that are extremely problematic to dispose of at this time in history. The nuclear proponents fail abysmally to provide us with honest factual information, and this is a matter clearly available to the public now. Nuclear advocates admit it is more costly than conventional forms of current electrical energy production, yet they say nuclear technology does not produce as much greenhouse gases or cost to society when nothing could be further from the truth and they know this to be the case and continue to lie about it anyway. Fukashima Japan proves otherwise, as did other global nuclear power plant disasters. Nuclear energy requires huge amounts of greenhouse gas production in the mining of the uranium and the processing of uranium, as well as huge needs for water which is a dwindling precious resource, and ultimately in the transport and storage of the resulting nuclear waste. Nuclear proponents plan to dispose of nuclear waste materials by putting them down deep holes in the ground, whereas for years the barrels containing nuclear contaminated materials were simply dumped various places, such as in the ocean, stored in large piles above-ground and in shallow underground pits. The record of how much radiation and toxic material contamination is related to the entire processes involved in the nuclear industry has never been made publicly available, yet we see the results in our deteriorating health and the degradation of many earthly environments as a direct and indirect result of this insanely vile form of energy production to enrich a few elite, well-entrenched, unscrupulous business people and their international companies. No mention whatsoever is given by nuclear advocates about the devastating health damage done to the unfortunate uranium miners who will suffer a drastically higher risk of developing and dying excruciatingly painful deaths from lung cancers and other aggressive diseases from their exposure to these toxic materials. Nor do these nuclear devotees bother to address the issue that nuclear accidents such as Chernobyl and 3 Mile Island are inevitable and the extensive nuclear radiation and contamination will be catastrophic and result in many unnecessary deaths, diseases and future birth defects from such accidents. Nor do they wish to admit that it is possible terrorists would decide to attempt to destroy nuclear power plants in nations they perceive to be enemies for religious, political or economic reasons, if the trends toward international conflict and intercultural disharmony are allowed to perpetuate and intensify. It is also likely that with ever increasing amounts of radioactive nuclear contaminated waste being produced, there will be accidents and potential terrorist attacks during the costly process of transporting the waste, disposing of the waste, at waste disposal sites and so on, as well as the likelihood that these zealots would obtain nuclear materials of various types to use in their weapons to create increased long term and immediate widespread destruction.

The USA is already admittedly using depleted uranium warheads in Iraq, which has debilitating effects on all life forms in that area. There is also no mention of what exceedingly damaging effects nuclear contamination will have in the likely result that earthquake and other naturally occurring forces in nature and 'fracking' will cause the ground water to become poisoned by the disposal, manufacture and processing of nuclear materials. We could list various other issues, yet you get the idea that the whole truth is being intentionally withheld from the public by those few greedy, insanely corrupted people that support and promote the use of nuclear technologies.

Therefore, at least in the short term, there should be an immediate internationally sanctioned United Nations moratorium mandated, whereby no new nuclear power plants are established anywhere in the world while other safer, cleaner, less polluting types of energies are given a real opportunity to prove what they can accomplish. Geothermal, solar, wind, air pressure, ocean wave and tidal energy generating technologies utilising water in various ways and many other less well-known, highly effective, efficient advanced technologies that generate safe non-polluting inexpensive energy now exist; such as various Tesla technologies which is now becoming known as 'plasma' (Earth's natural and very abundant) energies, instead of the toxic forms of fossil fuel and nuclear types of costly energy that is now so prevalent in earthly civilisation. These safe alternative energy producing sources have already been discovered, some have been proven to be viable now, as evidenced by their successful use in the world today. Additionally, there are numerous other unpublicised energy producing technologies being covertly developed and perfected in secretive locations around the world by quasi-government sponsored taxpayer funded organisations who are covertly working for the corporate multi-national power interests that we have discussed so thoroughly already. The existence of innumerable solutions to the so-called 'energy crisis' are already well-known, readily available, and this would include more effective energy conservation projects and processes. Many of these have been developed mostly from public tax payers' funding and subsequently been withheld and prevented from development by unscrupulous means from those vested interests that prefer the current inefficient, polluting technologies. To repeat, many innovative, advanced, safe energy producing technologies are being intentionally withheld and suppressed by those controlling interests who are seeking to earn massive fortunes from utilising the existing primitive 'çombustion' technologies that are now proven to be destroying our civilisation's environments. We are allowing this to happen and this must change soon, if our civilisation is to become truly productive and sustainable.

Our educational system must be radically improved to once again truly educate our children and the innumerable adults who wish and need to be properly and thoroughly literate and well-informed. There must be an improved, better-designed, intelligent restructuring of entire learning systems in society to address the real social and economic requirements for people to constructively and freely apply available knowledge. This must replace the increasing tendency toward a superficial level of education for the majority of the population while other people that can financially afford the lengthy education process are encouraged to become overly specialised in a particular field of study, often to the detriment of obtaining a balanced education encompassing diverse types of information. Many factors are prevalent in the education system whose subtle purpose is to adversely control and limit the full potential of people so they are receptive to various types of social programming. The result is our societies function below their potential because so many well-coordinated forces are serving in an integrated manner to prevent creative people and innovative small businesses from achieving meaningful, sustainable, profitable productivity in their preferred areas of activity.

Education must include a new course devoted entirely to the study of higher values, ethics, true justice, morality, global peaceful relationships and diplomacy that defines the nature of equitable, just behaviour in a secular, unbiased manner so that it is widely applicable in our daily lives and civilisation. It is the quality of our values, beliefs and motivations that serve to characterise and progressively build a truly civilised society. Therefore, we must aspire to manifest the very best within our character, rather than by exhibiting the most minimalist types of attitudes and actions to selfishly obtain our life's desires at the expense and often to the detriment of others. Educational learning of valuable knowledge must become the right of all people seeking to obtain it and education must be freely and widely available to people of all ages, not simply children. The associated cost of obtaining an education must be lowered or eliminated for all people globally, and especially those people unable to afford any cost for their education. For those who say it is impossible to finance such a system of education, then it is wise to mandate seriously cutting massive amounts of funding from international military budgets, since militaristic agendas are among the least productive, most destructive and most costly activities upon this planet.

Likewise, there must be a more equitable distribution of the roles that people seek to learn about and work at in our societies, so that too many people do not wish to unwisely and inappropriately become lawyers, architects, or any other profession that has excessive numbers of practitioners for various reasons primarily related to high rates of income. It is vitally important that greatly needed key occupational roles are extensively promoted and adequately rewarded because some of these job skills are a precious limited resource that humanity cannot afford being in short supply. This would include occupations with specialist knowledge and skills that we must not lose or be able to replace when those possessing these capabilities are finally gone from this earthly life. Wages must be adequate and even subsidised in some challenging, much needed, somewhat unpleasant occupations because many of these types of people quite rightly believe and feel that they do not earn sufficient income for the hard, publicly essential, usually thankless work that they do. Some people refuse to do some jobs that are not glamorous enough or sound like too much hard, work; such as farming for food utilising sustainable, non-toxic, healthy methods. All people must again begin to renew their inner respect and take true pride in whatever work or profession they choose to do, or are forced by external circumstances to do until they can find more fulfilling work to do. Taking joy in whatever we each do that is productive and good for our civilisation is essential because each of us thereby helps everyone progress through our combined actions.

We can see many examples where governments and bureaucratic institutions intentionally obstruct and pervert progressive developments within society for unarticulated, surreptitious, clandestine, deceptive reasons that are seldom as they appear to be as stated by these entities. These entrenched social forces often disguise and obfuscate their actual true ulterior furtive motives to falsely appear to be derived from their pretence of concern for public health, justice, equality, safety and prosperity. In many cases, nothing could be further from the truth, as we have already discussed. A recent example of exactly this type of situation occurred in the former Liberal Party Government in Australia in 2007 and serves to make my point clear for all to recognise. An engineer from another nation wrote various government agencies and requested to immigrate to Australia to manufacture an electric car and he was granted Australian Permanent Residency on that basis. The electric car would only require about one hundred and fifty dollars worth of electricity to operate the vehicle around the inner city for one year's worth of normal distance driving. The electricity would be available from a normal electric outlet located in one's home or could also be supplemented by electrical energy generated by solar photovoltaic panels. He already had developed the working prototype which was capable of speeds up to one hundred and sixty kilometres per hour and it appeared like any normal, small-sized petrol driven car, so it was definitely not a 'toy car'. He immigrated to Australia; shipping to Australia the components that would be required to manufacture about one hundred of these electric vehicles, which had no toxic emissions and were quite safe to drive in their construction and design qualities. This well-intentioned capable man in 2007 found himself upon a plane leaving Australia permanently because the state governments that had agreed in writing to authorise him to develop and manufacture this exceedingly efficient electric car refused to authorise him to drive the vehicle upon Australian roads, among other arbitrary limitations they imposed upon him over several years. Therefore, he was unable to have the vehicle approved for use on Australian roads, contrary to what he had been promised in writing before immigrating to Australia to conduct his final development of the vehicle and begin manufacturing operations here. He then moved to England, where ideally his experiences will be much better than they were here; however, he may find similar attitudes exist in England too, which I am unable to confirm at this time. What is wrong with this picture of earthly reality? Greedy, self-serving, corrupted people obviously now still control governmental policies. This is now in the early stages of positive change in 2016.

  These issues reveal the frustrating experiences of millions of capable, intelligent, well-motivated people around the planet in all nations upon Earth who are simply attempting to make a positive, constructive impact on the present, less than ideal situation. For another, we have an example of a man that is able to provide a viable, cost-effective alternative to expensive, polluting, inefficient fossil fuelled vehicles that would serve as an unwanted competitor to the existing major vehicle manufacturers. Multi-national vehicle manufacturers have already been proven to enjoy various types of governmental protection and special treatment within most nations of the world, partly due to their involvement in these nation's political party processes. The indirect result is many governments appear to be intentionally preventing the activities of such 'independent operators' from competing internationally with the major vehicle manufacturers. Consider the similar situation in the suppressed technologies related to improved fuel efficiencies in standard vehicle engines and we can perceive intentional counter-productive decisions being perpetuated from the highest levels within our civilisation. Another example would include the suppression of hydrogen being used as a fuel source, with oxygen being the only emission.

In health related issues, we see known carcinogens and addictive substances being intentionally added to most tobacco products that result in disease and addiction among millions of people without any serious remedial action being undertaken by governmental health authorities. Microwave radiation is known to be toxic and yet in most nations these harmful radiations are legally used to cook and preserve our foods, as well as being used in communication devices such as mobile phones and many other health damaging applications. This is an unacceptable situation that must change for the better. Likewise harmful electromagnetic radiations (EMFs) and these include radar devices used to monitor at 'speed cameras', which exist in increasing profusion while road and traffic flow improvements are minimal in comparison to increased law enforcement activities.

In 1996-7 I was elected in Queensland to serve in the unpaid, voluntary capacity as the federal president of the largest, oldest inventors' organisation in Australia. In that role I learned firsthand about a great many interesting and somewhat disturbing realities related to innovation development internationally. Australia, per capita of population, or person for person in relation to the percentage of the total population, is clearly by far the most inventive, innovative nation on Earth. The year I became the president, the Australian federal government publicly propagandised about providing about one hundred million additional dollars toward developing innovation. That year our twenty year old inventor's organisation received absolutely nothing financially from the federal government. As federal president, I had simply requested our inventor's association be given some old dis-used Australian government computers so that we could to link all of the individual State inventors' organisation's databases together. Our intention among the other state presidents was to be able to coordinate the efficient listing of the information required to develop and manufacture of our member's more worthy inventions and innovations.

However; alternatively to our actual requirements that same year all of the state presidents of the inventor's organisation, including myself as the state (and federal) president of Queensland, were invited at taxpayer's expense to travel to Canberra, the national capital. There we did nothing more than to hold a conference with the Patent Office Representatives and the only agenda item was to encourage the state presidents to recommend to our members that they file provisional patents ('patent pending'), patents, registered designs, and other such costly documents that fully disclose the nature of our inventions with complete disregard for the status of our member's best interests. There was absolutely no genuine interest demonstrated that any government representatives cared at all about any of our needs or capabilities in that or any governmental meetings I ever attended. Let's briefly consider a few of the relevant issues in regard to this matter just to provide a little 'window' into the situation, since it is a global travesty of reasonable justice that now dissuades and eliminates the effective development of many good innovations.

A Patent is an extremely expensive document to obtain and retain for most normal inventors and it is intended to grant the Patent holder with the right to exclusively produce the item and/or sell the Intellectual Property Rights to others by License, and so on. The full final Patent comprehensively and accurately discloses every aspect that makes the idea unique to the entire world, through publicly available documents available 'online' from any computer. Therefore, anyone wishing to obtain ideas about its nature and intent can freely accomplish this, if they have a computer with internet facilities or wish to go to the patent office holding those documents and request to see them. If the idea or product is publicly disclosed before the Patent is granted, then one cannot obtain a Patent. If one cannot continue to pay the costs to maintain the Patent, then it is lost. After being assessed by the National Patent Office in each nation that the Patent is applied for as being something new, novel and different and paying the necessary fees, when a Patent is finally granted to the owner of the intellectual property; then any person or corporation can initiate a law suit to overturn the Patent if they believe it violates their own Patented Intellectual Property or products in some manner. If the owner of the Patent is unable to afford the legal expenses to defend the law suit over the many years that the process can take, then they lose the Patent, plus could be forced to pay the legal costs of the opponent in some circumstances. This does not imply that those who decide for some reason to sue the Patent holder must truly possess or present a valid case to the Court or Patent Office in order to begin their court proceedings. If anyone aside from the Patent holder or legal licensee makes the patented object and makes it publicly available for sale (or it could be freely made available as well if someone wished to do so, I assume) then the Patent holder is obligated under law to sue in court the entity that is in breach of their patent rights, or they lose the Patent protection. Are you beginning to get the idea of what is happening here? A Patent is a full public disclosure of one's intellectual property to obtain a 'license' that opens one to the legal obligation to sue others in the court system and potentially to be sued by others located anywhere in the world, in order to obtain and retain an exclusivity of some idea or innovation.

Very few inventors can afford this process in competition with large, well-financed international corporations. To see the misleadingly deceptive encouragement being given to the leaders of our inventor's organisations to knowingly recommend this entire process to our mostly poverty stricken inventors seemed to be relatively poor advice, all things considered. I reflected upon the fact that all we really wanted or needed were about eight old computers to begin to confidentially database our members, the basic description of their innovations and at what level of development they had obtained in order for our inventor's associations to assist our members in the ongoing development processes. We were attempting to integrate inventors with capable business people, equitable genuine financiers, and receptive ethical corporations so that the best of these inventions could be professionally developed and marketed internationally.

Subsequently, apparently because I looked presentable in my business suit and could string a few reasonable sounding sentences together, the Australian Federal Government decided in its boundless wisdom to send me to Tokyo, Japan as a representative of the Australian inventors association to attend the APEC Intellectual Property Conference. Again at Australian tax payer's expense, in Tokyo I met many governmental representatives, numerous multi-national corporate top executives, and national inventors' organisation representatives, such as myself. I also was fortunate to be invited to attend the Japanese Inventors Association's annual national awards ceremonies, which were most illuminating in numerous ways. Foremost among these realisations was that it became abundantly clear that globally all non-corporate inventors and innovators are constantly confronted by the same extremely daunting, almost impossibly competitive set of financially onerous, constricting circumstances. The Japanese inventors were willing to explain the difficulties they faced in commercialising their ideas and products with very little real assistance from their government or the business community, unless they gratefully accepted to work on behalf of large internationally active corporations and thereby willingly gave up and lost all control over the applications of their ideas, products and technologies.

Do you believe peace-loving scientists such as Albert Einstein or the many others who personally abhorred war, willingly and knowingly did their research that assisted ultimately in the development of atomic weapons so that it could be misapplied in this manner by the leaders of our civilisation's military? No, that would be quite unlikely. Therefore, this is only one of the many reasons why scientists, inventors, innovators and creative people are employed by multi-national corporations to do their product development. These inventive people are not usually provided with the full set of information on how their technologies will be utilised. Intellectual Property (IP) developed while employed by others normally becomes the property of the employer, which in today's international business community is usually a corporation, a 'think tank', research organisation, government institution, university, medical facility or so on. Generally, the resulting ideas and products are totally owned and controlled by those corporations, institutions, or entities that employ them; and definitely not by the originators of the ideas who are unable to financially cope with the entire set of circumstances required to properly develop and market innovations. Joint Venture Agreements to jointly possess intellectual property are becoming more common between innovators and those entities with which they interact, yet again one must be an expert in law and be able to defend potential violations of such agreements to make them enforceable internationally. It is important to also point out the proven fact that most privately owned, falsely so-called 'inventors' assistance organisations' are usually actually simply 'front' organisations that are intended to primarily devoted to obtaining ideas for corporations. These organisations commonly intentionally or 'naively' mislead inventors in various ways, as well as charge them excessive fees for mostly ineffectual services and poor advice that usually does not help the inventor to achieve success. There are some exceptions to this observation, yet they are in the distinct minority.

In Australia there were several such inaccurately termed 'inventor's assistance organisations' that were referred to us by the public and our members as not properly serving the innovators that sought to utilise their services. We then intentionally sent some of our members to inquire about the services a couple of these organisations purported to offer inventors, determine their fee structures, their business procedures and unfortunately found them to be unreliable, unprofessional, unethical. I also tested one of my own products with such an organisation to see what they recommended so that we could determine for ourselves the nature of their services and advice in order to better inform our own inventor's associations' members nationally. Suffice to say, be very careful in providing one's money for services that are made upon a 'best efforts' basis. A book could easily be written just on innovation development issues.

Not long after this memorably revealing experience in Canberra and Tokyo, I was told that because I sought to 'help inventors' through the activities of a private company that I owned as a sole Director; I was informed that my private activities to assist inventors were an unacceptable 'conflict of interest' with my role as the state and federal president of the inventor's association. This was apparently deemed to be the case by external, unidentified 'interested observers', in spite of the fact that I never once charged any inventor any fees for my observations because there was so little I could truly do to assist them within my company due to its own financial limitations. Nor had I disclosed anyone's confidential information to anyone, or any businesses or corporations. I was then 'asked' or more accurately 'told', not to seek re-election, which I accepted with some frustration. My purpose in sharing this experience is to be informative on several levels; some of which may not be so obvious to you now, yet in passing time you may glean some important information from various aspects of this story. Then I willingly 'walked away' from innovation development, just as I had earlier 'left behind' my formal, private UFO research activities a decade earlier than this particular time. Both were excellent decisions and many useful realisations reside within me now through those experiences.

We seem to be distracted from our topical matter, yet this is not the situation from my perspective. You will be consciously and unconsciously entertaining new thoughts, feelings and intuitive inputs about what truly meaningful, enjoyable, uplifting activities you will do with the reminder of your earthly life, in preparation for the much more important and productive eternal journey that comes when your present physical body ceases to function here. To know that we can simply 'walk away' from situations that are irreparable or no longer productive aspects of our lives is a vitally necessary realisation and many people are reaching this stage in our lives, both in a material, earthly sense and also in an immortal spiritual sense. So, build courage in your realisations and make firm your commitments to do what is best for you, your family, your community and our entire world, in your own unique special ways. Do it all and enjoy the process! Make whatever adjustments and changes that are required or desired as you proceed; knowing it is you and perhaps your family, who will live with the consequences of those decisions.

Therefore, it is wise to deliberate wisely and choose well before you act. To fail to act decisively with all the information available to you is less than your best effort and you may regret such attitudes in the future. We will discover that sometimes it is better to do nothing than to do 'the wrong thing';

whereas in other circumstances it is better to do almost anything than to continue to do virtually nothing, or whatever one has habitually already been doing that may not be working well. This is where your personal discretion, intuition, inspiration and valour arise to manifest themselves within your mind and life, for the betterment of yourself and the world.

We will now resume our consideration of the processes involved in our eternal existence after our present earthly life is completed with the death of our physical body. Some people have great difficulty in developing the faith and confidence that their individualised intellect or personal consciousness continues to remain functional after their body and brain cease to be alive here on Earth. We will use a couple of basic analogies and experiences to attempt to clarify these processes. However, ultimately this is an issue that will reveal and resolve itself progressively in various ways that you will personally perceive and comprehend. You can acquire the conscious realisation that your consciousness exists independent of your physical body while on Earth, yet in the final analysis the most conclusive proof will be found after you have left this system of earthly reality. The progressive, consciously-aware transition from our present human earthly state of consciousness; whatever relative level it may be upon, to a non-earthly level of 'higher' existence on any one of the innumerable possible destinations within cosmic existence is something we wish to experience while living on Earth in our normal state of consciousness. There are many unanticipated benefits inherent in acknowledging that we, as individuals, are able to become active and creative participants on higher levels of reality beyond the physical plane of existence while we are still living in our human body. In other words, we intend to consider that it is and will become increasingly possible and likely for each and all of us to experience real life situations that prove the reality of our eternal conscious existence while you are still aware within your human physical state of being. This may seem to you to be an unusual, odd or curious realisation process to accomplish, yet please allow me to assure you this is a natural development and one in which you are now very actively participating already, on both unconscious and conscious levels. The fact you have reached this point in our complex, unusual, often debateable and sometimes quite distastefully forthright discussion proves your persistence and capability in some definitive ways. If your normal human consciousness was firmly in total control of all of your mental and spiritual processes, then you would have likely never begun to read this book or would have set it aside long ago for many reasons.

We have already discussed many aspects of this topic previously, so we will resume with the analogy of physical death being somewhat akin to our normal conscious mind's suspension of our ordinary thought processes when we sleep at night. Dreams definitely reveal and serve to characterise key qualities of our immortal levels of consciousness in ways that we can understand, reproduce, study, creatively control, progressively develop and utilise to demonstrate our ability to shift the focus of our conscious attention onto higher planes of existence on a daily and nightly basis. We are also now learning to acquire the talent and capability to exhibit some of these states of mind and being while remaining wide awake and alert within our daily waking lives in various ways.

Our motives in this developmental process are to enable the more robust comprehensive expression of our increasingly integrated total states of being; definitely not to prove to ourselves or others that we can occasionally accomplish what to some may naively appear to be 'magic tricks' or 'minor miracles'. These are absolutely and definitively not areas where one seeks to play 'silly games' or do 'party tricks'. If your current personality or character seems inclined to violate spiritual principles; then you will need to please adjust your attitude now, or avoid these conscious efforts because you can be detrimentally affected in many ways for choosing to display such an inappropriate attitude in your conduct and motivation. I have already provided a few examples where I foolishly, ineptly and unjustifiably sought to either unknowingly or knowingly contradict various spiritual principles and suffered accordingly. I am not an especially 'enlightened' human being, nor am I a guru of any sort, nor would I even consider myself to be an especially 'advanced' or wise person in some senses. However, there are many areas of life and character in which I perceive a considerable positive progression in my attitudes and abilities.

We all are here on Earth for countless reasons and we are all identical in having numerous lessons to learn and illuminating realisations to discover in this earthly life. This process facilitates our progression into future reality systems that will become increasingly available to those who are willing and able to continually adjust and consciously develop their improving states of being to benefit themselves and others from enhanced awareness of these advantageous 'higher' reality systems. Please be aware we are not seeking to develop these perceptive abilities to use them unwisely to control, or influence others, or to gain material advantage, or other such short-sighted, materialistic, inappropriately motivated goals; as we all could be tempted to do from time to time, based upon our broad range of human nature issues that we are seeking to improve upon here. We are often tested by life, others and ourselves, in spontaneous unexpected unique ways. In such instances, we seek to be honest, truthful, reasonable and pragmatic in our responses and consider the perspectives, feelings, and best interests of others just as much as ourselves. That is a real challenge for us, which reveals where this entire earthly process is leading us all.

This is among the many reasons why we have considered so many diverse human nature issues as examples and topics of frustratingly tedious, onerously divisive and incalculably counter-productive human attitudes and activity, to identify the lower characteristic displays that we, as individuals and as a civilisation, seek to improve and incrementally resolve. Our own state of mind is our own internal 'territory' and this is where our truest responsibility and opportunity exists, initially and continually. Our consciousness can be developed swiftly for the better or we can vacillate endlessly, as fluctuating external circumstances influence and affect us adversely; pulling, pushing and throwing us about mercilessly, just as severe ocean waves and currents would buffet and disadvantage a poor swimmer.

Let's return to our analogy that our dreams can reveal higher aspects of reality to us on a regular basis. Dreams, be they delightful blissful sojourns into beautiful realities, or horrible unavoidable nightmares, or anywhere in between those hypothetical extremes of experience; are just as real and deeply meaningful as are our ordinary earthly experiences, thoughts, feelings and realisations. Some types of dreams, known as 'lucid dreaming', are likely to be even vastly more 'real' and intensely memorable than some of the daily experiences we have ordinarily in our waking lives on Earth. I will not explain how or why this is true, yet after experiencing some of these lucid dreaming events yourself, you will clearly recognise that the magnitude and purpose of some of these incredibly realistic, often astoundingly amazing vivid dreams are far more significant and memorable than anything you did in your waking life on a quite forgettable, ordinary average day last week. The more acutely consciously aware that we can become of our normal nightly dream experiences and be more able to bring a portion of this dream recall, knowledge and experience back with us into our waking earthly lives for the upliftment of our overall consciousness; the better for us in our waking lives and upon our immortal journey.

There are many methods to recall one's dreams and getting plenty of sleep is one very good beginning point. When one is well-rested it is far easier to waken after a vividly memorable dream, to consciously recall it and place it into one's normal memory to remember upon awakening the following morning before getting out of bed. Another ideal method is to keep a dream journal beside one's bed and when a vivid dream occurs, attempt to awaken yourself when it is completed to briefly record a few descriptive words or sentences primarily to fix the dream's events within your conscious mind's memory. Upon wakening in the morning, try to recall the primary dream details and record them in written form in your dream journal, and then reflect upon them to consider what relationship, if any, that you may perceive within the dream's events that may be relevant in your daily or spiritual life. Periodically review the dream journal to determine if there are any patterns or key issues that seem to be revealing themselves to your conscious mind over passing time. The fact you are actually consciously intentionally seeking to become progressively more and more aware of the incredibly numerous, deeply meaningful, interactive events that are continuously occurring within your life upon the 'dream levels' of reality will serve greatly to integrate your human consciousness with your eternal higher levels of consciousness. To repeat, please understand and come to acknowledge for yourself through your own internal processes and realisations that 'dream levels' of reality are every bit as real in some ways as are your normal ordinary waking life on this Earth.

As Soul, your true 'home' is the higher planes of reality beyond the physical and other 'lower' planes of existence. Therefore, to become continuously more aware of your diverse 'higher levels' of experience within other reality systems is helpful in ways we cannot adequately explain here. We have discussed the fact that all planes of existence actually co-exist simultaneously, yet each plane or level of reality has distinct qualities that are extremely fundamental to that particular level of reality, as well as to the entire nature of cosmic existence. The Casual Plane of existence is the level of reality where one can access and review all of one's physical existences, if the opportunity is presented for reasons to educate one on lessons and realisations that could not be learned in other ways. A brief, very simple example of this situation in a dream was provided to me in my early teen years. The event stood out occasionally throughout my present life to periodically remind me that in this life I have spiritually vowed not to start fights or to ever be knowingly become responsible for the death of other human beings in combat that I initiate. This is among the reasons why I never wanted to serve in military service. At the time I was unaware of the full meaning of the lucid type dreams.

As a youngster of about ten, in the dream it was as though I was participating directly in the action of the event and experienced the very vivid, quite memorable death of my life in a previous lifetime as a Viking warrior. In this intensely real, life-like seeming dream, I was involved in savage hand to hand combat with long swords and other weapons upon the deck of a ship full of combatants. The dream was relatively short in duration, yet in it I knew we were attacking or being attacked by another ship and found ourselves unexpectedly seriously outnumbered. Our crew of warriors were being overwhelmed by a capable enemy, who was determined to kill us all without mercy. Later once awake in my normal life as a young boy at that time, I ardently recalled the clarity and unforgettable emotions involved in truly fighting for the preservation of my life, a powerful memory which served me quite well from time to time in later life. As I struck one enemy down directly in front of me, I did not see another opposing attacking warrior behind me. As I struck my fatal own blow upon my opponent in front of me, with my head held high, I never saw the vicious sword stoke that completely severed my head from my body. I did intensely experience and later dramatically recalled of bizarre feeling as my head left my shoulders and went bouncing a short distance across the deck, ending up facing my falling, decapitated body. The memory was a vividly etched in my mind in that last conscious moment in that particular lifetime. I clearly recognised my headless body and wondered what it was doing 'over there'. I was not an observer in the dream; rather I was actually allowed to forcefully relive and re-experience that event with all the clarity that had occurred in that individual life in my distant past existence as a ruthless raider and bloodthirsty Viking killer. In that dream I was able to again be provided an opportunity to clearly recall my last few moments of conscious awareness, as I realised I would not be seeing my family again and that my chosen way of life was proven to be a mistake.

Then, I awakened suddenly, perspiring, heart pounding and consumed by mixed emotions from the dream; astounded and perplexed by the poignant memory, which then triggered a number of conscious realisations and commitments that my spirit had made after that life and other similar physical existences, to choose to act in as civil and peaceful a manner as possible throughout my life. I have stayed true to that spiritual pledge and I have not attacked any person unless I was first attacked by them and was unable to avoid the situation in defending myself. One notable exception occurred when I punched a concrete wall as a youngster while trying to hit a local bully for abusing his much weaker younger brother. I clearly recall going to the jewellery store where the bullied man was the owner about forty years later while visiting my parents' home in Roswell in order to apologise for my also being unkind to him as a youngster by teasing him due to his large ears. He kindly graciously accepted my apology and amazed me by thanking me as he fondly recalled that exact event and surprisingly replied that he always appreciated me highly, because it apparently was the only time anyone had 'stood up' for him in his very challenging life as a youngster. I still have those scars on my right thumb as a reminder to never throw the first punch", unless first attacked.

In some parts of this book it may seem that I have been exceedingly critical and overly condemning of some aspects of our human civilisation and our leadership, which could be interpreted by some as being a verbal or philosophic act of hostility upon my part. Well, as my boys debate the issue of joining the Australian military to go to war to defend our society's version of so-called 'freedom', I have a few very hard complex choices to make myself, just as my own father did when he unnecessarily volunteered to do a one year tour of duty in Viet Nam in 1967-8. In this life we either say what we believe in our hearts, minds and spirits to be true from the experience and evidence before us, or we are not being true to our real selves, especially in historical times of testing like these are for humanity. It is not that I wish to appear to be inadvisably overly critical of our civilisation's choices; instead it is my personal responsibility at this moment in my life to attempt to share my perspective with those willing to consider it; be it right, wrong or indifferent from other people's viewpoints and beliefs. If you disagree with some or even much of what stated here, then that is your prerogative and duty to assert your opinions. Ideally, you too will have experience and factual proof to substantiate your beliefs, knowledge, and facts, just as I do from my perspective.

These previous remarks are intended to preface one of the most uplifting, illuminatingly memorable experiences of my entire life. This following event directly relates to clarifying our subject matter in this chapter and within this book. How do we truly know for a definitive fact that eternal life upon other levels of reality will await us when this earthly life is completed? That is indeed one of the ultimate answers we all will provide uniquely to our selves over passing time through an infinite variety of diverse experiences. This event has been selected because unlike a 'near death experience' which was briefly discussed in an earlier chapter; this personal experience subtly illustrates how natural a process transition from earthly life to physical death and focusing levels of consciousness can be for those of us who are able to travel the higher planes 'at will', based upon the capabilities we have developed throughout our eternal existence.

About 18 years ago, my father was diagnosed with terminal multiple cancers; quite likely resulting indirectly from his many years spent in the military in proximity to nuclear weapons, intense electrical fields, as well as the defoliant 'Agent Orange' and other weapons systems in Viet Nam. We knew Dad would soon be travelling to 'the other side of life' and while we wanted him to remain with us, we could see this was not going to be possible. I spent one very memorable month living with my mother and him, as he prepared to enter the next stage of life. We grew especially close during that special, emotionally challenging and most loving time together. I had often been 'at odds' with my father, who was a relatively stern disciplinarian that expected much of himself and those around him. As I mentioned previously, I was quite fortunate that he literally 'beat the lies out of me' as a youngster. As I matured sufficiently to attempt to raise my own children to be honest, responsible youngsters, I gained an excellent level of heightened appreciative awareness of the wonderful example that my mother and he had provided me with over the years of my childhood upbringing and later while I was, technically speaking, presumed to be 'an adult', a concept that still seems somewhat elusive to me at times.

Dad and I had the opportunity to privately recall and fondly share many old times alone together and also with my mother, who was deeply affected by these difficult times when her much beloved life partner would soon be leaving her behind to face life alone, or so she believed at the time. Dad and I happily relived the times when I would return home for Christmas after being away from the family for a year at university or later when I graduated and began working far from their home in Roswell, New Mexico, or later when I immigrated to Australia. Usually within a few days of my coming home, we would naturally find ourselves coming into unwanted, unavoidable verbal conflict over emotional differences of opinion about many life issues or personal situations. After we expressed our opinions, we always soon shared a spirit of mutual understanding, even if we 'agreed to disagree' with one another. In some cases there would also be a sense of forgiveness and respect after the emotional 'heat' of those moments had passed away into almost forgotten memories, vastly overwhelmed by our mutual love for one another.

I reminded him of the time I came home from university, living a thousand miles away, standing together at the kitchen sink peeling potatoes as Dad and I often did, while sometimes superficially helping Mom prepare dinner, before we quickly disappeared upstairs to watch the football and basketball games on television. I recalled about my third year of university, after a few of my psychology classes had encouraged the students to 'share our inner feelings', I did so a bit apprehensively with Dad while we stood together peeling potatoes at the kitchen sink. Understand, Dad was almost two metres tall, a powerfully built man, and not one to suffer what he perceived to be rudeness or foolishness gladly. It was the mid-70s, so such open honest communication between a retired military man and his apparently 'hippie looking', non-military prone elder son was still a relatively new and potentially volatile activity in our family life. It was a time in history when one was lucky to consciously acknowledge some of one's innermost feelings, much less be silly enough to try to share them openly with our parents, who were usually incorrectly perceived as some type of 'human dinosaurs' that were never able to really understand of our perspectives. There was a tendency to perceive the younger generation as being better educated and more knowledgeable, in spite of our parents' abundant life experience. Tentatively I made my 'little speech' in one abrupt sentence as quickly, clearly and pleasantly as possible, without looking at Dad as we peeled the last of our potatoes before putting them onto the fire to boil to make mashed potatoes, as was customary.

I said, "Dad, I think I resent you in some ways." I was waiting for the verbal tirade to begin when instead Dad turned to look at me eye to eye at one foot apart and softly with love in his eyes, he said, "Son, I am really glad you could share that with me." Neither he nor I said anything more and we finished peeling our potatoes in mutually accepted silence, with my experiencing considerable relief about his unexpected loving reply, and then went up to watch our sports together with a feeling of some mutual peace of mind being openly and then silently shared between us.

It was only many years later that I realised some of the reasons for his surprisingly accepting response. My Dad had never been able to express such feelings with his own father; who was a very aggressive, difficult, intensely private and demanding man that was raised under brutal circumstances as an orphan on a farm. After seldom seeing his father after he joined the US Air Force, Dad's father and his mother visited our home when I was about twelve years old. Unexpectedly, Dad's father died in his sleep in our spare bedroom. I could vaguely recall observing Dad's inexplicable turmoil at the time and remembered him rhetorically quietly muttering to my mother words to the effect, "Why did he have to come here to die?" In my later years, I realised that my Dad was much loved and respected by his father, who could never verbally express love for any of his eight children, and perhaps not even privately to his loving patient wife, who he had often been very unkind to in various ways. Much later, after Dad was on 'the other side' of earthly life, I finally realised why he had such a positive response to my seeming accusation about him as a brash, yet respectful twenty year old. Dad was well-aware that he was never able to openly express such an inaudible thought to his own father, yet somehow I had aroused the courage to do so myself; regardless of the turbulent results that such an act could quite potentially have brought about if he had responded differently.

Periodically over the following year, I thought occasionally about my unsolicited brief, somewhat negative comment to my Dad, realising that I loved him very much no matter what had happened during my childhood. In Dad's response I could more clearly see his true love for me, especially in being able to acknowledge and reply to me in a caring, understanding way. I was most impressed that he could accept such a seemingly vindictive remark without any provocation by him being made to me at the time to elicit it and then respond to me in a positive loving manner. Through those reflections in that year away from home at university, I realised it was not my Dad himself that I resented. Instead, I came to understand that it was more the volatile behaviours that he periodically demonstrated that frightened me so, since I was often punished for numerous transgressions, only a relative few of which did I then rationalise as being truly justified, from my own perspective as a child or youngster.

The very next Christmas, we were again standing alone in the kitchen, peeling potatoes as though only a few days had passed since our previous conversation. Once again I said without preliminary 'lead up' remarks or warning, looking down at my potatoes, which were once again nearly finished and ready to be boiled, "Dad, I've been thinking about it and I do not really resent you, so much as I do some of your behaviours as I was growing up." Again, Dad turned to look at me eye to eye about one foot away and softly with love in his eyes said, "Son, I am really glad you could share that with me." Again nothing more was said and no mention was made of the comment for well-over ten years and a great many Christmases were spent at that same sink peeling potatoes together.

Almost twenty years later, after raising my three young children for a number of years, we all were visiting them in the USA from Australia. Once again Dad and I were alone at the same kitchen sink, both peeling potatoes as though virtually no time had lapsed at all. That time I had the courage to look at Dad and said words to the effect that, "Dad, you know that I am trying to raise my own family now, so I much better understand the reasons why you did everything you did and I much appreciate your efforts." Again, Dad just looked intently at me eye to eye about one foot away and softly with love in his eyes said, "Son, I am really glad you could share that with me. I am glad to hear that is how you feel now" So am I.

Well, as Dad and I spent those emotional final four weeks of his life together, we grew closer than we had ever been before. All of the past upsets, emotional pain, petty resentments and mutually critical thoughts were sincerely forgiven between us, understood, and truly appreciated for the many lessons provided to us both in our life's learning processes and experiences together. It was only looking back that I began to more deeply and thoroughly discover and better comprehend how truly wise and spiritual Dad was, since I do not recall him ever speaking to us about religious or spiritual matters. At Mom's insistence we did attend church for many years and we never heard any complaints about it from Dad, who accompanied us to the Sunday services when he was home from his flying trips with the General.

We laughed as we reminisced about the times when I refused to do as I was told or caused trouble in various ways, which as a youngster tended to greatly frustrate my parents and sometimes created much discord in the home while growing up, especially if my parents began arguing about my punishment. I reminded him of the time he and I were travelling alone across country to move the family to New Mexico. I was eighteen at the time and Dad finally allowed me to drive the moving truck on a broad open almost deserted four lane highway. He made me repeatedly promise him to maintain a speed of fifty five miles per hour so we would reach our destination, since he had exactly calculated our fuel consumption. Of course as soon as he went to sleep, I 'accidentally' drove sixty five miles per hour for almost an hour and about twenty miles from the next small town we ran naturally out of fuel. When he asked me if I had gone too fast, I wanted to lie and say no, yet by then he and I had developed an understanding that the truth would be told, no matter what the circumstances. Of course I lied anyway and said, No Dad", I would not drive more than fifty five." Certainly he knew I was lying and he was not a happy man at that time, out in the blistering Texas desert, with many of their valuables stored in that truck that they would quite rightly not trust the ordinary movers to safely take in their much larger load of our family's possessions.

He wanted so much to discipline me at that time, yet I was genuinely apologetic and tried to deny that I had gone fast for very long. Apparently he thought I had learned my lesson related to increased speed meant increased fuel consumption and he kindly allowed the matter to 'rest'. Then I hitchhiked into town to get fuel while he remained to protect the truck from potential thieves or passing vandals on the nearly deserted section of highway.

We recalled another time when he had taught my brother and I how to change the oil in our two family cars. As he finished the oil change on the second car and reversed it away from us, he became distracted by my brother and me. We waved frantically at him to stop, further distracting him, and he reversed the one car into the other, badly damaging the door and smashed the window. Again, in this instance he was not at all a happy man. Of course my brother and I were almost sick with fits of laughter and we desperately tried to stop laughing which only made matters much worse, causing him to give the steering wheel a really vigorous pummelling, as he sought to internally deal with the issue. Another time Dad towed the same car which had been previously damaged to have its clutch replaced that I had somehow broken. I was driving the car being towed with my brother as a passenger. While we approached a traffic light at a major New Orleans intersection, it turned yellow. Dad always stopped at yellow lights and knowing this I was fully prepared to stop with him without hitting the car he was driving. Unfortunately, in the rear view mirror to him it must have appeared to him as though I was going to crash into the back of him, so he accelerated abruptly. Like a rubber band, the smaller car being towed by a strong rope was catapulted into the larger car, completely crushing in the front of the car I was driving, yet not even marking the older, heavier, quality car. My brother and I were absolutely hysterical with uncontrolled fits of laughter as the two vehicles sat in the middle of the intersection in busy New Orleans traffic, as once again we watched with impish foolish unconcerned amusement as Dad momentarily sat in the other car pounding upon the steering wheel in total frustration. There was no way we could stop laughing. We were both laughing so hard that we were almost sick to our stomachs. Even his livid rage could not make us stop laughing with tears running down our faces due to our hysterical fits of laughter, although we desperately tried in vain with all our might to wipe the silly smiles off our totally out-of-control faces, as we resumed our journey without further incident. With attitudes like these, you can understand why Dad tended to get upset with my younger brother and I quite often? I would as a youngster on long summer trips to periodically and repeatedly kick the back of Dad's seat as he drove and always sat directly behind him and would blame it on my brother who would then be in striking range as Dad would turn around in his fits of anger, thereby amusing me greatly. Does this begin to explain some things about the challenges of parenting an unusual child such as myself?

We spoke of many good times as well, as Dad and I enjoyed that time together as no other, in spite of the difficult painful circumstances he was enduring. We all agreed that I should return to Australia before Dad passed away, so that he and Mom would have some special last private time together, as he refused to go to the hospital. It was mutually agreed that I would not attend the funeral because of the distance in travelling from Australia. We had been fortunate enough to say all of our loving goodbyes while he was alive, although he was in such poor health from the consumptive cancers that were spreading rapidly throughout his pain-racked infirmed body. One day before I left for Australia, I asked "Dad, if you get over to the other side of life, can you let me know you are there?" Dad replied with the usual poise of a reliable, dedicated, peace-loving military man, Son", it's a mission!" About ten days after I left Mom rang me to say Dad had died. It was understandably a very emotional time for us all. Now this story gets quite astounding and encouraging, at least from my perspective.

The next morning after I learned of Dad's passing from earthly life, I went outside to take the children to school. In Australia, we lived in a beautiful rural hilltop location with many trees of various sizes on our property and on the private unoccupied land nearby. As I went to the car, I noticed a youngish seeming small hawk darting around our rather large yard and quickly among the surrounding trees, although not too expertly. The bird was apparently a young bird, not too long out of the nest, as characterised by its somewhat clumsy flight techniques and immature plumage. Its species indicated in our bird books was what they call in Australia a 'Little Falcon' or in America it is called a Peregrine Falcon, one of the fastest, most agile birds on the planet. As this somewhat awkward young bird flew wildly around the yard, it was squawking, squeaking and making other shrill calling noises as it flew and at first I thought it was looking for its parents. The children and I had no alternative except to take special notice of this amazing bird's antics because it dove very nearby us several times and finally settled upon a very low branch in a tree that I could reach easily myself. Imagine my total surprise when I slowly and carefully approached this unusual bird that was then sitting quietly on the low branch making soft calling noises seemingly at us. Of course I expected it to fly away as I approached, yet incredibly it allowed me to gradually reach upwards to softly stroke its breast feathers. At my request one the children ran to ask my wife to get the camera. She took some photos of me petting this unexpectedly friendly amazing bird that we had never previously seen before that morning, since no one would ever believe such a thing could happen.

Over the next two days the bird was always in the yard whenever we went outside. It very rapidly improved its flying skills and soon learned to become vastly more adroit at snatching tree frogs, lizards, and insects from the surrounding trees and bushes in such profusion that were we quite dumfounded by its astounding appetite and ability to find food everywhere. We almost never saw the little live morsels before it swooped at enormous speeds to deftly capture and then eat the poor unsuspecting tiny creatures. Any time we would come out of the house, it would call loudly to us and immediately begin to put on quite an entertaining aerial show for us, which it did not seem to do to any great extent when we watched it from inside the house. My wife even commented that perhaps it could somehow be related to my Dad's passing from this earthly life, yet initially at that time I was fairly dubious of even considering that possibility. After all, how could Dad's human spirit, in some incomprehensible disincarnate manner, manage to enter some bird's body or possibly locate us here in Australia, over ten thousand miles from the USA? The idea was too absurd for me to contemplate until the following completely unbelievable event occurred.

On the third consecutive morning I was walking out of the house with my old style large-sized mobile phone held in my left hand when the most fascinating, astonishing, perplexing, marvellous, wonderful event happened without any warning. The falcon was perched upon the top of the tall electric pole about thirty metres from our front door. As soon as I stepped out onto the upstairs landing to go down the stairs, it called once loudly and launched itself into a power dive at me like a speeding blur of feathers. I was frozen at the unexpected sight and at the last possible moment it pulled extremely sharply out of the dive and very smoothly landed with its sharp claws gripping the top of the leather case of my mobile phone. The beautiful falcon then looked at me quizzically, while making some soft bird noises and turning its head from side to side and was having a good look into my eyes. In my right hand I held a partially eaten green 'granny smith' apple. The children were right behind me ready for school and one of them again scampered to get their mother to bring the camera to capture the most ideal, inconceivably improbable photo opportunity because no one would believe such a wild tale otherwise. The bird sat perched upon my mobile phone looking from my face and then focusing its sharp gaze upon the green apple, which was my Dad's favourite type of apple, and then back to look piercingly into my eyes again. I slowly moved the apple close to the bird's head and to my complete dumbfounded amazement, it began to eagerly peck off fairly substantial size pieces of the apple and immediately swallow them, flicking its head from side to side as it did, splattering some of the apple's juice in all directions. I asked for some sardines because no predatory bird I ever heard of chooses to eat green apples. The bird took absolutely no notice of the sardines or the small bits of meat that we also offered him over the approximately ten minutes that it sat upon my mobile phone, which I kept grasped firmly in my left hand. Instead, it took quite a few more little bites of the green apple before flying upwards in one of the most splendid aerial displays of aerobatic flying and diving we had yet witnessed, calling loudly in differing ways throughout the entire time it performed for us. The children were quite late going to school that particular day. We all were left almost speechless with bewildering awe, possessing no possible doubt that somehow my then deceased Dad, the children's grandfather Lt. Col. 'Doc' Wonders, the retired famous United States Air Force pilot, had managed to travel all the way to Australia to see us one last unforgettable time. The falcon's attitudes and actions to us all on that special memorable day were as if to say in a very clear visual manner that we could understand and not ignore, "I'm still around, and so long, until I see you all again." Nothing like that has happened since that time, yet my mother shared her own meaningful stories with me in regard to her knowing that Dad's spirit seems to be available to her, especially in times of extreme loneliness, pain, sadness or need.

The most emotionally uplifting event that Mom related to me occurred upon their wedding anniversary about five years after Dad had moved on to the next stage in his immortal life. While at times she believed strongly that she could feel Dad's presence around their home, on this special wedding anniversary occasion, she was feeling especially lonely and missing him intensely. For no conscious reason, she suddenly felt a very strong inner impulse to go up to an antique desk she had and look inside a drawer that had remained locked for decades because the key had been lost. Something inspired her to do whatever was required to open the locked drawer and finally with the use of a letter opener, she managed to pry the lock open without damaging the desk drawer. She looked into the drawer and there to her sheer delight was one of the best of the relatively few wedding anniversary cards that Dad had ever given her. Dad was not one to give flowers or cards, regardless of the occasion or circumstances, since he seemed to believe demonstrating love was the best way to behave where romance was concerned. Mom read the card and told me that as she did so, it was as though Dad was saying the words along with her as she read them, which expressed his eternal love and appreciation for Mom. She felt absolutely positive and was adamant that Dad's spirit had somehow encouraged her to go to that desk and open the drawer to find that unexpected lost card written to her many decades earlier. To some people this story may seem a simple matter of unconscious memory or sheer coincidence. However; to my mother, this incredibly poignant enchanting experience was a marvellously gratifying, heart-warming event that proved to her my father's continued ability to make a subtle, yet definitive interconnection with her, the truest love of his life, just as the falcon's fantastic antics were conclusive proof of Dad's love for us all and his continued existence upon higher levels of reality for my family in Australia. We never saw that bird again after that day. I would expect that after the third day when an aspect of Dad's spirit departed the bird for higher realms, it would have then become much like any other wild Little Falcon in Australia, or anywhere else Peregrine Falcons exist.

    Occasionally, I can quite literally 'feel' my Dad's spiritual presence on a subtle intuitive level where he is usually quietly expressing both his appreciation of my strong supportive relationship with my Mom and to reassure me that things are going well, in spite of appearances to the contrary at times. I have experienced many dreams with my father, although none that I wish to share here. Recently, I felt the need to ask Dad's spirit "How has it been going for these 18 years?" Dad replied with words to the effect, "Son, you would not believe what can be accomplished on this side of eternal infinite life as Soul in that length of time." He then added, "All of the old peace loving military men who died in all the unwanted wars and all of the innocent victims of warfare and violence are now united together here against the continuation of warfare on Earth, with the vast legions of angels and Divine Beings and God Itself, to manifest peace on Earth, so do not worry about the forces of darkness succeeding. They are already defeated, although they have not yet surrendered to this realisation; they will do so soon." I was amazed by these clear intuitive comments. Additionally, in the past six months I have seen a most unusual white hawk about eight or nine times at relatively close range on my rugged rural land in Australia where I now live alone surrounded within nature, 'off the grid'. I do not contend this white hawk represents my father's spirit; however, this unique bird did recently intentionally fly relatively slowly at very low level within 3 metres of me, very unexpectedly.

Suffice to say, I am confident that Dad's Spirit as Soul is still vibrantly alive and doing very well, living upon the higher planes of reality. Peace of a global nature is now in the process of developing here on Earth, in spite of the unlikely seeming possibility to war-mongering people and 'dark entities' wanting to promote warfare here.

There is absolutely no doubt whatsoever in my mind that these higher levels of reality intimately co-exist with our physical levels of reality in a way that significantly surpasses normal human understanding. It is impossible from the normal perspective of ordinary human consciousness to perceive or comprehend how highly evolved life forms, including human beings that are actually manifestations of

Soul, can function upon multiple levels of existence simultaneously with full consciousness and capability. One's higher levels of Soul awareness provide clues through all types of phenomenal experiences and gradually we unfold spiritually enough to acquire various ascendant perceptive and creative capabilities to manifest enhanced expressions of our inner divinity. Obviously, some of these spiritual qualities are developed over the eons through countless lifetimes in the 'lower' planes of existence, so some manifestations of Soul are more developed in some people and life forms than in others, depending upon the rate of their progression. It is absolutely essential to fully realise and understand that every part of eternal infinite existence, including the physical plane and Earth, are manifestations of God's cosmic reality system. Therefore, every aspect is divinely created and functions with an incomprehensibly intricate compassionate, benevolent, intent throughout the entire scheme of cosmic reality systems that are established specifically to enable consciousness to creatively express itself and unfold into progressively higher and more refined, capable, sublime, loving states of Divine awareness and being.

Your own thoughts, experiences and realisations regarding the continued existence of human consciousness after it leaves the earthly body at death may possibly be far more dramatic or conclusive than these events have been for my family. You may be fortunate enough to know someone that experienced a 'near death experience' (NDE) and knowingly travelled in full vivid conscious awareness as their physical body technically 'died', and they clearly recalled going into the higher planes of existence, and then later their Spirit returned to their body to report their memorable experiences while being there. You may be extremely blessed to have done so yourself or perhaps had a lucid dream at some time in your life that vividly proved the nature of higher realities to you in an unforgettable manner. Within the Global Mission of Peace Family there are more than 20 people that have openly shared that they experienced a wide variety of 'near death experiences' (NDEs), so among this closely affiliated, peace loving people from many nations internationally; we all share a great respect, appreciation and knowing lucid direct personal undeniable experience regarding the reality of 'life after death' of their physical body in the heavenly 'higher' realms. In every case, they soon consciously decided to return to their physical body for many reasons, to continue their earthly lives with renewed confidence and purpose. These uniquely miraculous events have certainly resulted in a greater spiritual awareness within this wonderfully loving, cooperative, close knit group of divinely inspired people who openly 'share a loving heart' of affinity between us all within this exceptionally positive international organisation with people of every race, religion and many nations as its' members.

These real events are shared for your consideration, as dubious as they may seem to a uniformed person that never experienced such amazing and undeniable events themselves. You may dramatically know at the deepest levels of your comprehensive being about the undeniable reality of these types of spiritually confirming events and concepts. Your acknowledgement of your own illuminating, awareness-increasing, fantastic, miraculous life experiences serve to influence and uplift your entire life and the lives of those around you in both obvious and sometimes very subtle ways. This shared fact is exceedingly important to us all. Alternatively, you may have never knowingly experienced anything that illustrated to you that human consciousness can continue to exist beyond the earthly levels of reality after the death of one's physical body. The ample evidence abounds around us, if we care to look for it. When one seeks this profound realisation through our own unique inner self, then these amazing experiences and awareness will be provided to you in conclusive unexpected ways that will surprise and delight you.

One factor is absolutely certain and that is that all of us will have the opportunity to experience the death of our physical body at some point in time. At that most special and wonderful of moments, realise that you are not so much dying as actually being re-born into the higher realms of existence where you can become vastly more aware of your full nature and capabilities to experience joy, divine love, and meaningful abundance that are characteristic of the higher levels of divine reality systems. Ideally at your death in this physical earthly life, you will experience no fear or regrets because then you truly realise that you are an immortal being that will everlastingly exist upon various levels of reality, guided by your own conscious free-will and eternal evolving Soul. I am and we all are exceedingly fortunate to be sharing life's journey now within this fantastic 'family by choice' as happy members of the Global Mission of Peace (GMOP), who will be and are now manifesting peaceful productive solutions cooperatively together. Join us if you wish, as a Volunteer or with a project that will help our world become a better place to live for all Earth's people and life forms here.

Please be encouraged to seek your own conclusive experiences to verify the fact that you can become consciously aware and integrated with these higher levels of eternal reality while you are alive and well, living upon this beautiful Earth. In this manner you will familiarise yourself with these co-existent reality systems in a fashion that is natural and ideal for you, depending upon your attitudes and circumstances at the time. Surely, I never envisioned or dreamed of the possibility of these unexpected and miraculous experiences and realisations, nor to hear about these similar events being openly and lovingly shared with others in such a wonderful manner as occurs within GMOP and Eckankar. In your own life's incredible and undeniable processes, it is likely to be the same is true for you and others you know. God is so amazingly creative that it boggles the mind to attempt to contemplate on how and why these exceptionally special, unique events and realisations occur for so many of us here now. We are joining with those who are receptive, spiritually prepared, and totally committed to making this immortal blessed journey of discovery cooperatively together now. Welcome, we are delighted you are with us all now !!!

Chapter 12

Focus Upon the Positive

Throughout life we are enormously benefited by doing our best to maintain one's entire focus upon the positive, as much as is humanly possible. There is a wise saying, "You become what you focus upon; relative to positive/negative states of mind". Basically, whatever you focus upon, you tend to attract and manifest into your life with regard to yourself and others. Therefore, if you habitually seek to sustain and express relatively positive states of mind and retain predominantly pleasant emotional attitudes, then this establishes a definite tendency for an increased likelihood that primarily good things will happen in your life. Likewise, the converse is also applicable, to some extent. Unpleasant, unwanted and unhappy events will happen to all of us at times, regardless of our attitudes, so to respond in a positive, perceptive, calm, reasonable manner is a most helpful attribute to develop.

There is every reason to be fully aware when perceiving reality, regardless of whether it seems to be positive or negative from the observer or involved participant's perspective. For example, if one is working full-time at a job and earning a low wage that cannot pay for all of one's most meagre costs of living, then it is reasonable to observe this reality and ideally to remedy the situation if possible in a constructive manner. Alternatively, the perspective of an employer who is attempting to remain profitable in a competitive financial environment, the relatively low wages paid to a worker may seem to be quite an appropriate and even generous form of remuneration, when compared to no employment, partial employment or bankruptcy. Often one's situation and perspectives are linked in an integral manner and those who have not experienced one's reality system for themselves may often have little comprehension or empathy with other viewpoints than those they personally hold themselves. Therefore, one person's reality may seem to be another person's fiction, just as most of our political and business leaders seldom have an accurate perception of the nature of the lifestyles of the lower income segments of society, or the challenges the under-employed or unemployed confront every day of their lives. Another example would be living in an abusive relationship as a spouse or child, when compared to the attitude of the aggressive abusive person, who may feel justified in their actions and not perceive a problem with their own attitudes or behaviour. So, when we focus upon the positive, we do not ignore any aspects of reality in our mindset. A key factor is to also attempt to understand those who experience different types of lives and attitudes than we ourselves do.

We all notice that when we are kind, happy and considerate in our interactions with others, then we generally receive similar friendly treatment from them. It is fairly easy to observe that when we do not experience pleasant interactions with others, then we can usually determine whether it is primarily due to their state of mind, our own, or that we both are partly responsible for the non-harmonious situation. Once we are able to recognise the exact circumstances, then we are in an ideal position to respond in a way that will improve matters or perhaps to simply avoid further interactions, if that is a reasonable possibility. Life may seldom seem to be that simplistic, yet if we are able to develop patterns of thought, emotion and behaviour that adjust to the circumstances around us, then we can enhance our skills to cope with and make the best of all types of challenging situations.

A quite basic real life example was observed by me recently in a nice restaurant where I seemed to be the person who was learning an excellent lesson through someone else's astute realisations and quality behaviour. Initially one lady arrived for dinner and immediately from my perspective, she began to be somewhat 'difficult', especially after her friend arrived. It could be said they were being relatively unpleasant in various subtle ways with a very friendly, polite waitress. It seemed to me that the couple were behaving exactly as was customary for them, based upon the 'vibe' they exuded as I perceived the situation developing from when they arrived. At the time, I noted to myself that it could be an inaccurate perception on my part and partly due to my own 'sensitive' state of mind, in that I was not in the best possible mood myself due a few stressful situations occurring in my life and was already well-aware of that fact. I discretely took special care to observe the events as objectively as possible, since the reasonably good mood we had been enjoying (in spite of our own life stresses) changed abruptly as soon as the first lady was seated within a few feet of our table. This situation intensified as time passed, from my perspective.

This story is shared because it reveals how people with numerous differing states of mind interact constantly in earthly life. It is through many ordinary events the opportunity exists to achieve realisations, lessons and progressive developments, if one allows and enables this process to occur. I was provided with a valuable lesson by being privileged to witness the remarkable attitudes demonstrated by the restaurant staff that immediately assessed the situation and made a series of wonderful adjustments in rapid sequential order. The flawless quality of their perceptions and consummate conduct in smoothly handling the entire situation was accomplished in a most professional and spiritually evolved manner that amazed me. They did far better than I could have done under those particular circumstances, considering my state of mind at the time.

The first member of the couple arrived before the other and chose to seat herself outside at a table next to ours' without consulting the waitress. Once seated the lady immediately asked us if it looked as though it would rain, to which I replied that I did not think so. She responded that the weather report predicted rain. So I said, "Well, I hope not." since we were also seated out of doors so we could enjoy the summer breeze in full view of the nearby beautiful river. The lady then ordered a wine. Soon after receiving the glass of wine, her dinner guest arrived. I was somewhat interested to see the seemingly flamboyant greeting ritual the two people shared, as the first lady stood up and bowing slightly, quickly greeted her friend in a most friendly and cordial manner and asked if the table location was acceptable. She replied that it looked like possible rain and it was a bit too windy, yet sat down saying it was unlikely they would stay for dinner anyway. When asked if it was going to rain, the waitress was quite cute about it and said, "The rain is not invited for dinner." and then chatted pleasantly with them. Unexpectedly, the first arrival told the delightfully friendly, happy waitress, "I'll have some of whatever you are on", inferring the waitress was on some sort of drugs or mood altering substance, when in reality she was simply being very genuine and joyful with the customers. The waitress just smiled sweetly at that comment, making no response and then asked the new arrival if she would like to order a drink. The lady replied that she would like wine, but had not brought her own bottle and stood up to go to a local bottle shop to get one, then realising it was about two blocks away, she quickly sat back down and asked about the house wines. When asked if she would like a glass, she responded that she did not want a glass from a bottle that had already been opened. The waitress suggested a nice bottle of red wine and the other lady who had already received her glass of wine complained that she would prefer that wine to the one she already had ordered. The waitress said that was fine and her glass would be 'on the house' (free) if she wished to drink it, or it could be taken away. She decided to keep her now complementary (free) glass of wine; the bottle of wine was selected, brought and shown to both ladies, who again asked if it was unopened for some incomprehensible reason, since it was clearly a new unopened bottle. Unfazed, the waitress smiled broadly, giggled a bit and showed them that it was unopened and placed it to her cheek momentarily and posed with it, as if in a photo opportunity. Then they could not decide for a minute or so if they really wanted the bottle of wine after all, yet finally decided that it was acceptable. The waitress poured a small bit for the lady to taste to determine if it was acceptable to her, which it was. She then poured a glass for the second arrival who had ordered the bottle. Then she poured the second glass for the first arrival, who had not wanted the glass of wine that she had ordered, yet chose to drink it anyway. After the second glass was poured, the lady immediately complained to the waitress that she had poured it too quickly and at the incorrect angle, saying, "You got too many bubbles in my wine." The waitress apologised and said, "Thank you for pointing that out to me. We learn things from the customers all the time." I noted the waitress had titled the glass at about 45% which is standard for most situations, so to me her method of pouring the wine was quite normal. The waitress then asked if she could leave the bottle on the table to breathe, knowing it was a relatively inexpensive 'screw top' wine anyway, so they could pour it in any manner that suited them, which was fine with the customers.

A few other similar exchanges occurred, with the waitress always being very charming, polite and genuinely hospitable. Then in an urgent mood, they then insisted upon moving inside, in spite of fact the popular restaurant was filling up rapidly, they had no reservation, and still had not committed to eating a meal there yet. The waitress responded that it would be fine and she would find them a nice table indoors so they could still look out onto the lovely river nearby.

The entire experience of observing these ladies' attitudes and their seemingly persistent attempts to goad the waitress into demonstrating anything aside from a delightfully polite attitude; which they were unable to accomplish, had begun to seriously distract me from my own nice time, which annoyed me and my dinner partner a bit. Since we had finished eating, I went to pay our bill. The waitress who was serving the couple accepted the payment for our meal and I briefly had a polite quiet word with her about the events that I had witnessed, commending her on her kindly pleasant responses to avert a potentially awkward set of situations. She just laughed and said it was common and that she refused to allow them to upset her in any way, as she had six hours of busy work ahead of her, inferring she was determined to retain her positive state of mind. I went to the bathroom to wash my hands and by the time I returned the couple had been moved inside the restaurant. I went back to our table and our own equally delightful waitress returned to farewell us, since we went to that restaurant often. Being the odd character I am; I could not resist commenting quietly about the events we had witnessed and observed that it must be difficult to deal with such people on a regular basis. She smiled widely and then could not help but laugh; seeing how their attitude had adversely influenced me. She very briefly explained that all the staff recognised and accepted the fact that many customers are not particularly happy or polite people with the restaurant employees, so they were all firmly committed to maintaining a quality attitude that was relatively impervious to being disturbed by such antics. I realised the staff had exhibited a high standard of spiritualism, whereas I had immediately become somewhat reactive to the negative mindset of the couple that were somewhat displeased with whatever was said or done by the waitress, as was their prerogative. The event allowed me to realise how easily I can be drawn into responding to the attitudes of others in a debilitating manner, when alternatively the simple step to respond in a positive manner was available to me, just as it was for the waitress. In a sense, I clearly failed 'the test' in some ways, yet in the process I learned a valuable lesson that I should already know quite well. Some may say, "Don't sweat the small stuff" while others are oblivious to the motivations and resultant effects their own attitudes and actions. I would say, be selective in deciding what truly matters in one's life and respond to the best within your character, regardless of how other people choose to think or act.

We do not need to respond negatively to other people's states of mind, as I did to some degree in the example provided previously, especially when we are already so well-aware of their potential to adversely affect us in various ways. We can expect the best for ourselves, exemplify the highest aspects of ourselves, and simply allow others to be whatever they wish to be, so long as they are not especially unpleasant or aggressive toward us. If they are, then we can do exactly as the waitress did; basically 'turn the situation around' and choose to retain and express our pleasant polite demeanour, regardless of other people's attitudes and actions. This to me seems a most valuable, simplistic lesson that all of us can benefit from, if we apply this wisdom in our lives in multitudinous ways. Of course life is not ideal sometimes and there will be circumstances when we must assert ourselves and this is a matter for one's own discretion, wisdom and experience.

Life is divinely designed to challenge us in the exact ways that will potentially be of most benefit to us. Our goal is to become increasingly able to respond in a positive, active, self-responsible fashion and learn throughout these processes to progressively achieve character growth and solutions in our life, rather than to repeat the habitual reactions that persistently perpetuate further unpleasant human nature issues and difficult circumstances. However, unfortunately earthly life for most of us replicates habitual attitudinal patterns of behaviour that cause us to repetitively entangle our lives within redundant situations. Once we are able to more clearly recognise how our particular beliefs and attitudes create the circumstances for these conditions to exist, then we are far more able to make the necessary adjustments to our intellectual and behavioural patterns, in spite of the fact it requires perceptive awareness and sincere commitment. This process can be so obscure, arduous, formidable, complex and laborious that one may tire of the efforts and can become prone to complacency or a lack of patience and empathy. The solution is to be patiently persistent with yourself, remain well-aware of your various successes, and be especially considerate of the progress that you are making over the longer term. It is often by reflecting upon how exacting this transformation process is that one more fully appreciates the many achievements that have already been accomplished which will assist and inspire you to steadfastly pursue the personal developmental goals that you seek to achieve. Again and again you may need to remind yourself that spiritual unfoldment is not a race; rather it is a vitalised spontaneous living path of continual miraculous discovery that one travels throughout their eternal existence.

Because this is an endless journey of conscious Soul development, it does not imply that one is benefited by a lackadaisical attitude or that progress is something one need not strive to achieve, since it will occur inevitably someday. Such a complacent attitude can lead to some very unpleasant life conditions. Instead, our aspiration is to nurture the skills and attributes that enable us to retain focus and intent to consistently improve our attitudes and conduct in incremental ways as these opportunities become available every day. This attitude and behaviour pattern is the best way to create a mindset that is most able to deal with the inevitable setbacks, fluctuations and disappointments that naturally accompany this earthly life. We choose to set our standards high for ourselves and do our best to attain them. If we do not always succeed in our efforts then we remind ourselves of our errors in judgement and inappropriate actions and we resume our course. There are many characteristics contained with each of us as human beings and from time to time, depending upon the circumstances, all of these traits will likely seek some form of expression and fulfilment. This fact is one of the key reasons that we seek to identify our character with the very best aspects of our overall comprehensive state of being because if we willingly choose to identify with the lower aspects of ourselves and untruthfully attempt to justify and rationalise our unwise, inappropriate, unkind behaviours and attitudes then we will find life and eternal life to be a very long, often cruel and inevitably quite a painfully hard road to travel for ourselves and others.

We have not addressed many negative issues that could be relevant to our discussion, such as mental illness, suicide, the seriously negative potentiality that exists within some people, the suffering that noxious people will ultimately endure for their short-sighted and unkind actions, and many other such factors. This has been the situation because generally we have been focusing upon the positive, in spite of the many appearances to the contrary in addressing numerous human nature issues that we need to resolve, as individuals and as a civilisation. People whose personalities can often be characterised by an inordinate proportion of adverse emotional volatility, and who continually experience conflicted lives dominated by turmoil and various types of physical maladies have three primary influences to consider. First, they are being spiritually strengthened in this process. Second, they are likely to be resolving karmic issues from both their present and past lives. Third, but definitely not the last reason, is that they are slow to implement the necessary changes into their current lives to improve matters in significant ways. When one has paramount issues that require attention, which are ignored or intentionally not resolved, then generally these challenging situations can gradually or quickly worsen; sometimes intensely so. We can see these fundamental processes being pervasively revealed in people's lives that seem to do an excessive amount of suffering, who often express a wide range of negative emotions or hostile opinions, that are prone to having an inordinately frequent number of unusual accidents, those which knowingly create problems for others or are rude and abusive, who thrive on drama, gossip, the criticism of others and so on. There are always exceptions to such over-generalisations; however, if we could look throughout peoples' many lifetimes of existence upon the lower planes of reality, then we would begin to perceive that there is an exceptionally effective system of eternal justice functioning throughout cosmic reality. On Earth we are fortunate to be able to vividly witness and intimately experience these immutable wheels of karmic process functioning in ways that all can recognise, understand and benefit from, once we comprehend how these factors affect us all.

The accurate recognition of one's inner spiritual status, as contrasted with our external material earthly appearances, is an essential attribute to develop with the assistance of our higher aspects of immortal being. We do not wish to overly complicate the factors involved, yet our tendency while existing within the lower Planes can be to become relatively unaware of many of the higher realities while simultaneously misperceiving our spiritual level of development, as well as that of others. For example, we may become likely to exaggerate our own spiritual unfoldment and perhaps do likewise for others, in assuming them inaccurately to be highly evolved spiritually when in cosmic eternal terms this would not be true. For example, to some people I may seem to be quite an aware person, yet in my present state of human consciousness I am quite underdeveloped spiritually in some senses; relative to those much more highly evolved life forms existing within the physical universe, as well as many of those existing upon the higher levels of reality, even below the Soul Plane. This fact is not something that any of us who are doing our best in life should be ashamed or embarrassed about. Instead, we simply wish to obtain a relatively truthful, accurate image of our basic level of development so we do not ever overestimate our status to become arrogant, egotistical, vain, haughty and self-satisfied, even in a kindly way. We seek to remain genuinely humble and deeply appreciative for any spiritual progress and enlightenment that we are fortunate to receive or develop. We want to always be grateful for the precious gift of life itself, which allows us the opportunity to enjoy all of life's multitudinous realisations and lessons, which can sometimes be rather emotionally tormenting, unpleasant, painful, embarrassing, revealing and thought provoking. Other times, life's realisations can be joyous, delightful, sublime, humorous, and result in a state of comfort that encourages a peaceful inner existence in spite of the complex issues that are likely to be occurring externally. In earthly life, we are extremely fortunate to experience the entire scope of consciousness through this ingenious system of multifaceted reality; where one's imagination, dreams, plans, attitudes, attributes and efforts all coalesce to attain ever greater levels of achievement and awareness.

Because the eternal quest of spiritual unfoldment and illumination is so obscure, nebulous and incomprehensible to our ordinary human intellect and perceptions, we greatly benefit by assuming an attitude characterised by inner joy, peace of mind and heightened awareness. One of our major life goals is to engender the continual development of our numerous perceptive abilities and enhanced inner self-control of our emotions. No matter what happens externally in daily earthly life, we do our best to remain in relative control over our emotions and responses to life's complex and unexpected situations; accepting graciously whatever life presents to us as being another opportunity to grow spiritually, intellectually and emotionally in multitudes of ways. This is one of the most important creative abilities and life lessons that we can possibly learn in this earthly lifetime. We seek to sincerely improve our commitment to recognise the full inherent wisdom being expressed through life's varied circumstances while augmenting our own capabilities to handle almost any situation with poise, clarity, self-control, compassion, responsibility, honesty and inner peace of mind. This evolving ability will become one of your greatest attributes and remain with you throughout eternity as one of the crucial aspects of your true wealth of character.

It is quite possible to develop these skills in everyday life. Regardless of the nature of your daily life's events, you can become determined in a patient, persistent, kindly manner to manifest the best of your personal qualities. This activity has enormous value and benefits because as your state of mind rises to meet life's challenges in an ideal fashion, you become an inspiration to yourself as well as many other people. Life is largely defined by the choices we make in our beliefs, attitudes and behaviours. Obviously, we already are aware of this to a considerable extent because we are so often tested by life's situations to think and behave in a manner that is not totally in our favour; so most of us already automatically restrain ourselves unconsciously or consciously from exhibiting various negative, unkind, unwanted, thoughtless or inappropriate behaviours. We currently recognise that such negative states of mind, once expressed outwardly, seldom accomplish anything positive, so in such cases we ideally allow our conscience to guide our actions. What we are intent upon doing is to develop increased perceptive and intellectual habitual states of being that allow us to obtain a broader, more in-depth, detailed perception of all life's experiences and our own resultant thoughts, feelings and responses so that we gain ever greater inner control and better outcomes from all of our actions. This goal is among our foremost essential qualities as human beings and immortally as Soul, so the process provides extremely significant meaning and true purpose in our lives.

Please consider a variety of intensely challenging life circumstances that you have faced and resolved in various ways throughout your childhood and as an adult. Attempt to visualise the numerous difficult, exceedingly complex situational dilemmas that you have experienced with all sorts of apprehension, confusion, frustration, determination, persistence, emotional turmoil characterised by conflicting mixed feelings, and even many seemingly unresolvable conundrums. Through it all, you have managed to reach decisions that have served to illuminate your mind and influence your heart's feelings to uplift and enlighten your overall state of being in incremental progressive ways. Many times we have no easy simple solutions available to us, especially when so often other people's best interests and emotions are directly or indirectly involved in our decision making processes. The vital thing to realise and acknowledge is that whatever your decisions have been; some being much better or worse than others, the key factor is all these choices have ultimately served to create progress in your life and developed your character in various ways. We do not need to avoid arduous deliberations in consciously adjusting the flow of events in our lives. Nor do we especially benefit by being overly critical of our poor judgements or mistakes, so long as we are genuinely doing our best to assess all the information available to us in making the right decisions for ourselves and those other people for whom we are responsible at the time. The focal issue is to recognise that some of our greatest mistakes in life can lead us toward making the required adjustments in our attitudes and actions that subsequently function as our most noble strengths of character. Another aspect to recall are those memorable times when our perceptions and judgement were relatively limited in scope and did not include the diverse array of relevant variables that would have been helpful in assisting us to make more informed, more appropriate, better decisions. In this evaluative process, we will realise the productive usefulness of creating sensible deductive solutions by utilising our full range of capabilities, intellect and the inclusion of intuitive perception. We intend to cease decision making through impulsive, arbitrary, superficial, self-focused actions that are primarily based upon limited information. We seek to consider vastly more information that will become available to our inquiring, open mind.

This developmental process reveals the higher levels of conscious motivation that we can access. Reflecting upon this mode of behaviour will identify some of the reasons we will be benefited by initiating a more thorough, discriminating, careful analysis of the full scope of related factors in any particular situation, especially when making our more important judgements. We all fully realise that once some types of decisions have been made, and then they cannot be annulled or otherwise rescinded, even if we desperately wish and need to do so. Therefore, the much better, preferable activity pattern is to be quite selective and very deliberate in regard to one's evaluative and decision making processes in all areas of one's life. Some choices are relatively simplistic and easy to reach a conclusion with minimal time required in analysis of the available information. Alternatively, other types of decisions require considerable forethought, exploration, research, contemplation, intuition, and the use of the full range of one's perceptive and intellectual capabilities. The reason for this is we quite literally usually end up 'living with' our life's many decisions; be they in our relationships, occupation, driving style, health, attitudes, beliefs and even our dreams of our future destiny.

Consciously analysing one's habitual decision making patterns of behaviour and then progressively adjusting them to become increasingly proficient and wisdom driven is an ideal choice in how one applies their daily efforts in earthly life and in immortal life as well. Recall that both aspects of reality co-exist simultaneously and are intimately interrelated with one another in mostly unobservable ways for earthly humans. By sincerely enlivening one's overall awareness to comprehensively include all manner of possible perceptions and information in making one's life choices, regardless of how seemingly minor or mundane they may appear to be, we are able to develop the good skills and habits that will create constantly improving circumstances for us in most cases. When things do not go as we wish they would, which can be quite frequently in this earthly life, then we have the glorious opportunity to focus our attention and efforts on responding with the best possible attitudes and expressions of our overall character in spontaneous, yet deliberate, productive, positive activity patterns. If we see that things are still not working out as hoped or planned, then we can make various adjustments to improve the situation or simply persist in doing our best to obtain the ideal ultimate result. We also need to learn to accept when something we want is unlikely to be forthcoming and in those situations we are benefited by 'letting go' or mentally and emotionally releasing that desire to direct our attention into other more productive activities. Choosing this process in my own life over many years has resulted in this book being slowly produced in my spare time and finally being internationally published after almost a ten year waiting period for the prevailing international circumstances to change for the better. It was a wise uplifting decision to shift my attention toward accomplishing activities that were truly meaningful and quite enjoyable to me in regard to producing this book, aside from researching, writing and editing the 'human nature issues' sections in this book, which were often quite upsetting and even painful to endure.

    The focal point in this part of our discussion is determining how we make the best possible decisions to create an ideal life for ourselves and those people that are important in our personal lives, while also having a productive positive effect upon our community and larger reality within which we exist. The level of our functionality as a human being and as Soul manifests this in innumerable ways. There is always room for improvement in our states of mind and being, yet there is also good cause to rejoice and be exceedingly grateful for the reality of our conscious existence and the progress that we have already accomplished in our earthly and immortal life.

    Your eternal journey of discovery is a uniquely individual pilgrimage and this particular lifetime on Earth is definitely an opportunity to nurture and portray some of the best personal qualities that are inherent within your comprehensive character. The more committed you are in focusing your attention upon eliciting the highest aspects of yourself, the better things will ultimately be in your life and the more positive influence you will have upon others, as well as yourself. It is an odd thought to realise that we can actually positively influence our own self by the way we choose to think, yet it is quite a natural reasonable fact of life that we already well-recognise, if we simply consider the relevant issues involved. We currently exert enormous control and restraint over our minds and actions, so this process is very well understood by us, as individuals and collectively as a civilisation. We are now seeking to evoke the latent, immanent divinity already existing within our innate human consciousness by establishing the mental, emotional, and circumstantial conditions to inwardly and externally demonstrate these fine qualities in ways that uplift and transform our daily life, as well as our immortal existence.

There are infinite methods to achieve this transcendence of ordinary mind to attain the manifestation of the higher aspects of Soul through one's earthly life. One of the best progressive developments is to attempt to keep your mind focused upon the positives you wish to exemplify, while not becoming oblivious to the events around yourself. We do not cease to become involved in the world as we are now; rather we primarily adjust our attitudes and actions so that the events of the world do not exert undue external pressures upon us to think and act in ways that are contrary to our highest nature. This is inherently a challenging process in earthly life, so we must remain patient, persistent, and committed in our loyalty to one's higher aspects of character to the best of our ability under all types of changing circumstances. There are enormous benefits derived from remaining true to this basic course in life because it also influences one's higher aspects of innate being, Soul, to increasingly reveal Itself within the privacy of one's mind, spirit, emotions, perceptions and beliefs. This ongoing process enables and encourages Soul levels of awareness and capability to assume a much more active, prominent role in one's life in ways that are relatively incomprehensible to the normal human intellect. What we all can clearly comprehend are the wonderful, delightfully joyous results of these types of activities occurring within our mind and lives. The uplifting nature of this process is detectable and becomes increasingly obvious to one's self and others, since it is revealed in many spontaneous, miraculous events and realisations. Life takes on an entirely new, superior level of meaning and purpose. We obtain our truth, love, wisdom, peace and pleasure from innumerable sources and experience the obvious fact that it is not what one accomplishes in their material lives that matters most, rather what one is and becomes as a human being, Soul. Once this process begins to gather momentum, you will discover that your life is progressively being enriched with fantastic peak experiences that are derived from some fairly ordinary life events. You will rediscover depth, joy and meaning in life's fundamental realities. This is a very good thing.

You may quite rightly ask, "Where to from here?" The key realisation is this 'where' is obviously not a location; it is a state of conscious being in which one is devoted to becoming the best person that is humanly possible for you at this time in your immortal progressive development as Soul. The real vehicle of expression and realisation is your human self, your personality. Your total self now serves as the mode of self-conscious awareness that enables you to introspectively define and determine the course of your earthly life's purpose; to in a sense 'do it all properly this time'. You can realise in the deepest possible ways that you are Soul, an eternally super-conscious being of incredible dimension and capability that vastly surpasses human comprehension and perception. This is the essence of what and who you are. You will never ever forget this monumental realisation when it finally occurs. We are all on the path toward the realisation that we are Soul and many in earthly life have been divinely blessed to have been granted and worked very diligently to earn the precious gift to experience this indescribably blissful, awesome state of being. A Soul Realisation experience is so far beyond normal human levels of awareness that we will not discuss it here any further. Suffice to say, to experience the inner manifestation of Soul levels of awareness is an experience that leaves absolutely no doubt about many of life's larger realities and proves dramatically the factual existence of our inner eternal consciousness that animates us and provides us with conscious awareness.

It is interesting to consider the diverse scope of attitudes and activities that lead us continually toward achieving ever greater levels of realisation, perception and awareness. As we believe we are reaching our goal, we find that reality expands again to become inclusive of far more potential, meaning and substance than appeared to be possible from our previous perspectives. The only tool available to us throughout this eternal journey is our consciousness, which is both the participant and the observer in this complex, joyous, unanticipated process of ongoing discovery and eternal mystery. The more functional the nature of our consciousness, the better we are able to traverse the territory that we perceive as earthly reality, which is surrounded by and permeated by the infinite expanses of cosmic reality within, through and around us upon many levels of existence. Anything we can do to expand, advance, augment, intensify, magnify, enrich, strengthen and elevate our levels of consciousness is an excellent development that enhances our opportunities for further transformative progress. This is your quest and you are in absolute total control over your destiny, regardless of any appearances to the contrary in an arbitrary seeming universe. If you make choices unwisely, then be assured that life will at some stage begin to abuse you unmercifully. Choose well and you, as Soul, are completely impervious to any negativity and there is nothing that material reality can do to you to diminish your immortal essence, once you are truly aware of this fact and live accordingly.

When we say we seek to focus upon the positive, this primarily refers to keeping alert within one's conscious awareness to the fact that you are actually Soul, an evolving divine spark of God's conscious energy. This is the paramount reality for you to recognise as an individual. The events in our external daily life, as well as some aspects of our lower mental and emotional processes, are secondary to this superlative realisation. All earthly activity is derived from the functional results of this fundamental innate immortal level of conscious reality. When we discuss remaining 'focused upon the positive' in life, we are not predominantly referring to earthly daily events and experiences, although we surely do attempt to maintain as positive an attitude and behaviour in these circumstances as well. We are well-aware that our earthly events are intended by divine design to 'push our buttons' in diverse ways to test, provoke, frustrate, strengthen, motivate, upset and encourage us to experience the full range of human possibilities. Our various spiritual responses to these multifarious experiences are of vast significance to us in transcending our present level of conscious being to progressively unfold and evolve into manifesting the higher divine aspects of our innate inner reality. We must acknowledge and fully accept that earthly life is always going to be challenging in numerous unexpected ways. Therefore, our attempt to focus spiritually upon the positive is actually committed almost exclusively to retaining our dignity and higher life purpose through consciously envisioning and manifesting our powerful, loving, incredibly perceptive sense of inner true self as being Soul. This visualisation process helps to enable us to successfully meet all life has to offer us through its lessons, realisations and quite diverse scope of experiential reality. In short, we gratefully make the best of whatever life presents to us. We know that change is inevitable and that we must simply continue to do our part, which is to be well-aware that all life's experiences assist us in various, often incomprehensible ways. I often appreciate and give thanks for a challenge since it can "fast track" our development, if we take the time to carefully consider our responses and options.

One of the best methods for enjoyably familiarising one's human levels of consciousness with the divine aspects of Soul is to develop a state of gratitude and deep appreciation for your very existence. The fact that you are a conscious being that is self-aware, alive, alert, able to move, experience life itself, do things in your environment, possess and exert your free-will, create your own reality through your thoughts and actions, influence your own states of consciousness, perceive reality clearly, interact with all types of other conscious beings, be an immortal form of consciousness that can uplift and improve its lifestyles and awareness; love, be happy or sad, as well as innumerable other such capabilities and potentialities is really quite an astounding reality that we are very fortunate to experience.

To attempt to consider the possibility that you, your conscious self that is self-aware and active in life, could possibly NOT exist is a great place to begin this realisation process. In other words, seriously attempt to contemplate upon the possibility or even the likely probability that your conscious mind and self did not exist within cosmic reality or earthly reality upon any level of existence. If this were possible, then you would obviously not be at all aware of anything, as you would not exist, as though you had never been born into earthly life, or into any other form of reality as a self-conscious aware being or life form. You would then not need to perceive anything or in any way concern yourself with anything, since you simply would not exist. You would have no mind, no body and no conscious awareness. You would not exist. You see where we are going with this line of realisation? How would you feel about the possibility of you not existing at all?

Alternatively, you may consider how you would address a situation where if you were quite unhappy in life that you could request that God simply terminate your Soul awareness. If that were to occur, then you as Soul, a spark of

God energy, would be dissolved to subsequently be redistributed to other life forms; so that you, or more accurately your immortal consciousness would simply cease to exist so far as your conscious perceptions were concerned for all of eternity. You would have no opportunity to reconsider your decision, no second chances, no apologies available, no requests possible to God for another existence as Soul, since physical and eternal life would then become permanently, forever over, and terminated completely for you and your self-aware, perceptive consciousness. No more awareness; no more difficulties, no more joys, no more love, no more daily events, no more anything.

The reason this idea is so challenging and uncomfortable to contemplate is because it is an unusual concept to consider in that you would not have a consciousness available to consider or perceive anything at all. There would no longer be 'you', the observer and perceiver, nor any physical body to inhabit. Therefore, from your non-existent perspective, the Earth, universe and all of cosmic reality would not exist, as you would have no consciousness to perceive it 'from'. This obviously would not in any way negate the ongoing existence of the realities that other life forms would all experience; rather, you would simply not be around to share this eternal journey with the rest of us. You would not be lonely or confused by this fact since you would not be aware of anything or that you were missing out on life, as you would not exist. Are you getting quite sick at the thought of such a possibility yet? I hope so, because we must realise that without consciousness we are nothing, we have nothing, we do nothing, we perceive nothing, we simply do not exist, end of the story of life on Earth and anywhere else. The 'game', 'set', and 'match' of life is over and there is never ever anything else to replace it; it is over, the end.

Considering the realisation that such a thing could happen to us is a painful, almost traumatic experience if it is seriously evaluated from the perspective that it could actually happen. For example, hypothetically we could theorise that God could decide that it is getting frustrated with these useless, self-serving, evil-minded, greedy, violent, corrupted types of human beings and universal 'dark creatures' existing within Its' physical and cosmic reality systems. God could at some time arbitrarily decide that those Souls who had not demonstrated a genuine love of life and a real affection or respectful appreciation for others did not belong in Its' systems of reality any longer.

Please allow me to digress momentarily. Making this hypothetical, inaccurate, artificial mental distinction is intentionally designed to create a temporary inner feeling of separation from God. We actually are greatly benefited by acknowledging that each and all of us are an integral aspect of God. In reality, none of us are a separate entity to God. Therefore, God cannot decide that it doesn't want conscious life forms around anymore because then God would also cease to exist on some levels. In a very real sense, as Soul, I am an eternal aspect of God through the reality of the Holy Spirit or ECK energies and so are you. However, for the point in our discussion please consider the following set of circumstances to provide us with a better appreciation of our eternal existence.

Now please further assume that God did not feel like creating or sustaining an alternative system of reality for learning intense life lessons, such as the awful place that the traditional religionists describe as being Hell. Some sick and depraved people unwisely believe they would enjoy living within a reality system like the traditional Biblical version of Hell, regardless of their suffering or that which they inflicted upon others in their eternal lifetimes of damnation there. They would soon realise the errors in their judgement and perceptions, yet let's assume that God, in Its' infinite wisdom and competence, had anticipated this possibility may occur. Therefore, an all knowing God would design a process of divine judgement whereby every Soul was provided an opportunity to evolve for a given number of physical and other types of existences within varied cosmic reality systems. If after a specified amount of physical time passed without any appreciable development, or if that Soul had intentionally created great misery for other life forms, then at some arbitrary time that Soul would be permanently terminated. Then Its' divine energies would be purified, reclaimed, and redistributed in the creation of new Souls that would begin their immortal journey of development within the physical and other reality systems throughout the infinite duration of God's existence. In conclusion, then it would be either a situation of evolve, progress, be loving or altruistic or eventually be terminated as a conscious eternal life form, Soul, which would be a really serious 'loss' for one to suffer if God our Creator were to decide to 'un-create' or terminate us as Soul, due to our own poor attitudes, evil ways and the pain we intentionally inflicted upon other life forms through our multitudes of physical existences.

While I am clearly NOT suggesting this is the manner in which divine reality actually functions, in some senses it could be a distinct possibility. In life we are not provided a handbook on cosmic systems of reality, or a rule book of divine spiritual laws; aside from the scriptures humans have written themselves, often with the intent to control one another and justify certain attitudes and practices. Therefore, we are all learning through this process of life together and it is wise to appreciate the opportunity to progress together.

Genuine gratitude is a mental characteristic, an attitude and a very pleasing, satisfying, uplifting emotional state of being. By nurturing one's feelings of gratitude, such as by visualising the indescribable importance of one's immortal conscious existence within cosmic systems of reality, we can better apprehend and appreciate the true meaning of our lives. We could also consider the fantastic relevance that love has in our lives. We often confuse human love with the far less comprehensible divine love that enabled us, as Soul and as human life forms, to be created and sustained by God, our Creator. Human love has many complicated mental, emotional associations and expectations attached to it. We actually do not yet truly comprehend the full nature and relevance of God's divine love for all creation. Therefore, my suggestion is to concentrate your attention upon learning to more fully explore and experience thoughts, realisations and emotions of gratitude for every aspect of your earthly life, physical and mental abilities, the role of love in your life, your opportunity to develop your character over eons of time, and especially the fact of your immortal existence as Soul.

There are so many things that we can and should be grateful for that it would require a book to list and discuss them all. Even then, it would be an incomplete effort because there are so many factors in cosmic reality that serve to establish this comprehensive existence that we as humans could never be aware of at our present level of reality. We can and must begin to be far more grateful for the countless good things in our lives and levels of consciousness, as well as the infinite cosmic reality systems within which we are privileged to exist throughout eternity. Many of us already experience considerable gratitude for the blessings in our lives. However, we all would benefit from setting aside quiet times and 'make time', even if it is while sitting at a traffic light on our way to or from work, to give special thanks to God and Soul for their uplifting, sustaining influences upon us that are such essential prerequisites to our ongoing survival. By focusing one's total attention upon vividly experiencing gratitude at a deep fundamental conscious level through one's ordinary human consciousness in a graphically emotional, intensely feeling manner; to intellectually acknowledge the incredible magnitude of our countless opportunities, gifts, capabilities, blessings, joys, challenges, and longevity in our eternal existence, then we grow spiritually closer in harmony with Soul and God. To become more harmonious with Soul and God by the application of our free-will as human beings is the true purpose of our earthly and cosmic lives. It is a delightful, wonderfully vibrant feeling that contains peace of mind and spirit and many other idyllic emotions and realisations. This enhancement of one's harmonious relationships with Soul and God are progressively augmented by consciously experiencing gratitude upon all levels of one's being. Please try to experience gratitude far more often so that it becomes as natural as breathing. You will like and even love the eventual results enormously, as your life begins to blossom in innumerable unexpectedly beautiful ways.

Life is like a big 'fruit salad' and sometimes our 'grapes' have sour tasting, hard crunchy seeds amongst the sweeter, softer, more delicious fruits, yet even these 'bitter hard seeds' are very good for us in various ways, just as are life's more difficult challenges and some of our unhappy experiences.

The primary initial resultant development of living life with an attitude of gratitude is that Soul feels more 'at home' within your human level of consciousness. Genuinely felt, private, inner expressions of true gratitude serve to encourage Soul to be more welcome and comfortable in manifesting Its' presence through revealing experiences that you will very much enjoy and benefit from enormously. We do not choose to immerse ourselves in a self-serving type of publicly displayed pseudo-gratitude that we can see exhibited so dramatically in some religion's group gatherings, which is fine for them if it makes them happier and more connected with Soul and God. Rather, we seek to sincerely commune with Soul in the privacy of our quiet contemplative times, as well as throughout our daily lives. This is a way of life; an eternal life path, because we genuinely are exceedingly grateful for our existence and seek to demonstrate the fact in real life, not an occasional activity that we do simply to obtain benefits or feel good within ourselves. Pseudo-gratitude can be characterised by one's hypocritical actions and attitudes that reveal we are wilfully and intentionally failing to adjust our lives in the necessary ways to become more worthy of Soul and God's manifestation and expression through our lives, minds and hearts.

This spiritual path in life is all about true meaning and has virtually nothing to do with external appearances or what others may think of us. Inwardly acknowledging and expressing one's gratitude with Soul and God for their existence is a most private experience because unexpected and inexplicable things will definitely happen, many dramatic realisations will occur, and sometimes miracles reveal themselves to us in unexpected magical seeming events. We must be extremely discerning in whether or not we discuss our most special private experiences with others. One must evaluate carefully if, why, with whom and how we choose to share these sanctified experiences with other people. This is partly why I have very deliberately chosen not to disclose many of my own private spiritual beliefs and most of the more sublime spiritual experiences that have occurred in the last thirty years, especially those since becoming a member of Eckankar. One aspect of our spiritual journey involves what could be defined as the 'law of silence' regarding spiritual matters. This spiritual principle basically addresses the fact that some divinely inspired experiences are monumental in the context of your inner spiritual unfoldment, and these are privately provided for your own exclusive benefit. It is intended that no other people are ever told about some of these more superlative types of events and realisations; including one's own family who would not fully understand or appreciate the experiences. This is not to categorically say that all such events are 'secrets' in the human sense of the term. Generally speaking, they are simply the private communion and communication between your human self, Soul and God Consciousness, or the Holy Spirit, or the ECK depending upon the terminology you prefer to use.

Jesus is reported to have said words to the effect of, "Do not cast your pearls before swine." My interpretation of this wise comment is that we are well-advised to not disclose the true inner treasures of our spiritual essence to those who would not understand our sublime experiences, and that may be prone to gossip about us maliciously, or even condemn us for our beliefs and honesty. Some people would naturally develop personal resentments toward us because they were unable to experience such similar events themselves and they may incorrectly perceive us as being braggarts, who believe ourselves to be superior to them or others in spite of this not being the situation. There is much more that could and should be said on this subject, yet we will not do so here now. Soul will communicate about these countless other realities within the sanctuary of your own precious consciousness.

Another two key attributes we seek to develop are genuine humility and true compassion. Like gratitude, these essential qualities of character establish the ideal fertile mental, emotional and spiritual environment for our advancement. The reason this is so important is due to the sometimes unrecognised fact that as one makes incremental spiritual progress, life's internal and external challenges can often fluctuate significantly in scope and intensity quite spontaneously. To successfully cope with and resolve these situations requires expanding one's strength and integrity of character across a diverse spectrum of traits that serve to temper, purify and refine one's states of being. Humility is among the necessary noble qualities that help to achieve and maintain a temperance of one's personality so that while one's capabilities, perceptions and opportunities are progressively enhanced, then there are similar incremental advancements in the qualities of one's spiritual character. Compassion is among these required to manifest noble actions in life to inwardly self-govern one's various thoughts, deeds and influences. As we discussed in our basic assessment of the many human nature issues that now so severely plague our civilisation; we are able to perceive that some of the diverse outcomes of rapid technological development have been accomplished without a parallel progression in humanity's spiritual and ethical state of being. This global situation is analogous to our own individual personal development. If our capabilities, perceptions and opportunities all have the potential to substantially progress through the enhanced evolutionary unfoldment of our comprehensive level of consciousness, then it is vitally important that we experience a parallel increase in the superlative spiritual qualities exemplified by the higher aspects of Soul within and through the expression of our normal human character.

In daily earthly life we can easily see people in the public around us that have been somewhat overwhelmed by their status, capabilities and other opportunities to such an extent that it retards their personal character's qualities to the point that they can become somewhat 'low minded' and even repulsive to more refined, spiritually aware people. Please allow me to digress briefly to observe that a truly highly spiritually evolved person would be unlikely to respond to other people with revulsion, no matter what their attitudes and conduct were, because their superlative state of consciousness would simply observe the facts with little or no emotional distain. So here I am referring to spiritually inclined people, like myself, who are less able to 'detach' their perceptions and emotions from the personality choices made by people around them. To continue, the arrogance, greed, ignorance, intolerance, haughty abuse of material power and other unattractive inappropriate character traits become the norm for people that lose empathy and compassion for others. Such afflicted people demonstrate the unfortunate results that occur if one becomes vain and so 'full of one's (lower) self' that the negative, lesser aspects of one's overall human nature begin to dominate their character. Such negative people are often prone to overly exaggerate and overtly display their relatively modest character attributes in such a theatrical manner that they become a detriment to themselves and others. We see many such people rising to prominent positions of governmental and economic power in the world today, as we have discussed at length already so we will not repeat these issues again. Conversely, we see a few fantastic examples of people at the height of social prominence and wealth who clearly demonstrate the best possible qualities, so these dichotomies are evident for us to observe on Earth today.

It is imperative that we examine the resultant affects of not focusing upon the inner divinity that is the true source of all consciousness and capability. We cannot afford to complacently disregard the fact that as we spiritually progress, there will be numerous advancements in all areas of our life. If we allow ourselves to lose or even diminish the conscious awareness that the fundamental cause of all of our progression is due to Soul influences, then we are severely degraded in our ability to maintain our current developmental status and significant setbacks ultimately become quite likely. Therefore, it is essential that we focus upon encouraging the development of our best spiritual attributes because otherwise we will have great difficulty in responding properly to life's challenges as the tests of character become increasingly more prevalent and intense. These spiritual tests of character, the resulting lessons, and subsequent realisations can become vastly more focally directed specifically at our fewer remaining weaknesses as we evolve spiritually. This unexpected testing process is quite likely to occur in unanticipated ways.

    Basically, potentially one day we are doing just fine and then suddenly one or more of life's divine tests of character or faith will unexpectedly confront us, often in our most vulnerable, 'unseen' or unconscious areas of character or life experience. We may not even be aware of our hidden proclivity to succumb to such a situation in our life or we can be challenged at a time when we are quite rightfully feeling ourselves to be at our strongest and most spiritually developed level. As one progresses 'upwards' upon the spiritual 'ladder' of Soul's evolutionary development, the various 'tests' of one's comprehensive human and spiritual character become increasingly greater. We are making an artificial distinction between our human character and our spiritual nature because in earthly life we so easily sometimes forget about or ignore our spiritual nature that it must occasionally assert Itself to influence our thoughts and actions. This process of Soul asserting itself can be incredibly disruptive to one's earthly life, as some of us will likely be well-able to attest by recalling examples from our own life's experiences. We are very serious, in a fun and light-hearted way, about developing, maintaining, enhancing and continually expanding these superlative qualities of character throughout our earthly and eternal lives. The alternatives are nothing short of periodic personal devastation. However, the positive is that if we 'fall' or we do 'the wrong things', as we all do from time to time; then we can and do gain important realisations. At those illuminating moments in our lives, we must simply accept our lessons graciously and do our best to 'recover our losses', which in some cases may not occur again in this earthly lifetime; and move forward and upwards again, hopefully the wiser for our errors in judgement for manifesting our more feeble aspects of lower character in making the unwise or inappropriate decisions.

To resume the assessment of why humility and compassion are among our most important spiritual qualities, we must identify, recognise and accept the important fact that these two attributes enable us to create strength of character that is based upon true divine love, not earthly power. True divine love is by far the greatest real power in every cosmic system of reality, including this Earth. This situation seems confounded and distorted here upon this planet, yet this too is an essential part of our eternal tests of character. We need to be able to discern the many actual spiritual realities that are co-existent within a contorted chaos of conflicting value systems. Here on Earth we experience many incredibly complex situations where real meaning and purpose is divinely and intentionally complicated so that we are able to learn to discern, then willingly choose the correct path and freely demonstrate our innate higher qualities of character in all types of experiences, throughout our earthly lives. This process properly prepares us for the sequential stages of unfolding reality upon other planes of cosmic reality throughout our immortal existence.

Humility is the spiritual quality that tempers human arrogance and haughty self-serving attitudes and behaviours that can easily destroy one's life and adversely influence others. Humility can serve as a self-governing mechanism within our conscience that gently reminds one to refrain from exerting one's increasingly significant personal abilities to the detriment of others. In other words, as we progress spiritually, we develop capabilities and perceptive abilities that many other people and life forms do not possess. Therefore, it is essential to conscientiously seek to remain humble and thankful for life's blessings, treating all other life forms with compassion; and not to foolishly become arrogant, vain, and dictatorial, among other such negative attitudes that could subtly develop over time through changed circumstances, based upon one's relative progress.

There is no disputing that some truly noble, genuinely loving, kind, giving, compassionate, humble people manifesting Soul awareness are now serving as 'vehicles' for the distribution of God's energies and divine love into this world. Such people can quite rightly become perceived as being akin to spiritual 'giants' among the 'pigmies' of humanity. Mother Teresa was exactly such a person who was among the simplest, most caring, unassuming, humble, sincere, peaceful, and truly loving of humans during her time on Earth. Outwardly she appeared and considered herself to be a relatively small and insignificant aspect of divine expression, whereas inwardly she epitomised the latent spiritual aspirations existing within each of us, so that we all easily and clearly recognised her as being a spiritual giant among humanity. Mother Teresa exemplified genuine humility and true compassion among many other spiritual virtues we seek to inspire and manifest within ourselves over passing time. There may be those people around Mother Teresa who would unfairly seek to cast aspersions upon various aspects of her character, whether actual or illusionary fabrications of resentful minds, it matters not. My point here being that Mother Teresa's expression of humility did not overly concern itself too much with what others believed her motives were or what her rewards would be for her dedicated work on behalf of the underprivileged actually were;

she simply got on with her self-chosen work in a way that was evident to us all. Those people she helped knew best about her motives and attributes, so this is the true test of character in doing things because they need to be done and they are the right things to do, not because there is a good material or status role attached to the activity. This should become a valuable lesson for us all to learn. *"In this life we cannot all do great things. We can only do small things with great love." Mother Theresa*

Who am I to suggest what specific improvements one can make to one's self, when I am so imperfect myself? Well, this is not particularly my concern here because these issues are things I am able to work on in the privacy of my own mind and life. This discussion is all about your unique journey of self-discovery. Anything I am able to do or say here to assist you on your path toward your ultimate eternal destination, which is the same as mine, is the better for us both and all. We each have the opportunity and spiritual obligation to improve ourselves according to our own methods, at the pace that suits us and this continuous process is within your own private domain and personal control.

Therefore, humility is a personal attitude that says we, as individuals, are no better and no worse than any other human being in our innate potentiality. Humility is a developmental aspect of one's character that prevents one from becoming overly impressed with one's progress and somewhat reduces the almost unavoidable tendency for us to periodically self-destruct our lives in various ways, intentionally or unconsciously. It is somewhat painfully obvious that in our assessment of these spiritual qualities and many others we could have chosen to identify and discuss in considerable detail, yet have not; that we all are naturally prone to turn our attention to the perceived benefits and positive results of nurturing and manifesting these divine attributes. The actual fact is we should seek to exemplify divine virtues because they are innately the 'right' way to be, think and behave; not because there are a great group of associated beneficial 'perks' involved in acting and thinking in such positive ways. Do any of us really believe that any of history's greatest people thought about what others would think of them if they devoted themselves to what we now know to be noble, just necessary causes that at the time were incorrectly perceived to be rebellious, heretical, contentious personal philosophies? Did Martin Luther King, Mother Teresa, Nelson Mandela, Jesus, Joan of Arc, Ghandi or other such people think to themselves, "How can I become famous, make some money doing what I like and have a good easy life?" No, not at all; rather these people and countless others like them were inwardly driven to express and demonstrate their inner beliefs and resolve to act to improve their world to the very best of their ability, each in their own unique special ways. Such virtuous people sought to manifest their inner divinity and their moralistic, just and equitable philosophies of life in spite of any and all potential opposition. Mankind has often sought to silence, undermine, or destroy those who serve as the conscience of humanity, yet even this does not dissuade the truly gifted among us from expressing and demonstrating their inner truths in external reality. Therefore, genuine humility and deep compassion are essential prerequisites for those of us who aspire to manifest our innate inborn divinity and true "love for all and hatred for none", as Mr. Ambassador says.

Throughout our discussion we have identified many more spiritual virtues that characterise those who manage to quell the incessant demands of the lower aspects of our human self. We could continue to specify and discuss them, yet one can feel the need to conclude our discussion here to get on with the magnificent job at hand.

"Soul exists because God loves It." says Sri Harold Klemp. We are indeed privileged to have many magnificent Human Beings 'leading the way' by divinely inspired examples in our earthly lives at this beautiful special time of enhanced spiritual progress in our long human history.

We now go forward characterised by inner peace, with love, appreciation, mutual acceptance and respect for one another; and committed to accomplishing our cooperative plans to create a better future, one day and way at a time. Regardless of our various beliefs and life paths, we will achieve what we came to Earth to do. Look inwardly for inspiration, for divine love, true eternal peace and harmony within Soul and God, our Creator. May the Blessings Be.

OUR New Beginning ...

Bliss In ALL !!!

www.ingramcontent.com/pod-product-compliance
Lightning Source LLC
Chambersburg PA
CBHW070450120526
44590CB00013B/636